THE NEW PUBLIC GOV

'Stephen Osborne is to be congratulated for assembling an impressive array of contributors and producing a text which makes a major contribution to the debates about this emerging paradigm.' Robert Pyper *Glasgow Caledonian University, UK*

'This book showcases the best writing on "public governance", bringing together new research in institutional analysis, policy dynamics, and government–society relationships. It provides a good balance of conceptual insights and empirical analysis grounded in the large changes evident in advanced countries in recent decades.' Brian Head *University of Queensland, Australia*

'This text, edited by Stephen Osborne, may do as much for critical insight to Europe's public service delivery as the David Osborne and Ted Gaebler text on Reinventing Government did for the United States in the 1990s in refocusing the public sector for improvement.' Dean F. Eitel *DePaul University, USA*

Despite predictions that 'new public management' would establish itself as the new paradigm of Public Administration and Management, recent academic research has highlighted concerns about the intra-organizational focus and limitations of this approach. This book represents a comprehensive analysis of the state of the art of public management, examining and framing the debate in this important area.

The New Public Governance? sets out to explore this emergent field of research and to present a framework with which to understand it. Divided into five parts, it examines:

- Theoretical underpinnings of the concept of governance, especially competing perspectives from Europe and the US
- Governance of inter-organizational partnerships and contractual relationships
- Governance of policy networks
- Lessons learned and future directions

Under the steely editorship of Stephen Osborne, and with contributions from leading academics including Owen Hughes, John M. Bryson, Don Kettl, Guy Peters and Carsten Greve, this book will be of particular interest to researchers and students of public administration, public management, public policy and public services management.

Stephen P. Osborne is Professor of International Public Management and Director of the Centre for Public Services Research at the University of Edinburgh, UK. He is President of the International Research Society for Public Management (IRSPM) and Editor of *Public Management Review* (PMR).

THE NEW PUBLIC GOVERNANCE?

Emerging perspectives on the theory and practice of public governance

Edited by Stephen P. Osborne

LONDON AND NEW YORK

First published 2010
by Routledge
2 Park Square, Milton Park, Abingdon, Oxon OX14 4RN

Simultaneously published in the USA and Canada
by Routledge
270 Madison Ave, New York, NY 10016

Routledge is an imprint of the Taylor & Francis Group, an informa business

Transferred to Digital Printing 2010

Typeset in 10/12pt Times NR MT by Graphicraft Limited, Hong Kong

British Library Cataloguing in Publication Data
A catalogue record for this book is available
from the British Library

Library of Congress Cataloging in Publication Data
The new public governance? : emerging perspectives on the theory and practice of public governance / edited by Stephen P. Osborne.
p. cm.
Includes bibliographical references and index.
1. Public administration. 2. Public-private sector cooperation.
3. Organizational change. I. Osborne, Stephen P., 1953–
JF1351.N44 2009
352.01–dc22
2009027964

ISBN10: 0-415-49462-1 (hbk)
ISBN10: 0-415-49463-X (pbk)
ISBN10: 0-203-86168-X (ebk)

ISBN13: 978-0-415-49462-5 (hbk)
ISBN13: 978-0-415-49463-2 (pbk)
ISBN13: 978-0-203-86168-4 (ebk)

IN LOVING MEMORY OF MY FATHER,
FRANK OSBORNE

CONTENTS

TABLES

FIGURES

CONTRIBUTORS

Beatriz Acevedo is a researcher on international drugs policy at Anglia Ruskin University.

Taco Brandsen is Associate Professor at Radboud University Nijmegen.

John M. Bryson is McKnight Presidential Professor of Planning and Public Affairs at the University of Minnesota.

Celine Chew is Lecturer in Marketing and Strategy at Cardiff University.

Richard Common is a Senior Research Fellow at the University of Manchester.

Barbara C. Crosby is Associate Professor in Public and Non-profit Leadership at the University of Minnesota.

Federica Farneti is Assistant Professor at the Alma Mater Studiorum University of Bologna.

Carsten Greve is Professor of Public Management at Copenhagen Business School.

Jean Hartley is Professor of Organizational Analysis at the Institute of Governance and Public Management, University of Warwick.

Graeme Hodge is a Professor of Law at Monash University, and Director of the Monash Center for Regulatory Studies.

Owen Hughes is Professor of Public Management at Monash University.

Chris Huxham is Professor of Management at the University of Strathclyde Business School.

Menno Huys is a PhD student at the Faculty of Policy and Management at Delft University of Technology.

Tobias Jung is ESRC Research Fellow within the Centre for Charitable Giving and Philanthropy, and based at the University of Edinburgh Business School.

Patricia Kennett is Reader in Comparative Policy Studies at the University of Bristol.

Donald F. Kettl is Dean of the School of Public Policy at the University of Maryland.

Erik-Hans Klijn is Professor of Public Administration at Erasmus University.

Jan Kooiman is now retired. He was Professor of Public Organisations at Erasmus University.

Joop Koppenjan is Associate Professor of Public Management at the Delft University of Technology.

Laurence E. Lynn, Jr, is the Sydney Stein, Jr, Professor of Public Management at the University of Chicago.

Kate McLaughlin is now retired. She was Senior Lecturer in Local Governance at the University of Birmingham.

Ronald W. McQuaid is Director of the Employment Research Institute at Edinburgh Napier University.

Steve Martin is Professor of Public Management at Cardiff University.

Kenneth J. Meier is the Distinguished Professor of Political Science at Texas A. & M. University, and Professor of Public Management at Cardiff University.

Mark Moore is Hauser Professor of Non-profit Organizations, J. F. Kennedy School of Government, at Harvard University.

Stephen P. Osborne is Professor of International Public Management at the University of Edinburgh Business School.

Laurence J. O'Toole, Jr, is the Margaret Hughes and Robert T. Golembiewski Professor of Public Administration at the University of Georgia.

Emanuele Padovani is Associate Professor at the Alma Mater Studiorom University of Bologna.

Victor Pestoff is Guest Professor both at the Institute for Civil Society Studies, Ersta Sköndal University College, Stockholm, and at the European Research Institute on Cooperative and Social Enterprise, University of Trento.

B. Guy Peters is Maurice Falk Professor of Government at the University of Pittsburgh.

Steven Rathgeb Smith is the Nancy Bell Evans Professor of Public Affairs at the University of Washington.

Judith Smyth is director for public governance and commissioning with OPM, England.

Melissa M. Stone is a member of the Humphrey Institute of Public Affairs, University of Minnesota.

Siv Vangen is a senior lecturer at the Open University, England.

David W. Young is Emeritus Professor of Management at Boston University.

1

INTRODUCTION

The (New) Public Governance: a suitable case for treatment?[1]

Stephen P. Osborne

Introduction

More than a decade has passed since the publication of Christopher Hood's influential piece that codified the nature of the *New Public Management* (NPM) paradigm (Hood 1991). At that time it seemed likely, certainly within the Anglo-American research community, that this paradigm would sweep all before it in its triumphal recasting of the nature of our discipline – in theory and in practice. A hundred-odd years of the hegemony of Public Administration (PA) in the public sphere seemingly counted for nothing in this momentous shift. Since then, though, the debate on the impact of the NPM upon the discipline, and indeed about whether it is a paradigm at all (Gow and Dufour 2000), has become more contested.[2]

This introductory chapter is intended to move this debate forward. It considers, somewhat provocatively, that the NPM has actually been a transitory stage in the evolution from traditional Public Administration to what is here called the *New Public Governance.*[3] A note upon terminology is important here. The term "public policy implementation and public services delivery" is used here to denote the overall field of the design and implementation of public policy and the delivery of public services. Within this, Public Administration, the NPM and the New Public Governance (NPG) are then denoted as policy and implementation *regimes* within this overall field – thus neatly skirting the above, rather redundant, argument as to whether these regimes are actually paradigms or not.

The argument advanced here is that public policy implementation and public services delivery have passed through three design and delivery regimes: a longer, pre-eminent one of PA, from the late nineteenth century through to the late 1970s/early 1980s; a second one, of the NPM, through to the start of the twenty-first century; and an emergent third one, of the

NPG, since then. The time of the NPM has thus in fact been a relatively short-lived and transient one between the statist and bureaucratic tradition of PA and the embryonic plural and pluralist tradition of the NPG. The remainder of this chapter will first expound upon the extant natures of PA and the NPM. It will then explore the nature of public governance and the NPG before considering the new challenges that it poses for both the theory and the practice of public policy implementation and public services delivery.

Inevitably, such a tripartite regime model is a simplification – elements of each regime can and will coexist with each other or overlap. Many network governance systems often operate in the shadow of, or in spite of, the dominant regime of hierarchy – for example, both PA and public governance contain strong, if differentiated, elements of hierarchy (Klijn 2002). The intention here is to tease out three "archetypes", in the Weberian tradition, that will assist and promote analysis and discussion of the conceptual and practical development of public policy implementation and public services delivery.

It must be emphasized that this book is not meant to propose "the NPG" as a new paradigm of public services delivery. It is neither that normative nor that prescriptive. The question mark in the title is deliberate. Rather, this book is a critical examination of the concept of "public governance". Offering a range of perspectives, the book questions whether or not public governance is a new paradigm for the delivery of public services in the twenty-first century, and offers a range of critical perspectives upon it – both in theory and in practice.

In entering into this discussion, it is useful to bear in mind a distinction made by Dawson and Dargie (1999) in their work on the NPM. They urge the necessity to differentiate between the NPM as a political ideology, as an academic field of study and as a body of managerial practice. The latter two elements are of especial importance and need to be held distinct. The analysis of the workings and impact of any regime is distinct from the normative assertion of "how best" to manage within it.

The shadow of the past . . .

Public Administration

The key elements of PA[4] (Hood 1991) can be defined as

- The dominance of the "rule of law";
- A focus on administering set rules and guidelines;
- A central role for *the bureaucracy* in making and implementing policy;
- The "politics–administration" split *within* public organizations;

- A commitment to incremental budgeting; and
- The hegemony of the professional in public service delivery.

Developing out of the early years of the public sector in the late nineteenth and early twentieth centuries, PA, as an academic field of study, has been a strongly "grounded", rather than theoretical, discipline in the UK – the classic early statement being Robson 1928 – and at variance with its cousins in mainland Europe and the US, which are more firmly located within administrative theory.

As a field of practice, it reached its high point in the UK in the 1945–79 era of the welfare state, when the state was confidently expected to meet all the social and economic needs of the citizenry, "from the cradle to the grave". PA was to be the instrument of this brave new world, with a focus on administrative procedures to ensure equality of treatment. Predictably, perhaps, such a vision was doomed to failure – public needs inevitably outstripped the public resources available to meet them. In the latter days of their hegemony both the welfare state and PA came under increasing fire – first from their academic critics (for example, Dunleavy 1985) and eventually from the political elite (see Mischra 1984 for an overview of these critiques). Most damagingly, Chandler (1991) argued that PA had now entered terminal decline as a discipline, whilst Rhodes (1997) asserted that it had become a "bystander" to the practice of public policy implementation and public services delivery. This paved the way for the rise of the NPM.

New Public Management (NPM)

The spread of the NPM, from the late 1970s onward, saw the growth of a new discourse of public policy implementation and public services delivery. In its most extreme form, this asserted the superiority of private-sector managerial techniques over those of PA, with the assumption that the application of such techniques to public services delivery would automatically lead to improvements in the efficiency and effectiveness of these services (Thatcher 1995). The key elements of the NPM can be summarized as:

- An attention to lessons from private-sector management;
- The growth both of hands-on "management" – in its own right and not as an offshoot of professionalism – and of "arm's length" organizations where policy implementation was *organizationally distanced* from the policy-makers (as opposed to the "interpersonal" distancing of the policy–administration split within PA);
- A focus upon entrepreneurial leadership within public service organizations;
- An emphasis on inputs and output control and evaluation, and upon performance management and audit;

- The disaggregation of public services to their most basic units and a focus on their cost management; and
- Within the Anglo-American and Australia/New Zealand regions at least, the growth of use of markets, competition and contracts for resource allocation and service delivery within public services.

In the research community, this led to a focus upon the management of public services and of public service organizations (PSOs) as a distinct field separate from the public policy process – public management as opposed to public administration. At a practical level, it led to the evolution of management as a coherent and legitimized role and function within PSOs, in contrast to (and often in conflict with) the traditional professional groupings within PSOs.

In the years since it first contested the territory of public policy implementation and public services delivery with PA, though, the nature and/or success(es) of the NPM have been questioned on a range of grounds (see McLaughlin et al. 2002 for an overview of these critiques). Critics have argued *inter alia* that:

- The NPM is not one phenomenon or paradigm, but a cluster of several (Ferlie et al. 1996) – and has a number of distinct personae, dependent upon the audience, including ideological, managerial and research-oriented personae, as discussed by Dawson and Dargie (1999) above;
- The geographic extent of the NPM is limited to the Anglo-American, Australasian and (some) Scandinavian arenas, whilst PA continues to remain dominant elsewhere (Kickert 1997; see also Hood 1995);
- The nature of the NPM itself is also geographically variegated – with, for example, the British and American variants actually being quite distinct from each other in their focus and locus (Borins 2002);
- In reality, the NPM is simply a subschool of PA that has been limited in its impact by the lack of a real theoretical base and conceptual rigor (Frederickson and Smith 2003);
- The benefits of the NPM are at best partial and contested (Pollitt and Bouckaert 2004); and
- That the NPM was a "disaster waiting to happen" (Hood and Jackson 1992) and was a failed paradigm (Farnham and Horton 1996).

Similarly, in the dedicated textbooks on this topic, one will find both advocates of the NPM (Hughes 2002) and critics (Flynn 2002).

The NPM has been criticized most devastatingly for its *intraorganizational focus* in an increasingly plural world and for its adherence to the application of outdated private-sector techniques to public policy implementation and public services delivery – and in the face of evidence about their inapplicability (Metcalfe and Richards 1991).

The state of the art

Increasingly, then, both PA and the NPM have begun to look like partial theories, at best. The strength of PA is in its exploration of the essentially political nature of public policy implementation and public services delivery, and of the complexities and nuances of the public policy making and implementation process. However, the extent to which the implementation studies literature within PA has been able to unpackage the differential influences upon public policy implementation has been disappointing. There is a tendency for implementation to be seen simply as a "black box" with no apparent will to explore the complex subprocesses of the management of the outputs of the policy process – public services themselves (Schofield 2001; Hill and Hupe 2003). At worst, public managers and management are portrayed as the villain(s) of the piece, thwarting the resolve of their political masters and often subverting the intentions of new policy to their own ends.

By contrast, the strength of the NPM has been in its ability to address precisely the complexities of this "black box", now recodified as the management of change and innovation (Osborne and Brown 2006). However, it has suffered with an equally limiting tendency to see the public policy process as simply a "context" within which the essential task of public management takes place. In its most extreme form, the NPM has even questioned the legitimacy of public policy as a context for public management, arguing that it imposes unreasonable democratic constraints on the management and provision of public services (Meier 1997). Most damagingly, though, is the argument that the NPM is limited and one-dimensional in its ability to capture and contribute to the management and governance of public services and of PSOs in an increasingly fragmented and interorganizational environment (Rhodes 1997).

The argument made here is hence that both PA and the NPM fail to capture the complex reality of the design, delivery and management of public services in the twenty-first century. Given such criticisms of both paradigms, therefore, it is time to question whether there is a pressing need now for a more sophisticated understanding of public policy implementation and public services delivery – one that moves beyond the sterile dichotomy of "administration versus management" and that allows a more comprehensive and integrated approach to the study, and practice, of public policy implementation and public services delivery. The intention in this volume is to explore whether the NPG has the potential or actuality to be this overarching theoretical framework for the study and the practice of public services delivery.

. . . And the shadow of the future

The New Public Governance (NPG)

At the outset, it is important to be clear, once more, about two points. First, that the NPG is being presented here neither as a normative new paradigm to supersede PA and the NPM nor as "the one best way" (Alford and Hughes 2008) to respond to the challenges of public policy implementation and public services delivery in the twenty-first century. Rather it is being presented both as a conceptual tool with the potential to assist our understanding of the complexity of these challenges and as a reflection of the reality of the working lives of public managers today.

Second, "governance" and "public governance" are not new terms – they come with considerable prior theoretical and/or ideological baggage. Critics have differentiated three broad schools of governance literature: corporate governance, "good" governance, and public governance.

Corporate governance is concerned with the internal systems and processes that provide direction and accountability to any organization. In public services it has most often been concerned with the relationship between the policy-makers and/or trustees of public organizations and the senior managers given the task of making these policies a reality (for example, Cornforth 2003).

"Good" governance is concerned with the promulgation of normative models of social, political and administrative governance by supranational bodies such as the World Bank (Leftwich 1993; Rhodes 1997). Invariably this has placed a premium upon market-based approaches to the allocation and governance of public resources (see, for example, Osborne and Kaposvari 1997).

Public governance, which is the focus here, can itself be broken down into five distinct strands:

- *Socio-political governance*, concerned with the over-arching institutional relationships within society. Kooiman (1999) argues that these relationships and interactions must be understood in their totality in order to understand the creation and implementation of public policy. In this approach, government is no longer pre-eminent in public policy but has to rely upon other societal actors for its legitimacy and impact in this field.
- *Public policy governance*, concerned with how policy elites and networks interact to create and govern the public policy process. Marsh and Rhodes (1992), Börzel (1997) and Klijn and Koppenjan (2000), building upon the work of Hanf and Scharpf (1978), are good examples of such explorations of the workings of policy communities and networks. Most recently, Peters (2008) has explored "meta-governance" instruments

as a way by which to reassert political direction within multi-stakeholder policy networks.

- *Administrative governance*, concerned with the effective application of PA and its repositioning to encompass the complexities of the contemporary state. Thus, for example, Salamon (2002) uses governance almost as a proxy term for the generic practice of public policy implementation and public services delivery, whilst Lynn et al. (2001) also use it as a catch-all term to try to create a holistic theory of public policy implementation and public services delivery in conditions of the "hollow state" (Milward and Provan 2003). More provocatively, Frederickson (1999) contends that governance, taken together with the theory of "administrative conjunction", is in fact a way to reposition PA as the continuing pre-eminent discipline for the realities of the modern world.
- *Contract governance*, concerned with the inner workings of the NPM, and particularly the governance of contractual relationships in the delivery of public services. In this vein, Kettl has argued that public agencies in the modern contract state have become "responsible for a [public service delivery] system over which they [have] little control" (Kettl 1993: 207; see also Kettl 2000).
- *Network governance*, concerned with how "self organizing inter-organizational networks" (Rhodes 1997; see also Kickert 1993) function both with and without government to provide public services. In contrast to public policy governance, this is focused upon those networks that implement public policy and deliver public services (for example Denters and Rose 2005; Entwistle and Martin 2005).

All of these theoretical perspectives on governance make an important contribution to our understanding of public policy implementation and public services delivery. The intention here is to argue that, from being an element within the PA and NPM regimes of public policy implementation and public services delivery, public governance has become a distinctive regime in its own right – the NPG. The intention here is to suggest and explore a distinctive niche for the NPG that captures the realities of public policy implementation and public services delivery within the plural and pluralist complexities of the state in the twenty-first century.

Working with the above definitions of public governance, therefore, and building upon the insights of Peters and Pierre (1998), it is argued here that it is possible, indeed desirable, to develop a theory of the NPG that does capture these realities and complexities. This theory is not integral to PA or to the NPM but is rather an alternative discourse in its own right. It is predicated upon the existence of a *plural state* and a *pluralist state*, and it seeks to understand the development and implementation of public policy in this context.[5]

As outlined above, therefore, PA is situated firmly within the political studies discipline. Influential theorists include Woodrow Wilson (1887) and William Robson (1928). It has at its core a concern with the unitary state, where policy making and implementation are vertically integrated as a closed system within government. It focuses upon the policy making and implementation cycle, with an assumption that effective PA is comprised of the successful implementation by public managers of policies decided "up stream" in this system by democratically elected (and, it is implicitly assumed, accountable) politicians. Because of its vertically integrated nature, hierarchy is the key resource-allocation mechanism for PA, with a focus upon vertical line-management to ensure accountability for the use of public money (Day and Klein 1987; Simey 1988). The value base is one based in an explicit assumption of the hegemony of the *public sector* for the implementation of public policy and the delivery of public services.

Some writers, of course, have long recognized the fallibility of the PA paradigm without entirely dismissing it as a framework for the design and delivery of public services. The theory of "street level bureaucrats" (Lipsky 1979), for example, seeks to explain the breakdown of the "policy-maker–administrator" divide in conditions of resource shortage, but without dismissing in its entirety the framework of PA for the provision of public services (see also Schofield 2001 for a good overview of this range of arguments).

By comparison, the NPM[6] is a child of neo-classical economics and particularly of rational/public choice theory. Influential writers include Tiebout (1956) and Niskanen (1971). It is concerned with a disaggregated state, where policy making and implementation are at least partially articulated and disengaged, and where implementation is through a collection of independent service units, ideally in competition with each other. The key role of the state here is regulation, often within a principal–agent context (Vickers and Yarrow 1988). Its focus is almost wholly upon *intraorganizational processes and management.*[7] Drawing upon open rational systems theory, it models the production of public services as an intraorganizational process that turns inputs into outputs (services) within a mediating environment, and with an emphasis upon the economy and efficiency of these processes in producing public services. As already noted, it assumes competitive relationships between the independent service units inside any public policy domain, taking place within a horizontally organized marketplace – and where the key resource-allocation mechanism is a variable combination of competition, the price mechanism and contractual relationships, depending upon which particular variant of the NPM one chooses to expound. Its value base is formed around "the logic of accounting" and is contained within its belief that this marketplace, and its workings, provides the most appropriate place for the production of public services. An extreme form of this argument is made by Pirie (1988).

In contrast to both of the above, the NPG, if it is to be situated as a paradigm of public services delivery, is rooted firmly within institutional and network theory, and draws much from the influential work of Ouchi (1979), Powell (1990), Powell and DiMaggio (1991), and Nohria and Eccles (1992). It posits both *a plural state*, where multiple interdependent actors contribute to the delivery of public services, and *a pluralist state*, where multiple processes inform the policy-making system. Drawing upon open natural systems theory, it is concerned with the institutional and external environmental pressures that enable and constrain public policy implementation and the delivery of public services within such a plural and pluralist system. As a consequence of these two forms of plurality, its focus is very much upon interorganizational relationships and upon the governance of processes, stressing service effectiveness and outcomes that rely upon the interaction of PSOs with their environment. The central resource-allocation mechanism is the interorganizational network, with accountability being something to be negotiated at the interorganizational and interpersonal level within these networks (Osborne 1997). Importantly, such networks are rarely alliances of equals but are rather riven with power inequalities that must be navigated successfully for their effective working. Hence the value base in such networks is often dispersed and contested.

The NPG is thus both a product of and a response to the increasingly complex, plural and fragmented nature of public policy implementation and service delivery in the twenty-first century. Its key elements in relation to PA and the NPM are summarized in Table 1.1.

Now, significant work has already taken place that might legitimately be said to fall within the boundaries of the emergent regime of the NPG. This includes work upon the nature and governance of the policy process (Klijn and Koppenjan 2000, 2004), the issue of "managing outward" for PSOs and managers (Moore 1995; O'Toole et al. 2005), the development of key management skills in an interorganizational context (Getha-Taylor 2008), expanding the nature and impact of accounting within PSOs to embrace a more holistic approach to their environment (Ball and Seal 2005; Marcuccio and Steccolini 2005), and the governance of interorganizational relationships themselves (Hudson 2004; Huxham and Vangen 2005). Invariably, though, the focus has been at the organizational rather than the service system level.

However, it has become increasingly apparent that the public policy implementation and public services delivery research agenda, certainly within the UK, is one where its parameters and questions have been set within the previous regimes – and particularly within that of the NPM. This research agenda is asking the old questions about public policy implementation and public services delivery. These questions are epitomized within the ESRC Public Services Programme in the UK. This program has been important for the research community and has produced some outstanding research findings. Nonetheless, as a research agenda, it is characterized precisely by these "old

Table 1.1 Core elements of the NPG, in contrast to PA and the NPM

Paradigm/key elements	*Theoretical roots*	*Nature of the state*	*Focus*	*Emphasis*	*Resource allocation mechanism*	*Nature of the service system*	*Value base*
Public Administration	Political science and public policy	Unitary	The political system	Policy creation and implementation	Hierarchy	Closed	Public sector ethos
New Public Management	Rational/public choice theory and management studies	Regulatory	The organization	Management of organizational resources and performance	The market and classical or neo-classical contracts	Open rational	Efficacy of competition and the marketplace
New Public Governance	Institutional and network theory	Plural and pluralist	The organization in its environment	Negotiation of values, meaning and relationships	Networks and relational contracts	Open closed	Dispersed and contested

questions" of intraorganizational efficiency and effectiveness. These old questions can be summarized as:

- How do we manage public policy implementation to ensure that the political will is carried out in practice? *(the policy implementation question)*
- How do we ensure organizational and individual service performance? *(the audit and targets question)*
- How do we ensure that individual PSOs can work in partnership most effectively? *(the partnerships question)*
- How do we hold public managers accountable? *(the scrutiny question)*
- How do we "incentivize" staff for optimal productivity? *(the rewards question)*
- How do we ensure organizational sustainability? *(the change and innovation question)*

The argument here is that, if we are going to develop the NPG as a conceptualization of public policy implementation and public services management, it is necessary to move toward an integrated body of knowledge about the NPG. This requires our research community to start asking a series of "new questions" about the fundamentals of the NPG. These questions are focused upon the underlying principles of public services delivery in the plural and pluralist state and upon the public service system, rather than upon individual PSOs. These new questions are, it is argued here, sevenfold:

- What should be our basic unit of analysis in exploring public policy implementation and public services delivery – and what are the implications of this for theory and practice? *(the fundamentals question)*
- What organizational architecture is best-suited to delivering public services in the plural state? *(the architectural question)*
- How do we ensure sustainable public service systems – and what does sustainability mean? *(the sustainability question)*
- What values underpin public policy implementation and services delivery in such systems? *(the values question)*
- What key skills are required for relational performance? *(the relational skills question)*
- What is the nature of accountability in fragmented plural and pluralist systems? *(the accountability question)*
- How do you evaluate sustainability, accountability and relational performance within open natural public service delivery systems? *(the evaluation question)*

It should be emphasized that these new questions are not a simple replacement for the old ones. The imperative for effective intraorganizational and service management remains – and so the "old questions" still remain pertinent. However, such effectiveness by itself will not engender the delivery of successful public services in the contemporary plural and pluralist state. In order to contribute to such delivery, the NPG needs to encompass *both* an active research agenda that will explore the efficacy and limitations of the regime *and* a developing body of capable and beneficial managerial practice within this plural and pluralist context. These questions will be returned to in the conclusions of this present volume, with a discussion of their implications both for a research agenda and for policy practice.

Structure of this book

This volume is in five parts. The first part will provide a series of theoretical perspectives upon public governance and question the applicability of the concept of the "NPG". Parts 2–5 will then explore the nature of public governance in a series of key, and indeed overlapping, areas: interorganizational collaboration, contractual relationships, interorganizational networks for services delivery, and public policy networks. The conclusions to the volume will then consider the implications of public governance for public services delivery research over the next decade and beyond.

Notes

1 This chapter builds upon and expands the arguments made previously by this author in two prior pieces: S. Osborne (2006) "The New Public Governance?", *Public Management Review*, 8 (30): 377–88, and S. Osborne (2009) "Delivering Public Services: Are We Asking the Right Questions?", *Public Money and Management*, 29 (1): 5–7.
2 As one mainland European colleague remarked somewhat humorously to this author recently, the tradition in the UK is to see every change of national government as the start of a new paradigm of public management and administration.
3 Ever since Hood's influential essay on the New Public Management, there has been a tendency to herald every shift in public services provision as the "New Something-or-other". Whilst there are clear limitations to this approach, it is nonetheless the one adopted here – primarily to differentiate it from the other diverse approaches to "governance" and "public governance" discussed below.
4 Brint Milward has made the point in a personal communication to this author that there is an inevitable national variance in the nature of public administration, and of the other regimes. The "politics–administration" split, for example, is perhaps a particularly European, and especially British, emphasis within PA. Moreover, all the elements are liable to buckle under extreme stress – the incrementalism of PA was clearly put on hold during the two world wars of the twentieth century, for example.
5 These concepts of the *plural state* and *pluralist state* are reviewed further below.
6 NPM, as discussed here, is very much the market-driven variant that emphasized the efficacy of interorganizational competition in the delivery of public services.

It is the model prevalent across the UK, the US, and Australia and New Zealand in particular. An alternative version, which is common across mainland Europe, does not place such an emphasis upon external competitive environment. Rather, it emphasizes contractual mechanisms *within* rather than *without* government (Schrijvers 1993).

7 Though Ostrom and Ostrom (1971) do offer a more explicitly *interorganizational* approach to public choice theory as a basis for the NPM.

References

Alford, J. and Hughes, O. (2008) "Public Value Pragmatism as the Next Phase of Public Management", *American Review of Public Administration*, 36 (2): 130–48.

Ball, A. and Seal, W. (2005) "Social Justice in a Cold Climate: Could Social Accounting Make a Difference?", *Accounting Forum*, 29: 455–73.

Borins, S. (2002) "New Public Management, North American Style", in K. McLaughlin, S. Osborne and E. Ferlie (eds) *The New Public Management: Current Trends and Future Prospects*, London: Routledge.

Börzel, T. (1997) "What's So Special about Policy Networks? An Exploration of the Concept and Its Usefulness in Studying European Governance", *European Integration online Papers (EIoP)*, 1 (16), http://eiop.or.at/eiop/texte/1997-016a.htm.

Chandler, J. (1991) "Public Administration: A Discipline in Decline", *Teaching Public Administration*, 9: 39–45.

Cornforth, C. (ed.) (2003) *The Governance of Public and Non-profit Organisations. What Do Boards Do?*, London: Routledge.

Dawson, S. and Dargie, C. (1999) "New Public Management: An Assessment and Evaluation with Special Reference to Health", *Public Management Review*, 1 (4): 459–82.

Day, P. and Klein, R. (1987) *Accountabilities*, London: Tavistock.

Denters, D. and Rose, L. (2005) *Comparing Local Governance*, Basingstoke: Palgrave Macmillan.

Dunleavy, P. (1985) "Bureaucrats, Budgets and the Growth of the State", *British Journal of Political Science*, 15: 299–328.

Entwistle, T. and Martin, S. (2005) "From Competition to Collaboration in Public Services Delivery: A New Agenda for Research", *Public Administration*, 83 (1): 233–42.

Farnham, D. and Horton, S. (eds) (1996) *Managing the New Public Services*, Basingstoke: Macmillan.

Ferlie, E., Ashburner, L., Fitzgerald, L. and Pettigrew, A. (1996) *The New Public Management in Action*, Oxford: Oxford University Press.

Flynn, N. (2002) *Public Sector Management*, London: Prentice Hall.

Frederickson, G. (1999) "The Repositioning of American Public Administration", *Political Science and Politics*, 32: 701–11.

Frederickson, G. and Smith, K. (2003) *The Public Administration Primer*, Boulder, Colo.: Westview Press.

Getha-Taylor, H. (2008) "Identifying Collaborative Competencies", *Review of Public Personnel Administration*, 28 (2): 103–19.

Gow, J. and Dufour, C. (2000) "Is the New Public Management a Paradigm? Does It Matter?", *International Review of Administrative Sciences*, 66 (4): 573–97.

Hanf, K. and Scharpf, F. (eds) (1978) *Interorganizational Policy Making*, London: Sage.

Hill, M. and Hupe, P. (2003) "The Multi-layer Problem in Implementation Research", *Public Management Review*, 5 (4): 471–90.

Hood, C. (1991) "A Public Management for All Seasons?", *Public Administration*, 69: 3–19.

Hood, C. (1995) "The New Public Management in the 1990s: Variations on a Theme", *Accounting, Organizations and Society*, 20 (2–3): 93–109.

Hood, C. and Jackson, M. (1992) "The New Public Management: A Recipe for Disaster", in D. J. Parker and J. W. Handmer (eds) *Hazard Management and Emergency Planning: Perspectives on Britain*, London: James and James.

Hudson, B. (2004) "Analysing Network Partnerships: Benson Re-visited", *Public Management Review*, 6 (1): 75–94.

Hughes, O. (2002) *Public Management and Administration*, Basingstoke: Palgrave.

Huxham, C. and Vangen, S. (2005) *Managing to Collaborate*, London: Routledge.

Kettl, D. (1993) *Sharing Power: Public Governance and Private Markets*, Washington, DC: The Brookings Institution.

Kettl, D. (2000) *The Global Public Management Revolution*, Washington, DC: The Brookings Institution.

Kickert, W. (1993) "Complexity Governance and Dynamics: Conceptual Explorations of Public Network Management", in J. Kooiman (ed.) *Modern Governance*, London: Sage.

Kickert, W. (1997) "Public Governance in the Netherlands: An Alternative to Anglo-American 'managerialism'", *Public Administration*, 75 (4): 731–52.

Klijn, E.-H. (2002) "Governing Networks in the Hollow State: Contracting-out, Process Management or a Combination of the Two", *Public Management Review*, 4 (2): 149–66.

Klijn, E.-H. and Koppenjan, J. (2000) "Public Management and Policy Networks: Foundations of a Network Approach to Governance", *Public Management Review*, 2 (2): 135–58.

Klijn, E.-H. and Koppenjan, J. (2004) *Managing Uncertainties in Networks*, London: Routledge.

Kooiman, J. (1999) "Social–political Governance: Overview, Reflections and Design", *Public Management Review*, 1 (1): 67–92.

Leftwich, A. (1993) "Governance, Democracy and Development in the Third World", *Third World Quarterly*, 14: 605–24.

Lipsky, M. (1979) *Street Level Bureaucracy*, New York: Russell Sage Foundation.

Lynn, L., Heinrich, C. and Hill, C. (2001) *Improving Governance: A New Logic for Empirical Research*, Washington, DC: Georgetown University Press.

McLaughlin, K., Osborne, S. and Ferlie, E. (eds) (2002) *The New Public Management: Current Trends and Future Prospects*, London: Routledge.

Marcuccio, M. and Steccolini, I. (2005) "Social and Environmental Reporting in Local Authorities: A New Italian Fashion?", *Public Management Review*, 7 (2): 155–76.

Marsh, D. and Rhodes, R. (1992) *Policy Networks in British Government*, Oxford: Clarendon Press.

Meier, K. (1997) "Bureaucracy and Democracy: The Case for More Bureaucracy and Less Democracy", *Public Administration Review*, 57 (3): 193–9.

Metcalfe, L. and Richards, S. (1991) *Improving Public Management*, London: Sage.

Milward, B. and Provan, K. (2003) "Managing the Hollow State: Collaboration and Contracting", *Public Management Review*, 5 (1): 1–18.

Mischra, R. (1984) *The Welfare State in Crisis*, Brighton: Wheatsheaf.

Moore, M. (1995) *Creating Public Value: Strategic Management in Government*, Cambridge, Mass.: Harvard University Press.

Niskanen, W. (1971) *Bureaucracy and Representative Government*, Chicago, Ill.: Aldine-Atherton.

Nohria, N. and Eccles, R. (eds) (1992) *Networks and Organizations: Structures, Form and Action*, Cambridge, Mass.: Harvard Business School Press.

Osborne, S. (1997) "Managing the Coordination of Social Services in the Mixed Economy of Welfare: Competition, Cooperation or Common Cause?", *British Journal of Management*, 8: 317–28.

Osborne, S. and Brown, K. (2006) *Managing Change and Innovation in Public Service Organizations*, London: Routledge.

Osborne, S. and Kaposvari, A. (1997) "Towards a civil society? Exploring its meanings in the context of post-communist Hungary" in *Journal European Social Policy*, 7(3): 209–222.

Ostrom, V. and Ostrom, E. (1971) "Public Choice: A Different Approach to the Study of Public Administration", *Public Administration Review*, 31: 203–16.

O'Toole, L., Meier, K. and Nicholson-Crotty, S. (2005) "Managing Upward, Downward and Outward: Networks, Hierarchical Relationships and Performance", *Public Management Review*, 7 (1): 45–68.

Ouchi, W. (1979) "Markets, Bureaucracies and Clans", *Administrative Science Quarterly*, 25: 129–41.

Peters, G. (2008) *The Two Futures of Governing: Decentering and Recentering Processes in Governing*, HIS Political Science Series Paper 114, Pittsburgh, Pa.: University of Pittsburg Press.

Peters, G. and Pierre, J. (1998) "Governance without Government? Rethinking Public Administration", *Journal of Public Administration – Research and Theory*, 8: 227–43.

Pirie, M. (1988) *Privatization: Theory, Practice and Choice*, London: Wildwood House.

Pollitt, C. and Bouckaert, G. (2004) *Public Management Reform: A Comparative Analysis*, Oxford: Oxford University Press.

Powell, W. (1990) "Neither Market nor Hierarchy: Network Forms of Organization", *Research in Organizational Behaviour*, 12: 295–336.

Powell, W. and DiMaggio, P. (1991) *The New Institutionalism in Organizational Analysis*, Chicago, Ill.: University of Chicago Press.

Rhodes, R. (1997) *Understanding Governance*, Buckingham: Open University Press.

Robson, W. (1928) *Justice and Administrative Law*, London: Macmillan.

Salamon, L. (2002) *The Tools of Government: A Guide to the New Governance*, New York: Oxford University Press.

Schofield, J. (2001) "Time for a Revival? Public Policy Implementation: A Review of the Literature and an Agenda for Future Research", *International Journal of Management Reviews*, 3 (3): 245–63.

Schrijvers, A. (1993) "The Management of a Larger Town: Outcome Related Performance Indicators and Organizational Control in the Public Sector", *Public Administration*, 71: 595–603.

Simey, M. (1988) *Democracy Rediscovered: A Study in Police Accountability*, London: Pluto Press.

Thatcher, M. (1995) *The Downing Street Years*, London: HarperCollins.

Tiebout, C. (1956) "A Pure Theory of Local Expenditures", *Journal of Political Economy*, 64 (5): 416–24.

Vickers, J. and Yarrow, G. (1988) *Privatization: An Economic Analysis*, Cambridge, Mass.: MIT Press.

Wilson, W. (1887) "The Study of Administration", *Political Science Quarterly*, 2.

Part I

THEORETICAL PERSPECTIVES ON PUBLIC GOVERNANCE

2

GLOBAL PERSPECTIVES ON GOVERNANCE

Patricia Kennett

Introduction

The concepts of globalization and governance are firmly established within public policy debates. However, the dynamics, nature and implications of the relationship between globalization and governance are fiercely contested. This chapter will begin by examining various definitions of the concepts and the linkages between them. It will then go on to consider the spaces and practices of governance under the condition of globalization. It will focus particularly on the emergence of the institutional structures of global governance, the key actors, dynamics and practices of public governance. The remainder of the chapter will consider whether new forms and layers of decision-making and participation herald the arrival of a new multi-layered public governance.

Governance and globalization

New forms of relationship and interaction between state and society, governments and citizens, and state and not-state institutions have emerged in the context of what Jessop refers to as an arena of "unstructured complexity" (Jessop 2004) and Rhodes characterizes as "a differentiated polity" (Rhodes 1997). These novel forms have been captured in the concept of governance (Swyngedouw 2005; Rhodes 1996; Daly 2003; Newman 2005; Kjaer 2004; Jessop 2004; Stoker 1998). Governance facilitates an understanding of the ways in which power penetrates policy spaces, processes and practices, and the formal and informal institutional arrangements which contribute to a "matrix of governance" (Lieberthal 1995) or "choreographies of governance" (Swyngedouw 2001), the ensemble of norms, patterns of behavior, networks and other institutions, and the power-play between them. As Koenig-Archibugi (2003) explains, within governance systems "problem solving is not the preserve of a central authority able to impose solutions on subordinate agencies and individuals, but the result of the interaction of a plurality of actors, who often have different interests, values, cognitive orientations, and power resources" (p. 319).

Governance, as Daly (2003) asserts, is fundamentally about change. In much of the literature, it is mainly concerned with the idea of a change from the realist perception of old government and the Westphalian system, whereby the world is organized into territorially exclusive, sovereign nation-states, each with an internal monopoly of legitimate violence, to new governance. The former is characterized as having a governing administration which is regarded as the key dominant actor in the policy arena. Internally there exists a clear hierarchy of authority, and governing is seen as a top-down, hierarchical process, with the nation-state taking centre stage. However, with the change from government to governance, the governing administration is now only one player amongst many others in the policy arena. Thus, the policy arena has become visibly more crowded and contested, there are more actors involved, the boundaries between the public and the private spheres are less precise, and the government's command over the policy process is said to have been transformed (Kjaer 2004; Newman 2005).

Globalization has become an essential context in which to locate the analysis of public policy. Whilst the concept has generated enormous debate regarding the substance, extent and nature of the phenomenon, it is interpreted here as an economic, ideological, political and institutional project facilitated and enabled through a technological revolution, an ideological and policy shift, a strengthening of the role of international financial institutions, and a changing geopolitical landscape (Giddens 1999; Held and McGrew 2000, 2002). Increasing competition in global markets, pressure from international institutions, domestic policy decisions to reduce national barriers to international economic transactions, combined with the impact of new technologies, "created the enabling conditions for the onset of globalisation" (Biersteker 1998: 24).

Globalization has given rise to a stronger and more influential institutional transnational and supranational element of a new public order which goes beyond the traditional boundaries of the state. The concepts of global governance (Rosenau and Czempiel 1992) and, more recently, global public policy (Stone 2008) have emerged to refer to the interaction of "multiple and fluid regimes and to . . . the role of actors, events, laws, and policies that fall outside the traditional boundaries of the state" (Macrae 2006: 527). For Rosenau (1995), "global governance is conceived to include systems of rule at all levels of human activity – from the family to the international organization – in which the pursuit of goals through the exercise of control has transnational repercussions" (p. 13). Whilst Dingwerth and Pattberg (2006) argue that the term "global governance" has become a catch-all phrase for "almost any process or structure of politics beyond the state – regardless of scope, content or context" (p. 185), they state nevertheless that "the study of global governance acknowledges that a plethora of forms of social organization and political decision-making exist that are neither directed toward the state nor emanate from it" (p. 191).

An important dynamic in understanding the relationship between globalization and governance is the recognition that, despite apparent differences, governance is best-understood not only as a "general phenomenon" (Krahmann 2003: 223), occurring across different levels of analysis with governance arrangements at the national, regional and global levels displaying important similarities, but also as integrated and dialectical. Whilst global public policy is distinct from the national process of policy-making, it is not detached from it. Although national public institutions no longer serve as the sole organizing center for policy in the context of networks and the rise of the new "relational rationality" as opposed to a traditional rule-based universal rationality linked to the rise of the modern state and modern law (Ladeur 2004), the state is by no means in retreat (Weiss 2005) or withering away. Rather, government power has been dispersed and reconstituted across new sites of actions augmented through new strategies and technologies (Jessop 2004; Kennett 2008). As Sassen (2004) argues, the realm of the national and the realm of the global are not two mutually exclusive domains. The state is neither an autonomous actor constrained only by the structural anarchy of the international order, nor is it being dismissed as irrelevant in the context of the emergence of a new cosmopolitanism. Drawing on Robertson's (1995) earlier work, Holton (2008) refers to "methodological glocalism" as a way of "retaining a sense of the significance of nation-states and institutions whilst also incorporating transnational processes in the global field" (p. 46). Rather than a single nested scalar hierarchy, Brenner (2001) refers to "a mosaic of unevenly superimposed and densely interlayered scalar geometries" (p. 606). For Holton (2008), the global and the national are co-present, and interact and intersect in a range of ways. According to Held (2000), we are witnessing a new regime of government and governance "which is displacing traditional conceptions of state power as an indivisible, territorially exclusive form of power". Far from globalization leading to "the end of the state", it is stimulating a range of government and governance strategies, a more activist state (Held 2000: 422), and in some fundamental ways a new public governance.

The shaping of global governance

The idea of transnationalism and a transnational sphere of social action has emerged as a major way of understanding globalization and generally refers to a range of phenomena that are seen as transcending the boundaries or sovereignty of nation-states, such as the growth of transnational corporations and the globalization of production, the emergence of a capital class and new social movements. The proliferation of NGOs, and their increasing visibility in world politics and policy, has generated powerful debate at a time when traditional, nationally based channels of participation have been in decline. For Lipschutz (1992), an increasing role for civil society in the global arena "represents an ongoing project of civil society to reconstruct, reimagine, or re-map world politics" (p. 291).

The shift to the globalization of production and finance represented a new social structure of production and power relations (Cox 2004), and an international institutional structure that, according to Wilkin (2000), conformed "to the political-economic interests of, broadly speaking, the G7 core capitalist states and their corporations" (p. 22). The emergence of this new social structure of production and power relations has been sustained through a dominant-rationalist-knowledge structure (Cox 1987) through which "the activities of transnational corporations, transnational investment, global restructuring and the creation of global markets have been legitimized by dominant discourses of globalization, modernization, and social progress" (Steans 2004: 30). Rosenau (1990) refers to the increasing relevance of private "sovereignty-free actors", multi-national corporations, transnational societies, and international governmental and nongovernmental organizations. The United Nations Global Compact Initiative, for example, embraces and further promotes these developments through an ambitious example of global cooperation among private companies, governments, multi-lateral organizations and NGOs (Woods 2003), with over 4,700 corporate participants and stakeholders from over 130 countries. Actors from all sectors are brought together to "advocate and promulgate" ten core principles drawn from the Universal Declaration of Human Rights, the ILO's Fundamental Principles on Rights and Work, the Rio Principle on Environment and Development, and the United Nations Convention Against Corruption. It seeks to promote these core values through the "development, implementation, and disclosure of environmental, social and governance policies and practices" (http://www.unglobalcompact.org).

However, as Sholte (2000) appropriately points out, it is the IFIs, the World Trade Organisation, and the OECD which have overshadowed agencies such as the ILO and UNESCO on questions of managing globalization. The dominance of market-driven approaches to stimulate growth and competitiveness has, according to Wilkinson (2005), "recast transnational corporations into mobilisers of capital, generators of technology and legitimate international actors with a part to play in an emerging system of global governance" (p. 37). This is evident in the development of the World Economic Forum (WEF), "which brought together the top representatives of transnational corporations and global political elites" (Robinson and Harris 2000) and the Transatlantic Business Dialogue (TABD) (Farnsworth 2008).

The economic crisis of the 1970s had already increased dependence of many countries on international financial institutions such as the IMF and the World Bank, and by the 1980s the expansion of capitalist markets and the deregulation of financial markets, and the undermining of Keynesian demand management and the "industrial settlement" established in many older Western nations marked the emergence of the political, ideological and institutional context of globalization. Consumer sovereignty was promoted and implemented through monetarism, the minimal state and new public management, and through notions of contract and choice. Pierre (2000) refers to these developments in Western democracies during the 1980s as representing a challenge to the state "from within" as the institutional arrangements, industrial settlement and citizenship regime of the postwar era were perceived as the sources of poor economic performance, and barriers and impediments to effective competition within states and in the increasingly important international markets. The neo-liberal agenda, which had had little influence, increasingly took center stage, expanding from its initial stronghold of Chile, to Great Britain and the United States, becoming the focal point around which the logics of transnational diffusion were articulated.

An essential ingredient in establishing and legitimating the political, ideological and institutional context was the rise of "economism". For Kay (2008), the ascendancy of economic modes of thinking has been a key aspect of new governance structures and has impacted on the way that governance is constructed and practiced. He uses the term "economism" to refer to "governance structures where economic logic or economically inspired advice is institutionally embedded, normalized and held as necessary in the determination of policy choices" (p. 19). Carriers and channels of diffusion include organizational carriers such as the International Monetary Fund, the World Bank and the World Trade Organisation, as well as private firms and multinational corporations. These classical organizations have played a significant part in the global spread of neo-liberalism, and more recently good governance and active citizenship, as the "fracturing of economic consensus" (Thirkell-White 2007) has seen a shift from the discursive neo-liberalism and market fundamentalism of the 1980s to one of "inclusive neo-liberalism" (Porter and Craig 2004).

By the 1990s, governance and the context of diffusion was changing as neo-liberal fundamentalism, new public management and global institutions were being called into question by civil society and national governments. Concerns began to emerge regarding the lack of accountability and transparency, the democratic deficit, the negative impact of IFI's strategies and policies, particularly for people in less developed and emerging societies, and fragmentation in policy and provision resulting from the implementation of the New Public Management. In the national arena, particularly in Great Britain, Germany and the USA, the changing political landscape saw the emergence of "Third Way" politics (Giddens 1994) and the "Communitarian Turn", the central themes of which included participative governance and public deliberation as well as "joined-up government" and interorganizational collaboration to address the diverse needs of the public. This was supported by a discourse and policy agenda promoting active citizenship, decentralization, local participation, self-help and partnership, and the development of new forms of governance.

The transnational business, political and intellectual elite, consisting of "globalizing bureaucrats, politicians, and professionals" as well as consumer elites from the media and commercial sectors, and chief executives of transnational corporations (Sklair 1995, 1998), has played a key role in transforming, strengthening and shaping the political and economic dimensions of international institutions and networks. Thus, the global elite as well as hierarchical forms of global governance have been important conveyors of ideational norms and practices, discussed later in this chapter. In addition, as Robinson and Harris (2000) argue, "Studies on building a global economy and transnational management structures flowed out of think tanks, university centres, and policy planning institutes in core countries" (Robinson and Harris 2000) and have been particularly successful in promoting a neo-liberal rationality (Cammack 2008) cohering around the themes of market liberalization, culminating in the well-known package of policy measures referred to as the "Washington Consensus" in the 1990s and, more recently, the "Post-Washington Consensus", one of the cornerstones of which has been "good governance".

Global governance as a multi-actor perspective

Globalization and governance are interconnected dialectically in terms of scale (Brenner 2001), form, process and practice. Integrating the concepts analytically facilitates an understanding of the changing relations of space and power (Macrae 2006: 52), and the ways in which power penetrates the spaces, processes and practices of governance. As Newman (2005) explains, "the image of a hierarchical relationship between state and citizenry . . . is displaced by the idea of multiple parallel spaces in which power is encountered and negotiated" (p. 4). Exploring the context, dynamics and discourse in and through which global governance has emerged and evolved highlights the relationship and interaction between different spatial scales and various actors and institutions.

The concept of global governance engages with a multi-actor perspective and embraces a plurality of mechanisms that horizontally and vertically link the activities of various actors such as politicians, civil servants, international governmental organization committees and representatives, interest group and non-governmental organization representatives, and experts (Dingwerth and Pattberg 2006; Kennett 2008). For Kooiman (1993), the concepts of diversity, dynamics and complexity are central features of governance itself. The socio-political system is increasingly differentiated, characterized by multiple centers, and is one in which "Actors are continuously shaped by (and in) the interactions, in which they relate to each other" (Kooiman 2003: 2). Kooiman (2003) argues that it is the role of government to enable interactions, encourage many and varied arrangements for coping with policy, and ensure equitable distribution of services between actors through self- and co-regulation and public–private partnerships, or what Kooiman calls "types of societal interactions" and "modes and orders of governance". However, for Kooiman, no single governing agency is able to realize legitimate and effective governing:

> No single actor, public or private, has all knowledge and information required to solve complex, dynamic and diversified problems; no actor has sufficient overview to make the application of needed instruments effective; no single actor has sufficient action potential to dominate unilaterally in a particular governing model.
>
> (Kooiman 1993: 4)

Thus, there has been a shift from direct forms of governance to a process of governance exercised through a plurality of actors, sites, spatial scales, and processes, with an increasing reliance by governments on informal forms of power and influence rather than on formal authority.

Within this "differentiated polity", a new form of coordination is required which, according to Rhodes (1997), emerges through networks. Within increasingly complex multi-level global governance, these networks, involving a more diverse range of actors, have become increasingly influential. Stone refers to the multiple and varied transnational policy spaces where global public policies occur as "agora" (Stone 2008). The term is drawn from Greek history and refers to "a marketplace or a public square", a place for social, political and economic interaction, where borders are ill-defined and fluid, which Stone (2008) equates with the relationship between the commercial and the public domain in the modern global era. According to Stone, utilizing the idea of the agora is useful

> to identify a growing global public space of fluid, dynamic, and intermeshed relations of politics, markets, culture, and society. This public space is shaped by the interactions of its actors – that is multiple publics and plural institutions.
>
> (Stone 2008: 21)

According to Ruggie (2004), "the very system of states is becoming embedded in a broader, albeit still thin and partial, institutionalized arena concerned with the production of global public goods" (p. 500), or what Yeates (2008) refers to as "embedded transnationalism". National public domains of countries have become more interlocked, and essentially nationally provided public goods have become "globalized", such as financial codes and standards, human rights, labor standards and health (SARS and HIV) (Kaul et al. 2003; Kaul 2005). The increasingly transnational character of a range of policy issues has, according to Stone (2004), provided the rationales for "research collaboration, sharing information and co-operation on other activities that creates a dynamic for the international diffusion of ideas and policy transfer" (p. 38). Processes of interaction among the various actors in international politics are now more frequent and intense, giving rise to what Ladeur (2004) refers to as "flexible institutions" (p. 5) taking place beyond the state. These "flexible institutions" have become increasingly influential in the global arena, in contrast to the Westphalian international system whereby, as Ruggie (2004) points out, the public domain was constituted by states that were "the decision-makers and executors of their joint decisions and actions, which were authoritative to the extent they were so recognized by states" (p. 505). The hierarchical international institutional architecture enshrined within the Bretton Woods system established after World War II comprised territorially distinct units engaging in "external" transactions.

As Holton (2008) argues, networks have become a characteristic mode through which the transnational is organized. Thus, a crucial element of global governance is the shift from markets and hierarchies toward networks and partnerships as modes of coordination (Marsh and Smith 2000), involved not only in influencing policy decisions but also in the business of government itself. Both the scope and the intensity of global networks have expanded rapidly since the mid-1980s. Holton (2008) describes networks as "forms of multi-social organisation that are distinct from . . . Markets and hierarchies" (p. 4), involving more enduring forms of social commitment and trust than markets, but more flexible and less centralized than hierarchies. Global hierarchies are seen as undemocratic and remote, whilst markets are unable to respond adequately to the new environment.

Transnational governance is characterized by a move toward non-binding "soft" rules such as standards and guidelines, benchmarking and monitoring, in contrast to the Westphalian world where rule-making was expressed in "hard laws". Djelic (2006) argues that compliance is increasingly reliant on societalization, acculturation, and normative pressures, access to membership and resources as well as with the threat of sanction and through mechanisms of conditionality. In this context, social interaction through "various forms of direct interface and exchange that often takes place within and across social networks" (Djelic 2006: 70) has become an influential carrier of diffusion logics, as structuration and socialization processes define the rules of the game and "reflect a particular ideology and associated practices" through which normative and symbolic systems, rules and ideological frames are established shaping behavior and interaction. As Scott (2003) argues, carriers are not neutral vehicles "but mechanisms that significantly influence the nature of the elements they transmit and the reception they receive" (p. 879). Nor are they bounded and self-contained entities, but overlapping and multi-scalar. As MacRae (2006) argues, scales are not fixed but are both fluid and interconnected in terms of processes and actors. Agents do not act only within their respective policy spaces, and are therefore not confined to a singular role and identity and a singular spatial scale. The European Union, for example, provides opportunities for domestic actors in the policy process and vice versa. Transfer does not simply occur in a unilinear hierarchical process from supranational to national to subnational but is ongoing and multidirectional, and spatial scales are perceived as "overlapping areas of policy, norms, values, power relations, and social interaction, where actors are not confined to a single scale" (p. 528).

Within the transnational policy community, Stone (2008) identifies three types of "carriers of global policy processes involved in the diffusion of ideas, standards, and policy practice" (p. 30). The "internationalised public sector official" operates in transnational executive networks. These are individuals who derive their authority from their official positions within their nation-state. The "international civil servant" is employed by an international organization and, in theory, is impartial and non-partisan. However, the role of these actors in terms of innovation and implementation in global policy is difficult to discern, but where national interests continue to be pursued these individuals have "considerable capacity to shape (or delay) policies because of their expertise, routines, and positions of power" (Stone 2008: 30). The "transnational policy professionals" represent the growing community of consultants, business leaders, scientific experts, NGO executives whose network or association is often receiving public funding. These groups of actors interact within and across a range of policy networks, often playing different roles at different spatial scales, contributing to what Ladeur refers to as the "broadening of the perspective of the participants through the commonality of interchanging roles" (Ladeur 2004: 5). Thus, different types of networks may overlap in both functions and activity, intensifying the diffusion of policy and discourse.

The limits to global governance

Global governance implies that, through various structures and processes, actors can coordinate interests and needs through multi-centered structures and processes that are flexible and appropriate for achieving policy objectives and responding to policy issues on a global scale. However, there is no one mode of decision-making within the international arena, and indeed the trend is toward an increasing fragmentation of governance architecture. Stone (2008) points out that this can lead to a "policy vacuum" in relation to the "ownership" of public problems and the delegation of responsibility.

Global environmental governance, for example, has grown "tremendously and uncontrollably", with some 500 international agreements that now influence the governance of environmental problems. The proliferation of multilateral environmental agreements, the development of a substantial body of international law, and the creation and diffusion of norms have few equivalents in other areas of global governance (Green and Thouez 2005). However, some critics argue that the "crazy quilt" (Charnovitz 2005) of global environmental governance has become "unmanageable in size and intractable in its complexity" (Green and Thouez 2005: 4).

Also evident is the creation of a growing body of international law concerned with the protection and enforcement of human rights. There are at least twenty-nine international conventions and declarations related to discrimination, including United Nations conventions on basic universal human rights and rights of excluded groups such as women, children and racial/ethnic minorities, as well as International Labour Organisation (ILO) conventions on the rights of workers, and declarations on race and racial prejudices (Marquez et al. 2009). As Spiro (2002: 3) argues:

> International law in general is assuming greater consequentiality as a determinant of state behaviour. States are increasingly willing to pass human rights agendas against other states, even in the absence of geopolitical gains; and non-state actors, and interested publics, now garner power independent of states with which to advance compliance with international law.

However, it is still the case that the acts of states feature centrally in how the human rights issues impact and are played out. The country of which you are a citizen must be a signatory of the particular treaty. Most human rights conventions within the UN system do not create legally enforceable binding obligations which individuals can impose on states. Mechanisms for protection and enforcement take the shape of progress reports by country governments, international conventions and meetings. Indeed, although a state might be a signatory to the various human rights conventions, ratification is permitted subject to reservations – for example on the ground that national law, tradition, religion or culture are not congruent with convention principles. The Convention on the Elimination of All Forms of Discrimination against Women (CEDAW) adopted in 1979 by the UN General Assembly has been particularly controversial, as the extended list of country declarations, reservations and objections to CEDAW indicates. According to the UN Department of Economic and Social affairs, "Some reservations are drawn so widely that their effect cannot be limited to specific provision in the Convention" (www.un.org/womenwatch/daw/cedaw/reservations.htm). Whilst national governments have been increasingly willing to sign up to international conventions and treaties, albeit with numerous reservations, there is still a reticence not only to recognize the precise obligations that they have assumed in terms of social rights, but also to extend and strengthen the international human rights framework (Novitz 2008).

The global arena is a highly contested terrain, and fraught with asymmetries of power and tensions around particular policy issues. Brenner (2001) refers to a "kaleidoscope effect" to refer to the qualitative differences in the organization of scalar patterns and the nature of interaction at different spatial scales across policy areas. There are also problems relating to the implementation of public policy in a global context when both formal and informal institutions of global governance often "lack both the authority and the means to enforce policy compliance" (Stone 2008: 27).

More recent concerns have emerged around the legitimacy, representativeness and effectiveness of the IFIs, and the inadequacies of global financial governance and regulation in the context of the meltdown of global financial markets and economic recession. Although these concerns were initially highlighted following the Asian Financial Crisis, only limited reform was enacted and, indeed, the role of international and supranational organizations was enhanced through the provision of financial and technical assistance. During the current economic recession, the IMF has had an opportunity to reassert its role in the international economy in terms of immediate crisis management and with the long-term reform of the international financial system. At the time of writing, the IMF has agreed a $2.1 billion two-year loan with Iceland, a $16.5 billion agreement with Ukraine and a $15.7 billion loan to Hungary. Other countries are currently negotiating potential loans from the IMF. The International Finance Corporation (IFC), the private-sector lending arm of the World Bank, has also announced that it will launch a $3 million fund to capitalize small banks in poor countries that are battered by the financial crisis.

In terms of internal reform, the IMF allocates a country quota to each member based on the relative size of its economy. This determines the country's financial contribution to the IMF, its voting power, and ability to access IMF financing. A two-year reform programme of the system of quota shares was introduced in 2006 to address their unfair, "misaligned" (IMF 2008) distribution and to increase the voting share of emerging market and developing economies: 135 countries will see increases in their voting power, with an aggregate shift of 5.4 percentage points (Figures 2.1 and 2.2).

Another central element of the reform package has been the attempt to increase "the voice of low-income countries" through an increase in basic votes. Basic votes are provided to all members on an equal basis. The agreement reached endorsed a tripling of basic votes, the first such increase since the IMF was established in 1945. Additionally, the Articles of Agreement will be amended so that the share of basic votes in total voting power does not decline in the event of future quota increases. However, in spite of reforms and financial assistance, the question of whether or not these key institutions are "fit for purpose" was raised at the first international summit on the financial crisis held in November 2008. Issues to be addressed included the reform of the global financial architecture, strengthening coordination, consistency and quality among actors and regulatory standards, and increasing regulation and transparency of financial instruments and institutions. One

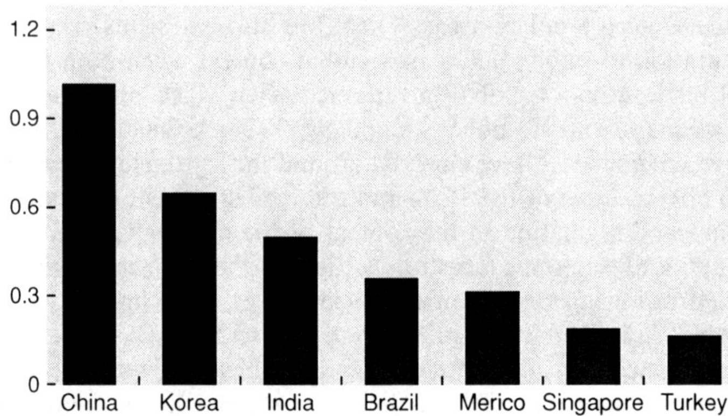

Figure 2.1 Who gains?
Source: IMF, Finance Department.

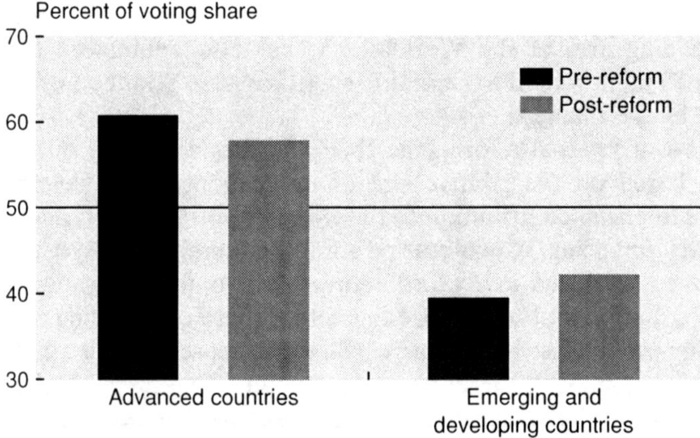

Figure 2.2 Shift in voting power toward developing countries.
Source: IMF, Finance Department.

of the major goals was to begin to improve coordination at global level, review the role of international institutions in financial market surveillance and to adjust global governance structures for the future. A major overhaul of the international institutions based on the key principles of efficiency, transparency and accountability, and representation was considered essential.

Whilst international and supranational institutions have a role to play in this current economic crisis, it has also revealed their limitations and the necessity for reform and improved international coordination. Although the European Union has been slow to react, governments in Europe and beyond have shown an increasing willingness to intervene in their economies. It is national governments who have been the key players in the "socialization of losses" (UNCTAD 2008) as "the threat of a meltdown has brought governments back onto centre stage" (p. 1). The US administration instituted a $700 billion bailout in October 2008, and the US Senate accepted a further economic stimulus of around $900 billion in January 2009 (News Daily 2009). In the UK a second bank-rescue package totaling at least £50 million was also announced in January 2009. Whether or not this increased enthusiasm shown by national governments for intervention can be characterized as the end of the neo-liberal consensus and a resurgence of Keynesianism, as some suggest, only time will tell as norms, procedures, practices and discourses of governance are developed and diffused across different spatial scales and policy fora. What is clear, however, is that national governments have recognized that, in a global world, national bailouts alone are inadequate strategies not only for addressing the current crisis but also for promoting sustainable, equitable and more effective new public governance.

Conclusion

Internationalization is not a new phenomenon, but over the last thirty years the nature and scope of transnational links and networks have broadened and intensified. Governance in a global world is being shaped and reshaped in constellations of public and private actors that include states, international and regional organizations, professional associations, expert groups, civil society groups and business corporations. New political structures and policy spaces beyond the state have multiplied as new issues arise and networks of actors mobilize to be involved. Innovative layers of governance, strategies of operation have emerged, along with new technologies of governance.

Regulation has increasingly shifted from the national level to policy levels beyond the state, but this is not an indication of the demise of the state. The shaping of global governance has often occurred as a result of state encouragement or, as Thompson (2003) puts it, "under the shadow" of either hierarchy of market. As Jessop (2004) argues, there is still substantial scope for the reconstituted state "to mediate between the increasing numbers of significant scales of action" (p. 18). However, within the differentiated myriad of networks of formal and informal institutions the increasing involvement of non-state actors in norm- and rule-making processes, and compliance monitoring, confirms the arrival of a global public governance.

Contemporary global public governance is a complex, fragmented, unstable and highly contested arena. However, rather than anarchic and unruly, it is framed through norms, practices and discourses which are shaped, stabilize and change over time. As Isin and Wood (1999) point out, late modernity cannot be associated only with fragmentation and disruption but also with the emergence of new social movements and of "numerous social, political, cultural and social groups in search of new kinds of identification, politicization and solidarity" (p. 154). Governance in a global age is characterized by novel fora and channels for participation and resistance as well as by new forms of stratification and exclusion. There are different conduits and spatial scales through which nations and peoples are enmeshed in the global arenas, rights and claims expressed. In the context of an established yet still evolving globalization and governance architecture, new forms of politics, representation and layers of governance are emerging, both internationally and locally, constituting multi-layered public governance.

References

Biersteker, T. J. (1998) "Globalization and the Modes of Operation of Major Institutional Actors", *Oxford Development Studies*, 26 (1): 15–32.

Brenner, N. (2001) "The Limits to Scale? Methodological Reflections on Scalar Structuration", *Progress in Human Geography*, 25 (4): 591–614.

Cammack, P. (2008) "Poverty Policy and the Politics of Competitiveness", in P. Kennett (ed.) *Governance, Globalization and Public Policy*, Cheltenham: Edward Elgar.

Charnovitz, S. (2005) "A World Environment Organization", in W. B. Chambers and J. F. Green (eds) *Reforming International Environmental Governance: From Institutional Limits to Innovative Reforms*, Tokyo: UNU Press.

Cox, K. R. (2004) "Globalization, the Class Relation and Democracy", *GeoJournal*, 60: 31–44.

Daly, M. (2003) "Governance and Social Policy", *Journal of Social Policy*, 32 (1): 113–28.

Dingwerth, K. and Pattberg, P. (2006) "Global Governance as a Perspective on World Politics", *Global Governance*, 12: 185–203.

Djelic, M.-L. (2006) "Marketization: From Intellectual Agenda to Global Policy Making", in M.-L. Djelic and K. Sahlin-Andersson (eds) *Transnational Governance: Institutional Dynamics of Regulation*, Cambridge: Cambridge University Press.

Farnsworth, K. (2008) "Governance, Business and Social Policy", in P. Kennett (ed.) *The Handbook of Comparative Social Policy*, Cheltenham: Edward Elgar.

Giddens, A. (1994) *Beyond Left and Right,* Cambridge: Polity Press.

Giddens, A. (1999) *Runaway World: How Globalization Is Reshaping Our Lives*, London: Profile Books.

Green, J. F. and Thouez, C. (2005) *Global Governance for Migration and the Environment: What Can We Learn from Each Other?*, Global Migration Perspectives No. 46, Geneva: Global Commission on International Migration.

Held, D. (2002) Regulating Globalization? In Held, D. and McGrew, A. (eds) *The Global Transformations Reader*, Cambridge: Polity Press.

Held, D. and McGrew, A. (2000) *The Global Transformations Reader*, Cambridge: Polity Press.

Held, D. and McGrew, A. (2002) *Governing Globalization*, Oxford: Polity Press.

Holton, R. J. (2008) *Global Networks*, Basingstoke: Palgrave Macmillan.

International Monetary Fund (2008) "Governance: Country Representation", http://www.imf.org/external/about/govrep.htm [accessed 9 December 2008].

IPES (2008) Outsiders? The Changing Patterns of Exclusion in Latin America and The Caribbean. 2008 Report Inter-American Development Bank.

Isin, G. E. and Wood, K. P. (1999) *Citizenship and Identity*, London: Sage.

Jessop, B. (2004) "Hollowing out the 'Nation State' and Multi-level Governance", in P. Kennett (ed.) *A Handbook of Comparative Social Policy*, Cheltenham: Edward Elgar.

Kaul, I., Conceicao, P., Le Goulven, K. and Mendoza, R. U. (2003) (eds) *Providing Global Public Goods; Managing Globalization*, New York: Oxford University Press.

Kaul, I. (2005) "Private Provision and Global Public Goods: Do the Two Go Together?", *Global Social Policy*.

Kay, A. (2008) "Economism and Public Policy", in P. Kennett (ed.) *Governance, Globalization and Public Policy*, Cheltenham: Edward Elgar.

Kennett, P. (2008) "Governance, the State and Public Policy in a Global Age", in P. Kennett (ed.) *Governance, Globalization and Public Policy*, Cheltenham: Edward Elgar.

Kjaer, A. M. (2004) *Governance*, Cambridge: Polity Press.

Koenig-Archibugi, M. (2003) "Global Governance", in J. Mitchie (ed.) *The Handbook of Globalisation*, Cheltenham: Edward Elgar.

Kooiman, J. (1993) "Social–political Governance", in J. Kooiman (ed.) *Modern Governance*, London: Sage.

Kooiman, J. (2003) *Governing as Governance*, London: Sage.

Krahmann, E. (2003) "National, Regional, and Global Governance: One Phenomenon or Many?", *Global Governance*, 9: 323–46.

Ladeur, K.-H. (ed.) (2004) *Public Governance in the Age of Globalization*, Aldershot: Ashgate.

Lieberthal, K. (1995) *Governing China: From Revolution through Reform*, New York: W. W. Norton.

Lipschutz, I. (1992) "Reconstructing World Politics: The Emergence of Global Civil Society", *Millennium*, 21 (3): 300–420.

Macrae, H. (2006) "Rescaling Gender Relations: The Influence of European Directives on the German Gender Regime", *Social Politics: International Studies in Gender, State and Society*, 13 (4): 522–50.

Marsh, D. and Smith, J. J. (2000) "Understanding Policy Networks: Towards a Dialectical Approach", *Political Studies*, 48: 4–21.

Marquez, G., Chong, A., Duryea, S., Mazza, J., and Noro, H. (2009) *2008 Report. Outsiders? The Changing Patterns of Exclusion in Latin America and the Caribbean* Inter-American Development Bank, Washington, USA.

News Daily (2009) "Government Add to Rescue Plan", www.newsdaily.com.tre467me-us-financial/ [accessed 28 January 2009].

Newman, J. (ed.) (2005) *Remaking Governance: Peoples, Politics and the Public Sphere*, Bristol: Policy Press.

Novitz, T. (2008) "International Law and Human Rights in the Context of Globalization", in P. Kennett (ed.) *Governance, Globalization and Public Policy*, Cheltenham: Edward Elgar.

Pierre, J. (ed.) (2000) *Debating Governance: Authority, Steering, and Democracy*, Oxford: Oxford University Press.

Porter, D. and Craig, D. (2004) "The Third Way and the Third World: Poverty Reduction and Social Inclusion in the Rise of 'Inclusive' Liberalism", *Review of International Political Economy*, 11 (2): 387–423.

Rhodes, R. A. W. (1996) "The New Governance: Governing without Government", *Political Studies*, 44: 652–67.

Rhodes, R. A. W. (1997) *Understanding Governance: Policy Networks, Governance, Reflexivity and Accountability*, Buckingham: Open University Press.

Robertson, R. (1995) "Glocalization, Time-space and Homogeneity", in M. Featherstone, S. Lash and R. Robertson (eds) *Global Modernities*, London: Sage.

Robinson, W. I. and Harris, J. (2000) "Towards a Global Ruling Glass? Globalization and the Transnational Capitalist Class", *Science and Society*, 64 (1): 11–54.

Rosenau, J. (1990) *Turbulence in World Politics: A Theory of Change and Continuity*, Princeton, NJ: Princeton University Press.

Rosenau, J. N. (1995) "Governance in the 21st Century", *Global Governance*, 1 (11): 13–43.

Rosenau, J. N. and Czempiel, E.-O. (eds) (1992) *Governance without Government: Order and Change in World Politics*, Cambridge: Cambridge University Press.

Ruggie, J. (2004) "Reconstituting the Global Public Domain: Issues, Actors and Practices", *European Journal of International Relations*, 10 (4): 499–531.

Sassen. S. (2004) "De-nationalized State Agendas and Privatized Norm-making", in Ladeur, K.-H. (ed.) *Public Governance in the Age of Globalization*, Aldershot: Ashgate.

Scholte, J. A. (2000) *Globalization: A Critical Introduction*, Basingstoke: Palgrave Macmillan.

Scott, W. R. (2003) "Institutional Carriers: Reviewing Modes of Transporting Ideas over Time and Space and Considering Their Consequences", *Industrial and Corporate Change*, 12 (4): 879–94.

Sklair, L. (1995) *Globalization and World Society*, Cambridge: Polity Press.

Sklair, L. (1998) "Globalization and the Corporations: The Case of the California Fortune 500", *International Journal of Urban and Regional Research*, 22 (2): 195–215.

Spiro, P. J. (2002) "Mandated Membership, Diluted Identity: Citizenship, Globalization, and International Law. Available at SSRN: http://ssrn.com/abstract = 322360 [accessed on 28 April 2008].

Steans, J. (2004) "Globalization, the State and Welfare: Gendering the Debate", in P. Kennett (ed.) *Handbook of Comparative Social Policy*, Cheltenham: Edward Elgar.

Stoker, G. (1998) "Governance as Theory: Five Propositions", *International Social Science Journal*, 50 (155): 17–28.

Stone, D. (2004) "Think Tanks beyond Nation States", in D. Stone and A. Denham (eds) *Think Tank Tradition: Policy Research and the Politics of Ideas*, Manchester: Manchester University Press.

Stone, S. (2008) "Global Public Policy, Transnational Policy Communities, and Their Networks", *The Policy Studies Journal*, 36 (1): 19–38.

Swyngedouw, E. (2005) "Governance Innovation and the Citizen: The Janus Face of Governance-beyond-the-state", *Urban Studies*, 32 (11): 1991–2006.

Thirkell-White, B. (2007) "The International Financial Architecture and the Limits to Neoliberal Hegemony", *New Political Economy*, 12 (1): 19–41.
Thompson, G. (2003) *Between Hierarchies and Markets: The Logic and Limits of Network Forms of Organisation*, Oxford: Oxford University Press.
UNCTAD (2008) "The 'Crisis of a Century' . . .", *Policy Brief*, no. 3, October, Geneva.
Weiss, L. (2005) "The State-augmenting Effects of Globalization", *New Political Economy*, 10 (3): 345–53.
Wilkin, P. (2000) "Solidarity in a Global Age – Seattle and Beyond", *Journal of World Systems Research*, VI, 1 (200): 20–65.
Wilkinson, R. (2005) "The Commission on Global Governance in a New World", in R. Wilkinson (ed.) *The Global Governance Reader*, London: Routledge.
Woods, N. (2003) "Global Governance and the Role of Institutions", in D. Held and A. McGrew (eds) *Governing Globalization: Power, Authority and Global Governance*, London: Polity Press.
Yeates, N. (2008) *Understanding Global Social Policy*, Bristol: The Policy Press.

3

META-GOVERNANCE AND PUBLIC MANAGEMENT

B. Guy Peters

The reforms that have been implemented in the public sector over the past several decades have had a very wide range of motivations, and have had an equally wide range of consequences for the public sector for the citizens of the countries in which they are being implemented. In almost any country one can identify, the public sector is now significantly different from that which was to be found several decades ago, and indeed in some cases the public bureaucracy would be hardly recognizable to civil servants who had previously worked in government. The idea of many political leaders has been that the bureaucracy was the problem, not the solution, and that fundamental changes were required.

What is clear in all this change is that the traditional public sector is no longer the model of first and last recourse for individuals responsible for governing. The traditional model of bureaucratic governance involved a range of assumptions about how to govern, although the traditions of governing were not the same in all countries. Walsh and Stewart (1992), for example, described that mode of governance for the United Kingdom. This model emphasized the autonomy of the public sector, the separation of public-sector employment from the private sector, and hierarchical authority within the administrative system. Other administrative systems, such as in France and Germany, emphasized that hierarchical control perhaps even more, but also accepted closer relationships between the administrative system and the civil society, and political parties.

This chapter will first describe, if briefly, the changes that have been implemented in governing over these past decades.[1] This description will argue that, although there are different styles of reform, the fundamental consequence of these reforms has been to move governing out of the center of the conventional, politically driven public sector and to empower a range of actors including (but not limited to) senior public servants, lower-echelon public employees, and members of civil society. The rhetoric and the reality of governing were transformed in this process, and many conventional styles of governing were delegitimated.

These reforms, however, have produced a number of significant problems in governance that I shall detail. Finally, I shall argue that there is an emerging style of governing from the center that can be described as meta-governance (see Sorenson 2006). It recognizes the need for some delegation and devolution of governing but at the same time recognizes the need for greater central direction. This paper will take the classic newspaper reporter's approach, and ask "Who, What, Where and Why" about meta-governance, and especially about meta-governance directed at devolved public organizations and to networks. Meuleman (2008) and others have also documented the need to consider meta-governance of more conventional components of the governance process, but I shall focus more on the rather recent changes in the administrative process. Further, I shall invest more time and space in explaining the "why" of creating meta-governance, given that this aspect of the story being told here is crucial for understanding the choices being made by politicians and by public servants.

What is meta-governance?

I shall be using the term "meta-governance" to describe the process of steering devolved governance processes. In other terms, it is the "governance of governance". The notion of meta-governance is that a number of organizations and processes within the public sector have attained a substantial degree of autonomy – a condition often described as governance – and that there may be a need to impose some control over those components of governing. As argued below, the changes within the public sector during the past several decades have been a major source of the perceived need for meta-governance; but in some cases, e.g. the United States (Carpenter 2001), there have been significant requirements for meta-governance within the political system for some time.

Whether the administrative process has been altered because of the acceptance of managerialist reforms or because of more participatory styles of governing is largely irrelevant; the real or perceived requirement for meta-governance will be roughly the same. That requirement will be to provide direction to the administrative system, but to do so through mechanisms that maintain the virtues that have been produced by delegated and devolved forms of governing, while providing central direction and control. Governing has always involved some balancing of control and autonomy for public organizations, and for individual public servants, but that balance becomes more apparent when decisions must be made about reasserting greater management controls over devolved systems.

As governance has become of much greater importance in the academic literature on the public sector, as well as in the real world of governing, scholars have begun to develop the concept of meta-governance. For example, Louis Meuleman (2008) has provided the most extensive discussion of the concept of meta-governance now available, focusing on its relationship to the three conventional modes of governance: hierarchies, markets and networks. Bob Jessop (2002; see also Bell and Park 2006) has also provided a series of discussions of meta-governance, focusing attention on governance failures and the need to develop strategies for coping with those failures. Also, Sorenson (2006) has emphasized the need to reassert political controls over the devolved governance processes.

The available literature does an adequate job of developing the concept of meta-governance, but has been less effective in examining the instruments that may be available for providing the steering needed. To some extent, the instruments available to would-be meta-governors are much the same as those available to any actor available in the public sector, that range of instruments described by Christopher Hood (1976) as NATO (nodality, authority, treasure and organization). These tools are almost entirely generic, so may be adapted to cope with the meta-governance requirements, but they do not provide any specific analytic advantage for understanding the issues. The logic of the tools of the "new governance", as described by Salamon (2001), are more closely aligned with the needs for meta-governance, but still do not provide specific assistance for meta-governance.

The particular issue differentiating instruments for meta-governance from other instruments for governing is that these "tools" are directed at the internal control of the public sector itself, rather than at influencing the economy and society. While much of the same logic is involved, there may be some important differences as well. In particular, when attempting to impose controls over organizations within government itself there is an implicit, or explicit, understanding that those organizations should accept the authority of the controllers. This assumption may be incorrect, and many public organizations do attempt to evade authority, but the "shadow of hierarchy" is clearly darker within government than without.

Finally, meta-governance can be conceptualized as directed at controlling the environment of action in the public sector, rather than controlling that action directly. Theodore Lowi (1972), for example, argued that controlling the environment of action could be used more generally to classify public policies.[2] Further, if the would-be governor is faced with difficult more-control situations, attempting to frame action indirectly may be the most effective manner of governing. For example, regulations tend to shape the environment of public action, as has been further elaborated through regulation theory (Scott 2004).

Reforms: toward the decentered state

The numerous and varied reforms in the developed democracies are difficult to summarize, but in this chapter I shall focus on two of the more important strands of change (see also Peters 2001). As already noted, these two versions of reform have tended to move the public sector away from the more or less bureaucratic nature of governing. They both attempt to find ways of involving a wider range of actors – from the market and from civil society – in the processes of governing. These transformations, unlike many other attempts at reform in the past, involve a clear theory of governing and of the public sector, and are also more coherent than many previous attempts at reform. That said, there are several alternative conceptions which have some common elements but which also have rather different assumptions about the way in which the public sector functions.

The most familiar of these reforms have been captured in the phrase New Public Management (NPM).[3] The basic idea of these reforms has been to transform the public sector so that it looks and acts a good deal more like the private sector. Hood (1991) and others (Christensen and Laegreid 2007) have pointed to a number of internal differences within NPM, although at the same time recognizing that there is some core to the patterns of change. The use of market principles within NPM has been conceptualized as a means of enhancing the efficiency and effectiveness of the public sector, by opening up the public sector to more competition and using more business-like instruments for management. That competition was to be from outside government as well as among organizations and employees within government.

As well as being an approach to management, the NPM is a theory of governing more generally. One of the fundamental arguments, if generally made implicitly, is that political domination of governing is likely to be inefficient and therefore governing will be improved if as many things as possible are removed from the hands of the political class. The tendency to move activities out of the center of government into agencies, and to use a variety of alternative service-delivery mechanisms, has tended to reduce the number of levers that political leaders can pull to achieve the results they desire, and the results they promised in elections. Those structural and procedural reforms, in turn, appear to have allowed managers to make more decisions about the content of policy as well as about its implementation.

The principal alternative to the NPM has been a series of participatory reforms designed to enable not only citizens but also lower-level public servants to have greater influence over policy and implementation. These reforms have been justified largely on democratic terms, in contrast to the efficiency and effectiveness associated with NPM. That said, a number of scholars of public administration, as well of organizations more generally, have argued that involving the lower echelons of organizations and members of civil society more directly in decisions provides more information about the actual functioning of programs.

One important extension of the participatory reforms has been the development of "governance"[4] as the means for delivering services, and often for deciding on policy, in a number of developed democracies. The logic of the governance reforms has been that the conventional hierarchical models of bureaucracy, and the conventional representative models of democracy, have become outmoded. The public appear to be losing faith in political parties and in elections (Dalton and Wattenberg 2000; Mair and van Biezen 2001), so that contemporary states are increasingly legitimated by their outputs rather than by the democratic processes that have in the past legitimated them. In addition, the bureaucratic processes through which governments have delivered public services are seen as clumsy, ineffective and unresponsive.

Those conventional models of governing have not recognized their own failures, nor the development of elements in the civil society that are capable of providing a substantial amount of self-steering in their own policy areas. As networks of social actors have come to take more responsibility for aspects of governing, the emergence of the concept, and the reality, of governance has meant that the state can be relieved of many of its more difficult tasks. Some scholars (Rhodes 2000) have made the extreme argument that societies can be governed almost entirely by self-organizing networks of social actors. Even in less extreme views, however, it is clear that social actors – interest groups, NGOs, and perhaps some individuals – are providing governance in a wide range of policy areas.

The governance argument, and again its reality, is not viable in all political systems. The heartland of this style of governing is Northern Europe, especially Scandinavia and the Low Countries, although there are notable examples from the United States (Milward and Provan 2000). The dichotomy between state and society in the Anglo-Saxon world has made this style of governing more problematic, and often the close relationship between the public sector and groups may be considered corruption. Further, in the less-developed world and in transitional regimes there may not be a civil society with sufficient strength to provide an alternative to formal governance through the public sector. Despite these caveats, there has been a sense that the basic logic of network governance has become ever more widely spread, in practice as well as in academic discourse.

The need for meta-governance

The reforms of the public sector associated with both NPM and "governance" have tended to produce a number of benefits but have also produced a number of unintended and largely negative consequences. These consequences tend to affect not only the management of public programs but also the political process itself. One can identify a wide range of problems arising from network governance, but I shall discuss only four of the more significant ones here: decision-making, coordination and accountability. Also, while I am discussing these problems as if they are self-evident, they may not be; and a good deal of the politics of contemporary network governing reflects attempts to overcome these issues.

Decision-making

The rather clumsy bureaucratic institutions associated with conventional governing do have their problems but they do have the capacity to make decisions. In representative democracy, majority rule and other constitutional conventions ensure that decisions can be made.[5] Likewise, implementation through public bureaucracies is done following legal constraints, so that again there can be decisions. These words of praise do not mean that the decisions taken are high-quality decisions, only that a decision can be made.

Making decisions in the networks associated with "governance" is not as easy as it is sometimes assumed to be. Unlike formal institutions, most networks, or other types of structures involving social actors in governing, do not have clear decision-rules. The implicit norms are to bargain to consensus, but that bargaining may produce decisions by the lowest common denominator (Scharpf 1988) unless there are other norms in place concerning checking one's self-interest at the door.[6] Without either *ex ante* rules or strong informal norms, governance is likely to produce no decisions, or relatively poor quality decisions. While the advocates of network governance may be excessively optimistic about the self-organizing nature of those structures, they do seek to provide an alternative to hierarchical control.

The above discussion of networks can be extended to include some market-oriented versions of service delivery associated with NPM. For example, contracts and public–private partnerships involve agreement among the parties involved, and can therefore result in no deal being struck, or in a deal being made that does not move much beyond the lowest common denominator. Further, part of the logic of NPM has been to infuse the public sector wth private-sector values, and therefore the decisions being made may not reflect as strong a sense of the public interest as might be desirable.[7] Again, to make these arrangements function in the public interest may require infusing them with values that go beyond the interests of the separate parties involved.

Participation

A major democratic issue involved in the development of governance through networks and other more informal mechanisms is simply whether democracy is actually advanced through mechanisms that are purportedly more democratic. Part of the logic of developing networks of social actors is that conventional representative democracy is failing as a means of translating public wishes into action. If nothing else, there is substantial evidence that public involvement with political parties and in conventional modes of participation has been declining markedly (Mair and van Biezen 2001). Further, networks are designed to involve more actors in processes of governing and also to involve them in governing on a more continuous basis, so that democracy is not just at election time.

Despite the problems inherent in representative democracy, it is not clear that networks will do that much better in representing social interests in governing. The network models of democracy depend upon the involvement of the full range of interests and individuals in society, but the very people who may be excluded from effective participation in representative institutions may also be excluded from participation in the networks. Being involved in a network for governance involves, at a minimum, some level of organization; and the socially excluded in societies are, almost by definition, those with minimal organizational skills. Even if somehow included in networks, those same people would have, on average, fewer persuasive skills and would, again on average, be less capable of influencing decisions.

Coordination

Governments have had difficulties in coordinating their activities as long as there have been governments. Individual organizations and programs pursue their own goals, often at the expense of broader goals for government as a whole. The absence of effective coordination in the public sector generally reduces the efficiency and effectiveness of public programs, and also enhances the familiar public perception of the incompetence of government. Further, a failure to coordinate effectively will produce lacunae, with some important public problems not being addressed adequately.

Although poor coordination is a familiar problem, it has been exacerbated by the reforms of the past several decades. For example, the use of the agency model for service delivery has created an even greater number of autonomous organizations that then have to be coordinated. Likewise, networks and public organizations closely linked with networks may be more difficult to coordinate than organizations within the public sector. Finally, senior managers have been empowered to make more of their own decisions, so that they, too, may be more difficult to coordinate through the usual mechanisms.

The general strategy for decentering reforms has been to focus on good management and efficiency within a single organization or policy area. That strategy has had numerous successes, but at the same time it weakens the capacity of governments to impose general policy initiatives and priorities. For example, the creation of a large number of autonomous or quasi-autonomous agencies has created many more organizations that need coordinating.

Accountability

Finally, the principal issue that arises in the development of NPM and of governance styles in the public sector is accountability for the decisions that are taken in the name of the public. Both these alternatives to traditional forms of governing tend to attenuate the linkages between public action and political organizations, and to assume that those political linkages are perhaps less important than had been thought conventionally. There are further assumptions about alternative forms of accountability (see Mulgan 2000, 2009) and control, but these alternative mechanisms may not substitute in a democratic system for the primacy of politics and ministerial responsibility for public action.

Accountability is often conceptualized as a mechanism for enforcing control over public organizations and programs, but it is also a means of guiding the improvement of programs. The structural and procedural elements contained in the reforms over the past several decades not only weaken the capacity to control government; they also limit the error-correction elements of accountability. The logic is much the same, with the breaking or attenuation of the linkages between the political leaders and program delivery implying that any learning or control also will be broken.

Summary

The use of both NPM and the governance approaches to organizing and managing the public sector have produced some clear benefits for the public sector and for citizens; but, as with any set of reforms, there are also costs involved. These costs have been minimized by the advocates of these reforms, and have also been less obvious because there have been some real benefits created and also because these reforms were compatible with the general neo-liberal ideology of the era in which they were implemented. In addition, the reform process has been supported and advocated by a range of international organizations that have legitimated and diffused these changes in the public sector.

It is to some extent obvious what problems have been created by these reforms, but it is less clear what the most appropriate solutions to these problems would be. The simplest response to these changes might be to attempt to return to the *status quo ante*. That is almost certainly not possible, although probably more for the participatory and network reforms than for the NPM reforms. Having permitted greater involvement of both employees and social actors, it would be difficult to eliminate that participation. Therefore, political or administrative leaders who want to be able to steer effectively must find ways of using the gains achieved through prior reforms while still overcoming the problems that have been created.

Meta-governance strategies: when should we meta-govern?

The final question to be considered when dealing with the meta-governance of public programs is when, within the policy process, to emphasize meta-governing. The traditional approach to public management relied on controlling administrative processes and using *ex ante* rules to ensure that decisions conform to law and to the directions coming from the political leadership. That hierarchical style of governing has been the target of a great deal of the reform efforts already described. The reforms described above have tended to reverse much of the hierarchical nature of governing, permitting individual public organizations as well as networks to make more of their own decisions and to be held accountable for those decisions after the fact.

The implications of the changes in management are that any attempts to restore control over implementation will have to be *ex post*, attempting to detect problems after the fact and asserting control largely through error correction. To some extent, accountability has always relied upon error correction and punishment, and even more contemporary instruments for control such as performance management (see below) may depend heavily upon detecting poor performance after the fact. That error correction is valuable but may also be inefficient in permitting the misuse of resources and the waste of time. Therefore, attempts at meta-governance that only correct errors should not be dismissed entirely, but they are perhaps less efficient at altering steering than are more direct instruments. Governments are far from perfect in governing, as an extensive literature documents, but having them overseeing other actors still provides for redundancy in controlling policy.

Instruments for meta-governance

The choice of instruments for meta-governance represents an answer to the question of "How" to meta-govern. Instrument choice is an important question for any attempt at governance, but is perhaps more difficult for meta-governance because of the numerous challenges already discussed. The task is to find instruments that can provide effective steering while at the same time permitting the targets of the control to retain a good deal of their capacity to make autonomous decisions concerning a range of activities.

Performance management

Performance management has been one of the most common instruments associated with NPM. The basic logic of performance management is to develop suitable measures of the outputs and outcomes of public action, and by using those measures to drive improved service delivery by the public sector. Making this method effective in turn requires the identification of the goals of government and making the linkage between those goals and the indicators of public-sector activity. Although there are numerous problems in the identification of appropriate measures, the basic idea can be helpful in both managing organizations and in holding those organizations accountable.

Performance management can also be seen in the context of meta-governance. Setting the goals enables senior managers and/or political leaders to determine what the organization should be doing, while allowing the organizations to shape the actual means through which those goals would be reached. The latitude that the organizations may actually have in that implementation may actually be constrained to some extent by the goals, but even then there is some ability for a public organization or a network of actors. If performance is indeed what matters, then the organizations and networks should be able to make many of their own decisions about the actual provision of the services.

Strategic management

Much of traditional management within the public sector has been detailed, and has tended to specify procedures and the details of programs. Further, much of that management has been conducted within individual programs and organizations, and, even if successful in improving performance, does not contribute to overall governance of a political system. Indeed, enhanced performance within the single organizations may reduce the overall performance of a system by reducing the probability of coordination among the various components of the system.

Therefore, one important strategy for improving the governance of that entire system of governance is to focus on policy coordination. The focus on coordination, in turn, should proceed from negative coordination through to positive coordination (Scharpf 1994) and finally through to strategic management. The more strategic approach would continue to emphasize coordination among the actors, but would do so around the principal goals for the political system and the society as a whole. This would be in contrast to beginning with the limited, disparate goals of the individual organizations and programs, and attempting to build coherent policies from them.

Strategic management can be thought of as meta-governance because, although it posits the central values and goals for the policy process, it does not need to specify the means of achieving those goals. As already noted for performance management, establishing goals and then permitting choices about attaining the goals provides substantial controls over policy directions, and even about the style of implementation, but also preserves some aspects of the autonomy of organizations and networks. If, indeed, this meta-governance functions within the shadow of hierarchy, then the center can always pull the power back and impose more direct controls; but the initial efforts at meta-governing could be more indirect.

Budgets, personnel and the golden thread

In addition to the other reforms implemented within the public sectors, a number of political systems have engaged in extensive internal deregulation (see DiIulio 1994). This deregulation has weakened rules in areas such as procurement, personnel management and the budget. Further, public budgeting more generally has been reforming to provide managers with greater latitude in making decisions about the use of money. "Bulk budgeting" provides managers with a global budget, which they can use rather freely to make their programs perform as well as they can, within the bounds of law (see Scott 1996).

Contracting and the use of networks also provide a great deal of managerial freedom. The managers responsible for monitoring contracts and partnerships are also being given substantial latitude, and require that latitude to be able to be effective in more complex governance situations. Given that almost necessary latitude for managers, maintaining some thread of control is essential for asserting the primacy of political control over the activities of the public sector. The control need not be extensive but still is necessary, so therefore relying upon a relatively simple instrument or indicator may be crucial for meta-governing and much less disruptive than more direct instruments for control.

While controlling the budget is perhaps the most obvious means of meta-governing, controlling other basic inputs into the system may accomplish the same purpose. For example, controlling personnel allocations can also provide a relatively simple source of control over individual organizations, albeit perhaps not as direct as it might have been when a greater share of public-sector activity was provided directly, by career public servants. Controls over secondary legislation also function as powerful means of controlling seemingly autonomous public organizations, although these are less effective for networks or other more devolved forms of public governance.

Soft law

Much of the process of governing is conceptualized as the use of law and formal authority. This style of governing has a number of positive features and has served most governance systems very well. However, just as increasingly true for governance (Salamon 2001) more generally, these formal instruments appear less acceptable to people working within government. Much of the logic of the NPM has been that public managers should have greater independence from these types of controls, while the logic of the more participatory style of governing has been that lower levels of government should also have greater autonomy. Both of these approaches therefore have tended to lessen central controls without replacing them with establishing compensatory governance systems.

The idea of soft law has been applied primarily in international governance (Abbott and Snidal 2000) and within the European Union (Mörth 2004). In these settings there has been a marked absence of formal authority and legitimacy that is central to traditional institutional settings of governance.

The European Union has been able to use soft instruments to address policy areas that are formally outside its competence. By shifting from formal instruments associated with the "Community Method" to the softer instruments based on negotiation, goals were reached that could not have been reached through the more conventional means. The Open Method of Coordination in the EU (Borras and Jacobssen 2004) and the European Social Dialogue (Smismans 2008) are two of the more evident examples of the use of soft law in the multi-national setting.

The lessons derived from the experiences in international settings are applicable to the national and subnational levels. While these governments may be functioning within their area of competence, they may still confront an increasing range of barriers to the use of formal instruments for control. Certainly networks and other forms of informality in the public sector present resistance to hierarchical controls, as do autonomous organizations within the public sector itself. These organizations also tend to have a stronger political base than do those in the international environment, and hence may be more capable of resisting efforts to impose stronger forms of control than are the organizations in the international setting.

Perhaps the most important difference between actions within the international system and national policy-making is that there is at least some vestige of a shadow of hierarchy at the national level, regardless of the decisions that have been made that tend to lessen the level of control within those largely hierarchical systems. Thus, while soft law may be the only option for many dimensions of international governance, for domestic policy soft law may just be a convenient and efficient instrument, or set of instruments, for coping with potential political resistance to imposition of central policy decisions.

Trust and values

The above instruments for meta-governance depend upon relative formalistic and structural approaches, albeit ones that do not rely exclusively (if at all) on hierarchy. Using formal solutions is the natural reaction for most people working in the public sector, but a softer approach to governing (or meta-governing) may be to attempt to build values that can steer the range of organizations. There may be some common political values in societies (Painter and Peters 2009), as well as common administrative values (Hofstede 2001), that can shape the implementation of public programs and facilitate achieving public purposes.[8]

The use of trust and values corresponds to the idea of shaping behavior through shaping the environment of action described in the introduction. Governing through these instruments represents one of the cheapest and most effective approaches to meta-governance, and to governance more generally. If the would-be meta-governors can shape the values and the incentives to which the individuals making decisions respond, then the outcomes desired may be reached with little investment of resources, and with a continuing effect. The difficulty comes, of course, if the meta-governors change – e.g. there is a change in the governing coalition and there is a new set of values to guide decisions.

In the context of network governance and other more informal styles of governing, the use of values to steer requires to some extent that those values represent strongly the importance of the public interest. Scholars such as Moore (1995) have emphasized the importance of public values within the public sector itself, but those same values need to be extended to the other structures providing public services. Indeed, those values are more crucial for these devolved structures that are inherently more impacted by the values of the private actors (market or non-market) that are contained within them. Further, if these basic values about the publicness of the public sector are institutionalized well, then even changing the operating premises of policy – again, as when there is a change in government – can be accomplished more readily.

Summary

Meta-governance, and the perhaps more basic concern with governance, reflects the need to provide direction to economy and society, as well as the difficulty of providing that steering. Attempts to provide less direct mechanisms for steering society, and granting greater autonomy to actors within the public sector, have generated numerous managerial benefits. These reforms, however, have also created managerial problems within the public sector. These reforms have also created many political problems by reducing the levels of control that political leaders can exercise over public policies.

While reducing the levels of direct political involvement in the details of policy may have been desirable from the perspective of increasing efficiency, it was less desirable from a democratic perspective, and many politicians (and their constituents) have sought greater control by those elected representatives. As already noted, meta-governance strategies provide a way of providing that direction while at the same time preserving some of the efficiency gains from decentering reforms of government. The choice of meta-governance strategies, then, is an attempt to reassert some balance of power within the policy-making systems of the public sector, and to continue to involve non-state actors in the process while recognizing the primacy of politics.

One administrative reform tends to beget the next, as the difficulties created by one set of changes tends to create demands for additional changes. The question now is what will be the reaction to meta-governance reforms that are being implemented. One option might be to make the state role in governance even stronger, especially when having to confront the probability of a long and severe economic downturn. The other option might be to find new ways of involving the market and civil society in governing and to weaken further the role of the political aspects of governing.

These choices will not be easy, and may be country-specific. Much of the research on reform in the public sector has tended to assume rather common patterns of change, but we may now expect somewhat greater divergence among these systems. Coping with a major economic crisis, as well as with other major policy challenges such as climate change, may cause states to revert to more traditional patterns of governing. That would mean that more liberal states would rely heavily on the market, and more *étatiste* states would reassert more direct state dominance. The observed pattern to date has been to some extent the reverse of that, with liberal Anglo-American systems becoming heavily involved with steering and some European states such as Germany being more laissez-faire. Still, coping with a crisis can be a spur for reform and can help reveal future patterns of governing.

Notes

1 One suitable date for marking the beginning of the transformations would be the election of Margaret Thatcher in 1979. See Savoie (1994).
2 In many ways, Lowi was writing about meta-governance without doing so explicitly. See Nicholson (2002).
3 These reforms are hardly new, they emphasize the private more than the public, but they are indeed about management.
4 Governance is used to describe a variety of different aspects of the general process of governing. Here it is being used in a somewhat restrictive sense to mean the use of networks of social actors to do some parts of the work of governing that might once have been done by formal public organizations.
5 The major exception to that generalization would be presidential systems in which the conflicts between relatively equal branches of government can produce "gridlock". Some of the same gridlock may be produced in parliamentary systems that have the possibility of being "divided" because of second chambers (Elgie 2001).
6 Network structures may therefore reflect the classic problem of the commons, in which the pursuit of individual interest may undermine the collective good. The evolution of rules and norms as described in Ostrom's work (1996) appears to represent the exception rather than the rule in these cases. In particular, the cases of developing rules autonomously tends to occur primarily in smaller settings rather than in situations involving powerful national actors. What is the foundation of this remark? I would argue the reverse. A lot of work exists on the role of rules and institutions in networks.
7 That said, having the common values may facilitate making the decision.
8 Of course, those same virtues about the public sector may make political change more difficult and may require cultural change as well as (relatively) simple changes of structures and procedures.

References

Abbott, K. W. and Snidal, D. (2000) "Hard and Soft Law in International Governance", *International Organization*, 54: 421–56.

Bell, S. and Park, A. (2006) "The Problematic Metagovernance of Networks: Water Reform in New South Wales", *Journal of Public Policy*, 26: 63–83.

Borras, S. and Jacobssen, K. (2004) "The Open Method of Coordination and New Patterns of Governance in the EU", *Journal of European Public Policy*, 11: 185–204.

Carpenter, D. P. (2001) *Forging Bureaucratic Autonomy*, Princeton, NJ; Princeton University Press.

Christensen, T. and Laegreid, P. (2007) *New Public Management: Transformation of Ideas and Practice*, Aldershot: Ashgate.

Dalton, R. J. and Wattenberg, B. (2000) *Parties without Partisans*, Oxford: Oxford University Press.

DiIulio, J. J. (1994) *Deregulating Government*, Washington, DC: The Brookings Institution.

Elgie, R. (2001) *Divided Government in Comparative Politics*, Oxford: Oxford University Press.

Hofstede, G. (2001) *Culture's Consequences: Comparing Values, Behaviors, Institutions and Organizations across Nations*, Thousand Oaks, Calif.: Sage.

Hood, C. (1976) *The Tools of Government*, Chatham, NJ: Chatham House.

Hood, C. (1991) "A Public Management for All Seasons?", *Public Administration*, 69 (1): 3–19.

Jessop, B. (2002) "Governance and Meta-governance: On Reflexivity, Requisite Variety and Requisite Irony", in H. Bang (ed.) *Governance, Governmentality and Democracy*, Manchester: Manchester University Press.

Lowi, T. J. (1972) "Four Systems of Policy: Politics and Choice", *Public Administration Review*, 32: 314–25.

Mair, P. and Biezen, I. van (2001) "Party Membership in Twenty European Democracies, 1980–2000", *Party Politics*, 7: 5–21.

Milward, H. B. and Provan, K. G. (2000) Managing the Hollow State, *Journal of Public Administration Research and Theory*, 10: 359–80.

Moore, M. (1995) *Creating Public Value: Strategic Management in Government*, Cambridge, Mass.: Harvard University Press.

Mörth, U. (2004) *Soft Law in Governance and Regulation*, Cheltenham: Edward Elgar.

Mueleman, L. (2008) *Public Management and the Metagovernance of Hierarchies, Networks and Markets*, Heidelberg: Physica.

Mulgan, G. (2000) "Accountability: An Ever-expanding Concept", *Public Administration*, 78 (3): 555–73.

Mulgan, G. (2009) "Accountability", in *IPSA Encyclopedia of Political Science*, Thousand Oaks, Calif.: Sage.

Nicholson, N. (2002) "Policy Choices and the Use of State Power: The Work of Theodore J. Lowi", *Policy Sciences*, 35: 163–77.

Ostrom, E. (1996) "Covenants, Collective Action and Common Pool Resources", in K. E. Soltan and S. L. Elkin (eds) *The Constitution of Good Societies*, University Park, Pa: Penn State University Press.

Painter, M. A. and Peters, B. G. (2009) *Administrative Traditions and Administrative Change*, Basingstoke: Palgrave Macmillan.

Peters, B. G. (2001) *The Future of Governing*, 2nd edn, Lawrence, Kan.: University Press of Kansas.

Salamon, L. M. (2001) "Introduction", in L. M. Salamon (ed.) *Handbook of Policy Instruments*, New York: Oxford University Press.

Savoie, D. J. (1994) *Reagan, Thatcher, Mulroney: In Search of the New Bureaucracy*, Pittsburgh, Pa.: University of Pittsburgh Press.

Scharpf, F. W. (1988) "The Joint Decision Trap: Lessons from European Union Integration and German Federalism", *Public Administration*, 66 (2): 239–78.

Scharpf, F. W. (1994) "Games Real Actors Could Play: Positive and Negative Coordination in Embedded Negotiations", *Journal of Theoretical Politics*, 6: 27–53.

Scott, C. (2004) *Regulation in the Age of Governance*, Cheltenham: Edward Elgar.

Scott, G. (1996) *Government Reform in New Zealand*, Washington, DC: International Monetary Fund.

Smismans, S. (2008) "The European Social Dialogue in the Shadow of Hierarchy", *Journal of Public Policy*, 28: 161–79.

Sorenson, E. (2006) "Metagovernance: The Changing Role of Politicians in Processes of Democratic Governance", *The American Review of Public Administration*, 36: 98–124.

Walsh, K. and J. Stewart (1992) "Change in the Management of Public Services", *Public Administration*, 69: 499–518.

4

INNOVATIONS IN GOVERNANCE

Mark Moore and Jean Hartley

Introduction

This chapter explores a special class of innovations – innovations in governance – and develops an analytical schema for characterizing and evaluating them. To date, the innovation literature has focused primarily on the private rather than on the public sector, and on innovations which improve organizational performance through product and process innovations rather than on public sector innovations which seek to improve social performance through reorganizations of cross-sector decision-making, financing and production systems. On the other hand, the governance literature has focused on social coordination but has not drawn on the innovation literature. The chapter uses four case studies illustratively to argue that innovations in governance deserve greater theoretical attention. Further, it argues that five inter-related characteristics distinguish public sector innovations in governance from private-sector product and process innovations. Innovations in governance: go beyond organizational boundaries to create network-based financing, decision-making and production systems; tap new pools of resources; exploit government's capacity to shape private rights and responsibilities; redistribute the right to define and judge value; and should be evaluated in terms of the degree to which they promote justice and the development of a society as well as by their efficiency and effectiveness in achieving collectively established goals.

Innovations in governance as an emerging research domain

Recently, there has been a great deal of both professional and scholarly interest in "innovation" in the public sector (Altshuler and Behn 1997; Borins 1998; Hartley 2005; Moore 2005; Mulgan and Albury 2003; Albury 2005; National Audit Office 2006). Among professionals, innovation is seen as a critical method for improving the performance of government, and enhancing government's legitimacy with citizens. Nothing other than an innovative government can keep pace with citizen aspirations for a government that is both efficient and effective in its core operations, and capable of responding to the diverse and changing needs of a modern society.

For their part, public management scholars (Hartley 2005, 2006, 2008; Osborne and Brown 2005; Landau 1993; Walker et al. 2002; Koch and Hauknes 2005; Moore 2005) have focused on the kinds of changes in government[1] that should count as important innovations, how much innovation occurs, what structures and processes promote or retard innovations, and whether current institutional structures and processes support enough innovation for government to respond to or anticipate societal demands for change.

Our focus in this chapter is on what we claim is a distinct class of public sector innovations that deserve special attention: a class of innovations that we characterize as "innovations in governance". These innovations differ from standard intraorganizational innovations in products, services and production processes in at least two obvious ways. On the one hand, the innovations are conceived and implemented *above the organizational level*: they involve networks of organizations, or the transformation of complex social production systems rather than changes solely within a particular organization. On the other hand, these innovations focus not only on concrete changes in what particular things are produced through what particular production processes, but also on the *ways in which productive activity is financed (or, more broadly, resourced), the processes that are used to decide what will be produced, and the normative standards used to evaluate the performance of the social production system.*

We focus on this class of innovations for two different reasons. On the one hand, we argue that these innovations are theoretically interesting because they challenge conventional ideas about what constitutes an important innovation, where and how innovations are produced, and how they might best be evaluated. On the other hand, these innovations are important in practical terms. Those innovations in the public sector that are brought to public attention, or which win awards, often have the characteristics of being important or significant because they change where and how innovation is produced, as noted above. For both theoretical and practical reasons, then, we suggest that this class of innovations deserves close attention.

We want to be clear, however, that our approach to this subject is exploratory. We suggest but cannot confirm that we have identified a set of public sector innovations that are both similar enough to one another and different enough from other kinds of innovations to be considered as a coherent class of innovations. And our suggestion that, in practice, this class of innovations is both common and important among all public sector innovations requires further investigation. All that we are sure of is that there are some kinds of innovations now being developed in the public sector that do not resemble the standard picture of product and process innovations that occur in manufacturing and service-delivery firms in the private sector, or the standard picture of program innovations in public-sector organizations. We suggest, however, that it is likely that in explaining how such innovations occur, how to evaluate their impact, or how to teach people how to do more of them or make them more successful, we shall have to go beyond existing theories of innovation. This chapter is part of the journey of discovery about such innovations, their explanation and impact.

Evidence that "innovations in governance" have been an important part of the overall level of innovation in government is not hard to find. Most descriptions of important innovations in the public sector tend to focus on these kinds of innovations as well as on more traditional product and process innovations. Evidence that innovations in governance have given the academics trouble comes from the fact that when the theoreticians seek to categorize different kinds of innovations they often start with the familiar product, process and technology categories, but end up having to create some kind of residual category. Walker et al. (2002), for example, include the concept of "ancillary innovation", defined as that which involves "organization–environment boundary innovations". Mulgan and Albury (2003) talk about "systemic innovation", which results from or is based on the development of new underpinning technologies (or production systems) and/or organizational forms necessary to sustain and guide these new production systems. Only Hartley (2005, 2008) mentions the concept of governance innovations, in an outline of the dimensions (not categories) of innovation. These include changes to institutional forms of government (such as the devolution of power from national government to newly established governments for Wales and Scotland) and changes in organizational form and arrangements for the planning and delivery of services (e.g. privatization, new collaborative arrangements between the public and private sectors) as well as those innovations that provide for greater public and/or user participation in service design and delivery, and in the use of boards to govern particular choices and services (e.g. school governing bodies).

Importantly, when we turn to the literature for guidance about how to understand such innovations, we find a gap. The innovation literature (for both private and public sectors) helps us understand what counts as an innovation. That literature makes it clear that innovations have to be more than mere ideas: innovations are *new ideas and practices brought into implementation* (e.g. Bessant 2005; Tidd et al. 2005; van de Ven 1986; Wolfe 1994). They are therefore different from inventions (Bessant 2003). Some commentators also add that an innovation is different from continuous improvement or other minor changes. For example, Lynn (1997) argues that "Innovation must not simply be another name for change, or for improvement, or even for doing something new lest almost anything qualify as innovation. Innovation is properly defined as an original, disruptive, and fundamental transformation of an organization's core tasks" (p. 154). In this formulation, innovation is a step change for the organization (see also Utterback 1996). Moore and colleagues (1997) argue that innovation is "large enough, general enough and durable enough to appreciably affect the operations or character of the organization". Innovation may also include reinvention or adaptation of an innovation in another context, location or time period (Rogers 2003; Thompson 1965).

But all of this discussion of innovation focuses on innovations within organizations – important changes in what organizations produce and deliver. It does not focus on changes in structures and processes operating above the level of a single organization, and on financing, decision-making, and evaluations of performance as well. If, then, a public-sector innovator had made changes above the level of a given organization that transformed social conditions by changing the social structures and processes that generated resources to deal with the problem, or changed who was responsible for doing the work, or allowed individuals to make voluntary contributions to the social purposes in exchange for more control over what was being produced with social resources, the existing literature on public sector innovation seems to have relatively little to offer. The public sector literature on innovation will need to conceptualize and theorize innovations in governance as well as innovations in government organizations.

When we turn to the governance literature, in contrast, we find a literature that is attuned to an analysis of the broader social systems that guide, finance and produce large social outcomes. Kooiman (2003), for example, has defined governing as "The totality of interactions, in which public as well as private actors participate, aimed at solving societal problems or creating societal opportunities; attending to the institutions as contexts for these governing interactions; and establishing a normative foundation for all these activities" (p. 4). Government, as an important governance institution, is able to use its powers to convene actors from different sectors, and both to regulate and to finance their activities might play an important role in introducing innovations in the (social-level) governance of the social production systems. But this literature has not focused on how to analyze particular changes made in governance processes, and their implications for the transformation of both social conditions and the redistribution of the burden of producing those social conditions, or on the methods that were used to bring this new governance system into existence and to sustain its operations. In short, the governance literature misses the detailed operational focus that characterizes the innovation literature.

The gap in the academic literature on innovations in governance, noted by Hartley (2005), is unfortunate, for the practical world seems to be producing a great many innovations of this type. Indeed, we seem to be going through a revolution in the governance of public production systems as governments seek to reach beyond their borders to find additional resources, additional operational capacity, and even additional legitimacy to achieve their assigned goals. Some of the innovations involve changes in organizational-level governance – for example, a school is required to establish a parent's council that can oversee its operations, or patients in public hospitals are given increased powers to voice their concerns about service quality. In other situations, the innovations involve new ways of knitting elements of different organizations together to create a more effective problem-solving approach to a given problem (Skelcher 2005). Hill and Lynn (2005) argue that "the focus of administrative practice is shifting from hierarchical government towards greater reliance on horizontal, hybridized, and associational forms of governance" (p. 173). These shifts, in line with other changes associated with "networked governance" (Benington 2000; Newman 2001), have implications for management, both in terms of organizational and inter-organizational processes, and potentially for performance.

Hierarchical government has been able to harness the use of state authority as well as resources to achieve outcomes, sometimes coercively (e.g. through legislation about taxation and military powers) and through its claim to have a democratic mandate. The shift to achieving societal goals through partnerships with the private, voluntary and community sectors means that influence becomes a significant strategy as well as (sometimes instead of) formal hierarchical authority (Hartley and Allison 2000). This has implications for the ways in which managers undertake their tasks and for the organizations, partnerships and networks within which they do this. Hence innovations in governance become important to analyze as well as service innovations.

The gap in the literature is not hard to fathom. Both academics and professionals who have sought guidance about how to produce value-creating innovations have generally turned to the private sector for inspiration and guidance. They do so for two reasons. First, the private sector tends to give innovation a more prominent place in improving performance than government has done. Second, there is simply more scholarship on private than on public management. Consequently, in seeking scholarly guidance about the role of innovation in improving governmental performance, and the processes that can foster value-creating innovation, one naturally turns to the private sector literature. However, the private-sector literature has not examined innovations in governance, and there are few studies which have examined innovation above the firm level (Hartley 2005). Many of the innovations which concern the public sector are not the process and product innovations that have been the meat and potatoes of innovation in the private sector. They are, instead, innovations designed to reshape a broader social system that not only produces public goods and services (and, in doing so, to transform aggregate social conditions in socially desirable ways), but also provides the financing and material to produce these results. They also shift the location of decision-making authority over the new system to determine how the benefits and burdens of that new system will be distributed.

Method of inquiry

The purpose of this chapter is to initiate a more sustained, detailed investigation into this particular class of innovation that seems to be both very important in government and less well understood by the private sector literature.[2] The method is to look closely at a small number of public sector innovations (based on documentary evidence, obtained from teaching cases and from official reports and the media) that seem to fall within the broad set of innovations in governance, taking care to ensure that the selection of the cases includes some important variants. We do not offer these cases as reliable histories of events, nor as complete evaluations of their social impact. Nor do we offer these cases as a representative sample of innovations. We offer them, instead, as particular instantiations of innovations in government that do not seem to fit the accepted frame of product and process innovations discussed in relation to the private sector. They provide an opportunity to explore these apparently anomalous forms of innovation. The value of the cases lies in their ability to challenge our conceptual thought, not in their historical accuracy or representativeness. From the cases we develop five propositions about how innovations in governance are distinctive from product and service innovations.

Innovations in governance: some illustrative and challenging examples

Contracting with community groups for child protection services

The Massachusetts Department of Social Services was experiencing considerable difficulties in achieving the goals of their Child Protection Services (CPS) programme. Preventing abuse and neglect of children had to be addressed within financial constraints and with due regard for the privacy of families and the rights of parents. As the agency sought to balance the interests of the care of children, on the one hand, and the rights of families and parents, on the other, it made decisions with negative consequences of two kinds: failing to intervene where abuse or neglect was subsequently found, and intervening where the cases turned out not to require action. The difficulty of making the appropriate response in circumstances that are inherently complex, dynamic and unpredictable (cf. Hoggett 2006), together with the sensitive and ambivalent nature of the issues involved, meant that the CPS suffered from a chronic threat to its legitimacy and effectiveness.

Such problems were particularly marked among immigrant communities of Boston. Many did not trust the intentions, methods or procedures of the CPS. They thought that the CPS did not adequately understand the culture of local communities, which affected what constituted good and bad parenting in that context. They did not think the agency obtained accurate information from individuals about family conditions or interpret it properly. They did not think the agency had much to offer them when there were instances of abuse and neglect.

Faced with this perceived crisis in the performance and legitimacy of the CPS, which was also in serious financial difficulty, the Massachusetts Department of Social Services developed an "innovative" approach which was based on contracting out the service and which implicitly shifted the governance arrangements through delegating the responsibility for receiving and responding to complaints about child abuse and neglect to community-based organizations because they enjoyed much closer connections to, and much greater legitimacy with, immigrant communities. This seemed innovative not least because it tapped into a wider set of capacities and resources than the agency possessed: local knowledge of the customs and mores of parenting, ability to obtain and interpret information about conditions within a family, and a capacity to make interventions that would feel appropriate and useful to the affected.

However, behind this change lay some troubling questions for the observer. For example, was the state delegating either the *de facto* or *de jure* right to define what constituted abuse and neglect to a community-based organization? If not, what decision-making and administrative systems would ensure that the community-based organizations applied CPS standards accurately and consistently? What would happen to the legitimacy and effectiveness of the community-based organization if it was required to enforce CPS standards of care and intervention? Would such a move undermine exactly the kind of innovativeness that the state was seeking through this contract?

To make the arrangement workable, both organizations had to learn to recognize their own and the other party's interests and negotiate differently. The government agency had begun with the goal of contracting out child protection services, defined largely in terms of hearing and responding to complaints about child abuse and neglect. The community-based organization defined its interest in persuading the CPS to give it money for the provision of services to clients, without taking responsibility for setting and enforcing standards. In fact, these views dominated the actual negotiations and led to a contract that was somewhat cynical on both sides: the CPS claimed to have widened responsibility for abuse and neglect services (while actually shifting its responsibilities and lowering its costs), and the community-based organization accepted this responsibility but without really taking the full responsibility for doing the work or accurately pricing the level and activities required. The inadequacy of the contract was exposed later when a child in the care of the community-based organization was found to have been seriously abused. A formal investigation showed that the community-based organization had not, in fact, taken the kind of consistent responsibility for the care of children that the CPS claimed to have contracted for.

This case illustrates that innovation does not necessarily lead to improvement (see also Hartley 2005 for this distinction). There was potential for an innovation which would have enhanced public value (Moore 1995; Benington and Moore forthcoming) by paying explicit attention to the governance as well as the service innovation. Such an innovation would need the community-based organization to organize a community-based discussion about problems of abuse and neglect and ways to address child protection. It might have orchestrated such a discussion either on its own, or with the CPS and possibly other interested stakeholders. Then, following that community-based discussion, a whole system of prevention and intervention involving individual and collective, community-based and governmental action might have been developed. The difficulty for the CPS was that it had been unable to focus on this as an innovation in governance arrangements because they would only contract for service or process innovations in child protection.

Private partnerships to support New York City's parks

The New York park system was once one of the glories of life in New York. Initially conceived in the mid-nineteenth century by Frederick Law Olmsted as oases from urban squalor, and then extended as a wide network of easily accessible green spaces, New York's parks had long been a refuge for city-dwellers. By the late 1960s, however, the parks were falling into disrepair. The gardens were trampled; trees were vandalized; the greenswards were dusty and littered; the recreational equipment was broken. They were less often and less widely used because they seemed, and actually were, increasingly dangerous.

The city government parks organization had become overwhelmed, with insufficient financial and staff resources to run the city's parks. It could not rely on citizens to use the parks well nor could it generate public commitment to the parks. Senior managers decided on a new approach. Instead of the organization acting as though it was the only body responsible for the parks, they decided to reach out for partnerships with citizen groups, to encourage a greater interest in the parks in exchange for somewhat greater control over what happened within them. The partnerships they created took different forms in different parks, but in each case citizen groups were invited to contribute direct resources to the park. This was not through taxation (which ensures that the costs of park maintenance are fairly distributed amongst all citizens, but which reduces the perception of a personalized effect of contributions). Instead voluntary contributions of time and money to particular parts of, or particular activities within, each park were solicited. From one perspective, such partnerships might be viewed as "selling" a piece of the public park to a particular set of users in exchange for an additional voluntary contribution of labor or money. In practice, the newly renovated parks and the new, jointly sponsored activities were not exclusively for the contributors; because they were (at least in principle) still available to all. The volunteers may have felt particularly attached to the park renovation, and they may have felt some special entitlements to use the space and to host those who came to use the parks. But the parks retained their public character in that they were free to all and the overall set of uses for the parks did not change.

Through these partnerships, the New York City parks bloomed again. They became prettier, safer, and much more widely used without costs to government increasing. Arguably, the public value of the parks had been enhanced. On the other hand, the commitment of voluntary time and resources created a certain degree of informal moral agency and claim over influencing the debates over public purpose, as we shall explore later.

Congestion charging in London

London is widely viewed as a world city, the powerhouse of the British economy, and an international gateway for investment and tourism. Yet it has been dogged by an inadequate transport system, which is seen as limiting economic growth and the quality of life of its citizens, workers and tourists. A combination of problems (underinvestment in public transport, deterioration of the railway system following privatization, fragmentation of decision-making about infrastructure including transport planning and provision) had left London at the turn of millennium with major traffic-congestion problems. Private and commercial vehicle use in central London had become slow and unpredictable, affecting business and leisure time. Public transport was unreliable, giving car-drivers little incentive to use public transport instead.

The development of an innovative solution, partly in the form of congestion charging, came from a particular combination of circumstances. The Transport Strategy was developed in recognition by politicians and managers that four factors coincided in a way which meant that it was possible to start to resolve London's transport crisis. First was the innovation in governance of the establishment of devolved government for London as a city. The new Greater London Authority, with a directly elected mayor with a manifesto about improving transport and travel, gave a strong democratic mandate to tackle transport problems. In addition, at the same time, London's transport services were integrated through the establishment of a new organization, Transport for London (a strategic innovation which underpinned part of the governance innovation). Third, the central government, still newly elected, provided a level of financial resources which helped to tackle chronic underinvestment. The fourth element was the hiring of key senior international managers with a proven track record of tackling transport problems. Each of these elements can be considered an innovation in its own right, and they were used together to develop an innovative strategy for reducing congestion in central London. A charge was introduced, from February 2003, for using a vehicle (other than taxis) in the central eight square miles of London during the day. This was the first time for generations that roads in London had been subject to a toll for use.

Initially, this approach faced a number of political and technical/operational problems. Establishing a consistent and fair way of warning travellers of imminent entry into the charging area, and monitoring road use so that the charge could be applied were important. So was ensuring that payment and enforcement was effective, efficient and feasible, with travellers having access to information about other forms of travel. There was also a challenge to ensure longer-term viability of the scheme, and to encourage behavioral changes in the travel habits of the millions who lived and worked in London.

The political challenge was to create a vision and mobilize for the proposed changes, with long-term commitment to the innovation. When the policy was first proposed by the mayor, chaos and disaster were predicted by the opponents of the scheme, and even ordinary Londoners were sceptical about whether it would work. Civil disobedience, traffic gridlock in the area just outside the charge zone, and intolerable pressure on the bus, Underground and rail networks were all predicted. The plans of the elected mayor and the newly devolved Greater London Authority, along with Transport for London, were all put under the spotlight by the media and by lobbying groups, though some groups were supportive. Politicians took time and care to outline London's problems, to explore options and to listen to concerns about the new scheme. Managers held consultation events around London to learn about the ways in which different groups might be affected. An important issue was to ensure that congestion charging shaped travel behavior in fundamental ways, not merely raised funds for the city. In other words, citizens and visitors had to learn to adapt to the new system. Since the introduction of charging, car traffic has reduced by about 30 percent, business has benefited from shorter and more reliable journey times, public transport has (largely) coped, and cycling has increased.

Elder care in Singapore

Singapore's highly centralized national government is committed to, and has achieved, dramatic economic growth fueled by foreign direct investment. Among the conditions that attracted investment was a government that protected private property rights and that could promise labor peace. Partly to achieve this, government guaranteed access to high-quality housing, which was highly prized by families.

Economic development gradually produced strains on the social and governmental structures. There was an increasing demand for governmental processes that were more open and democratic – that allowed or encouraged debates about public policy, and made governmental actions more accountable. Also, as society became exposed to more individualistic Western cultures, social relationships in families were altered, and concern arose about an aging population. Longevity was increasing; and, despite the decades of economic growth, it was possible that those who had created that growth would not be financially secure in retirement.

To many, the aging population was not a problem because a well-established social custom located responsibility not on the individual or the state but on offspring. They had a duty to attend to their parents' needs which had been strong enough to produce both reliable care from the vast majority of Singaporeans and vigorous informal criticism of anyone who seemed to abandon their aging parents.

However, the customary system had always been incomplete (for example, what about elders with no children?). It had always been imperfectly enforced (there were some children who neglected their parents, and those parents had no formal right of action against their children). In addition, there was concern in government that customary duties were weakening under the influence of both Western ideas and a sense that the state would provide. It was conceivable that this customary system would break down, leaving many elderly people exposed to penury and loneliness.

This issue was taken up by an appointed legislator as his particular cause. He proposed a new public law to underpin the customary duty. The law required children to care for their parents in kind or by financial contribution, and gave neglected parents recourse to the law. It also allowed the state to pursue children who failed in their duty of care. The shift from the customary system to backing with statutory requirement and a right of action was a significant innovation.

Preliminary considerations

We think it is fair to say that these sorts of innovations differ from the product/service/process innovations that have been the focus of such extensive attention in the private sector literature. But many of the most widely remarked and celebrated innovations in the government sector seem to be of these broader, more structural types where production, financing and decision-making are all moved around in a new configuration to reshape the system that determines what is produced, how it is financed, and whose values are given emphasis in guiding the process of social production.

How are we to understand these innovations? They seem to work (to varying degrees) in practice, but where do they fit in our theories of innovation? How might the analytic frameworks we use for characterizing and evaluating innovations have to be changed to accommodate these broader, more structural types?

Are innovations in governance really innovations?

Let us start by asking whether changes like the ones above deserve to be called innovations and, if so, why. We can then turn to the question of what, if anything, makes them different from product/process innovations.

The innovations described above may logically entail or create the conditions under which many different process and product innovations can occur. For example, it is quite likely that the new governance arrangements in New York's Central Park will generate a wider variety of uses of the park ranging from gardening, to bird-watching, to ethnic festivals. Further, for each of these new uses (or services) a different production and financing system might be generated.

Similarly, the new system for governing the rationing of the roads in London might require the development of many new products and activities that permit the charging of individuals for travel – the technical arrangements that allow us to make what was once a freely used resource one where use is more exclusive through noting who is using the product/service and charging them for it. But, while each of the governance innovations has dimensions of production and service innovation, that is not the whole story.

One can also raise doubts about the degree to which these ideas are genuinely new. The fact that these innovations seem to reach out to private associations and private individuals to accomplish public purposes does not seem particularly new. Society, acting with or without the help of government as its agent, has always relied on or been shaped by charity and civic action with or without the financial encouragement and direction of government. Similarly, we have long been accustomed to the idea that prices can be used not only to raise revenues for the seller, and to divide the value of creating a product or service that is desired by a customer between the producer and the user of that product and service, but also to ration limited supplies of a given product, and to channel the products and services to those who want it most (conditional on their ability to pay). We have used this idea not only in the private marketplace, but also in managing the level and distribution of production for such utilities as water, electricity and communications. So it does not seem such a big innovation to use it as a device for rationing road use. And we have long understood that public purposes such as elder care could be advanced by requiring individuals to act in accord with public laws as well as by relying on existing moral commitments to induce individuals.

Still, what makes the cases interesting as innovations is that they do, in fact, change the location and financing of social production, and the level and distribution of things that could reasonably be called social or public goods and services. The level, character and distribution of child protection services change as community-based groups are drawn into the process with government authorization and contracts. The fact that they are drawn into the production process gives them at least *de facto* and perhaps *de jure* roles in deciding what will be produced, for whom, and in what ways, with important consequences for both the parents (whose conduct is now monitored differently) and the children (whose welfare depends so much on the actions of parents). The level, character and distribution of park services change as the new partnerships are initiated and sustained – and with those changes an alteration in the observed character and utilization of the New York City park system. The level, character and distribution of the London roads service changes when congestion charging is introduced. The level, character and distribution of aid to aging parents is altered when legislation imposing this duty on children is discussed, passed and enforced through private and public means. And so on.

It is because these innovations change what is produced, how the new products and services are distributed, how the burden of producing the services is borne, and what happens to the material conditions in society that these "innovations in governance" deserve to be taken seriously as innovations. If they did not produce these material changes in what is produced for whom, and how the aggregate social conditions are changed as a consequence, then they would not be interesting as an important class of social innovations.

Five ways in which these innovations are different

The fact that these self-consciously constructed and introduced measures change the material processes through which society seeks to deal with particular problems makes them innovations that are worth noting as innovations. From the point of innovation theory, however, what makes them particularly interesting is all the ways in which they are *not* like the innovations in products and services. They seem to differ in at least five, highly inter-related ways.

Bursting the boundary of organizations/creating network-based production systems

First, the innovations described above seem to burst the boundaries of any particular organization, and to relocate and redistribute where and how socially productive activity occurs. The contracts with community-based organizations shift the production of child protective services from a state bureaucracy to a network of community-based groups. The invitation to private agencies to contribute their efforts to the maintenance of the parks shifts both the production and use patterns of the parks from one that was set by the Parks Department to one that is set by the Parks Department working in a network of partnerships. London's congestion pricing system invites drivers in London to find other means for meeting the objectives they pursue by using London's streets.

In each of these innovations, a particular organization stops being the sole locus of change. Further, the organization's future success stops being the sole focus of evaluation. Instead the focus of attention shifts from the analysis of what happens inside an organization to an analysis of a production system that crosses organizational boundaries, and sometimes (as in the case of both congestion pricing and the law mandating the care of aging parents) reaches to the mobilization of millions of decentralized individuals. The way in which the innovation is evaluated, then, is not in terms of whether it increases the productivity or success of a given organization, but of whether it succeeds in altering the broad social conditions that have become the focus of some collective concern. That collective concern could have previously been seen as the exclusive responsibility of a given governmental organization, but has now been transformed by the innovation into a problem to be solved by a much wider production system that stretches well beyond the resources that can be directly controlled by any given government organization.

Indeed, it is precisely this move to burst the boundary of an organization's hold on a given (and complex) problem that represents an important part of the innovation. As long as a given problem was held within a given organization, and as long as society relied on that bounded organization to solve the problem, the problem could not be fully addressed. It was only when the society, acting through the agency of government, decided to invite other actors into the solution of the problem that an important change could be made. These innovations are less organizational innovations, then, than system innovations that reconfigure production systems for achieving a given social result.

Tapping new pools of financing, material resources and human energy

Second, in many cases, innovations in governance focus not only on changing production systems, but also on tapping new wellsprings of resources. Those new resources that are tapped can come in quite different forms. Some of the new resources involve specific bits of specialized operational capability that turn out to be valuable in achieving a particular purpose the government has in mind. In the case of the community partnerships for Child Protective Services, the State Agency hoped to tap into an asset that a community program has naturally, and has further developed over time: namely, its established knowledge of, and legitimacy with, the local community. In the case of elder care in Singapore, the innovation is to strengthen a voluntarily contributed private capacity to care for the elderly with a legal obligation that will, ideally, add force and consistency to a voluntary customary practice.

At other times, the new resources come in a more fungible form; namely financial contributions. In the case of the New York City parks, for example, an important part of the innovation seems to be allowing relatively wealthy New Yorkers who want their parks to be nice to make voluntary contributions of money. (The donors can make their contributions a bit less fungible than they first appear by conditioning their availability on an agreement that the government will use them in a particular way. But the specialization in the use of the resources comes via institutional agreements rather than as material aspects of the resources.)

Regardless of whether the resources come in the form of money, labor or material, and regardless of whether the resources are highly fungible or are specialized to some very specific purposes, one way that these innovations seem to work in helping to solve public problems is by locating and mobilizing resources that were previously on the sideline or not fully exploited in the public effort.

Exploiting government's capacity to convene, exhort, and redefine private rights and responsibilities

Third, in seeking to mobilize more heavily resourced and more effective production systems than it could when it was operating only through existing government organizations with existing governmental resources, government relies on different instruments to accomplish its ends. In the classic form of government-led public problem-solving, government assumes the full responsibility for defining a public purpose, mobilizing resources to solve it, and deploying those resources in the most efficient and effective way through a government agency. The principal operating instrument of the government is the taxes used to sustain the operations of a government bureaucracy. In the innovations described above, government uses different instruments to achieve its results.

In the case of the CPS, it uses finances not only to support a government agency, but also to contract with a private organization. It does so partly because the organization already has some capacity that the government needs and cannot easily develop, and partly because it might be able to use moral suasion and the felt responsibility of the community group to make a greater contribution than it could buy from more professionalized or more commercial enterprises.

In the case of the parental support bill in Singapore, government uses state authority to compel those who might be tempted to stray from their customary duty to their parents, and gives vulnerable parents a right to action against neglectful children. The creation of such an obligation has to be accompanied by sufficient resources to ensure that cases brought by parents can be heard in state courts. But the principal asset of the state that is engaged is its authority to direct private action, and to mobilize the forces of informal social control to help enforce the obligation, a force that might be strengthened or weakened through the passage of the law.

In the case of the New York City parks, the government attracts primarily money and some voluntary labor to improve conditions in the parks, and it does so by allowing private parties to make the contributions they wish to make and to earmark their funds for those purposes and places. The important and interesting change here is that the Parks Department gives up its reliance solely on tax revenues in preference for accepting voluntary contributions to the parks and, in doing so, gives up its exclusive power to decide how the public parks will be maintained and used. As the price of accepting voluntary contributions, government must negotiate with private parties, and accept their ideas of what particular things they would like to do with the parks, as well as make decisions on their own about what the best or fairest use of the park resources would be.

In these innovations, then, government not only uses its money to animate and direct activity of its own employees or contractors but also uses its direct regulatory authority and its hortatory moral power to mobilize private actors to make contributions to public purposes. It also allows individuals to make contributions to what were previously wholly government-controlled operations and, in doing so, allows the contributors to begin to make changes to the results of the public system.

Redistributing the right to define and judge the value of what is being produced

Fourth, the innovations described above seem to change the locus of "decision rights" over the use of particular assets in society. This seems to come as an almost inevitable consequence of changing organizational boundaries and reaching out for private resources. When the state recruits private money and community organizations to its purposes, it seems to give up at least some of its power to define what should be produced, for whom, and in what way. The New York City Parks Department loses some of its iron control over what happens in the parks. The CPS loses its iron control over what happens in the handling of instances of abuse and neglect. Because it seeks some voluntary help in both cases, those who provide the help can negotiate the terms under which their help is offered. Because they have the power to "exit", their "voice" becomes more powerful in shaping governmental policy and action. They do not have to remain "loyal" to the government and its purposes.

On the other hand, the locus of decision-making and judgments about value have shifted in emphasis away from the individual to the state in relation to choices over free access (London) and the duty of care to elderly people (Singapore). Decision rights that used to be held by individuals in a private domain had been powerfully reconditioned by government authority.

Evaluating the innovations in terms of justice, fairness and community-building as well as of efficiency and effectiveness

Fifth, because these innovations use government authority as well as government money, and because they redistribute decision rights over the use of both publicly owned and privately owned assets, they invoke a different normative framework for evaluating the innovations we observe. In the classic case of private-sector product/process innovations, the innovations are evaluated largely in instrumental, utilitarian terms. The important questions are whether the new production processes resulted in lower costs, or higher quantity or quality per unit of cost; whether the new product or service positioned an organization more effectively in its preferred markets; and therefore whether it increased the prospects for maximizing shareholder wealth (as revealed in increased public valuations of its stock price).

In the cases considered here, where the innovations seem to relocate either responsibilities for producing publicly valued results, or rights to decide what constitutes publicly valued results, or some combination of the two, one is forced, we think, to evaluate the innovations not only in terms of efficiency and cost-effectiveness, but also in terms of what might be considered right relationships in the society – some notion of justice and fairness. After all, when a collective policy-decision is taken to move some established responsibility from the private domain to the public domain – as occurred when the Greater London Authority assumed the right to charge drivers for using certain London streets, or when the Singapore government legislated the obligation to provide elder care to the children – we are as interested in the question of whether that is a just and fair allocation of responsibility in the society as we are in the question of whether it will work to transform material conditions in desired directions. Conversely, when a collective public policy-decision is taken to give private parties more power in shaping what were previously governmentally dominated operations – when, for example, the CPS decides to give community-based organizations increased rights to shape the local response to child abuse and neglect, or the New York City Parks Department allows private groups the right to make financial and labor contributions to the parks that are conditioned on their particular ideas of what would be a good use of that public asset – we are also motivated to ask whether such a move is proper or not, and what the implications will be for the overall fairness and justice of a particular public production system.

Conclusion: innovations in governance as a challenge to innovation theory

In these five respects, then, the innovations in governance seem quite different from the innovations in products, services and production processes that we have, until recently, associated with innovation in the private sector. These innovations change production systems that cut across the boundaries of organizations, not just those of a single organization. They enlarge the range of resources that can be tapped to enlarge and improve the performance of the production system. They involve changes in what instruments government uses to animate and direct the production system for achieving the desired goals. They alter the configuration of decision-making rights with respect to how private and public resources will be used. And they raise important questions about the distribution of burdens and privileges in the society. Precisely because they involve changes such as these, it does not seem unreasonable to describe these as innovations in the governance of society and social conditions, not simply as innovations in government operations.

In considering the future of innovations in the public sector, innovations in governance are a significant part. It is possible that innovations will continue to evolve in ways which go to the heart of democratic government – the processes by which a community *discovers* its own interests, and begins to speak coherently as a collective about its aspirations of justice, prosperity, social relations and ecological sustainability. John Dewey (1927) wrote in *The Public and Its Problems* that the most important problem facing the public is discovering itself and identifying its own true interests. We argue that this challenge will only be solved by more practice with, and innovations in, the processes of democratic deliberation itself.

Acknowledgment

This is a revised and developed version of Mark Moore and Jean Hartley (2008) "Innovations in Governance", *Public Management Review*, 10 (1): 3–20.

Notes

1 In this chapter, we use "government" to refer to both government organizations (e.g. federal and national government, local government, etc.) and public service organizations which may have a degree of autonomy from central government, such as health services, criminal justice services, and agencies concerned with the environment, public health, etc., but which are funded and regulated as part of the public service sector.

2 Note: there is an equivalent issue in the private sector: namely, when private firms construct new contractual relations or, more ambitiously, new governance relations to improve their individual firm performance (see Tidd et al. 2005). This includes mergers and acquisitions, which are evaluated in terms of the impact they have on the market position of the firms involved in the mergers. It also includes the complex bundles of ownership rights and responsibilities that have integrated high-tech bio-med firms. It may even include choices that socially conscious enterprises make about whether and how to form working partnerships with nonprofit organizations. For our purposes here, however, we will focus most attention on these activities in the public sector where government is one of the important actors in creating or acting within a particular governance scheme.

References

Albury, D. (2005) "Fostering Innovation in Public Services", *Public Money and Management*, 25 (1): 51–6.

Altshuler, A. and Behn, R. (eds) (1997) *Innovations in American Government*, Washington, DC: The Brookings Institution.

Benington, J. (2000) "The Modernization and Improvement of Government and Public Services", *Public Money and Management*, 20 (2): 3–8.

Benington, J. and Moore, M. (forthcoming) *In Search of Public Value*, Basingstoke: Palgrave Macmillan.

Bessant, J. (2003) *High-involvement Management: Building and Sustaining Competitive Advantage through Continuous Change*, Chichester: John Wiley.

Bessant, J. (2005) "Enabling Continuous and Discontinuous Innovation: Learning from the Private Sector", *Public Money and Management*, 25 (1): 35–42.

Borins, S. (1998) *Innovating with Integrity*, Washington, DC: Georgetown University Press.

Dewey, J. (1927) *The Public and Its Problems*, Athens, Ohio: Swallow Press/Ohio University; reprinted 1988.

Hartley, J. (2005) "Innovation in Governance and Public Services: Past and Present", *Public Money and Management*, 25 (1): 27–34.

Hartley, J. (2006) *Innovation and Its Contribution to Improvement: A Literature Review for Policy-makers, Policy Advisors, Managers and Academics*, London: Department of Communities and Local Government.

Hartley, J. (2008) "The Innovation Landscape for Public Service Organizations", in J. Hartley, C. Donaldson, C. Skelcher and M. Wallace (eds) *Managing to Improve Public Services*, Cambridge: Cambridge University Press.

Hartley, J. and Allison, M. (2000) "The Role of Leadership in Modernisation and Improvement of Public Services", *Public Money and Management*, 20 (2): 35–40.

Hill, C. and Lynn, L. (2005) "Is Hierarchical Governance in Decline? Evidence from Empirical Research", *Journal of Public Administration Research and Theory*, 15 (2): 173–95.

Hoggett, P. (2006) "Conflict, Ambivalence and the Contested Purpose of Public Organizations", *Human Relations*, 59 (2): 175–94.

Koch, P. and Hauknes, J. (2005) *Innovation in the Public Sector*, Oslo: Publin.

Kooiman, J. (2003) *Governing as Governance*, London: Sage.

Landau, J. (1993) "Organizational Change and Barriers to Innovation: A Case Study in the Italian Public Sector", *Human Relations*, 46 (12): 1411–29.

Lynn, L. (1997) "Innovation and the Public Interest: Insights from the Private Sector", in A. Altshuler and R. Behn (eds) *Innovation in American Government*, Washington, DC: The Brookings Institution.

Moore, M. (1995) "Creating Public Value", Cambridge, MA: Harvard University Press.

Moore, M. H. (2005) "Break-through Innovations and Continuous Improvement: Two Different Models of Innovative Processes in the Public Sector", *Public Money and Management*, 25 (1): 43–50.

Moore, M. H., Sparrow, M. and Spelman, W. (1997) "Innovation in Policing: From Production Line to Jobs Shops", in A. Altshuler and R. Behn (eds) *Innovation in American Government*, Washington, DC: The Brookings Institution.

Mulgan, G. and Albury, D. (2003) *Innovations in the Public Sector*, London: Cabinet Office.

National Audit Office (2006) *Achieving Innovation in Central Government Organizations*, London: The Stationery Office.

Newman, J. (2001) *Modernising Governance: New Labour, Policy and Society*, London: Sage.

Osborne, S. and Brown, K. (2005) *Managing Change and Innovation in Public Service Organizations*, London: Routledge.

Rogers, E. (2003) *Diffusion of Innovations*, 5th edn, New York: Free Press.

Skelcher, C. (in press) "Does Governance Perform? Concepts, Evidence, Causalities, and Research Strategies", in J. Hartley, C. Donaldson, C. Skelcher and M. Wallace (eds) *Managing to Improve Public Services*, Cambridge: Cambridge University Press.

Thompson, V. (1965) "Bureaucracy and Innovation", *Administrative Science Quarterly*, (10): 1–20.

Tidd, J., Bessant, J. and Pavitt, K. (2005) *Managing Innovation: Integrating Technological, Market and Organizational Change*, 3rd edn, Chichester: John Wiley.

Utterback, J. (1996) *Mastering the Dynamics of Innovation*, Cambridge, Mass.: Harvard Business School Press.

Van de Ven, A. (1986) "Central Problems in the Management of Innovation", *Management Science*, 32 (5): 590–607.

Walker, R. Jeanes, E. and Rowlands, R. (2002) "Measuring Innovation: Applying the Literature-based Innovation Output Indicator to Public Services", *Public Administration*, 80: 201–14.

Wolfe, R. (1994) "Organizational Innovation: Review, Critique, and Suggested Research Directions", *Journal of Management Studies*, 31 (3): 405–31.

5

GOVERNANCE AND GOVERNABILITY

Jan Kooiman

1. Introduction

This chapter is not about governance in general. There are several introductions available giving a fair picture of the many approaches to the concept (e.g. Schuppert 2005; Kjær 2004; Pierre 2000). Three features are common to them: they reflect the growth of social, economic and political interdependencies; governance is a matter of public as well as private actors; and dividing lines between public and private sectors become blurred. They differ mainly by directing themselves at a particular level, such as local, European or global governance, or by focusing on a particular form or aspect, such as network, multi-level, or participatory governance. The governance perspective discussed in this chapter fits more in the second group looking at governance as a societal phenomenon to be studied at all levels. In this sense Osborne is correct in saying that it can be considered as "most expansively . . . social-political governance as an over-arching theory of institutional relationships within society" (2006: 381).

In its theoretical framework, interactions are given a central place as it takes as its (normative) starting point that the solving of major problems and the creation of major opportunities in modern societies are a combined responsibility of state, market and civil society together – be it in different and shifting combinations of interactions between actors and institutions within and between them (Kooiman 1993, 2003).

The more detailed elaboration of the governance approach now becomes part of the broader governability concept consisting of a system-to-be-governed (SG), a governing system (GS) and the interactions between the two (GI). The first part of the chapter is devoted to the interactive governance perspective as such, and the governability framework forms the second part of this chapter (Kooiman 2008).

2. Interactive governance

In accordance with other approaches, the interactive governance perspective proceeds from the assumption that societies are governed by a combination of governing efforts (Kooiman 2003). These governing mixes are "answers" to ever-growing societal diversity, dynamics and complexity, and responses to major societal issues such as poverty and climate change.

The main concept here is that of "interactive governance", defined as *the whole of interactions taken to solve societal problems and to create societal opportunities; including the formulation and application of principles guiding those interactions and care for institutions that enable and control them.*

The emphasis on "interactions" constitutes the main innovation in this approach. Interactions are specific forms of action, undertaken in order to remove obstacles and to follow new paths, whereby the definition of a problem or an opportunity depends on the issue at hand as well as on the position and understanding of the observer. The adjective "societal" is best-understood by way of its antonym, "private", and is often replaced by the word "public" – it is everything that has a common, social and collective component. Institutions are also included in the definition as they are considered to be vital for any governance interaction. So, too, are principles according to which interactions take place and institutions function. The assumption is that governance arrangements lacking a normative basis suffer from ineffectiveness and illegitimacy in the long run.

Theoretically the interactive perspective on governance proposes that societies are made up of large numbers of governance actors, who are constrained or enabled in their actions by structures. Actors, in this perspective, are any social unit possessing agency or power of action. These include individuals, associations, leaders, firms, departments and international bodies. Structure refers to the frameworks within which these actors operate; these limit or widen their action potentials, and must therefore be taken into account. These frameworks include culture, laws, agreements, material and technical possibilities. According to sociological reasoning, actors are continuously making changes to these structures while at the same time being subjected to their influence (Giddens 1984; Berger and Luckmann 1966). The analysis of governance requires attention to both dimensions.

Present-day societies derive their strength from their diversity, complexity and dynamics.

Diversity calls attention to the specific and varying qualities of actors and other entities in a societal system. It is a source of creation and innovation, but also carries the danger of disintegration. Complexity invites examination of societal structures, interdependencies and inter-relations, and is a condition for combining interdependencies. The difficulty is how to reduce it in an effective and responsible manner. By introducing dynamics of systems we call attention to the regularity or irregularity with which societal developments, often combined with tensions, take place. Dynamics create the potential for change, but can have disruptive consequences.

These features continuously present societies with problems, but also with opportunities. These opportunities and problems themselves are also complex, dynamic and diverse. After all, they reflect the strengths and weaknesses of these societies. This also applies to the institutional conditions under which opportunities are created and seized, and problems formulated and solved. To satisfy governance standards, such as being effective, efficient, legitimate and social-political or interactive, governance itself has to reflect the diverse, dynamic and complex character of the challenges it faces. Often problem definitions are too simple, policies too static, and audiences too generalized: this might be one of the primary reasons why so much governance does not satisfy governance criteria as stated.

3. Governability

Governors, the governed and the nature of interactions among governors and the governed all contribute to the governability of societies or parts thereof. In other words: governability is not considered as something primarily due to the quality of those governing or governance entities – as in older concepts of governability often was argued (for an overview of this aspect, see Kooiman 2008); in the interactive governance perspective, governability is considered to be a quality of societal systems as wholes. For that reason, it can be defined as *the overall capacity for governance of any societal entity or system as a whole.*

The interactive governance approach assumes that the condition of governability of any system is continuously changing in response to external and internal challenges. What may be high governability at a given time may be low governability at another. Similarly, what may be effective governance in one place may be ineffective in another. Acts of governance may influence governability as a whole or any of its components. However, many external factors influence governability as well, some of which cannot, or only incompletely so, be handled neither by those governing or those governed at the scale this is applied. This often enhances uncertainty with respect to the governability of a societal system or entity in its human as well as its natural parts. One may state that governability is a condition fluctuating on a continuing scale without ever reaching the extremes; it is never total or complete.

Systems

Systems are usually defined as the whole of inter-relations among a given number of entities. Societal systems are "rich" in the sense that their components and their inter-relations have many facets, will overlap in many ways, all have their own histories and identities. Systems show properties which cannot be derived from simply adding properties of the constituting components. What a system looks like, how it can be broken down, and what its boundaries and other qualities might be depend on the perspectives of its observers. Any system – societal, natural, or combinations of the two – can be seen as part of a set or hierarchy of nested systems. Where in this set one wants to locate a particular system also exists in the eyes of its beholders. The more beholders with comparable ideas about a system, the stronger the concept becomes, for study and for practical purposes. The flexibility of defining systems, their parts, their boundaries and environments for particular research purposes is one of its attractions. This general observation also applies to societal systems.

The diversity, complexity and dynamics of the inter-relations between parts characteristic for systems (societal and natural) make for uncertainties and unpredictability in systems behavior. There is nothing secretive about these qualities; they simply are the consequence of actors, elements or parts of systems acting or interacting without having the possibility of knowing what the results of their actions or interactions are for systems behavior as a whole. Systems theorists such as Jervis (1997), Gell-Mann (1994) and Cilliers (1998) all put great emphasis on this aspect.

Mechanisms like these have consequences for those (inter)acting in a societal system, but also for the study of them, because basically reductionist approaches focusing on actors or interactions by themselves must fail because the larger (system) picture misses (see, e.g., Mayntz 2004). But a purely holistic one, where the system as such is the unit of analysis, does not work, either. Combinations are necessary. By stressing the role of interactions as we do, one step toward a better understanding of governance behavior can be set.

Important is the conceptual relation between scale, level, hierarchy and nestedness as we see the analysis of governance and governability of a specific system as a choice of level in a set of nested systems. Scale is seen as the spatial, temporal, quantitative, or analytical dimensions used to measure or study any phenomenon and level as a unit of analysis located at the same position on a scale. Scales and levels can serve different analytical or theoretical purposes.

To understand what a system might look like, it must have boundaries in one way or another. Societal systems with natural components or resources included are open systems – up to a point. This is of importance not only theoretically but also at a fundamental level. Completely closed systems, according to the laws of entropy, will die in the long run, because every system needs outside energy and/or information to survive. On the other hand, completely open is not an option, either. Societal systems derive their existence from a recognizable identity, and identity assumes or requires distinction from its environment. So one might say that systems and their environments together "constitute" these boundaries.

Subsystems

One of the possibilities within system approaches is to define subsystems together forming the system as a whole. It seems logical in the context of the interactive governance of societal systems to take as a choice criterion these interactions, defined as a subsystem (GI) between, on the one hand, the subsystem-to-be-governed (SG) and, on the other hand, the governing subsystem (GS). [For sake of presentation we delete the addition "sub"; instead we speak of societal system and the three subsystems SG, GS and GI.] So we might extend the definition of governability by seeing it as the overall capacity for governance of any societal entity or system consisting of SG, GS and GI. In practice this means that we consider the concept of governability as an integrated whole, while explaining that each of its components (SG, GS and GI) has a conceptual basis on its own. All three components also have their own governability aspects. The SG we see as all societal processes and structural arrangements, activities that form and surround what we call societal primary processes, such as creating a family, taking care of the sick, producing cars and catching fish. We do not intend to develop general theories for them, but our interest is in focusing on governability issues they may raise. The governing system (GS) consists of actors, entities and parties having varying potentials available for their governance roles and tasks with regard to the SG. GI we see as the subsystem where all relations and interactions between SG and GS are concentrated. Although GI is to a large extent dependent on the way GS and SG are able and willing to interact, they may develop characteristics of their own, which in the interactive governance perspective will receive special attention.

For governance or governability purposes, all aspects of systems, including scales, levels, boundaries and nestedness, can be "problematized" and considered relevant depending on the research purpose or practical application. It does make a difference from a governance point of view where a boundary can be imagined as resilient or fluid, a boundary can be considered as soft, hard or permeable, and the influence of other system levels in the nested hierarchy taken into consideration or not.

4. Governability and the system-to-be-governed (SG)

The key consideration with any SG is to determine where and what makes it more or less governable. So we have to specify and narrow down what we see as relevant for conceptualizing SG in such terms, and the best way to do this is to find one or more good theories or conceptual approaches. These have to be of an interdisciplinary nature as we want to look at SG in broad terms as long as we don't know where to find such potential governability factors.

It speaks for itself that we take the central concepts we have developed so far as our analytical point of departure. This is in the first place the interaction concept used at the actor and system level as a central one as well as the idea that modern societies are being characterized by the features diversity, complexity and dynamics, and preferably as a combination.

Using the interaction and the system concept as two main concepts for conceptualizing SG, we might take two analytical roads, comparable to the "old-time" distinction between micro and macro. One is building up from a micro-societal situation, using interactions around a societal activity or primary societal process such as teaching a class, selling a car, building a bridge or catching a fish as a starting point. One can look out for the diversity, complexity and dynamics of such processes and broaden their scope till a level has been reached where asking governability questions starts to make sense. The second one is to begin with a macro-system situation such as a whole fishery, an education or industrial system and break this down into smaller components, find out about their diversity, complexity and dynamics, again until a level has been reached where governability issues one wants to pursue arise.

Now, we can think ourselves lucky that there is a body of literature where both approaches have been practiced ("system-down" and "actor-up"), and in fact we used this ourselves in earlier research on the governance of fisheries. This is the chain concept, where a commodity, in our case fish, is followed from the eco-system to the consumer, enabling analysis not only of ecological, social, economic, cultural, ethical and political aspects of fish chains by scholars from different disciplines but also of their diversity, complexity and dynamics (Kooiman et al. 1999; Kooiman et al. 2005). We shall now discuss these two analytical strategies.

Commodity chains as an example of conceptualizing SG

Although any type of primary process could be chosen, we shall focus on what have come to be known as commodity chains. Other terms and analyses are global value chains, commodity networks, circuits and, in the French tradition, *filières* – all having special meanings, research communities, ideological and political backgrounds (for an overview, see Bair 2005). Of those we take two as they show nicely a system-and-actor approach to an SG: the world-system and the global (value) chain.

World-systems studies of commodity chains are the most macro, stressing their role in the structuring and reproduction of capitalist society and international division of labor. Commodity chains are the units of analysis of contraction and expansion processes over time (many of the studies are historical analyses), with notions of competition at their basis. In the last few centuries such cyclical patterns in commodity chains have taken place several times, according to this theory. Globalization, according to it, is not a recent phenomenon; there has been a world economic system since the sixteenth century. A recent study shows that commodity chain analysis "not only can chart the growing disjuncture between global economic activity and global income distribution, but also can provide causal explanations for this outcome" (Kaplinski 2001: 117).

Global commodity (value) chain (GCC) studies emphasize the organizational character of the economic integration taking place around commodities under the influence of globalization. In an authoritative definition, a GCC consists of

> interorganizational networks clustered around one commodity or product, linking households, enterprises, and states to one another within the world-economy. These networks are situationally specific, socially constructed, and locally integrated, underscoring the social embeddedness of economic organization.
>
> (Gereffi and Korzeniewicz 1994: 2)

Value chain studies have contributed much to the knowledge of chain processes. An important distinction is between producer-driven, e.g. automobiles, or buyer-driven, mainly agricultural products chains where the influence of supermarket giants and retailers is great. To this set of two a third was recently added, trader-driven chains, "where international trading companies . . . are able to procure continuously specific volumes and quality mixes" (Gibbon 2001: 351).

These two examples of chain studies show the possibility of studying a particular SG in ways where their actor as well as their structural aspect can be taken into account. In this case different chains show different types of governability characteristics, where world-system approaches show broad patterns of governability issues in a longer time perspective, such as who gets what at a global scale, while value chain studies show such issues more related to specific chains, such as who controls and governs them. It speaks for itself that other societal systems such as public health or international finance can be analyzed in actor-up or structure-down terms, and show their particular governability issues depending on the scale or level one wants to pursue.

5. Governability and the governing system (GS)

Governability from the point of view of the GS is the capacity to bring about, organize and carry out governance activities in the face of societal and natural diversity, complexity and dynamics. In the interactive governance approach, a conceptual framework has been developed for this purpose from which we shall present two attributes here: orders and elements of governance

(Kooiman 2003; the attribute modes will discussed under the heading of GI, as in the context of governability they fit better there). This capacity applies to all three of the major components – state, market and civil society – and to the hybrid forms among them as subsystems of GS.

Governability and subsystems of GS

States are still the most central and omnipresent societal governance subsystems. They steer and control from local to international levels in diverse and complex ways. For all practical purposes, the concept of a homogeneous societal institution, denoted as "the state" and governed by uniform rules, has to be replaced by other models, allowing variety and differentiation as well as certain degrees of independence and interdependence. Changes also show the dynamics of the modern state, and "[w]hilst the state . . . may be in retreat in some respects, its activity may be increasing in others. And nowhere . . . has its key decision-making role been seriously undermined" (Müller and Wright 1994: 1).

Markets, as governance institutions, also have their own diverse, complex and dynamic features. Williamson's view of governance (1975), in which institutional economics provide the institutional framework, consists broadly of markets, hierarchies and mixed forms of them, through which transactions are channeled. This amounts to getting away from general economic laws explaining market interactions, but showing some of their governance aspects. Next to this the field of economic sociology is the main contributor to insights into the market as a governance institution and its societal characteristics in a broad sense (e.g. Swedberg 2005).

The governance roles of *civil society* can be conceived of as a societal institution for which the term "public domain" has been coined; interactions between the media, interest groups, universities and social movements discussing, criticizing and mobilizing more informal governance forces. There is a massive literature on the subject, e.g. about what belongs to it or not, what its societal contributions are, differences between north and south. The dynamics and balance between state and civil society are in constant flux such that "neither of the two can monopolize public life without provoking a reaction from the opposite realm to retain political space" (Biekart 1999: 36–7).

Hybrids between the three societal institutions receive much attention today. Where the state withdraws and leaves some of its servicing tasks to the market, companies with private or mixed ownership are also common. For governability this hybridization of institutions and the way they are institutionalized on the borderline between state, market and civil society are important and are challenging issues to assess (Van Tulder and Van der Zwart 2006).

Governability and attributes of SG

Elements of governance

In the interactive governance theory, three governing elements are distinguished: images, instruments and action. All three play a role: images as sets of ideas where those governing want to go, instruments giving these ideas substance and making them operational, and action potential needed to support these instruments and let them do their work.

Images constitute the guiding lights for the how and why of governance. Images come in many types: visions, knowledge, facts, judgments, presuppositions, hypotheses, convictions, ends and goals. They not only relate to specific issues but also contain assumptions about fundamental matters such as the relationships between society and nature, the essence of humankind, and major societal trends. For governance and for governability, it is important that images help in understanding the diversity, complexity and dynamics of the subjects and issues they are facing. A distinction between types of images/knowledge might be helpful: ideas, arguments and data. The more these three support each other, and the more other actors are able to assess the validity of governance images from their perspective and to add to or modify it, the more they are shared, the more governance images can contribute to governability. The same type of reasoning can be developed for the instrumental and action component of governance (see further Kooiman 2003, 2008).

The governance elements images, instruments and action are highly interrelated. It is the fit between the three elements of governance that can be seen as the major contribution of these elements to governability.

Orders of governance

The theoretical framework developed here also relates to orders of governance. These can be imagined as three concentric circles nested as in the peel of an onion. The three orders are closely related and always – even when they are not made explicit – available.

First-order governance takes place wherever people and their organizations interact in order to solve societal problems and create new opportunities. It provides the means of solving the constant stream of problems which surface in the system-to-be-governed – problems of supply, price, market, employment, work satisfaction, etc. In diverse, complex and dynamic societies, first-order governance faces special challenges. It starts with the identification of problems, a process which takes place first of all in the minds of societal actors. The first step in the governance process is therefore the identification and formulation of societal problems, whereby the latter are distinguished from private problems by their scale and shared nature. Once problems, and problem systems, have been identified, attention shifts to the solution space.

It is important throughout to retain in the analysis the diversity, complexity, dynamics and scale of situations, as only then will images remain close to reality.

Second-order governance focuses on the institutional arrangements within which first-order governing takes place. Here the term "institution" denotes the agreements, rules, rights, laws, norms, roles, procedures and organizations that are applied by first-order governors to make decisions. Institutions provide the framework within which first-order governance takes place, and constitute the meeting ground for those being governed and those governing. Second-order governance implies the reconsideration and adaptation of the parameters of first-order governance.

Meta- or third-order governance feeds, binds and evaluates the governing exercise. Many principles govern activities. For example, the principles responsibility and sustainability are recognized almost universally. In meta-governance, governors and governed alike take each other's measure in formulating norms by which to judge each other and the measuring process, too.

For governability, the three orders have special importance: together they form the backbone of the capacity of a GS to govern in the three dimensions sketched. Not only each by itself but crucially are the three governing orders or differentiated tasks connected with them in a societal system: are they complementary to one another, or are they at odds?

It will be quite clear that this discussion of the three subsystems of GS and the choice of a few attributes is only the very beginning of analyzing and assessing GS. The attributes presented are from earlier work in the field of governance, and can be worked out and added to at will. The potential literature on these subjects is almost unlimited, and for each special case reasonable choices can be made. Basic, however, is the idea that the governance capacity of SG and its contribution to the governability of a specific society or societal field has to include all three subsystems and, as we proposed for SG, has to include structural- as well as action-level variables, preferably in their mutual relation.

6. Governability and governance interactions (GI)

Interactions between SG and GS are crucial for governance, and thus important for studying and assessing governability. Those governed, through their participation, try to exert influence on those governing, and governing entities try to influence those governed through their policies and management efforts. Above, the centrality of the interaction concept for our governance perspective has been put forward; here we continue this presentation of our ideas at this point.

In the reality of modern governance, an enormous variety of interactions can be observed. From the GI perspective, they can be ordered in a few major types: participatory, collaborative and policy or management interactions (see Kooiman 2003 for the conceptual basis of this distinction).

For governability, it is important to know how social-political entities – such as individuals, organizations, groups, movements or other forms of collective action – *participate* in governing interactions. Where does such participatory action come from? Who acts and who reacts? I see participatory interactions as directed from SG to GS. The character of the interaction is determined by the responsiveness of those governing, on the one hand, and what has been called the "repertory" of resources and activities which the governed command, on the other (Barnes and Kaase 1979). This repertory is wide and varies: voting, letter-writing, and protesting in sit-ins and boycotts, participating in a movement or being a member of a focus or action group, and many more. Social movements are the classical example of this kind of spontaneous, loosely organized form of governance interaction. As these interactions are the least systematically organized, I call them *interferences.*

The importance of *collaborative* forms of governance interactions is growing. Why, for governance purposes, are groups, organizations and authorities willing to share their activities and aim to do things together instead of doing them alone? Often mutual interdependencies are mentioned as the main reason for such collaborative or co-operative interactions. Partnerships between public and private entities are a popular form of such collaboration. But collaborative interactions between companies and NGOs can also be found in many fields (see, for a recent overview, Glasbergen et al. 2007). As these collaborative interactions are mainly of a horizontal nature, they are indicated as *interplays.*

Policy and management interactions are the collective variables for all interventionist interactions by GS aimed at having an impact on SG. Public authorities at all levels have numerous interactions, dressed in policy terms, at their disposal to bring about politically preferred societal changes (Mayer et al. 2005). Management is seen as a way to organize these interactions according to criteria of efficiency and effectiveness. Stake-holder identification, for example, has become a popular (interventionist) tool in this respect (Bryson 2004: 32–3). As basically these interactions are formally organized, I call them *interventions.*

Social-political cultural traditions and power relationships also find their expression in governance interactions. For example, it is often said that "Anglo-Saxon" social-political culture does not stimulate formal interactions between governors and governed, in contrast to the "Continental" tradition, where those are enabled and often institutionalized. Such differences may also explain why co-governing interactions, such as co-management schemes in fisheries, are more common in some political cultures than in others (Wilson et al. 2003).

This points to the analytical distinction in governance interactions made for interactions generally: an action or intentional level and a structural or contextual level. This distinction, although the subject of heated social science debates, such as in terms of agency-structure, is a useful one. Any conceptualization of the constituent actors in a governance interaction necessarily involves an idea of its structural component.

At the structural level, three modes of governance can be distinguished: self-, co- and hierarchical governance. These three modes roughly correspond to the three interaction modes at the action level of governance: interferences with self-governance, interplays with co-governance, and interventionist ones with hierarchical governance. All societies demonstrate mixes of these three governance modes, and all three modes contribute in specific ways to the role governance systems and governance interactions play in governability.

In modern society, *self-governance* refers to situations in which actors take care of themselves, outside the purview of government. Liberal political thinking typically highlights societal self-governing capacities, while socialist-oriented ones downplay them. It must be emphasized here that self-governance is not necessarily a government-created capacity, but comes about of its own accord. In fact, if a capacity for self-governance is not sustained, societal governance is an impossible task. The collective-action school has made the most systematic analysis of self-governance with regard to the exploitation of common-pool natural resources, such as capture fisheries (Ostrom 1990).

The essential element of *co-governance* is that societal parties join hands with a common purpose in mind, and stake their identities and autonomy on this process. Much attention has been devoted to co-governance and to the opportunities that it offers. In capture fisheries, a form of co-governance called co-management has been particularly influential (Wilson et al. 2003). Governance theory contains numerous manifestations of co-governance, including communicative governance, public–private partnerships, networks, regimes and co-management (Kooiman 2003).

Hierarchical governance is the most classical mode, and is characteristic for the interactions between a state and its citizens, but also for companies with their personnel. It is a top-down style of intervention, expressing itself in policies, rules and regulations. Steering and control are the key concepts here. In recent years, perceptions of hierarchical governance have become redefined under the influence of market ideas and concepts like managing and client orientation (e.g. Ferlie et al. 2005).

Systems of GI

Combining the action and structural level of governance, interaction systems of them come into sight. For analyzing governability, it is important to get an idea what the features of GI systems might be next to those of GS and SG. To understand what is going on in these GIs, again we might use insight into diversity, complexity and dynamics. There is an important argument for taking the *diversity* of values, goals and interests of those involved in interactions into account. This points to processes of ordering and re-ordering of aspects of diversity. The complexity of GIs can easily be understood if one takes a closer look at all the groups and organizations involved in specific governance fields. And their dynamics can be seen as a composition of forces which sometimes turn into gradual developments, but more often result in nonlinear patterns of change. Insights in societal dynamics have direct or indirect relevance for governance and an assessment of the role of the GI in governability. For example, in his study of interactions between state and society, De Vries (2005) distinguished four (macro) types of policy interactions between government and society in the Netherlands by cross-tabulating (dis)parity of power and authority (vertical, horizontal) and perceived interests (antagonistic, congruent). These four types were characteristic only for a certain period during the last fifty years, and after some time changed into another system of policy interaction – a transition which expresses the dynamic nature of governance interactions.

7. Conclusion

In this essay I sketched the main contours of the governability concept based upon the interactive perspective on governance. In other publications some of its aspects have been dealt with more extensively, and interdisciplinary activities evolved to work with and test it in the study and practice of fisheries, coastal zones and aquaculture (see papers in special issue of *Journal of Transdisciplinary Environmental Studies*, 2008: Kooiman et al. 2008; Chuenpagdee et al. 2008; Mahon 2008; Bavinck and Salagrama 2008; also Jentoft 2007; Mahon et al. 2009; Jentoft and Chuenpagdee 2009). There are still many conceptual questions not answered. However, a systematic beginning has been made to release it from its earlier scholarly isolation by an unfortunate pseudo-political use of the concept. So far it has shown its utility in actual research in the field of aquatic resources, and there is no immediate reason why it could not be applied in other societal fields as well.

References

Bair, J. (2005) "Global Capitalism and Commodity Chains: Looking Back, Going Forward", *Competition and Change*, 9 (2): 153–80.

Barnes, S. H. and Kaase, M. (1979) *Political Action*, Beverly Hills, Calif.: Sage.

Bavinck, M. and Salagrama, V. (2008) "Assessing the Governability of Capture Fisheries in the Bay of Bengal: A Conceptual Exploration", *Journal of Transdisciplinary Environmental Studies*, 7 (1).

Berger, P. L. and Luckmann, T. (1966) *The Social Construction of Reality: A Treatise in the Sociology of Knowledge*, Garden City, NY: Anchor Books.

Biekart, C. H. (1999) *The Politics of Civil Society Building*, Utrecht: International Books.

Bryson, J. M. (2004) "What to Do when Stakeholders Matter: Stakeholder Identification and Analysis Technique", *Public Management Review*, 6: 21–54.

Chuenpagdee, R., Kooiman, J. and Pullin, R. (2008) "Assessing Governability in Capture Fisheries, Aquaculture and Coastal Zones", *Journal of Transdisciplinary Environmental Studies*, 7 (1).

Cilliers, P. (1998) *Complexity and Postmodernism*, London: Routledge.

De Vries, M. S. (2005) "Generations of Interactive Policy-making in the Netherlands", *International Review of Administrative Sciences*, 71: 577–91.

Ferlie, E., Lynn, L. E., Jr, and Pollitt, C. (eds) *The Oxford Handbook of Public Management*, Oxford: Oxford University Press.

Gell-Mann, M. (1994) *The Quark and the Jaguar*, London: Little, Brown.

Gereffi, G. and Korzeniewicz, M. (eds) (1994) *Commodity Chains and Global Capitalism*, Westport, Conn.: Praeger.

Gibbon, P. (2001) "Upgrading Primary Production: A Global Commodity Chain Approach", *World Development*, 29 (2): 345–63.

Giddens, A. (1984) *The Constitution of Society*, Berkeley, Calif.: University of California Press.

Glasbergen, P., Bierman, F. and Mol, J. P. A. (eds) (2007) *Partnerships, Governance and Sustainable Development*, Cheltenham: Edward Elgar.

Jentoft, S. (2007) "Limits to Governability? Institutional Implications for Ocean and Coastal Governance", *Marine Policy*, 4: 360–70.

Jentoft, S. and Chuenpagdee, R. (2009) "Fisheries and Coastal Governance as a Wicked Problem", *Marine Policy*, 4: 553–60.

Jervis, R. (1997) *System Effects: Complexity in Political and Social Life*, Princeton, NJ: Princeton University Press.

Kaplinski, R. (2001) "Globalisation and Unequalisation: What Can Be Learned from Value Chain Analysis", *Journal of Development Studies*, 327 (2): 117–46.

Kjær, A. M. (2004) *Governance*, Cambridge/Oxford/Boston, Mass.: Polity.

Kooiman, J. (ed.) (1993) *Modern Governance*, London: Sage.

Kooiman, J. (2003) *Governing as Governance*, London: Sage.

Kooiman, J. (2008) "Exploring the Concept of Governability", *Journal of Comparative Policy Analysis*, 10 (2): 171–90.

Kooiman, J., Bavinck, M., Chuenpagdee, R., Mahon, R. and Pullin, R. (2008) "Interactive Governance and Governability: An Introduction", *Journal of Transdisciplinary Environmental Studies*, 7 (1).

Kooiman, J., Bavinck, M., Jentoft, S. and Pullin, R. (eds) (2005) *Fish for Life*, Amsterdam: Amsterdam University Press.

Kooiman, J., Vliet, M. van and Jentoft, J. (eds) (1999) *Creative Governance*, Aldershot: Ashgate.

Mahon, R. (2008) "Assessing Governability of Fisheries Using the Interactive Governance Approach: Preliminary Examples from the Caribbean", *Journal of Transdisciplinary Environmental Studies*, 7 (1).

Mahon, R., Fanning, L. and McConney, P. (2009) "A Governance Perspective on the Large Marine Ecosystem Approach", *Marine Policy*, 2: 317–21.

Mayer, I., Edelenbos, J. and Monnikhof, R. (2005) "Interactive Policy Development: Undermining or Sustaining Democracy", *Public Administration*, 83: 179–99.

Mayntz, R. (2004) "Mechanisms in the Analysis of Social-macro Phenomena", *Philosophy of the Social Sciences*, 34 (2): 237–59.

Müller, W. C. and Wright, V. (1994) "Reshaping the State in Western Europe", *West European Politics*, 17: 1–11.

Osborne, S. (2006) "The New Public Governance?", *Public Management Review*, 8 (3): 381.

Pierre, J. (ed.) (2000) *Debating Governance*, Oxford: Oxford University Press.

Schuppert, G. F. (ed.) (2005) *Governance-Forschung*, Baden-Baden: Nomos.

Swedberg, R. (2005) *Principles of Economic Sociology*, Princeton, NJ: Princeton University Press.

Van Tulder, R. and Van der Zwart, A. (2006) *International Business–Society Management*, London: Routledge.

Williamson, O. E. (1975) *Markets and Hierarchies*, New York: Free Press.

Wilson, C. D., Nielsen, J. R. and Degnbol, P. (eds) (2003) *The Fisheries Co-management Experience*, Dordrecht: Kluwer.

6

DOES GOVERNANCE EXIST?

Owen Hughes

The question in the title has a fairly obvious answer. Of course governance exists, so the question posed is moot from the very start. Consult any dictionary, and the word appears. That there is a noun "governance" is undoubted; precisely what it means is contested – so contested that the word has lost much of its utility. Much has been written about governance, particularly since its relatively recent rediscovery in the political science/public administration literature. As Frederickson has noted, "because governance is a power word, a dominant descriptor, and the current preference of academic tastemakers, there has been a rush to affix to it all of the other fashions of the day" (2005: 285). Governance in some usage becomes somewhat mysterious; meanings are assigned that have relevance only for a *cognoscenti* socialized and imbued into the mystery, with everyone else excluded. This is problematic.

Much of what follows is about the word "governance", and its meanings and usage. It is argued here that it is the standard dictionary meanings of "governance" that have resonance, utility and acceptability, and to attach special meanings to an ordinary word is unhelpful. Governance is about running organizations, about setting up structures to enable the organization to be run. Although words may change meaning over time, to ascribe obscure meanings to a word that has a commonplace meaning that is different is to invite irrelevance. Aside from some fashionable usage, "governance" is a good word; it is a simple word with simple meanings, and should be used accordingly.

Standard meanings of governance

It is beyond doubt that "governance" is used more than it was in the political science and public management literatures. However, as Pierre and Peters argue, "the concept of governance is notoriously slippery; it is frequently used among both social scientists and practitioners without a definition which all agree on" (2000: 7). A lack of definitional clarity may not be that unusual in the social sciences – does anyone agree on a single definition for "justice" or "democracy"? – but usage of such terms is understood as requiring some explanation or qualification when they are used. For some reason, "governance" has become a word for which, despite the innate slipperiness of the concept, there are attempts – often wildly different – at precision in definition or ascription of uses. It is argued here that these attempts do not add much to understanding; the major reason being that, alongside the more abstruse recent usages, there are standard meanings that are clear, generally used and well understood.

At base, there is, in English, the verb "govern", which derives from the Latin *gubernare*, meaning "steer, direct, rule"; and this, in turn, derives from the Greek *kubernan*, meaning "steer". The verb "govern" can then attract the well-known and common suffix "-ance" in order to transform the verb to a noun, in exactly the same way that "perform" becomes "performance". "Governance" is but one of many nouns deriving from "govern"; others include "government", "governor" and "governability". After this start, though, there is little agreement about governance.

The *New Shorter Oxford* lists three related meanings for governance: the first meaning is "the action, manner, or fact of governing; government" and also includes "controlling or regulating influence, control, mastery" and "the state of being governed; good order". The second meaning is "the function or power of governing; authority to govern" and "a governing person or body"; and the third meaning is "conduct of life or business, behaviour". These meanings are not inconsistent with each other, nor with other dictionaries. They have also been reasonably settled for several centuries: the first meaning is from Middle English, the second from later Middle English to the late sixteenth century, and the third from late Middle English to the mid-seventeenth century.

The dictionary meanings are also quite consistent with ordinary usage, especially "controlling or regulating influence, control, mastery" and the "conduct of life or business". Governance is about running organizations, about steering as in the original derivation, how to organize, and how to set procedures for an organization to be run. In what follows, this meaning is referred to as the standard, dictionary sense. In ordinary parlance, it is quite normal and correct to refer to the governance of schools and golf clubs, corporations, universities and even entire societies.

Not only is governance most often used in this steering and running organizations sense, it is also used this way in academic circles. Kjaer, for instance, sees governance as "the setting of rules, the application of rules, and the enforcement of rules" (2004: 10). Donahue argues that accountability underpins civilization and that "one broad model of accountability is governance – the rules and institutions for the authoritative organization of collective life" (2002: 1). Here, governance is taken in its broad meaning and is entirely consistent with the standard dictionary definition and usage.

Kooiman, too, is quite careful in his usage of terms. What he terms "social-political governance" is defined as "all those interactive arrangements in which public as well as private actors participate aimed at solving societal problems, or creating societal opportunities, and attending to the institutions within which these governing activities take place" (1999: 70). Kooiman also distinguishes between governance and governability; governance "can be seen as the total effort of a system to govern itself; governability is the outcome of this process – not an 'end state' but a stock-taking at a particular moment in time of complex, diverse and especially dynamic processes" (1999: 87). Regarding governance as "interactive arrangements" and as "the total effort of a system to govern itself" is entirely consistent with the standard meaning, and with "social-political" setting the context. In a later work, Kooiman draws a distinction between governing and governance, as follows:

> Governing can be considered as the totality of interactions, in which public as well as private actors participate, aimed at solving societal problems or creating societal opportunities; attending to the institutions as contexts for these governing interactions; and establishing a normative foundation for all those activities.
>
> Governance can be seen as the totality of theoretical conceptions on governing.
>
> (2003: 4)

This does provide an additional layer of abstraction in that there are clearly meanings of governance that do not require them to be about theoretical conceptions. However, Kooiman's work is argued to draw quite explicitly from the "steering" meaning of governance through the Dutch *besturen* and is entirely consistent.

Government and governance

As mentioned earlier, there is one, perhaps rare, point of some agreement among commentators and this is that "government" and "governance" now have different meanings. As Rhodes argues, "current use does not treat governance as a synonym for government" (1996: 652). Pierre and Peters, too, argue that government and governance may have the same derivation, but "they need not, and indeed, should not, be taken to mean the same thing" (2000: 29). However, some works do conflate the two.

An OECD paper defines governance as "the formal and informal arrangements that determine how public decisions are made and how public actions are carried out, from the perspective of maintaining a country's constitutional values in the face of changing problems, actors and environments" (2005: 16). This definition is only about *public* governance and is, therefore, already an unsatisfactory definition for governance as a whole. The paper then argues:

> The 30 member countries of the OECD share core governance elements. These have emerged with the evolution of the modern state and include: democracy and citizenship; representation; a constitution; the rule of law; competitive party and electoral systems; a permanent civil service; separation of powers between the executive, the legislature and the judiciary; and secularity.
>
> (OECD 2005: 15)

A footnote here says "drawn from Finer (1997)". Now, it is the case that Finer does mention all these things, but quite clearly in the context of *government* – the focus of his magisterial work. Finer's work is explicitly about the state, the authoritative forces of the police and the military.

In an earlier work, Finer found four meanings for "government". The first is "the activity or the process of governing, i.e. of exercising a measure of control over others"; the second is "a condition of ordered rule"; the third is "the people charged with governing"; and the final one is "the manner, method or system by which a particular society is governed" (Finer 1970: 3–4). And, as he continues, "this is all fairly straightforward because each of these meanings is well accepted and the only problem is to sort out the different usages and keep them separate" (1970: 4).

There are two points that follow. First, "government" is indeed about control, about authority, about ordered rule, as well as about those people able to do the ordering and the ruling. This part is quite clear. Second, the last meaning of Finer's, "the manner, method or system by which a particular society is governed", would, in current usage, be "governance" rather than "government" (see Rhodes 1996).

A government is the formal apparatus of society and can impose its will on the society. Governments have force at their disposal; they can require compliance through laws, and the coercion implied by those laws can be carried out. In societies with some pretence at democracy, the use of force may be muted – the Army and the police are nowhere near large enough to maintain the regime through force alone – and the legitimacy of government maintained by some kind of popular sovereignty. But the key point about government is that force is ultimately behind it; no other lawful authority but government can compel people to act in ways that it prescribes. Government and governance are not the same; that much can be agreed. There can, indeed, be governance without government.

Rhodes (1996) and Bevir and Rhodes (2003)

Usages of governance, consistent with standard meanings, exist alongside far more esoteric ones. The question that follows is: Do these add to understanding about governance as opposed to that obtained from ordinary, standard usage? While there are many formulations, one of the most widely cited formulations on governance is that of Rhodes (1996), who found what was termed "six separate uses of governance". These are:

- as the minimal state;
- as corporate governance;
- as the new public management;
- as "good governance";
- as a socio-cybernetic system; and
- as self-organizing networks (Rhodes 1996: 653).

In a later formulation by the same writer as a co-author (Bevir and Rhodes 2003), there are seven meanings; now – significantly – termed "definitions" rather than "uses" as in the earlier work. Most are the same as the Rhodes (1996) list, although the minimal state "use" is no longer present, and two new definitions have been added: "governance as international independence" and "governance as the new political economy" (Bevir and Rhodes 2003: 45–53). Some of these provide real insight, but others are neither meanings nor definitions. Using the earlier, dictionary definition of governance as running things and organization to run things, many are simply not required, that is, they are ordinary uses of the ordinary meanings of governance.

To start with the original Rhodes (1996) list, governance "as the minimal state" is argued by Rhodes to be about redefining public intervention and using markets to deliver services. He quotes Stoker approvingly that "governance is the acceptable face of spending cuts" (1996: 653). Rhodes argues that this kind of governance encapsulates the ideological preference for less government, but that this "says little else being an example of political rhetoric" (1996: 654). It is difficult to see any definition of governance in this point; indeed, it is dismissed by Rhodes, and it is hardly surprising that the notion did not survive to the Bevir and Rhodes (2003) list.

Similarly, the "governance as good governance" definition is really an ordinary use of the term with a commonplace qualifying adjective. Bevir and Rhodes argue that good governance refers to international agencies such as the World Bank in their promoting of better governing, and that "good governance tries to marry NPM to the advocacy of liberal democracy" (2003: 47). Presumably this means that good governance is about international agencies packaging up NPM with liberal democracy and selling it to developing nations under the guise of good governance. It is an odd claim given that there has been great caution in the application of NPM in such contexts and that building institutional capacity has been the main emphasis (Minogue et al. 1998). More apposite here is Kettl's argument that the management reform movement "builds on the notion that good governance – a sorting out of mission, role, capacity, and relationships – is a necessary (if insufficient) condition of economic prosperity and social stability" (2005: 6).

However, it is argued there is no new *definition* of governance in the notion of good governance. Certainly, the World Bank and other international institutions have become more interested in how countries, particularly countries receiving aid, organize and run themselves. They have become interested in good governance, that is, that societies are well run. But, again, all that is happening here is that the ordinary meaning of governance is being used.

Governance "as international independence" is similarly not a meaning and even less a definition. For Bevir and Rhodes, this involves the weakening of the nation-state's capacities for governance, through hollowing out of the state and multi-level governance (2003: 47). While there is extensive discussion of governance issues by scholars of international relations, there is no need for a special usage or meaning to be attached to the use of governance in such a context. Rosenau, for instance, from this international relations literature, argues that governance refers to "mechanisms for steering social organizations toward their goals" (1997: 40), also "the process of governance is the process whereby an organization or society steers itself" (1997: 146). Both points use the ordinary "steering" definition of governance and apply it to the running of entire societies and nation-states. It is argued that governance "as international independence" is not a useful definition.

Rhodes and Bevir and Rhodes argue that the power available to central-government actors has declined and that one definition of governance resulting is "as a socio-cybernetic system". In this definition of governance, "there is no longer a single sovereign authority and blurred boundaries between public, private and voluntary sectors", with examples cited including "self-regulation and co-regulation, public–private partnerships, co-operative management, and joint entrepreneurial ventures" (2003: 48). There may be a valid point here, but it does not add up to a *definition* as such. It is rather a recognition that governance needs to be looked at in its wider and original sense of steering, rather than as a synonym for government. Also, it is an unhelpful term that Rhodes has invented for the purpose. Given that "cybernetics" derives from the same Greek and Latin as does "governance" (Rosenau 1997: 146), calling governance "a socio-cybernetic system" is an obvious tautology. It is also unhelpful to define governance in relation to another term – cybernetics – that similarly evades agreed definition.

It is also difficult to see a distinction between this definition and that of governance "as the new political economy" which "re-examines both the government of the economy and the boundaries between civil society, state and the market economy as they become increasingly blurred" (Bevir and Rhodes 2003: 48–9). With blurred boundaries in this definition and the socio-cybernetic one, surely there is no separate meaning, either. In both of these, the site for governance cannot be located with certainty. As Kennett argues, "with the change from government to governance the governing administration is now only one player amongst many others in the policy arena" (2008: 4). There may be a real point to some of the ideas in "socio-cybernetic governance", but it is not a *definition* of governance, nor is it necessary to have one. Even if "socio-cybernetic" can be accepted as being meaningful, it is no more than a qualifying adjective to the standard meaning of governance. Other actors may well exercise governance functions, but such activities can co-exist within the normal meaning of governance as setting up a set of rules to run organizations.

There are other parts of the Rhodes (1996) and the Bevir and Rhodes (2003) lists of definitions that do warrant further discussion: governance as corporate governance; governance as the new public management (NPM); and governance as networks.

Corporate governance

One of the Rhodes and Bevir and Rhodes definitions of governance is "as corporate governance" (Bevir and Rhodes 2003: 45–6). A minor point is that a word should not be defined in terms of itself; but, more broadly, it is argued that this is not a definition at all, rather an ordinary usage of running things and steering, in this case involving corporations.

There is a large and important literature on corporate governance. There are many academics writing and researching issues about the running of corporations, in particular their accountability structures, principal–agent issues and the like (Jensen 2000; Keasey et al. 2005b). Moreover, there has been more action, more serious theorizing in corporate governance in the private sector than in public-sector governance in recent years. From principal–agent theory to transaction–cost theory to Enron and Sarbanes/Oxley, questions of corporate governance have dominated management in the private sector. Of course, there may be a tangential government involvement here in that the corporation's legal environment as set out by government is a key consideration in issues of corporate governance. But it is not the only consideration and neither is it necessarily the most important. The more recent concerns about corporate governance have been mainly about designing internal and external structures of accountability that lead to good managerial performance. The motivation is mainly to maintain and enhance shareholder and investor confidence rather than to satisfy any direct requirements from government.

However, corporate governance does not require a separate definition of governance. Its usage in this context is simply "governance" being used in its standard meaning. For instance, the Cadbury report in the UK in 1991 defined corporate governance as "the system by which companies are directed and controlled" (Keasey et al. 2005a: 21). An Australian government report defines corporate governance as encompassing "the arrangements by which the power of those in control of the strategy and direction of an entity is both delegated and limited to enhance prospects for the entity's long-term success, taking into account risk and the environment in which it is operating" (Australia 2003: 2). The paper continues by arguing that a good governance framework "should guide the actions of individuals by providing clarity of direction as to appropriate behavior and decision-making" (Australia 2003: 2). Governance is also seen as being about accountability in that "a robust governance framework should, through transparency and accountability mechanisms, link power and responsibility to performance and review" (Australia 2003: 2–3).

Not only are these points a good exposition of corporate governance; they are also entirely consistent with the standard meanings of governance outlined earlier. Applying governance to a corporate context does not require another definition at all; it is still about steering mechanisms but in a different context – the corporation rather than the society.

Governance as the new public management (NPM)

Another definition of governance in Bevir and Rhodes is "as the new public management". The key example used by them is the distinction made in a key work between steering and rowing, as they argue:

> Osborne and Gaebler distinguish between "policy decisions (steering) and service delivery (rowing)". They argue bureaucracy is a bankrupt tool for rowing. In place of bureaucracy, they propose "entrepreneurial government" which will stress competition, markets, customers and measuring outcomes. This transformation of the public sector involves less government (or less rowing) but more governance (or more steering).
>
> (Bevir and Rhodes 2003: 46)

Two questions follow from this. First, does governance as used by Osborne and Gaebler or NPM constitute a new definition of the word "governance"; and, second, has governance been a major concern of NPM, sufficient for an entire new definition to apply?

First, the distinction between steering and rowing was actually made by Savas (1987) and is duly attributed by Osborne and Gaebler (1992). Even if the latter's use has had more currency, it is misleading to characterize them as simply being about steering and rowing. Also, at no point do Osborne and Gaebler even mention NPM. Their ten principles of "entrepreneurial government" are quoted by Rhodes, who then argues "clearly, NPM and entrepreneurial government share a concern with competition, markets, customers and outcomes" (1996: 46). There may be similarities, but it is simplistic to conflate the two.

Moreover, when Osborne and Gaebler do use "governance" it is done in quite a standard way. For instance, they argue (with original emphases):

> Our fundamental problem is that we have *the wrong kind of government*. We do not need more government or less government, we need *better* government. To be more precise, we need better governance. Governance is the process by which we collectively solve our problems and meet our society's needs. Government is the instrument we use. The instrument is outdated, and the process of reinvention has begun.
>
> (1992: 23–4)

At another point, Osborne and Gaebler (1992) argue that privatization for ideological reasons is selling snake oil:

> Services can be contracted out or turned over to the private sector. But *governance* cannot. We can privatize discrete steering functions, but not the overall process of governance. If we did, we would have no mechanism by which to make collective decisions, no way to set the rules of the marketplace, no means to enforce rules of behavior.
>
> (1992: 45)

There is no new use of the word "governance" in Osborne and Gaebler, no novelty, certainly no definition, only the use of the word in its standard dictionary sense. Both Rhodes and Bevir and Rhodes argue that NPM is relevant to the discussion "because steering is central to the analysis of public management and a synonym for governance" (Rhodes 1996: 655; Bevir and Rhodes 2003: 46). This could be argued to prove the point that governance itself is about steering; Osborne and Gaebler are doing nothing more than using the term quite correctly according to its standard dictionary definition.

The second point to look at is the extent to which NPM is or was about governance in any case, sufficient for NPM then to be a definition of governance. It is argued here that, while there may be some system design aspects of NPM involving governance, these have not been anywhere near as substantial as the concerns in NPM about managing within government.

The most profound change resulting from NPM-type reforms has been the recognition that public managers are themselves responsible for achieving results and must take personal responsibility for doing so (Hughes 2003). From this change alone comes the need to decide if results have been achieved – performance measurement in its various permutations – as well as changes in accountability and much else. These are largely internal. As Kickert argues:

> Management in the public sector has to deal with more value patterns than business-like effectiveness and efficiency criteria, such as legality and legitimacy, social justice, and equal rights. So, we need to broaden the concept of public "management" to "governance".

> This concept is not restricted to internal management and organization but explicitly encompasses external relations between public organizations and their socio-political environment.
>
> (Kickert 1997: 197)

NPM was always more about the inside of the organization as well as enhancing the personal responsibility of managers. This was to occur with the governance structures largely unchanged; the governance part of NPM was minor and tangential rather than central. Therefore, governance "as NPM" is neither necessary nor helpful in a terminological sense.

To complicate the issue further, there are major problems in deciding exactly what is involved in NPM. It is often naïvely and incorrectly seen as a program. Not only is there no agreed set of points constituting NPM; neither is there anyone who puts the so-called program forward. And, as Hood and Peters argue, "Like most divinities, NPM turned out to be somewhat mystical in essence, as no two authors of that era listed exactly the same features in enumerating its traits" (2004: 268). Fountain describes NPM as "a loose collection of policy and management initiatives" (2001: 19); Christensen, Lie and Lægreid similarly argue that NPM "is actually a rather loose concept encompassing several different administrative doctrines" as well as being "rather contradictory" (2007), and Van Thiel, Pollitt and Homburg argue:

> NPM is like a chameleon: it constantly changes its appearance to blend in with the local context. . . . Such adaptability is possible, because NPM is not a coherent set of ideas and tools. The ideas might be the same, but the underlying story differs all the time.
>
> (2007: 197)

All of these writers admit, at least implicitly, that they cannot define NPM. What we have is a theory without a theorist, a program without an advocate and an agenda without anyone putting it forward. In so far as there is any agreement as to what is involved in NPM, the most salient points are within the organization and not in system-wide changes to governance.

Two other uses of "governance" in the context of public management need to be mentioned. These are put forward as replacements for NPM – one from Dunleavy et al. (2006) and the other from Osborne (2006).

Dunleavy et al. (2006) argue that NPM is dead and has been overtaken by what they term "digitally enhanced governance" (DEG). This is characterized by "reintegration", "holism" and "digitalization". Reintegration means rolling back the disaggregation of NPM to include such points as joined-up governance and "re-governmentalization". Holism is to include client-based or needs-based reorganization, one-stop provisions, ask-once processes, interactive and "ask-once" information-seeking, data warehousing, pre-emptive needs analysis, end-to-end service re-engineering and agile government processes. Digitalization elements include electronic service delivery and e-government, new forms of automated processes, radical disintermediation, active channel-streaming, customer segmentation, mandated channel reductions in order to move toward co-production of services, quasi-voluntary compliance, do-it-yourself forms and tax-paying and open-book government. But, even if there is no real explanation as to how digitally enhanced *governance* is different from *government*, there is no inkling that Dunleavy et al. are using governance in an unusual way that requires any new definition.

Another paper, by Osborne (2006), argues for something new called New Public Governance (NPG). Osborne argues that the time of NPM is "a relatively brief and transitory one between the statist and bureaucratic tradition" of public administration and "the embryonic plural and pluralist tradition" of what is termed New Public Governance. NPG posits "both a plural state, where multiple inter-dependent actors contribute to the delivery of public services and a pluralist state, where multiple processes inform the policy making system" and as a "consequence of these two forms of plurality, its focus is very much upon inter-organizational relationships and the governance of processes, and it stresses service effectiveness and outcomes" (Osborne 2006).

Even if NPG is thus far diffuse and ill-defined, it may well provide a way forward, particularly with its clear complementarity with Kooiman's "social political governance". However, NPG does need to avoid a programmatic approach. In the same way that failure to establish what the NPM program was doomed it as a movement, a similar fate may well occur for NPG. But, for present purposes, Osborne, too, does not need a new definition of governance that relies on meanings beyond the standard dictionary definition.

Governance, networks and markets

One particularly contentious definition of governance is that it is all about networks. Rhodes argues that "governance has too many meanings to be useful, but that the concept can be rescued by stipulating one meaning. . . . So, governance refers to self-organizing, inter-organizational networks" (1996: 660). Two points follow from this. First, the governance-as-networks definition must be all-encompassing and sufficiently robust to capture all behaviors involving what was previously known as governance. Second, if there is to be only one meaning, then there is a presumption that all others need to be discarded, including the standard dictionary definitions discussed earlier.

On the first point, networks are argued by Rhodes to be a new form of organization, a third way of organizing, and that "to markets and hierarchies, we can now add networks" (1996: 653). Governance is now to be defined "as networks":

> From this perspective, governance consists of self-organizing, inter-organizational networks. These networks are characterized, first, by interdependence between organizations. Changes in the role of the state mean the boundaries between the public, private and voluntary sectors are shifting and opaque. Second, there are continuing interactions between network members, caused by the need to exchange resources and to negotiate purposes. Third, these interactions resemble a game with actors' behavior rooted in trust and regulated by rules that are negotiated and agreed by network participants. Finally, the networks have a significant degree of autonomy from the state. Networks are not accountable to the state; they are self-organizing.
>
> (Bevir and Rhodes 2003: 53)

Networks are argued to be a means for co-ordinating and allocating resources – a governing structure – in the same way as markets and bureaucracies. This is contrary to the usual distinction made between two forces: bureaucracy and markets (Ostrom 1974).

Adding a third player is an important claim, and part of an ongoing discussion of the relative importance and interactions of governance, networks and markets. Where the network model is of some utility is in describing the political machinations, the interest groups, the individuals and the interactions that lead to either an edict or a contract. Depending on point of view, the locus of government could be in the politicking before that point or the exercise of power itself.

Mintzberg argues that in the network model "government is viewed as one intertwined system, a complex network of temporary relationships fashioned to work out problems as they arise, linked by informal channels of communication" (2000: 76). Kamarck also sees three actors, with the market as the third:

> In entrepreneurial government the public's work is done by people who work for the government; in networked government the public's work is paid for by the government even though it is performed by people who do not work for the government. In the third emerging model of government – market government – the work of government involves no public employees and no public money. In market government, the government uses its power to create a market that fulfills a public purpose.
>
> (Kamarck 2002: 249–50)

Bevir and Rhodes argue that "although the state does not occupy a privileged, sovereign position, it can directly and imperfectly steer networks" and the "key problem confronting government is, therefore, its reduced ability to steer" (2003: 53). The reduced ability to steer is somewhat overstated. It is the case that "government action depends increasingly on nongovernmental partners, from nongovernmental organizations that deliver public services to private contractors who supply important goods" (Kettl 2005: 6). But this does not mean any necessary decline in the power of government at all, rather an increased realization that the formal, rational bureaucratic model is no longer appropriate and that it actually suits governments to involve a wide range of actors in what they do. This involvement may be aimed at making government more efficient and effective rather than ceding any real power to the outside at all.

Take, for example, a police force or a tax office as a governmental organization that has substantial, real power to force citizens to comply with rulings. Once, during the apogee of the traditional bureaucratic model, such organizations operated with little regard for the outside. The bureaucratic model assumes that all information is held inside and the traditional bureaucrat makes a decision in an entirely rational way. But agencies that act in a high-handed manner can lose public support even as they act entirely within their legal powers. And an agency that loses support may lose its "authorizing environment" (Moore 1995) and have its status and standing decline in the public mind.

Those in charge of the tax office now realize that the views of clients, accountants and other players are quite valid inputs and, without changing its powers one iota, actively solicit opinions from outside players. There may be a network operating here; but the point is that, far from the network being in a position of governing, it is rather that the exercise of power by government can be better-directed with active outside involvement. As Kettl argues:

> In order to embrace the large and complex networks responsible for service delivery, many reformers now speak of *governance* instead of government. As these networks have become more important, government officials have increasingly reached out to sweep them into the reform movement as well. Improving government services requires more than managing government agencies.
>
> (Kettl 2005: 6)

On a contentious issue such as accounting standards, the outside professional body may have substantial input into legislation, but rather than the government conceding power it is rather exercising its unchanged power more judiciously. It is no concession of power to a network to involve it in decision-making. Other organizations are assisting government in doing what it wants done and, "despite the view of some who persist in seeing networks as a weakening of the state, networked government can also be looked at as a different way of implementing the goals of the state" (Kamarck 2002: 246).

Pollitt is not overly impressed by the network approach, finding it "unsatisfying, indeed, at times, frustrating" (2003: 65). He does not like the "ahistorical assumption" that networks are new; nor the assertion that there are now more networks or that these are somehow more democratic; nor the methodological and theoretical weaknesses (2003: 65–6). As he argues, the biggest disappointment for the public manager is "the paucity of interesting and tested propositions for action coming from network theory" (2003: 66). This is a particularly important point. If networks are to be a form of governance, more needs to be demonstrated than that there is a lot of interaction going on between interests and governments. In sum, Pollitt argues:

> This is not to say that network theory has nothing to offer. Rather, I see it as just somewhat overblown. At its worst it offers a romantic vision of a whole new way of governing, pivoted on a disparate bunch of case studies, usually drawn from a limited number of sectors. At its best, though, it reminds us of the (longstanding) importance of informal relationships *between* organizations and groups, and how these organizational dynamics can set the context for more formal and specific processes of decision-making.
>
> (2003: 67)

Mintzberg, too, argues that reliance on the network model "can be overdone" and refers to France where "both public and private sectors have long been dominated by a powerful and interconnected élite that moves around with a freedom and influence that is proving increasingly stifling to the nation" (2000: 78–9). The same general point could be made for other European countries.

It is quite obvious that there is a lot of political bargaining at all levels in governments and societies. Networks exist and do have influence. But there is some distance from seeing the bargaining in action, influencing public policy as a result, to saying that networks are running the government. Nor is there any evidence that governance means self-organizing networks and that this now needs to be the sole meaning of the word.

The second point is whether or not the case has been made for discarding all other definitions of governance than governance as networks. Even with due allowances for hyperbole, the network model is not sufficiently robust to have moved the English language away from the ordinary dictionary meanings of governance discussed earlier. To regard networks as governance or governance as networks is to see the two terms as entirely synonymous. Rhodes argues that only one meaning of governance is to be accepted, that is governance as self-organizing, interorganizational networks. This means that other usages, the several hundred years of reasonably settled meaning, the ordinary usage in terms of a school or a tennis club, the ordinary usage in a specialized context, such as corporate governance, or good governance, all need to be discarded. There is some utility to the network approach either as an organizing principle or as one approach to governing, but to say that there is only one meaning of governance and that is as networks is, indeed, overblown.

A search for meanings

Social science is replete with words that seemingly defy clear meaning. In his 1970 book on comparative government, Finer argued that the study of comparative government "still wallows in semantic confusions":

> Some of the most commonly used words are homonyms – one identical word with several meanings. Others are stipulatory: whether one knows it or not, the writer is using the term in a special and often highly personal way. Some terms are both.
>
> (Finer 1970: 3)

Some current uses or definitions of "governance" are clearly stipulatory, some are highly specialized. Also, in the same era as Finer, Mills argued against those he termed "grand theorists" who "never get down from the higher generalities to problems in their historical and structural contexts" leading to "unreality so noticeable in their pages" and

> One resulting characteristic is a seemingly arbitrary and certainly endless elaboration of distinctions which neither enlarge our understanding nor make our experience more sensible. This in turn is revealed as a partially organized abdication of the effort to describe and explain human conduct and society plainly.
>
> (Mills, 1970, p. 42)

Whatever else their contribution might be, some theorists of governance have quite certainly not obeyed the imprecation to plain explanation. For instance, Bevir and Rhodes state "we use an anti-foundational epistemology and an interpretive approach to understand changes in British governance" (2003: 1). This is hardly about explaining human conduct and society plainly. Further into their book, the abstraction goes further. As they argue:

> Our decentred approach to governance casts a new light . . . because it treats bureaucracy, markets and networks as meaningful practices created and constantly recreated through particular, contingent actions. In many ways, therefore, networks are an integral part of our social and political life, they are characteristic of bureaucracy and markets as well as governance. . . . Once we stop reifying institutions, bureaucracies and markets, we find many of the

> characteristics allegedly specific to networks are widespread aspects of political structures. Our decentred approach encourages a shift of focus from networks, now recognized as an integral part of social life, to the beliefs held by actors and to the stories told by political scientists. Governance is new because it signifies an important change in these beliefs and stories.
>
> (Bevir and Rhodes 2003: 68)

The words are recognizably English but are stipulatory and lead to lots of subsequent questions. What does a decentered approach mean here, and how does it cast a new light – and on what? What are "meaningful practices created and constantly recreated through particular contingent actions"? Exactly who "reifies institutions, bureaucracies and markets", and to what purpose? What are the "beliefs held by actors", and what kinds of "stories told by political scientists" are to be read? More importantly, what does any of this say about governance in Britain or anywhere else? It is hard to see what the student of governance will get from this, particularly public managers looking for assistance to solve real problems (Sparrow 2000). Such use of language is more likely to widen the gulf between public management theory and practice, and to separate political science from public management further.

Conclusion

"Governance" is a good word, one with many uses, but it is a word in need of rescue. It risks being so burdened with meaning that its ordinary standard dictionary definition – entirely appropriate for many current uses – becomes lost. Governance is about running organizations, public and private; it is about steering; it is about solving societal problems. Governance cannot be confined to the public sector; indeed, its greatest current usage is in terms of corporate governance rather than of public governance. Some definitions of governance pay insufficient attention – often none – to its usage and meaning in other contexts. Again, governance needs to be able to include the rules for a tennis club or how the board of a company or a school is to operate.

The definitions of governance as networks, as new public management, as socio-cybernetic systems, as the new political economy, to name but a few, do not add to understanding of governance as a word, although they might have other utility. Governance should be used, governance should be discussed, but let the purpose be clear and the explanation considered.

References

Australia (2003) *Review of Corporate Governance of Statutory Authorities and Office Holders*, Canberra: Commonwealth of Australia.

Bevir, Mark and Rhodes, R. A. W. (2003) *Interpreting British Governance*, London: Routledge.

Christensen, T., Lie, A. and Lægreid, P. (2007) "Still Fragmented Government or Reassertion of the Centre?", in T. Christensen and P. Lægreid (eds) *Transcending New Public Management: The Transformation of Public Sector Reforms*, Aldershot: Ashgate.

Donahue, John D. (2002) "Market-based Governance and the Architecture of Accountability", in John D. Donahue and Joseph S. Nye, Jr (eds) *Market-based Governance: Supply Side, Demand Side, Upside and Downside*, Washington, DC: The Brookings Institution.

Dunleavy, Patrick, Margetts, Helen, Bastow, Simon and Tinkler, Jane (2006) "New Public Management Is Dead – Long Live Digital-era Governance", *Journal of Public Administration Research and Theory*, 16 (3): 467–94.

Finer, S. E. (1970) *Comparative Government*, Harmondsworth: Penguin.

Finer, S. E. (1997) *The History of Government from the Earliest Times*, Oxford: Oxford University Press.

Fountain, Jane (2001) *Building the Virtual State: Information Technology and Institutional Change*, Washington, DC: The Brookings Institution.

Frederickson, H. George (2005) "Whatever Happened to Public Administration? Governance, Governance Everywhere", in Ewan Ferlie, Laurence E. Lynn, Jr and Christopher Pollitt (eds) *The Oxford Handbook of Public Management*, Oxford: Oxford University Press.

Hood, Christopher and Peters, Guy (2004) "The Middle Aging of New Public Management: Into the Age of Paradox?", *Journal of Public Administration Research and Theory*, 14 (3): 267–82.

Hughes, Owen E. (2003) *Public Management and Administration*, 3rd edn, Basingstoke: Palgrave Macmillan.

Jensen, Michael C. (2000) *A Theory of the Firm: Governance, Residual Claims, and Organizational Forms*, Cambridge, Mass.: Harvard University Press.

Kamarck, Elaine Ciulla (2002) "The End of Government as We Know It", in John D. Donahue and Joseph S. Nye, Jr (eds) *Market-based Governance: Supply Side, Demand Side, Upside and Downside*, Washington, DC: The Brookings Institution.

Keasey, Kevin, Short, Helen and Wright, Mike (2005a) "The Development of Corporate Governance Codes in the UK", in Kevin Keasey, Steve Thompson and Mike Wright (eds) *Corporate Governance: Accountability, Enterprise and International Comparisons*, Hoboken, NJ: John Wiley.

Keasey, Kevin, Thompson, Steve and Wright, Mike (eds) (2005b) *Corporate Governance: Accountability, Enterprise and International Comparisons*, Hoboken, NJ: John Wiley.

Kennett, Patricia (2008) "Introduction", in Patricia Kennett (ed.) *Governance, Globalization and Public Policy*, Cheltenham: Edward Elgar.

Kettl, Donald F. (2005) *The Global Public Management Revolution*, 2nd edn, Washington, DC: The Brookings Institution.

Kickert, W. (1997) "Public Governance in the Netherlands: An Alternative to Anglo-American 'managerialism'", *Public Administration*, 75: 731–52.

Kjaer, Anne Mette (2004) *Governance*, Cambridge: Polity.

Kooiman, J. (1999) "Social–political Governance", *Public Management*, 1 (1): 68–92.

Kooiman, J. (2003) *Governing as Governance*, London: Sage.

Mills, C. Wright (1970) *The Sociological Imagination*, Harmondsworth: Penguin.

Minogue, Martin, Polidano, Charles and Hulme, David (1998) "Introduction: The Analysis of Public Management and Governance", in Martin Minogue, Charles Polidano and David Hulme (eds) *Beyond the New Public Management: Changing Ideas and Practices in Governance*, Cheltenham: Edward Elgar.

Mintzberg, Henry (2000) "Managing Normatively", in Henry Mintzberg and Jacques Bourgault, *Managing Publicly*, Toronto: Institute of Public Administration Canada.

Moore, Mark (1995) *Creating Public Value: Strategic Management in Government*, Cambridge, Mass.: Harvard University Press.

Organization for Economic Cooperation and Development (2005) *Modernising Governance*, Paris: OECD.

Osborne, David and Gaebler, Ted (1992) *Reinventing Government: How the Entrepreneurial Spirit Is Transforming the Public Sector*, Reading, Mass.: Addison-Wesley.

Osborne, Stephen (2006) "Editorial: The New Public Governance?", *Public Management Review*, 8 (3): 377–87.

Ostrom, Vincent (1974) *The Intellectual Crisis in American Public Administration*, revised edn, Tuscaloosa, Ala: University of Alabama Press.

Pierre, Jon and Peters, Guy (2000) *Governance, Politics and the State*, Basingstoke: Palgrave Macmillan.

Pollitt, Christopher (2003) *The Essential Public Manager*, Maidenhead: Open University Press.

Rhodes, R. A. W. (1996) "The New Governance: Governing without Government", *Political Studies*, 44 (4): 652–67.

Rosenau, James N. (1997) *Along the Domestic–Foreign Frontier: Exploring Governance in a Turbulent World*, Cambridge: Cambridge University Press.

Savas, E. S. (1987) *Privatization: The Key to Better Government*, Chatham, NJ: Chatham House.

Sparrow, Malcolm (2000) *The Regulatory Craft: Controlling Risks, Solving Problems and Managing Compliance*, Washington, DC: The Brookings Institution.

Van Thiel, S., Pollitt, C. and Homburg, V. (2007) "Conclusions", in C. Pollitt, S. Van Thiel and V. Homburg (eds) *New Public Management in Europe*, Basingstoke: Palgrave Macmillan.

7

WHAT ENDURES? PUBLIC GOVERNANCE AND THE CYCLE OF REFORM

Laurence E. Lynn, Jr

In the field of public administration and management, something is always new. In America, proclaiming "the new" has long been popular among academics. John Gaus announced the "new administration" in the early 1920s; Leonard White celebrated the "new management" and John Pfiffner the "new public administration" in the 1930s. Participants in a historic conference at Minnowbrook unveiled a new "new public administration" in the 1970s. And the habit has spread to Europe. A "new public management" was famously identified by Christopher Hood in the early 1990s and a "new city management" was born in the Netherlands.

As New Public Management (NPM) lost amplitude in the academic issue-attention cycle (Downs 1972) – pronounced "dead" by Patrick Dunleavy and colleagues not two decades after its birth (Dunleavy et al. 2006) – increasing prominence has been given to the "next new thing": the "new (public) governance". As R. A. W. Rhodes has observed, the coming and going of intellectual fashions is "often fun, sometimes instructive, rarely long-lived" (Rhodes 2000: 54). As such, new fashions might be little more than manifestations of the sociology of academia. More charitably, they might be viewed as heuristics that stimulate critical thought and investigation, and innovations in practice, although often at the cost of distorting history for effect.

Worth taking more seriously, however, is the implicit assumption that institutions of governance are relatively malleable.[1] "Each generation redesigns government," claimed a group of experts associated with America's National Academy of Public Administration (DeWitt et al. 1994: 175). This assertion collides with a widely held contrary view that institutional evolution is generally path-dependent and incremental. How might we reconcile seemingly conflicting claims of malleability and stability?

In taking up this issue, the meaning of terms is important. Define "institutions" as "stable sets of commonly recognized formal and informal rules that coordinate or constrain" behavior (Weimer 1995: 2–3); a "paradigm" as habits of thought or mind shared by policy-makers concerning how to resolve problems of governance (Margolis 1993); and "path dependence" as a process of narrowing the range of political and economic choices in a way that links decision-making through time (North 1990). Using these definitions, the proposition that a new public governance is replacing whatever preceded it can be restated as follows: The habitual reactions of policy-makers – legislators, elected executives, judicial officers, and administrators – to problems of governance are shifting irreversibly as a result of changes in the contexts of governing, and the result is or will be new, at least temporarily stable institutions. The conceptual questions raised by this proposition are: What endures and what does not in national institutions of governance? and How and why do the answers matter? The related empirical question is: What kinds of evidence are necessary to sustain claims that "the new" is upon us?

This chapter addresses these questions and offers some speculative conclusions. The following section considers the stories of two historical issue-attention cycles (Downs 1972) involving claims concerning the advent of something new in state–society relations: American claims concerning the emergence of a new (public) administration at every level of government in the 1920s and 1930s, and the claims first heard in the early 1990s concerning the emergence of a new (public) governance – a story that is ongoing. There follows a comparison of the arguments sustaining the two stories, raising the question of whether the second story might end as the first did: in the emergence of a genuinely new paradigm of administrative thought and action. The paper concludes with reflections on what can be said about what endures and what does not as fashions in public administration and management reform succeed one another.

"The new": old and new

An American penchant to proclaim or advocate "the new" had its first important expression following decades of Progressive-era reforms in American institutions: the beginnings of a professional civil service; economic regulation; an income tax; the executive budget; new forms of direct democracy; the direct election of US senators; and women's right to vote. Fifteen years later, the term "new" had been dropped, and "public administration" had become an accepted paradigm of thought and action.

Beginning in the twentieth century's final decade, many on both sides of the Atlantic began claiming that a "new (public) governance" is replacing public administration as the profession's foundational paradigm. For a time, this term competed for attention with the seemingly more resonant and popular NPM. Within a decade, however, the new (public) governance in various and diverse guises was ascendant.

Though this more recent discourse concerning "the new" has distinctive national versions and has yet to run its course, comparing these two episodes of the field's intellectual and institutional history can be instructive. Unlike the reform cycle associated with NPM, the new (public) governance has a reasonable but uncertain prospect of ending like the earlier American story: in a new paradigm of thought and action.

The "New (Public) Administration"

In the latter decades of the nineteenth century, a modern administrative state began to replace America's largely pre-bureaucratic, agrarian, populist institutions. Beginning with civil service reform in the 1880s, the pace of change accelerated, and government at all levels grew in scope, size and influence. The landmark Budget and Accounting Act of 1921 institutionalized modern executive government in America.

New problems

Leonard White summarized the context in which the American administrative state emerged:

> After the echoes of the Civil War had died away a new society was perceived to be emerging from the rural–small town economy of the first eighty years of our national existence. Invention was working its transformation through the industrial revolution and leading to an urban civilization based on the machine from the factory. This new civilization attracted millions of persons from other countries who came with different backgrounds of government and different standards of life. The new regime thus created new problems of public order, public health, housing, protection of safety standards, recreation, care of the unfortunate and the delinquent, regulation of utilities, and regulation of conditions of employment, and necessitated the development of new programs of government service. . . .
>
> (White 1933: 3)

Those who observed and participated in the reform process believed themselves to be responding to unprecedented and dynamic social, economic, technological and political change that rendered nineteenth-century institutions ramshackle and obsolete, not only in America but throughout the industrializing world (Bertelli and Lynn 2006). Frederick Cleveland wrote in 1913: "A wave of organized democracy is sweeping the world, based on a broader intelligence and a more enlightened view of civic responsibility than has ever been obtained" (1913: 438). In the preface to his seminal 1926 textbook, *An Introduction to the Study of Administration*, White referred to administration as "this enormous terrain, studded with governmental problems of first magnitude" (White 1955 [1926]: xvi). During the administration of President Franklin D. Roosevelt, White and his co-authors Marshall Dimock and John Gaus wrote:

> The student of public administration is now confronted with a literally overwhelming torrent of new administrative agencies and new problems to be assimilated and appraised. . . . [That] [s]o many currents of experience from industry, from psychological research, from the study of comparative government . . . to name but a few – are adding their contribution to the main stream require[s] both improvements in administrative technique and equally more accurate ideas concerning the nature of administration.
>
> (Gaus, White and Dimock 1936: vii–viii)

A solution: public administration

In "The New Problem of Administration", published in the early 1920s, John Gaus argued that, faced with issues that were "technical, detailed, involved, [and] requiring special knowledge and expertise" (Gaus 1923–4: 220), political parties and legislatures tended "to leave difficult problems to administrative agencies for solution" (Gaus 1923–4: 218). To the perfectly serviceable term "administration", Gaus added the term "new", defining "the new administration" as a flexible instrument endowed with "a wide share of policy formulation . . . a large measure of discretion . . . [and] wide exemption from judicial review", a transformation analogous to the creation of the "modern national state" by European monarchs (p. 220). Gaus noted that the "new administration" had emerged "so suddenly that many of us are still unaware of its implications or problems or challenges" (p. 230).[2]

The cumulative result of these various transformations at local, state and federal levels of American government was dramatic, wrote Harold Laski in the new British journal *Public Administration* in the same year. "A state built upon *laissez-faire* has been transformed into a positive state. Vast areas of social life are now definitely within the ambit of legislation; and a corresponding increase in the power of the executive has been the inevitable result" (1923: 92). Pre-bureaucratic nineteenth-century patronage administration, fragmented and decentralized, had been replaced by a modern, managerial and professional bureaucratic state with significant delegated authority to make policy, to regulate private activity, and to promote public welfare.

In 1933, White defined what he termed "the new management", which, he said, emerged from 1900 to 1930, as "a contemporary philosophy of administration" favoring consolidation of administrative power at all levels of government. The changes in administrative institutions during that period, claimed White, were "primarily dedicated to greater efficiency, toward improved methods, better and more extensive services and the elimination of waste and irresponsibility" (White 1933: 4). Joining White in proclaiming "the new" was John Pfiffner. In his 1935 textbook, he wrote: "the new public administration is essentially democratic in spirit and practice. . . . [It] combines power with responsibility" to political officers who are under popular control (1935: 19). Administration is "society working through government to solve the collective problems of a technological age" (p. 20).

By the mid-1930s, public administration had achieved a level of maturity that no longer required the qualifier "new"; indeed, it was often referred to as "the" public administration. The field's leading scholars and practitioners expressed what had become "habits of mind", a professional reasoning process that was concerned with a new agenda concerning

> the interrelationships among the values of democracy; the dangers of an uncontrolled, politically corrupted, or irresponsible bureaucracy; the corruptibility of legislative processes; the imprecision of popular control of administration; and judicial and executive institutions that can balance capacity with control in a constitutionally appropriate manner.
>
> (Bertelli and Lynn 2006: 43)

The field could now identify itself with a literature evincing a subtle, pragmatic wisdom concerning administrative practice that was, at the same time, infused with democratic idealism and a keen awareness, if not a complete conceptual grasp, of the challenges created by America's constitutional separation of powers.

The "New (Public) Governance"

In the early 1990s, many of public administration's leading scholars and practitioners began, once again but this time on an international scale, to proclaim "the new", which was simultaneously available in two distinct brands: NPM, which emphasized "markets", and the new (public) governance, which emphasized "networks". The story of NPM has been often told and, as argued earlier, is of less interest than the new (public) governance, which remains ascendant and possibly transformative.

Dutch, American and British experts separately asserted the proposition that advanced democracies are moving toward new forms of governance; indeed, some suggested "governance without government", a mode of societal steering that has been de-bureaucratized in favor of emergent hybridized and consociational institutions of civil society. These emergent discourses were necessarily influenced by national and regional institutional histories and contexts; Anglophone, American, Nordic and Continental ideas had their own flavors (Klijn 2008). Common themes and emphases soon became evident, however.

New governance in Europe

Introducing his 1993 edited symposium volume *Modern Governance: New Government–Society Interactions*, Jan Kooiman discussed "new patterns of interaction between government and society" and "new ways of governing and governance" that he termed "social-political governance" (1993: 2, 3). In response to the increasing complexity, dynamics and diversity of societies, the public and private sectors are, he said, engaging in continuous interactions and acting in conjunction with one another rather than separately. The result has been new structural forms of interactive steering, managing, controlling and guiding in certain sectors.

R. A. W. Rhodes, writing in 1996 of the changes he perceived in British government, redefined, in the manner of Gaus in the early 1920s, the heretofore generic and descriptive term "governance" as signifying "a change in the meaning of government, referring to a *new* process of governing; or a *changed* condition of ordered rule; or the *new* method by which society is governed" (Rhodes 1996: 652–3). Specifically, Rhodes argued, to markets and hierarchies (bureaucracies) as governing structures can now be added networks characterized by trust and mutual adjustment. Later Mark Bevir, Rhodes and Patrick Weller, organizers of a symposium similar to Kooiman's a decade before, used "governance" to encapsulate "the changing form and role of the state in advanced industrial societies", especially focusing on public-sector reform and on "the changing boundary between state and civil society" (2003: 13).

Subsequently, Stephen Osborne proposed that we are entering a new stage in the profession of public administration and management. The first stage, traditional public administration, while emphasizing politics, gave short shrift to management. The next stage, NPM, focused on management while relegating democratic institutions to the status of mere context if not of outright impediment. From an intellectual perspective, New Public Governance (NPG) corrects the theoretical and practical shortcomings of its predecessors, encompassing the contemporary complexities and realities of governing by drawing on organizational sociology and network theory rather than on political science or public-choice economics in order to overcome the fragmentation and uncoordinated character of twentieth-century managerial practice.

The "new (public) governance" has been proposed elsewhere in the Anglophone world. In Canada, Gilles Paquet spoke of "a shift from a somewhat 'defensive,' anti-democratic, centralizing, homogenizing and hierarchical former regime ruled by elites *toward* a more 'open,' communitarian, non-centralizing, pluralistic and distributed governance regime" (1999: 73). Of Australian social policy, Tim Reddel says that "a new governance discourse offers some promise as a policy framework that can re-conceptualize the state–community (and market) relationship and deliver improved community outcomes, particularly in the context of place-based or spatial policies and programs" and featuring "dialogue, deliberation, and association" and "engagement with a strong civil society" (Reddel 2002: 50–1, 54, 60).

In his 2008 assessment of the European literature on governance, Erik-Hans Klijn concluded that the term "governance", in so far as it identifies a departure from traditional emphasis on the internal functioning of governments, refers to governance networks, that is, to government's "relationships with other actors and the process of handling complex decisions and implementation processes" (Klijn 2008: 510–11). "Governance", he says, "is the process that takes place within governance networks", that is, within "a web of relationships between government, business and civil society actors [which are] based on interdependencies [that] are not necessarily equitable" (p. 511). Thus, in contrast to those, such as Rhodes and Kooiman, who have viewed the new governance as traditional structures *plus* networks, Klijn views it as networks alone.

New governance in America

In 1994, American scholars associated with the National Academy of Public Administration identified a "cluster of ideas and symbols" they termed "new governance" (Dewitt et al. 1994). Inspired by books such as David Osborne and Ted Gaebler's *Reinventing Government* (1992) and Michael Barzelay and Babak Armajani's *Breaking Through Bureaucracy* (1992), "new governance" was said to encompass "[n]ew ways of doing the public's business", driven primarily by policy specialists and already being experimentally introduced by state and local governments, and soon to be attempted at the federal level (by the Clinton administration). "New governance" anticipated and advocated further changes in the participants, purposes, means and politics of government. Participants, they believed, would come to include alliances and collaboration in lieu of fragmentation and decentralization of decision-making. Citizens would be empowered rather than being merely the passive objects of government initiatives.

In 2000, American political scientist Lester Salamon defined the "new governance" as having two distinctive features: its collaborative nature and its recognition that this form of governance involves challenges as well as opportunities. As Salamon sees it, each of a "dizzying array" of new administrative forms or tools had its own skill requirements, its own delivery mechanisms, and its own political economy (2000: 1612, 1613). Most of the new tools are highly "indirect", involving the sharing with non-governmental actors of discretion over the exercise of public authority and the allocation of public resources. His initial term for this phenomenon – he began writing about it in 1980 – was "third party government". In support of his claims, he quotes Donald Kettl as having observed that "[e]very major policy initiative launched by the federal government since World War II . . . has been managed through public–private partnerships" (Salamon 2000: 1615, citing Kettl 1993: 4). A similar phenomenon, under such rubrics as "pillarization" and "subsidiarity", has, he notes, been occurring in Western Europe.

A new governance discourse has arisen in specific policy domains as well. Robert Durant argues that traditional command-and-control regulation is inadequate for non-point source pollutants such as greenhouse gases, and that regulatory management concerning environmental and natural-resource policies must reconnect with stakeholders and give greater flexibility to both regulators and regulated communities (Durant 2004). American public administration scholars have viewed national and state rural development councils as an example of a new governance featuring reduced federal direction in favor of intergovernmental collaboration and increased involvement of state, local and private agencies (Radin 1996). Americans Lisa Bingham, Tina Nabatchi and Rosemary O'Leary (2005) discuss a "different face" of the "new governance", which will be the "watchword for the next millennium".

> Practitioners are using new quasi-legislative and quasi-judicial governance processes, including deliberative democracy, e-democracy, public conversations, participatory budgeting, citizen juries, study circles, collaborative policy making, and alternative dispute resolution, to permit citizens and stakeholders to actively participate in the work of government.
>
> p. 547

The stories compared

Both of the stories sketched above feature claims about a changed world: the institutional status quo has been, or is being, replaced by something so different that it constitutes a new way of thinking and addressing public issues. However, a convincing argument of any kind, but certainly a scholarly one, requires not only a claim concerning what is (probably) true but also four additional elements: reasons, evidence, a warrant (authorizations or justifications based on theory or principle) and, finally, qualifications (limits of applicability).[3] What are the arguments central to each of the two stories? Are they equally convincing? If not, why not? If so, what are the implications for thought and practice?

The arguments offered on behalf of both the new (public) administration and the new (public) governance generally include the required elements. Their respective claims are easy to identify: "a new (public) administration based on new government institutions has emerged over the last thirty years" in the first story, and "new modes of governing involving networks and the sharing of authority with civil society institutions are replacing traditional reliance on public authority" in the second. Reasons are similar in both arguments and take the form: "traditional institutions proved to be inadequate for addressing problems of increasing complexity associated with changes in society, technology, and the economy".

When it comes to the evidence and the warrants supporting the claims and reasons, however, the quality of the two arguments diverges. One reason may be that new governance ideas are still being formulated and contested. Another reason goes directly to the quality of the arguments being put forward for the new (public) governance: their normative, theoretical and empirical dimensions are not always clearly distinguished, and are often conflated. While disentangling these strands has not been attempted here, it is important to identify problems of evidence, theory and qualifications.

The problem of evidence

During the emergence of the American administrative state, academic public administration and public administration as codified professional practice were largely inchoate and emergent. The political scientists, municipal research-bureau staff, and activist reformers who created both the reality and the historical record of institutional transformation were themselves participants in the historical process. As a result, evidence was predominantly based on experience, direct observation and official data. When first articulated, the new public administration was regarded as a *fait accompli*; its examples constituted evidence of a new reality, a new paradigm in the literal meaning of that term.

Now, given the existence of a mature profession, so-called cycles of administrative reform can run their course largely in the academic imagination and in the specialized precincts of technocrats and consultancies. Thus, examples of a new (public) governance are often carefully selected harbingers of a reality possibly in the making rather than constituting a balanced assessment of the range of actual changes in state–society relations. Many contributors to the new governance literature offer broad generalizations concerning institutional change or examples of new forms of goverance without saying much about whether habits of thought among policy-makers have changed. Moreover, contending as it is with still other claims on behalf of "the new", such as the "new city management" (Hambleton 2002; Hambleton and Gross 2007) and the "new public service" (Denhardt and Denhardt 2002, 2003), in which there is as much advocacy as analysis, it is not yet clear whether the new (public) governance reflects just another cycle of intellectual fashion stimulated as much by who desires reform as by intellectual curiosity or the emergence of what will eventually be seen as a self-evident new reality based on new habits of thought, the evidence for which is everywhere at hand.

However, the difference in the evidentiary bases for the two stories and their claims should not be overstated. Of the established American administrative state, White noted that "[w]ithout any adequate proof of the superiority of the new institutions at hand, it is clear that they have by and large commended themselves to the voters. As soon as adequate measures of success or failure are at hand, their contribution may be made more clear" (1933: 236). The new (public) governance literature, moreover, features increasing empirical depth. Salamon's claims concerning the new reality of third-party government, for example, are supported by data on the expanding role and size of the nonprofit sector in publicly financed service delivery and also by a growing body of official data and scientific research. The literature on the new governance in the European Union and on new forms of citizen participation in governance features a good deal of experiential reflection and some scientific investigation. Research such as that of Radin (1996) and Durant (2004) use the new governance as a frame for analyzing institutional change in rural economic development and in environmental and natural resource management respectively. Studies such as that of Taylor (2002) demonstrate the extent of government influence in new governance structures. Empirical knowledge is accumulating.

In summary, empirical evidence supporting claims that a new (public) governance is redrawing state–society boundaries is contested and, in quality and extent, as yet unconvincing.

The problem of theory

Proclaiming "the new" in both stories depends for intellectual leverage and salience on a more principled warrant, that is, on a theory that justifies the logic of linking claims, reasons and evidence.

Claims on behalf of the new (public) administration were thought to be vindicated by the needs of the polity in a modernizing and industrializing society as expressed through America's constitutional scheme of governance. The warrant can be stated more generally. The cumulative and combined effects of several historical developments over three centuries – the advent of the nation state, the transformation of mercantilism into capitalism, democratic and specifically republican revolutions, industrialization, modernization and urbanization, and international conflicts – resulted in the emergence in the developed world of centralized, hierarchically organized, politically accountable administrative states founded on the rule of law (Aucoin 1997; Dahl and Lindblom 1953: 511; du Gay 2000; Goodsell 1983; Meier 1997; Peters and Pierre 2003).

In contrast, most arguments for a new (public) governance are primarily analytical rather than theoretical, featuring classification and generalization rather than a causal logic rooted in democratic principles. In many of these arguments, a necessarily selective body of evidence is, in effect, assumed to speak for itself. The fact that numerous countries are making reforms with a family resemblance to one another is often presumed to suggest inevitability and a global convergence of governing paradigms (cf. arguments for NPM). Advocates for new paradigms might be forgiven for omitting such theorizing; their goal is an immediate and practical one: to alter the thinking of policy-makers, stakeholders and administrators in support of new, arguably better forms of governance. Such omissions are less forgivable in scholarly discourse, however, which is, and ought to be, held to more rigorous standards for claims and for the logic of the reasons and evidence that support them.

What might be the warrant for the argument that a new (public) governance is, within a generation, replacing centuries-old institutional expressions of republican rule? Why might it be in the interests of the stakeholders of representative democracy – citizens, elected representatives, and legal institutions – to dispense with bureaucracy and the types of accountability mechanisms associated with it in favor of more dispersed, diffuse and ambiguous accountability? And why now?

The most popular warrant is the vague notion of "globalization". The triumph of more aggressive forms of capitalism (at least until the global financial crises beginning in 2008), of border-erasing technologies, and of competition-based, performance-oriented social allocation, that is, of the global marketplace, over socialism, state-directed social allocation, and social democratic welfare statism was, it is asserted, bound to affect all states in similar ways. Globalization, in other words, represents a disruptive historical discontinuity, the significance of which for state–society relations is as great as the emergence of the nation-state, of market capitalism and of representative democracy.

Fred Riggs and Judith Merkle have articulated the basis for a more principled warrant for the new institutional developments. The basic principle of democracy as an aspect of modernity, in Riggs's account, involved the replacement of top-down monarchic authority with bottom-up representation: dominated subjects were replaced by free citizens able to participate in governance, choose their governors, and hold them accountable through periodic elections. But, he says, "[i]t has never been easy in even the most democratic countries for the organs of representative government to sustain effective control over their bureaucracies" (1997: 350), and it became more difficult as those bureaucracies were being rationalized in order that they might approach industrial reliability and efficiency.

Merkle offers a similar type of reasoning (1980). In her account, future president Woodrow Wilson initiated a new idea: "power wielded without regard to persons [either monarch or the people] but rather to attain social ends whose usefulness and means of attainment could eventually be determined by science itself" (1980: 280). She continues: "It was a theory of politics that proclaimed the victory of the experts and defined 'politics,' or the contest for power, as obsolete" (p. 281). An implication of Merkle's reasoning is that all the pathologies of bureaucracy that were coming to be widely recognized will influence the premises of political choice.

> All of these modes of influence [by bureaucracies] tend to break down the ability of the political system to control bureaucracy, while at the same time they introduce the values and the vested interests of the state's own administrative "servant" into the political process itself.
> (Merkle 1980: 282; cf. Karl 1976)

Attempts at democratic control, as Riggs also notes, only undermine the effectiveness of administrative action, ensuring a fundamental tension between them.[4]

Based on these types of reasoning, the warrant for a new (public) governance might be that civil society institutions, governing elites and other stakeholders are coming to the view that the inevitable tensions between representative democracy and nonrepresentative bureaucracy should be ameliorated by redrawing the state–society boundary so as to enlarge the role of civil society – a political preference which will come to be accepted by policymakers and judges as consistent with republican principles and therefore legitimate.

Of interest at this point is an integrative concept originating in sociological theory, that of an "organizational field", that is, a "recognized area of institutional life . . . involving the totality of relevant actors" (DiMaggio and Powell 1991: 64–5).[5] Paul DiMaggio and Walter Powell argue that "[b]ureaucratization and other forms of organizational change occur as the result of processes that make organizations more similar without necessarily making them more efficient". Three forces that induce isomorphism, that is, convergent structural/functional arrangements, are *coercive*, i.e. political influence (operating as an exogenous influence on organizations) that ensures legitimacy; *mimetic*, i.e. standardization of responses to uncertainty; and *normative*, i.e. standardization reflecting professional beliefs and values (DiMaggio and Powell 1991: 67). In other words, choices of administrative arrangements may be a resultant of socialized rather than rational choice within organizational fields, of imitation, coercion, or ideology rather than of calculation and analysis. We should not be surprised to find convergence on a functional or specific policy institution even if not on a whole-of-government scale.

Elaborating on this line of reasoning is Powell's (1990) elucidation of the conditions that give rise to network forms of organization. Under certain circumstances, he argues, exchange relationships may be governed by reciprocity and collaboration rather than by (complete, incomplete, or implicit) contracts or structures of formal authority. In general, says Powell (1990: 326–7),

> networks appear to involve a distinctive combination of factors – skilled labor, some degree of employment security, salaries rather than piece rates, some externally-provided mechanisms for job training, relative equity among the participants, a legal system with relaxed antitrust standards, and national policies that promote research

> and development . . . which seldom exist in sufficient measure without a political and legal infrastructure to support them.

Cross-national variation in the frequency of network forms may be explained, Powell suggests, by variations in state policies that support and sustain collaborations. Differentiating among administrative forms in this way may help in identifying the underlying dynamics of change.

Finally, R. L. Jepperson and J. W. Meyer, also sociologists, adduce a framework of explanation that views the evolution of the formal organization of society as governed by the modern polity, by which they mean

> the system of rules conferring societal authority in pursuit of collective ends, establishing agents of collective regulation and intervention. . . . We have in mind processes such as monetarization and democratization – the construction of markets and rights – and the institutionalization of goals such as collective progress and justice.
> (Jepperson and Meyer 1991: 206)

Their framework accommodates global influences.

> Our line of argument proposes that a wider polity (often worldwide) of universalistic collective definitions plays a governing role, combined with an expanding set of subunit national societies competing and copying each other within this frame.
> (1991: 209)

These authors, then, suggest the possibility of a mimetic isomorphism that allows for degrees of convergence on a new (public) governance that are consistent with path dependence.

The new skepticism

The earlier American story attracted little fundamental criticism; virtually no one argued that a new administrative state was not in fact emerging, although many noted in qualification that change was proceeding gradually. But qualifications and outright skepticism abound in the story of new (public) governance. Johan Olsen (2006: 2) quoted Hood (1996: 268) that many reform proposals are "repackaged versions of ideas that have been in public administration since its beginnings" and that "new" approaches frequently rehash old ideas (Kettl 1993: 408). Olsen also notes that Rhodes (1994; see also Davis and Rhodes 2000) predicted a return to bureaucracy ten years ago, and Peters (1999: 104–5) sees "a possible return to Weber's organizational archetypes". Based on comparative analysis, Pollitt and Bouckaert say that "The idea of a single, and now totally obsolete, ancient regime is as implausible as the suggestion that there is now a global recipe which will reliably 'reinvent' governments" (2004: 63). Even Kooiman, a progenitor of the governance perspective, concedes that "the state is still very much alive" (Kooiman 2003: 130).

Of particular interest is the analysis of governance reforms in Anglophone and European states by Bevir, Rhodes and Weller. They ask: "What is the plot of our story?" The complex plot comprises twelve points. Notable among them is the following: "the beliefs and practices of elite actors [engaged in reform] originate in the traditions they have inherited. They construct issues or dilemmas out of experiences infused with these traditions" (2003: 202). Further, "[g]overnance is constructed differently and continuously reconstructed so there can be no one set of tools" (p. 203). Moreover, specific reforms have different meanings in different countries; new governance in the Netherlands will differ from new governance in the UK. There is "no universal process of globalization driving public sector reform" (p. 203). The primary elites, moreover, remain central agencies. Thus, the new (public) governance is, at best, a highly nuanced and qualified story.

New (Public) Governance: a new paradigm?

Comparing a completed story with a work in progress is problematic. There is value in the effort, however, if the question is posed as follows: Might the story of new (public) governance have the same ending as the story of the new (public) administration? That is, might the qualifier "new" eventually be dropped and "public governance" replace "public administration" as the general term that encompasses all forms of state–society interactions that we study and practice?

A deeper issue lurks beneath this question, however: whether the bases of legitimacy for state-sponsored action will shift decisively toward more open and transparent civil society institutions. Ultimately this is a political question. The discussion in the preceding section sketched one political path toward such a result: pressure on elected officials from citizens disaffected by strong-state traditions that persuades them to advocate and authorize altogether different forms of societal steering, as did indeed take place in America in the decades from 1890 to 1930.

However, skepticism concerning such a political development is warranted. Any paradigm which requires political actors to change fundamentally their ways of viewing their roles *without* concomitant changes in constitutions and political institutions is arguably doomed to become just another academic fashion that will run its course. Of Salamon's approach to new governance, for example, Guy Peters has argued that there are more fundamental considerations than "tools of governance" at work in American politics. Indeed, there are more fundamental issues at work in democratic politics worldwide.

One of those fundamental considerations is constitutional governance. With all that has been new over centuries of state development, what has endured has been those institutions that guarantee the legitimacy of delegated authority: legislatures and judicial bodies along with norms of public service (Lynn 2006). In America, and in other countries as well, to the extent that electoral politics involves the direct engagement of interest groups and other constituencies, elected officials will continue to be under pressure, when the legitimacy of the uses of delegated authority is called into question, to enforce traditional modes and concepts of accountability. If there was any doubt about the truth of this proposition, the responses of governments worldwide to the financial and economic crises that engulfed the world beginning in 2008 should have dispelled it.

Constraining managerial tools and practices, and in a sense transcending them, then, are the law and legal institutions and their derivative checks and balances. "State power is the great antagonist against which the rule of law must forever be addressed," says H. W. Jones (1958: 144). As Anthony Bertelli notes, administrative law regimes exist to police the delegation of powers from sovereign authority to bureaus. "The commitment to uphold administrative law is made credible in most of the world by a third party[, notably] the courts" or by other arrangements, such as ombudsmen or inspectors-general or other entities possessing independent authority to review and report (Bertelli 2005: 151). Note Walter Kickert and Jan Hakvoort (2000: 251), the "all-pervasive dominance of administrative law, combined with the rational, deductive, comprehensive, systematic way of legal thinking, must have serious implications for the form of 'public management' that is adopted" in Continental countries dominated by civil law and in other countries as well.

Constitutions and constitutional institutions will continue to frame the evolution of states and, as a consequence, their managerial institutions. The overthrow of current constitutional arrangements is not in prospect. Within these institutional frameworks, institutions will continue to evolve, and we shall see, perhaps even anticipate, patterns of interaction that are new. But the narrative of differentiation that emerges from comparative research presages distinctive futures, not convergence, for national administrations. These futures may, over time, come to look different from the contemporary reality of public governance, but only in so far as the central problematic of democratic governance, accountability to representative institutions, is resolved in ways that sustain the constitutional legitimacy of state action. Whatever may be new will be rooted in soil that is very old indeed.

Notes

1 American public administration scholar Nicholas Henry (2007) has identified six paradigms in the field's first century, the last of them being governance.

2 He noted, however, that the new administration had been anticipated by British essayist Walter Bagehot, whose admiring biographies of Victorian administrators prefigured the challenges of the modern administrative state.
3 This paragraph is based on Toulmin (2003) as interpreted by Booth, Colomb, and Williams (2003).
4 Argues Riggs (1997: 347), "No bureaucracies, modern or traditional, are democratic; they are instead administrative and hierarchic." Of the emergence of the American administrative state, Barry Karl (1976: 503) notes that "the professionalization of administration created national interests among administrative specialists themselves, separating them from the local attachments their [Jacksonian] predecessors had understood so well," thus deepening the problems of democratic accountability. The consequences of professionalization may be even more evident in European democracies.
5 This part of the discussion is adapted from Lynn (2006).

References

Aucoin, Peter (1997) "The Design of Public organizations for the 21st Century: Why Bureaucracy Will Survive in Public Management", *Canadian Public Administration* 40 (2): 290–306.

Bertelli, Anthony M. (2005) "Law and Public Administration", in Ewan Ferlie, Laurence E. Lynn, Jr and Christopher Pollitt (eds) *The Oxford Handbook of Public Management*, Oxford: Oxford University Press.

Bertelli, Anthony M. and Laurence E. Lynn, Jr (2006) *Madison's Managers: Public Administration and the Constitution*, Baltimore, Md: Johns Hopkins University Press.

Bevir, Mark, Rhodes, R. A. W. and Weller, Patrick (2003) "Comparative Governance: Prospects and Lessons", *Public Administration*, 81 (1): 191–210.

Bingham, Lisa Blomgren, Nabatchi, Tina and O'Leary, Rosemary (2005) "The New Governance: Practices and Processes for Stakeholder and Citizen Participation in the Work of Government", *Public Administration Review*, 65 (5): 547–58.

Booth, Wayne C., Colomb, Gregory G. and Williams, Joseph M. (2003) *The Craft of Research*, 2nd edn, Chicago, Ill.: University of Chicago Press.

Cleveland, Frederick A. (1913) *Organized Democracy*, New York: Longmans, Green.

Dahl, Robert A., and Charles E. Lindblom (1953) *Politics, Economics, and Welfare: Planning and Politico-economic Systems Resolved into Basic Social Processes*, New York: Harper Torchbooks.

Davis, G., and Rhodes, R. A. W. (2000) "From Hierarchy to Contracts and Back Again: Reforming the Australian Public Service." In *Institutions on the edge: Capacity for governance*, ed. M. Keeting, J. Wanna, and P. Weller, 74–98. St. Leonards, Australia: Allen and Unwin.

Denhardt, Robert B. and Denhardt, Janet Vinzant (2002) "The New Public Service: Serving Rather than Steering", *Public Administration Review*, 60 (6): 549–59.

Denhardt, Robert B. and Denhardt, Janet Vinzant (2003) *The New Public Service: Serving, Not Steering*, Armonk, NY: M. E. Sharpe.

DeWitt, John, Kettl, Donald F., Dyer, Barbara and Lovan, W. Robert (1994) "What Will New Governance Mean for the Federal Government?", *Public Administration Review*, 54 (2): 170–6.

DiMaggio, Paul J. and Powell, W. W. (1991) "The Iron Cage Revisited: Institutional Isomorphism and Collective Rationality in Organization Fields, in W. W. Powell and Paul J. DiMaggio (eds), *The New Institutionalism in Organizational Analysis*. Chicago, IL: The University of Chicago Press.

Downs, Anthony (1972) "Up and Down with Ecology: The Issue-Attention Cycle", *The Public Interest*, 28: 38–50.

du Gay, Paul (2000) "In praise of Bureaucracy: Weber–Organization–Ethics", Milton Keynes, UK: Open University Press.

Dunleavy, Patrick, Margetts, Helen, Bastow, Simon and Tinkler, Jane (2006) "New Public Management Is Dead – Long Live Digital-era Governance", *Journal of Public Administration Research and Theory*, 16: 467–94.

Durant, Robert F. (2004) "Toward a New Governance Paradigm for Environmental and Natural Resources Management in the 21st Century?", *Administration and Society*, 35 (6): 643–82.

Gaus, John (1923/24) "The New Problem of Administration", *Minnesota Law Review*, 8: 217–31.

Gaus, John M., Leonard D. White, and Marshall E. Dimock, eds. (1936) *The Frontiers of Public Administration*. Chicago: University of Chicago Press.

Goodsell, Charles T. (1983) *The Case for Bureaucracy: A Public Administration Polemic* 2d ed., Chatham, NJ: Chatham House Publishers.

Hambleton, R. (2002) "The New City Management", in R. Hambleton, H. V. Savitch and M. Stewart (eds) *Globalism and Local Democracy: Challenge and Change in Europe and North America*, Basingstoke/New York: Palgrave Macmillan.

Hambleton R. and Gross J. S. (eds) (2007) *Governing Cities in a Global Era: Urban Innovation, Competition and Democratic Reform*, Basingstoke/New York: Palgrave Macmillan.

Henry, Nicholas (2007) *Public Administration and Public Affairs*, 10th edn, Upper Saddle River, NJ: Pearson Prentice-Hall.

Hood, Christopher (1996) "Beyond 'Progressivism': A New 'global paradigm' in public management?" *International Journal of Public Administration*, 19: 151–177.

Jepperson, R. L. and Meyer, J. W. (1991) "The Public Order and the Construction of Formal Organizations", in W. W. Powell and P. J. DiMaggio (eds), *The New Institutionalism in Organizational Analysis*, Chicago, IL: The University of Chicago Press.

Jones, H. W. (1958) "The Rule of Law and the Welfare State", *Columbia Law Review*, 58: 143–56.

Karl, Barry (1976) "Public Administration and American History: A Century of Professionalism", *Public Administration Review*, 36: 489–503.

Kettl, Donald F. (1993) *Sharing Power: Public Governance and Private Markets*, Washington, DC: The Brookings Institution.

Kickert, Walter J. M. and Hakvoort, Jan L. M. (2000) "Public Governance in Europe: A Historical–Institutional Tour d'Horizon", in Oscar Van Heflin, Walter J. M. Kickert and Jacques J. A. Thomassen (eds) *Governance in Modern Society: Effects, Change, and Formation of Government Institutions*, Dordrecht: Kluwer.

Klijn, Erik-Hans (2008) "Governance and Governance Networks in Europe: An Assessment of Ten Years of Research on the Theme", *Public Management Review*, 10: 505–25.

Kooiman, Jan (ed.) (1993) *Modern Governance: New Government–Society Interactions*, London: Sage.

Kooiman, Jan (2003) *Governing as Governance*, London: Sage.

Laski, Harold J. (1923) "The Growth of Administrative Discretion", *Journal of Public Administration*, 1: 92–100.

Lynn, Laurence E., Jr. (2006) *Public Management: Old and New*, London/New York: Routledge.

Margolis, Howard (1993) *Paradigms and Barriers: How Habits of Mind Govern Scientific Beliefs*, Chicago, Ill.: University of Chicago Press.

Meier, K. J. (1997) "Bureaucracy and Democracy: The Case for More Bureaucracy and Less Democracy", *Public Administration Review*, 57 (3): 193–99.

Merkle, Judith A. (1980) *Management and Ideology: The Legacy of the International Scientific Management Movement*, Berkeley, CA: University of California Press.

Merriam, Charles E. (1940) "Public Administration and Political Theory", *Journal of Social Philosophy*, 5: 293–308.

North, Douglass C. (1990) *Institutions, Institutional Change, and Economic Performance*, New York: Cambridge University Press.

Olsen, Johan P. (2006) "Maybe It Is Time to Rediscover Bureaucracy," *Journal of Public Administration Research and Theory*, 16: 1–24.

Paquet, Gilles (1999) "Innovations in Governance in Canada", *Optimum*, 29 (2–3): 71–81.

Peters, B. Guy (1999) *Institutional Theory in Political Science*, London and New York: Pinter.

Peters, B. Guy and Jon Pierre (2003) "Introduction: The role of Public Administration in Governing", in *Handbook of public administration*, ed. B. Guy Peters and Jon Pierre, 1–9, London: Sage.

Pfiffner, John M. (1935) *Public Administration*, New York: Ronald.

Pollitt, Christopher and Geert Bouckaert (2004) *Public Management Reform: A Comparative Analysis*. 2d ed., Oxford: Oxford University Press.

Powell, W. W. (1990) "Neither Market nor Hierarchy: Network Forms of Organization", *Research in Organizational Behavior*, 12: 295–336.

Radin, Beryl (ed.) (1996) *New Governance for Rural America: Creating Intergovernmental Partnerships*, Lawrence, Kan.: University Press of Kansas.

Reddel, Tim (2002). "Beyond Participation, Hierarchies, Management and Markets: 'New' Governance and Place Policies", *Australian Journal of Public Administration*, 61 (1): 50–63.

Rhodes, R. A. W. (1994) "The Hollowing-out of the State", *Political Quarterly*, 65: 138–51.

Rhodes, R. A. W. (1996) "The New Governance: Governing without Government", *Political Studies*, 44 (4): 652–67.

Rhodes, R. A. W. (2000) "Governance and Public Administration", in J. Pierre (ed.), *Debating Governance*. Oxford: Oxford University Press, pp. 54–90.

Riggs, Fred W. (1997) "Modernity and Bureaucracy", *Public Administration Review*, 57: 347–53.

Salamon, Lester M. (2000) "The New Governance and Tools of Government Action: An Introduction", *Fordham Urban Law Journal*, 28: 1611–74.

Taylor, Andrew (2002) "'Arm's Length but Hands On': Mapping the New Governance. The Department of National Heritage and Cultural Politics in Britain", *Public Administration*, 75 (3): 441–66.

Toulmin, Stephen Edelston (2003) *The Uses of Argument*, Cambridge: Cambridge University Press.

Weimer, David L. (1995) "Institutional Design: Overview", in David L. Weimer (ed.) *Institutional Design*, Boston, Mass.: Kluwer.

White, Leonard D. (1933) *Trends in Public Administration*, New York: McGraw-Hill.

White, Leonard D. (1955) *Introduction to the Study of Public Administration*, 4th edn, New York: The Macmillan Company.

Part II

GOVERNANCE AND INTERORGANIZATIONAL PARTNERSHIPS TO DELIVER PUBLIC SERVICES

8

THEORY OF ORGANIZATIONAL PARTNERSHIPS: PARTNERSHIP ADVANTAGES, DISADVANTAGES AND SUCCESS FACTORS

Ronald W. McQuaid

Promoting "partnership" and greater interagency cooperation between government departments, public agencies, private companies and the third sector has become a staple of strategies to promote social and labor-market inclusion at national and supranational levels, for instance internationally (CEC 2003, 2001: 6; OECD 2008) and the UK (DWP 2006). Area-based strategies to tackle social and labor-market exclusion have particularly used partnership approaches involving different organizations and forms of relationship – for the UK government, "renewal relies on local communities", and non-public bodies have a leading role to play in promoting employability, regeneration and inclusion (SEU 2001; McQuaid and Lindsay 2005; McQuaid et al. 2007).

Across and beyond the EU, policy-makers are turning to new forms of partnership and seeking to include a wider range of stakeholders in the design, planning and delivery of policies. In the case of employment policies, this reflects an acceptance that, in order for employability policies or interventions to address the range of complex and multi-dimensional problems faced by unemployed and economically inactive people, multi-agency approaches are required. For instance, as governments refocused their welfare-to-work strategies on those claiming long-term income-based benefits in many European countries (Lindsay and McQuaid 2008, 2009) and incapacity benefits in the UK (Lindsay et al. 2008), they also "opened up" employability services to a wider range of stakeholders, in an attempt to extend their quality and reach, and to access specialist knowledge and expertise.

Different types or organization of partnerships are appropriate in different circumstances, and a key strategic issue is to identify and choose an appropriate type. Some of the main dimensions of partnership are: what the partnership is seeking to do, i.e. its purpose and whether it is strategic or project-driven; who is involved, i.e. the key actors and the structure of their relationship in the partnership; when, i.e. the timing or stage of development of the partnership process and changing relationships and activities over time; where, i.e. the spatial dimension; and how the activities are carried out, i.e. the implementation mechanisms (McQuaid 2000).

This chapter considers a number of conceptual and policy issues surrounding partnership working, including interagency cooperation, mainly using examples in the areas of employability and local regeneration policy. Following this introduction the chapter addresses: definitions of "partnership"; potential benefits associated with partnerships/interagency cooperation; limitations and problems with partnerships/interagency cooperation; critical success factors in effective partnerships; some implications for governance; and conclusions.

Definitions of partnership

The term "partnership" covers a multi-dimensional continuum of widely differing concepts and practices, and is used to describe a variety of types of relationship in a myriad of circumstances and locations. Some, such as public–private partnerships, often refer to specific forms of contractual relationships, although this chapter is concerned with wider formal and informal interagency cooperation. Such is the rhetorical power of the language of "partnership" that concerns have been raised that the concept has become little more than a buzzword to "sprinkle liberally through funding applications" (Osborne 1998); or an idea so ubiquitous in major policy initiatives that it defies definition (Rowe and Devanney 2003) and risks losing its analytical value (Miller 1999). Lankshear et al. (1997: 88–9) suggest that key terms like "partnership" are

> words that cross discursive boundaries, spanning multiple world-views, interests and value systems. They all carry positive connotations and name ideals to which people who embrace different – and often incompatible – aspirations, purposes, interests and investments claim allegiance.

The concept of partnership in service delivery arose, during the 1980s and 1990s, as a canon of public policy and private enterprise (Knox 2002). The OECD (1990: 18) has defined partnerships as:

> Systems of formalised co-operation, grounded in legally binding arrangements or informal understandings, co-operative working relationships, and mutually adopted plans among a number of institutions. They involve agreements on policy and programme objectives and the sharing of responsibility, resources, risks and benefits over a specified period of time.

Further to this very broad definition, a number of more context-specific definitions of partnership have been articulated. Harding (1990: 110) sets out a general definition of "private–public partnership" as "any action which relies on the agreement of actors in the public and private sectors and which also contributes in some way to improving the urban economy and the quality of life". Bailey et al.'s (1995: 293) more specific definition of partnerships for urban regeneration speaks of "the mobilisation of a coalition of interests drawn from more than one sector in order to prepare and oversee an agreed strategy for regeneration of a defined area".

It is useful to distinguish partnerships at different levels of organization, such as at strategic or project levels, or geographically at regional and local levels. Snape and Stewart (1996) are interested in different levels of inter-agency cooperation – they distinguish between three ideal-typical forms of partnership working in social-inclusion policy: *facilitating partnerships*, which manage longstanding strategic policy issues; *coordinating partnerships*, which are concerned with the management and implementation of policy based on broadly agreed priorities; and *implementing partnerships*, which are pragmatic and concerned with specific, mutually beneficial projects. To this can be added more strategic-goal agreement partnerships which seek to identify key directions and aims, and how these might be achieved through partnership working.

Drawing on a number of existing approaches, Hutchinson and Campbell (1998: 9) suggest that there is a consensus around a number of defining features: partnerships bring together a coalition of interests drawn from more than one sector to generate agreement; partnerships have common aims and a strategy to achieve them; partnerships share risks, resources and skills; partnerships achieve mutual benefit and synergy.

This discussion demonstrates that partnership remains a varied and ambiguous concept. In the UK context, the debate has been further complicated by the government's application of the language of partnership to programs and relationships that in fact involve the allocation of resources on the basis of competitive tendering to provide services. These include public–private partnerships (and private finance initiatives, or PFIs, in the UK) (McQuaid and Scheerer 2010). Government departments and funders are required to fulfill the dual role of acting as strategic partners, working with other government agencies and stakeholders to shape the general framework for local policy implementation, while also acting as a funder, contracting out services often through some of the same stakeholders.

Increasingly important are partnerships between different public-sector bodies which link different types of services (e.g. the linking of welfare allowances, health, and job search, etc.). There may be tensions between organizing activities along specific functions and tasks (e.g. providing welfare benefits in a cost-effective way) and more client-centered approaches where the full range of issues facing a client need to be dealt with in order to help them to move on (e.g. to employment). For example, it may be important to train a person to manage their health condition first, and to remove their fear of losing welfare benefits if they take a job, as well as improving their vocational and job-seeking skills, etc. The question arises as to how best to maintain economies of scale and other efficiencies in each of the different supports given to a client while making them coordinated and flexible enough to meet the needs of the clients realistically, in the right time, place and manner. Is it best through merging the different services, or through better joint working (partnership) between different agencies (in which case the incentives must promote the flexibility required for effective joint working, while not introducing significant inefficiencies)?

While organization providing training and support for unemployed people under contract to the UK government Public Employment Service, Jobcentre Plus (under the policy during the 2000s termed "New Deal", which targeted different groups of unemployed people), tend to be referred to as "partners", the differential financial power, and control of resources and policy direction that characterize these providers' relationships with the Public Employment Service raise questions about models of partnership, and the potential benefits and problems associated with different approaches (Lindsay and McQuaid 2008). Nevertheless, previous analyses of various models of partnership working and interagency cooperation generally point to a number of benefits and limitations associated with such processes (see Mosley and Sol 2005). It is to these issues that we now turn.

Benefits of partnership and interagency cooperation

Partnership-based approaches to dealing with social and labor-market exclusion have become increasingly popular among policy-makers. A review of the literature suggests that there are a number of benefits associated with interagency cooperation (Hutchinson and Campbell 1998; McQuaid 2000; Dowling et al. 2004; McQuaid et al. 2005).

Flexible and responsive policy solutions

Perhaps the most regularly deployed argument in favor of partnership-based approaches is that problems such as urban regeneration or labor-market exclusion are complex and multi-dimensional, requiring a range of inputs from stakeholders involved in delivering on social, economic and physical development (Rhodes et al. 2003). The individual barriers (e.g. lack of skills), personal circumstances (e.g. caring responsibilities) and socio-economic context (e.g. living in an area of multiple deprivation and low job opportunities) faced by people with low employability are often inter-related, overlapping and mutually reinforcing. Hence policy solutions aimed at one factor, or part of the support system, are unlikely to be fully successful owing to the counteracting impacts of other factors. Partnerships between key actors or service providers are therefore essential in order to tackle the various causes as well as the symptoms of low employability. In terms of labor-market policies, local partnerships arguably facilitate the tailoring of the program and its delivery to the specific problems and opportunities of local labor markets (Nativel et al. 2002).

Facilitating innovation and evaluation

Partnerships arguably have greater scope to test new and innovative approaches, as stakeholders coming together from a range of different policy perspectives can, in itself, produce greater dynamism through the sharing of ideas, expertise and practice, and risks can be contained. They also allow individual partners to test new approaches and, if necessary, withdraw from unsuccessful or difficult experiences. Effective partnership working therefore challenges existing approaches by bringing to bear experience from other sectors and organizations, and developing new ways of working (Nelson and Zadek 2000). Under employability programs to assist unemployed people, policy-makers in the UK have sought to encourage the development of a flexible program that can operate slightly differently across delivery areas, promoting experimentation and innovation, and the emergence of new ideas and solutions at the local level (DWP 2004). Beyond the obvious benefits of such an approach, the flexible nature of localized partnerships facilitates a process of comparison and appraisal, so that best practice can be identified and alternative options and design features can be evaluated.

Sharing knowledge, expertise and resources

A defining feature of any interagency partnership is the manner in which skills, knowledge and expertise are shared in order to maximize the appropriateness, quality and efficiency of provision. By engaging with private and third-sector providers with expertise in specific areas of service provision, or with experience in engaging particularly disadvantaged client groups, public agencies can expand the reach, diversity and quality of their services.

Pooling of resources, synergy

At the most basic level, partnership-based approaches can increase the total level of resources brought to bear on problems, by increasing the number of budget-holding organizations involved in delivering solutions (Conway 1999; McQuaid 1999). Synergy may also be achieved through combining complementary resources from different organizations and from them operating in more appropriate ways compared to their normal organizational approach. In addition, targeting or altering mainstream expenditure on specific shared goals (i.e. "mainstreaming" or "bending the spend") and achieving synergies, and so maximizing the impact of resources, are issues that partnerships potentially have great impact.

Hence supporters of partnership-based approaches are particularly committed to the idea that an effective partnership amounts to "more than a sum of its parts". Miller (1999), drawing on the example of effective local regeneration programs in England, enthuses about the potential for partnership to provide: "added value through the synergy of joint working" and a "transformational" learning process where stakeholders learn from each other and often alter their own approach accordingly. "Effective partnerships can be expected to generate: information sharing; improved communication; a better understanding of what each stakeholder can offer; the avoidance of duplication and inefficiencies; and the identification of opportunities for effective sharing of resources" (Miller 1999: 349).

For Nelson and Zadek (2000), the achievement of this synergy or "partnership alchemy" depends upon five key factors: context, the socio-cultural environment and key drivers (systemic and specific triggers) that shape the creation of partnership; purpose, the complexity and scope of partnership goals and activities, including the level of agreement on a common agenda; participants, the leadership characteristics, resources, capacities and competencies of different participants; organization, the organizational and legal structure, governance principles and communication, consultation and conflict resolution mechanisms; outcomes, the ability to identify and evaluate outcomes and adapt the partnership accordingly.

Finn (2000) argues that national-government initiatives have often been structured in order to access the experience of working in the community and engaging certain client groups held by local authorities and community stakeholders (including the former's experience as large employers in many areas). By engaging with private and third-sector providers with expertise in specific areas of service provision (e.g. mentoring or literacy training) or with experience in engaging particularly disadvantaged client groups, public agencies can expand the reach, diversity and quality of their services.

Developing a coherent service

Partnership working at the strategic level can ensure that policy initiatives in major areas of government activity are "aligned". The drive to achieve coherent local and regional frameworks linking regeneration and employment policies has been a major theme of recent reforms in the UK. The integration of policies under shared strategic priorities can ensure that – for example – supply-side and demand-side labor-market strategies try to compliment each other, and that supply-side interventions are informed by an understanding of the long-term needs of communities and local labor markets. There are a number of examples of national employability policies being linked to local demand-led strategies and regional regeneration initiatives (Lindsay and Sturgeon 2003; Gore 2004), but progress in this area has been uneven.

Improving efficiency and accountability

One of the key benefits associated with effective interagency cooperation is that it can lead to more efficient policy delivery, by eliminating the duplication of effort and improving communications. Within partnerships, interagency bodies have the capacity to be more democratic – at best they can open up decision-making processes and gain the input and "buy-in" of organizations representing a broad range of constituencies and interests. However, there are often concerns that it is not clear "who is in charge" (see below).

Capacity-building

Examples of best practice in regeneration projects in England have demonstrated that local partnerships can build community capacity and engender a sense of community ownership (Rhodes et al. 2003). For the voluntary sector, interagency cooperation (particularly with government) offers new opportunities to have a practical impact on the policy agenda, enabling organizations to fulfill the key objectives of representing the community and giving voice to the concerns of disadvantaged groups (Miller 1999). Becoming "delivery partners" has also helped these organizations to access long-term and stable funding. At the strategic level, cooperation between government agencies and departments can lead to a sharing of knowledge and practice across different areas of expertise, and result in joint working toward a seamless multi-faceted service for clients.

Gaining legitimization and "buy-in"

The tapping of "local knowledge" through the involvement of community-level stakeholders can contribute to the development of approaches that are able to engage disadvantaged communities and address specific localized problems. Engaging community-level stakeholders can also result in the legitimization of, and mobilization of local support for, new policy goals. This can be particularly important in geographical areas characterized by severe disadvantage, where public agencies may be viewed with skepticism by residents who have previous experience of unsuccessful employability and regeneration interventions. By using local people to help in the development and implementation of policies, there can be greater ability to get the target client group to help the recruitment and retention of "hard to reach" individuals, etc. (McQuaid 1999). At the planning level, where lead agencies are willing to cede and share decision-making, budgets and responsibilities with partners, they can engender a sense of shared ownership, helping to legitimize their policy aims.

The benefits discussed above may be achievable where effective structures for interagency cooperation and/or partnership working are in place. However, there are considerable challenges in achieving these positive outcomes which are now discussed.

Partnership and interagency cooperation: potential problems and limitations

Partnerships may not achieve the potential for synergy owing to inertia or other reasons (e.g. Huxham 2003). Some of the challenges in achieving effective and efficient partnerships are now discussed: a lack of clear and/or consistent goals; resource costs; impacts on other services; and differences in approach between partners. The specific issue of community participation is then discussed.

Conflict over goals and objectives

A lack of clear, specific aims or goals is often cited as a major cause of the failure of partnerships. Many partnerships have agreed broad aims, but their detailed goals may be unclear or the partners may have differing understandings of what the goals mean (Mitchell and McQuaid 2001). This can rapidly lead to misunderstanding, lack of coordination, and possible conflict between the partners. This may be accentuated if some partners have undeclared or "hidden" agendas. At the strategic level, conflicting priorities and "turf wars", where different agencies fight over control of an issue or service, can undermine attempts at developing collaborative approaches. At the operational level, gaining the commitment and engagement of private and third-sector partners, and community representatives, can be complicated by organizational barriers and inflexibilities, and localized problems in relation to limited community capacity.

Resources costs

There are considerable resources costs, for instance in terms of staff time in meetings and discussions and making agreements, and in delays to decisions owing to consultation with partners. It may also be difficult to close an inefficient or unsuccessful partnership, or even one whose objective has been achieved, if all partners do not agree, as this may "sour" relations elsewhere.

Accountability

There can also be problems of accountability as no single partner feels fully accountable for the actions of the partnership owing to the split between responsibility and control (e.g. no single body takes full responsibility for problems or for ensuring that overall the policy is effective and efficient). It may not be clear "who is in charge". If each partner "claims" the full success of the partnership (e.g. in an initiative to help unemployed people seeking work) but only considers its own costs, this may distort decisions, and efficiency and value for money will be difficult to measure. The opportunity or direct costs of staff time in participating in the partnership also needs to be accounted for. The full social costs of the partnership need to be aggregated and compared with the full social benefits, rather than each partner focusing upon its own costs and benefits (e.g. possibly through a form of social return on investment).

Impacts upon other services

Partnerships (especially those with stand-alone implementation units) may be seen as an alternative to re-aligning mainstream services to deal with particular issues. But the scale of, and integration between, mainstream services may have a far more significant impact, especially in the long term. Conversely, partnerships may draw resources from other mainstream services or confuse the services in the minds of users, so reducing their effectiveness (i.e. there may be a significant opportunity cost in economic terms).

Organizational difficulties

Organizational difficulties inhibiting successful coordination of programs and approaches, and overcoming the specialist concerns of disparate organizations, is a key implementation problem faced by agencies working together. Within this context, barriers to effective partnership working include: organizational (these include differing missions, professional orientations, structures and processes of agencies); legal/technical (statutes or regulations set down by higher authority, and the technological capacity and practice of the organization); and political (the external political environment but also internal bureaucratic politics).

At the strategic level, effective interagency cooperation may be undermined by the rigidity of institutional and policy structures. Government departments and agencies have arguably traditionally operated in narrowly focused "policy silos" (see above), with resources and expertise concentrated in specialized areas of policy. Breaking out of these policy "silos", to develop multi-policy interagency solutions, can be difficult owing to institutional arrangements that regulate the use of funding and deployment of manpower resources. There is also a danger that strategic-level partnerships can be drawn into the minutiae of process, rather than focusing on implementing change – the actual outcomes achieved by partnership working can be difficult to measure, which can lead to the partnership being seen as an end in itself rather than a means of implementing policy change (Ball and Maginn 2005).

Capacity-building and gaps

There can be difficulties when government seeks to engage different sectors in delivering policy, if key stakeholders lack the professional, organizational or financial capacity to contribute. There have been problems where governments have sought to outsource provision before sufficient private- or voluntary-sector capacity is available. In many localities a lack of "community capacity" (i.e. of the local people in the community) consistently undermines the ability of local stakeholders to engage in partnerships. Where local partnership structures are weak, a considerable commitment of time, effort and resources is likely to be required in order to build capacity. As noted above, even with such a commitment, building trust may prove difficult in disadvantaged communities where public-service providers can be viewed with suspicion. Preparation of local communities (and others, such as local employers) to participate effectively in partnerships often needs a clear strategy that is adequately resourced (and includes practical aspects such as being prepared in advance to deliver quick "wins" without waiting for the usual long timescale of public-sector decision-making). Even at a professional level there is often a capacity gap in terms of specific skills and attitudes that hinders partnership development and implementation.

Differences in philosophy among partners

There may be significant differences in philosophy between the partners, such as in the degree to which they feel the market can solve problems around a particular policy (e.g. employability) or the legitimate role of different stakeholders. There are a variety of related factors that have affected the development and implementation of partnerships, such as differing value and ethical systems between the public- and private-sector actors (OECD 2008; McQuaid 2000). Problems may arise in combining public and private management practices, philosophies and language within one partnership organization, while the extent to which formal contracting is a sound basis for partnership has been debated. Contractualism offers benefits associated with accountability and clarity in responsibilities and reward structures. However, where stakeholders are required to be both actors within a purchaser–provider contract and strategic partners there may be a confusion of roles and incentives. It has also been suggested that the strict obligations associated with contractual relations (and even Service Level Agreements in the public sector) can stifle some innovation. More generally, an integrated "policy culture" shared by agencies and groups involved in delivery is important if partnerships are to be effective. Where policy culture becomes fragmented – for example, owing to conflicting priorities over financial resources or tensions over the differential power of partners to "drive the agenda" – partnership working can quickly disintegrate (Dobbs and Moore 2002).

Power relations

The handling of differences in the relative power of different bodies or individuals in a partnership is important to its success. In most partnerships there is a degree of unequal power. The presence of unequal power should not imply that all partners should necessarily have equal power. Some may have greater legitimate claim, due for instance to their greater involvement in the project or local area, or have greater political legitimacy in the case of elected bodies. Although there are different types of power, greatest power generally rests with those controlling resources. In the case of local regeneration partnerships, they are likely to dominate those in the local area who may have a considerable understanding of what is relevant and effective, albeit from a local rather than macro-perspective, and whose feeling of "ownership" can be crucial to the initiative's success. At different stages of a partnership there will be different balances of power between actors. To illustrate, in the early stages when an initiative is being developed, all those "around the table" will have potentially large influence as their involvement will often be considered important for getting the initiative started. However, the environment within which the key funders operate is very influential (for instance, in ruling certain approaches out of discussion). When the initiative is agreed, then the views of the main funders are likely to become relatively more important, i.e. there may be a shift from the influential power of some actors (such as local voluntary groups). As McDonald (2005) argues, power relations remains an area for greater theoretical development.

Community participation

In regeneration partnerships, a lack of "community capacity" consistently undermines the ability of local stakeholders to engage in partnerships (Dobbs and Moore 2002). Where local partnership structures are weak, a considerable commitment of time, effort and resources is likely to be required in order to build capacity (Rhodes et al. 2003). Carley (2006) notes the importance of an integrated "policy culture" shared by agencies and groups involved in the delivery of local inclusion strategies.

The inclusion of community and voluntary-sector stakeholders can also raise issues surrounding the changing role of such organizations. McLaughlin and Osborne (2000) argue that the increasing involvement of the voluntary sector as a delivery partner "risks subverting the legitimate role" of community organizations by attaching them to "labyrinthine" contractual processes of regeneration programs. Osborne (1998) has also warned against the danger of community-level actors becoming the "puppets" of government agencies, which may be attracted to indulging in tokenistic forms of local consultation rather than less comfortable discussions with street-level groups representing the full diversity of community interests. The concern here is that local authorities and other governmental stakeholders tend to be reluctant to cede authority, and seek "safe" forms of local engagement in which their decision-making autonomy is not challenged (Rowe and Devanney 2003).

Miller (1999) discusses the problems of government–community-sector cooperation from the opposite perspective, noting that the introduction of new stakeholders presents new potential problems beyond the familiar tensions between the state and private sectors. Miller distinguishes between the formalized professional nonprofit sector and the "community sector" of local, informal and citizen-based organizations. He further distinguishes between primarily service-oriented organizations and those seeking to "enhance local democracy" (i.e. those with a political agenda). The former prioritize the extent to which the partnership enables the delivery of services; the latter will be more interested in strategic action and the partnership process in itself.

It is crucial that advocacy groups engaged in practical partnerships are persuaded to commit to constructive debate within the boundaries of the relevant policy agenda, and to consider their contribution to the delivery of outcomes. Without such a commitment, community-level stakeholders risk acting as a brake on progress, "putting themselves between regeneration agencies and local people" (Sanderson 1999). There can also be questions of legitimacy in the engagement of community-level stakeholders – government agencies seeking to build partnerships are understandably attracted to established community organizations, but these "usual suspects" may not always reflect the diversity of interests within local areas (Geddes 1998).

Some key success factors in partnership working

The above discussion highlights some of the advantages, problems and issues around partnership working and other approaches to interagency cooperation. Much of the literature on interagency cooperation emphasizes questions of partnership structure, strategy and internal regulations (e.g. Hudson and Hardy 2002). Although this provides a useful overview to the question of partnership, it is perhaps lacking in specific examples of how successful partnerships have emerged. Coupar and Stevens (1998: 145) state that partnership "is not so much about institutions or methods, as about attitudes and culture. It is a question of building mutual trust, of recognising differences and finding common ground". This section identifies lessons from successful partnerships and interagency initiatives, in which a number of recurring features can be identified.

A clear strategic focus

Successful models of interagency cooperation tend to be governed by: a detailed, clearly defined strategy; a commitment to shared objectives and clear targets informed by an overarching strategic vision; a transparency of operations; and strategic interests being given priority over local or sectional interests. Rhodes et al. (2003), reviewing Single Regeneration Budget partnerships, emphasize the need for "formal sign-up" to an agreed strategy and approach from all relevant partners. Establishing "shared values" has been a positive characteristic of local employability partnerships (Blaxter et al. 2003), although Miller (1999) suggests that this is more likely to succeed if cooperation is based around clearly defined, specific and limited objectives.

Strategic leadership and support

It is essential that there is clear strategic leadership and support for partnership within each partner organization. Staff on the ground must be confident of such support and be able to "speak for the organization" at main partnership meetings. This requires confidence in, and support for, staff from senior management and decision-makers to allow staff to make the partnership work effectively and efficiently. There must be a genuine willingness to make the partnership work, which may help to counteract the common tendencies to retreat into "policy silos" based on professional discipline or organizational structure.

The importance of trust, organizations and people in partnerships

The importance of trust (between organizations and between individuals in partnerships) is often highlighted (Gambetta 1988). Effective delivery partnerships need: the right mix of skills and expertise; certainty within each partner organization regarding roles and responsibilities; continuity of approaches and membership in order to maintain "trust and certainty"; and a recognized and legitimate role for all partners, with no one actor dominating. Referring to regeneration partnerships, Rhodes et al. (2003) suggest that all immediately relevant policy actors must either directly sign up to the specific project or be linked through wider partnership bodies for interagency cooperation to be effective. However, it is important for partnerships to be clearly focused – Blaxter et al. (2003) and McQuaid et al. (2005) reflect on innovative local employability projects, noting that only appropriate stakeholders with the power, skills or resources (including networks of influence) to add value to the partnership were included.

Capacity for cooperation and mutualism

Effective partnership or interagency cooperation operates through strong and established networks of communication and joint working at the local level, and – where external actors are involved – the inclusion of organizations with the capacity and resources to engage effectively in partnership relations and add value to the partnership process. It is essential that organizations, and individual representatives, involved in partnerships have both the authority and the institutional flexibility to engage in mutual decision-making and resource-sharing. Training staff to participate effectively and efficiently in partnerships is essential for those involved in either the development or the implementation of partnerships. Specific practical training should be provided to all staff involved (preferably jointly involving staff from the relevant partners so that they can develop a common vocabulary and understanding and agreements on how to operate). Given the highly structured institutional framework of many public agencies, this can be problematic, but successful local employability partnerships have seen actors such as the Public Employment Service work creatively to ensure maximum flexibility in the sharing of information and resources (McQuaid et al. 2005).

Organizational complementarity, co-location and coterminosity

The engagement of organizations that compliment each other's resources and expertise is important to maximizing the benefits of partnership working. Employability is a multi-dimensional issue, affected by individual factors, personal and family circumstances, and external barriers (McQuaid and Lindsay 2005). It is therefore essential to ensure that there is a good "match" between the organizations represented in partnerships, so that a range of issues affecting the employability of different individuals and communities can be addressed. At a practical level, there are benefits associated with the individuals represented within partnerships holding similar levels of budgetary and policy responsibility, and (where possible) operating within coterminous – or at least similar – geographical boundaries. Halliday and Asthana (2005), drawing on the example of Health Action Zones in rural areas of the UK, note how a lack of coterminosity and problems of physical distance can combine to constrain the development of the organizational capacity necessary to support community-based change. Co-location for the delivery of services may also be beneficial in many cases.

Incentives for partners and "symbiotic interdependency"

If partnerships are to be effective, then mutual benefit and reciprocity are usually important. Actors must believe that there are benefits for their own organization set against the costs of involvement (benefits could include financial leverage, expansion of competencies and influence, achievement of organizational goals, positive public relations, or the opening of new markets). The presence of common or complementary goals is important, as is the degree of symbiotic interdependency – the extent to which benefits for one partner agency produce mutually beneficial outcomes for other partners (Fenger and Kok 2001). This contrasts with competitive interdependency, where the action of one actor interferes with another actor's ability to take action or achieve his goals, potentially generating conflict. Systematically building and strengthening the "shadow of the future", whereby future relationships are important and so influence current reciprocity, can reinforce partnership working and the sharing of current benefits.

For example, effective employability partnerships tend to be built upon evidence of mutual benefits related to (for example) securing markets, and addressing recruitment and retention issues (for employers); and the extension of partnership working and areas of influence and competence, and the achievement of positive outcomes for target groups (for policy actors and service providers). Where the interdependency of mutual goals and benefits is unclear, individual agencies may resist moves toward new cooperative structures.

The value of action and outcome-oriented procedures

Effective partnerships tend to focus on outcomes rather than merely on evidence of activity (Rhodes et al. 2003). In terms of the delivery of local employability services, there is a need for: an emphasis on the quality as well as the quantity of outcomes; clear decision-making procedures, with management close to service provision; and an action- and results-oriented approach, with measurable goals clearly defined and evaluated (McQuaid et al. 2005). However, we should finally acknowledge that measuring the value of effective interagency cooperation is likely to prove difficult. There are considerable problems in seeking to identify the specific impacts of any one model of cooperation. Nickell and Van Ours (2000: 219), referring to Dutch and UK labor-market policies, note the problems associated with comparing the impact of different "configurations of institutions":

> First, there is no empirical basis to disentangle the separate contribution of each policy change. Second, some policy changes are time consuming and therefore time lags may be substantial. . . . Third, policy changes are complimentary. The effect of one policy depends

on whether or not a different policy is implemented as well. A change of institutions in the labour market is a package deal.

In general, outcome-oriented partnerships are characterized by: an emphasis on the quality as well as the quantity of outcomes; responsiveness and clear decision-making procedures, with management close to service provision; and a consistent approach to reviewing results, with measurable goals clearly defined and evaluated at regular, appropriate intervals.

"New Governance" and "New Public Management"

Geddes and Benington (2001), reviewing social-inclusion strategies across the EU, suggest that specific institutional configurations are particularly associated with certain types of welfare state. Statist, interventionist welfare states, such as those found in Nordic states, are less likely to develop broad multi-agency partnerships with nonstate organizations, and more likely to deploy government agencies as the main or sole provider of activation employment policies. However, shifts toward new "state–market–civil society" mixes in the provision of welfare and employability services are common to a range of different welfare state models (Van Berkel and Van der Aa 2005; Lindsay and McQuaid 2008).

These shifts to some extent reflect a more general move toward new forms of public-sector governance. Governance can be defined as the framework through which political, economic, social and administrative authority is exercised at local, national and international levels. This framework consists of a wide variety of mechanisms, processes, institutions and relationships (including partnerships) through which individual citizens, groups and organizations can express their interests, exercise their rights and responsibilities, and mediate their differences (Nelson and Zadek 2000). Governance is increasingly about balancing the roles, responsibilities, accountabilities and capabilities of: different levels of government – local, national, regional and global; and different actors or sectors in society – public, private and civil society organizations and individual citizens.

Moves toward what has been termed the "new governance" – characterized by a shift in the roles and responsibilities bureaucracies, and the involvement of private agencies in service delivery – stem partly from concerns over budget constraints on the public sector, higher client expectations and therefore the demand for better-quality services, the drive for efficiency through "least cost, best performance" approaches, and the belief that private-sector management systems can deliver these benefits (Considine 2000).

Rhodes (1997) argues that New Public Management (NPM) is one manifestation of these new forms of governance. NPM is characterized by the deployment of business principles and management techniques, and the use of private enterprise to deliver public services, partly to gain associated efficiencies. This may be done through partnerships combining public- and private-sector bodies or through quasi-markets and purchaser–provider splits in the organization of public services. Exponents have seen NPM as offering a solution through more flexible organization, flattened management hierarchies, and the decentralization of decision-making (Hood 1991).

Such approaches emphasize the importance of choice for the provider of a public service and the implementation schemes to exploit possible efficiency gains in the provision of public services. This, however, is a more restricted view of partnerships than has been taken in this chapter. In the case of Private Finance Initiatives (repackaged as Public–Private Partnerships in the UK after the new government of the late 1990s), there may be no increase in choice of service or product for the ultimate user of the service. This partly reflects the outcomes of the debates since the 1980s concerning whether the public sector should have an enabling role, determining the form and level of public services but not primarily delivering them, or a role as sole provider of services (see, for instance, Giloth and Mier 1993).

There remain questions of accountability, with one argument being that local authorities and government departments are more clearly and publicly accountable than multi-agency quangos and contracted providers. Others argue that the introduction of quasi-markets, in an attempt to stimulate market-type competitive behavior, is problematic, as such behavior emerges only from the operation of genuinely open markets, but the product monopolies and single state purchasers of public services that characterize "internal market" arrangements do not provide such an environment (Drechsler 2005). The critique of NPM is that it attempts to replace poor public management with private-sector inputs rather than with better public management (Bevir et al. 2003), and marks an attempt to reduce costs (with implications for services) by taking elements of public spending "off the books" (Newman and McKee 2005).

With the expansion of this contractualism through competitive tendering in employment and other policy areas, it has been suggested that the manner in which service providers have been required to engage in such processes of compulsory competitive tendering has created new rivalries, which have the potential to undermine the ethos of partnership (Peck 2001). The form, power structure and implementation of partnerships is key. In the case of UK employment policy in the late 1990s and the 2000s, there is some evidence that the process of strategic delivery plan development early in the program's rollout was undermined by the competitive arguments made by organizations in favor of an expansion in their own role in the delivery process (Mason 2007). However, despite some early claims that the extension of the private sector's role into unfamiliar areas of employability provision under the UK's policies to assist unemployed people initially has proved to be problematic, there is no consistent evidence of differences in quality as a result of private-sector inputs (Hasluck 2001), while Dunleavy et al. (2006) have argued that NPM is in decline. More generally, the future of wider non-contractual-based partnerships and intergovernmental working may be more assured, for the reasons discussed previously.

Conclusions

The above discussion highlights the complexity and diversity of the issues surrounding the development and implementation of partnership approaches and other forms of interagency cooperation. The chapter provides a framework for considering the advantages and problems of partnership working, particularly in the context of regeneration and employability policies. It also discussed "critical success factors" in terms of: strategic focus; the participation of key individuals and organizations; a shared capacity for cooperation and mutualism; incentives and symbiotic interdependency; organizational complimentarity and coterminosity; and outcome-oriented procedures. A number of specific issues have emerged from the above analysis, which revolve around lessons we can learn concerning how partnerships can be improved (in terms of strategic direction, structure, operation, etc.) and when are they appropriate.

If we are better to understand, and theorize on, when and how to improve partnership working, then further research is needed into several sets of questions, relating to why have partnerships and what form they should take. First, there is a need to identify the balance between a body carrying out its activities largely alone (with potential benefits of clearer accountability, speed of action and reduced transactions costs associated with partnerships) or in a partnership with other agencies (with potential costs and benefits discussed above) or somewhere on the multi-dimensional spectrum between these. Second, for what reasons and under what circumstances are different forms of partnership most appropriate, and what are the implications of different forms of partnership working? It is important to identify the different types of partnership based upon such factors as motivations, benefits and costs. We need to consider how, and to what extent, interagency cooperation has facilitated the development of innovative and locally responsive policy solutions and what forms of partnership organization most facilitate this in different macro- and micro-circumstances. Third, what benefits and problems have been associated with the implementation of New Public Management type approaches to specific areas such as employability and regeneration policies, and what are the implications of different models of private-sector participation? To what extent do different models of partnership working, or contracting out, contribute to effective interagency cooperation and, crucially, outcomes, and what are the tensions between contractualism and strategic partnership working?

Given the complexity of issues concerning partnerships, there is a need to: clarify our typologies of partnerships working; develop a greater understanding of the issues concerning the implementation of partnerships on the ground; and create more nuanced general theoretical analyses of partnerships.

Acknowledgments

Many of these ideas were developed through discussions with Colin Lindsay and other colleagues, including Matthew Dutton and Malcolm Greig, at the Employment Research Institute, and this is gladly acknowledged.

References

Bailey, N., Barker, A. and MacDonald, K. (1995) *Partnership Agencies in British Urban Policy*, London: UCL Press.

Ball, M. and Maginn, P. J. (2005) "Urban Change and Conflict: Evaluating the Role of Partnerships in Urban Regeneration in the UK", *Housing Studies*, 2 (1): 9–28.

Bevir, M., Rhodes, R. A. W. and Weller, P. (2003) "Traditions of Governance: Interpreting the Changing Role of the Public Sector", *Public Administration*, 81 (1): 1–17.

Blaxter, L., Farnell, R. and Watts, J. (2003) "Difference, Ambiguity and the Potential for Learning: Local Communities Working in Partnership with Local Government", *Community Development Journal*, 38 (2): 130–9.

Carley, M. (2006) "Partnership and Statutory Local Governance in a Devolved Scotland", *International Journal of Public Sector Management*, 19 (3): 250–60.

Commission of the European Communities (CEC) (2001) *Strengthening the Local Dimension of the European Employment Strategy*, Luxembourg: Office for Official Publications of the European Communities.

Commission of the European Communities (CEC) (2003) *The Future of the European Employment Strategy: A Strategy for Full Employment and Better Jobs for All*, Luxembourg: Office for Official Publications of the European Communities.

Considine, M. (2000) "Contract Regimes and Reflexive Governance: Comparing Employment Service Reforms in the United Kingdom, the Netherlands, New Zealand and Australia", *Public Administration*, 78 (3): 613–38.

Conway, M. (1999) *Partnerships, Participation, Investment, Innovation: Meeting the Challenge of Distressed Urban Areas*, Dublin: European Foundation.

Couper, W., Stevens, B. (1998) "Towards a New Model of Industrial Partnership", in Sparrow, P., and Marchington, M. (eds), *Human Resource Management: The New Agenda*, London: Financial Times Pitman Publishing, pp. 145–59.

Department for Work and Pensions (DWP) (2004) *Building on New Deal*, Sheffield: DWP.

Department for Work and Pensions (DWP) (2006) *A New Deal for Welfare: Empowering People to Work*, London: DWP.

Dobbs, L. and Moore, C. (2002) "Engaging Communities in Area-based Regeneration: The Role of Participatory Evaluation", *Policy Studies*, 23 (3–4): 151–71.

Dowling, B., Powell, M. and Glendinning, C. (2004) "Conceptualising Successful Partnerships", *Health and Social Care in the Community*, 12 (4): 309–17.

Drechsler, W. (2005) "The Rise and Demise of the New Public Management", *Post-autistic Economics Review*, 33 at: www.paecon.net/PAEReview/

Dunleavy, P., Margetts, H., Bastow, S. and Tinkler, J. (2006) *Digital Era Governance: IT Corporations, the State and E-government*, Oxford: Oxford University Press.

Fenger, M. and Kok, P. J. (2001) "Interdependency, Beliefs, and Coalition Behavior: A Contribution to the Advocacy Coalition Framewoork", *Poplicy Sciences*, 34 (2): 157–170.

Finn, D. (2000) "Welfare to Work: The Local Dimension", *Journal of European Social Policy*, 10 (1): 43–57.

Gambetta, D. (1988) "Can We Trust Trust?", in D. Gambetta (ed.) *Trust: Making and Breaking Cooperative Relations*, Oxford: Blackwell.

Geddes, M. (1998) *Local Partnership: A Successful Strategy for Social Cohesion?*, Dublin: European Foundation.

Geddes, M. and Benington, J. (2001) "Social Exclusion and Partnership in the EU", in M. Geddes and J. Benington (eds) *Local Partnerships and Social Exclusion in the European Union: New Forms of Local Social Governance?*, London: Routledge.

Giloth, R. and Mier, R. (1993) "Co-operative Leadership for Community Problem Solving", in R. Mier et al. (eds) *Social Justice and Local Development Policy*, Newbury Park, Calif.: Sage.

Gore, T. (2004) "The Open Method of Co-ordination and Policy Mainstreaming: The European Employment Strategy and Regional Conversion Programmes in the UK", *European Planning Studies*, 12 (1): 123–41.

Halliday, J. and Asthana, S. (2005) "Policy at the Margins: Developing Community Capacity in a Rural Health Action Zone", *Area*, 37 (2): 180–8.

Harding, A. (1990) "Public–Private Partnerships in Urban Regeneration", in M. Campbell (ed.) *Local Economic Policy*, London: Cassell.

Hasluck, C. (2001) "Lessons from the New Deal", *New Economy*, 8 (4): 230–4.

Hood, C. (1991) "A Public Administration for All?", *Public Administration*, 69 (1): 3–17.

Hudson, B. and Hardy, B. (2002) "What Is Successful Partnership and How Can It Be Measured?", in C. Glendinning, M. Powell and K. Rummery (eds) *Partnerships, New Labour and the Governance of Welfare*, Bristol: Policy Press.

Hutchinson, J. and Campbell, M. (1998) *Working in Partnership: Lessons from the Literature*, DfEE Research Report RR 63, London: Department for Education and Employment.

Huxham, C. (2003) "Theorizing Collaborative Practice", *Public Management Review*, 5 (3): 401–23.

Knox, C. (2002) *Review of Public Administration: Partnerships*, Belfast: Office of the First Minister and Deputy First Minister.

Lankshear, C., with Gee, J. P., Knoebel, M. and Searle, C. (1997) *Changing Literacies*, Buckingham: Open University Press.

Lindsay, C., and McQuaid, R. W. (2008) "Inter-agency Co-operation in Activation: Comparing Experiences in Three Vanguard 'Active' Welfare States", *Social Policy and Society*, 7 (3): 353–65.

Lindsay, C., McQuaid, R. W. and Dutton, M. (2008) "New Approaches to Employability in the UK: Combining 'Human Capital Development' and 'Work First' Strategies?", *Journal of Social Policy*, 36 (4): 539–60.

Lindsay, C. and McQuaid, R. W. (2009) "New Governance and the Case of Activation Policies: Comparing Experiences in Denmark and the Netherlands", *Social Policy and Administration*, 43 (5): 445–63.

Lindsay, C. and Sturgeon, G. (2003) "Local Responses to Long-term Unemployment: Delivering Access to Employment in Edinburgh", *Local Economy*, 18 (2): 159–73.

McDonald, I. (2005) "Theorising Partnerships: Governance, Communicative Action and Sport Policy", *Journal of Social Policy*, 34 (4): 579–600.

McLaughlin, K. and Osborne, S. P. (2000) "A One Way Street or Two Way Traffic? Can Public–Private Partnerships Impact on the Policy-making Process?" in S. P. Osborne (ed.) *Managing Public–private Partnerships for Public Services: An International Perspective*, London: Routledge.

McQuaid, R. W. (1999) "The Role of Partnerships in Urban Economic Regeneration", *International Journal of Public–Private Partnerships*, 2 (1): 3–28.

McQuaid, R. W. (2000) "The Theory of Partnerships – Why Have Partnerships?", in S. P. Osborne (ed.) *Managing Public-private Partnerships for Public Services: An International Perspective*, London: Routledge.

McQuaid, R. W. and Lindsay, C. (2005) "The Concept of Employability", *Urban Studies*, 42 (2): 197–219.

McQuaid, R. W., Lindsay, C., Dutton, M. and McCracken, M. (2007) *Best Practice in Inter-agency Co-operation on Employability*, report for the Department for Employment and Learning, Northern Ireland, Belfast: DELNI.

McQuaid, R. W., Lindsay, C. and Greig, M. (2005) "Job Guarantees, Employability Training and Partnerships in the Retail Sector", *Local Economy*, 20 (1): 67–78.

McQuaid, R. W. and Scherrer, W. (2010) "Changing Reasons for Public Private Partnerships", *Public Money and Management*, 30 (1): 27–34.

Mason, M. (2007) "Collaborative Partnerships for Urban Development: A Study of the Vancouver Agreement", *Environment and Planning A*, 39 (10): 2366–82.

Miller, C. (1999) "Partners in Regeneration: Constructing a Local Regime for Urban Management?", *Policy and Politics*, 27 (3): 343–58.

Mitchell, I. and McQuaid, R. W. (2001) "Developing Models of Partnership in Economic Regeneration", in L. Montanheiro and M. Spiering (eds) *Public and Private Sector Partnerships – the Enterprise Governance*, Sheffield: Sheffield Hallam University Press.

Mosley, H. and Sol, E. (2005) "Contractualism in Employment Services: A Socio-economic Perspective", in E. Sol and M. Westerveld (eds) *Contractualism in Employment Services*, The Hague: Kluwer, http://www.ilo.org/public/english/bureau/inst/download/dp15604.pdf

Nativel, C., Sunley, P. and Martin, R. (2002) "Localising Welfare-to-work? Territorial Flexibility and the New Deal for Young People", *Environment and Planning C: Government and Policy*, 20 (6): 911–32.

Nelson, J. and Zadek, S. (2000) *Partnership Alchemy: New Social Partnerships in Europe*, Copenhagen: Copenhagen Centre.

Newman, J. (2001) *Modernising Governance: New Labour, Policy and Society*, London: Sage.

Newman, J. and McKee, B. (2005) "Beyond the New Public Management? Public Services and the Social Investment State", *Policy and Politics*, 33 (4): 657–73.

Nickell S. and Van Ours J. (2000) "Why Has Unemployment in the Netherlands and the United Kingdom Fallen So Much?", *Canadian Public Policy*, 26 (1): 201–20.

Organisation for Economic Cooperation and Development (OECD) (1990) *Partnerships for Rural Development*, Paris: OECD.

Organisation for Economic Cooperation and Development (OECD) (2008) *Public–Private Partnerships: In Pursuit of Risk Sharing and Value for Money*, Paris: OECD.

Osborne, S. (1998) "Partnerships in Local Economic Development: A Bridge Too Far for the Voluntary Sector?", *Local Economy*, 12 (4): 290–5.

Osborne, S. P. (ed.) (2000) *Managing Public–private Partnerships for Public Services: An International Perspective*, London: Routledge.

Peck, J. (2001) *Workfare States*, New York: Guilford.

Rhodes, J., Tyler, P. and Brennan, A. (2003) "New Developments in Area-based Initiatives in England: The Experience of the SRB", *Urban Studies*, 40 (8): 1399–1426.

Rhodes, R. A. W. (1997) *Understanding Governance*, Buckingham: Open University Press.

Rowe, M. and Devanney, C. (2003) "Partnership and the Governance of Regeneration", *Critical Social Policy*, 23 (3): 375–97.

Sanderson, I. (1999) "Participation and Democratic Renewal", *Policy and Politics*, 27 (3): 324–41.

Snape, D. and Stewart, M. (1996) "Keeping up the Momenton – Partnership Working in Bristol and the West of England", Bristol: Bristol Chamber of Commerce.

Social Exclusion Unit (SEU) (2001) *Preventing Social Exclusion*, London: SEU.

Van Berkel, R., and van der Aa, P. (2005) "The Marketisation of Activation Services: A Modern Panacea? Some Lessons from the Dutch Experience", *Journal of European Social Policy*, 15 (4): 329–345.

9

PUBLIC–PRIVATE PARTNERSHIPS AND PUBLIC GOVERNANCE CHALLENGES

Carsten Greve and Graeme Hodge

Abstract

Public–private partnerships (PPPs) come in many different institutional forms, including those which use private finance and create long-term contracts for public infrastructure projects. This chapter reviews briefly the empirical experience with infrastructure PPPs in the OECD countries. The chapter then proceeds to examine what kinds of challenges PPPs pose to the theory and practice of public governance. In the discussion there is special emphasis on consequences of PPPs for democratic governance and for the prospect of genuine collaboration between the public sector and the private sector in the future.

Introduction

How do public–private partnerships (PPPs) fit into the new public governance regime? And what are the public governance challenges associated with the rise of PPPs? PPPs can be loosely defined as institutionalized cooperative arrangements between public-sector actors and private-sector actors. There have been numerous attempts to classify, order and characterize PPPs in the literature (Hodge and Greve 2007). While a broad conception of PPPs might be appropriate in some circumstances, this chapter examines a specific kind of PPP that occurred from the mid-1990s: long-term infrastructure contractual-type PPPs or, as the European Union terms them, "institutionalized PPPs". PPPs as long-term infrastructure projects are one prominent understanding of PPPs that will be used here. These types of PPPs were introduced in the United Kingdom from the 1990s onwards (although there are historical examples: see Wettenhall 2003, 2005; Kettl 1993), and soon caught the attention of various governments around the world, notably Australia. The PPP institution has been a small but important part of government reform in most OECD countries as well as in developing countries (for overviews, see Osborne 2001b; Deloitte 2006; Hodge and Greve 2005; Ghobadian et al. 2004; OECD 2008).

This chapter discusses how PPPs became a part of the new public governance regime as they allowed governments to engage with a number of private agents in often complex and contractually sophisticated relationships. Governments have been using PPPs for various activities in order to tackle cross-border challenges through private partners. In a democratic context, the role of PPPs remains debatable. PPPs mean that governments may be in danger of detaching themselves from the wider electorate and democratic constituencies at the grassroot levels because the PPP deals appear so complex and inaccessible that PPPs have become an elitist game – a game played by economists, lawyers, consultants and financial experts.

The chapter is structured in the following way. The first part provides a brief overview of the recent PPP evolution and debate, and traces the development of PPPs from their primarily UK origin to the global attention they are enjoying currently. The second part discusses the challenges that PPPs present for new public governance structures. The third part discusses if there is a democratic gap between the PPP deals and the democratic institutions. The fourth part concludes the chapter by assessing the role of PPPs in future public governance regimes.

Public–private partnerships for infrastructure

PPPs in their modern-day incarnation as long-term infrastructure contracts are now a commonplace factor in political, administrative and economic reform discussions throughout the world. In a PPP, the government interacts with a number of private-sector companies to design, finance, build, own and operate infrastructure projects, and maybe transfer them back to the government again. There is a great variety in how these elements can be used, for example Design Finance Build Operate (DFBO) or Build Own Operate Transfer (BOOT). The contractual periods are often long – up to thirty or forty years, or even longer. There can be considerable risk involved. But there is also possibility for innovation and gain-sharing. The key argument has been that the government and the private sector work together toward a common purposeful objective. One definition sees PPPs as "cooperation of some sort of durability between public and private actors in which they jointly develop products and services and share risks, costs and resources which are connected with these products" (Van Ham and Koppenjan 2001: 598). There has been a discussion whether PPPs represent a genuine modernization effort, or if PPPs are just a mere excuse on the road to more privatization. The US scholar Stephen Linder's (1999) early survey of the main arguments related to PPPs mentioned the possibility that "PPP" was just another word for privatization. While that discussion is not completely dead, PPPs have emerged in their own right in the public governance literature as one recognizable organizational and institutional form and something more than just marketization (Bovaird 2006).

The sectors in the UK where most PPPs have been located include health, defence, education and transport (HM Treasury 2003). The UK emerged as the primary exponent for the PPP phenomenon (Osborne 2001b). PPPs were a part of the John Major government's reform program in the UK in the early 1990s. It started life as the Private Finance Initiative (PFI) at the time. There were several objectives with the Major government's policy for private involvement in public infrastructure (Terry 1996). One objective was to reduce the need for public-sector borrowing by letting private finance come in. Another objective was to shift the balance between the public sector and the private sector in favor of the latter sector. The PFI scheme was clearly a part of the Conservative government's agenda for the public sector in the 1990s. In 1997, however, the New Labour government was elected in the UK. One option for the new government could have been to abolish the PFI scheme at the time. Instead, the New Labour government chose to keep the PFI scheme. Why? Two reasons have been mentioned in the literature (Flinders 2005). First, New Labour needed the private finance to help finance the welfare services that New Labour had promised as part of its broader modernization agenda. As New Labour had committed itself not to raise taxes, they needed a way to finance the modernization agenda. Second, New Labour could exploit the PPP theme to signal to the private sector that the party was not anti-business and nothing like the old Labour party. Whatever the cause, the PPP agenda received a boost with the election of the New Labour government in the UK.

There has been a steady rise in the number of projects. In 2008, there were 625 PPPs in the UK with a total capital value of £58.87 billion (HM Treasury 2008: 6). The Treasury has been the key driver in the UK PPP policy. The policy has been laid out in several key documents on the PFI scheme (HM Treasury 2003, 2006). The UK National Audit Office has followed the policy closely, and evaluated many of the projects as well as the policy (National Audit Office 2003). The evaluations made by the National Audit Office are probably some of the most thorough evaluations one is likely to find about PPPs in the world.

The debate in the UK has ranged from the early assessment of the Institute for Public Policy Research (2001) report (which to a certain extent endorsed PPPs but also warned against the notion that PPPs were the only show in town) to the present controversy over the financial implications and current high-profile projects (Pollock et al. 2007). For Flinders (2005), PPPs changed with the different political priorities of the New Labour government during the 2000s. The arguments changed from being about economics to being about innovation. For Broadbent and Laughlin (1999), PPPs were a part of the ongoing UK modernization process in the public sector. The academic assessment of whether PPP has been good value is a theme where there are some disagreements. Some reviews of the UK experience have cast PPPs in a favorable light (Pollitt 2005). Others have remained more skeptical (Shaoul 2005). Recently, researchers have begun to question the validity of the presumed savings about which the UK Treasury has been boasting (Pollock et al. 2002, 2007).

Australia was another place where PPPs caught on from the late 1990s. Many projects have been initiated in Australia, ranging from a tunnel in Sydney harbor to a motorway and tunnels in Victoria – the Citylink project. The Australian PPP experience has generally lived up to many of the official policy expectations (Allen 2007; Hodge 2005). But there have also been failures along the way – in the hospital sector, for example (English 2005).

In the rest of Europe, such as Germany, Spain and Italy, PPPs have also been prolific. In Germany new hospitals and roads are being built as PPPs. In Spain, new transport facilities are being constructed as PPPs. In the new European member states, PPPs have become an option to be considered (Bovaird 2004; Teisman and Klijn 2001). In the US and Canada, PPPs have been an important part of the strategy to renew infrastructure (Bloomfield et al. 1998; Rosenau 2000) (see the recent OECD 2008 overview of what countries are doing in relation to PPPs).

In international reviews from advocates in consultancy firms (see, for example, Deloitte 2006; PriceWaterhouseCoopers 2005), PPPs are being praised. International organizations such as the European Union and the OECD are making cautious endorsements of PPPs. The international organizations admit that PPPs are viable tools to use, but they refrain from being overly enthusiastic. The OECD states that PPPs are one policy option out of many. Perhaps the international organizations have learned the lessons of the 1980s and 1990s where privatization was being lauded, with subsequent problems occurring in the aftermath.

Summing up, the PPP has become an important new institution in the world of infrastructure policy. While some countries, notably the UK and Australia, have been at the forefront of developments, other countries and international organizations have followed suit more reluctantly. Many countries and also international organizations are being cautious about the PPPs' long-term perspectives, and are careful not to become too enthusiastic. Meanwhile, the bulk of scholars have been skeptical about the economic promises about PPPs, although some of the academic reviews to date have acknowledged the specific economic and financial results obtained by using PPPs in particular countries and sectors.

Public–private partnerships and public governance challenges

In many ways, PPPs contribute to the new style of governing emphasized in the *New Public Governance*. As we have learned in the introduction to this book, the new public governance puts emphasis on different factors from those emphasized by New Public Management. In a governance framework, authority is spread among a number of actors (Heinrich and Lynn 2001). No one is quite in charge, and the governance responsibilities are dispersed (Kettl 1993). Governments have used PPPs to build relationships with the private sector and to reach public goals through private means. PPPs grew out of the privatization era, but PPPs could also be seen as a genuine new way of bonding between public-sector and private-sector organizations that would allow for more sophisticated use of private-sector expertise. Governments can tap into private-sector knowledge in order to innovate, share risks with private-sector organizations, and realize gains and share them with private-sector organizations in a way that was not possible in the privatization era. And they can make use of private-sector organizations when public-sector organizations are not capable of handling the tasks themselves. Whether new hospitals or new primary schools were being built, or new bridges or tunnels constructed, governments could use the private-sector expertise in innovative hospital-building, tunnel construction and school-building to get higher-quality projects, the argument went. One key factor in aligning private-sector means with public-sector goals was to tie the success of the projects closely to private finance. Private-sector investors would see public infrastructure projects as safe and reliable investments. Public-sector organ-izations could use the private finance made available to them, and also use it to make sure that private-sector firms kept an interest in the projects.

There are, however, many challenges to public governance that occur because of PPPs, and here we shall restrict ourselves to five of them.

The first challenge in governing through PPPs is complexity. PPPs have come to be seen as increasingly complex deals. PPPs are long-term contracts, so they are shielded by sudden political interference. They are as such mainly accessible to experts in finance and law, and can be very difficult for lay people to understand. Often the deals and contracts are not documents that engage publics in debates over the future governance challenges. PPP deals rely on consultants to formulate and to check the deals. There are complex negotiations leading up to a PPP contract, and there is very seldom a process of inviting the public or other stakeholders to have their say in the process. More often than not, the emphasis has been to seclude the negotiations and keep them for the partners to the contract themselves. There is the related criticism that PPPs are often not transparent. The deals are kept as secret as commercial contracts. They are rarely open for outside scrutiny. The institutional variety of PPPs adds to the complexity of the deals themselves. A special organizational unit that embodies the partnerships is often established as PPPs are set up, and in the UK this is known as the Special Purpose Vehicle. Often the Special Purpose Vehicle consists not only of two distinct organizations, but also of a number of organizations on each side of the negotiation table. A public-sector part may consist of several ministries and agencies working together on a particular project. A private-sector part may consist of a lead agency with many other organizations under contract to the lead agency. Add to that the financial institutions (banks and finance investors), the lawyers who oversee the contracts, and the various consultants who are drafted in to solve various technical issues, and there is a host of organizations involved in the partnership (Hodge 2004a,b).

A second challenge is the number of roles governments adopt in PPP relationships. A key organization is often the Treasury/ministry of finances as the organization in charge of the process. But, as with privatization, there is a certain double act appearing here. A ministry of finance is both an advocate of the PPP policy and a key guardian of the public purse. Often these two roles would be expected to collide. The organizations that should sound cautions are also often highly involved in policy development of some sort, such as the national audit offices that are supposed to check the government's policy, but also are involved in evaluations and recommendations to governments on PPP policy. Hodge (2005) notes how governments have moved from their traditional stewardship role to a louder policy-advocacy role concerning PPPs. As a consequence of this, we might reflect that government now finds itself in the middle of multiple conflicts of interest, acting in the roles of policy advocate, economic developer, steward for public funds, elected representative for decision-making, regulator over the contract life, commercial signatory to the contract, and planner.

A third challenge is when to choose a PPP over an alternative governance form. A PPP is one option as a governance form, but there are others. Other alternatives are hierarchy through a traditional public-service organization, contracting out/outsourcing, and finally a more or less loosely structured network. Choosing among the different governance forms is not always a deliberate action by governments. How to weigh up the advantages and disadvantages is often given too little thought. The closest alternative to a PPP arrangement would be contracting out/outsourcing. Some researchers believe that there is really no difference between the two, and that most of what passes for PPPs actually is contracting out (Klijn and Teisman 2005). Whether governance forms could be matched to the governance forms in the way that Williamson (1985) suggests, or as Karmarck (2007) in her analysis of different governance forms for public policy challenges might envisage, is a topic of some controversy; but there may be a need for discussing PPPs in this light instead of advocating PPPs for every policy area (see also the British Institute of Public Policy Research in 2001).

A fourth challenge for the government is how to manage partners from the private sector that follow their own strategic agenda. Many governments do not possess enough capacity to govern the new PPPs; or, put in other terms, the private sector as agents acts strategically in order to avoid the scrutinizing moves by the public-sector principals. Private-sector companies may try to outsmart governments, and other governmental partners, and not be able to fulfill the contracts and the obligations into which they have entered. This kind of analysis would suggest a closer look at the market conditions for private-sector organizations entering into PPP arrangements. Private-sector organizations may be interested in PPPs in several ways, one of them being that they seek to exploit weaknesses in the public sector, and try to get lucrative deals on behalf of their owners and stockholders. Governments should be able to oversee the ecology of a market (Frumkin 2002); but, if they cannot do so, private-sector agents may find ways to bypass government intentions and rules.

A fifth challenge is that a PPP is a long-term contract. A PPP is a particularly tricky institutional form because its long-term contracts (up to thirty or forty years) make it almost by definition impossible to foresee which factors can influence the governance environment in the long run. More attention in the literature on public governance is being paid to developments over time (Pierson 2004; Pollitt 2007). PPPs are good examples of that. Although over 600 PPP projects in the UK, for example, have been established, it is difficult to evaluate the output and the outcome of these projects because of the duration of the contractual period.

Added to this challenge has been the first peer review of the impressive on-time and on-budget figures reported by Mott Macdonald (2002). The review of Pollock et al. (2007) was unequivocal in its judgment of these figures, stating:

> there is no evidence to support the Treasury cost and time overrun claims of improved efficiency in PFI . . . [estimates being quoted are] not evidence based but biased to favor PFI . . . only one study compares PFI procurement performance, and all claims based on [this] are misleading.

Boardman, Poschmann and Vining (2005), for instance, noted the difficulty of capturing transaction costs in any comparison between partnership and traditional project delivery, and catalogued seventy-six major North American PPP projects. They noted that less than half included a significant private financing role. They presented five transport, water provision and waste projects, showcasing a series of “imperfect” partnership projects with high complexity, high asset specificity, a lack of public-sector contract-management skills and a tendency for governments to be unwilling to "pull the pin" on projects once under way. They particularly point to private entities being "adept at making sure, one way or another, that they are fully compensated for risk-taking" and to strategic behavior such as declaring bankruptcy (or threatening to) in order to avoid large losses. There are clear tensions for governments here, having to hold their nerve and watch commercial failures materialize when risks are borne by the private sector, despite their yearning to be viewed as successfully governing a growing and vibrant market. PPPs encompass different accountability and governance arrangements compared to traditional procurement – indeed, these arrangements are one of the claimed advantages of this provision method. Interlinked financial incentives across a consortium of players, the sharing of risks through carefully contractualized legal relationships, and more flexible decision-making processes between executive government and service provider all feature as improvements over traditional procurement arrangements. The progressive contractualization of the state's services and activities has been accompanied by the general assumption of increased accountability in all its forms, although this has rarely been tested. Whilst contractualization may have increased managerial accountability, it may have been at the expense of reduced public accountability in its various forms.

Summing up, PPPs present challenges to the traditional forms of public administration in terms of the complexity of the deals and the number of actors involved; the government's capacity to steer; the choice between governance forms; possible strategic behavior by the private-sector organizations; and the duration of contracts which makes evaluation difficult. In that way, PPPs share many of the same features associated with the emergence of the new public governance as described in this book.

Discussion

These challenges remind us that it might take some time before PPPs are fully compatible within an elaborate public governance structure. The challenges point to a broader issue of the place of PPPs within a public governance framework. These issues have to do with the democratic aspects of public governance. The danger is that, if the challenges are not addressed, the PPPs will be difficult to align with democratic concerns.

PPPs shift the responsibility for some of the traditional steps associated with public policy-making in a democracy. It is commonplace to distinguish between policy formation, decision-making, implementation and results. When a PPP is established, the private sector is given the responsibility to implement the policy and to create results. Decision-making about PPPs is mainly a technical matter, once the decision to propose a partnership option has been taken. Governments are often required to oversee a competitive bidding round for the contract before deciding who can become the private partner in the PPP. In Europe, choosing among the bids must follow the criteria set out in the European Union public procurement rules, including the special rules for "a competitive dialogue". After the contract to become a partner has been awarded, the government leaves the implementation responsibility to the partnership organization, often called the Special Purpose Vehicle. Through the contract that binds the partners together, the partnership organization is then responsible for achieving the desired result – for example, financing, building and operating/maintaining a new hospital, a primary school or a sports facility. The private sector is given more responsibility, and now for a longer period than through ordinary competitive contracts.

The follow-up in terms of democratic regulation is not in place in all countries that have introduced PPPs. Whilst we have instituted a "regulatory state" of independent regulators, ombudsmen and audit review bodies in order to disperse power away from political quarters after the privatization of state businesses (Hodge 2004c), this has not yet occurred with PPP deals. They have continued to be essentially two-way government–business deals rather than also involving the community or any other independent accountability body to protect the public's interests. They have also been handled on a case-by-case basis, by the government itself, in the face of multiple conflicts of interest. The potential for the interests of the advocating government and business partners to dominate the public interest is palpable here. For example, early drafts of the Australian state of Victoria's PPP guideline materials did not even mention the "public interest" notion and treated government solely as if it were a contractual partner in a commercial deal. In many ways this is reminiscent of past centuries.

Communities seem to need far more discussion and debate as to how they might better ensure that the public interest is met through PPP deals, as well as meeting the needs of the contracting parties. To the extent that new infrastructure contract delivery arrangements have reduced existing accountability arrangements and altered longstanding governance assumptions without democratic debate, new partnership arrangements lack legitimacy (Hodge 2006).

A key point is if the criticisms aimed at PPPs can be remedied in the long run. Or is there something inherently difficult in aspiring toward a "genuine" partnership between public-sector organizations and private organizations? One view could be that it is just a matter of more analysis needed which will improve the basis for decision-making and eventually secure the potential benefits (US Government Accountabiliy Office 2008). Recalling the old saying that the "public and private management is alike in all unimportant aspects" (see the discussion in Alison 1992), the question is if the two sectors can genuinely work together or if the competing interests are simply too great to overcome. Money is the end of private business while money is a means in the public sector to achieve a social outcome (Moore 2000). It cannot be denied that a lot of the literature on PPPs in the beginning was of a hopeful nature that emphasized the opportunities of cooperation. In recent years, as we acquire more empirical analysis on PPPs, the verdict becomes more nuanced. A proper way forward for research on PPPs is to rely even more on empirical investigation that can bring fresh insights to the question of whether PPPs work in practice and how they fit into the institutions of public governance and the wider democratic context in which they are embedded.

It would seem that these aspects of democratic governance should be investigated more in the PPP debate. So far much of the literature has been preoccupied with the performance of PPPs and the legal aspects of PPPs, but seems to pay less attention to the governance challenges faced by democracies if they were to use PPPs more systematically. Of course, many governments may not, in fact, make use of PPPs that much; and, if that is the case, PPPs are confined to a special corner in the public governance discussion.

The global financial crisis that occurred in the late 2000s sparked off a new round of debate as to how PPPs are appropriate in a new public governance framework. The promise of transfer of knowledge and know-how from the private partner to public organizations is probably still an attraction to governments around the world (Moszoro and Gassorowski 2008). But the uncertainty connected to the long-term impact of the financial crisis may cast a shadow over the future attractiveness of the PPP model. One of the first reports on the topic estimated that the global financial crisis offers both governments and the private sector a chance to review the risk allocation schemes (Regan 2008).

Conclusion

PPPs for infrastructure projects came on to the policy scene in a big way from the 1990s onward. The UK and Australia were among the first countries to adopt PPPs, although PPPs had been known in North America and other places under different names in earlier times. PPPs offered what the privatization policy before could not offer: close cooperation between public-sector partners and private-sector partners, risk-sharing, and long-term contracts for infrastructure projects.

PPPs are but one of several options in the various governance forms available. Much emphasis has been laid on "from public to private" while the real question is that governments often find that they can choose among governance forms. PPPs offer some qualities, but are not seen as universally attractive as governments may find inside production or complete outsourcing a better alternative. The shift or not to PPPs does not always occur automatically, as Williamson's (1985) theory of transaction costs anticipates, but requires empirical analysis to see why governments in certain countries chose or abandoned the PPP policy option.

PPPs have usually been discussed in terms of their economic and financial benefits or drawbacks, and PPP debates are often dominated by legal experts or financial experts. In this chapter, we have sought to highlight the governance challenges associated with PPPs. There are a number of challenges connected with using PPPs. These include the complexity of the deals, the role of the ministry of finance or key government sponsor of PPP deals, choice between governance forms, government steering capacity, and the time question (long-term contracts). How well these challenges are met is likely to influence how the PPP model fits into a democratic framework. PPP means involvement of the private sector in public policy-making to a greater degree than before, and questions also concern the robustness and readiness of regulatory institutions to deal with PPPs. A key point of discussion is if genuine partnerships are possible within the PPP model, or whether the deeper interests between public-sector organizations and private organizations will remain an obstacle to greater collaboration. More PPP literature is focusing on empirical results which are likely to cast light on some of the questions. The discussion on PPPs appears to be moving from promises of PPPs to a more evidence-based discussion of what works and what does not work in practice. The improved empirical evidence is likely to influence the policy dialogue on the place of PPPs in the future institutions of public governance.

References

Alison, Graham T. (1992) "Public and Private Management: Are They Fundamentally Alike in All Unimportant Aspects?", in Jay Shafritz and Albert Hyde (eds) *Classics in Public Administration*, Belmont, Calif.: Wadsworth.

Allen Consulting Group (2007) *Performance of PPPs and Traditional Procurement in Australia*, Final Report to Infrastructure Partnerships Australia, 30 November 2007.

Bloomfield, Pamela, Westerling, David and Carey, Robert (1998) "Innovation and Risks in a Public–private Partnership: Financing and Construction of a Capital Project in Massachusetts", *Public Productivity and Review*, 21 (4): 460–71.

Boardman, Anthony, Poschmann, Finn and Vining, Aidan (2005) "North American Infrastructure P3s: Examples and Lessons Learned", in Graeme Hodge and Carsten Greve (eds) *The Challenge of Public–private Partnerships: Learning from International Experience*, Cheltenham: Edward Elgar.

Bovaird, Tony (2004) "Public–private Partnerships in Western Europe and the US: New Growths from Old Roots", in Abby Ghobadian, David Gallear, Nicholas O'Regan and Howard Viney (eds) *Public–private Partnerships: Policy and Experience*, Basingstoke: Palgrave Macmillan.

Bovaird, Tony (2006) "Developing New Forms of Partnership with the 'Market' in the Procurement of Public Services", *Public Administration*, 84 (1): 81–102.

Broadbent, Jane and Laughlin, Richard (1999) "The Private Finance Initiative: Clarification of a Future Research Agenda", *Financial Accountability and Management*, 15 (2): 95–114.

Deloitte (2006) *Closing the Infrastructure Gap: The Role of Public–private Partnerships*, London: Deloitte.

English, Linda (2005) "Using Public–private Partnerships to Deliver Social Infrastructure: The Australian Experience", in Graeme Hodge and Carsten Greve (eds) *The Challenge of Public–private Partnerships: Learning from International Experience*, Cheltenham: Edward Elgar.

Flinders, Matthew (2005) "The Politics of Public–private Partnerships", *British Journal of Politics and International Relations*, 7: 215–39.

Frumkin, Peter (2002) "Service Contracting with Non-profit and For-profit Providers: On Preserving a Mixed Organizational Ecology", in John Donahue and Joseph Nye (eds) *Market-based Governance*, Washington, DC: The Brookings Institution.

Ghobadian, Abby, Gallear, David, O'Regan, Nicholas and Viney, Howard (eds) (2004) *Public–private Partnerships: Policy and Experience*, Basingstoke: Palgrave Macmillan.

Heinrich, Carolyn and Lynn, Laurence (eds) (2001) *Governance and Performance*, Washington, DC: Georgetown University Press.

Her Majesty's Treasury (2003) *PFI: Meeting the Investment Challenge*, London: The Stationery Office.

Her Majesty's Treasury (2006) *PFI: Strengthening Long Term Partnerships*, London: The Stationery Office.

Her Majesty's Treasury (2008) *Infrastructure Procurement: Delivering Long-term Value*, London: The Stationery Office.

Hodge, Graeme (2005) "Public–private partnerships: The Australian Experience with Physical Infrastructure", in Graeme Hodge and Carsten Greve (eds) *The Challenge of Public–private Partnerships: Learning from International Experience*, Cheltenham: Edward Elgar.

Hodge, Graeme (2006) "Public–private Partnerships and Legitimacy", *University of New South Wales Law Journal, Forum*, 12 (2).

Hodge, Graeme and Greve, Carsten (eds) (2005) *The Challenge of Public–private Partnerships: Learning from International Experience*, Cheltenham: Edward Elgar.

Hodge, Graeme and Greve, Carsten (2007) "Public–private Partnerships: An International Performance Review", *Public Administration Review*, 67 (3): 545–58.

Institute of Public Policy Research (UK) (2001) *Building Better Partnerships*, London: IPPR.

Karmarck, Elaine (2007) *The End of Government as We Know It: Making Public Policy Work*, Boulder, Colo.: Lynne Rienner.

Kettl, Donald F. (1993) *Sharing Power*, Washington, DC: The Brookings Institution.

Klijn, Erik-Hans and Teisman, Geert (2005) "Public–private Partnerships as the Management of Co-production: Strategic and Institutional Obstacles in a Difficult Marriage", in Graeme Hodge and Carsten Greve (eds) *The Challenge of Public–private Partnerships: Learning from International Experience*, Cheltenham: Edward Elgar.

Linder, Stephen (1999) "Coming to Terms with the Public–private Partnership: A Grammar of Multiple Meanings", *American Behavioral Scientist*, 43 (1): 35–51.

Moore, Mark H. (2000) "Managing for Value: Organizational Strategy in For-profit, Nonprofit and Governmental Organizations", *Nonprofit and Voluntary Sector Quarterly*, 29 (1), supplement: 183–204.

Moszoro, Marian and Gasiorowski, Pawel (2008) *The Optimal Capital Structure of Public–private Partnerships*, International Monetary Fund Working Paper WP 08/1, Washington, DC: International Monetary Fund.

Mott Macdonald (2002) *Review of Large Public Procurement in the UK*, London: Mott Macdonald.

National Audit Office (2003) *PFI: Construction Performance*, HC 371, London: The Stationery Office.

Organisation for Economic Cooperation and Development (OECD) (2008) *Public–private Partnerships: In Pursuit of Risk Sharing and Value for Money*, Paris: OECD.

Osborne, Stephen (ed.) (2001b) *Public–private Partnerships: Theory and Practice in International Perspective*, London: Routledge.

Pierson, Paul (2004) *Politics in Time*, Princeton, NJ: Princeton University Press.

Pollitt, Christopher (2007) *Governing with the Past*, Oxford: Oxford University Press.

Pollitt, Michael (2005) "Learning from the UK Private Finance Initiative Experience", in Graeme Hodge and Carsten Greve (eds) *The Challenge of Public–private Partnerships: Learning from International Experience*, Cheltenham: Edward Elgar.

Pollock, Allyson, Price, David and Player, Stewart (2007) "An Examination of the UK Treasury's Evidence Base for Cost and Time Overrun Data in UK Value-for-money Policy and Appraisal", *Public Money and Management*, April: 127–33.

PriceWaterhouseCoopers (2005) *Delivering the PPP Promise: A Review of PPP Issues and Activities*, available at www.pwc.com

Rosenau, Pauline Vaillancourt (ed.) (2000) *Public–private Policy Partnerships*, Cambridge, Mass.: MIT Press.

Shaoul, Jean (2005) "The Private Finance Initiative or the Public Funding of Private Profit", in Graeme Hodge and Carsten Greve (eds) *The Challenge of Public–private Partnerships: Learning from International Experience*, Cheltenham: Edward Elgar.

Teisman, Geert and Klijn, Erik-Hans (2001) "Public–private Partnerships in the European Union: Official Suspect, Embraced in Daily Practice", in Stephen Osborne (ed.) *Public–Private Partnerships*, London: Routledge.

Terry, Francis (1996) "The Private Finance Initiative: Overdue Reform or Policy Breakthrough?", *Public Money and Management*, January–March: 9–16.

United States Government Accountability Office (2008) *Highways Public–private Partnerships: More Rigorous Up-front Analysis Could Better Secure Potential Benefits and Protect the Public Interest*, GAO 08–44, Washington, DC: Government Accountability Office.

Van Ham, J. C. and Koppenjan, Joop (2001) "Building Public–private Partnerships: Assessing and Managing Risks in Port Development", *Public Management Review*, 4 (1): 593–616.

Wettenhall, Roger (2003) "The Rhetoric and Reality of Public–private Partnerships", *Public Organisation Review: A Global Journal*, 3: 77–107.

Wettenhall, Roger (2005) "The Public–private Interface: Surveying the History", in Graeme Hodge and Carsten Greve (eds) *The Challenge of Public–private Partnerships: Learning from International Experience*, Cheltenham: Edward Elgar.

Williamson, Oliver (1985) *The Economic Institutions of Capitalism*, New York: Free Press.

10

INTRODUCING THE THEORY OF COLLABORATIVE ADVANTAGE

Siv Vangen and Chris Huxham

This chapter looks at some key governance tensions that are a consequence of the increasingly interorganizational nature of public management. The focus is on the potential for collaborative advantage arising out of interorganizational partnerships. We introduce the *theory of collaborative advantage* and explain, through some illustrative examples, its ability to aid understanding about the management of collaboration in practice.

A theme-based theory of collaboration

The theory of collaborative advantage was developed from research which has been ongoing since 1989, in which we have worked with and collected data from very many and varied types of collaborative situations, involving individuals with various roles including partnership managers, representatives of participating organizations and senior managers whose organizations are involved in collaboration. This has included supporting individuals who are aiming to drive particular collaborations forward, design and facilitation of development events for collaborative partners, design and delivery of collaborative leadership development events, contributions to practice seminars and conferences, direct participation in collaborations, both as participants and as initiators and leaders, and contributing to policy development. The collaborations have ranged from "dyads" (two-party collaborations) to international worldwide networks. They have touched almost every aspect of the public and nonprofit sectors, and include public-private partnerships (PPPs) that also span the commercial sector. Their areas of concern take in, for example, a wide range of focuses on health and on education, anti-poverty, substance abuse, community development and planning, careers development, policing, economic development, and so on.

The theory has two organizing principles. First, it is structured around a tension between Collaborative Advantage – the synergy that can be created through joint working – and Collaborative Inertia – the tendency for collaborative activities to be frustratingly slow to produce output or uncomfortably conflict-ridden. It is also structured around issues that tend to energize those

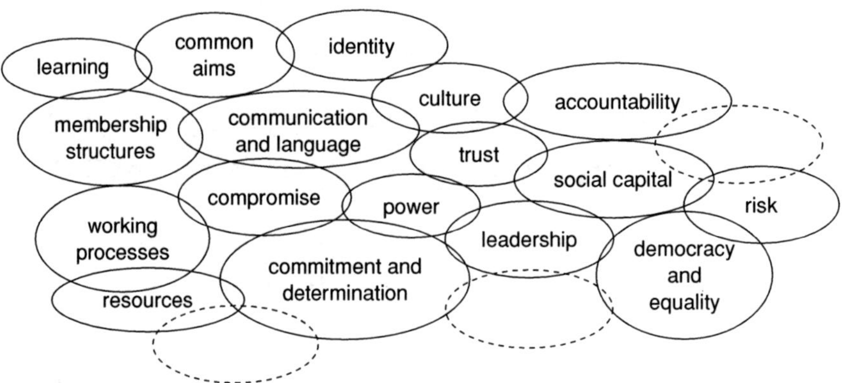

Figure 10.1 Themes in collaboration practice.

who manage collaborations – their anxieties and rewards. It seeks to depict what underpins the anxiety and reward in each area. We call these issue areas themes in collaboration practice (see Figure 10.1). Over the years, we have also added topics that stem from our own observations, from policy considerations and from other researchers. The themes overlap with each other, so issues underlying each theme cross-relate with issues underlying others.

The theory itself is descriptive because it illustrates the complexity that underlies collaborative situations and the resulting challenges that are intrinsic to them. It is also prescriptive because it describes the issues that must be managed but without providing precise recipes for managerial action. It thus recognizes the idiosyncratic nature of collaborative situations and that there are positive and negative sides to alternative ways of managing. It provides conceptualizations and frameworks that can be used as "handles for reflective practice" (Huxham and Beech 2003) – that is, pointers to aspects of collaborative situations that need deep consideration and management – thus enabling managers to think through and find ways of managing their own collaborative situations.

This chapter provides brief overviews of four of these conceptualizations and frameworks relating to agreement on aims, trust-building, cultural diversity and attitudes to knowledge transfer. In so doing, we introduce some of the issues, tensions and challenges that generate collaborative inertia and some ways for considering how to turn these around in order to gain the advantage. In conclusion, we indicate how these four "themes" integrate with others that we do not have space to cover here, to provide an overall sense of the nature of collaborative practice (see Huxham and Vangen 2005 for a fuller holistic exposition of the theory of collaborative advantage). We also introduce some alternative conceptions of successful practice and discuss their relevance for understanding how to achieve collaborative advantage.

Managing aims

Seeking agreement on aims is essential yet the notion of congruent aims is fundamentally paradoxical.

Looking specifically at the aims of a collaboration is helpful because difficulties associated with agreement on aims frequently engage those who manage collaboration in practice. The gist of the argument is that developing clear, common or agreed aims is essential if partners are to make any joint progress (Hudson 2004; Oliver 1990). Yet the notion of congruent aims in collaborative situations is fundamentally paradoxical. The paradox arises because the possibility for achieving advantage usually rests on drawing synergy from heterogeneous partners with different resources, experiences and expertise. These differences, however, stem partly from partners having different purposes and visions, which lead them to seek dissimilar involvements and benefits from collaborating. This paradox makes seeking agreement on aims problematic in practice.

One way of understanding this problematic is to look closely at how aims may be conceptualized. In collaborative situations, it is possible to distinguish aims that influence actions and directions across six dimensions: level, origin, authenticity, relevance, content and overtness, as illustrated in Figure 10.2. Let us elaborate on this a little further.

(i) Level

The first dimension relates to the level at which aims are recognized and distinguishes between those that are about the collaboration, those that are about organizational purposes and those that individuals wish to achieve. Aims expressed at the collaboration level relate to participants' views of what the collaborating partners aspire to achieve together. They are the public declaration of the sought-after collaborative advantage. In contrast, organizational- and individual-level aims relate to the aspirations for the collaboration of each of the organizations and individuals involved. This

Types of aims	
Level	Collaboration's, organizations' and individuals' aims
Origin	External Stakeholders, members
Authenticity	Genuine and pseudo
Relevance	Process and substance
Content	Collaboration dependent/independent
Overtness	Explicit, unstated and hidden

Figure 10.2 Aims in collaboration practice.

distinction thus recognizes that aims at both the organizational and individual levels motivate and influence the actions of those who enact the collaboration in practice.

(ii) Origin

The aims in the first dimension mostly relate to the concerns of members of the collaboration. However, aims formulated by members are sometimes strongly influenced by the aims of organizations or individuals external to the collaboration. Government is perhaps the most common organizational stakeholder exerting pressure on collaborations, and it frequently influences and shapes them. Whether collaborations are mandated or constrained by government, nationwide policies as well as local priorities and interests tend to have an effect on the aims of the collaboration.

(iii) Authenticity

Aims expressed by members and external stakeholders may be genuine statements about what they aspire to achieve. However, there are many reasons why members may not identify with aims that are nevertheless publicly stated. For example, they may not seriously subscribe to aims that have been imposed upon them by external pressure, or changes in the situation may have altered the relevance of previously genuine aims. Organizations may, for example, invent a jointly owned substantive aim that satisfies the specifications of a funding-provider and which effectively disguises their real aim. Similarly, individuals may invent aims for their organizations to legitimize their own personal involvement in the collaboration. We characterize such possibilities as pseudo-aims.

(iv) Relevance

The identification of specific aims for each of the parties involved as well as the joint purpose is acknowledged as important if the collaboration is to succeed. Recognizing which organizational aims can reasonably be pursued through the collaboration is, however, not always straightforward. Other related aims remain to be addressed by the organization alone or perhaps through other collaborations. The fourth dimension thus distinguishes those aims that should or are intended to relate specifically to the collaborative agenda from those that are closely related but not explicitly a part of it.

(v) Content

Many of the aims expressed by individuals are essentially concerned with what the collaboration is about, such as gaining access to resource and expertise, sharing risk, improving coordination in service provision and increasing efficiency. They relate to substantive outcomes and are obviously important in all collaborations. However, participants also – often implicitly – express aims that relate to how the collaboration will be undertaken. These aims can relate to any aspect of collaborative processes, so might, for example, relate to modes of communicating, to the kind of relationship between members or to a myriad other possibilities.

(vi) Overtness

Finally, aims may be openly discussed and explicitly stated, but there are also many reasons why they may knowingly not be revealed to other participants, even if there is genuine goodwill between partners. Hidden agendas are endemic in collaboration. Deliberate concealing of aims is, however, not the only reason why they may not be clearly stated. In practice, there may be limited opportunities to discuss explicitly all potentially relevant aims in open forum; many aims go unstated even when there is no intent to hide them.

Taken together, these dimensions thus indicate that the aims relevant to collaborative situations will relate to aspirations not only for the collaboration but also for the organizations and individuals involved; may have been generated by those involved but may also have been imposed or suggested by external stakeholders; may be genuine but can also be manufactured to provide a reason for involvement in collaboration; do not always relate to the activities of the collaboration; can relate to substantive or processual concerns; and do not all appear overtly in the discourse of the collaboration.

Conceptualizing the aims across these six dimensions may help facilitate better understanding of the variety of aims that are relevant to collaborations, and the ways in which multiple and conflicting aims can prevent agreement and progress. When faced with the task of managing collaborations, trying to identify aims across the dimensions, as they may be perceived by all partners, can be very enlightening, whether it is done as a quick and easy or a more thorough investigative exercise. Such an exercise can, for example, reveal difference between aims at the organizational level, which has the potential to cause conflicts of interest and misunderstandings. Similarly, whilst it is not possible to know others' hidden agendas, it is possible to speculate that they may exist and even have a go at guessing what they may be. There are a multitude of other types of insights that may be gained from applying the aims dimensions to real collaborative situations. The type of insights that may thus be gained can be very helpful in understanding and judging how best to work collaboratively with partners.

At the general level, the obvious conclusion to be drawn from this conceptualization is that agreeing on aims is frequently problematic in practice and that discussion aimed at establishing clarity of purpose can easily unearth irreconcilable differences. Arguably, it may be prudent to get started on some tangible actions without fully agreeing on aims. Instead partners should seek to gain enough agreement to allow them to make progress. Exactly what constitutes enough depends on partners' assessment of the particular situations. Time set aside for incremental collaborative achievements can help build trust between partners which can then form the basis upon which difficult discussions about aims can be held.

Managing trust

Trust is a prerequisite for successful collaboration yet many situations are characterized by suspicion and mistrust.

As with the issue of aims, trust is also seen as a necessary condition for successful collaboration (Lane and Bachmann 1998) yet the reality of many collaborations suggests that trust is frequently weak – if not lacking altogether. This particular paradox then suggests that there is a need to look at how trust can be built and maintained between partners in the context of collaboration.

One way of conceptualizing trust-building is through the loop depicted in Figure 10.3. This argues that two factors are important in initiating a trusting relationship. The first concerns the formation of expectations about the

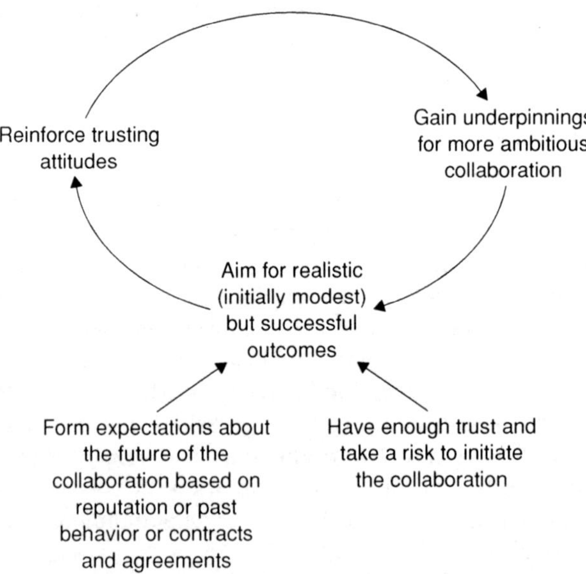

Figure 10.3 The trust-building loop.

future of the collaboration; these will be based either on reputation or on past behavior, or on more formal contracts and agreements (Gulati 1995). Given the difficulties of agreeing aims, as discussed above, this is a nontrivial starting point. The second starting point involves risk-taking: partners need to trust each other enough to allow them to take a risk to initiate the collaboration (Gambetta 1988). If both of these initiators are possible, then, the loop argues, trust can be built gradually through starting with some modest but realistic aims that are likely to be successfully realized. This reinforces trusting attitudes and provides a basis for more ambitious collaboration.

This conceptualization of trust-building aligns itself well with a "small wins" approach (Bryson 1988) within which trust can be built through mutual experience of advantage gained via successful implementation of low-risk initiatives. Trust can be developed over time, moving gradually toward initiatives where partners are willing to take greater risks because a high level of trust is present. When risk and uncertainty levels are high, a strategy involving incremental increases in resource commitments may indeed be the preferred strategy. In many situations, however, the collaborative advantage aimed for requires the collaborating partners to be more ambitious, and hence to adopt a higher-risk approach. The small-wins approach may, for example, be in contradiction to the need to address major social issues rapidly or meet the requirements of external funding bodies for demonstrable output. More comprehensive ways of managing trust have different implications for initiating and sustaining the trust-building loop. We shall elaborate further on this below.

Initiating the trust-building loop

(a) Forming expectations

Two structural features – ambiguity and complexity – that tend to characterize collaborations can act as barriers to the initiation of trust-building. Whilst researchers have argued that "explicit" membership where the parties "know and agree on who is involved and in what capacity" is a key definitional element of collaboration, the surprising reality of many situations is the ambiguity about who the partners are. Typically, there are differences in views about who the central members are and what their roles or membership status are with respect to the collaboration. In practice it can be difficult to be certain about what organization, collaboration or other constituency (if any) individuals represent. Simply identifying with whom to build trust therefore can be very difficult and time-consuming.

Working out with whom trust should be built is not the only challenge in getting started in the trust-building loop. As we have already discussed above, practitioners continuously raise concerns over the establishment of joint aims.

Seeking agreement on aims to initiate the trust-building loop effectively can be problematic in practice.

(b) Managing risk

Gradually, as trust develops, it becomes a means for dealing with risk. In situations where the small-wins approach is not feasible, however, the risk associated with the collaboration has to be managed as an integral part of trust-building. Risk is usually associated with opportunistic behavior and vulnerability relating to apprehensions that partners will take advantage of collaborative efforts by, for example, claiming ownership of joint efforts. When the aim is to build trust, however, risk management cannot be concerned with guarding against opportunistic behavior, e.g. via sanctions set out in contractual agreements. Instead risk management must ensure that any future collaborative advantage can realistically be envisaged and is shared. This requires efforts associated with aims negotiation, structural ambiguity, clarification of expectations, willingness and ability to enact the agreed collaborative agenda in view of associated power and influence relationships, and so on. These activities are extremely resource-intensive and time-consuming, and their management requires a great deal of skill and sensitivity. Hence the effort is only recommended where trust cannot be built incrementally.

Sustaining the trust-building loop

(c) Managing dynamics

Many collaborations are initiated, so it must be presumed that expectations can be formed on the basis that either a minimal level of trust is present and/or there is a willingness to bear the associated risk. Sustaining the trust-building loop then requires the participants to work together, gradually becoming more ambitious, over time, in their joint endeavors. Unfortunately, while all organizations are dynamic in nature, collaborations are particularly so because they are sensitive to transformation in each of the partner organizations and therefore may change very quickly. Effort put into building mutual understanding and developing trust can be shattered, for example, by a change in the structure of a key organization or the job-change of a key individual. Sustaining the trust-building loop therefore requires continuous attention to trust relationships.

(d) Managing power imbalances

Even when careful and continuous attention is paid to trust-building, the inherent fragility of the loop is evident. Alongside the issues relating to the dynamic nature of collaboration, power issues in particular seem to challenge efforts aimed at sustaining the loop. Imbalance in power, and the inevitability that some partners will be more central to the enactment of the collaborative agenda than others, tends to dictate behaviors that get in the way of trust-building. An appreciation of the inevitability of power imbalances as well as the ability to interpret any actions that members take in response to them may help prevent loss of trust. Furthermore, an understanding of the way in which balances of power tend to change during the life of a collaboration, and indeed whether and how power imbalances can and should be deliberately shifted, seems essential in sustaining the trust gained.

(e) Nurturing the collaborative relationships

Issues pertaining to the identification of partners, complexity and multiplicity of aims, risk and vulnerability, complexity and dynamics of collaborative structures and power imbalances clearly all pose serious management challenges for building and sustaining trust. If not managed effectively, any one of these issues can prevent trust from developing or even cause loss of trust. Ideally, therefore, all these issues need to be managed simultaneously and, owing to the dynamic nature of collaboration, in a continuous manner. Failing to do so may cause the trust loop to fracture.

This framework has sought to illustrate in broad terms the contrast between two different approaches to the management of trust: small wins versus comprehensive management. Both approaches have their merits. The illustration of each intends to provide insight to inform the managerial judgment about the kind of trust-building activities that are appropriate to collaborative situations.

Managing culture

Cultural diversity is a source of advantage and inertia.

We argued above that the bringing together of difference in terms of partners' resources, experiences and expertise provides the potential for collaborative advantage. A significant part of this difference can be attributed to cultural diversity. In that sense, perceptions of difference are typically rooted in the national, organizational and professional cultures with which the various partners identify. A paradox arises because cultural diversity is seen both as a source of stimulation and reward, and as a source of potential conflicts of values, behaviors and beliefs (Bird and Osland 2006; Cray and Mallory 1998). The gist of the argument is that partners' culturally embedded differences interact to cause tensions. These tensions can be conceptualized as pertaining to three areas in particular: encountering otherness, interaction order and harnessing difference (see Vangen and Winchester 2007 for a fuller elaboration on culture in collaboration).

(i) Encountering otherness

Encountering otherness involves the integration of different ways of being, interacting and working that are akin to specific cultures and which affect individuals' orientation toward others in the collaboration. Expectations of others' behaviors tend to be based on perception of similarity – or even stereotyping – of individuals within a culture. These expectations, research suggests, tend to lead to misaligned expectations and perceptions of superiority potentially affecting every strategic and operational aspect of a collaboration (see e.g. Bird and Osland 2006; Walsh 2004).

Encountering otherness, therefore, gives rise to a particular managerial tension. On the one hand, it is necessary to build cultural awareness to tackle misaligned expectations and perceptions of superiority and, on the other hand, it is essential to avoid the pitfalls of stereotyping. The tension arises because the act of building cultural awareness necessarily implies a need to conceptualize and generalize; thus, the danger of stereotyping is inherent in the learning. In any event, as each collaborative situation is unique in its configuration of cultural communities of belonging, the generic learning cannot capture the specific confluence of cultural diversity within each specific setting. Hence the requisite understanding is not necessarily transferable from one situation to another.

Working effectively with otherness involves knowing how to manage the idiosyncratic nature of each individual situation. Yet individuals will enter new situations with embedded "ways of being" which may not feasibly be revisited with every new or significantly changed collaborative situation.

(ii) Interaction order

Whilst encountering otherness is concerned with individuals' embedded perceptions and expectation of their partners, other cultural differences are manifested in the working practices and interaction between partners. We use the term "interaction order" to refer broadly to partners' working practices.

The most important aspect is communication. Most obviously, the confluence of different natural and professional languages and organization-specific jargon increases the tendency for misinterpretations and misunderstandings. Furthermore, culturally determined etiquette generates issues concerned with initiating, managing the content and managing the style of communication. In terms of initiation, partners frequently have different views about whether formal titles should be used or not, what formal level or organizational position individuals need to hold to represent their organization in communication with their partners, and so on. Similarly, the content of communication can be influenced by differences in the formality of a culture in terms of, for example, whether specific guidelines are required or not. Lastly, styles of communicating vary across cultures, so that some partners, for example, prefer to be succinct and to-the-point whereas others like to engage in lengthy negotiations.

The need to establish an interaction order thus points to a particular management tension; cultural sensitivity is necessary to interact across different communities yet a generic form of communication is necessary to enact the joint agenda. The tension arises because different cultures encompass different natural and professional languages and culturally determined etiquettes, which impact on both the process and the content of communication. Paying attention to these differences may be essential in securing effective communication. At the same time, any generic form of communication, necessary to enact the joint agenda, may not accommodate all the cultural diversity present in any specific collaboration.

(iii) Harnessing difference

Harnessing individuals' embedded perceptions, behavioral characteristics and professional expertise alongside differences in organizations' systems and procedures is essential if the advantage is to be gained. This points to a further three inter-related managerial tensions:

(A) FLEXIBILITY VERSUS ESTABLISHED ORGANIZATIONAL PROCEDURES

Flexibility – at the individual and organizational level – is necessary to accommodate the encounterment of otherness and differences in interaction order. Organizations' structures and procedures, for example, reflect the nature of their individual remits, and their ability to collaborate is associated with their ability to adapt to the needs of the joint agenda. Yet organizations' contribution to the collaboration is typically rooted in their unique resources and expertise, so that any alteration – to structures and procedures – is done at the risk of upsetting those that work. Thus, whilst flexibility is necessary to enact the collaborative agenda, this is most likely in tension with retaining those established procedures that enable organizations to make a contribution in the first place.

(B) AUTONOMY VERSUS ACCOUNTABILITY

In many situations, then, harnessing difference entails working within systems that are ill-fit for the purpose. Individual managers typically lack discretion, power and authority to act on behalf of their organization. This can make it difficult for them to employ appropriately their understanding of their partner's culturally embedded perceptions, behavioral characteristics and professional expertise. This tension between autonomy and accountability can play out in several ways. To harness differences effectively, individuals undoubtedly need enough autonomy to act on behalf of their organizations; yet at the same time they need to protect their organizations' interest. Managers may thus end up compromising either their need to accommodate cultural difference at the level of the collaboration or their accountability for their actions back to their organizations.

(C) RETAINING CONTROL VERSUS GRAPPLING WITH COMPLEXITY

Working within ill-fitting structures and procedures with insufficient amounts of autonomy will not render the accommodation of cultural differences simple. The greater the diversity of partners involved, the greater the complexity that needs to be managed. Two common responses to handling complexity are to seek partners where there is a greater degree of similarity or to control, via communication, the activities of the collaboration as a whole. There is a real opportunity cost associated with simplifying cultural diversity in this way. The potential strength, and hence the real potential for collaborative advantage, rests on the collaboration's ability to tap into the expertise and experiences of all involved. Limiting the number of individuals involved in communication, for example, implies that the potential for collaborative advantage is limited to the strength of communication between those individuals. There is thus a real tension in dealing with the complexities stemming from the number of stakeholders that are involved: whilst retaining control is a necessary element of steering the joint agenda forward, grappling with complexity is necessary if the collaboration is to harness the expertise of those who hold the potential to creating advantage.

The tensions that we have conceptualized seek to illustrate that cultural differences – whether rooted in nations, organizations or professions – can impact on all aspects of collaboration. Successfully managing cultural diversity involves paying careful attention to the plurality of issues arising from cultural interaction. The managerial tensions outlined in this section, as summarized in Figure 10.4, define key areas where attention is required.

Managing knowledge transfer

Attitudes to knowledge-sharing vary.

While there may be many reasons for collaborating, "interorganizational learning" is a key aspect of all (Hartley and Allison 2002). For example, in the case of a collaboration over care of the elderly between a health agency and a social services department, social services staff might learn how to carry out some of the care tasks previously carried out by health staff, and health staff might learn how to advise patients about possible state benefits

MANAGERIAL TENSIONS		
Encountering otherness		
i) **Misaligned Expectations**	⟺ *Versus*	**Sophisticated Stereotyping**
Learning aimed at building cultural awareness is necessary to tackle misaligned expectations and perceptions of superiority.		Generic learning cannot capture the specific confluence of cultural diversity within a specific setting. The act of building cultural awareness necessarily implies a need to conceptualize and generalize, inherently incorporating the pitfalls of sophisticated stereotyping.
Interaction order		
ii) **Cultural Sensitivity**	⟺ *Versus*	**Generic Communication**
Cultural sensitivity is necessary to effectively interact across different communities.		Any specific form of communication, necessary to enact the joint agenda, may not accommodate all the cultural diversity present in any specific collaboration.
Harnessing difference		
iii) **Flexibility**	⟺ *Versus*	**Established Organizational Procedures**
Flexibility in structures and processes is necessary to accommodate the encounterment of otherness and differences in interaction order.		Established structures and procedures may be what enable organizations to make a contribution to the joint agenda in the first place.
iv) **Autonomy**	⟺ *Versus*	**Accountability**
Individuals need autonomy to act on behalf of their organizations to take the agenda forward.		Accountability is necessary to protect organizations' interests and their inherent contribution to the collaboration.
v) **Retaining Control**	⟺ *Versus*	**Grappling with Complexity**
Retaining control is a necessary element of steering the joint agenda forward.		Grappling with complexity is necessary if the collaboration is to harness the expertise of those who hold the potential to creating advantage.

Figure 10.4 Tensions in the management of culture.

for which they might be eligible. "Substantive learning" (Huxham and Hibbert 2008) of this type generally relates to *knowledge transfer* where knowledge embedded in one organization eventually also becomes embedded in a partner organization. Knowledge transfer may be an explicit reason (or part of the reason) for setting up a collaboration. For example, an aim of a community substance-abuse partnership might be that police and health workers learn to understand each other's perspective and expertise on the issue. More often than not, however, knowledge transfer happens alongside pursuit of the explicit reason for collaborating. Substantive learning may also, however, relate to *knowledge creation* in which the partners jointly work together to create something that neither previously had. Collaborative knowledge creation is an important concept in the context of innovation management.

Conventional accounts of interorganizational learning tend to construct it in one of three ways. Sometimes partners are construed as having a *selfish* attitude, acquiring knowledge from a partner exclusively for their own use in an exploitative manner (Ingram 2002). Sometimes they are seen as having a *sharing* attitude, which leads them either to exchange knowledge with partners or to go further and explore innovative solutions to problems at hand collaboratively (Inkpen and Tsang 2005). Quite often, however, no consideration is given to substantive learning at all, in which case the attitude to it is essentially one of *sidelining*, although learning is very likely to happen alongside whatever other activities the collaboration holds (Spekman, Isabella and MacAvoy 2000). These stereotypical attitudes can be characterized as follows:

Selfish: we take from you without giving to you;

Sharing – exchanging: we take from you and we give to you; you take from us and give to us;

Sharing – exploring: we take from you and we give to you; you take from us and give to us – and we learn together to create knowledge;

Sidelining: learning from or with partners is not something we think about.

The first three are characteristically *active* stances in which the partners are deliberate about the attitude they take, but sidelining is inherently *passive* in nature.

These conventional, stereotypical views of learning do indicate something about the nature of learning in collaboration. It certainly does include selfish, sharing and sidelining elements. However, in reality it is more complex than that. To understand more about the attitudes to learning that participants actually bring to collaborations, it is helpful to break them down into stances toward the giving and taking of knowledge from a partner. In each case, there are many possibilities. We shall look at them in turn.

(i) Stances to giving knowledge

Here are two examples of *giving* stances:

Protective: we don't trust you, therefore we don't give to you;
Unconfident: we don't trust our knowledge, so we shall not give it to you.

In both cases, members of the organization seek to avoid giving away knowledge and may therefore be viewed by partners as selfish. But in neither case is the motivation selfish. In the first case, the protectiveness is born out of fear that partners will appropriate the knowledge to the detriment of the organization – for example, by encroaching on their territory. It is a *reactive* stance. In the second case, the *active* refusal to give knowledge comes from a lack of faith in the validity of the knowledge – some statistical data, for example.

However, stances to giving do not always embody an unwillingness to pass knowledge to partners. Sometimes participants give willingly and may therefore appear to the receiver to have a sharing attitude. This may, however, mask underlying motives that are less than altruistic. For example:

Force feeding: when we need you to have understanding, we give to you;
Parenting: when we deem it to be good for you, we give to you.

The attitude behind the first might be considered as *pro-actively* selfish. The receiving partner is being manipulated for the benefit of the giving one. The second may be seen as an *active*, positively helpful attitude toward supporting and developing a partner; but it is nevertheless instrumental and controlling, so there is an element of selfishness about it.

(ii) Stances to taking knowledge

Attitudes to taking knowledge are equally divergent. Here are two examples:

Careless: we didn't intend to take from you but since we now have the knowledge we shall use it (without considering the consequences for you);
Discretionary: we take from you only if we choose to.

The first case might occur, for example, when potential partners share ideas in order to see whether they might form a joint bid to a funding agency. If they decide to make the bid independently, one may use ideas generated by another. In this type of situation, participants in the taking organization are acting reactively to an opportunity that unexpectedly presents itself. There was no original intent to act selfishly, but that is what happens *reactively* and often unwittingly. The original motivation is not selfish, but the consequences of carelessness for the idea-giving organization may be severe. The second case represents the situation when participants take an *active* stance against taking knowledge from a partner for purely selfish reasons linked to an assessment of the value of the knowledge to their organization. This kind of stance gives no consideration to whether their having the proffered knowledge would help the partner.

(iii) Stances in combination

These example stances are a few of the many that occur in collaborative situations; many more examples are provided in Figures 10.5 and 10.6. Each partner's attitude to learning with or from their partners is made up of attitudes to giving and taking (which are sometimes sidelined in the sense that they are enacted unconsciously). These can vary depending on the type of knowledge that is being transferred or created and will vary over time as the relationship changes and develops. Obviously attitudes to knowledge transfer are linked to the aims that partners bring to the collaboration, and their interpretation of each other's attitudes will have an important bearing on their ability to develop trusting relationships. The important point for managing collaboration is that participants' behavior may appear selfish but not derive from selfish motivations; and, equally, many appear sharing but are actually derived from selfish motivations. Taking a stereotypical view of attitudes in the way described at the start of this section can thus lead to misinterpreting partners' behavior. Misunderstandings of partners' cultural norms may add significantly to the potential for this. Gaining the skill to "read a partner correctly" is therefore an important part of managing collaboration.

Conclusion: understanding collaborative success

The above four example themes indicate some of the challenges inherent in achieving collaborative advantage. They each present a slice of the overall picture – a perspective on the challenges of collaboration – and, as we have indicated, they interact, with each affecting the others. The theory of collaborative advantage is constructed around many more of these themes. We do not have space to describe them all here, but we can summarize the most important of them. In terms of power, for example, the issue is that power-sharing is important yet there are often both real and perceived power imbalances between partners that tend to have a negative impact on behaviors. Membership structures are frequently ambiguous, complex and dynamic, which render issues to do with agreement on aims, building trust, managing power relationships and cultural diversity infinitely hard. Leadership is likely to be beyond the scope of any one individual to tackle,

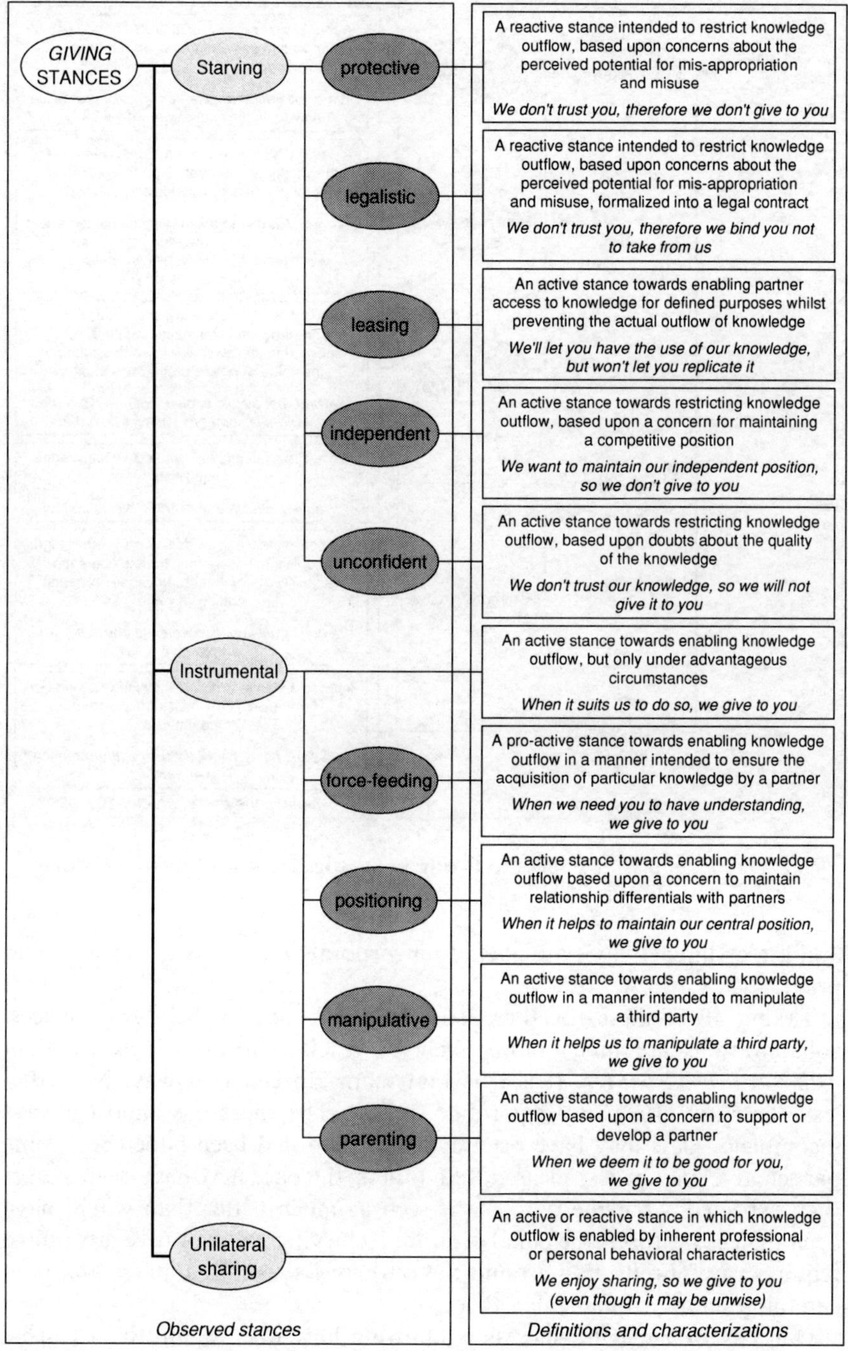

Figure 10.5 Examples of stances to giving knowledge (reproduced from Huxham and Hibbert 2008).

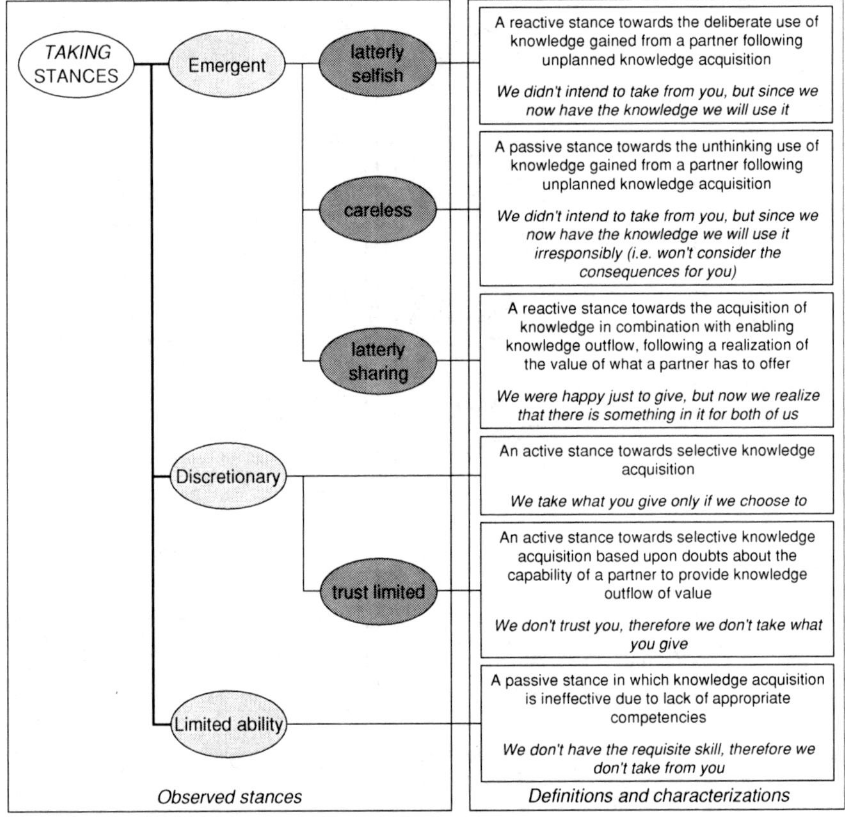

Figure 10.6 Examples of stances to taking knowledge (reproduced from Huxham and Hibbert 2008).

and leadership activities are likely to incorporate dilemmas of ideology and pragmatism.

Taking all of these together, it is clear that, left to their own devices, collaborations are much more likely to reach *collaborative inertia* than *collaborative advantage*. It is true that many do end that way. Nevertheless, there are also many reports of success. The success is almost always incomplete – less may have been achieved than had been hoped for, some participants may be less pleased than others, the pace may have been slower than expected – but the outcome is seen as much better than would have been the case without the collaboration. Achieving collaborative advantage requires careful reflection around the types of issues raised above and then careful attention to managing them.

One key to achieving success is knowing how to recognize it; it can be much broader than the achievement of any substantive targets set out at the start. Five perspectives on success are important (Huxham and Hibbert 2007). The first does indeed relate to *substantive outcomes* of the collaboration, but these can be highly varied in type. They may relate to financial or resource gains – for example, better use of public funds – improvements in service provision or much smaller "products" such as raised awareness, training or learning. They may be beneficial for the organizations, for the individuals involved in a collaborative initiative or for the clients or citizens at whom they are targeted. They may be short- or long-term outcomes. And they are almost always relative gains; relative to what might have happened without the collaboration or to how well other organizations in similar situations are doing, for example.

The second perspective on success relates to the *process of collaborating*. Sometimes a successful process is just seen as a means to a substantive end. However, good processes can also be in themselves viewed as a measure of success. Like successful substantive outcomes, processes that have become good vary in type considerably. In some cases, the mere act of using respectful language to each other marks a successful process development. At the other end of the scale, a collaboration may be working well at an advanced level, being highly pro-active, making good decisions and taking joint action.

The third perspective overlaps to some degree with the first two. *Emergent milestones* are not targets planned from the start, but semi-serendipitous achievements that arise along the way. They are signals that the collaboration actually achieved something, however great or small. Also highly varied, they are located on a continuum of tangibility. At the least tangible extreme, milestones relate to the resolution of process issues; for example, it might be the point at which partners start to take account of each other's interests. At the most tangible extreme, they relate to physical artifacts; for example, the co-location of partners into the same building. Between these two extremes, emergent milestones include the production of a joint report or the holding of a jointly organized event for a wider audience. Emergent milestones are important success-indicators partly because achieving major final targets can take a very long time, and partly because they often indicate something that turned out to be more significant than would have been expected in advance. They are often good trigger-points for helping the collaboration to move on to greater things.

The fourth perspective is concerned with *recognition*. Recognition of a collaboration by those not involved – for example, by articles in the press or receipt of an award – is clearly a good – independent and verifiable – indicator of substantive success. However, recognition can also be valued in its own right. For example, recognition often comes in the shape of a request to help another collaboration to achieve similar process or substantive ends. Recognition of individuals in a collaboration, in whatever form, can be seen as evidence of the skills they bring to the collaborative team.

The final perspective on success relates to personal *pride*. Statements of success are often wrapped up in language that promotes a positive personal identity for the speaker; people who claim success sometimes go so far as to portray themselves as heroes. Being in a position to take pride in "a job well done" and identify with the collaboration is an important form of success. As with the other perspectives, success personified through pride can be expressed in a variety of ways. An individual might claim positive output from the collaboration as her own doing, or portray herself as pivotally pro-active or as having important personal qualities such as willpower or experience. The pride perspective signifies collaborative success through personal fulfillment. In that sense, it is different from the other perspectives because the main beneficiary is the speaker herself. However, pride-success can be argued to be more than just a personal indicator. Reaching the point where individuals are willing to acknowledge overtly – and even promote – their own role in a partnership is significant.

The five perspectives on success provide a basis for developing realistic, rather than idealistic, expectations of what success in collaboration might look like. They emphasize that what is achieved is not necessarily predictable. They are also useful for demonstrating success, to stakeholders – participants, constituents, customers, staff or policy-makers – even when a substantive outcome is not (yet) forthcoming. Most usefully, the five perspectives can be used as a framework to facilitate development of collaborative practice. They suggest signifiers that it is appropriate to watch out for and be positive about, even within a context where success is less than absolute.

Summary: using the theory of collaborative advantage

In this chapter we have introduced the theory of collaborative advantage through providing overviews of a selection of conceptualizations and frameworks pertaining to the management of aims, trust, cultural diversity and knowledge transfer. Our aim was to explain its ability to aid understanding about the management of collaboration in practice. The various conceptualizations and frameworks are intended for use as handles for reflective practice, which assumes real experience of collaboration.

The theory conveys that managing collaborations is a highly complex endeavor. It prescribes – through a focus on themes – the kinds of issues that need attention. However, it does not tell the user which of these themes to focus on, when to do so and how to use the information captured in them to guide them in their management actions. Knowing how to use the theory is in itself a matter for managerial judgment. Themes such as aims, trust and cultural diversity or attitudes to knowledge transfer provide sensible starting points for consideration of managerial action. However, it may be equally prudent first to seek to get a sense of what success might look like.

This can in turn help identify the themes that are likely to yield valuable insights. Similarly, in using these conceptualizations and frameworks as handles of reflective practice, the nature of success envisaged may influence decisions about alternative ways of managing.

Acknowledgments

We wish to thank our colleagues who allowed us to use our joint work in this chapter: Nik Winchester for his work with Siv on "culture", Paul Hibbert for his work with Chris on "learning" and "success", and Pam Hearne for her work with Chris on "success". Chris also wishes to thank the Advanced Institute for Management Research, grant number RES-331-25-0016.

References

Bird, A. and Osland, J. S. (2006) "Making Sense of Intercultural Collaboration", *International Studies of Management and Organisation*, 35 (4): 115–32.

Bryson, J. (1988) "Strategic Planning: Big Wins and Small Wins", *Public Money and Management*, 8 (3): 11–15.

Cray, D., Mallory, G. R. (1998) "Making Sense of Managing Culture", International Thomson Business Press.

Gambetta, D. (1988) "Can We Trust?", in D. Gambetta (ed.) *Trust: Making and Breaking Cooperative Relations*, Oxford/New York: Blackwell.

Gulati, R. (1995) "Does Familiarity Breed Trust? The Implications of Repeated Ties for Contractual Choice in Alliances", *Academy of Management Journal*, 38 (1): 85–112.

Hartley, J. and Allison, M. (2002) "Good, Better, Best? Inter-organizational Learning in a Network of Local Authorities", *Public Management Review*, 4: 101–18.

Hudson, B. (2004) "Analysing Network Partnerships", *Public Management Review*, 6 (1): 75–94.

Huxham, C. and Beech, N. (2003) "Contrary Prescriptions: Recognizing Good Practice Tensions in Management", *Organization Studies*, 24: 69–94.

Huxham, C. and Hibbert, P. (2007) "Hit or Myth?: Stories of Collaborative Success", Partnership Sourcing Ltd (ed.) *Partnering for Profit*, London: PSL.

Huxham, C. and Hibbert, P. (2008) "Manifested Attitudes: Intricacies of Interpartner Learning in Collaboration", *Journal of Management Studies*, 45: 502–9.

Huxham, C. and Vangen, S. (2005) *Managing to Collaborate: The Theory and Practice of Collaborative Advantage*, London: Routledge.

Ingram, P. (2002) "Interorganizational Learning", in J. Baum (ed.) *The Blackwell Companion to Organizations*, Oxford: Blackwell.

Inkpen, A. C. and Tsang, E. W. K. (2005) "Social Capital, Networks and Knowledge Transfer", *Academy of Management Review*, 30: 146–65.

Lane, C. and Bachmann, R. (1998) *Trust Within and Between Organizations: Conceptual Issues and Empirical Applications*, Oxford: Oxford University Press.

Oliver, C. (1990) "Determinants of Interorganizational Relationships: Integration and Future Directions", *Academy of Management Review*, 15 (2): 241–65.

Spekman, R. E., Isabella, L. A. and MacAvoy, T. C. (2000) *Alliance Competence: Maximizing the Value of Your Partnerships*, New York: John Wiley.

Vangen, S. and Winchester N. J. (2007) "An Exploration of Culture in Cross-national Collaborations", presented to the BAM annual conference, Warwick, 11–13 September. Available from authors.

Walsh, K. (2004) "Interpreting the Impact of Culture on Structure", *Journal of Applied Behavioral Science*, 40 (3): 302–22.

Further reading

Cropper, S., Ebers, M., Huxham, C. and Ring, S. P. (2008) *The Oxford Handbook of Inter-organizational Relations*, Oxford: Oxford University Press.

Huxham, C. and Vangen, S. (2005) *Managing to Collaborate: The Theory and Practice of Collaborative Advantage*, London: Routledge.

11

RELATIONSHIP MARKETING, RELATIONAL CAPITAL AND THE GOVERNANCE OF PUBLIC SERVICES DELIVERY[1]

Stephen P. Osborne, Kate McLaughlin and Celine Chew

Marketing in public services – an opportunity missed?

As government and voluntary and community organizations (VCOs) increasingly work in partnership to make public policy, and to design and deliver public services, new challenges are raised for the practice of marketing within public service organizations (PSOs)[2] and for assessing its fitness for purpose within the "new regulatory state" (Jayasuriya 2004). However, this task is complicated by the considerable ambiguity surrounding the role of marketing within PSOs. Indeed, the very existence of a "marketing function" within PSOs is contentious in its own right. Based on English experience, this chapter seeks to develop clear conceptual foundations to guide the placing and practice of this functional discipline within such organizations.

It argues that marketing activity has been embraced by PSOs, albeit with considerable reluctance, as an inevitable corollary to the NPM reform agenda of the past thirty years – with its dominant notions of consumerism and the "marketization" of public services, and rather than as a desirable management discipline in its own right (Walsh 1994; Burton 1999). In doing so, it has neglected the opportunities offered for its development by alternative conceptualizations of marketing that take institutions, networks and governance, rather than consumers, as the central unit of analysis.

We argue that public services marketing practice over this period has been dominated by transactional models of marketing (Laing 2003) that have belied the growing relational complexity of the above trends. Nowhere is there any evidence of a willingness to test the suitability and/or robustness of alternative models of marketing that might meet the needs of PSOs operating within the current plural public policy environment, with its emphasis on partnerships and relational contracting and governance (Erridge and Greer 2002; Schwartz 2005; Bovaird 2006).

This chapter is in three parts and seeks to address this gap by exploring the utility of precisely such an alternative model for practice (*relationship marketing*) by situating this within a broader model of relationship management that encompasses the associated concept of *relational capital*. It commences by arguing that the model that has underpinned the development of public services marketing to date is an inappropriate one. Second, it validates this argument by presenting three "micro-cameos" of the recent application of marketing activity to public services management. Third, it introduces the alternative model of relationship marketing and evaluates what such an alternative framework might contribute to the practice of marketing within PSOs.

Modeling PSO marketing behavior: the genesis of "public-sector marketing"

In the 1960s, marketing was predominantly presented as the key managerial discipline across *all* sectors of society. For example, Kotler and Levy (1969) argued that marketing was

> . . . a pervasive societal activity [and that all organizations] are concerned about their "products" in the eyes of certain "consumers" and are seeking to find tools for furthering their acceptance.
>
> (Kotler and Levy 1969: 10–12)

This position has subsequently been assumed by many marketing scholars and practitioners, and has become the starting point for drawing marketing into the public domain – such as through social change and public education programs (social marketing), and debates about the rationing of public services (demarketing) and about the acquisition of resources by PSOs through fundraising (Kotler and Zaltman 1971; Kotler and Andreason 1975; Laing and McKee 2000; Donaldson and O'Toole 2002).

However, this predominant perspective has increasingly been subject to an evolving ambiguity about the boundaries of marketing for PSOs. Having argued previously for marketing as a generic organizational function, key advocates have subsequently shifted their ground to introduce an element of *marketing conditionality* into the debate. In this perspective, five assumptions are held to constrain the universality of the marketing concept:

- there are at least two parties to the exchange;
- each party has something of value to offer to the other party;
- each party is capable of communication and delivery;
- each party is free to accept or reject the offer; and
- each party believes it is appropriate or desirable to deal with the other party (Kotler and Keller 2005).

These five conditions challenge the applicability of marketing to many public-service contexts. It is argued here that PSOs are not always free to accept or reject public-policy initiatives instigated by politicians, for example, nor can their clients/users always be free to accept or reject a particular public-service offering (social control and primary/secondary education services being the most obvious examples of this).

Crucially, these early ideas about the conditionality of marketing exchange are rooted in classical economics and a model of exchange theory that supports a purely *transactional* view of marketing, with the firm as a unitary entity operating in isolation from other organizations. This perspective on marketing is based upon a model of discrete transactions that have "a distinct beginning, short duration and sharp ending by performance" (Morgan and Hunt 1994: 1). However, it has been criticized latterly in the management literature through the concepts of the "new competition" (Best 1993) and "new institutionalism" (Powell and DiMaggio 1991). Drawing upon the work of Benson (1975) on resource-dependency theory and Williamson (1985) on transaction-cost analysis, these new conceptualizations posit a model of network-based organizations that paradoxically compete by collaborating with other organizations, in order to lever in information, resources and capabilities. Such a model introduces new levels of complexity to exchange relationships that are perhaps beyond the scope and competencies of traditional transactional models of marketing and which, it is argued here, are highly relevant to the practice of marketing for PSOs operating within the New Public Governance regime.

The marketing function and PSOs in England

This has a comparatively recent history. It was not until the 1980s, when the "marketization" of public services under the then Conservative government commenced in earnest, that attention was turned to the potential benefits of marketing for PSOs operating in market and quasi-market conditions (Le Grand 1993; Scrivens 1991; Sheaff 1991; Walsh 1991). This marketization was thus a core driver for the growth of the marketing function within British PSOs. As such it has had a profound influence upon its trajectory since then. Central to this influence was the classical economic principle of exchange discussed above, which assumes market relations to be based upon discrete and autonomous transactions and with little thought to the governance of reciprocal or ongoing transactions (Hindmoor 1998; Walsh 1991).

As a consequence of these assumptions, the marketing behavior of individual PSOs has invariably been highly individualistic in nature and self-seeking, arguably to the detriment of the whole public service system. Further, individual PSOs, and especially VCOs, have often been drawn into market scenarios for public services that have privileged competition and adversarial relationships over collaboration both *between* PSOs and *within* them (Palmer 2001).

Three "micro-cameo" examples will illustrate this argument. First, the creation of the internal market in healthcare in the 1990s created competition between newly created "Trust" hospitals (service providers) and the primary care referral agents, usually general practitioners (service purchasers). The response of many individual Trust hospitals to this was to look to the marketing function to develop their competitive position within these newly created markets (Kitchener and Whipp 1995). The archetypal "4Ps" model, where organizations sought to strengthen their competitive position by varying dimensions of the *product*, its *promotion*, *price* and *place of distribution* (Kearsey and Varey 1998; Sheaff 1991), informed marketing practice over this period. As a consequence, individualism, interhospital rivalry and competitive behavior flourished in many areas. Individual Trust hospitals succeeded by pursuing their own corporate objectives and financial security – but at the cost of scant attention being paid to overall healthcare policy or the holistic health needs of the local community (Fillingham 1994).

As a result of such behavior, marketing as a profession within PSOs became subject to damning critiques that it had led to goal displacement and strategic drift in healthcare (Sheaff 1991; Scrivens 1991; Walsh 1994). How could either local or central government steer health policy, it was argued, when individual healthcare actors were more preoccupied with their own survival than with the health outcomes of patients?

A second example can be found in the field of the personal social services. The NHS and Community Care Act 1991 required local-authority Social Services Departments to create a "mixed economy of care" for their services (Wistow et al. 1994). In their early attempts to create this new mixed economy, these departments saw VCOs as a natural choice as preferred providers – both because of the perception of them as sympathetic to the needs of vulnerable people (Brenton 1985) and because of their perceived (though unproven) institutional advantages, including cost efficiency, flexibility and consumer responsiveness (Knapp et al. 1990).

As a consequence, relationships between local government and VCOs were transformed. The previous "grant-funded" relationship between local government and the VCO sector was replaced by a performance-based "contract culture" and the development of, often fractured, principal–agent relationships. In 1996 the Deakin Commission (Commission on the Future of the Voluntary Sector 1996) emphasized that a serious breakdown in relations between the governmental and VCO sectors in England had resulted from this adversarial model and needed to be addressed by a shift into more explicitly relational approaches – leading to the development of the Voluntary Sector Compact and later to Compact Plus (Osborne and McLaughlin 2002; Osborne 2003). This represented an emergent policy framework for building relationships across organizations that emphasized inter- rather than intra-organizational management and governance.

As a result of this debate, some initial attempts were made to develop and test alternative models of the marketing function in PSOs (for example, Laing and McKee 2000; Laing and Hogg 2002; Wright and Taylor 2005). Notwithstanding these, though, the discrete transactional model of marketing has continued to dominate practice within PSOs.

Finally, clients of the social security system in England are mandatory "customers" of the Benefits Agency – no alternative provider exists. As such, the Agency has been encouraged by central government to promulgate a "customer focus" as its dominant paradigm of behavior. In addition, though, it is also required by government to implement competing policies that challenge the notion of "claimants as customers" (Pheysey 1993).

Specifically, the alternative concerns of central government – to tackle the perceived negative impact of the benefit system on the work incentive and to minimize fraudulent claims – have produced a competing discourse of claimant behavior, as "workshy" and "fraudulent claimant" respectively. In this instance, therefore, the preferred marketing model of the agency, which was attempting to design consumerist choice into the system, was challenged by this alternative policy trajectory. Consequently, the limited transactional model of the marketing function employed by the Agency was unable to cope with this level of policy complexity and paradox (Falconer and Ross 1999).

These micro-cameos throw up two important challenges for the future of the marketing function in PSOs. First, that its originating context of transactional and operational management has constrained the development of marketing within PSOs to a focus on *intraorganizational and operational debates*. This has crowded out consideration of more sophisticated models of it as a basis for exploring its possible role in shaping the *strategic behavior* of PSOs.

Second, that the place of marketing within PSOs has become a highly contested one. In VCOs, for example, the remit of the marketing function can often be limited to fundraising alone, rather than integrated into their strategic positioning activity (Chew 2003, 2006). Similarly, inside governmental organizations, marketing professionals have often had to "sail under another banner" in order to have an impact on strategic direction and positioning (Piercy and Cravens 1995; Laing and McKee 2000).

It is contended here that the conventional transactional notion of marketing, above, fails to accommodate such policy and system complexity, and offers an incomplete basis for guiding marketing behavior within PSOs. What is required, therefore, is new, policy-relevant models of marketing that can assist PSOs in developing strategic responses to the growing relational complexity of implementing public policy in the plural state. This returns us to the relational approaches to marketing and organizational management now evolving – but that to date have been little applied to PSOs.

Relationship marketing

Within the broader marketing literature it is increasingly acknowledged that relationship marketing (RM) represents an archetypal shift for marketing practitioners (Payne and Ballantyne 1993; Sheth and Parvatiyar 2000; Veloutsou et al. 2002). This shift acknowledges that sustainable competitive advantage increasingly requires collaborative activity rather than rivalrous competition, as discussed above, and that relationships are often the most valuable resource of a firm (Sharma and Patterson 1999; Helfert et al. 2002). This is the core of RM, which Harker (1999: 16) has defined as an organization engaging in

> . . . proactively creating, developing, and maintaining committed, interactive and profitable exchanges with selected customers over time.

Gronroos (1994, 1999), in seminal papers, has argued that a marketing strategy continuum exists. At one end of this continuum is transactional marketing, rooted in classical economics, and that deals with one transaction at a time. At the other end is RM, which focuses upon building relationships. The core of this relationship-building is *trust*. Drawing upon transactional economics, Selnes (1998: 308) notes that

> . . . the importance of trust comes about . . . because of the difficulty or impossibility of acquiring information about future events or defining a contract that covers such future events.

Other authors have defined trust as a "willingness to rely on an exchange partner in whom one has confidence" (Moorman et al. 1993) and have, crucially, specified its two core dimensions:

- trust in the *honesty* of a partner to fulfill obligations; and
- trust in the *benevolence* of a partner to be genuinely interested in your welfare, to be motivated to seek joint gains and not to seek opportunistic benefit.[3]

Trust is argued to be at the core of RM. It both facilitates the adaptation process that is often necessary to complete an exchange within an ongoing relationship (Brennan and Turnbull 1999) and provides the basis for mutual commitment that "reduces the uncertainties associated with opportunistic behaviour" in a volatile environment or market (Sheth et al. 2000). Given the present emphasis in public policy upon trust as a governance mechanism within the evolving plural state (Davis and Walker 1997; Osborne 2006), it is surprising therefore that RM has made only a marginal contribution to marketing practice and organizational governance for PSOs. This chapter now presents the case for a more significant contribution.

Building the contribution of RM to public-policy implementation and public-services delivery

Within the confines of this brief chapter, it is not possible to undertake a comprehensive exploration of the potential contributions of RM to public management and public governance. However, examples of three specific benefits will suffice for our purpose.

Performing in the plural and pluralist state

In the introduction to this volume, Osborne argued that the dawn of the twenty-first century has seen the evolution of the "new public governance" in public management, where the negotiation of both plural (involving multiple actors) and pluralist (involving multiple processes) public policy making and implementation is the dominant paradigm. Further, he has argued that traditional approaches to public policy implementation and public services delivery have failed to provide substantive guidance to public managers struggling to cope with this level of complexity – public administration invariably relegates the actual implementation of public policy to a "black box" that is subservient to the greater task of policy formulation whilst public management portrays the policy process as simply the context for the actual practice of public management. Both views are partial and flawed. RM offers PSOs and public service managers an opportunity to move beyond this simple bipolar opposition and to engage with the policy process in a way that enhances pro-active interorganizational management and governance.

Morgan and Hunt (1994) have argued that RM actually comprises three levels of marketing activity:

- the *micro*, organization–consumer, level (Berry 1983);
- the *macro*, organization–organization, level (Arndt 1983); and
- the *meso*, organization–society, level (Moorman et al. 1993).

This approach can offer PSOs a conceptual framework to move to a new plane of marketing sophistication. The micro-level concerns the exploration of co-production with the recipients of public services – both an essential element of good services management (Ravald and Groonroos 1996) and a core component of contemporary public policy in the UK and Europe (Brandsen and Pestoff 2006). The macro-level focuses attention upon both boundary-spanning and boundary-maintenance activities for PSOs – both essential for effective interorganizational collaboration (Kale et al. 2000; Tsai 2000). Finally the meso-level involves the engagement of PSOs in the policy formulation and implementation process as cognizant, purposive actors rather than as passive recipients (Ring and Van de Ven 1992; Gulati et al. 2000). By conceptualizing marketing activity across these three levels, PSOs can clarify its overall contribution to organizational performance. This is an essential first step in articulating a clear formulation of the place and role of the marketing function within PSOs and in replacing the current ambiguity and confusion.

Understanding and managing trust

Trust is at the heart of any interorganizational relationship and governance, including in public services provision (Osborne and Murray 2000; Huxham and Vangen 2000). Often, though, "trust" appears in the literature as a reductive self-defining concept. RM offers a different, dynamic perspective upon it, and one more suited to the challenges of PSOs within the plural state. The first of these challenges is the "principal–agent" problem (Vickers and Yarrow 1988). This concerns the asymmetry of information that exists in relationships between two or more parties to a task. At its extreme, the principal to a partnership must employ a range of instruments in order to monitor and control the behavior of their agent. Within a more relational context, however, both can use their trust in each other to monitor the outcomes of their relationship rather than relying upon costly and bureaucratic performance management systems, with all their implied transaction costs (Waterman and Meier 1998; Bachmann 2001). RM provides a clear basis upon which to build and maintain such trust – as well as warnings against its misuse and potential lack of transparency (Morgan and Hunt 1994; Palmer et al. 2000).

The second challenge is that of dealing with risk, and its associated costs, in service innovation – a notoriously difficult activity in the risk-aversive culture of PSOs (Erridge and Greer 2002; Osborne and Brown 2005). A relational approach based upon trust allows these risks and costs to be shared, minimizing the danger and sharing the benefits of a venture to each party to the relationship. It also allows opportunistic behavior to be minimized, and the dedicated skills and knowledge base of an organization to be protected (Lorenzoni and Lipparini 1999; Kale et al. 2000).

Thus, and third, trust is an *input* into relationship-building in the sense that it is one of the core resources of any relationship. No ongoing relationship will survive without it. It is an *output* in the sense that working successfully together in a relationship reinforces and develops further the trust between the parties involved – successful relationships breed deeper, and more successful, relationships (Ring and Van de Ven 1992; Gulati et al. 2000). Another key to successful performance in the plural state, therefore, is the effective governance of interorganizational relationships through mechanisms based upon trust. RM offers a framework for PSO practitioners to understand and mediate these trust-based relationships.

Table 11.1 illustrates the challenge of moving toward such "relational governance", when much of the marketing and managerial practice of the

Table 11.1 Commissioner–provider inter-relationships in public services provision (developed and adapted from the work of Ring and Van de Ven 1992: 490)

		Interaction between service commissioner and service provider	
		Low	*High*
Level of pre-existing trust between service commissioner and service provider	*Low*	Market governance: discrete (classical) transactions	Hierarchical governance
	High	Market governance: recurrent (neo-classical) transactions governance	*Relational governance*

recent decades has been based on a marketization model that has encouraged discrete transactions and low trust levels between commissioners and providers, as discussed above. Many current relationships are still bound by the classical and neo-classical governance of such individual transactions, whilst the policy trajectory, and the insights of RM, increasingly emphasizes relational governance. At the core of this challenge, therefore, is how to make the shift between these competing modes of governance. The concept of *relational capital*, from the associated field of organizational strategy, provides further assistance here for PSO managers.

Relational capital – the heart of relationship governance

Donaldson and O'Toole (2002) argue persuasively that RM cannot stand alone in the development and governance of productive interorganizational relationships. It has to go alongside other activity to optimize such relationships. One of the most significant concepts that the associated field of organizational strategy can thus offer to such holistic *relationship management* by PSOs is that of "relational capital" (RC).

Kale et al. (2000) define RC as

> . . . the level of mutual trust, respect and friendship that arises out of close interaction *at the individual level* between alliance partners.
>
> (p. 218; our emphasis)

The key insight for PSO managers in this literature is to focus upon the import of *individuals and individual relationships and their interaction with the organizational level of relationships*. Too often it seems that, in the public administration and management field, relationships are reified to the organizational level alone – the neo-corporatist assumptions of the Voluntary Sector

Compact in the UK are a good example of this (Osborne and McLaughlin 2002). The RC approach does recognize the import of organizational factors for effective interorganizational working. However, it also makes explicit that these organizational factors are dependent upon key relationships at the *individual level* (where organizational staff interact with the staff of other PSOs, policy-makers and service recipients) for this import.

The most recent research from the private-sector research has shown that 30–70 percent of all private-sector partnerships fail (Duysters et al. 1998; Park and Ungson 2001; Overby 2006) – and that RC is one of the strongest safeguards against such failure (Morgan and Hunt 1994; Gulati et al. 2000). Thus, partnerships built upon RC become key strategic resources of an organization and enable it to gain a competitive advantage over its rivals not embedded in such partnerships (Kale et al. 2000; Tsai 2000; Sarkar et al. 2001). The key to deriving this advantage lies in the ways in which the key individuals in organizations learn to manage the balance between trust and distrust and conflict between their respective organizations:

> A firm derives its competitive strength from its proprietary assets and will be protective about losing them to alliance partners. Partnerships are fraught with hidden agendas driven by the opportunistic desire to access and internalize the partner's core proprietary skills. . . . [Relational capital creates] a mutual confidence that no party to an exchange will exploit others' vulnerability even if there is an opportunity to do so. . . . [This confidence] arises out of the social controls that [relational] capital creates.
>
> (Kale et al. 2000: 222)

Finally, the private-sector literature also warns of the "dark side" of RC. Just as it can strengthen organizational performance, so it can undermine it, by tying in a firm to an unproductive or damaging relationship or by reducing its openness to new and potentially productive relationships (Parkhe and Miller 2000; De Weaver et al. 2005). As a consequence, it is essential to manage the creation, sustenance and impact of RC upon an organization (Sarkar et al. 2001; Sawhney and Zabin 2001).

Conclusions

This chapter has argued that the practice of marketing in PSOs over recent decades has been based within a classical model of marketing that has emphasized both transactional relationships and rivalrous competition. This has been contrasted both with the current public policy trajectory toward the governance of complex relationships and with best practice within the private sector that has emphasized the need for the governance of plural relationships in order to perform most effectively in contemporary interorganizational fields. It has argued that the concepts of relationship marketing and relational capital have significant insights to offer to marketing and organizational management within PSOs, precisely because they examine the practice and challenges of interorganizational management and governance in the plural state. It is not our case that "good marketing" is a substitute or proxy for "good management". It certainly is not. But it does have an important contribution to make to good *governance* and particularly to the extent that it can focus attention upon essential strategic decisions about interorganizational relationships within the plural state.

Two insights are especially important. First, RM and RC offer a framework within which to locate and articulate the position of the marketing function within PSOs and that emphasizes its strategic rather than its operational significance. This should help clarify the current confusion and obfuscation about the positioning of this function. Second, they also offer a framework for the practice of marketing in PSOs that emphasizes the challenges of the plural state and some guidelines as to intra- and interorganizational management and governance within it. This chapter is a contribution to commencing a debate about these contributions as part of the development and critique of the public governance paradigm.

However, an important concluding caveat must be entered here. Almost all of the theory and evidence underpinning both RM and RC have been developed from private-sector experience. The task now is to take these insights to develop a model of relationship management that is more firmly rooted in public administration and management, and that offers real insight to PSO managers about the contribution that RM and RC can make to public services management. It will also need to acknowledge the limitations both of these conceptual tools and of RM in the real world. No concept or tool is inherently positive. The limitations and dangers of RM and RC need to be explored as well as their positive contributions. Becoming too deeply embedded within a relationship or network can risk being drawn into an unproductive exchange or precluding the opportunity of developing new and alternative relationships, as discussed above.

The key task for PSO managers, and with which relationship marketing can help, is thus to be able to make strategic choices about the extent and nature of organizational relationships and their import for organizational performance. Central to this is the place of relational capital in making a reality of these relationships for staff and managers within PSOs, so that they can control and govern these relationships rather than be controlled by them. What the regime of public governance requires, it is suggested, is a new generation of *relational capitalists* who are adept not only in the core skills of their field or industry but also in facilitating, governing and sustaining the interorganizational relationships that are now at the heart of public services provision.

Notes

1 This chapter is a revised version of K. McLaughlin, S. Osborne and C. Chew (2009) 'Relationship marketing, relational capital and the future of marketing in public service organization,' in *Public Money and Management*, 29(1): 35–42.

2 *Public Services Organizations* are any organizations from across the governmental, VCO and business sectors that are involved in the provision of public services.

3 See also, *inter alia*, Morgan and Hunt 1994; Lorenzoni and Lipparini 1999; and Gulati et al. 2000.

References

Arndt, J. (1983) "The Political Economy Paradigm: Foundation for Theory Building in Marketing", *Journal of Marketing*, 47: 44–54.

Bachmann, R. (2001) "Trust, Power and Control in Trans-organizational Relations", *Organization Studies*, 22 (2): 337–65.

Benson, J. (1975) "The Interorganizational Network as a Political Economy", *Administrative Science Quarterly*, 20: 229–49.

Berry, L. (1983) "Relationship Marketing", in L. Berry, G. Shostack, and G. Upah (eds) *Emerging Perspectives on Service Marketing*, Chicago, Ill.: AMA.

Best, M. (1993) *The New Competition*, Cambridge, Mass.: Harvard University Press.

Bovaird, T. (2006) "Developing New Forms of Partnership with the 'Market' in the Procurement of Public Services", *Public Administration*, 84 (1): 81–102.

Brandsen, T. and Pestoff, V. (2006) "Co-production in the Third Sector and the Delivery of Public Services", *Public Management Review*, 8 (4): 493–502.

Brennan, R. and Turnbull, P. (1999) "Adaptive Behavior in Buyer–seller Relationships", *Industrial Marketing Management*, 28 (5): 481–95.

Brenton, M. (1985) *The Voluntary Sector in British Social Services*, Harlow: Longman.

Burton, S. (1999) "Marketing for Public Organizations: New Ways, New Methods", *Public Management*, 1 (3): 373–85.

Chew, C. (2003) "What Factors Influence Positioning Strategies in Voluntary Non-profit Organizations? Towards a Conceptual Framework", *Local Governance*, 29 (4): 288–323.

Chew, C. (2006) "Positioning and Its Strategic Relevance: Emerging Themes from the Experiences of British Charitable Organizations", *Public Management Review*, 8 (2): 333–50.

Commission on the Future of the Voluntary Sector (1996) *Meeting the Challenge of Change: Voluntary Action into the 21st Century*, London: Commission on the Future of the Voluntary Sector.

Davis, H. and Walker, B. (1997) "Trust-based Relationships in Local Government Contracting", *Public Money and Management*, 17 (4): 47–54.

De Weaver, S., Martens, R. and Vandenbempt, K. (2005) "The Impact of Trust on Strategic Resource Acquisition through Interorganizational Networks: Towards a Conceptual Model", *Human Relations*, 58 (12): 1523–43.

Donaldson, B. and O'Toole, T. (2002) *Strategic Market Relationships: From Strategy to Implementation*, Chichester: John Wiley.

Duysters, G., De Man, A. and Wildeman, L. (1998) "A Network Approach to Alliance Management", *European Management Journal*, 17: 182–7.

Erridge, A. and Greer, J. (2002) "Partnerships and Public Procurement: Building Social Capital through Supply Relations", *Public Administration*, 80 (3): 503–22.
Falconer, P. and Ross, K. (1999) "Citizen's Charters and Public Service Provision: Lessons from the UK Experience", *International Review of Administrative Sciences*, 65 (3).
Fillingham, D. (1994) "Health in the Marketplace", in H. Tam (ed.) *Marketing Competition and the Public Sector*, Bath: Longman.
Gronroos, C. (1994) "From Marketing Mix to Relationship Marketing: Towards a Paradigm Shift in Marketing", *Asia–Australia Marketing Journal*, 2 (1): 9–29.
Gronroos, C. (1999) "Relationship Marketing: Challenges for the Organisation", *Journal of Business Research*, 46 (3): 327–35.
Gulati, R., Nohria, N. and Zaheer, A. (2000) "Strategic Networks", *Strategic Management Journal*, 21 (3): 203–15.
Gutch, R., Kunz, C. and Spencer, K. (1990) *Partners or Agents*?, London: NCVO.
Harker, M. (1999) "Relationship *Marketing* Defined? An Examination of Current Relationship *Marketing* Definitions", *Marketing Intelligence Planning*, 17 (1): 13–20.
Helfert, G., Ritter, T. and Walter, A. (2002) "Redefining Market Orientation", *European Journal of Marketing*, 36 (9–10): 1119–39.
Hindmoor, A. (1998) "The Importance of Being Trusted: Transaction Cost Theory and Political Network Theory", *Public Administration*, 76 (1).
Huxham, C. and Vangen, S. (2000) "Leadership in the Shaping and Implementation of Collaboration Agendas", *Academy of Management Journal*, 4: 1159–77.
Jayasuriya, K. (2004) "The New Regulatory State and Relational Capital", *Policy and Politics*, 32 (4): 487–501.
Kale, P., Singh, H. and Perlmutter, H. (2000) "Learning and Protection of Proprietary Assets in Strategic Alliances", *Strategic Management Journal*, 21 (3): 217–37.
Kearsey, A. and Varey, R. (1998) "Managerialist Thinking on Marketing for Public Services", *Public Money and Management*, 18 (April–June).
Kitchener, M. and Whipp. R. (1995) "Quality in the Marketing Change Process", in M. Martinez and I. Kirkpatrick (eds) *The Politics of Quality*, London: Routledge.
Knapp, M. et al. (1990) "Public Money, Voluntary Action: Whose Welfare?", in H. Anheier and W. Seibel (eds) *The Third Sector*, Berlin: De Gruyter.
Kotler, P. and Andreason, A. (1975) *Strategic Marketing for Non-profit Organizations*, Englewood Cliffs, NJ: Prentice Hall.
Kotler, P. and Keller, K. (2005) *Marketing Management*, New York: Prentice Hall.
Kotler, P. and Levy, S. J. (1969) "Broadening the Concept of Marketing", *Journal of Marketing*, 33 (January): 10–15.
Kotler, P. and Zaltman, G. (1971) "Social Marketing: An Approach to Planned Social Change", *Journal of Marketing*, 35: 3–12.
Laing, A. (2003) "Marketing in the Public Sector: Toward a Typology of Public Services", *Marketing Theory*, 3 (4): 427–45.
Laing, A. and Hogg, G. (2002) "Political Exhortation, Patient Expectation and Professional Execution: Perspectives on the Consumerization of Health Care", *British Journal of Management*, 13 (2): 173–88.
Laing, A. and McKee, L. (2000) "Structuring the Marketing Function in Professional Service Organisations", *European Journal of Marketing*, 34 (5–6): 576–97.
Le Grand, J. (1993) *Quasi-markets and Social Policy*, London: Macmillan.

Lorenzoni, G. and Lipparini, A. (1999) "The Leverage of Interfirm Relationships as a Distinctive Organizational Capability: A Longitudinal Study", *Strategic Management Journal*, 20 (4): 317–38.

Moorman, C., Deshpande, R. and Zaltman, G. (1993) "Factors Affecting Trust in Market Research Relationships", *Journal of Marketing*, 57 (1): 81–101.

Morgan, R. and Hunt, S. (1994) "The Commitment–trust Theory of Relationship Marketing", *Journal of Marketing*, 58: 20–38.

Osborne, S. (2003) "A Dance to the Music of Time: Evolving Relationships between Government and the Voluntary and Community Sector over Time", *Local Governance*, 29 (4): 227–43.

Osborne, S. (2006) "The New Public Governance?", *Public Management Review*, 8 (3): 377–88.

Osborne, S. and Brown, K. (2005) *Managing Change and Innovation in Public Service Organizations*, London: Routlege.

Osborne, S. and McLaughlin, K. (2002) "Trends and Issues in the Implementation of Local 'Voluntary Sector Compacts' in England", *Public Money and Management*, 22: 55–64.

Osborne, S. and Murray, V. (2000) "Understanding the Process of Public–private Partnerships", in S. Osborne (ed.) *Public-Private Partnerships: Theory and Practice in International Perspective*, London: Routledge, pp. 70–83.

Overby, S. (2006) "Big Deals, Big Savings, Big Problems", *CIO Magazine*, 1 February.

Palmer, A. (2001) "Co-operation and Collusion: Making the Distinction in Marketing Relationships', *Journal of Marketing Management*, 17 (7–8): 761–84.

Palmer, A., Barrett, S. and Ponsonby, S. (2000) "A Behavioural Analysis of Co-operative Marketing Organisations", *Journal of Marketing Management*, 16: 273–90.

Park, S. and Ungson, G. (2001) "Interfirm Rivalry and Managerial Complexity: A Conceptual Framework of Alliance Failure", *Organization Science*, 12: 37–53.

Parkhe, A. and Miller, S. (2000) "The Structure of Optimal Trust: A Comment and Some Extensions", *Academy of Management Review*, 25 (1): 10–11.

Payne, M. and Ballantyne, D. (1993) *Relationship Marketing: Bringing Quality, Customer Service and Marketing Together*, Oxford: Butterworth-Heinemann.

Pheysey, D. (1993) *Organisational Cultures: Types and Transformations*, London: Routledge.

Piercy, N. and Cravens, D. (1995) "The Network Paradigm and the Marketing Organization: Developing a New Management Agenda", *European Journal of Marketing*, 29 (3): 7–34.

Powell, W. and DiMaggio, P. (1991) *The New Institutionalism in Organizational Analysis*, Chicago, Ill.: University of Chicago Press.

Ravald, A. and Groonroos, C. (1996) "The Value Concept and Relationship Marketing", *European Journal of Marketing*, 30 (2): 19–31.

Ring, P. and Van de Ven, A. (1992) "Structuring Cooperative Relationships between Organizations", *Strategic Management Journal*, 13 (7): 483–98.

Sarkar, M., Echambadi, R., Tamer Cavusgil, S. and Aulakh, P. (2001) "The Influence of Complementarity, Compatibility and Relationship Capital on Alliance Performance", *Journal of the Academy of Marketing Science*, 29 (4): 358–73.

Sawhney, M. and Zabin, J. (2001) *Seven Steps to Nirvana: Strategic Insight into Ebusiness Transformation*, New York: McGraw-Hill.

Schwartz, R. (2005) "The Contracting Quandary: Managing Local Authority–VNPO Relations", *Local Government Studies*, 31 (1): 69–83.
Scrivens, E. (1991) "Is There a Role for Marketing in the Public Sector?", *Public Money and Management*, Summer: 17–23.
Selnes, F. (1998) "Antecedents and Consequences of Trust and Satisfaction in Buyer–seller Relationships", *European Journal of Marketing*, 32 (3–4): 305–22.
Sheaff, R. (1991) *Marketing for Health Services: A Framework for Communications, Evaluation and Total Quality Management*, Oxford: PsychoBabel.
Sharma, N. and Patterson, P. (1999) "The Impact of Communication Effectiveness and Service Quality on Relationship Commitment in Consumer, Professional Services", *Journal of Services Marketing*, 13 (2): 150–70.
Sheth, J. and Parvatiyar, A. (2000) *Handbook of Relationship Marketing*, Thousand Oaks, Calif.: Sage.
Sheth, J., Sisodia, R. and Sharma, A. (2000) "The Antecedents and Consequences of Customer-centric Marketing", *Journal of the Academy of Marketing Science*, 28 (1): 55–66.
Tsai, W. (2000) "Social Capital, Strategic Relatedness and the Formation of Intraorganizational Linkages", *Strategic Management Journal*, 21 (9): 925–39.
Veloutsou, C., Saren, M. and Tzokas, N. (2002) "Relationship Marketing: What if . . . ?", *European Journal of Marketing*, 36 (4): 433–49.
Vickers, J. and Yarrow, G. (1988) *Privatization: An Economic Analysis*, Cambridge, Mass.: MIT Press.
Walsh, K. (1991) "Citizens and Consumers: Marketing and Public Sector Management", *Public Money and Management*, June–August: 9–16.
Walsh, K. (1994) "Marketing and Public Sector Management", *European Journal of Marketing*, 28 (3): 63–71.
Waterman, R. and Meier, K. (1998) "Principal–agent Models: An Expansion?", *Journal of Public Administration Research and Theory*, 8 (2): 173–202.
Williamson, O. (1985) *The Economic Institutions of Capitalism: Firms, Markets, Relational Contracting*, New York: Free Press.
Wistow, G., Knapp, M., Hardy, B. and Allen, C. (1994) *Social Care in a Mixed Economy*, Buckingham: Open University Press.
Wright, G. and Taylor, A. (2005) "Strategic Marketing in Health Care", *Public Management Review*, 7 (2): 203–24.

12

LEADING ACROSS FRONTIERS: HOW VISIONARY LEADERS INTEGRATE PEOPLE, PROCESSES, STRUCTURES AND RESOURCES

Barbara C. Crosby, John M. Bryson and Melissa M. Stone

Within collaborations aimed at solving complex public problems, leadership is clearly important in achieving successful outcomes (Bryson, Crosby and Stone 2006; Ansell and Gash 2008). We are especially interested in better understanding how leaders work across sectoral, organizational and cultural boundaries to bring diverse groups of people together to work out sustainable remedies for such problems. We see the leadership practice of these leaders as integrative – that is, they help organizations integrate people, processes, structures and resources in semi-permanent ways. Integration is similar to collaboration, but we think the former term captures more directly the need for leaders and constituents to move back and forth across boundaries and build linking pathways and other commonalities.

This chapter explores the visionary practices of integrative leaders in a collaborative transportation initiative in the Minneapolis-St Paul region of the United States (Bryson, Crosby and Stone 2008). The focus is on visionary leadership practices because they are vital to helping diverse stakeholders develop a shared understanding of a public problem and potential solutions, as well as commit to work for new policy regimes (Crosby and Bryson 2005a). The chapter weaves together three theoretical strands – leadership, collaboration and cross-boundary work – to supply the basic fabric of our analysis. To begin, we explain our research design – including the theoretical strands, definitions and methods. The following section describes the Urban Partnership program developed in recent years by the US Department of Transportation (USDOT), and details the successful effort of a group of Minnesota transportation officials, local governments and policy advocates to secure one of the major grants (Urban Partnership Agreements or UPAs) awarded through the program. We then offer findings about how visionary leaders helped diverse stakeholders develop shared understandings and commitments that allowed the group successfully to compete for and implement an Urban Partnership project. Finally, we present lessons and conclusions.

Research design: theory and methodology

In order to understand how leaders exercised visionary leadership in this case, we draw theoretical strands from several bodies of work: Crosby and Bryson's work on how leaders inspire and mobilize diverse constituents to tackle complex public problems in shared-power environments where no one is wholly in charge (Crosby and Bryson 2005a, 2005b); Huxham and Vangen (2005) and their colleagues' studies of collaboration; and our own review of the literature on cross-sector collaboration (Bryson, Crosby and Stone 2006). We also consider the role of boundary objects, boundary experiences and boundary groups (Carlile 2002, 2004; Feldman et al. 2006; Kellogg, Orlikowski and Yates 2006; and Bryson, Crosby and Bryson 2009), and the role of technology (Orlikowski 2000) in facilitating the creation and maintenance of multi-stakeholder, multi-sector collaborations. (The attention to technology emerged from our study of the Urban Partnership case, because computer-assisted "intelligent transportation systems" were a key component.)

Our initial research on this case was aimed at testing and refining our cross-sector collaboration framework (Bryson, Crosby and Stone 2006) and understanding more concretely the factors that affect the success of cross-sector collaborations. The results of that research are reported in "Collaboration in Fighting Traffic Congestion: A Study of Minnesota's Urban Partnership Agreement" (Bryson, Crosby and Stone 2008). We explain our case-development methods after an in-depth consideration of our theoretical fabric.

Theoretical strands

Crosby and Bryson's *Leadership for the Common Good* framework is the organizing strand for this study. Strands focusing on cross-sector collaboration and cross-boundary work are woven in as we seek to illumine leadership aspects of this particular case of collaborative public problem-solving.

Leadership for the common good

Crosby and Bryson (2005) emphasize the importance of, and interconnections between, *visionary*, *political* and *ethical* leadership practices for helping diverse stakeholders make sense of a public problem, commit to doing something about it, obtain needed policy and implementation decisions, and enforce new shared-power arrangements. These practices are linked

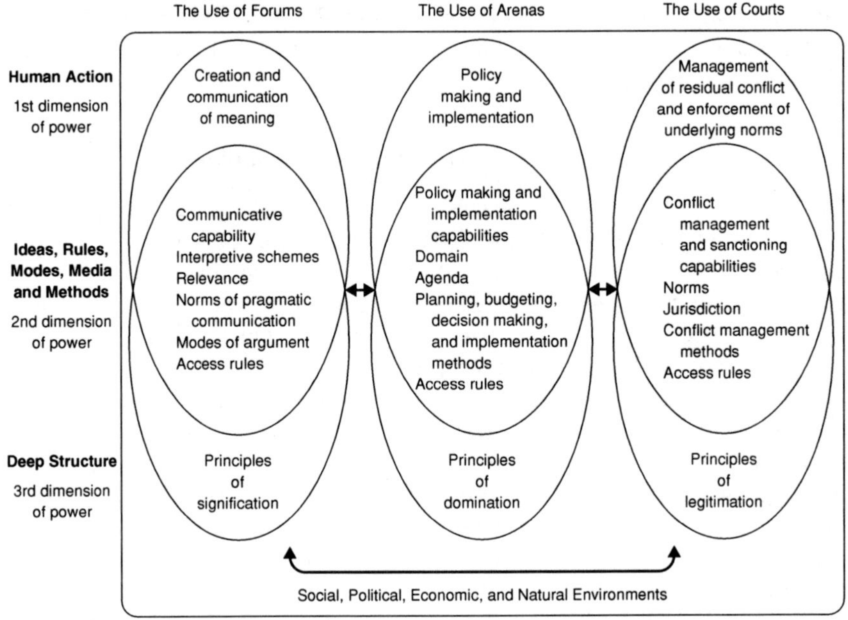

Figure 12.1 The triple three-dimensional view of power. From Crosby, B. and Bryson, J. (2005) Leadership for the Common Good, San Francisco: Jossey-Bass, p. 409

together in a multi-dimensional view of power (Figure 12.1) that highlights the creation and communication of meaning in formal and informal forums (the main practice of visionary leadership), policy-making and implementation in formal and informal arenas (the main practice of political leadership), and conflict resolution and normative regulation in formal and informal courts (the main practice of ethical leadership). Each of the practices has three dimensions: (1) observable action; (2) the rules, modes, media, methods that underpin action; and (3) the taken-for-granted, deep social structures of language and meaning (Crosby and Bryson 2005a; Giddens 1979, 1984).

We argue that, in order to operate effectively in environments in which the power to resolve a public problem is dispersed among many individuals, groups and organizations, leaders should direct their attention and energies to the middle dimension – that is, the rules, media and modes that draw on the deep structures in the third dimension and shape observable action in the first dimension. An especially important element of the middle dimension is the design of formal and informal forums, arenas and courts, the social settings in which observable action occurs. We argue that, in pursuing the common good, visionary leaders emphasize the design and use of forums, political leaders emphasize the design and use of arenas, and ethical leaders emphasize the design and use of courts.

Thus, visionary leaders who wish to develop common understanding or meaning around traffic congestion would focus on the rules, media and modes that shape communication in formal and informal forums. Perhaps they decide to hold a workshop highlighting different perspectives on traffic congestion. They will establish rules to ensure that some people are speaking during the debate and others are not. They will structure the workshop agenda and perhaps require that ideas be presented in a certain format. They will develop an invitation list and strategies for ensuring that certain people are or are not in the audience. They will use methods that winnow and synthesize disparate ideas.

Cross-sector collaboration

In addition to arguing for the necessity of visionary, political and ethical leadership for remedying complex public problems, we argue that remedying complex public problems is likely to involve cross-sector collaboration of some sort (Bryson, Crosby and Stone 2006), and thus leaders will need an understanding of what fosters successful cross-sector collaboration. Such collaborations are unlikely to get off the ground unless potential partners have some agreement on a need or opportunity that requires collaboration (Mattessich, Murray-Close and Monsey 2001). Collaborations are unlikely to get very far after that unless partners develop enough trust to continue working together, find ways to deal with power imbalances, cope with shifting membership, develop supportive processes and structures, and have a system of evaluating outcomes and fostering accountability (Winer and Ray 1994; Huxham and Vangen 2005; Bryson, Crosby and Stone 2006).

Our analysis of the literature on cross-sector collaborations indicated that initial conditions, process and structure, contingencies (such as power) and accountability mechanisms all have important effects on the formation, operation and outcomes of these initiatives (Bryson, Crosby and Stone 2006) (see Figure 12.2). Initial conditions that seemed to contribute to the formation of collaborations included turbulence in the environment, history of sector failure, supportive politics, pre-existing formal and informal networks, and general agreement on a problem or opportunity that would be the focus of the collaboration. Crucial process components seemed to be methods of building and exercising leadership, creation of various initial agreements among collaborating partners, development of the collaboration's legitimacy, creation and maintenance of trust, effective conflict management, and planning. Crucial structural components were governance arrangements, membership criteria and characteristics, and blend of hierarchy and network. Important contingencies included power imbalances and competing institutional logics. We concluded that a measure of cross-sector collaborations' success is the extent to which they produce "public value", a term coined by Mark Moore (1995) and which we define as fulfilling public purposes, mandates,

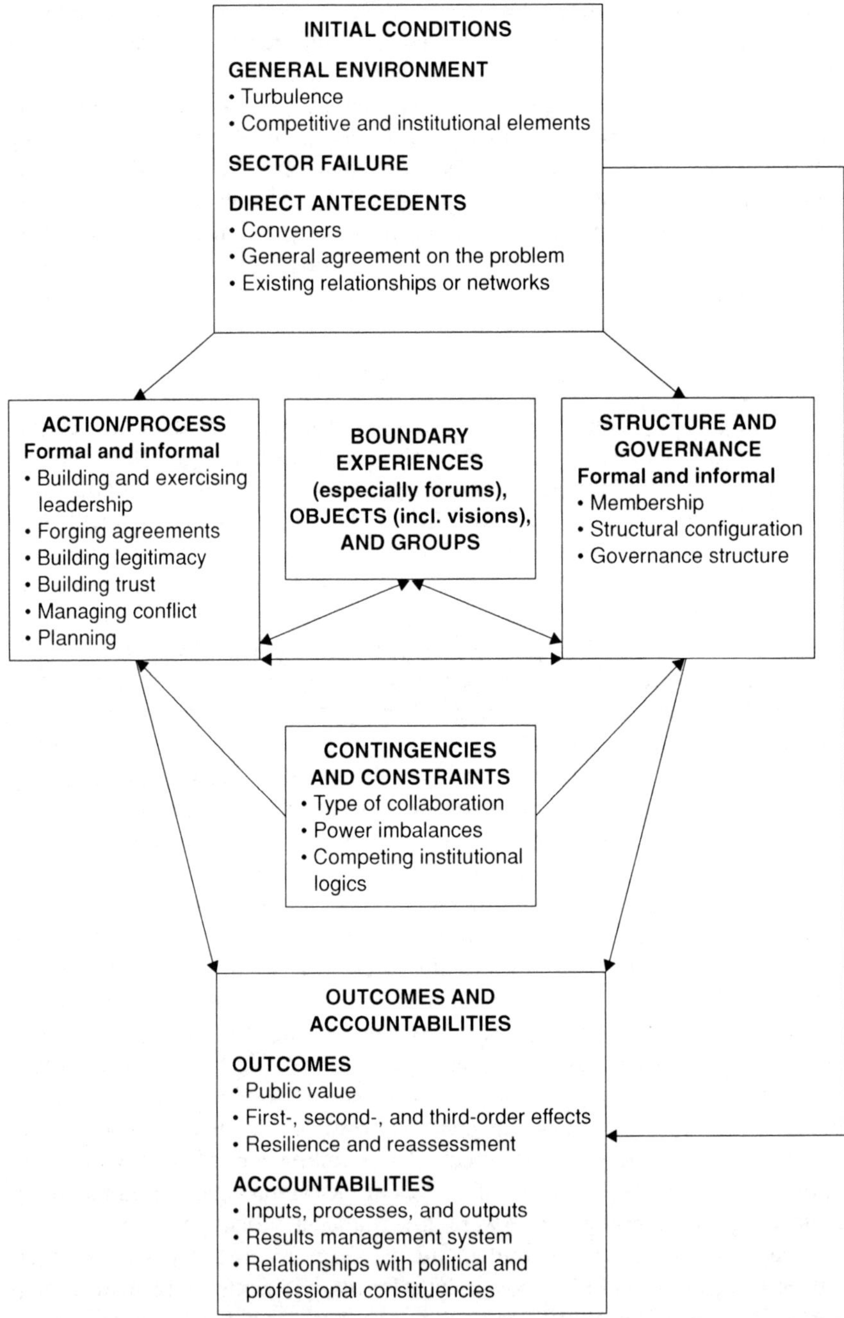

Figure 12.2 A framework for understanding leadership in cross-sector collaborations.

organizational missions and the expectations of the citizenry at reasonable cost. To construct a reliable picture of collaborations' outcomes, participants and analysts will need to rely on an accountability system that tracks inputs, processes and outcomes; uses a variety of methods for gathering, interpreting, and using data; and relies on strong relationships with key political and professional constituencies.

This chapter focuses on the process components, but also on their interaction with initial conditions, structure, contingencies and outcomes. Our questions specifically are: How do visionary leaders help collaborating partners from different sectors develop enough of a shared purpose to form the basis of initial agreements? How do they use planning processes to build shared understandings and commitments to craft and implement solutions? How do they use the design of settings (with their partially visible rules) to create a shared purpose and set of commitments, and to build trust, establish legitimacy and manage conflict? We think attention to the intermediate level of power – rules, modes, media and methods – can be very helpful in answering these questions, but we shall also use insights from the literature that emphasize the important role of boundary objects, boundary experiences and boundary groups in helping people connect with perspectives very different from their own and commit to a new, shared perspective. In this case, technology also appears to operate at the intermediate level of power as an integrative underpinning of observable action.

Boundary experiences, objects and groups

Boundary experiences are "shared or joint activities that create a sense of community and an ability to transcend boundaries among participants" (Feldman et al. 2006: 94; Feldman and Khademian 2007). UPA was forged out of the self-conscious design and use of such experiences; it continues, at least in part, because of them as well. Boundary objects are "physical objects that enable people to understand other perspectives" (Feldman et al. 2006: 95). Beyond that, boundary objects can facilitate the transformation of diverse views into shared knowledge and understanding (Carlile 2002; Kellogg, Orlikowski and Yates 2006). Attention to boundary objects first developed in a production or manufacturing context, where the objects often were scale models or mockups, but since then the idea has been extended to include less material objects. Boundary objects and their development help participants make sense of their world, what they may want to do with it, and why; and, in doing so, the exercise helps participants connect people, ideas and other kinds of actors into a way forward. Said differently, boundary objects act as a kind of "transitional object" (Winnicott 1953) or "facilitative device" (de Geus 1988) from here-and-now real possibilities to the there-and-then actualities. Boundary objects may be used to deal with what Carlile (2004) calls "syntactical" problems, or incompatible codes, routines or protocols; "semantic" problems, resulting from differences in meaning, assumptions or context; or "pragmatic" problems, caused by differing stakeholder interests that can be resolved only if people alter some of their existing knowledge or ways of doing things.

Boundary organizations or boundary groups are "collections of actors who are drawn together from different ways of knowing or bases of experience for the purpose of coproducing boundary actions" (Feldman et al. 2006: 95). Examples include cross-boundary networks, taskforces and teams; coordinating committees; and representative policy-making bodies. Minnesota's UPA is perhaps best-understood as a boundary organization; it is mostly a "virtual organization" comprised of many members, including the Minnesota Department of Transportation (MnDOT), Metro Transit (the regional transportation authority) and the City of Minneapolis, and a host of other organizations, groups and individuals participate.

Other theoretical threads

Theories about cross-cultural communication also may be important in this case, since cultures at the state and local level may be quite different from the culture of federal agencies. (Culture here refers to habitual ways of doing things, distinctive organizational and institutional rituals, core values, and routines and logics [Schein 2004].) The cultures of government agencies are likely to be quite different from those of nonprofits and business. A similar concept, "competing institutional logics", appears in organizational theory and neo-institutional views of the environment to emphasize the deep-seated and often contradictory norms and views of action embedded in the logics of bureaucracy, democracy, markets, and so forth (Friedland and Alford 1991).

Studies of collaboration have paid little attention to the role of computerized information technology in facilitating or hampering cross-sector collaboration. Orlikowski (2000) has offered a "practice lens" for studying technology in organizations, and we draw on her insights. Our analysis of the Minnesota UPA revealed that technology played several important roles: as its own driving force, as a solution, and as a motivator, facilitator and positive political force (Bryson, Crosby and Stone 2008).

Case-study methodology

Our extended study of the Minnesota UPA project used a simplified version of the framework presented in Figure 12.2 to develop the questions we posed to those closely involved in advocacy, conceptualization and management of the implementation of the project. We conducted semi-structured interviews with twenty-six individuals involved in Minnesota's UPA. In selecting our sample, we paid careful attention to gaining perspectives from individuals at multiple levels of government and with varying levels of responsibility and authority over the UPA implementation, including federal officials, state legislators, MnDOT and Metro Transit staff, policy advocates, legislators, and members of local transportation groups.

The interview protocol included questions related to the interviewee's background in the transportation field, the initial conditions leading up to the UPA collaboration, the structures and processes of decision-making, and the outcomes and accountability processes involved. A note-taker accompanied the interviewer to record the interviewee's comments verbatim on a laptop computer, and these notes were then imported into the qualitative analysis software program QSR NVIVO.

Important to our design and analysis was feedback from key practitioners in the local transportation field. We convened an Advisory Group comprised of leaders from each of the primary UPA partnership organizations to provide feedback on our initial findings and draft reports. Archival newspaper articles and other publications formed the basis of a secondary data-collection effort focused on capturing the story of UPA development and implementation as reported by local newspapers and publications in the recipient states, with particular emphasis on the legislative and political processes necessary for successful implementation of the UPA policy.

We developed a thematic coding structure based on our original cross-sector collaboration paper, input from the Advisory Group, and discussion among research-team members. The software also allowed us to disaggregate thematic results into categories based on the characteristics of interview participants, such as their work affiliation and job title.

Background of the Urban Partnership Agreement

Traffic congestion in US metropolitan areas has become an exceedingly complex, or "wicked", problem in the last four decades. The habitual approach to solving the problem – building more freeways – increasingly ran into limitations in the form of citizen protest and competing demands on public budgets. Plus, when new or expanded freeways or other roads were built they often did not reduce congestion in the long run. Soon the new lanes were also clogged with traffic as more people moved into the areas and low-density development continued to spread outward from city centers. By the 1960s transportation analysts with economics training were beginning to argue that the only way actually to reduce traffic congestion was to price the use of the roads during peak hours of use. Referring to the laws of supply and demand, they argued that demand would go down if drivers had to pay for access. The analysts argued that some drivers would pay the fee, but others would take alternative, uncongested routes, vary their driving time, take the bus, or stay at home. By the 1990s, policy entrepreneurs were imagining integrated transportation systems that relied on congestion pricing, transit, a variety of advanced technologies, and telecommuting.

From the 1960s through the 1990s, the idea of using pricing to manage traffic congestion had difficulty getting off the ground. Feasibility studies and a few pilot projects were tried, but elected officials and citizens generally were not convinced that the approach would work. Citizens also objected to paying a fee for facilities they felt they had already funded through their taxes. By the late 1990s, however, congestion was getting even worse in many urban areas, and a greater number of public officials were realizing that they could not build their way out of the problem.

Within USDOT during the George W. Bush Administration, Tyler Duvall, assistant secretary for transportation policy, began working with a few other top transportation officials to move from researching congestion pricing to mounting larger-scale demonstrations. One of his key allies was Mary Peters, the then administrator of the Federal Highway Administration, but there were a number of others in the department, including Patrick DeCorla-Souza, who was a long-time advocate of congestion pricing. Duvall tried to convince USDOT Secretary Norm Mineta to make congestion pricing a federal priority. Initially, Mineta was skeptical but after a top-level strategy meeting in 2006 agreed to make the shift, and congestion pricing was included in the department's 2006 Strategy Statement. Duvall, Peters, David Horner (the chief counsel of the Federal Transit Authority) and others then began designing a demonstration project to channel funding to major metropolitan areas that would tackle congestion with a set of complementary strategies called "the four Ts": transit, technology, tolling and telecommuting. The designers thought that integrating the four strategies would provide the biggest payoff in terms of congestion pricing. They were able to secure about $120 million in departmental discretionary funds to put into what became known as the Urban Partnership project, which was designed to demonstrate whether congestion pricing had a clear positive impact. The plan was to create a competitive request for proposal (RFP) process that would result in approval of a few highly promising projects.

Soon, however, a much larger amount of money became available when Congress suspended its usual practice of allowing members to earmark transportation funds. As a result, the pot for the project eventually grew to $1.1 billion. In addition, Mary Peters became US Secretary of Transportation, allowing her to champion the program from the top position in the department.

In Minnesota, congestion pricing advocates, state and local officials, and transit supporters began discussing participation in the Urban Partnership program, officially announced at the end of 2006. Minnesota, after all, was the site of one of the country's most successful congestion-pricing experiments, in the form of the MnPass project on highway I-394 – an Intelligent Transportation System (ITS) application of dynamic pricing to a segment of I-394 in the western part of the Minneapolis-St Paul metropolitan region.

Minnesota Department of Transportation (MnDOT) officials decided, after some initial reluctance, to submit a proposal for an Urban Partnership grant in collaboration with the Metropolitan Council, which operates the bus transit system (Metro Transit) for the Minneapolis-St Paul region. Soon after, the Citizens League (a nonprofit public-policy study group focusing on Minneapolis-St Paul), the University of Minnesota's Center for Transportation Studies, and the State and Local Policy Program at the university's Humphrey Institute featured the Urban Partnership program at their Road Pricing Summit on 1 February 2007. It was here that Rick Arnebeck from MnDOT announced that the department would seek a UPA grant. Tyler Duvall also spoke at the summit.

MnDOT project leaders assembled an interagency Steering Committee to oversee the proposal development process. In addition to individuals from MnDOT and the Metropolitan Council, the committee over time grew to include local officials from highly congested traffic corridors, county officials, and University of Minnesota experts. MnDOT hired SRF Consulting Group to prepare the actual grant proposal. John Doan of SRF played a key role in the drafting process; he was a former MnDOT employee who had worked on congestion pricing while there.

Since the proposal was due at the end of April, the Steering Committee members knew that they had to obtain agreement among numerous state and local parties about the main components of the proposal. For example: In which locations would congestion pricing be applied? What form would it take? What would be the implications for bus services and routing? What technological innovations would be emphasized? What role would telecommuting play?

The committee organized a half-day workshop in March and several subsequent meetings to help numerous stakeholders consider possible answers to these questions and develop a consensus about what should be included in the proposal. Additionally, project supporters worked behind the scenes to make sure that powerful legislators, the governor and the lieutenant-governor would support the form of tolling that would be included in the Minnesota UPA proposal.

At times, project advocates worried that disagreements about proposal components would sink the effort, but eventually the Steering Committee and outside advocates obtained enough consensus and compromise to be able to submit a strong proposal, focusing on the I-35W corridor south of Minneapolis and on downtown Minneapolis bus routes that linked to the corridor. Minnesota's proposal was selected as one of the nine semi-finalists announced by USDOT in June. The semi-finalists then were invited to present their plans to USDOT, and in August the nine were winnowed to five finalists – Minneapolis, Seattle, New York, San Francisco and Miami. (In the spring of 2008, New York would drop out, and Los Angeles and Chicago would be added.)

The total UPA grant to Minnesota was $133.3 million to be matched with $55.2 million in funds from the state legislature and Metropolitan Council. In addition to approving the match, state legislators would also have to approve tolling authority for the I-35W corridor. The UPA partners had approximately one year to assemble all components of the implementation plan.

Once Minnesota was chosen as a finalist, the UPA Steering Committee went into implementation mode. It became a smaller, more operations-oriented group, and MnDOT put Nick Thompson, operations manager, in charge of day-to-day oversight of the operational aspects of the project. At the same time, the Metropolitan Council transit officials and local government partners began working on their pieces of the project, while legislators and MnDOT senior officials worked on legislative strategy. Ultimately, the 2008 session of the Minnesota Legislature approved the required state matching funds as well as needed MnDOT authority for implementing the UPA.

How sponsors and champions exercised visionary leadership in the UPA case

Two main types of leaders – sponsors and champions – seem necessary for carrying out successful collaborative efforts to tackle public problems (Crosby and Bryson 2005a). Sponsors bring formal authority, financial resources and legitimacy to the endeavors. Champions typically bring tireless commitment, networking skills and often significant informal authority. They are willing to take risks in the service of potential payoff. They understand the policy-change process and take a long view. In this case, federal-level champions and sponsors worked together to construct the Urban Partnership program, and state and local champions and sponsors put together Minnesota's successful campaign to obtain and implement a UPA. Among the federal leaders, Mary Peters was initially a champion and became a sponsor. Tyler Duvall, Patrick DeCorla-Souza and David Horner were champions. In Minnesota, champions included Lee Munnich, Adeel Lari, Bob DeBoer, members of the I-35W Solutions Alliance (consisting of local officials in the 35W corridor) and a MnDOT middle manager. Senior executives at MnDOT and Metro Transit were important sponsors.

Our analysis focuses on how these champions and sponsors exercised visionary leadership in a way that integrated stakeholders, processes, structures and resources from different sectors and governmental levels to tackle a shared problem. As noted earlier, visionary leaders do the crucial work of helping constituents make sense of a public problem and commit to doing something about it. As these leaders assemble collaborations, they focus on developing agreement on the collaboration's purpose or mission, and securing commitment to producing and implementing strategies for carrying it out. In carrying out this work, visionary leaders emphasize the social practice of creating and communicating shared meaning in formal and informal forums.

Visionary leadership comprises three main tasks: interpreting the need or opportunity and giving direction about how to respond to it, offering compelling visions of the future, and adeptly designing and using formal and informal forums. Let us now consider the processes by which sponsors and champions in this case carried out those tasks in ways that integrated different government units and levels and government and nongovernment partners.

Seizing opportunities to provide interpretation and direction

Visionary leaders help make public problems real through a problem-definition process: they make social needs and opportunities visible, detail their causes and consequences, and frame them in ways that appeal to diverse stakeholders. They also engage in solution-seeking processes, chiefly eliciting and championing new ideas for dealing with the problems.

Making societal needs or opportunities visible

In this case, existence of the problem of urban traffic congestion was fairly widely known. Highway-users experienced the problem daily, government officials fielded complaints about it, academic and government reports detailed its pervasiveness and costs, and public-opinion surveys often put it high on the list of citizen concerns (Metropolitan Council 2007).

Detailing causes and consequences

Citizens and analysts alike tend to agree that a major factor in urban traffic congestion is too much reliance on cars and (possibly) highways and land-use patterns, especially urban sprawl. This discussion has been going on for decades.

In the interviews conducted for our UPA study, analysts at the federal level also pointed to the existence of federal transportation programs (and funding) in separate silos, marked "highways", "buses", "intelligent transportation systems" and "non-motorized transport". Analysts also realized that these arrangements provided little incentive for state and local transportation agencies and decision-makers to coordinate their work. Comprehensive and coordinated planning to ease a multi-faceted problem like congestion was difficult indeed. A more behind-the-scenes concern within USDOT was that federal highway programs in particular were not focused and data-driven.

The at-least-partially-shared problem diagnosis lowered barriers among prospective UPA partners in Minnesota. All agreed that urban congestion was bad and getting worse. They did focus on different parts of the problem: legislators tended to see the congestion located in their districts; the I-35W Solutions Alliance was fighting against congestion in a particular highway corridor. The Minnesota partners had enough agreement on the problem and the shared mission of remedying it that they could work together, in keeping with Huxham's finding that collaborations can proceed without complete agreement on aims (Huxham 2003).

Framing the problem and solutions

Stakeholders, including the general public, generally agreed that traffic congestion was a *public* problem and that therefore government has some responsibility for doing something about it. Government reports, citizen surveys, media accounts and scholarly reports portrayed traffic congestion as a *public bad* because of widespread and multiple harmful effects: pollution, personal stress, economic toll. An example would be the *Critical Issues in Transportation* report published by the Transportation Research Board (2007), a division of the nonprofit National Research Council.

As noted above, federal transportation analysts and other anti-congestion campaigners had begun to argue that congestion was a *complex problem* that required *comprehensive integrated solutions*. A fragmented approach was characterized as failure-prone, and an integrated approach was deemed potentially very effective. The integrative frame was expressed in the linking of the "4 Ts" (tolling, transit, technology and telecommuting) in the grant application process and public proclamations about it.

Money also helped convey the idea of an integrated system across boundaries. In the Road Pricing Summit sponsored by the Citizens League and in follow-up informal conversations, people who were not necessarily attracted to pricing or the 4-T idea did respond to the lure of major federal funding. The funding conveyed a sense of legitimacy (federal officials are willing to put big money behind this idea) and it also promised *significant* impact. This promise helped motivate potential partners to begin thinking how to align their goals and favored projects with what federal officials were proposing. It also helped overcome resistance from transportation-planners concerned about the possible need to rethink projects already underway. Additionally, Minnesota partners needed incentives to accept the risk that they would sink time and effort into something (the UPA grant application) that might not succeed. In other words, the large size of the grant was a powerful inducement (Stone 2002). Perhaps the use of the word *partnership* had positive impact in that it conveyed a sense that federal officials were willing to let state and local applicants come up with program specifics and that they would stay involved as the projects went forward.

Additionally, what might be called a transportation *corridor* frame had become a familiar way of thinking about transportation projects –

transportation planners and policy-makers had begun to think beyond rebuilding a highway or establishing a bus route, to considering the ways various modes of travel operated together in a corridor that included at least one major traffic route and feeder routes. The corridor idea helped link together modes and stakeholders along the corridor.

The prospect of integrating advanced technology throughout the project helped stakeholders see the UPA as an exciting opportunity to innovate. As one interviewee stated, people are attracted by the possibility of being innovators, because "[i]t's exciting to implement new technology". Another added that an incentive for MnDOT was "another opportunity to be cutting edge". The UPA was therefore a technology-assisted motivating or attractor force (Allen and Cherrey 2000).

A sticking point was the framing of tolling as a "public bad". The very word "tolling" has a negative connotation for many citizens. They object to paying tolls for something they see as a public good. They argue: "I've paid for the highway with my taxes. Why should I pay again?" The supporters of "tolling" or "pricing" in this case tried to replace this negative frame with a positive "public good" frame. Tax dollars, they suggested, simply guarantee that highways are universally available on demand as long as their capacity is not exceeded. After that users might legitimately pay a price for access to free-flowing lanes. Moreover, thanks to transponder technology, that price can be carefully calibrated to respond to high demand or peak periods. In effect, free flow becomes worth more when more people want it. The label "dynamic pricing" captured this argument.

Pricing advocates still had to overcome the perception that charging for the use of one or more lanes was taking those lanes away or subtracting capacity from the system. They countered that pricing actually increased the numbers of cars that a highway can accommodate. This argument is somewhat less straightforward than the argument for pricing. One advocate used the analogy of pouring rice into an hourglass: that is, if many grains of rice are poured rapidly into an hourglass they will soon overwhelm the capacity of the narrow neck, and almost no grains will get through after a certain point in time. Yet if the rate of entry is slowed enough, which presumably pricing would do, all the grains will get through. Advocates quite literally did this; in other words, they used the rice and hourglass as a boundary object to facilitate shared knowledge and understanding. Demonstration projects – such as MnPass on I-394, and the Stockholm and London experiences – that show the beneficial effects of pricing were also crucial for making this less-than-intuitive argument stick.

Championing new ideas for dealing with the problems

Congestion pricing was a relatively new idea for some stakeholders. The effectiveness of its use outside the US and in a few places inside the US helped champions make their case to different stakeholder groups. Effectiveness or efficiency arguments appeal across sectors and government levels. The idea of integration seemed to help as well. Supporters of telecommuting, bus rapid transit, congestion pricing and "intelligent systems" could all see how their favored part of the congestion solution could be advanced but also enhanced by being meshed with other solutions within the UPA program. Making funding contingent on an integrated UPA grant application was a means that federal transportation officials used to ensure that this idea would have traction. The federal designers of the UPA program also built in funding and mandates for evaluation so that the program appealed to rational planning advocates.

Federal and state champions had gotten their tolling idea fully developed in preparation for the policy window (Kingdon 1995) that opened when traffic congestion emerged as a priority transportation-policy focus in the final two years of the Bush administration, and the transportation secretary picked up substantial discretionary funding because of the impasse over earmarking. They instituted a competitive process that required complementary, silo-busting strategies and "forced creative thinking", as one interviewee said. They even took a bit of comfort from any resistance they encountered – they interpreted it as a sign of innovativeness. Meanwhile, the RFP, competitive grant process was a well-known routine for most players. So it fitted within their normal frames of reference.

Perhaps in their enthusiasm for alliteration, the federal policy entrepreneurs slipped up. In Minnesota, tolling raised the hackles of the governor, many legislators, and citizens. Paying to use a road already paid for by taxes seemed anathema to them. Indeed, any tolling on Minnesota highways had to be expressly permitted by the state legislature. Arguments that congestion pricing added capacity were not enough to win the governor's support. To win him over, the assemblers of Minnesota's UPA application had to apply dynamic pricing to a shoulder lane, so that existing lanes were not "taken away" by tolling. Now the shoulder lane idea is being considered in other states. Meanwhile, USDOT decision-makers had to be willing to move away from their desire to price existing lanes, if they were to approve the Minnesota application. They ultimately selected Minnesota as a UPA finalist because transportation agencies in the state had a reputation for competence, plus success with congestion pricing, and thus federal officials viewed them as legitimate and trustworthy partners.

Technological advances made "dynamic pricing" possible as a solution to traffic congestion and allowed motorists to use transponders rather than toll booths to pay. According to one interviewee, technology allows "road pricing without significant transaction costs". He also noted that technology improves transit services because it allows "buses to travel with shorter headways" and makes transit service more predictable and reliable by, for example, providing "real-time" traveler information. All of this enhances the attractiveness of Bus Rapid Transit (BRT) and "thereby creates a virtuous cycle for transit – the more appeal, the more demand for it, the greater the frequency with which it's provided, the better the economies of scale, the lower the cost per traveler [and therefore the more demand for it]".

Offering compelling visions of the future

Sponsors and champions engage in translation and construction processes as they attempt to make an alternative future "real" in the minds of constituents. To be persuasive, they must translate abstract ideas like congestion pricing into accessible and appealing words and imagery that can provide a clear pathway from current conditions to a desirable future. Elements of the path and the future state must be constructed or woven together in a plausible and compelling way. In this case, the vision communicated explicitly and implicitly by sponsors and champions of the UPA program included smooth-flowing highways on which substantial numbers of vehicles use transponders to take advantage of priced lanes, technologically sophisticated side-boarding buses operate a lot like light rail trains, commuters continually are fed up-to-date information about travel times, park-and-ride facilities are available, new commercial and residential development springs up around bus hubs, and more people use the Internet to work from home or hook up to carpools. The vision was communicated through verbal imagery, cross-boundary objects (like the RFP, drawings, maps and reports) and groups (like Minnesota's UPA Steering Committee) that made it potentially real and thus believable. This may be where trust comes in – perhaps visionary leaders foster shared interpretation of others' motives, competencies and commitments.

Designing and using formal and informal forums

Structure and process come together in the design and use of formal and informal forums, the settings in which leaders and constituents engage in the dialogue, discussion and debate that may result in shared understandings of public problems and solutions – in this case, urban traffic congestion and integrated arrangements of transit, tolling, technology and telecommuting. UPA sponsors and champions put together a number of cross-boundary forums at the national, state, regional and local levels. For example, in January 2006 about eighty leaders of transportation agencies that comprise USDOT participated in an offsite planning retreat, where they identified metropolitan highway congestion as the nation's biggest transportation problem deserving priority. An urban congestion working group was formed to come up with an action plan in sixty days. In these high-level forums, an economics/pricing frame was defensible because congestion-pricing initiatives had succeeded in the US and abroad and because other solutions clearly were not having much effect. What emerged from these forums was the vision of an integrated system, branded with the "4 Ts" label. The "4 T" label was itself a kind of boundary object, or at least a summary term that carried somewhat shared meaning across audiences.

Once the UPA program was defined, federal and local champions used follow-up forums to alert potential applicants to the program's existence and its potential to provide significant remedies for the problem. Bridging across the boundaries between national and local was facilitated by the existence of individuals and groups in the Minneapolis-St Paul area who had participated in national transportation forums, supported and publicized Minnesota's successful MnPass program, and shared the economics pricing frame. Some had worked together on corridor projects. Some MTA and MnDOT employees had collaborated as partners in a group called Team Transit. Several interviewees pointed to the pre-existing relationships among stakeholders as being a key contributor to their willingness to get involved in shaping the UPA. This finding reinforced our previous study (Bryson, Crosby and Stone 2006) indicating that pre-existing networks and relationships were an important initial condition affecting the formation of cross-sector collaborations.

Stakeholder forums convened during Minnesota's application process included disparate groups, and facilitators used methods designed to foster inclusion and balance power. The I-35W Solutions Alliance was powerful in these settings because members had their act together. A sense of urgency was supplied by the short timelines that USDOT had imposed for submitting Urban Partnership applications. Agreements from these forums and Steering Committee meetings solidified into the actual grant application.

Forums may be thought of as structures that mediate between deep social structures such as language and observable action such as the debate and discussion that occurs in a workshop. Forums convened as part of a cross-sector collaboration are shaped by and also facilitate collaborative processes to carry out the work of the collaboration. They can be boundary experiences, produce boundary objects and often result in formation of boundary groups, such as taskforces and steering committees. Recalling the syntactical, semantic and pragmatic functions of boundary objects, we conclude that syntax was not much of an issue in this case, since most of the partners, regardless of their government level or sector, spoke "transportation-ese". They did have semantic differences – for example, over tolling or intermodal approaches. They had to work out what integration across modes meant. They had to grapple with how much change would be needed if different professional groups associated with different modes had to work together. Pragmatics would require building a coalition, and boundary objects could be something around which people could coalesce and make their own meaning and align their interests. The proposal that was submitted and won contained all of these elements. Supporters quite literally had to agree on the syntax in the proposal; they had to agree on what the words meant; and the proposal itself represented a shared agreement or treaty that reconciled interests and committed the signers to alter some of what they knew and how they would do things.

Another important boundary object was the USDOT request for proposal (RFP), eliciting applications for the UPA program. The RFP was a boundary object that conveyed meaning from federal officials to state and local applicants. The RFP addressed the syntactical, semantic and pragmatic problems inside USDOT, and then presented applicants with the need to solve the same problems in their proposals, which the Minnesota proposal did, as did the final agreement between Minnesota and USDOT. Understanding the proposal and RFP as boundary objects adds to our previous finding that forging sound initial agreements is an important process element in cross-sector collaborations (Crosby and Bryson 2005a; Bryson, Crosby and Stone 2006).

Planners of stakeholder forums during the formulation of Minnesota's UPA application used what Lee Munnich calls a "grasstops" approach. They invited stakeholders from local governments, state agencies, regional government agencies, academic programs and nonprofit advocates. They did not extend their invitation to the grassroots – commuters or residents surrounding candidate corridors. This approach, used successfully in planning for MnPass, kept disagreements among stakeholder groups from expanding much beyond the forums themselves. It also was probably appropriate for the tight timeline that UPA applicants had for obtaining consensus among key stakeholders about the contours of the proposed project. A more problematic result is that UPA implementers will need to invest time and effort in selling their vision to the wider population expected to use the new integrated system.

Communications technology provided important, though less visible, cross-boundary forums. Telephone conversations obviously were important; but one interviewee also noted that, without email and the ability to include attachments, the proposal could not have been done on time. From this perspective, the Internet and email also may be seen as media for assembling and revising boundary objects.

Using political leadership on behalf of the vision

As noted earlier, political leadership – the making and implementing of policy decisions in formal and informal arenas – is a necessary concomitant of visionary leadership aimed at tackling complex public problems. The most important process is building a sustainable coalition that can convince decision-makers to approve proposed policies and that can protect them during implementation. Structure and process come together in the design and use of arenas, the settings in which policy advocates vie with each other to obtain desired decisions from executive, legislative and administrative decision-makers. In this case, several champions helped organize the necessary coalition by crossing political boundaries at the state level to obtain high-level support for the Urban Partnership process. Because MnDOT and the Met Council decision-makers were not fully on board, champions from the university and the Citizens League met with these people to stress the opportunity represented by the Urban Partnership program. They did the same with key legislators. The legislators, in turn, helped MnDOT and Met Council change their minds by threatening to submit an Urban Partnership proposal if MnDOT and Met Council did not. Later the university and Citizens League champions controversially transgressed normal decision-making paths by putting pressure on the governor to support the emerging contours of the Minnesota application. Ultimately, the governor and his lieutenant-governor (who also was transportation commissioner) became sponsors once they were assured that congestion pricing would only be applied to existing high-occupancy-vehicle (HOV) lanes and shoulders. The successful Minnesota grant application thus was backed by a coalition of congestion-fighting advocates from the academic and nonprofit sectors, along with state, regional and local officials and transportation planners. The Minnesota coalition remained largely intact after federal officials approved its UPA project, though some initially supportive legislators began to grumble that they were not kept fully informed as the Steering Committee proceeded with planning the multiple projects that composed the agreement.

Extensive coalition-building also occurred at the federal level, where pricing advocates like Duvall and DeCorla-Souza convinced top administrators to put their clout behind the approach. US Transportation Secretary Peters persuaded White House staff that the Urban Partnership program was a good idea. Horner ensured that needed administrative decisions were aligned within various USDOT areas and that the program was protected from attack in formal courts. The federal sponsors and champions recognized that the next president could go back to a siloed approach, so they reached out to governors in order to build political support at the state level that would outlast the Bush administration. They reported that some states not included in UPA adopted the "4 T" approach; they believe that it may be "reaching critical mass in the states". They are trying to get the integrated multimodal approach included in next federal surface transportation re-authorization bill.

During the first year after federal officials approved Minnesota's UPA project, the state legislature became the most important arena, because the legislature had to approve the $55.2 million in matching funds as well as authority to impose dynamic pricing on project roadways. Here a key supporter was the chair of the Minnesota Senate transportation committee, who emphasized the safety benefits of reducing congestion and helped convince skeptical legislators that the program was worthwhile even if it did not directly improve transportation in their districts.

Lessons

Analysis of integrative visionary leadership in the case of Minnesota's Urban Partnership Agreement produces several lessons for those who aspire to practice integrative leadership.

1. Enough shared agreement about a problem permits diverse stakeholders to collaborate on remedying it, but diverse frames are still likely to need reconciling.
2. Academic champions are important. They have access to expertise outside government agencies and can be somewhat neutral conveners and analysts who have more freedom to espouse good, evidence-based ideas.
3. A well-defined competition is an effective way to elicit good ideas that accomplish the organizers' goals.
4. A competitive process that promotes flexibility and local adaptation within an overall strategic framework makes collaboration or partnership more attractive to the local partners.
5. Advanced technology can be an important solution component but also a magnet for participation.
6. Substantial funding provides a strong incentive and may provide legitimacy.
7. The prospect of having substantial impact may help partners sign on despite substantial risk.
8. Solution ideas should be well developed so they are ready for prime time when a window of opportunity opens.
9. Integrative leaders may be wise to link a vision for change to what stakeholders already want or intend to do. They should consider integrating collaborative structures and major system innovation with regular routines and decision-making channels, so that the changes are not interpreted as renegade endeavors. They are likely to need to blend collaboration and hierarchy.
10. Cross-boundary forums are crucial. Leaders can take advantage of existing ones to push ideas and create new ones to develop shared understanding of a problem and potential solutions as well as commitment to agreed-upon actions.
11. The production of boundary objects and agreement on the structure of needed cross-boundary groups and organizations seem to be important outcomes of cross-boundary forums.
12. A grasstops approach has advantages for developing solutions to complex public problems, but at some point leaders will have to focus on developing needed shared understandings and commitments at the grassroots, too.

Conclusions

In keeping with our prior research, we identified a number of sponsors and champions who provided essential visionary leadership in crafting a so-far-successful collaboration to remedy a complex public problem. Their partially shared agreement on the nature of the problem and its causes helped bridge differences among stakeholders from different levels of government and non-governmental organizations. They did apply a variety of competing frames to potential problem solutions. The integrative frame pushed by the federal advocates ultimately dominated because it was backed up by substantial funding and a promise of substantial impact, and because it offered ways for regional and local stakeholders to see how their pre-existing projects might fit within it. The technology requirement made the Urban Partnership program exciting to potential partners. Still the Minnesota Urban Partnership application might have foundered if pricing advocates had not succeeded in winning over the governor with a combination of using high-occupancy and shoulder lanes to meet the tolling requirement and if federal officials had not been flexible enough to allow this despite its being an "impure" form of congestion-pricing.

This case underscores important ways that visionary leaders can champion new and improved ideas for dealing with a public problem. Tying the ideas to effectiveness and efficiency arguments appealed across stakeholder divisions. The competitive RFP process and demonstration projects were especially effective in ensuring that the best ideas surfaced and accomplished what the initiators hoped they would.

The analysis of this case reveals the usefulness of understanding the role of forums in cross-boundary integration. We expect that viewing them as boundary experiences that produce boundary objects and groups and organizations may be a helpful perspective for integrative leaders. Our study of the Minnesota UPA collaboration highlights the importance of particular kinds of objects central to the process. These material artifacts have functioned as "boundary objects" (Carlile 2002, 2004; Kellogg, Orlikowski and Yates 2006). Of particular importance in the UPA case was the creation and use of boundary objects in the form of various proposals, agreements, maps and timelines by key stakeholders. These objects and the process of creating them were crucial to developing shared understandings, and the coalition needed to move forward. The role of boundary objects thus clearly merits further investigation.

Technology was a source of innovation via its enabling of congestion-pricing and telecommuting. Intelligent systems linked elements of the vision together. Technology was an exciter that appealed to people across governmental levels and across sectors. Technology was a facilitator in allowing disparate groups to use a common medium to assemble and revise boundary objects. We also conclude that further study of the role of technology in facilitating or hampering leadership across boundaries is merited.

References

Allen, K. E. and Cherrey, C. (2000) *Systemic Leadership: Enriching the Meaning of Our Work*, Lanham, Md: University Press of America.

Ansell, C. and Gash, A. (2008) "Collaborative Governance in Theory and Practice", *Journal of Public Administration Research Theory*, 18 (4): 543–71.

Bryson, J., Crosby, B. and Stone, M. M. (2006) "The Design and Implementation of Cross-sector Collaborations: Propositions from the Literature", *Public Administration Review*, 66 (s1): 44–55.

Bryson, J., Crosby, B. and Stone, M. M. (2008) *Collaboration in Fighting Traffic Congestion: A Study of Minnesota's Urban Partnership Agreement*, ITS Institute Publication no. CTS 08–25, Minneapolis, Minn.: Center for Transportation Studies.

Bryson, J., Crosby, B. and Bryson, J. K. (2009) "Understanding Strategic Planning and the Formulation and Implementation of Strategic Plans as a Way of Knowing: The Contribution of Actor-Network Theory". *International Public Management Journal*, 12 (2): 172–207.

Carlile, P. R. (2002) "A Pragmatic View of Knowledge and Boundaries: Boundary Objects in New Product Development", *Organization Science*, 13 (4): 442–55.

Carlile, P. R. (2004) "Transferring, Translating, and Transforming: An Integrative Framework for Managing Knowledge across Boundaries", *Organization Science*, 15 (5): 555–68.

Crosby, B. C. and Bryson, J. M. (2005a) *Leadership for the Common Good: Tackling Public Problems in a Shared-power World*, San Francisco, Calif.: Jossey-Bass.

Crosby, B. C. and Bryson, J. M. (2005b) "A Leadership Framework for Cross-sector Collaboration", *Public Management Review*, 7 (2): 177–201.

de Geus, A. P. (1988) "Planning as Learning", *Harvard Business Review*, March–April: 70–4.

Feldman, M. S., Khademian, A. M., Ingram, H. and Schneider, A. S. (2006) "Ways of Knowing and Inclusive Management Practices", *Public Administration Review*, 66: 89–99.

Feldman, M. S. and Khademian, A. M. (2007) The Role of the Public Manager in Inclusion: Creating Commitments of Participation. *Governance*, 20 (2): 305–24.

Friedland, R., and Alford, R. (1991) Bringing Society Back In: Symbols, Practices and Institutional Contradictions. In W. W. Powell, & P. J. DiMaggio (Eds.), *The New Institutionalsm in Organizational Analysis* ( ). Chicago: University of Chicago Press.

Giddens, A. (1979) *Central Problems in Social Theory: Action, Structure and Contradiction in Social Analysis*, Berkeley, Calif.: University of California Press.

Giddens, A. (1984) *The Constitution of Society: Outline of a Theory of Structuration*, Berkeley, Calif.: University of California Press.

Huxham, C. (2003) "Theorizing Collaboration Practice", *Public Management Review*, 5 (3): 401–23.

Huxham, C. and Vangen, S. (2005) *Managing to Collaborate : The Theory and Practice of Collaborative Advantage*, New York: Routledge.

Kellogg, K. C., Orlikowski, W. J. and Yates, J. (2006) "Life in the Trading Zone: Structuring Coordination across Boundaries in Postbureaucratic Organizations", *Organization Science*, 17 (1): 22–44.

Kingdon, J. W. (1995) *Agendas, Alternatives, and Public Policies*, revised edn, Boston, Mass.: Little, Brown.

Mattessich, P., Murray-Close, M. and Monsey, B. (2001) *Collaboration: What Makes It Work*, St Paul, Minn.: Amherst H. Wilder Foundation.

Metropolitan Council (2007) *2007 Metro Residents Survey*, St Paul, Minn.: Metropolitan Council.

Moore, M. H. (1995) *Creating Public Value*, Cambridge, Mass.: Harvard University Press.

Orlikowski, W. (2000) "Using Technology and Constituting Structures: A Practice Lens for Studying Technology in Organizations", *Organization Science*, 11 (4): 404–28.

Shein, E. H. (2004) Organizational Culture and Leadership. San Francisco: Jossey-Bass.

Stone, D. A. (2002) *Policy Paradox and Political Reason*, New York: W. W. Norton.

Transportation Research Board (2007) *Critical Issues in Transportation*, Washington, DC: Transportation Research Board.

Winer, M. and Ray, K. (1994) *Collaboration Handbook: Creating, Sustaining, and Enjoying the Journey*, St Paul, Minn.: Amherst H. Wilder Foundation.

Winnicott, D. W. (1953) "Transitional Objects and Transitional Phenomena", *The International Journal of Psycho-analysis*, 34 (2): 89–97.

13

PUBLIC GOVERNANCE AND THE THIRD SECTOR: OPPORTUNITIES FOR CO-PRODUCTION AND INNOVATION?

Victor Pestoff and Taco Brandsen

1. Introduction

In the opening chapter to this volume, Stephen Osborne presents an editorial overview of developments from New Public Management to the emergence of New Public Governance. He notes the increasingly interorganizational nature of public management in a clearly plural and pluralist world, where the number of actors involved in policy formulation and implementation have grown dramatically. This chapter will focus on one type of actor: the third sector. Is it good to involve the third sector in public governance? Arguments and counter-arguments are often based on normative assumptions rather than on empirical evidence, which remains fragmented and thin on the ground. The literature mentions several specific qualities or contributions that third-sector organizations could theoretically have, as compared to state or commercial organizations. We shall here explore the nature of those potential contributions.

The issue is especially relevant at a time when many countries in Europe have been searching for new ways in which to include the third sector in the provision and governance of social services. Of course, state–third-sector collaboration is not a new phenomenon and goes back a long way. What we now call the "third sector" provided public services before the state ever did, and in many countries its involvement in the welfare state dates back as far as the nineteenth century. Public governance implies that multiple parties are involved in the delivery of healthcare, care of the elderly, education, housing, welfare, safety and other public goods. Recent decades have been marked by a rearrangement of the relationships between the state and third-sector organizations that supply public goods and services like education, housing, healthcare and community services. New third-sector organizations have been drawn into public service provision; in other words, there has been an increase in co-management between third sector and state. In addition, those third-sector organizations already in the public services have faced the challenges of quasi-marketization and/or performance measurement. Long-term relationships based on trust have been replaced by short-term, contract-based relationships, changing the nature of the government–third-sector partnership.

At a general level, the reasons for involving the third sector in public service delivery are similar throughout Europe. First is the challenge of an aging population, second is the growing democracy deficit at all levels – local, regional, national and European – and third is the semi-permanent austerity in public finances. In any given EU member state, the reasons will vary and may be more specific. However, taken together, they imply a major legitimacy crisis for the public sector as a provider of welfare services. It is in this context that the third sector came back into the spotlight as a provider of public services in welfare states where it traditionally did not have a major role; in those where it did, its role has been changing. As a result, third-sector research has become increasingly intertwined with public management research, witnessed by various publications on the topic in the relevant journals and book series.

Another reason for the surge of interest in the third sector, paradoxically, is questions over its distinctiveness. The third sector comes under various other names, such as the voluntary sector, the (private) nonprofit sector, the social economy, civil society, all with slightly different defining characteristics and with a large degree of overlap. When we here refer to the third sector, we include all those groups and organizations grouped under other labels, accepting that it is a "loose and baggy monster" (Kendall and Knapp 1995) without trying to cage it in. This has not deterred politicians from various backgrounds from embracing the sector as one of the cures for the welfare state's ills. Yet the third sector is (in the context of public services) increasingly hard to get into focus. As a result of its involvement in public service delivery, and the contracting out and performance measurement that followed it, the traditional boundaries between market, state and third sector have been breaking down to the point where a class of indeterminate organizational hybrids has emerged (Evers 2005; Brandsen et al. 2005). It means that the third-sector organizations have taken on more characteristics of state organizations (e.g. in terms of formalization) and of market organizations (e.g. maximizing their income, but without maximizing their profit). Although no organization can be regarded as "pure", many organizations now reach the point where the ideal types – state, market or third sector – no longer help us truly to understand them.[1]

Within this context, we shall explore what role the third sector can play in the public services. None of these roles is exclusive to the third sector, and there are good grounds to challenge whether it has a specific contribution to make – indeed, whether the third-sector concept is truly useful. This chapter will argue that, if we are to judge the distinct contribution of the third sector to service delivery, an analysis should take account of the institutional framework within which it operates. Blanket statements on the specific nature of the third sector tend to be simplistic, and this is why further comparative work is needed. In the current chapter, we shall lay out some basic concepts along which a comparative analysis could be organized.

In the next section, we shall discuss the state of the art in research on this topic and conclude that there are two possible benefits of third-sector involvement in public service delivery. We examine the first in section 3, exploring the concept of co-production and its potential to democratize service delivery. In section 4 we go on to describe the potential contribution of the third sector, which is as a generator of innovation within the structure of service provision. In both cases we shall illustrate our point with empirical evidence, though we should emphasize that we do not claim to present a comprehensive literature review. The chapter ends with suggestions for future research.

2. The different roles of the third sector

2.1. The state of the art

Various theoretical traditions have addressed the role of the third sector in public service delivery, each with its own strengths and drawbacks. We shall here briefly describe the three main traditions: third-sector research, public management research and comparative welfare state research, including references to some key literature on the topic.

What is called "third-sector research" is a very mixed bag. Assumptions and theories about the specific strengths of third-sector organizations in relation to service delivery have been manifold. They generally concern four roles: (*a*) in community integration; (*b*) in giving the respective groups a voice; (*c*) in pioneering innovations in service provision that address groups, situations and/or needs neglected by states and markets; (*d*) their complementary role in enhancing the qualities of established public services (Zimmer and Stecker 2004; Evers and Laville 2004; Nyssens et al. 2006). Past research has demonstrated convincingly at the macro-level that state–third-sector relationships may benefit both sides (Gidron et al. 1992; Salamon 1995), and there is now a diverse body of theory on the topic (Smith and Grønbjerg 2006). There is also a good working knowledge on specific issues of third-sector management, such as the management of volunteers and board composition (Cornforth 2003). However, third-sector research has been less successful in demonstrating that, within these arrangements, the distinctive strengths of the third sector have really been addressed. Has its output differed qualitatively from that of other types of organizations?

Research in public management has by now examined quite extensively how service delivery by non-governmental organizations is organized and how this affects the nature of the relationships. For example, there is work on the effects of national compacts, the effects of contracting out services, and the role of these organizations in networks of service provision (Brandsen 2004; Osborne 2008). There has also been much attention to specific issues of concern to public management within the context of third-sector involvement, such as accountability (Kumar 2003), innovation (Osborne et al. 2008) and partnership (Carmel and Harlock 2008). This literature has been useful in clarifying the dynamics of government–third-sector relationships, with more attention to processes at the meso- and micro-level. Yet, as in third-sector research, only some of it has been explicitly comparative (e.g. Bode 2008), between sectors and/or between welfare systems, which makes general statements on the functions of the third sector rather tricky.

Mainstream welfare-state research has for the past decades largely ignored the third sector, as it has come to be dominated by the concept of welfare regimes (Kuhnle and Selle 1992). This has been beneficial in encouraging comparative research, but the third sector was left out of the original typologies formulated by Titmuss that were subsequently revised by Esping-Andersen (cf. Titmuss 1974; Esping-Andersen 1990). The Esping-Andersen typology distinguished liberal, conservative and social-democratic welfare states. Research on regimes tends to focus on national income transfer, whereas most government–third-sector partnerships concern services at the local level. Finally, the regime approach has mostly disregarded the issue of service quality, where the third sector's distinctive characteristics are more likely to be relevant. In short, what this tradition of research leaves us is a good understanding of the macro-context with rather implicit assumptions about why third-sector inputs are not so important, but little of the micro-dynamics (Pestoff et al. 2006).

Each of these traditions can contribute to an analysis of the functions of the third sector in relation to public service delivery. As noted above, several potential benefits of third-sector involvement emerge from the literature. Please note that we are not necessarily stating that these benefits always occur and that involving the third sector is always good. That would be an altogether normative perspective. Our purpose is to specify the supposed benefits and encourage research into the conditions under which they materialize.

On the basis of previous third-sector research, one could roughly classify the possible benefits of involving the sector in public service provision in terms of two main functions: democratization and innovation. This is where third-sector organizations may have an edge over their public or commercial counterparts. However, one cannot simply transplant the abstract functions as posited by third-sector research to public governance. They need to be reinterpreted within the specific context of public service delivery, where they take on a meaning that overlaps, but is not necessarily the same as, that within a purely voluntaristic context. For instance, the third sector supposedly contributes to the good functioning of democracy, but what does that mean when it is working within a system governed by representative democratic institutions? Or, if certain organizations improve their services for their particular clients, and differences in quality emerge, how does that fit in systems where everyone is entitled to services of the same quality?

2.2. Co-production and collective innovation

This is why we have reinterpreted the potential contributions of the third sector in two ways. Democratization will be understood in terms of *co-production* – direct participation by citizens in service delivery. *Innovation* will here be understood as the ability to renew the collective structure of service provision, whether it be in terms of skills, activities or even the underlying paradigm. These are the two distinctive contributions to service delivery identified by third-sector research.[2] Public management research has helped to understand better the effect of government policy on each of these two types of contributions. Comparative welfare state research can help us to understand, within their macro-institutional context, which institutional conditions favor which functions, and where does the third sector have which role. The role of citizens and of the third sector will vary among welfare regimes, with their different emphasis on individual or collective provision of social services and with different policies that focus on public-, private- or third-sector provision of welfare services. Let us now explore this variation, in relation to the two functions of co-production and innovation.

Co-production is one of several mechanisms that can be used to increase the influence of citizens over the services that are delivered to them. Evers (1998) argues that there are four concepts for strengthening the position of users in service delivery. They are: (*a*) representative political democracy, (*b*) participative democracy, (*c*) consumerism, and (*d*) involvement of the co-producer. The first concept relies on the indirect power of citizens as voters and their elected representatives. This refers to shaping the service sector according to the interests of society as a whole, not for a particular group. The second concept stems from a long history of self-organization, linked to the church, cooperatives, the labor movement, and other types of self-help groups and new social movements. This helps to offset the limits of parliamentary democracy and reinvigorate established voluntary organizations providing social services. There might, however, be a conflict between representative and participative democracy, and between a public interest with its universal rules and the concerns of particular groups striving for a specific solution for their needs. The third concept, consumerism, claims to bring more democracy through market-like arrangements in social services. Given time limits, it can provide a quick fix, rather than requiring citizen involvement in providing public services. Finally, it is the involvement of co-producers, like parent participation in schools and day care, which promises to empower consumers and reduce the gap between the professionals and their clientele (ibid.: 43–6).

Evers argues for a pluralistic or mixed approach of using several different pathways for democratizing the delivery of services (ibid.: 47–50). All welfare regimes and government policy can in their own way facilitate greater citizen participation and a greater role for the third sector in the provision and governance of social services. Yet the differences between welfare regimes and differences in the sectoral context are important in how this is done and where the role of the third sector is most distinctive – in other words, where it has a clear added benefit in relation to democratization. This is particularly the case in social-democratic welfare states where the third sector is least integrated in the established system of public service delivery as compared to its position in other regimes, and therefore paradoxically in a better position to be responsive to specific demands than governments.

Innovation, the ability to bring something new to service delivery, has been one of the chief justifications for involving the third sector. But what is innovation exactly? We shall here define it as a significant change in the process of the "production" of services. Whereas co-production refers to who is involved in the process, innovation concerns the qualities (in a neutral sense) of the service itself. It is of course possible to distinguish different kinds of innovation, depending, for instance, on the aspects of the service that are changed or the structure of the process of change.[3] We shall here keep matters simple, for reasons of space. We should also note that innovation is not necessarily always good: sometimes it is better to maintain the status quo and not allocate resources to changes that are not needed.

An important point is that innovation itself is not sufficient in the context of public services. There must also be a process that makes such innovations accessible to a broader range of users. After all, the major disadvantage of the third sector (at least from the perspective of *public* service delivery) is its particularistic nature, restricting improved quality to a select group of users. Indeed, this was historically one of the chief arguments for supporting a greater role of the state in financing and delivering welfare state services. In other words, whether innovation is a useful function of third-sector organizations depends not only on the performance of single organizations, but also on the ability of the overall field of organizations to transfer and adopt it. We shall therefore conceptualize innovation as a *collective* process.

We shall now proceed to discuss these two themes in more detail, describing the basic concepts and sketching some of the empirical evidence relating to them. Please note again that we are not making prior assumptions concerning the value of the third sector's contribution, but rather whittling down the variety of its potential contributions toward manageable and measurable concepts, for the systematic empirical research on the topic that is so badly needed.[4]

3. Co-production: citizen participation in service delivery

3.1. The co-production concept

Hirst (2002) argued that big organizations on either side of the public/private divide in advanced post-industrial societies leave little room for democracy or citizen influence. This is due to the lack of local control and democratic processes for internal decision-making in most big organizations. Evers (2006) maintained that user involvement in welfare services is a general concern throughout Europe and that there are at least five different approaches to involvement. They are partially overlapping and partially conflicting. They range from welfarism and professionalism, through consumerism and managerialism to what he calls participationalism. They are based on different values and promote different degrees of user involvement. These approaches will vary among sectors and over time. Their mix will probably differ among countries. Welfarism and professionalism are closely associated with each other, and neither leaves much room for user involvement. Rather, clients are viewed as people with little competence of their own. Consumerism and managerialism call for giving users greater choice through more exit options, and argue that the public sector needs to learn from the private sector (ibid.). However, they leave little room for voice or participation.

Participationalism encourages on-site participation by users of welfare services, based on the belief that citizens should engage personally in shaping the welfare services they demand. It emphasizes multi-stakeholder organizations and requires that users become co-producers. Welfarism and professionalism are usually promoted by social democratic governments, while consumerism and managerialism are normally championed by rightist governments. However, participationalism – or, more simply, co-production – lacks clear political proponents in most EU countries. In a service democracy of either the social democratic or rightist variety, citizens are the consumers of public-financed social services provided by municipal authorities, regional governments and private companies. They vote every fourth year and in the mean time they choose between various public or private service providers. This contrasts with views of participative democracy in which citizens are engaged in the provision of some of their own social services.

This is the background against which the concept of *co-production* has developed. The notion of citizen involvement in the provision of public services generated much interest among public administration scholars in America in the 1970s and the 1980s (see Parks et al. 1981 and 1999 for a good overview). It experienced somewhat of a revival with the publication at the turn of the century of a paper on incentives structures for co-production in Australian public services (Alford 2002) and in recent work on the Swedish welfare state (notably Pestoff 2006; Vamstad 2007). It was originally developed by the Workshop in Political Theory and Policy Analysis at Indiana University. During the 1970s they struggled with the dominant theories of urban governance underlying policy recommendations of massive centralization. Scholars and public officials argued that citizens as clients would receive more effective and efficient services if they were delivered by professional staff employed by a large bureaucratic agency. But this group of researchers found no empirical support for such claims promoting centralization (Ostrom 1999: 358).

They did, however, stumble on several myths of public production. One was the notion of a single producer being responsible for urban services within each jurisdiction. In fact, they normally found several agencies, as well as private firms, producing services. More important, they also realized that the production of a service, in contrast to goods, was difficult without the active participation of those receiving the service. They developed the term *co-production* to describe the potential relationship that could exist between the "regular" producer (street-level police officers, schoolteachers, or health workers) and "clients" who want to be transformed by the service into safer, better-educated or healthier persons. In complex societies there is a division of labor, and most persons are engaged in full-time production of goods and services as regular producers. However, individual consumers or groups of consumers may also contribute to the production of goods and services, as consumer-producers. This mixing may occur directly or indirectly. Co-production is, therefore, noted by the mix of activities that both public service agents and citizens contribute to the provision of public services. The former are involved as professionals or "regular producers", while "citizen production" is based on voluntary efforts of individuals or groups to enhance the quality and/or quantity of services they receive (Parks et al. 1981/1999). Co-production is one way in which a synergy could occur between what a government does and what citizens do (Ostrom 1999).

3.2. Empirical evidence

There is a lot of work on citizen participation, but relatively little in the context of service delivery. The TSFEPS Project[5] examined the relationship between parent participation in the provision and governance of childcare in eight EU countries (Pestoff 2006/2008). It found different levels of parent participation in different countries and in different forms of provision, i.e. public, private for-profit and third-sector childcare. The highest levels of parent participation were found in third-sector providers, like parent associations in France, parent initiatives in Germany and parent cooperatives in Sweden. Different kinds of parent participation (i.e. economic, political and social) were readily evident in third-sector providers of childcare services, while both economic and political participation were highly restricted in municipal and private for-profit services (ibid.). Later, Vamstad (2007) confirmed the existence of these three dimensions of co-production in Swedish childcare and underlined clear differences between types of providers concerning the saliency of these dimensions in providing welfare services (Pestoff 2008). This provides parents with unique possibilities for active participation in the management and running of their child(ren)'s childcare facility and for unique opportunities to become active co-producers of high-quality childcare services for their own and others' children. It is also clear that other forms of childcare allow for some limited avenues of co-production in publicly financed childcare, but that the parents' possibilities for influencing the management of such services remain rather limited.

In other words, existing empirical work appears to indicate that participation by individual citizens is best-facilitated by third-sector providers. What is less clear is why exactly this is the case and under what conditions co-production is most likely to be effective. So far, research on the topic has been conducted primarily (though not exclusively) in the context of social-democratic welfare regimes where service delivery is dominated by state provision. In such regimes, the third sector is least integrated within the structure of public service provision, which is arguably why co-production appears to function best within third-sector organizations. Sweden seems to be fertile ground for co-production (interestingly, this is the same country where the IKEA model of production originated, although there is no obvious connection). The objective for future comparative research is to determine how well co-production functions in other kinds of welfare-state regimes.

4. Innovations in public service delivery

4.1. The nature of innovation

Earlier, we defined innovation as a significant change in the process of production. A lot of third-sector literature appears to assume that the organizations in this domain are innovative by nature. After a review of the literature, Osborne (1998) concluded that studies on this topic relied on normative argument rather than on empirical data, were insufficiently aware of mainstream innovation-studies literature and failed to understand the contingencies of innovation, especially the impact of the public policy environment upon innovativeness. He argued that innovation emerges from the interaction of third-sector organizations with their institutional and policy environments. As we shall show, there is some evidence to support the latter claim.

A favorable institutional environment may be necessary not only to engender innovation within particular organizations but also to make sure that it spreads across to all other organizations. In this context, is worth turning to DiMaggio and Powell's (1991) classic study on isomorphism. They suggested that, once organizations are structured into a field, forces come into play which encourage similarity. In each organizational field there are a few true innovators who have the desire and the capacity to improve their performance by coming up with innovations. Other organizations will copy the ideas of these innovators, rather than innovate themselves. Particular innovations will thus gradually spread throughout the field. The aggregate effect of change will be diminished diversity, if not outright homogeneity, in the community that shares the innovations. One of the mechanisms through which this drive toward homogeneity occurs is imitation. Organizations voluntarily copy strategic elements from other organizations in their field ("mimetic isomorphism"). Another way is for people with similar educational backgrounds to come to dominate within fields of organizations ("normative isomorphism"). As they become more widespread, the innovations become more legitimate simply because they are widespread. Finally, the state or other powerful bodies in the environment may force organizations to adopt particular changes ("coercive isomorphism"). Whether and how such mechanisms affect the third sector is a significant empirical question, because, as far as innovation is concerned, it determines their significance to the public sector.

4.2. Empirical evidence

There is little systematic empirical work on the innovative capacity of third-sector organizations. The study by Osborne which we quoted earlier examined organizations in social welfare in the UK and found that the "policy context created by central and local government encouraged innovative activity by VCOs rather than it being an inherent consequence of their organizational structure or culture" (Osborne et al. 2008). Public policy was an important determinant of the extent and nature of innovation. Future research should further investigate the conditions under which government policy can be conducive to innovation. Research from the Netherlands shows evidence of a link between hybridization and innovation. As service-providers become more hybrid, and given that they have sufficient autonomy, they appear to start taking initiatives to reconcile the tension between their market, state and community characteristics. Such initiatives may be presented as "a focus on communities", "demand-driven supply", "putting the customer central", borrowing from both market or third-sector discourse, or both. In terms of organizational theory, it comes down to a strategy of diversification, possibly (though not necessarily) accompanied by a cognitive change in how the problems they need to solve are framed. This implies that organizations start to expand into new areas of activity where they believed their clients could be served better. Such diversification may even lead to a revision of the organizational mission. In an earlier article (Brandsen and Van Hout 2006) we examined the example of social housing, where social landlords gradually moved from a classical role of merely renting out their property on the basis of individual contracts to being leading members in programs of urban regeneration and community investment. They went beyond their original (bureaucratically defined) function and adopted a more holistic perspective, in which they would "revitalise communities" or something similar, treating their housing stock as a means rather than an end. This diversification may constitute an innovation at the level of the structure of service provision, if it is adopted throughout the field.

The second dimension of innovation concerns whether such strategies can spread beyond single organizations. In the context of public services, it is obvious that governments play an important role in disseminating innovation, by imposing ("mainstreaming") desired changes in service provision through regulation. The role of coercive isomorphism hardly needs mentioning in this context. There are theoretical reasons to suppose that the other types of isomorphism are less strong in the third sector than among other types of organizations, because it generally has a lower level of professionalization and is less tightly organized. However, they may be at play where third-sector organizations are tightly integrated in local and/or functional networks of service delivery. If innovation is interpreted as a collective effort, then it is the outcome of networks rather than of organizations, in the same sense that it would be for complex technological innovation (Powell et al. 1996). For instance, a case study in social housing in the Netherlands demonstrated that, although most organizations lacked a basic capacity to develop new ideas, the organizational field as a whole could progress because innovations by frontrunners were massively copied (Brandsen 2004). Within such a type of analysis, the process of innovation is conceived of as an interaction between organizations and the networks to which they belong (just as co-production emerges from the interaction of the organization and individual citizens).

If integration into public service networks is conducive to isomorphism, then the third sector has been most important to innovation in those institutional regimes where it is best-embedded and where it traditionally plays a pivotal role. This applies primarily to Bismarckian or conservative welfare states and to a lesser extent to Anglo-Saxon ones (even though the role of the third sector in the latter has often been understated).

5. Conclusion

In public governance, the third sector has come to play a more important role in public service delivery. Yet, despite many popular assertions, there is as yet only limited empirical evidence on the actual contribution of the third sector. This is not to say that it has none, simply that the available material refers to case studies (e.g. Titmuss' famous work from 1970 on blood donations) and that few studies have systematically analyzed the performance of the third sector under different conditions and in comparison with other types of providers. Such work as there is shows mixed results. It is imperative to continue and expand these studies over the coming years.

The conditions for setting up such a comparative program are better than they have been for a long time. There are now various third-sector research centers throughout Europe, which are connected through various cross-national research networks. In public management research, the third sector has become an established subtheme and one that benefits from the interest in new public governance. This will hopefully result in systematic comparative research into the benefits and drawbacks of the third sector's involvement in public service delivery, and perhaps in a debate that is based more on evidence and less on normative assumptions.

Notes

1 Indeed, some authors have defined the third sector as essentially hybrid, an indefinable area that as yet lacks a distinct identity (Brandsen et al. 2005). It could even be argued that the third sector is better-understood in terms of certain aspects of public services, rather than as a distinct cluster of organizations (Evers 2005; Brandsen et al. 2009).

2 It is clear that these two benefits can be empirically related, but they differ conceptually in that the former relates to the community as the primary object of analysis, whereas the latter is foremost about the system that produces services.

3 Osborne (2008) distinguishes between total innovation (involving working with a new client group and providing new services), expansionary innovation (involving working with a new client group, but using the existing services/methods of work of the organization), evolutionary innovation (involving working with the same client group, but providing new services), and incremental development (involving working with the same client group and providing the same services, but incrementally improving them).

4 It might be argued that our presentation could be strengthened by separating the analysis of the third sector in instrumental terms as a service deliverer from participatory approaches, where the third sector can perhaps enhance democratic participation. Each approach could then be presented independently. However, we feel that these two approaches are often implicitly or explicitly linked and sometimes inseparable. Therefore, we introduce each concept separately and present some initial empirical evidence for each within the same presentation. We deem it feasible for readers to distinguish between the two; and choose, therefore, not to present these two streams of analysis separately in independent chapters, for reasons of space and clarity.

5 The TSFEPS Project, Changing Family Structures and Social Policy: Childcare Services as Sources of Social Cohesion, took place in eight European countries between 2002 and 2004. See www.emes.net for details and reports. The eight countries were: Belgium, Bulgaria, England, France, Germany, Italy, Spain and Sweden.

References

Alford, J. (2002) "Why Do Public Sector Clients Co-produce? Towards a Contingency Theory", *Administration and Society*, 34 (1): 32–56.

Bode, I. (2008) *The Culture of Welfare Markets: The International Recasting of Pension and Care*, London/New York: Routledge.

Brandsen, T. (2004) *Quasi-market Governance: An Anatomy of Innovation*, Utrecht: Lemma.

Brandsen, T., Dekker, P. and Evers, A. (2009) *Civicness in the Governance and Delivery of Social Services*, Baden-Baden: Nomos.

Brandsen, T., van de Donk, W. and Putters, K. (2005) "Griffins or Chameleons? Hybridity as a Permanent and Inevitable Characteristic of the Third Sector", *International Journal of Public Administration*, 28 (9–10): 749–65.

Brandsen, T. and van Hout, E. (2006) "Co-management in Public Service Networks: The Organisational Effects", *Public Management Review*, 8 (4): 537–49.

Carmel, E. and Harlock, J. (2008) "Instituting the 'Third Sector' as a Governable Terrain: Partnership, Procurement and Performance in the UK", *Policy and Politics*, 36 (2): 155–71.

Cornforth, C. (2003) *The Governance of Nonprofit and Voluntary Organisations*, London: Routledge.

DiMaggio, P. J. and Powell, W. W. (1991b) "The Iron Cage Revisited: Institutional Isomorphism and Collective Rationality in Organizational Fields" in W. W. Powell and P. J. DiMaggio, eds., The New Institutionalism in Organizational Analysis, University of Chicago Press, pp. 63–82.

Esping-Andersen, Gösta (ed.) (1996) *Welfare States in Transition: National Adaptations in Global Economics*, London/Thousand Oaks, Calif./New Delhi: Sage.

Evers, Adalbert (1998) "Consumers, Citizens and Coproducers – a Pluralistic Perspective on Democracy in Social Services", in Gaby Flösser and Hans-Uwe Otto (eds) *Towards More Democracy in Social Services: Models and Culture of Welfare*, Berlin/New York: Walter de Gruyter.

Evers, A. (2005) "Mixed Welfare Systems and Hybrid Organizations: Changes in the Governance and Provision of Social Services", *International Journal of Public Administration*, 28 (9–10): 737–48.

Evers, A. (2006) "Complementary and Conflicting: The Different Meaning of 'User Involvement' in Social Services", in Aila-Leena Matthies (ed.) *Nordic Civic Society Organizations and the Future of Welfare Services: A Model for Europe?*, Copenhagen: Nordic Council of Ministers, TemaNord.

Evers, A. and Laville, J.-L. (eds) (2004) *The Third Sector in Europe*, Cheltenham: Edward Elgar.

Gidron, B., Kramer, R. M. and Salamon, L. M. (1992) "Government and the Third Sector in Comparative Perspective: Allies or Adversaries?", in B. Gidron, R. M. Kramer and L. M. Salamon (eds) *Government and the Third Sector: Emerging Relationships in Welfare States*, San Francisco, Calif.: Jossey-Bass.

Hirst, Paul (2002) "Democracy and Governance", in Jon Pierre (ed.) *Debating Governance, Authority, Steering and Democracy*, Oxford: Oxford University Press.

Kendall, J. and Knapp, M. (1995) "A Loose and Baggy Monster: Boundaries, Definitions and Typologies", in J. D. Smith, C. Rochester and R. Hedley (eds) *An Introduction to the Voluntary Sector*, London: Routledge, pp. 66–95.

Kuhnle, S. and Selle, P. (1992) "Government and Voluntary Organizations: A Relational Perspective", in S. Kuhnle and P. Selle (eds) *Government and Voluntary Organizations*, Aldershot: Avebury.

Kumar, S. (2003) *Accountability: A Qualitative Study of Relationships between the Public Sector, the Voluntary Sector and Users of Health and Welfare Services in the Context of Purchase of Service Contracting*, Birmingham: University of Aston.

Nyssens, M., Adam, S. and Johnson, T. (2006) *Social Enterprise: At the Crossroads of Market, Public Policies and Civil Society*, London: Routledge.

Osborne, S. P. (1998) *Voluntary Organizations and Innovation in Public Services*, London: Routledge.

Osborne, S. (2008) *The Third Sector in Europe: Prospects and Challenges*, London/New York: Routledge.

Osborne, S. P., Chew, C. and McLaughlin, K. (2008) "The Once and Future Pioneers? The Innovative Capacity of Voluntary Organisations and the Provision of Public Services: A Longitudinal Approach", *Public Management Review*, 10 (1): 51–70.

Ostrom, E. (1999) "Crossing the Great Divide: Coproduction, Synergy, and Development", in Michael D. McGinnis (ed.) *Polycentric Governance and Development: Readings from the Workshop in Political Theory and Policy Analysis*, Ann Arbor, Mich.: University of Michigan Press.

Parks, Roger B. et al. (1981/1999) "Consumers as Co-producers of Public Services: Some Economic and Institutional Considerations", *Policy Studies Journal*, 9: 1001–11; and reprinted in Michael D. McGinnis (ed.) *Local Public Economies: Readings from the Workshop in Political Theory and Policy Analysis*, Ann Arbor, Mich.: University of Michigan Press.

Pestoff, Victor (2006/2008) "Citizens as Co-producers of Welfare Services: Childcare in Eight European Countries", *Public Management Review*, 8 (4): 503–20; and reprinted in Victor Pestoff and Taco Brandsen (eds) *Co-production: The Third Sector and the Delivery of Public Services*, London/New York: Routledge.

Pestoff, V., Osborne, S. and Brandsen, T. (2006) "Patterns of Co-production in Public Services: Some Concluding Thoughts", *Public Management Review*, 8 (4): 591–5.

Powell, W. W., Koput, K. W. and Smith-Doerr, L. (1996) "Interorganizational Collaboration and the Locus of Innovation: Networks of Learning in Biotechnology", *Administrative Science Quarterly*, 41: 116–46.

Salamon, L. M. (1995) *Partners in Public Service: Government–Nonprofit Relations in the Modern Welfare State*, Baltimore, Md/London: Johns Hopkins University Press.

Smith, S. R. and Grønbjerg, K. A. (2006) "Scope and Theory of Government–Nonprofit Relations", in W. W. Powell and R. Steinberg (eds) *The Nonprofit Sector: A Research Handbook*, 2nd edn, New Haven, Conn.: Yale University Press.

Titmuss, R. M. (1974) *Social Policy: An Introduction*, London: George Allen & Unwin.

Vamstad, Johan (2007) "Governing Welfare: The Third Sector and the Challenges to the Swedish Welfare State"; Östersund: Ph.D. Thesis, No. 37.

Zimmer, A. and Stecker, C. (2004) *Strategy Mix for Nonprofit Organisations: Vehicles for Social and Labour Market Integration*, New York: Kluwer/Plenum.

Part III

GOVERNANCE OF CONTRACTUAL RELATIONSHIPS

14

GOVERNANCE, CONTRACT MANAGEMENT AND PUBLIC MANAGEMENT

Donald F. Kettl

In the late 1970s and early 1980s, citizens throughout the world pressed their elected officials to shrink the size of government. It did not matter what the actual size of government was. From the large Scandinavian welfare states to the relatively smaller governments in the United States, the government-limitation movement ignited and spread (Pollitt and Bouckaert 2000). Citizens, of course, had little interest in reducing the services they received. They wanted substantial government programs but they wanted to spend less, because they were convinced that government had become too bloated and inefficient.

That created a dilemma for government officials: how to avoid enraging citizens by cutting services they liked, and how to devise new strategies to shrink government's size and cost. The central strategy was privatization: selling enterprises to the private sector, where they could find buyers, and expanding the contracting out of goods and services, where they could find willing partners (Savas 2000). Some governments sold airlines, railroads, telecommunications companies, utilities and the post. Other governments expanded their use of contracting out and other partnerships with the private and nonprofit sectors (Schick 1996; English and Guthrie 2003; Albalate, Bel and Fageda 2007). Getting a good fix on this vast collection of activity is notoriously difficult. Most governments do not keep good records on the variety or volume of activity that is outsourced, and what little data there are are often not comparative over time. For example, in the United States, the Federal Procurement Data System tracked contract data, but the database was often unreliable.

Of all the strategies, contracting out poses the most fundamental, ongoing governance and public management puzzles. Once a government sells an enterprise, its governance responsibilities do not end. Taxpayers might have seller's remorse about the good old days when taxpayers supported services. More important, governments typically retain a regulatory role in ensuring the quality and safety of the services. In the United Kingdom, for example, balancing government regulation of the railroads with relying on the profit motive has been an ongoing struggle. Separating rail infrastructure and maintenance has proved especially problematic (Preston 1996). Although critics argued that the UK reforms had undermined safety, there is no evidence that overall safety has deteriorated (Evans 2007). Heavy pressure to meet schedules tended to undercut long-term maintenance and, critics argued, managing government contracts poses the most complicated ongoing puzzle because it brings in fundamental boundary challenges – what is public and what is private – and a different combination of management puzzles – how the public sector can gain leverage over the performance of private organizations (Osborne 2002).

It is tempting to point to the government-limitation movement as the watershed of these challenges. In fact, contracting out stretches back millennia. Caesar's chronicles of his campaigns are full of tales of managing the procurement of supplies for his troops. He could, of course, have relied on an extended supply-line from Rome to the furthest reaches of the empire, but that would have been extremely difficult to create and maintain. Backed by the strongest army in the world, ready to take what it could not buy, Caesar found it easier simply to procure what he needed from the locals. Machiavelli wrote about the outsourcing of an entire army. Sometimes this came at the point of a lance, but it was part of a millennia-old government reliance on procurement from private suppliers. It has been called by a wide variety of names, from "contracting out" to "competitive tendering" to "outsourcing", but interest in the movement is strong and growing. Not only are governments relying on private suppliers of goods and services, from paper and pencils to trucks and buses; they are quite literally sharing power with their private-sector partners (Kettl 1993). While the modern contracting movement has grown rapidly in the United States and Australia, in particular, it has spread to many countries around the world, especially in Australia and Britain (Boston 2000; Pollitt and Bouckaert 2000).

Governments have sometimes relied on such procurement because it was more convenient, sometimes because it was cheaper, sometimes because it made pragmatic sense. Powerful armies can simply take what they need; but that is an expensive way to provision an empire, for it requires a large army to extract the goods and services and to maintain order. In the long run, it is easier for governments to buy what they need than to take it, and over time a body of procurement law has grown up to shape and govern the procurement system (Gellhorn et al. 2003).

In the United States, for example, contracting out goes back to the nation's first days. During the American revolution, the army contracted out for arms and provisions, and General George Washington constantly complained that his suppliers were defrauding the government and stealing the higher-quality goods from his troops. In fact, throughout American

Table 14.1 Presence of contractor personnel during US military operations

Conflict	*Estimated personnel (thousands)* Contractor[a]	Military	*Estimated ratio of contractor to military personnel*[a]
Resolutionary War	2	9	1 to 6
War of 1812	n.a.	38	n.a.
Mexican-American War	6	33	1 to 6
Civil War	200	1,000	1 to 5
Spanish-American War	n.a.	35	n.a.
World War I	85	2,000	1 to 24
World War II	734	5,400	1 to 7
Korea	156	393	1 to 2.5
Vietnam	70	359	1 to 5
Gulf War	9[b]	500	1 to 55[b]
Balkans	20	20	1 to 1
Iraq Theater as of Early 2008[c]	190	200	1 to 1

Source: Congressional Budget Office based on data from William W. Epley, "Civilian Support of Field Armies," *Army Logistician*, vol. 22 (November/December 1990), pp. 30–35; Steven J. Zomparelli, "Contractors on the Battlefield: What Have We Signed Up For?" *Air Force Journal of Logistics*, vol. 23, no. 3 (Fall 1999), pp. 10–19; Department of Defense, *Report on DoD Program for Planning, Managing, and Accounting for Contractor Services and Contractor Personnel During Contingency Operations* (October 2007), p. 12.

Note: n.a. = not available.

a. For some conflicts, the estimated number of contractor personnel includes civilians employed by the US government. However, because most civilians present during military operations are contractor personnel, the inclusion of government civilians should not significantly affect the calculated ratio of contractor personnel to military personnel.

b. The government of Saudi Arabia provided significant amounts of products and services during Operations Desert Shield and Desert Storm. Personnel associated with those provisions are not included in the data or the ratio.

c. For this study, the Congressional Budget Office considers the following countries to be part of the Iraq theater, Bahrain, Jordan, Kuwait, Oman, Qatar, Saudi Arabia, Turkey, and the United Arab Emirates.

Source: http://cbo.gov/ftpdocs/96xx/doc9688/08-12-IraqContractors.pdf, p. 13.

history, the government has relied heavily on contractors for fighting wars. In the Revolutionary War, launched against the British in 1776, there was a contractor employee for every six soldiers (see Table 14.1). That ratio held steady for the next century of conflicts. By the war in Iraq in early 2008, there was a contractor employee for every soldier, a ratio that proved important not only for logistical support but also for reducing political opposition. If the American army had relied on soldiers for operations contracted out, six times the number of soldiers would have been required. This would have been a force unsupportable except through a large-scale draft, and it would unquestionably have stirred insurmountable political opposition.

The contracting-out process thus has deep roots but a modern focus. Governments rely on contracts to obtain goods and services they cannot – or do not wish to – produce on their own. They contract out to reduce their costs and to create at least the appearance of smaller governments, because only rarely do they transparently track the number of contractors or the amount of money spent through them. Contractors allow government to expand without increasing their size – at least as measured by the number of government employees (Light 1999). Although obtaining good numbers on the contracting-out process is difficult in individual countries, and impossible on a global scale, all signs point to a dramatic increase in the use of this indirect tool of government since the tax-limitation movement began in the late 1970s (Pollitt and Bouckaert 2000). The contracting-out movement has rippled throughout the world, in part because governments have always contracted out and in part because an expansion of the movement provided a tactical solution to the cross-pressures governments have faced (McLaughlin, Osborne and Ferlie 2002). From more traditional government contracts to purchase goods and services to the use of public–private partnerships to fund transportation projects, the interpenetration of the public and private sectors is large and growing.

Public management puzzles

As contracting out has increased, however, government's capacity to manage the contracts has not kept pace. While many contracts have worked very well, serious problems have emerged with many contracts. The most notable catalog of problems comes from the "high-risk list" assembled by the US Government Accountability Office. The GAO identifies programs that, it believes, are especially susceptible to waste and mismanagement. In 2008, its high-risk list numbered twenty-eight programs, including the management of contracts for defense and space programs, and the modernization of information systems for tax collection and air traffic control. In fact, virtually all of the items on the GAO's list involve substantial contracting out – except for the management areas like human capital and information technology required to run the contracts (US GAO 2008a).

Moreover, many countries are reforming their regulatory strategies for overseeing private-sector contracts. For example, as contaminants have crept into the production chain for pharmaceuticals, the European Union and many other governmental bodies have sought to redefine how best to regulate the quality and safety of drugs. Thus, governments are not only relying more on contracting for producing their own goods and services; they are also finding themselves drawn inexorably into regulating the contracting processes of private companies whose products affect the public interest (Brown and Jacobs 2008).

These challenges frame a critical issue: contracts raise serious governance problems, and a failure to solve them brings major consequences. It is not so much that contracts are, by their very nature, harder to manage than other government tools. Rather, contracts must be managed *differently* from other tools, like direct tools, regulations and tax expenditures (Salamon 2002). What works well in managing direct government services, especially through the traditional approach of hierarchical authority, frequently does not work well at all for contracts. In direct provision of government services, superiors rely on authority to oversee their subordinates, who work underneath them in the agency's hierarchy. In contracts, by comparison, government officials oversee performance through the negotiated provisions of the contract, enforced by civil law. Governments have often encountered serious problems in managing their contracts because they have relied on the tools for managing direct contracts in seeking to steer the performance of contracts (Kettl 2002). When there is a mismatch of management tools and governance tactics, problems result – much as would be the case for using a hammer to drive a screw or a saw to loosen a bolt.

Governments frequently slide into this mismatch because the ideology promoting contracting out tends to presume that contracts will be self-executing. The argument is simple. Private markets are believed superior to governments, because of the discipline that the marketplace provides. The forces of supply and demand provide self-correcting forces for problems of price and quality. So turn government's work over to the private sector and the markets will ensure effective and efficient services. Of course, no private purchaser would blindly trust the market with piles of money when buying important goods and services. That is the central meaning of *caveat emptor*. Public antipathy toward government sometimes overpowers the lessons that smart private buyers know all too well. Contracts, of course, are not self-executing, and governments need to behave as smart private-sector buyers do: to know what they want to buy, to deal in markets that will provide what they need, and to ensure that what they get is what they wanted (Kettl 1993; Padovani and Young 2006, 2008).

Moreover, private market discipline depends on competitive markets, with large numbers of buyers dealing with large numbers of sellers about goods whose nature and performance are relatively straightforward. In many government services, however, these conditions of market discipline are lacking; that is, there are what economists call "market failures". Such market failures constitute an age-old case for government intervention. The paradox of the contracting-out movement, therefore, is that the expansion of contracting out, as part of a movement to shrink government, has built a case for stronger government action, but in a different mode for which governments sometimes are ill-prepared. As government's contracting out grows into new areas, these problems of market failure multiply and bring new governance challenges.

The nature of goods and services

Governments contract for a vast array of goods and services. Some are relatively homogenous goods and services, from custodial and food services to automobiles and trucks. In fact, in some countries, governments have largely eliminated the jobs of government employees who used to serve as janitors and cafeteria workers – even security staff – and have contracted out those positions. But governments also contract out for a wide variety of non-standard items. Contractors often pilot unmanned drones thousands of miles away from the battlefield while sitting next to military officials. Governments rely on contractors to process the claims for government-funded health benefits and for programs to provide job skills to unemployed workers.

The further the contracting-out process moves from relatively standard goods and services, the further the process moves from full market competition and the harder it is to rely on market discipline. Private companies, of course, know this. They do not simply pay for everything their suppliers want to sell them and they do not blindly accept the low bid. In fact, for even mildly unusual goods and services – and especially for important items on which their businesses depend – private companies often seek a predictable supply of high-quality goods as much as the lowest cost (Donahue 1989). An automobile assembly line will quickly break down if the lowest bidder cannot reliably deliver seats or if windows break as workers try to install them. The growth of contracting out has taken government deeper into more of these non-standard areas, including weapons production, environmental services, transportation systems, social services, and a host of other areas. The very nature of these goods and services has taken contractors deeper into the full range of government's goods and services, and farther from the basic assumptions of market discipline.

The lesson is that even private companies do not negotiate contracts solely on the basis of price. These considerations of quality and reliability often take government away from the underlying assumptions that drove the expansion of government contracting, and more into issues that require detailed contract provisions.

Monopoly

Analysts have long known that the virtues of markets quickly erode if buyers have few sellers from which to choose. For many government programs, that is precisely the case. When the American government sought to buy a new-generation fleet of aerial refueling tankers, it had only two options: Boeing and EADS, the manufacturer of Airbus. Contractors spend 90 percent of the budget for America's space shuttle, but NASA works through United Space Alliance, a consortium of the two biggest aerospace contractors, Boeing and Lockheed Martin, because neither company was big enough to manage the project on its own (NASA 2003: 104). In a host of cases, from fighter planes to aerial tankers, and from submarines to social-service programs, government often has limited choice for companies providing specialized goods and services.

In fact, because many of these programs would not exist were it not for public purchases, government must often first create the partnerships and then seek to manage them. Contracting out for relatively standard goods and services is one thing, but the expansion of government contracting has necessarily brought government into policy areas where there are relatively few contracts. This raises the fundamental warning of economists: if government is presumed inefficient because of its monopoly status, private monopolies are unlikely to be any better. After all, it is not the publicness or privateness of service provision that, according to the argument for privatization, promotes greater efficiency. It is competition and choice. When there is little of either, government is unlikely to reap big savings and is very likely to court governance problems in countering the market failures. This does not mean that contracting out does not make sense in monopoly conditions. Indeed, government might wish to rely on contractors for expertise in areas where it lacks specialized skills or does not wish to invest in building them. But, when it contracts with monopolistic suppliers, government must be on the alert for the dangers of market failure and must adjust its own strategies to counter it (Padovani and Young 2006).

Monopsony

Economic analysts have long recognized the failures that follow from markets where there are few suppliers. But there are also risks that occur in markets in which there are few buyers. For many goods and services for which the government contracts out, it is the only buyer. Government is the only purchaser of long-range bombers and attack fighters, of nuclear submarines and aircraft carriers, of nuclear weapons and anti-aircraft rockets (although government officials fear the creation of black markets among terrorists for some of these items). Worries about the spread of strategically important technology and about relying on suppliers in other countries for strategic goods often further reduce the number of potential suppliers. In functions like the provision of social services, government is not the only buyer. International nongovernmental organizations like the Red Cross also play a substantial role in such functions; but, as government's contracting out has increased, in many countries it has come to dominate the markets for the provision of such services.

The argument for outsourcing begins with the presumed superiority of market competition. However, when government is the only buyer, private suppliers become dependent on government for their sales, which in turn disrupts market competition. Governments have no way of determining from the market what a fair price or good performance means, because without their role as buyer there would be no price, no performance and no market. For many goods and services, the market failures multiply: government is often the only buyer and frequently must deal with a very small number of potential sellers for goods and services where the government marketplace often is the only one.

This is not to say that such imperfect markets, with limited numbers of buyers and sellers, are inherently problematic. Neither is it necessarily the case that the absence of market competition necessarily means that the government should not rely on private contractors. Rather, it means that the government's reliance on private markets for such goods and services is more likely to be based on pragmatism than on low price. In World War II, for example, the US government used private contractors throughout the country to build the first nuclear weapons, because it did not wish to build and manage the factories itself and because it wished to scatter production to protect the facilities from attack. Instead it relied on GOCOs – government-owned, contractor-operated plants – to provide the expertise and flexibility needed to produce such complex systems (Kettl 2002). That arrangement grew into an effective partnership that lasted sixty years. The relationship had little of the market competition that privatization advocates point to as the process's basic virtue. In fact, it was a relationship of both monopoly supply and monopsony purchase, yet it worked well.

At the state and local levels of government in the United States, for example, governments have contracted out the contracting out of social service provision. For example, in Philadelphia, the social service system was a complex maze of government employees and private contractors. The city spent US$612 million to provide services to 20,000 children, with 820 social workers managing the services through a network of 348 contracts. The quality of services depended ultimately on the ability of the public and private nodes of the network to connect. The New York City childcare system has likewise been plagued with the difficulty of managing hundreds of agencies to which the city outsourced services (Young 1974).

The lesson is that the expansion of government contracting into more areas has not necessarily reduced government's role. It has transformed its role from supplier to manager of its contracts and has increased the need for it to be alert to the risks of monopolistic supply. This is not necessarily a more difficult job than managing a traditional authority-based hierarchy. Overseeing the contracting out of cafeteria or custodial services, for example, is relatively straightforward (although ensuring high-quality services through a reliable workforce is always a tough job). However, managing a contract requires a fundamentally different skill set – negotiating a contract, overseeing its execution, and assessing its results – from that required for managing direct service provision by government employees. As we shall see, some contracted-out services are indeed more difficult to administer, but contracting out is not inherently more difficult to manage than direct service provision. It is, however, fundamentally different, and those challenges escalate when government must work with monopolies.

Service integration

The complexities of these systems have increasingly led governments to rely on service integration contractors. Instead of purchasing goods and services directly from suppliers, government contracts with a general contractor, who in turn contracts out with other suppliers for the production of the good or service. In many cases, the service integrator is responsible not only for general oversight of the project but also for designing many of its key elements (Kettl 2009). Many new systems, from space shuttles to military fighting vehicles, have become so complex that government finds it easier to contract out the entire system, from design through all of the production stages. United Space Alliance is an example of such a service integration contract, but it extends much farther into functions as broad as social services and defense projects.

Such service integration contracts stretch to other levels of government and into other functional areas. The US Marine Corps, for example, invested a decade's work and $1.7 billion into a new amphibious fighting vehicle. However, the system proved extremely trouble-prone. It broke down once every four and a half hours, leaked, and was hard to steer. The vehicle fell well short of the Marine Corps' expectations; but the contractor, General Dynamics, nevertheless received $80 million in bonuses for its work. The core of the problem, government investigators concluded, was that the Pentagon had insisted on an overly complex system and had contracted out much of the design and production work – it had contracted out the contracting out, and the Marines lacked sufficient expertise to oversee the process. Military planners feared that they might have to start over with a fresh design and a new system (US GAO 2008b).

The rise of these service-integration contracts has had important implications for the service system. As government has contracted out not only the production but also the design, intellectual capital has flowed to the managing contractors. The capacity of government agencies to understand fully what they are buying, how much the goods and services ought to cost, how well programs are working, and how to fix any problems erodes as expertise drifts to the private sector. NASA investigations into both the *Challenger* and *Columbia* accidents found that the agency had become heavily dependent on its contractors for life-and-death judgments. In the *Challenger* disaster, it was a private contractor that had the important expertise on the effect of cold weather on the rubber O-rings, the failure of which doomed the shuttle seconds after launch. In the case of *Columbia*, NASA had to rely on its contractors to assess the flightworthiness of the shuttle. It did not have sufficient expertise in-house to exercise independent final judgment (NASA 2003).

In all these cases, government employees played the role of contract manager. There was nothing inherently wrong with this role. The problem was that its employees typically were trained as functional specialists. In the Marines, contract managers supervised the paper flow but lacked the expertise to make and oversee the key technical decisions. In Philadelphia, the employees charged with overseeing the contracts were social workers, who went to work for DHS to do social work. As the private and non-profit service network expanded, they became contract managers. Even that could have worked – except that the workers were trained as social workers, they had not been trained as contract managers, and the mismatch proved fatal to a 14-year-old girl, Danieal Kelly, whose problems the system failed to solve.

This unfortunate tale surfaces a broader set of problems. Not only is contracting out increasingly problematic because of the strategic mismatch between its ideological rationale – rely on the presumed superiority of private-market competition for delivering public services – and its reality – contracting out in many areas with substantial market imperfections; there is also the tactical mismatch in its management, between government employees hired for their substantial knowledge, in understanding programmatic goals, and the functions these employees actually perform, in managing the contractors who work to achieve those goals.

Contracting out has thus drifted a long way from the original goals that drove its growth. Market competition might indeed produce high-quality goods at low cost; but in many areas in government contracting, especially in the most important growth areas, there is little real market competition. In the process, much of government's substantive work has drifted into the hands of government contractors, leaving government employees with contract management responsibilities for which they are poorly prepared. The problem lies not with the contracting-out strategy but with its execution – and with the faulty assumption that the magic of the markets will assure high-quality services at low costs. The result, too often, is like baking a cake without flour.

Public management strategies

Does this mean that the dramatic expansion of contracting out, both in the United States and in many other nations around the world, is a fundamental mistake in the search for democratic governance? Do the performance problems that flow from this double mismatch argue for retreating on the contracting-out movement?

Dependence on contractors

The first answer is that this is a hypothetical question. Governments have become so dependent on contractors that retreating on the strategy would demand a very large increase in the number of government employees – a decision that would be difficult indeed to support in a political era focused on limiting government's size and reach. Re-publicization is rare. For example, in the aftermath of the 11 September terrorist attacks, the federal government decided to shift responsibility for airline security screening from the private sector to the government. It took a major terrorist attack to prompt such a decision, and the move stands in stark contrast to the decision by many other nations to contract out security screening. In virtually all other cases, contracting out is expanding into new areas, in part because it sometimes is cheaper. It often allows governments to reduce the number of public employees, and thus to create at least the illusion of smaller government (Light 1999). Most important, it allows government to obtain additional operating flexibility and invaluable expertise that would be very difficult to build within government itself. Rolling back the contracting-out movement seems very unlikely.

Performance issues

Second, the performance problems that have come from the outsourcing movement are not necessarily inherent. Government cannot typically rely on self-regulating market competition to ensure high success and low cost, but it can strengthen its capacity to act as a "smart buyer". It is one thing to contract out the production of goods and services to private suppliers. It is quite another to contract out the basic decisions about what goods and services to buy, how those goods and services should be designed, and how well they work. No private automobile company would willingly surrender to another firm the basic questions about what its cars ought to look like, how the sound systems would perform, or what mileage the engine should get; yet in some cases governments have contracted out just such basic decisions. It is scarcely surprising that such strategies have developed problems, for they bring neither the discipline of the markets nor the authority of governmental expertise. It will be impossible in most cases to restore market competition to those areas where it is lacking. Government would not wish to encourage private buyers for some goods, like nuclear weapons, and in many areas private sellers would not want to enter the markets without some assurance from government that their investments would produce profits. Government faces the inescapable challenge of building the capacity to manage its contracts more effectively.

Human capital issues

Third, this implies that a central core of government's challenge in contract management is a human resources issue. If government wants to ensure better performance in its contract systems, it will need to create and train better governmental contract managers. This, of course, is an inherent problem. In most governments, contract management is not a high-prestige field, and few government employees enter the public workforce with contract management as a career goal. Social workers join government to do social work; environmentalists to work on the environment; space scientists to do space science. This creates the human resources dilemma of a government that relies more on contracting out: those who join the government to pursue their substantive interests often end up in jobs that require them to manage contracts instead, where others do the work for which they trained; and those with the skills to perform contract management find themselves in lower-prestige positions. The effective management of contracts requires government human-resource planners to focus more attention on contracting out and to ensure that the employees overseeing contracts have the skills needed to do so. If social workers end up overseeing contracts without the necessary competencies, they will be unhappy, and program management will surely suffer.

What competencies do contract managers need? They must have strong substantive backgrounds, so that they can understand the issues that bubble up from the contractors; and they must be quick students in complex areas, so that they can steer contracts in the direction that governmental policy requires. They must be adept negotiators. They must be good financial managers, for control of the money flow is typically the strongest control of programmatic results. They must be good auditors, to ensure that money ends up going where they intend. They must be able to evaluate the outcomes of these complex relationships among government, contractors and subcontractors, so that they can assess whether government is getting its money's worth. They must, in short, be experts in steering complex processes (US GAO 2009). These competencies, of course, are a long distance from the arguments, often ideological, that promote the spread of contracting out; but without these skills government is likely to be steered by the contractors instead of the other way around. Government does not need to know more than its contractors. If it did, it might well not need them (or, at least, not need as many of them). But it must know enough to ensure that the private contractors are held accountable to public policy.

Information issues

Fourth, government needs to build a far more effective information system for tracking how the money flows and what the contracts produce. In most countries, it is impossible for anyone – even top government officials – to know how much money contractors are spending, and what their role is in shaping each program. A product of the anti-government privatization movement is that its promoters believed at the core of their being that private provision of goods and services is so inherently superior and self-regulating that there was no need to manage or measure the process. Government, however, does indeed need to track where its money goes and what it buys. Sometimes the battle is over the basic assumption that government ought to behave more like the private sector. But no private company would give its suppliers a blank check and fail to track how the money was spent (Hatry 2007; Poister 2003). If government is going to rely more on the private sector and to be called on to act more like the private sector, then it needs to follow other parts of this mantra as well, including building its capacity to oversee the flow of its money (that is, of taxpayer's money).

Transparency

Fifth, the contracting-out process needs far more transparency. A side-effect of the contracting-out movement has been an increasing difficulty in determining just who is doing what on behalf of the people while spending the people's money. The rise of service-integration contractors has even further muddied the trail, for it has made it even more difficult to determine who is making the important decisions. Moreover, contracting out is, of course, more than just about accomplishing the public's business. For contractors, it is about getting, keeping and expanding business, and the contracting-out process has, not surprisingly, tended to create problems of corruption. For example, a former US Department of Defense official was indicted for steering the US$23.5 billion aerial tanker project to Boeing and then taking a job at the big aerospace contractor.

As more decision-making power has flowed to private-sector companies, the challenge of identifying, preserving and promoting the public interest has grown. Laws can prohibit corruption and reduce the chances of the appearance of corruption, but the conflicting incentives of a governance system with more contracting out requires an even higher standard of transparency, sometimes beyond the level that many private companies find comfortable.

This transparency can come in many ways. In the United States, for example, the federal government has created a database, USASpending.gov, that allows citizens to search for who gets how much money and where it goes. While a US Senator, Barack Obama was a prime architect of the website, and his work on the project gave powerful clues about his instincts for web-based, information-driven accountability strategies. At the federal level, the Government Accountability Office's "high-risk list" has focused its auditing and evaluation work on the programs most prone to fraud, waste and abuse. But these efforts have often fallen short of public expectations and have failed to direct public attention to the core of many problems. More transparency cannot solve these problems, but without it there can be no solution at all.

Governance challenges

The deep realities of contracting out are very different from the rhetoric that helped feed its growth and the public's expectations about how it works. While often portrayed as a new movement, it is in fact as old as government itself. While often argued as a way to reduce government's size and scope, it has often brought government more deeply into the fabric of private organizations. While often presumed superior to government action because of the power of private markets, it often operates in arenas with substantial market failure. While often thought to be self-executing, it requires a strong and transformed role for government.

This does not make it good or bad in itself – just different from the ways in which government has traditionally been structured and governed. Indeed, contracting out is neither good nor bad. Governments have embraced it because of important, probably irreversible political and pragmatic realities. Government's most fundamental governance challenge, therefore, is to discover more effective strategies to ensure it works well. There is an endless stream of tales of mismanagement that has come from poorly managed contracts. These tales will spread and worsen if the trend toward increasing government contracting grows without a simultaneous growth in its ability to manage and govern the system it has created.

The job is eminently doable, but doing it will require a fresh approach to governance – one that develops new approaches to govern the new realities of government contracting. Government will need to focus on performance, on the results that contracts produce, instead of on the processes along the way. It will need to develop human capital, especially inside public agencies, so that government has the capacity to oversee the contracts it negotiates. It will need effective information systems, reinforced by greater transparency, to provide more effective feedback. In short, it needs a government robust enough to govern the systems it creates. It needs twenty-first-century approaches to govern effectively the realities of its twenty-first-century governmental tools.

References

Albalate, Daniel, Bel, Germa and Fageda, Xavier (2007) *Privatization and Regulation of Toll Motorways in Europe*, University of Barcelona, Research Institute of Applied Economics, IREA Working Papers.

Boston, Jonathan (2000) "Organizing for Service Delivery: Criteria and Opportunities," in B. Guy Peters and Donald J. Savoie (eds) *Governance in the Twenty-first*

Century: Revitalizing the Public Service, Montreal: Canadian Centre for Management Development.

Brown, Lawrence D. and Jacobs, Lawrence R. (2008) *The Private Abuse of the Public Interest: Market Myths and Policy Muddles*, Chicago, Ill.: University of Chicago Press.

Donahue, John D. (1989) *The Privatization Decision: Public Ends, Private Means*, New York: Basic Books.

English, Linda M. and Guthrie, James (2003) "Driving Privately Financed Projects in Australia: What Makes Them Tick?", *Accounting, Auditing and Accountability Journal*, 16 (3): 493–511.

Evans, Andrew W. (2007) "Rail Safety and Rail Privatisation in Britain", *Accident Analysis and Prevention*, 39 (3): 510–23.

Gellhorn, Walter, Byse, Clark, Strauss, Peter L., Rakoff, Todd and Farina, Cynthia R. (2003) *Administrative Law, Cases and Comments*, 10th edn, Mineola, NY: Foundation Press.

Hatry, Harry (2007) *Performance Measurement*, 2nd edn, Washington, DC: The Urban Institute.

Kettl, Donald F. (1993) *Sharing Power: Public Governance and Private Markets*, Washington, DC: The Brookings Institution.

Kettl, Donald F. (2002) "Managing Indirect Government", in Lester M. Salamon (ed.) *The Tools of Government: A Public Management Handbook for the Era of Third-party Government*, New York: Oxford University Press.

Kettl, Donald F. (2009) *The Next Government of the United States: Why Our Institutions Fail Us and How to Fix Them*, New York: W. W. Norton.

Light, Paul C. (1999) *The True Size of Government*, Washington, DC: The Brookings Institution.

McLaughlin, Kate, Osborne, Stephen P. and Ferlie, Ewan (2002) *New Public Management: Current Trends and Future Prospects*, Abingdon: Routledge.

National Aeronautics and Space Administration (NASA) (2003) *Report of the Columbia Accident Investigation Board*, at http://www.nasa.gov/columbia/caib/PDFS/VOL1/PART02.PDF

Osborne, Stephen P. (ed.) (2002) *Public Management: Critical Perspectives*, Abingdon: Routledge.

Padovani, Emanuele and Young, David (2006) "Managing High-risk Outsourcing", *Public Management*, 88 (1): 29–32.

Padovani, Emanuele and Young, David (2008) "Toward a Framework for Managing High-risk Government Outsourcing: Field Research in Three Italian Municipalities", *Journal of Public Procurement*, 8 (2): 215–47.

Poister, Theodore H. (2003) *Measuring Performance in Public and Nonprofit Organizations*, San Francisco, Calif.: Jossey-Bass.

Pollitt, Christopher and Bouckaert, Geert (2000) *Public Management Reform: A Comparative Analysis*, Oxford: Oxford University Press.

Preston, John (1996) "The Economics of British Rail Privatization: An Assessment", *Transport Reviews*, 16 (1): 1–21.

Salamon, Lester M. (ed.) (2002) *The Tools of Government: A Public Management Handbook for the Era of Third-party Government*, New York: Oxford University Press.

Savas, E. S. (2000) *Privatization and Public–private Partnerships*, New York: Chatham House.

Schick, Allen (1996) *The Spirit of Reform: Managing the New Zealand State Sector in a Time of Change*, Wellington: State Services Commission.

United States Government Accountability Office (2008a) "GAO's High-risk Areas as of March 2008", at http://www.gao.gov/docsearch/featured/highrisk_march2008.pdf

United States Government Accountability Office (2008b) *Defense Acquisition: Assessments of Selected Weapon Programs*, GAO-08-467SP, Washington, DC: US Government Accountability Office, at http://www.gao.gov/new.items/d08467sp.pdf

United States Government Accountability Office (2009) *Human Capital: Opportunities Exist to Build on Recent Progress to Strengthen DOD's Civilian Human Capital Strategic Plan*, GAO-09-235, Washington, DC: US Government Accountability Office, at http://www.gao.gov/products/GAO-09-235

Young, David W. (1974) "Referral and Placement in Child Care: The New York City Purchase of Service System", *Public Policy*, 22 (3): 293–327.

15

GOVERNANCE OF OUTSOURCING AND CONTRACTUAL RELATIONSHIPS[1]

Federica Farneti, Emanuele Padovani and David W. Young

Many public sector organizations (PSOs) rely on outsourcing as a way of increasing their "value for money" in the provision of public services (Broadbent and Guthrie 2008). As a result, the topic of outsourcing has been addressed with some regularity in the public management literature for many years. Increasingly, attention is being directed toward the nature of the risk associated with an outsourced activity, and the resulting implications for (Considine 1999, 2001; Considine and Lewis 2003) PSO managers.

In this chapter, we present a framework that PSO managers can use to assess the nature of the risk they face in an outsourcing decision, and juxtapose it with alternative governance models. We argue that, as the risk associated with an outsourced service increases, so, too, does the sophistication of the governance model a PSO needs to use to manage it. Thus, the decision to outsource a high-risk service must depend, in part, on whether the PSO has the capability to use the requisite governance model.

We begin by discussing the roots of outsourcing, with a particular focus on Four-governance Model framework. We assess his framework in light of our empirical research in Italian PSOs that led to our model for assessing outsourcing risk, and we argue that a PSO does not need to have a single governance model, or even a highly sophisticated one. Rather, it may need several governance models operating simultaneously, each attuned to the risk associated with the outsourced service being managed.

The outsourcing context

In some countries, the impetus for outsourcing has been legislative. In the UK, for example, although competitive outsourcing had been taking place for some time, the Local Government Act of 1988 required it at the municipal level. Similarly, as part of its public-sector reform initiative, New Zealand required municipalities to use public–private competition to improve local public services. In Australia, where there has been rapid growth in public–private partnerships (PPPs), some states, such as Victoria, require that half of all local public service expenditures be submitted to competitive bidding. As a result, many public services are now provided not only by PSOs, but by private-sector firms as well (Broadbent and Laughlin 2003; English and Guthrie 2003). In part the shift has been due to the commonly acknowledged fact that private-sector organizations are almost always more efficient in service-provision than public-sector ones (Kulmala et al. 2006).

However, a move toward outsourcing does not need a legislative mandate. In Italy, for example, although local government reforms *encouraged* outsourcing, they did not require it; and yet, by 1999, between 56 and 93 percent of the most important local services (natural gas distribution, waste disposal and collection, water and sewerage) were being outsourced (Enea-Nomisma 1999). In the US, although there are no legislative mandates, outsourcing has been going on for some time (Anthony and Young 2003). In particular, it began to grow rapidly in the 1980s under the political pressure of President Reagan's "New Federalism".

Outsourcing and contemporary public management

Outsourcing is a logical consequence of efforts by PSOs over the last three decades to minimize waste and to promote efficiency and effectiveness (Nolan and Brendan 2001). It has been fostered in many PSOs by a shift toward greater managerial autonomy, a move toward private-sector management approaches, and the promotion of competition among private-sector firms with the dual goals of decreasing costs and increasing quality.

Outsourcing also has been driven by a PSO's desire to increase its flexibility (Hartmann and Patrickson 2000) as well as to transfer some of its risk in running a program to private entities, while simultaneously allowing it to maintain control over the program's essential elements (Quiggin 1996). And, finally, outsourcing has allowed a PSO to draw on expertise not available in-house (Young 2000), thereby permitting it to use private-sector innovation, technology and expertise (Ponomariov and Kingsley 2008). In effect, many PSOs have moved quite deliberately and systematically from the left side of Figure 15.1 to the right side. Moreover, in conjunction with its shift to PPPs, the state of Victoria (Australia) also began to outsource some activities, such as human services, that previously were considered to be in the exclusive domain of the public sector (Teicher et al. 2006). Similar shifts have taken place in other countries as well (Tremblay et al. 2008).

With its focus on the private sector, outsourcing has also become a key element of the New Public Management paradigm (Hood 1991, 1995) and, more recently, the New Public Governance model (Box et al. 2001; Pollitt 2002; Cabrero 2005; Osborne 2006). It is being used in efforts to transform

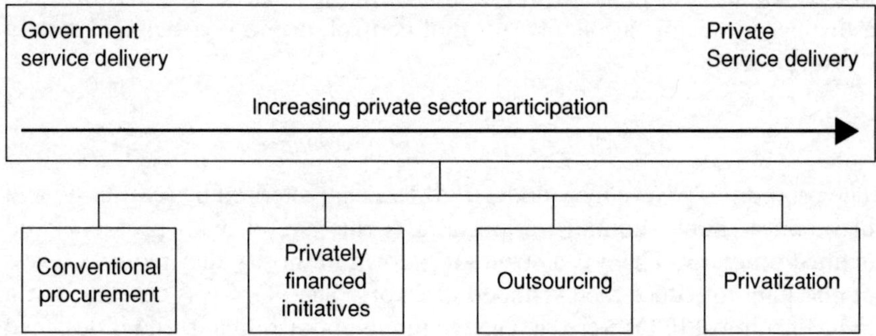

Figure 15.1 Public–private partnerships: the service delivery spectrum.
Source: Adapted from English and Guthire (2003).

governments into more effective and efficient entities that "can do more with less" (Osborne and Gaebler 1992; Koppenjan and Klijn 2004). Clearly, the effective management of outsourced services is essential for a PSO that wishes to provide its citizens with high value for money.

Outsourcing and the Four-governance Model framework

Outsourcing can be seen in the context of some broader changes that have taken place in PSO governance. One description of these changes is (Considine 1999, 2001; Considine and Lewis 2003) Four-governance Model framework. While there are other frameworks that could be used to view outsourcing (Hutt and Walcott 1990; Peters 1996; Pierre 1999; English et al. 2005), most are some variation of Considine's. As Figure 15.2 indicates, each

Model	*Source of rationality*	*Form of control*	*Primary virtue*	*Service delivery focus*
Procedural Governance	Law	Rules	Reliability	Universal treatments
Corporate Governance	Management	Plans	Goal-driven	Targets
Market Governance	Competition	Contracts	Cost-driven	Prices
Network Governance	Relationships	Co-production	Flexibility	Brokerage

Figure 15.2 The four governance models.
Source: Considine (2001).

of Considine's four models (procedural, corporate, market and network) has a distinct source of rationality, form of control, primary virtue, and service delivery focus.

Model 1: procedural governance

The procedural governance model (PGM) is characterized by centralized and hierarchical public administration, and is rule-bound, with protocols and defined practices. There is a strong top-down authority that requires layers of checking to reduce the likelihood of errors. The PGM was developed at a time when most PSOs were engaged in minimal outsourcing, and is designed to guarantee that standardized services are provided at the lowest per-unit cost.

Model 2: corporate governance

The corporate governance model (CGM) emerged because of a perception that the PGM did not fit with a variety of administrative requirements for successful outsourcing, mainly the need to maintain greater control over public expenditures (Pallot 1992; Pierre and Peters 2000). In addition, the PGM was not able to deal with the increasing complexity of government (Lapsley 1988) and the need to target some services for a subset of the citizenry.

In the CGM, considerable importance is given to planning, budgeting and reporting. A PSO using the CGM concentrates on outputs instead of on inputs, and it focuses on specific groups of citizens who are receiving services. In effect, its emphasis shifts from adhering to arbitrary rules to achieving results.

Model 3: market governance

In the market governance model (MGM), a PSO encourages competition among potential vendors, and develops contracts to define its relationships with the selected ones (English et al. 2005). These contracts stress quality as well as cost, and place considerable emphasis on meeting citizen needs (Pierre and Peters 2000).

The MGM may include arrangements with a commercial company, a public authority, a nonprofit organization, or all three (Goldsmith and Eggers 2004; Pollitt 2003). Its use of performance-based service contracting encourages vendors to be innovative and seek increasingly cost-effective ways to deliver services (United States General Accounting Office 2002).

In Australia, where the MGM began in the mid-1990s, PSOs at various levels of government have introduced "best commercial practices". In some instances, a PSO has used the "corporate form" for its business activities, and in others it has "privatized" a governmental unit by selling the relevant assets to an outside entity (Broadbent and Guthrie 2008).

By creating market dynamism and increased autonomy within the public context, the MGM can help to ensure accountable managerial behavior. However, for many PSOs, the MGM can also present some difficult managerial challenges (Osborne and Gaebler 1992). This is because, under the MGM, a PSO needs to be certain that it measures the vendor's outputs (rather than inputs), and structures an appropriate set of reporting and feedback relationships. For many PSOs, developing the requisite management-control system runs contrary to their longstanding, input-based managerial cultures, and therefore is a difficult transition to make (Padovani and Young 2008).

Model 4: network governance

Although the MGM strives to increase competition so as to help contain costs, its contracts generally focus on only one service. It therefore is inappropriate when some outsourced services need to be coordinated with others.

The network governance model (NGM) is designed to overcome this limitation. It does so, in part, by focusing on linkages among vendors; and, in so doing, responds to complex citizen needs. Indeed, because of the importance of managing the linkages among these needs, some researchers have argued that PSOs must move toward the NGM model if they are to serve their citizenry most effectively (Mandell 2001).

The goal of the NGM is to combine a high level of public–private collaboration (characteristic of the MGM) with a robust network of service providers. To achieve this goal, PSOs first establish long-term relationships with their vendors. They then use sophisticated information technology to connect the entire network of vendors (and other involved organizations) so as to give citizens a wide range of service-delivery options. Under the NGM, a key task of government is the management of these networks (McGuire 2002; McLaughlin and Osborne 2005; Klijn 2008).

The essence of the NGM, then, is cooperation among government, nonprofit and (sometimes) private-sector organizations to help ensure a high level of service coordination (Considine and Lewis 2003). In so doing, the NGM has spawned a stream of research that examines its impact on enhancing a community's social capital (Moran 2005). It also is conceivable that the NGM could influence a community's *relational* capital – a topic that has been explored considerably in the private sector (Sawhney and Zabin 2001) and has clear applicability to the public sector.

Relational capital is important if a PSO is successfully to outsource a complex set of activities, such as social services or pollution control, where it must develop partnership-like coordination among a wide network of vendors. These relationships can include "joint investments, shared research, common development ventures, and flexible methods for linking financiers, regulators and a host of public and private service providers" (Considine 2001: 30). They can also include the sharing of cost information with other public or private organizations in an effort to meet a complex set of citizen needs as cost-effectively as possible.

As with the MGM, many PSOs are not prepared for the challenges posed by the NGM. Because managing their networks frequently requires skills, knowledge and technology that they do not possess, PSOs have had varying degrees of success in attempting to use the NGM (Sørensen 2002; Goldsmith and Eggers 2004).

Moving from the PGM to the NGM

In all four governance models, PSOs are attempting to improve the quality and cost-effectiveness of their public services. However, movement from the PGM to the NGM entails developing new skills and implementing new technology so as to manage vendors differently. The result is an increase in the cost of governance as a PSO moves along the spectrum toward the NGM.

Given the possible higher costs of the more sophisticated governance models, the central question is not whether a PSO should be attempting to move as deliberately as possible from the PGM to the NGM, but rather which of the four governance models is appropriate for each service being outsourced. Thus, it is conceivable that a PSO could have several governance models operating simultaneously, each attuned to the nature of the service being outsourced.

A strategic framework for outsourcing

Before deciding on a governance model, a PSO must decide whether it will outsource a particular service or provide it itself. Part of this decision entails assessing the risk of low-quality and/or unduly expensive vendor performance, and considering what that might mean for the overall satisfaction of the citizenry. For example, if a city or town decides to have a youth program brochure prepared by an outside vendor, the citizenry most likely is unaware of, and unaffected in any significant way by, the vendor's performance.

By contrast, when a vendor provides a service directly to the citizenry, rather than to the PSO itself, there is a considerable potential for citizen dissatisfaction. Waste collection, snow removal and street repair are all examples of services where the citizenry is directly affected by the choices, able to assess their quality (however subjectively), and concerned about the resulting cost. In these latter instances, despite its potential for enhancing value to the citizenry, outsourcing can present difficulties in managing the provision of public services.

The need for risk assessment

Because of these differences in risk, a PSO that is considering outsourcing an activity must assess the risk associated with unsatisfactory vendor performance. In the case of printing a brochure, for example, the risk is low.

Clearly, quality specifications can be included in the contract, and the results can be easily monitored. But this is not the central issue. Rather, the question is: What are the consequences of poor vendor performance? In the brochure decision, the answer is that it will have little impact on the citizenry, and the vendor can be replaced easily, if necessary, for future printings.

On the other hand, services such as waste collection, water and sewerage provision, and traffic control have quality and service goals that are more difficult to measure and monitor. Moreover, poor vendor performance will directly affect the citizenry, and the PSO may have difficulty replacing a poorly performing vendor in a timely way. Clearly, the risk is higher.

A great deal of literature has emerged in recent years concerning outsourcing risk in both the public and the private sectors. In some instances, risk has been largely of a *financial* nature, and has been assessed in light of the difficulty of providing services within a set of budgetary constraints (Ball et al. 2003). In others, risk has been viewed in terms of a vendor's *capacity* to deliver the requisite services, or the *uncertainty* of the task to be performed (Venkateswar 2005). In still others, the focus has been on the *logistics* of managing the vendor (Steane and Walker 2000). In all of these areas, a central issue has been the information asymmetry between the vendor and the PSO, which can lead the PSO to assume more risk than it thinks it is (Demsetz 1968).

From the perspective of a PSO's outsourcing decisions, risk can be addressed more strategically than these uni-dimensional approaches. To do so, a PSO must focus on such matters as: (*a*) increased dependence on external suppliers, resulting in a potential loss of control over critical activities; (*b*) greater difficulty in cost management, especially when there are adversarial relationships; (*c*) loss of either essential competencies in the public entity or control over the resources that it would need to acquire in order to resume conducting the activity itself; and (*d*) loss of the flexibility to respond to changing needs of the citizenry (Kettl 1993; Quinn and Hilmer 1994; Domberger 1998).

Most of these latter concerns relate to a three-way juxtaposition of (*a*) the impact of the service on the citizenry, (*b*) the competitive nature of the market for vendors, and (*c*) the ease or difficulty of switching vendors (or returning to internal service provision) if a given vendor's performance is unsatisfactory (Padovani and Young 2006, 2008). With the preparation of a brochure, for example, there is a low potential for citizen dissatisfaction, the market is highly competitive, and the PSO would find it quite easy to switch from one vendor to another. By contrast, not only is a service such as waste removal highly important to the citizenry, but also there may be few other capable vendors in the marketplace, such that the PSO would have difficulty finding a replacement if the vendor's performance were unsatisfactory. Moreover, even if a replacement could be found, the cost of switching vendors might be high.

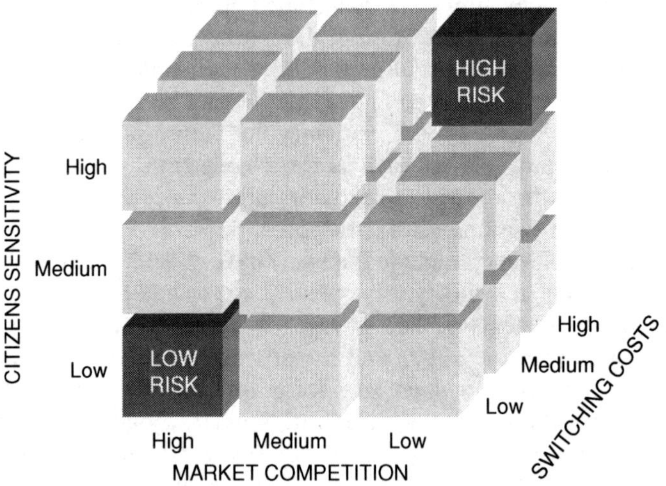

Figure 15.3 A framework for assessing risk.
Source: Padovani and Young (2006, 2008).

The interaction of these relationships is shown in Figure 15.3. As this exhibit indicates, from the perspective of our three dimensions of risk – citizen sensitivity, market competition, and vendor-switching costs – some services will rather clearly fall into the high-risk category while others will be low risk. Figure 15.4 shows how several different PSO services might be classified into this framework.

Relationship to the Four-governance Model framework

Juxtaposing our risk-assessment model in Figure 15.3 with Considine's Four-governance Model framework in Figure 15.2 gives rise to our contingency approach. With this approach, a PSO does not need to attempt to move along the spectrum from the PGM to the NGM. Instead, it needs to assess the risk of each service being outsourced, and select the most appropriate governance model for managing it.

Figure 15.5 shows how different outsourced services require different governance models. As it indicates, while some of a PSO's outsourced services may require the NGM, others may need only the low level of sophistication inherent in the PGM. For example, at the same time as a PSO is using the NGM for its social welfare services, it may use the PGM for very simple services, such as printing and mailing a brochure. Similarly, a PSO may need to use the CGM when it outsources services such as snowplowing, building or traffic-light maintenance, or landscaping. These services have a moderate risk of citizen dissatisfaction, but the market is robust, and the PSO can change vendors relatively easily if performance is unsatisfactory.

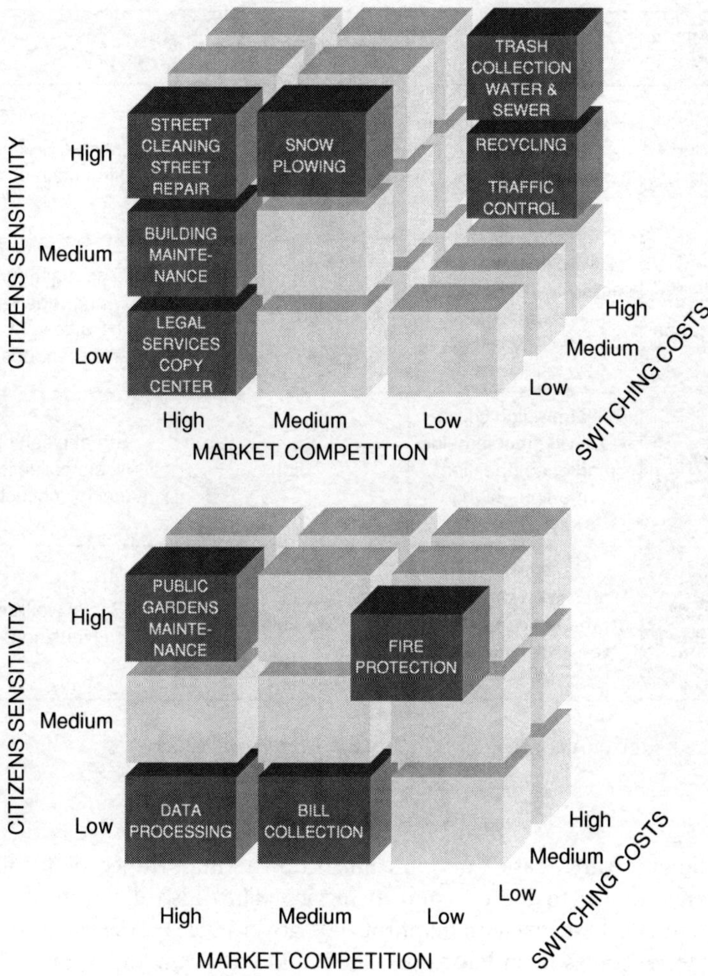

Figure 15.4 Examples of outsourcing risk.
Source: Padovani and Young (2008).

Even services with somewhat high citizen sensitivity and moderate difficulty in switching vendors, such as waste removal, may not require the NGM. If there is no need to coordinate the activities of multiple vendors, the MGM may suffice. Indeed, the NGM, with its requirement for highly skilled managers and sophisticated technology, is needed only for high-risk services that also are complex, such as social welfare, housing, healthcare, or pollution control. With all of these services, not only is citizen sensitivity high, but also the complex network of relationships means that changing vendors would be very disruptive to both clients and the other vendors.

Governance model	Kinds of risk	Overall level of risk	Examples
Procedural Governance	Low citizen sensitivity; high market competition; low switching costs	Low	Printing a brochure Routine maintenance
Corporate Governance	Low–medium citizen sensitivity; high–medium market competition; low–medium switching costs	Moderate	Building maintenance and repair Traffic-light maintenance
Market Governance	Medium–high citizen sensitivity; medium–low market competition; medium–high switching costs	High	Street cleaning Waste collection Local tax collection
Network Governance	High citizen sensitivity; low market competition; high switching costs	Very high	Social welfare Housing

Figure 15.5 Outsourcing risk and the Four-governance Model.

Case examples

The following three case examples illustrate the importance of fitting the governance model to the outsourced service. They also illustrate the difficulties that can arise when an inappropriate governance model is chosen. The case material comes from Padovani (2005) and Padovani and Young (2008).

Alpha Municipality

Alpha Municipality was a residential and tourism community of 22,000 inhabitants located in northeast Italy. Its town council had decided to engage in competitive bidding for trash collection and disposal services with the aim of reducing per-unit costs. The resulting contract specified the activities and procedures that the vendor needed to follow, rather than the results to be achieved. However, because of resource constraints, regular inspection by the contract manager of the vendor's adherence to the contract's terms was an all but impossible task. Moreover, the contract did not take into consideration several important vendor activities, such as responding to citizen complaints. As a result, assessment of the vendor's performance could only be measured by complaints, which typically were generated by tourists and were dealt with by the municipality's contract manager or its elected officials. Over the period of the contract there was a growth in complaints and considerable citizen dissatisfaction.

In this instance, the municipality's use of the procedural governance model was inappropriate. It resulted in a focus on regulating the vendor's *activities*, rather than on measuring its effectiveness in meeting citizen needs. It seems clear that either the corporate governance or the market governance model, with their emphasis on quality and citizen needs, would have been more appropriate.

Beta Municipality

Beta Municipality was a residential and industrial town of 30,000 inhabitants, also in northeast Italy but located inside a large metropolitan area. It faced many of the same issues as Alpha Municipality. Here, however, the contract with the vendor was results-oriented – the focus was on output targets to be accomplished by the vendor instead of on specific activities. On a daily basis, the contract manager inspected such output indicators as cleanliness of the streets, overflowing containers, and facility maintenance. Negative inspection-findings (as well as citizen complaints) were communicated to the vendor daily, and the vendor was required to notify the contract manager when each problem was resolved.

Structural deficiencies – instances when the same problems occurred repeatedly and needed to be solved more systemically – were discussed during bi-monthly meetings of a joint commission (composed of the contract manager, a vendor representative, and a citizen representative). The commission also levied penalties on the vendor for noncompliance.

As part of its MGM, Beta Municipality had a management control system that assisted the town's elected officials and senior managers in monitoring two very important performance indicators: percentage of recyclables and purity of recyclables. All other output indicators – such as street cleanliness, availability of solid-waste and recyclable containers, and the quality of facility maintenance – were delegated to the contract manager. With this governance model, there was considerable cooperation between the municipality and the vendor to meet citizen needs; and, as a result, the number of citizen complaints was minimal.

Gamma Agency

Gamma Agency was a public transportation entity that had outsourced the maintenance of its copy-center service – an internal service that provided flyers, timetables and other similar documents for citizens. The contract was procedural, with detailed specifications of activities to be delivered within specific deadlines (e.g. maintenance of specific parts of the machines at definite dates or after a specified number of copies had been printed) or on request (e.g. substitution of toners, repairing of damaged parts, etc.). In effect, Gamma Agency was using the PGM for a service where adherence to procedures was important.

Case comparisons

These three cases illustrate the importance of attaining a fit between the service being outsourced and the governance model used to manage the vendor. For example, because it employed the PGM model, Alpha Municipality was not able to address adequately the problems that arose with poor vendor performance. By contrast, in Beta Municipality, where the level of risk was the same as that of Alpha Municipality, use of the MGM helped to ensure that the service met the citizens' needs. On the other hand, Gamma Agency's use of the PGM was quite appropriate under the circumstances.

Conclusions

These three cases illustrate several important conceptual points. First, under the right circumstances, a simple governance model such as the PGM may be all that is needed to ensure adequate vendor performance.

Second, the use of an inappropriately simple governance model for a high-risk service can lead to problems with vendor performance, and thus can result in citizen dissatisfaction.

Third, from these case examples, one can conclude that choosing the most appropriate governance model is not a one-time event. If, for example, a PSO modifies its contract with a vendor to include a more complex mix of services, thereby creating an increase in its risk, it needs to assess the fit of its existing governance model with the new needs. Thus, as a PSO grows, as its outsourced services increase in complexity, and as the associated risk increases, it needs to shift to increasingly sophisticated governance models.

Fourth, before it decides to outsource a high-risk service, a PSO's senior management needs to be certain that it has the capability to use the requisite governance model; and, if that model is other than the PGM, the municipality needs a management control system that is sufficiently sophisticated to manage the vendor's activities.

Fifth, a PSO's management control system is an important element of the CGM, the MGM and the NGM. In Beta Municipality, for example, it was a key element in the effort to ensure adequate vendor performance.

Finally, given the above, it seems quite obvious that a PSO can have multiple governance models operating simultaneously. In part, the appropriate governance model for a given outsourced service depends on the degree of risk. Using the NGM for a low-risk service, for example, is excessively costly for the task at hand. At the same time, the decision to outsource a high-risk service must depend, in part, on whether the PSO has the capability to operate the requisite governance model. For example, to outsource a service that requires a high degree of coordination, but *without* possessing the managerial and technological capability for the NGM, may lead to redundant, conflicting and ineffective services. In the first instance, the cost of governance is excessive. In the second, insufficient (or inappropriate) resources are being devoted to the coordination effort, resulting in a potentially dissatisfied citizenry. Neither should be acceptable to a PSO's senior management team.

Note

1 This chapter expands upon and develops the argument in F. Farneti and D. Young (2008) "A Contingency Approach to Managing Outsourcing Risk in Municipalities", *Public Management Review*, 10 (1): 89–100.

References

Anthony, R. N. and Young, D. W. (2003) *Management Control in Nonprofit Organizations*, 7th edn, Burr Ridge, Ill.: McGraw-Hill/Irwin.

Ball, R., Heafey, M. and King, D. (2003) "Risk Transfer and Value for Money in PFI Projects", *Public Management Review* 5 (2): 279–290.

Box, R., Marshall, G., Reed, B. J. and Reed, C. (2001) "New Public Management and *Faux* Democracy, and the Challenge to Democratic Governance", *Public Administration Review*, 61 (5): 608–19.

Broadbent, J. and Guthrie, J. (2008) "Public Sector to Public Services: 20 years of 'Alternative' Accounting Research", *Accounting, Auditing and Accountability Journal*, 21 (2): 129–69.

Broadbent, J. and Laughlin, R. (2003) "Public Private Partnerships: An Introduction", *Accounting, Auditing and Accountability Journal*, 16 (3): 332–41.

Cabrero, E. (2005) "Between Public Management and New Public Governance: The Case of Mexican Municipalities", *International Public Management Review*, 6 (1): 76–99.

Considine, M. (1999) "Markets and the New Welfare State: Employment Assistance Reforms in Australia", *Journal of Social Policy*, 28 (2): 183–203.

Considine, M. (2001) *Enterprising States: The Public Management of Welfare-to-work*, Cambridge: Cambridge University Press.

Considine, M. and Lewis, J. M. (2003) "Bureaucracy, Network, or Enterprise? Comparing Models of Governance in Australia, Britain, the Netherlands, and New Zealand", *Public Administration Review*, 63 (2): 131–40.

Demsetz, H. (1968) "Why Regulate Utilities?", *Journal of Law and Economics*, 11: 55–65.

Domberger, S. (1998) *The Contracting Organization: A Strategic Guide to Outsourcing*, New York: Oxford University Press.

Enea-Nomisma (1999) *Rapporto Enea-Nomisma sui servizi pubblici locali*, Rome: Enea-Nomisma.

English, L. and Guthrie, J. (2003) "Driving Privately Financed Projects in Australia: What Makes Them Tick?", *Accounting Auditing and Accountability Journal*, 16 (3): 493–511.

English, L., Guthrie, J. and Parker, L. (2005) "Recent Public-sector Financial Management Change in Australia: Implementing the Market Model", in J. Guthrie, C. Humphrey, O. Olson and L. Jones (eds) *International Public Financial Management Reform: Progress, Contradictions and Challenges*, Greenwich, Conn.: Information Age Press.

Farneti, F., and Young, D. W. (2008) "A Contingency Approach to Managing Outsourcing Risk in Municipalities", *Public Management Review*, 10 (1): 89–99.

Goldsmith, S. and Eggers, W. D. (2004) *Governing by Network: The New Shape of the Public Sector*, Washington, DC: The Brookings Institution.

Hartmann, L. and Patrickson, M. (2000) "Externalizing the Workforce: Australian Trends and Issues for HRM", *International Journal of Manpower*, 21 (1): 7–20.

Hood, C. (1991) "A Public Management for All Seasons?", *Public Administration*, 69 (1): 3–19.

Hood, C. (1995) "The 'New Public Management' in the 1980s: Variations on a Theme", *Accounting Organization and Society*, 20 (2–3): 93–109.

Hutt, K. and Walcott, C. (1990) *Governing Public Organizations: Politics, Structure, and Institutional Design*, Pacific Grove, Calif.: Brooks/Cole Publishing Company.

Kettl, D. F. (1993) *Sharing Power: Public Governance and Private Markets*, Washington, DC: The Brookings Institution.

Klijn, E. H. (2008) "Governance and Governance Networks in Europe", *Public Management Review*, 10 (4): 505–25.

Koppenjan, J. and Klijn, E. (2004) *Managing Uncertainties in Networks*, London: Routledge.

Kulmala, H., Ojala, M., Ahoniemi, L. and Uusi-Rauva, E. (2006) "Unit Cost Behavior in Public Sector Outsourcing", *International Journal of Public Sector Management*, 19 (2): 130–49.

Lapsley, I. (1988) "Research in Public Sector Accounting: An Appraisal", *Accounting, Auditing and Accountability Journal*, 1 (1): 21–33.

McGuire, M. (2002) "Managing Networks: Propositions on What Managers Do and Why They Do It", *Public Administration Review*, 62 (5): 599–609.

McLaughlin, K. and Osborne, S. P. (2005) "The New Public Management in Context", in K. McLaughlin, S. P. Osborne and E. Ferlie (eds) *New Public Management: Current Trends and Future Prospects*, London: Routledge.

Mandell, M. (2001) "Collaboration through Network Structures for Community Building Efforts", *National Civic Review*, 90 (3): 279–87.

Moran, P. (2005) "Structural and Relational Embeddedness: Social Capital and Managerial Performance", *Strategic Management Journal*, 26 (12): 1129–51.

Nolan, Brendan C. (2001) "Introduction", in Brendan C. Nolan (ed.) *Public Sector Reform: An International Perspective*, Basingstoke: Palgrave: Macmillan.

Osborne, S. (2006) "The New Public Governance?", *Public Management Review*, 8 (3): 377–87.

Osborne, D. and Gaebler, T. (1992) *Reinventing Government: How the Entrepreneurial Spirit Is Transforming the Public Sector*, Reading, Mass.: Addison-Wesley.

Padovani, E. (2005) *Il governo dei servizi pubblici locali in outsourcing: Il controllo dell'efficacia* [*The Governance of Outsourced Local Public Services: Controlling the Effectiveness*], Milan: FrancoAngeli.

Padovani, E. and Young, D. W. (2006) "Managing High Risk Outsourcing", *Public Management*, 88 (1): 29–33.

Padovani, E. and Young, D. W. (2008) "Toward a Framework for Managing High-risk Government Outsourcing: Field Research in Three Italian Municipalities", *Journal of Public Procurement*, 8 (2): 215–47.

Pallot, J. (1992) "Elements of a Theoretical Framework for Public Sector Accounting", *Accounting Auditing and Accountability Journal*, 5 (1): 38–59.

Peters, G. (1996) *The Future of Governing: Four Emerging Models*, Lawrence, Kan.: University Press of Kansas.

Pierre, J. (1999) "Models of Urban Governance: The Institutional Dimension of Urban Politics", *Urban Affairs Review*, 34 (3): 372–96.

Pierre, J. and Peters, G. B. (2000) *Governance, Politics and the State*, London: Macmillan.

Pollitt, C. (2002) "The New Public Management in International Perspective: An Analysis of Impacts and Effects", in Kate McLaughlin, Stephen P. Osborne and Ewan Ferlie (eds), *New Public Management: Current Trends and Future Prospects*, London: Routledge.

Pollitt, C. (2003) *The Essential Public Manager*, Philadelphia, Pa: Open University Press.

Ponomariov, B. and Kingsley, G. (2008) "Applicability of the Normative Model of Outsourcing in the Public Sector: The Case of a State Transportation Agency", *Public Organization Review*, 8: 253–72.

Quiggin, J. (1996) "Competitive Tendering and Contracting in the Australian Public Sector", *Australian Journal of Public Administration*, 55 (3): 49–57.

Quinn, J. B. and Hilmer, F. G. (1994) "Strategic Outsourcing", *Sloan Management Review*, 35 (4): 43–55.

Sawhney, M. and Zabin, J. (2001) *The Seven Steps to Nirvana*, New York: McGraw-Hill.

Sorensen, E. (2002) "Democratic Theory and Network Governance", *Administrative Theory and Praxis*, 24 (1): 693–721.

Steane, P. D. and Walker, D. H. T. (2000) "Competitive Tendering and Contracting Public Sector Services in Australia – a Facilities Management Issue", *Facilities*, 18 (5–6): 245–55.

Teicher, J., Van Gramberg, B. and Holland, P. (2006) "Trade Union Responses to Outsourcing in a Neo-liberal Environment: A Case Study Analysis of the Australian Public Sector", *Asia Pacific Business Review*, 12 (2): 243–56.

Tremblay, M., Patry, M. and Lanoie, P. (2008) "Human Resources Outsourcing in Canadian Organizations: An Empirical Analysis of the Role of Organizational Characteristics, Transaction Costs and Risks", *The International Journal of Human Resources Management*, 19 (4): 683–715.

United States General Accounting Office (2002) *Contract Management: Guidance Needed for Using Performance-based Service Contracting*, GAO-02-1049, Washington, DC: US General Accounting Office.

Venkateswar, N. R. (2005) "Mitigating Operational Risk in Outsourcing", *DM Review*, 24 May 2005.

Young, S. (2000) "Outsourcing: Lessons from the Literature", *Labour and Industry*, 10 (3): 97–118.

16

THE GOVERNANCE OF CONTRACTING RELATIONSHIPS: "KILLING THE GOLDEN GOOSE"

A third-sector perspective

Steven Rathgeb Smith and Judith Smyth

Throughout the world, the role of third-sector organizations in providing public services is increasing, primarily through a sharp rise in government contracting with these organizations.[1] The result is profound changes in their governance, including the role of staff and boards, their programmatic focus and their internal operations. Moreover, some changes are fundamental and raise fears that through contracting governments may be "killing the golden goose". Contracting can also affect the motivation and characteristics of staff and board members and their accountability to stakeholders, including funders and service users. In many countries, the difference between traditional grants and contracts is declining as government commissioners increase the specificity and performance expectations on their grants, creating new governance and accountability challenges for third-sector organizations and their staff and volunteers.

The attraction of contracting with third-sector organizations – the "golden goose" – reflects many factors: pressure to contain costs, new attention to civil society organizations and their potential to build social capital and community, and the influence of the New Public Management, which seeks to improve the efficiency and effectiveness of public services through contracting, privatization and decentralization (see Hood 1991; Rhodes 1996; Considine 2003; Behn 2001; Kettl 2005). Given these factors, third-sector organizations offer at least the possibility of service innovation, lower costs, community and citizen engagement, voluntarism, and enhanced competition with the public sector. The community roots of many third-sector organizations also means that these organizations may have political support and influence, and represent politically important constituencies; thus, government contracting with these organizations may be a strategy for government to reach out and support a particular group or constituency. Over time, though, the potential benefits of contracting are often undermined by government policy, creating difficult choices and trade-offs for third-sector organizations and the individuals who use their services.

This government reform movement has had far-reaching effects on third-sector organizations and the relationship between government and these organizations. It has fueled the growth of a wide variety of organizations to provide an array of public services, especially in health, social services and housing. Indirectly, the government reform movement has facilitated the increased interest in voluntarism, citizen participation and community service. Over time, the sharp rise in contracting has also encouraged third-sector organizations to become more assertive politically, either directly through their own actions or indirectly through associations representing their interests. In the UK and the US, these infrastructure organizations have received government funding in order to support the capacity of their third-sector members to compete for contracts and rise to the challenges of regulation and inspection.

In the US and the UK, the increasing role of third-sector organizations in the last twenty years has also changed the role of government at all levels. Indeed, a key argument of this chapter is that the core principles of good public management – appropriate training and education of government managers, greater transparency and accountability, improved citizen engagement – drive all organizations that provide public services toward an increasingly standard offer regardless of the governance arrangements. These resulting effects are rarely raised or questioned whilst government and third-sector agencies wrestle with the knotty governance dilemmas raised by an increasingly complex policy process and service delivery system created by the growth of contracting.

An analysis of these governance challenges and dilemmas is the focus of this chapter, with an emphasis on the implications for public managers and third-sector staff and volunteers of the evolving contracting relationship. Thus, this chapter concentrates on third-sector organizations that receive substantial grants and contracts, with a particular emphasis on the impact of these contracts on the governance and programming of these organizations. The research on contracting practices informing the analysis and findings in this chapter is drawn primarily from the US and the UK in order to encourage international comparison and learning. These countries share similar trends in the overall growth of contracting with third-sector organizations and the increasing emphasis on achieving good performance through contract compliance, regulation and inspection, with its attendant effects on the governance of the third sector. Both countries illustrate more general issues of governance pertaining to contracting that are also applicable to other countries and regions with very different contracting arrangements and regulatory regimes. However, public policy toward the third sector in the UK diverges from the US owing to the Compact (2009), which is a formal structured process for the government and third-sector organizations in the UK to work together. Over time, the Compact has encouraged government to undertake other initiatives to support the third sector based upon this Compact framework.

Throughout the chapter, the term "third-sector organization" will be used instead of nonprofit organization, NGO and voluntary organization. Third-sector organizations refer to the diverse set of organizations that can provide an array of services including health and social care, education, conservation and recreation, and advocacy. These organizations may be entirely voluntary or they may receive substantial public subsidies and contracts. In general, the term "nonprofit organization" is most widely used in the US, while "third-sector organization" has emerged as the most common term to refer to these organizations in Europe, Australia and New Zealand. "NGO" is most widely used in developing countries and can refer to a diverse mix of intermediary organizations. In the United States, the term "NGO" has generally referred to nonprofit organizations that have a non-US focus. In the UK, a similar distinction exists between voluntary organizations and NGOs (see Harris and Rochester 2001), and in the last decade "third sector" has been replacing "voluntary organization" as the favored descriptor of the sector – for example, the UK government has established an Office for the Third Sector.

Importantly, the types of organization which regard themselves as part of the third sector are shifting. For example, the growth of hospices in the UK and the US creates new members of the third sector, but very few hospices formally involve themselves in the third-sector community or in their representative bodies such as the Independent Sector in the US or the National Council of Voluntary Organisations (NCVO) in the UK. Housing associations in the UK are in business and social terms very successful third-sector organizations but nowadays rarely involve themselves with general third-sector infrastructure work. In the UK, new forms of National Health Service (NHS) hospitals and schools have been established. Although they are not yet classified as third-sector organizations, they are in many ways constitutionally and positionally much more like third-sector providers than traditional public services. In the US, nonprofit hospitals are increasingly complicated mixed public and private entities, often with for-profit partnerships and subsidiaries. These emergent and changing forms of "ownership" should perhaps be seen as part of the third sector. Likewise, new social-enterprise organizations such as leisure services companies are assuming responsibility for the delivery of a range of services previously provided by government in the UK. For the most part, the traditional third sector has not embraced these new organizations into their fold, despite the income potential from membership fees locally and the potential to add to support for the sector nationally. Coming as they do from traditional public service governance, with very different psychological contracts and roots, these organizations appear to be on different journeys to more traditional third-sector organizations such as social service agencies.

The chapter initially chronicles the growth of contracting in different countries, followed by a discussion and analysis of the key challenges and developments affecting government and third-sector organizations involved in contracting. The focus in this section of the paper is on three key issues: performance management and accountability; self-regulation, inspection, accreditation and quality frameworks; and competition. Each of these challenges poses a threat to the "golden goose", thus the section examines the implications of these challenges for third-sector organizations, especially their governance. The chapter concludes with suggestions for research, policy and practice.

The growth of contracting

Government funding of third-sector organizations has a long history in many countries. In the United States, some of the oldest nonprofit organizations in the country, such as Massachusetts General Hospital and Harvard University, received government funding in the colonial period (Smith and Lipsky 1993; Salamon 1987). In many European countries, including the Netherlands, the United Kingdom, Germany, Denmark and Sweden, voluntary organizations emerged in the nineteenth century as crucial to providing important social and health services (Burger and Veldeer 2001; Lundstrom and Svedberg 2003; Henriksen and Bundesen 2004; Bode forthcoming). However, the growth of the welfare state in the early and mid-twentieth century in countries such as Denmark, the UK and Sweden resulted in a long-term decline in the role of third-sector organizations in providing services (Lundstrom and Svedberg 2003; Henriksen and Bundesen 2004; Gutch 1992). In these countries, local government tended to provide the bulk of social and health services, with voluntary organizations providing specific niche services such as emergency assistance. In the US, the situation was quite different. Public social welfare services were provided primarily by local government and were quite limited in nature. And the voluntary sector was quite small and narrow in scope. In the 1960s, government contracting grew sharply with the growth of the national government's role in health and social policy.

Subsequently, many governments shifted their initial funding of third-sector organizations to more formal contracts with competitive tendering and substantial regulation. This change, which began in the 1970s and then quickened in the 1990s and thereafter, was prompted by the search to reduce public spending and the growth of statutory services. Contracting with third-sector organizations offered the hope of lower costs. Also, conservative governments came to power in the UK, the US, New Zealand, Australia and elsewhere that were decidedly more skeptical of public services and more supportive of market approaches. Consequently, public agencies (usually local government in countries such as the UK, Australia and New Zealand) were pushed to transform their role into one of a purchaser and enabler rather than a direct provider of services (Gutch 1992; Considine 2003; Lyons forthcoming). This shift to the enabler role fit with the emergence of the "new public management" movement (Hood 1991; Rhodes 1996) that stressed "steering rather than rowing" for public agencies (Osborne and Gaebler 1993). To varying extents, this shift in policy is evident in many other countries such as the UK (Kirkpatrick et al. 2001; Gutch 1992), the US (Smith and Lipsky 1993; Gronbjerg 1993), Finland (Simonen and Kovaainen 1998), and Australia and New Zealand (Considine 2003; Lyons forthcoming). In these countries, this change to formal contracting has also entailed greater receptivity to government contracting with for-profit service agencies especially for long-term care and childcare.

In the UK, the government has pledged to increase the involvement of third-sector organizations in the provision of public services. Indeed, in 2006, the UK government formally asserted its intention to increase the involvement of the third sector in the delivery of public services (Cabinet Office 2006). This new target reflects a number of policy objectives:

- to introduce contestability and choice into public services by increasing the quality and range of organizations that can be commissioned to provide services;
- to ensure that the statutory sector is able to access the expertise of the third sector in delivering services to communities, particularly harder-to-reach communities and challenging client groups;
- to increase the capacity of public services as a whole to respond to growing demand for services and increased client choice; and
- to increase social capital within communities and facilitate the engagement of service users (Office of Government Commerce 2006).

In response, a new emphasis on commissioning as the central function of local government has developed, especially in England[2] as described in the Local Government Act of 2006. Commissioning, in this context, is the word used to describe the activities and processes used by governments to decide how best to use the total resources available to a population in order to improve outcomes. As applied to contracting, commissioning entails working with and through a range of different organizations, including third-sector organizations, to deliver better services for the public. At its core is an understanding that commissioners are purchasing services from public service teams within the local authority as well as from arm's-length provider organizations such as schools and hospitals, third-sector organizations, and for-profit provider businesses. Government policy-makers also hope that commissioning is an effective strategy to ensure that all providers of public services are contestible, even when formal competitive tendering has not been used (Audit Commission 2008). As articulated in the government's White Paper, local authorities should play a coordinating role, facilitating cross-agency collaboration and cooperation to produce innovative, joined-up services involving public- and third-sector organizations, especially for vulnerable people. Many policy-makers and practitioners in the UK are seeing the future role of local government as commissioning from a range of service providers – only including those provided from within the public sector if they are evidentially better and more efficient than potential competition.

In practice, though, the shift to contracting in many countries such as the UK and the US has not led to widespread privatization of public services. Many of the services provided by third-sector organizations are relatively new. Thus, contracting has been used to respond to innovation and create entirely new services, frequently in response to new social movements such as the women's movement. For instance, in the US, the UK and Canada, domestic violence programs are provided by voluntary agencies under government contract. Many other examples exist, including immigrant assistance and AIDS services. In the UK, national program such as Surestart, the Children's Fund and Connexions provided new opportunities for third-sector providers to offer new services, and in some areas the third sector increased its role as service provider quite considerably – although a frequent complaint of third-sector organizations is that they are used when funding streams are short-term and uncertain because it is easier to discontinue an external contract than to lay off government employees.

The political attractiveness of contracting and the use of contracting as a quick way to respond to new needs is evident in the growth of contracting among governments and large multi-national NGOs such as Save the Children, CARE and Oxfam. These third-sector organizations receive hundreds of millions of dollars in contracts to provide humanitarian relief and development programs. In addition, many countries in the developing world have contracts with locally based NGOs for a variety of important services. The extent of contracting in the developing world has exploded in the last twenty years owing to the changing character of foreign aid; recurring crises, wars and natural disasters; and political liberalization allowing the growth of the NGOs.

In the UK, these aspirations for greater engagement of the third sector in providing public services through contract has been generally welcomed by much of the third sector (Etherington 2006). Nonetheless, little evidence exists to suggest that significant redistribution of work from the public sector to the third sector has occurred despite specific targets for third-sector provision. For example, a Public Accounts Committee report published in 2006, *Working with the Voluntary Sector*, found that the government had failed to meet key targets to increase the third sector's involvement in public services (Public Accounts Committee 2006). The committee recommended that new targets should be established beyond 2006 to provide a real incentive for departments to increase their involvement in the sector. Indeed, the creation of children's and adult services authorities has resulted in work previously contracted out to the third sector transferring back into local authorities (including SureStart, the Children's Fund and Connexions services). And it should be noted that the UK government's targets to increase the proportion of services provided by the third sector are in conflict with government policy to develop local-authority commissioning capacity which is focused on choosing the best provider (in terms of willingness to change, efficiency and impact on outcomes), regardless of sector. Commissioners in England are being trained to focus on outcomes and to be sector-neutral. Arguably, the threat of privatization is acting as a spur for innovation and service improvement within the public sector as suggested by recent changes and reforms in adult and children's services in the UK.

One additional trend is evident in the relationship between government and the third sector. In the last ten years, many countries have implemented policies to individualize and personalize services. In some countries, the result is new consumer subsidies as a strategy to provide needed public services. Many countries offer childcare vouchers for eligible parents that the family can use to pay for childcare from any eligible provider (Adams, Rohacek and Snyder 2008; Simonen and Kovalainen 1998). And many countries increasingly employ housing vouchers to help the poor and disabled afford adequate housing (Priemus 2000).

Further, in the UK, the US and elsewhere, policy-makers, service-providers and consumers have individual budgets to personalize services for the aged and for people with disabilities through greater individual control over service decisions. Typically, the service recipient makes the decision on service providers with the help of a public service broker. Some recent studies show enormous benefits for individuals and considerable savings to the public purse.[3]

While both vouchers and individual budgets for social and child care and housing are not typically earmarked for third-sector organizations, they have had important direct and indirect effects on government–third-sector relationships. Individual budgets and vouchers call for new funding arrangements. Commissioners need to know the unit cost and overall value of services, producing an incentive for government administrators to create new contract forms including more spot purchasing for specific clients or circumstances and less reliance on potentially wasteful block contracts that provide funding for a group of clients and services. Skilled commissioners will need to understand how each provider is financed and the critical balance between fixed and variable costs. In general, individual budgets and vouchers encourage greater competition among service agencies and greater uncertainty among providers on receiving payments from government. However, individual budgets and vouchers tend to shine the spotlight on the quality and impact of services and encourage service providers to market their services directly to potential clients and the public in ways that could potentially lead to greater responsiveness to clients in the future.

Contracting in practice

The expansion of government contracting with third-sector organizations has created new challenges and opportunities for these organizations and, more broadly, the governance of public services. These challenges can be grouped into three broad categories: performance contracting and management; self-regulation, inspection, quality assurance and accreditation; and competition. Each of these factors has a substantial and enduring effect on the governance of services provided by third-sector organizations including the respective roles and responsibilities of public managers and the boards and staff of third-sector organizations. As will be discussed, these developments and challenges such as performance contracting can undermine the potential advantages of third-sector organizations that attracted public managers to engage these organizations in public service delivery through contracts. Also, these challenges and the effect on the third sector will also be evaluated at the end of each section with respect to the standards for good governance for the public services developed in 2004 by an independent commission jointly sponsored by the Office for Public Management (OPM) and the Chartered Institute of Public Finance and Accountancy (CIPFA).

Performance contracting and management

To varying degrees, the growth of government contracting with third-sector organizations has produced increasingly intensive efforts to hold these organizations to account. This effort began with the initial build-up of government contracting. Service agencies were expected to be accountable for their expenditure of public contract funds. However, this accountability tended to be in a line-item sense: Were the public funds spent according to the stipulations of the contract? This "process" or "regulatory" accountability typically involved reporting the number of clients served or meals delivered as well as a budgetary breakdown on the allocation of various expenditures (Behn and Kant 1999). Government also tried to increase the likelihood that the contract agency delivered a quality program by requiring staff and program standards even before any money was distributed. This objective is often achieved by a pre-qualifiying questionnaire in which evidence of accreditation, governance and financial solvency are required. In this initial period, accountability expectations tended to be relatively modest and/or informal.

Over time, many policy-makers became disenchanted with this process accountability, arguing that it provided little evidence of the effectiveness with which programs were achieving their desired outcomes. Further, government administrators worried about the potential mismatch between public- and third-sector priorities. As a result, public funders began to require that service agencies measure the impact they are having on outcomes for service users and taxpayers. Toward this end, government funding agencies instituted, to varying degrees depending upon the country and jurisdiction, performance-based contracting that strives to hold nonprofit (and for-profit) agencies accountable for reaching specific performance targets (Behn and Kant 1999; Forsythe 2001). Indeed, many governments, including the US, the UK, Australia and New Zealand, will not reimburse third-sector organizations unless they meet performance targets, although the extent and rigor of the performance contracting varies depending upon the service category and prevailing public policies (Smith forthcoming; Lyons forthcoming; Phillips forthcoming).

Outcomes-based contracting is being developed across the world. Rather than specifying activities and processes, commissioners are now working out how best to specify outcomes. Thus, third-sector service providers are increasingly expected to design the optimal service for the money available and demonstrate success through evidence of the impact on outcomes. Toward this end, in the UK, many policy-makers and administrators have embraced, the framework of Results Based Accountability by Marc Friedman (2005) and similar approaches that focus commissioners and service providers on outcomes. Friedman initially developed his ideas through work with federal and state governments in the US. His work is already beginning to be reflected in the nature of contracts in the UK and other countries, including New Zealand, which will over time change the way in which third-sector organizations measure and manage performance internally and the focus of attention of their boards.

Better performance by service agencies was of course a central goal of many policy-makers interested in expanding government contracting with nonprofit organizations; thus, the widespread application of performance management to third-sector organizations receiving public funds is a logical development. However, this heightened interest in performance has a number of implications for the governance of third-sector organizations, including the role of voluntarism within these agencies. This shift to outcome evaluation often involves a revolution in thinking for agencies and their overall management. Agencies need new investments in management information systems and monitoring in order to track and compile important programmatic and financial data, track outcomes (to the extent feasible), and better understand their cost structure. The effect is to "professionalize" the administrative infrastructure of third-sector organizations that can then create problems of mission and focus for an organization since a more substantial infrastructure can require new resources that may be at variance with the previous programmatic focus of the organization. However, professionalization can also be beneficial for the organization because it may allow the organization to manage its finances and programs more effectively. Overall, a more professionalized infrastructure may be required in order to sustain the organization and have a positive impact.

Moreover, in the UK, government is striving to standardize the assessment and referral forms used by all service providers in many services, including social housing, children's and adult services, in order to facilitate personalization and the collection of evidence of impact on outcomes from all the different service providers in these service categories. For example, children with additional needs will not be able to access the range of services without a Common Assessment Form (CAF) and a lead professional. Third-sector organizations will need to complete these forms and act as lead professionals, which will further standardize their work since compliance with these regulations will be required.

These adaptations can be an especially difficult challenge for smaller community-based organizations, given their relative undercapitalization and specialization. Many third-sector organizations started through community initiative often lack, at least initially, a highly trained professional or administrative staff. Some of these agencies originally emerge from an unincorporated group of people concerned about a social problem. A clear separation between the board and staff is absent, and many of these agencies do not have full-time executive directors. Government accountability measures, including performance-based contracts, often require these agencies to adopt new administrative procedures, add professionals, institute new financial management practices and, in some cases, modify existing physical structures. Consequently, the voluntarism that is the hallmark of many community agencies in their start-up phase is difficult to sustain in the current environment with the pressure to be more accountable to government and donors. Given this current emphasis on performance, third-sector organizations that continue to rely upon volunteers in direct service roles tend to be programs offering low-intensity services such as emergency assistance, crisis hot-lines, and tutoring.

Importantly, commissioners and third-sector organizations in the UK and the US have encouraged coalitions of third-sector organizations to come together for the purposes of contracting. This effort is challenging to the independence of third-sector organizations and can undermine their governance even when great care has been taken to agree clear accountability arrangements in writing.

This shift to professionalization and performance contracting can be especially consequential for the relationship between third-sector organizations and their clients. Many third-sector organizations emerge out of a desire of a "community" of people to address a problem or social need such as homelessness, arts education, or workforce development. These individuals create a service agency that regards its mission as logically being responsive to their community of interest (Smith and Lipsky 1993). Government, by contrast, tends to approach services and clients from the norm of equity, consistent with the need of government officials to treat groups and individuals fairly. Equity can be interpreted in a variety of ways, but in social and health services it usually means defining need in order to allocate resources by criteria deemed to be fair – e.g. income, geographic location, and severity of illness or need. Because of their emphasis on responsiveness, third-sector agencies may clash with government, especially on policy matters relating to services, clients and staff. This clash can be especially pronounced under a performance-contracting regime which can leave third-sector agencies little discretion on the performance targets to be met and may require the agency to shift its programmatic focus toward short-term goals and client groups at variance with their original community of interest (Smith and Lipsky 1993). Likewise third-sector organizations established to deliver a particular program of care (such as a "nine-step program" or particular form of therapy) will be challenged by outcome-focused contracts. In the past, they have won contracts from commissioners persuaded of the efficacy of the approach. In the future, they will need to demonstrate impact on outcomes, and in some cases they will have to consider a range of therapies in order to hit targets. If they fail to demonstrate target outcomes, they could be marginalized by commissioners who perceive that the third-sector providers are more concerned with process than with outcomes.

Another difficult program-related dilemma raised by performance contracting and contracting within competitive environments is that agencies may face incentives to "cream" the clients who have the greatest possibility of successful outcomes. For instance, performance-based job-training contracts may encourage agencies to work with clients who can succeed, especially since an agency will not be reimbursed unless clients are successful. In a competitive contract culture, agencies want a positive reputation in order to obtain new contracts or retain existing contracts. This incentive can promote the creaming of clients, even if it is counter to the overall objectives of the contract (see Considine 2003; Behn and Kant 1999).

The government–third-sector organizational relationship may be different if the contract is regarded as a one-time event. In the US, some federal contracts to third-sector agencies are awards for program innovation with no expectation of a continuing contract. However, even in these circumstances, the federal government increasingly requires extensive documentation of program services and finances by the agency. Also, the competition for contract funds means that, even if a contract is a one-time event, the agency may hope to replace a contract with another contract. For example, substance-abuse agencies have been able to obtain federal grants sometimes through the Department of Justice for innovative treatment programs for parolees. However, these agencies often hope that state government will assume the responsibility for funding these services or another federal contract will be awarded to take the place of the expiring contract (Sosin, Smith, Hilton and Jordan forthcoming).

Third-sector agencies may try to overcome some of the limitations imposed by government contracts by using private funds to cross-subsidize the cost of service. Or workers may essentially volunteer their own time to help particular clients in ways that go beyond the expectations of the government contracts. Yet the more recent shift in government funding toward performance contracting and standardization makes it more difficult for agencies to go beyond the expectations of the contract. Low vendor rates and greater competition also push agencies to be more bottom-line-oriented and reduce the "slack" in agency operations. As a result, agency staff are likely to interact with clients differently and focus even more directly on the specific expectations of the government funder.

Importantly, another key trend related to the heightened interest in performance is the growing interest and support among policy-makers and advocates for greater personalization of services. In the US, this trend is reflected in the creation of individual accounts for disabled children and adults that allow them or their guardians to choose their providers and thus direct their public funding.[4] Increased funding for vouchers in housing and childcare, rather than direct contracts to providers, also exemplifies this trend. In the UK, the Department of Children and Families (DCFS) is experimenting with lead practitioners or "brokers" with budget-holding authority who exercise choice in terms of services on behalf of children and families (DCFS 2006; Gillanders 2009). As in the US, the UK government is also establishing an individual budget for the disabled (Prabhakar, Thom, Hurstfield and Parashar 2008). However, this movement toward individual choice places even greater pressure on government to ensure the quality of local providers. Local commissioners and public managers will need to know that providers meet local standards of service and management, including safety and governance. Over time, the shift to vouchers and individual budgets will undermine the traditional contract relationship between government and third-sector providers. It has the potential to improve outcomes by creating more informed managers, purchasers and citizens, but it could also create greater financial and programmatic uncertainty among providers since they will now have to compete for funding with individuals and/or their guardians.

Interestingly enough, the advent of performance contracting and the more recent push for greater choice in services may encourage more community connections by many third-sector agencies. Many agencies founded in the last thirty years were started by individuals who were very passionate about addressing a specific problem, such as economic development, at-risk youth, substance abuse, housing, or mental health. The boards tended to be small, and government contracts tended to encourage passivity in board governance since many board members were not familiar with the intricacies of government contracts and joined the board for their commitment and support for the agency's clients and programs rather than for their funding expertise and connections. Further, since funding was initially adequate to support operations, agency boards had little incentive to seek broad-based community support. But the new pressure to be efficient and more accountable pushes third-sector community agencies to restructure their boards and their community relations in order to improve their competitive position for public contracts and to raise private funding. Agencies also want to have broad community support in order to enhance their profile and perceived legitimacy, particularly given the greater importance of client choice.

In conclusion, set against the six standards described in the Good Governance Standard for Public Services (Independent Commission 2004), the effect of performance contracting on governance is summarized in Table 16.1.

Self-regulation, inspection, accreditation and quality frameworks

The dilemmas and challenges of performance- or outcome-based contracting between government and third-sector organizations has encouraged governments and third-sector organizations across the world to develop new approaches to ensuring service quality and good performance, including greater emphasis on technical assistance and support, self-regulation, inspection and accreditation.

Broadly speaking, technical assistance is often delivered through a variety of different capacity-building initiatives. In the UK and the US, four different approaches to improving the capacity and professionalism of the third sector are evident. First, governments have specifically encouraged the broader application of accreditation policies. In the UK context, accreditation means that organizations or individuals are accredited to deliver a particular service, and that accreditation indicates that they have "*achieved a specified, minimum standard, laid out by the accrediting body*" (Department of Health 2006a: 34). Overall, an accreditation process is a one-off measure of current competence; if an organization is successfully accredited, then it may be awarded a "kitemark". For instance, the acquA accreditation process was developed by third-sector organizations in Herefordshire, UK, and is administered by the Health and Social Care Alliance. Commissioners from the NHS, and local government have agreed not to contract with any organization not accredited through acquA.

Second, in the UK, a strong tradition of regulation and inspection has developed. External bodies set standards and carry out inspections with the aim of assessing whether organizations are meeting the minimum standards required. Regulatory bodies and inspectorates for health and social care in the UK include the Health Care Commission and the Commission for Social Care Inspection (CSCI). In the US, these regulatory bodies such as the Commission on the Accreditation of Rehabilitation Facilities (CARF) and the Joint Commission that accredits healthcare organizations are also

Table 16.1 Impact of performance contracting on governance

Standard	*Effects on third-sector organizations*
Focusing on the organization's purpose and on outcomes for citizens and service users	If the focus is increasingly defined by commissioners, then board members may spend too little time discussing organizational purpose. Outcome performance measures may be set externally and may vary when there are a multiplicity of different contracts to satisfy.
Performing effectively in clearly defined functions and roles	New systems of delegation from the board to executives need to be developed to establish clarity about the lead responsibility for relationships with commissioners.
Promoting values for the whole organization and demonstrating the values of good governance through behavior	Boards need to decide where their values are incompatible with the requirements of commissioners and when to say no to new work. Boards need to review their key relationships and ensure probity through regular review of the interests of members in relation to commissioners. Paradoxically, this effort may have the effect of reducing the number and influence of public officials and politicians on TSOs. Commissioners often require evidence of ethnic and gender diversity on boards as well as the presence of people with financial qualifications.
Taking informed and transparent decisions and managing risk	Boards need to make decisions about their reliance on public contracts (which in many cases is very high). They need to be very clear about the use of charitable funds. Typically these funds are earmarked for innovation and work which is not funded by government contract, which requires separate accountability.
Developing the capacity and capability of the governing body to be effective	May need to include familiarization with commissioners' requirements and ability to represent the organization in public consultations.
Engaging stakeholders and making accountability real	Boards need to work diligently to understand the views of service users and feed these back to commissioners to influence the shape of future contracts. Managing multiple contracts increases the number of stakeholders to manage.

increasingly important as a way for government to encourage service quality and better performance by private providers.

Third, in the UK and the US, growing interest exists in developing quality frameworks specifically tailored for the third sector. A quality framework is a structure for examining the quality of an organization across a number of areas. For example, the UK's Charity Commission's *Hallmarks* describe six overarching principles of an effective charity that together creates a framework for effectiveness to guide charities in their work. Quality frameworks are often used to promote organizational learning and development. Good examples in the UK include Investors in People, Quality Counts and the Good Governance standard for public services which underpins the governance frameworks for local government, Children's Trusts, and wider public services in England and Wales (Audit Commission 2008). In the US, the Maryland Association of Nonprofits has developed the Standards of Excellence which detail good governance standards for nonprofits (Maryland Association of Nonprofits 2009). And the Panel on the Nonprofit Sector (2007) sponsored by the national organization, the Independent Sector, issued a report entitled *Principles of Good Governance and Ethical Practice* as a guide for self-regulation by nonprofits and foundations.

In the UK, peer review is also increasingly regarded as an important strategy to enhance the performance of third-sector organizations. These processes involve external experts in the relevant field assessing an organization's performance or providing challenge and support to an organization. For instance, the Improvement and Development Agency for local government (I&DeA) supports peer review to promote better performance in local government, including commissioning with the third sector (I&DeA 2008). Peer review may involve an individual or team of peer reviewers from within the third sector carrying out an assessment of how well an organization meets the requirements of a quality framework. Another variation that is gaining greater credence is peer referencing whereby individuals or teams of reviewers assess an organization and benchmark it against other comparable organizations in its sector or field. This type of formalized peer review within local government or the third sector tends to be less advanced in most other countries, including the US and Canada.

Peer review and the broad interest in quality standards and frameworks such as the Standards of Excellence are part of a widespread move to enhance the capacity of the third sector for *self-regulation.* For instance, the Charity Commission in the UK (2006) explicitly states a commitment to encouraging self-regulation and a reduced regulatory burden where possible in their Partnership strategy. The Commission states that work currently ongoing to help large umbrella charities review their quality standards tools to reflect the Commission's Hallmarks of an Effective Charity could lead the Commission to withdraw from conducting Review Visits to these charities.

As another indication of the commitment of the UK government to enhancing performance management and regulation in the third sector, the Treasury conducted a cross-cutting examination of the role of the third sector in service delivery as part of the 2002 UK government's Spending Review (HM Treasury 2002). The substantial contribution that the third sector already made to public service delivery underpinned the review, which then produced new government policies regarding the third sector and commissioning. First, new initiatives such as FutureBuilders and CapacityBuilders are designed to increase the capacity and professionalism of the third sector in order to help it meet the demand for more public service provision.[5] Second, government is trying to reduce the barriers in current procurement, commissioning and contracting regimes faced by third-sector organizations in accessing contracts or funds. (Similar initiatives have occurred in the US.) Third, government and third-sector organizations are at least rhetorically committed to the goal that third-sector organizations engaged in public service delivery should be well governed and managed, properly regulated, and meet at least the minimum programmatic, managerial and ethical standards (NCVO 2008).

The tension between government accountability expectations and self-regulation and control by third-sector organizations that is evident in many countries has been especially evident in the UK in recent years. For example, the 2002 UK Treasury review commented:

> in contracting with the voluntary community sector to deliver services, Government must ensure that regulation is proportionate and the independence of the sector is recognized; the greater the regulation, the greater the risk that the best features of the sector are smothered.
>
> (HM Treasury 2002: 17)

In more recent policy statements, such as the Report of the Third Sector Commissioning Task Force (Department of Health 2006), the Government stressed the need for the third sector to demonstrate their "fitness for purpose". However, the report also warns that "disproportionate and inconsistent demands of multiple regulators" presents a major barrier to increasing the involvement of the third sector in service delivery. The report also suggests that a simplification of the present regulation system is needed, commenting that:

> Regulation, licensing and accreditation of health and social care providers needs to be equitable, proportionate, risk-based and streamlined, so that it optimises the overall inspection and monitoring burden proportionate to the balance of users', providers', commissioners' and regulators' needs.
>
> (Department of Health 2006b: 17)

The report also highlights the merits of peer-review initiatives such as acquA to enable the third sector to meet the demands of contracting with public-sector organizations.[6]

To streamline regulation further, the UK government's Better Regulation Task Force (BRTF) (2005) issued a report entitled "*Better Regulation for Civil Society*", which recommended that the UK funding and regulatory government departments undertake a systematic measurement of the administrative burdens associated with third-sector contracts. The principle of proportionality in regulatory systems is particularly pertinent for the third sector, meaning that a regulatory system does not treat all organizations the same but is proportional to the organization's size and capability to respond to regulatory requirements.

Another vitally important influence on third-sector organizations in the UK is the Compact: a formal agreement negotiated between the government and leading third-sector organizations in 1998. It is intended to apply to the interactions between government at all levels including local government and the NHS and the third sector. After a slow start, most local commissioners are implementing the basic principles of the Compact whenever they are contracting with third-sector organizations. Indeed, the Commissioner for the Compact is considering plans to develop a potential accreditation for good Compact practice (Compact 2008).

The UK Compact has generated broad attention throughout the world from governments and third-sector organizations. Some countries, such as Australia, have experimented with local-level compacts (Casey and Dalton 2006). However, no country has yet developed as structured an agreement and relationship as the UK. The reasons for the divergence between the UK and the rest of world relate to its strong national government, extensive voluntary sector, and relatively weak local government. Further, many leading voluntary organizations in the UK are highly dependent upon state support – unlike in the US where the extent of government support varies widely. Other countries such as Germany and the Netherlands already have corporatist-like structures in place that permit and encourage bargaining between government and the voluntary sector, mitigating somewhat the pressure to create new institutions and structures like the Compact.

In sum, contracting in the UK, the US and other countries appears to be entering a new uncertain phase: greater interest in accountability and performance but also more support for decentralization, discretion and individual choice. In this sense, the tensions evident in contracting with third-sector organizations embody some of the inherent contradictions of the New Public Management more generally (Rhodes 1996) which promotes markets and better performance and more community and citizen responsiveness. The push for accountability is creating stricter standardization of expectations by government of third-sector organizations. Board members and staff of third-sector organizations may thus feel very disaffected because of the lack of independence and the burdens of compliance. One could argue that the endgame is the transfer of better governance practices to the board of third-sector organizations and the consequent reduction of external regulation and inspection. However, this shift seems unlikely. Meanwhile third-sector provider organizations in many countries, including the UK, the US, Australia and Canada, face the need to be increasingly compliant and accountable in everything they do.

In conclusion, set against the six standards described in the Good Governance standard for public services (Independent Commission 2004), the effect of increasing external regulation and inspection on governance is similar in some respects with the impact of performance contracting. These effects are summarized in Table 16.2.

Increased competition

The growth of performance contracts and the more general interest in enhanced accountability promotes greater competition for public contracts and private donations, although obstacles to effective competition and broader counter-trends at the street-level promoting collaboration also make the implementation of effective competition practices difficult. In the initial build-up of government contracting with third-sector organizations, most agencies did not really compete with other agencies for contracts. In the US and in other countries, most contracts were cost-reimbursement contracts that essentially paid agencies for their costs based upon the contract terms and budget. Reimbursement was not linked to outcomes, and most agencies recovered their costs (at least as specified in the contract). Little incentive existed for agencies to compete with other agencies for contracts since contracts were unlikely to be moved from one agency to another unless egregious problems existed. Moreover, outcome data were lacking that would provide a basis for changing contract agencies. The advent of performance contracting gives government much more information and justification for changing contract agencies if performance targets are not being met. At least some third-sector organizations also have an incentive to compete with their fellow agencies since they could potentially grow through additional contracts.

The increase in competition for public and private grants (and clients) is also related to other important trends affecting third-sector agencies. Public commissioners are seeking to provide a more level playing field for service providers from different sectors, creating more competition for third-sector organizations from for-profit and public-sector teams, although the extent of this competition varies greatly depending upon the jurisdiction.

Thus, for-profit firms now compete for contracts in service categories previously dominated by third-sector providers, including childcare, home care, and community programs for the mentally ill and developmentally disabled. For-profits may possess some advantages vis-à-vis nonprofits in the

Table 16.2 Impact of external regulation on governance

Standards	*Effects on third-sector organizations*
Focusing on the organization's purpose and on outcomes for citizens and service users	Boards tend to focus their time on preparation for and reaction to external judgments rather than on satisfying themselves that the organization is performing well. This emphasis can in turn distance the board from operations. Board members often feel that external judgments are unfair and do not reflect how the organization is working on the ground. This lack of understanding can be a serious threat to the third sector and its ability to recruit passionate and enthusiastic members. One of the purposes of self and peer review processes is to put boards back into the driving seat.
Performing effectively in clearly defined functions and roles	New systems of delegation from the board to executives need to be developed to establish clarity about the lead responsibility for relationships with inspectors and regulators. Chairs and board members are usually interviewed by external inspectors keen to judge the effectiveness of relationships with the executive and with stakeholders. Staff who have not been fully engaged before the inspection find this personally challenging, and it is a significant organizational risk.
Promoting values for the whole organization and demonstrating the values of good governance through behavior	Values and behavior are rarely the target of external inspections apart from issues of accountability for public money, probity and ethics. Areas for investigation may then come from members of the public or service users. External inspection puts considerable pressures on boards to ensure that their membership is ethnically and gender diverse. When the organization encounters financial and/or programmatic problems, inspection reports may require new board members with particular expertise (often financial) to be recruited.
Taking informed and transparent decisions and managing risk	Inspectors look for evidence of good business management through examination of agenda and minutes. Risk management is inspected.
Developing the capacity and capability of the governing body to be effective	Regulatory bodies often provide training and conferences for board members. This training then promotes standardization of board composition and behaviors within service sectors.
Engaging stakeholders and making accountability real	Boards need to produce evidence of the meaningful involvement of service users and other stakeholders and their influence on decision-making.

competition for contracts and government funding. First, for-profit chains have access to capital and a sufficient size that allows substantial economies of scale, allowing it to operate at least some programs more efficiently. Second, many third-sector organizations are mission-based and small and unwilling to serve certain type of clients or in specific regions, reducing the opportunities for them to cross-subsidize their operations through growth or a diversified client mix. Many community-based organizations may also be very ambivalent about expansion (or lack the capacity for growth). For-profits typically do not have these types of mission constraints and, consequently, may be more willing to serve a diverse mix of clients, including controversial clients. Third, for-profits tend to be newer entrants to the provision of some types of services such as home care or community programs for the mentally ill. As a new entrant, they may be able to obtain substantially higher rates for their services than a thirty-year-old community-based organization since rates for specific agencies tend to be quite dependent upon the date of founding (and the negotiating skill of the chief executive). Once established, rates tend to grow incrementally, and during periods of fiscal crisis or austerity actually decline.

The variation in the mix of for-profits and third-sector organizations in particular service categories in different localities reflects several factors. Some jurisdictions discourage or restrict the entry of for-profits. In some areas, the third-sector provider community is so large and entrenched that for-profits are themselves discouraged from entering specific service markets. For-profits may avoid financially risky services such as serving the homeless mentally ill. Further, rates for some services may be so low that for-profits may find it difficult to make a profit; hence nonprofits that can cross-subsidize their services with private donations or earned income may have a competitive advantage.

A second important trend facilitating greater competition is the push for greater client choice in the selection of service agencies, especially in community care for the aged and disabled. To the extent that clients have greater choice of services, agencies will need to adjust by marketing their services to citizens and competing with other agencies. The movement toward client choice varies significantly between countries and even within countries. Nonetheless, this trend is especially noticeable in services for the elderly, MR/DD clients, and the chronic mentally ill that offer them more independence and control over their own lives. While client choice in service providers remains limited in some service categories and jurisdictions, it is slowly building momentum and influence, so it is likely that greater choice will be available in the coming years.

The third factor promoting competition is the sheer number of third-sector organizations in many communities. Many are relatively small and young. So they are now at a point in their organizational life-cycle where some of the initial grants and contracts are expiring or maturing. So these organizations need to create a sustainable plan for the future that includes new sources of revenue. This planning often involves competing for public contracts and grants.

Finally, the increasingly intensive accountability measures including performance contracts can intensify the competitive pressure on nonprofits. Specifically, performance contracts raise the specter that an agency could lose its contracts if it did not meet specific performance targets. Relatedly, governments in the UK, the US (Smith forthcoming) and elsewhere have restructured many contracts from a cost-reimbursement to a fee-for-service, allowing government to exert greater fiscal and programmatic control over contract agencies (at least theoretically); in effect, contracts and funding from government (and private funders) is increasingly restricted, creating greater uncertainty and prompting agencies to be more aggressive in seeking new funding sources. This trend can be counter to other strands of government policy which stress the need for long-term partnerships in which contract relationships are open, transparent and characterized by continuous improvement on both sides.

The greater competition for public contracts (and private donations, depending upon the country) encourages third-sector organizations to tap earned income and fees more extensively as a source of revenues. In the context of social and health services, fees and earned income can involve a variety of diverse revenue options: the payment of fees by individuals, public and private insurance companies, and corporations; selling services such as technical assistance or cookbooks; earning money from client-run businesses, such as a restaurant staffed by the disadvantaged; real-estate development (including parking revenue); and selling food at a local festival.

Despite the broad attention to earned income and fees by third-sector organizations (Alter 2007), many third-sector organizations are not well positioned to raise substantial earned income through the sale of services (Foster and Bradach 2005). Many community organizations are, as noted, undercapitalized, limiting their ability to launch new projects or initiatives. They also tend to be very value-driven, with scant interest in expanding their earned income. Also, many agencies do not have any service that they can profitably sell on the "market".

The growing emphasis on earned income and competition raises a broader concern that many community-based organizations may feel pressure to be more competitive and emphasize services that generate adequate public and private revenues, thus shifting away from their commitment to supporting valued community services lacking adequate funding (Eikenberry and Kluver 2004; Alexander, Nank and Stivers 1999). In the process, nonprofits may change their governance structure through staffing and board changes that diminish their commitment to longstanding values and their historical mission. However, some third-sector organizations may deepen their connections to their community in response to competition since agencies have an incentive to broaden their community and political support to aid them in successfully winning contracts, obtaining private grants and donations, and developing earned income sources (which often need private grants for their initial capital).

Overall, the trend is certainly toward greater competition among contract agencies; however, other developments are encouraging nonprofits to consider greater collaboration with other public and private organizations. The economic crisis is forcing increased consideration of collaboration among service agencies to reduce costs – including, in more extreme cases, full-scale merger. Faced with fewer financially stable agencies, government officials may feel pressure to work more collaboratively with third-sector service providers. And some localities lack a sufficient number of third-sector providers to have effective market competition for government contracts. Also, contracts themselves have become more complex and may include requirements for collaboration among service agencies. For example, a program for at-risk youth may be delivered by a third-sector organization in collaboration with the local school district.

In conclusion, set against the six standards described in the Good Governance standard for public services (Independent Commission 2004), the effect of competition on governance is summarized in Table 16.3.

The politics of contracting

Prior to extensive contracting, agencies tended to focus on their own private set of concerns that were regarded as quite separate from the public sector, and government regulation was quite minimal. Consequently, agencies possessed little incentive to actively lobby government (especially since government was unlikely to respond with any substantial changes in policy). However, contracting profoundly changed the incentives faced by third-sector organizations regarding political activity and their interest in influencing government policy. The availability of contracts meant that agencies could obtain funds for new and existing programs. And agencies receiving government contracts were directly affected by government policy regarding contract rates, regulations and programmatic standards, referral policies and the overall budget climate. As a result, third-sector organizations are now in a different political position than prior to the contract era, with much greater incentive to engage in the political arena and to strive to influence public policy.

Nonetheless, third-sector organizations can face significant obstacles to political activity and advocacy. As noted, many agencies are quite small and lack the staff resources actively to participate in the political process. The board members of many third-sector organizations tend to be attracted to board service owing to their commitment to the agency's mission and services such as child welfare or homelessness; consequently, most board

Table 16.3 Impact of competition on governance

Standards	*Effects on third-sector organizations*
Focusing on the organization's purpose and on outcomes for citizens and service users	Faced with increasing competition, it is tempting for boards to chase work and to let mission drift. Competition can drive down costs, and then quality of service may suffer. The quality problems can then act as a disincentive for voluntary board members to serve. Outcome-focused contracting is in many ways difficult to manage when there are high levels of competition since outcomes are often only achieved by collaboration between several different agencies and attribution of results to a single agency is impossible.
Performing effectively in clearly defined functions and roles	Particularly when competitive tendering is underway, chairs, nonexecutives and executives need to be very clear about their relative roles and what they say to whom.
Promoting values for the whole organization and demonstrating the values of good governance through behavior	Collaboration is very often a core value of third-sector organizations, so that competition is a real challenge. Without the motivation of profit maximization, third-sector organizations find competition fundamentally challenging because they may need to reduce costs, compromise quality, stop using volunteers, and/or raise the qualification levels of staff in order to compete. Boards need to be very clear when to say no to new business because they can risk losing high-quality executive staff. Growing from a community-based service provider into a regional or national organization fundamentally changes governance and accountability, and usually results in considerable change in the types of people willing to serve on boards.
Taking informed and transparent decisions and managing risk	Competing for contracted work is inherently risky and time-consuming. Boards should spend time in making decisions about what to compete for and when. They need to ensure that there is the capacity and capability in the organization because winning a tender and then delivering it is resource-hungry and can deflect attention from other important matters.
Developing the capacity and capability of the governing body to be effective	Effective boards are more likely to contribute to winning and retaining work.
Engaging stakeholders and making accountability real	Boards who know their stakeholders are more likely to win and retain work.

members possess little experience with government policy. In many countries, the board and staff of the organization may also be concerned that political activity might jeopardize their relationship with government and, in the US, even their tax-exempt status.[7]

In response to these sometimes contradictory pressures, third-sector organizations have an incentive to construct their political strategies with a recognition of the potential impact on their relationships with government and the resource constraints facing these agencies. First, third-sector organizations in many different countries, including Canada, the UK, Australia and the US, have banded together to create coalitions and associations of providers to lobby government and advocate key agency priorities. These coalitions can be formally incorporated tax-exempt organizations with paid staff or more loosely organized associations with no formal legal status. Some coalitions are sizable enough to have paid staff while other coalitions have no paid staff by the coalition, although they may depend upon the in-kind contributions from the member agencies.

In the UK, two of the most widely known associations representing the third sector are the National Council of Voluntary Organisations (NCVO) and the Association of Chief Executives of Voluntary Organisations (ACEVO). In addition, there is a range of sector-specific bodies such as the National Housing Federation and an emerging group of infrastructure bodies representing, for example, hospices, foundation hospitals and academy schools. In the US, national-level associations include the Alliance for Children and Families and the National Council of Nonprofits. Many state-level coalitions and associations also exist, including the Minnesota Council on Nonprofits as well as subsector organizations such as the Massachusetts Association of Human Service Providers.

A second response of third-sector agencies to the politics of contracting is to hire staff or appoint board members with experience with government contracts. In many jurisdictions, third-sector agencies now have executive directors who previously held important government positions. Board members can now include prominent local leaders with credibility and legitimacy to influence government policy. Of course, individual agencies will vary in the extent to which they have staff with previous government experience; in general, the larger agencies with the more extensive resources are in a better position to compete for these highly desirable staff and executives.

Hiring staff with government experience is a very public acknowledgment that government contracting can be a long-term relationship for many third-sector organizations. Today, third-sector organizations provide an incredibly diverse array of services, often under very difficult circumstances. Many government contracts are for ongoing services such as child welfare, prisoner re-entry programs, community programs for the developmentally disabled and mentally ill, home care for the elderly, and workforce development. To be sure, the certainty of funding is often very unclear and unpredictable. Many agencies, especially larger agencies, may experience declines in some contracts and increases in other contracts in any particular year (Sosin, Smith, Hilton, and Jordan forthcoming; Allard 2008). However, agencies tend to have long-term relationships with government and are expected to be able to weather the cyclical nature of government funding. As a result, third-sector organizations need to invest in their staff with the goal of building productive long-term relationships with government in order to be effective and sustainable; staff with government experience can be of great assistance.

Thinking about the relationship with government as a long-term relationship is reflected in other organizational adaptations to contracting. Government contract administrators place great priority on several key management components: sound financial management, including regular audits; attention to performance management, including the use of current program evaluation models; up-to-date tracking of clients and services; and a good reputation in the local community. In order to meet government expectations on these important priorities, third-sector agencies with contracts (or interested in obtaining contracts) need to invest in expertise in financial management, program evaluation and information technology. Over time, then, government contracting tends to change the internal agency dynamics and management style profoundly.

The movement of professionals back and forth between government and third-sector contract agencies tends to encourage a consensus on programmatic standards in particular service categories. Over time, this consensus can become a characteristic of the "contracting regime" whereupon government and third-sector agencies develop a common set of assumptions to guide their relationships. The regime concept suggests that two parties are mutually dependent upon each other, so that each party cannot easily leave the relationship. However, an equally important aspect of regimes is that one party is typically much more powerful than the other. In the case of contracting regimes, government tends to be the more powerful partner and is in a position to dictate programmatic and financial expectations even in the face of opposition from their contract agencies (Smith and Lipsky 1993; also Considine 2003; Considine and Lewis 2003). For example, a public child welfare department and a set of third-sector child welfare agencies may develop specific norms about acceptable practice, referral policies and reimbursement rates. These norms then guide the behavior and strategic management of the government department and the providers. In this relationship, government is able to drive the evolution of these norms, given their resources and political influence and the relative absence of alternative funding sources for their programs.

Contracting regimes tend to operate based upon a certain level of trust among the two parties, despite this power imbalance. Contracts are often relational and long-term even in instances where competitive bidding is required (Smith and Smyth 1996). This "relational contracting" does not preclude differences of opinion or outright conflict but it does underscore the stability of many contracting arrangements and the importance of cooperation among the two parties (Deakin and Michie 1997; Ring and Van de Ven 1992; Van Slyke 2007). But this cooperation occurs within a framework established by the more powerful partner. Third-sector organizations may cooperate with government on a contract for community care for the chronically mentally ill; but the standards of care, financial regulations and outcome measures are still set largely by government. Put another way, a third-sector organization, by its decision to contract, indicates a willingness to cooperate with government on the implementation of a government program. Consequently, relational contracting does not capture the nature of typical contracting relationships since "relational" implies equity in decision-making and power.

In the process, third-sector organizations tend to adopt similar internal practices in order to compete effectively for government contracts, and they are in many cases required by the stipulations of the contract to abide by specific financial and programmatic regulations (Smith forthcoming; Sosin, Smith, Hilton and Jordan forthcoming). Organizations with certain cultures or histories may resist these isomorphic tendencies, especially if government contracts are a relatively small part of their overall revenue or if they provide low-intensity services where government regulations are less intrusive and extensive.

Overall, then, the governance of third-sector organizations changes quite profoundly as the contracting relationship evolves and develops, especially in terms of board governance, internal management practices, and external relations including political engagement. The politics of contracting encourages third-sector organizations to engage with government officials and build long-term relationships that position the organizations to obtain contracts and favorable policies and regulations. The ripple effect on the service provider is internal restructuring to ensure that the organization reflects the management priorities of government.

Conclusion

Contracting with third-sector organizations has grown, owing in part to the influence of New Public Management thinking on the value of markets, greater responsiveness, and decentralization. Indeed, commissioners and public managers in the UK, the US and elsewhere are under increasing pressure to get the best-possible value for money when they are deciding how best to commission and how far to involve the third sector in service design and delivery. Moreover, the increase in contracting for public services has brought a greater emphasis on performance and accountability. Yet, in order to achieve better performance, government commissioners have been pressured to depart from the classic market paradigm. In the UK, the central government is investing large sums of money in capacity-building and infrastructure development designed to improve the governance and management of the third sector. This same interest in capacity-building has been evident in many other countries including the US, Canada, New Zealand and Australia. Capacity-building has also promoted an investment approach to contracting that views the government–third-sector relationship as a long-term proposition.

Whilst this capacity-building aims to improve governance, the simultaneous increase in performance accountability and the development of more detailed regulation, inspection and quality assurance systems have in practice removed from the boards of third-sector organizations the immediate need to take direct responsibility for service quality. Increasingly, boards tend to use the results of external inspections and benchmarking systems to judge their own performance, rather than themselves taking a direct interest in what is going on. Board agendas can often be consumed with the reception of inspection reports done by others.

The growth of contracting, pressures to achieve economies of scale, and the sector's responses to competition will likely mean that increasing proportions of the work go to a smaller number of larger contractors, especially given the financial crisis affecting countries throughout the world. Large regional and national third-sector providers find that community and service-user involvement is increasingly difficult to do; yet inspectors and regulators spend more time than before looking for evidence of service-user and community involvement.

In a very real sense, we are in the midst of an important transition period in the third sector in the US, the UK and around the world as board members learn new behaviors individually and as groups, in response to wider changes in public policy pertaining to contracting and government regulation. However, a paucity of evidence exists of the relationship between good governance, impact and outcomes, and more research needs to be done on this significant topic across sectors. In addition, an urgent need exists perhaps to reclassify service providers so that the debate on quality and effectiveness can be moved away from the goals and priorities of a core of traditional third-sector organizations such as large social service providers toward a debate about which organizational forms and governance styles are evidentially better to provide really effective public services. This new debate would then enable objective comparison between traditional third-sector agencies and new social enterprises and quasi-autonomous service providers (in the UK, for example, city academies and foundation hospitals; in the US, charter schools and public development authorities) in a genuine attempt to learn which forms of governance really offer best value for public money. This reassessment should also include a review of the relative merits of small local community-based organizations, given their contribution to active civil society as well as the implications for policy and practice of the growth of large provider organizations. Inadvertently, current policies and practice on contracting may be "killing the golden goose" by undermining effective performance and sustainability and community and civic engagement in third-sector organizations. Board members and staff of third-sector organizations, policymakers, and advocates interested in improving the quality of services and strengthening social citizenship should welcome this inquiry and debate.

Notes

1 The authors would like to thank Putnam Barber, Mary Kay Gugerty, Margaret Harris, and Stephen B. Page for comments on an earlier draft of this chapter and the financial support of the Nancy Bell Evans Center on Nonprofits and Philanthropy at the Evans School of Public Affairs, the University of Washington, for research support in the preparation of this chapter.
2 Scotland and to an extent Wales have somewhat different policies.
3 See, for example, www.in-control.org.uk
4 In the US, the Bush administration, through its New Freedom Initiative (NFI), offered individuals more choice in service providers and helped facilitate more client independence and work opportunities. NFI has financed a variety of demonstration and pilot projects in support of these choice goals throughout the country.
5 For more information on Futurebuilders, see: http://www.futurebuilders-england.org.uk For information on Capacitybuilders, see: http://capacitybuilders.org.uk/
6 For example, the Department of Health Report praises the acquA (Acquiring Accreditation) initiative in Herefordshire as a good example of how third-sector organizations can effectively organize and regulate themselves to meet the more rigorous demands of entering into contractual relationships with public-sector providers for the delivery of health and social care service (p. 19).
7 For information on US experience, see Berry 2003; Bass, Arons, Guinane, and Carter 2007.

References

Adams, Gina, Rohacek, Monice and Snyder, Kathleen (2008) *Child Care Voucher Programs: Provider Experiences in Five Countries*, Washington, DC: The Urban Institute, http://www.urban.org/UploadedPDF/411667_provider_experiences.pdf

Alexander, Jennifer, Nank, Renee and Stivers, Camilla (1999) "Implications of Welfare Reform: Do Nonprofit Survival Strategies Threaten Civil Society", *Nonprofit and Voluntary Sector Quarterly*, 28 (4): 452–75.

Allard, Scott W. (2008) *Out of Reach: Place Poverty and the New American Welfare State*, New Haven, Conn.: Yale University Press.

Alter, Kim (2007) *Social Enterprise Typology*, Portland, Oreg.: Virtue Ventures, http://www.virtueventures.com/setypology.pdf

Audit Commission (2008) *Competition and Contestability: How Councils Can Improve Services through Competition and Contestability*, http://www.improvementnetwork.gov.uk/imp/core/page.do?pageId=1068494

Bass, Gary D., Arons, David F., Guinane, Kay and Carter, Matthew F. (2007) *Seen but Heard: Strengthening Nonprofit Advocacy*, Washington, DC: The Aspen Institute.

Behn, Robert D. (2001) *Rethinking Democratic Accountability*, Washington, DC: The Brookings Institution.

Behn, Robert D. and Kant, Peter A. (1999) "Strategies for Avoiding the Pitfalls of Performance Contracting", *Public Productivity and Management Review*, 22 (4): 470–89.

Berry, Jeffrey M. and Arons, David (2003) *A Voice for Nonprofits*, Washington, DC: The Brookings Institution.

Better Regulation Task Force (BRTF) (2005) *Better Regulation for Civil Society: Making Life Easier for Those Who Help Others*, http://archive.cabinetoffice.gov.uk/brc/upload/assets/www.brc.gov.uk/betregforcivil.pdf

Bode, Ingo (forthcoming) "Creeping Marketization and Post-corporatist Governance: The Transformation of State–nonprofit Relations in Continental Europe", in Susan Phillips and Steven Rathgeb Smith (eds) *Governance and Regulation in the Third Sector*, Abingdon: Routledge.

Burger, Ary and Veldeer, Vic (2001) "The Growth of the Nonprofit Sector in the Netherlands", *Nonprofit and Voluntary Sector Quarterly*, 30 (2): 221–46.

Cabinet Office (2006) *Partnership in Public Services: An Action Plan for Third Sector Involvement*, http://www.cabinetoffice.gov.uk/media/cabinetoffice/third_sector/assets/psd_action_plan.pdf

Casey, John and Dalton, Bronwen (2006) "The Best of Times, the Worst of Times: Community-Sector Advocacy in the Age of 'Compacts'", *Australian Journal of Political Science,* 41 (1): 23–38.

Charity Commission (2006) *Partnership Strategy*, http://www.charity-commission.gov.uk/spr/partner.asp

Compact (2008) *The Concise Compact Guide*, http://www.thecompact.org.uk/files/102396/FileName/TheConciseCompactGuide.pdf

Considine, Mark (2003) "Governance and Competition: The Role of Non-profit Organisations in the Delivery of Public Services", *Australian Journal of Political Science*, 38 (1): 63–77.

Considine, Mark and Lewis, Jenny M. (2003) "Bureaucracy, Network, or Enterprise? Comparing Models of Governance in Australia, Britain, the Netherlands, and New Zealand", *Public Administration Review*, 63 (2): 131–40.

Deakin, Simon and Michie, Jonathan (1997) "Contracts and Competition: An Introduction", *Cambridge Journal of Economics*, 21: 121–5.

Department of Children and Families (DCFS) (2006) *Budget Holding Lead Professional (BLHP)*, www.dcsf.gov.uk/localauthorities/_documents/content/SCYPG07_14-attach.doc

Department of Health (2006a) Report of the Third Sector Commissioning Task Force – Part II Outputs and Implementation. http://www.dh.gov.uk/prod_consum_dh/groups/dh/groups/dh_digitalassets/@dh/@en/documents/digitalassets/dh_4137568.pdf

Department of Health (2006b) *No Excuses. Embrace Partnership Now. Step towards change! Report of the Third Sector Commissioning Task Force* – Part Outputs and Implementation. http://www.dh.gov.uk/prod_consum_dh/groups/dh_digitalassets/@dh/@en/documents/digitalasset/dh_4137568.pdf

Eikenberry, Angela M. and Kluver, Jodi Drapal (2004) "The Marketization of the Nonprofit Sector: Civil Society at Risk?", *Public Administration Review*, 64 (2): 132–40.

Etherington, Stuart (2006) *Annual Conference Keynote Speech*, http://www.ncvo-vol.org.uk/press/speeches/?id=2465

Forsythe, Dall W. (ed.) (2001) *Quicker, Better, Cheaper? Managing Performance in American Government*, Albany, NY: The Rockefeller Institute Press.

Foster, William and Bradach, Jeffrey (2005) "Should Nonprofits Seek Profits?", *Harvard Business Review*, February: 92–100.

Friedman, Mark (2005) *Trying Hard Is Not Enough: How to Produce Measurable Improvements for Customers and Communities*, Victoria, BC: Trafford.

Gillanders, Gillian (2008) *The Budget Holding Lead Professional Pilots Have Lessons for All Children's Services Authorities*, London: OPM, http://myblog.opm.co.uk/?p=57

Gronbjerg, Kirsten (1993) *Understanding Nonprofit Funding*, San Francisco, Calif.: Jossey-Bass.

Gutch, Richard (1992) *Contracting Lessons from the US*, London: National Council of Voluntary Organisations.

Harris, Margaret and Rochester, Colin (eds) (2001) *Voluntary Organisations and Social Policy in Britain*, Basingstoke: Palgrave Macmillan.

Henriksen, Lars Skov and Bundesen, Peter (2004) "The Moving Frontier in Denmark: Voluntary–State Relationships since 1850", *Journal of Social Policy*, 33 (4): 605–25.

Her Majesty's Treasury (2002) *The Role of the Voluntary and Community Sector in Service Delivery: A Cross Cutting Review*, http://www.hm-treasury.gov.uk/d/CCRVolSec02.pdf

Hood, Christopher (1991) "A Public Management for All Seasons", *Public Administration*, 69 (1): 3–19.

Improvement and Development Agency (I&DeA) (2008) *Peer Review: Helping You Improve*, http://www.idea.gov.uk/idk/aio/8748019

Independent Commission for Good Governance in Public Services (2004) *The Good Governance Standard for Public Services*, London: Office for Public Management (OPM)/Chartered Institute of Public Finance and Accountancy (CIPFA), http://www.opm.co.uk/resources/papers/policy/Good_Gov_Standard.pdf

Kettl, Donald (2005) *The Global Public Management Revolution*, Washington, DC: The Brookings Institution.

Kirkpatrick, Ian, Kitchener, Martin and Whipp, Richard (2001) "Out of Sight, Out of Mind: Assessing the Impact of Markets for Children's Residential Care", *Public Administration*, 79 (1): 49–71.

Lundstrom, Tommy and Svedberg, Lars (2003) "The Voluntary Sector in a Social Democratic State: The Case of Sweden", *Journal of Social Policy*, 32 (2): 1–22.

Lyons, Mark (forthcoming) "Australia: A Continuing Love Affair with the New Public Management", in Susan Phillips and Steven Rathgeb Smith (eds) *Governance and Regulation in the Third Sector*, Abingdon: Routledge.

Maryland Association of Nonprofits (2009) *Standards for Excellence: An Ethics and Accountability Code for the Nonprofit Sector*, http://www.marylandnonprofits.org/html/standards/documents/Booket507Revised.pdf

National Conference of Voluntary Organisations (NCVO) (2008) *Governance Hub Stresses Need for Ongoing Collaboration and Investment in Governance Development*, http://www.politics.co.uk/opinion-formers/press-releases/ncvo-governance-hub-stresses-need-ongoing-collaboration-and-investment-in-governance-development-$1215533$364415.htm

Office of Government Commerce (2006) *Buy and Make a Difference: How to Address Social Issues in Procurement*, http://www.ogc.gov.uk/documents/Social_Issues_in_Public_Procurement.pdf

Osborne, David and Gaebler, Ted (1993) *Reinventing Government*, New York: Plume.

Panel on the Nonprofit Sector (2007) *Principles of Good Governance and Ethical Practice*, Washington, DC: The Independent Sector, http://www.nonprofitpanel.org/report/principles/Principles_Guide.pdf

Phillips, Susan (forthcoming) "Regulating for Relational Governance of the Voluntary Sector: Teetering toward Reform in Canada", in Susan Phillips and Steven Rathgeb Smith (eds) *Governance and Regulation in the Third Sector*, Abingdon: Routledge.

Prabhakar, Meera, Thom, Graham, Hurstfield, Jennifer and Parashar, Urvashi (2008) *Individual Budgets for Families with Disabled Children*, London: Department of Children and Families, http://www.dcsf.gov.uk/research/data/uploadfiles/DCSF-RR057.pdf

Priemus, Hugo (2000) "Housing Vouchers: A Contribution from Abroad", in C. Eugene Steuerle et al. (eds) *Vouchers and the Provision of Public Services*, Washington, DC: The Brookings Institution.

Public Accounts Committee (2006) *Working with the Voluntary Sector*, http://www.publications.parliament.uk/pa/cm200506/cmselect/cmpubacc/717/717.pdf

Rhodes, R. A. W. (1996) "The New Governance: Governing without Government", *Political Studies*, 44: 652–67.

Ring, Peter Smith and Van De Ven, Andrew H. (1992) "Structuring Cooperative Relationships between Organizations", *Strategic Management Journal*, 13 (7): 483–98.

Salamon, Lester M. (1987) "Partners in Public Service: The Scope and Theory of Government–Nonprofit Relations", in Walter Powell (ed.) *The Nonprofit Sector: A Research Handbook*, New Haven, Conn.: Yale University Press.

Simonen, Leila and Kovalainen, Anne (1998) "Paradoxes of Social Care Restructuring: The Finnish Case", in Jane Lewis (ed.) *Gender, Social Care and Welfare State Restructuring in Europe*, Aldershot: Ashgate.

Smith, Steven Rathgeb (forthcoming) "The Government–Nonprofit Relationship in the United States: New Challenges and Possibilities", in Susan Phillips and Steven Rathgeb Smith (eds) *Governance and Regulation in the Third Sector*, Abingdon: Routledge.

Smith, Steven Rathgeb and Lipsky, Michael (1993) *Nonprofits for Hire: The Welfare State in the Age of Contracting*, Cambridge, Mass.: Harvard University Press.

Smith, Steven Rathgeb and Smyth, Judith (1996) "Contracting for Services in a Decentralized System", *Journal of Public Administration Research and Theory*, 6 (2): 277–96.

Sosin, Michael, Smith, Steven Rathgeb, Hilton, Timothy and Jordan, Lucy P. (forthcoming) "Temporary Crises and Priority Changes: The Case of State Substance Abuse Systems", *Journal of Public Administration Research and Theory*.

Van Slyke, David M. (2007) "Agents or Stewards: Using Theory to Understand the Government–Nonprofit Contracting Relationship", *Journal of Public Administration Research and Theory*, 17 (2): 157–88.

Part IV

GOVERNANCE OF INTERORGANIZATIONAL NETWORKS

17

TRUST IN GOVERNANCE NETWORKS: LOOKING FOR CONDITIONS FOR INNOVATIVE SOLUTIONS AND OUTCOMES

Erik-Hans Klijn

1. Introduction: governance, governance networks and trust

Authors writing on the subject of governance have begun to acknowledge its new buzzword status. However, an old adage reminds us that if a concept is everything it is nothing (see also Frederickson 2005: 285). Frederickson (2005) asks what has become of public administration in recent years when every area of the field seems to have been subsumed under the broad umbrella of governance.[1] This chapter seeks to discuss the value of trust in governance or governance networks. But, before we do so, we must first assess the meaning of governance.

What is governance?

In his widely cited article, Rhodes (1997) provided six different interpretations of the word "governance". His overview of governance covered corporate governance, new public management, good governance as a socio-cybernetic system, governance as a self-organizing network, and other aspects. Others have added to Rhodes's definitions by including multi-level governance and market governance (see Frederickson 2005; Bekkers et al. 2007). Looking more closely at all the interpretations, I see the following four major definitions to be dominant in the literature (Kooiman 1993; Rhodes 1997; Pierre and Peters 2000; Frederickson 2005; Osborne 2006; Sorensen and Torfing 2007):

1. Governance as *good governance or as corporate governance.* In this view, governance refers to the principles of a properly functioning public administration. Such an administration is characterized by the fair treatment of

citizens and an unambiguous organization that adheres to the basic principles of the rule of law. The emphasis here is on the operation of government, rather than on the manner in which government is organized. However, this view of governance adds little to classical ideas of government or even bureaucracy.

2. Governance as *new public management*, a means of improving performance and accountability or a form of *market governance* (Osborne and Gaebler 1992; Bekkers et al. 2007). Under this definition, the role of governments is to steer rather than to row (Osborne and Gaebler 1992). The focus of government should be to set goals, and not to control the implementation process. Policy implementation is best left to separate public or private agencies which can be held accountable through the use of clear performance indicators and other market mechanisms. This definition of governance is similar to that of new public management, which stresses that governments should guide performance from a distance, using performance indicators and market mechanisms to arrange services and secure policy outputs. Governance under this definition is almost akin to "political functioning".

However, it is important to remember that governance is something completely different from the concept of New Public Management. While governance tends to emphasize the horizontal relationships between governmental organizations and other organizations, New Public Management can be considered an opposing paradigm to governance in many ways since it emphasizes central steering. In much of the New Public Management literature, one can find the assumption that the function of politics is to set clear goals, steer progress with clear and cleverly designed incentives, and then leave implementation to other organizations (Osborne and Gaebler 1992; Hood 1991).

3. Governance as *multi-level governance or intergovernmental relations.* In some studies in the governance literature, governance is described as multilayer government or intergovernmental governance. These are two separate strands of literature that are distinctly different from each other. Nonetheless, their common theme is the difficulty of achieving results in a multi-actor setting. Although not all studies explicitly use the network concept, this literature stresses that networks are needed to address all aspects of governance problems because these tend to cross public organization boundaries and their hierarchical levels. For example, governance issues such as those related to the economic regeneration of deprived areas or environmental and pollution issues tend to cross a number of organizational and hierarchical boundaries (Bache and Flinders 2004; Agranoff and McGuire 2003; Hooge and Marks 2004), and the literature in this area focuses on specific types of networks in which public actors from various levels have prominent positions.

4. Governance as *network governance* (both self-steering or non-self-steering). Governance and the network concept are strongly related in some parts of the governance literature (Kooiman 1993; Rhodes 1997; Kickert et al. 1997; Sorensen and Torfing 2007). Governance takes place mainly within the fluid network of public and non-public actors, and the interaction between these groups makes the processes of governance complex and difficult to manage. Consequently, the steering and management strategies required are different from that used in more classical approaches. The focus under this definition is on the complex interaction process, and the process of negotiation in a network of governmental organizations and other organizations that are both private and public (not-for-profit).

Looking at the four conceptualizations of governance, we can conclude that there is little reason to differentiate between governance and governance networks, since the two more interesting conceptualizations (3 and 4) of governance tend to stress that governance takes place within a networks of actors. At best, we can make a faint distinction by saying that governance relates to the interaction process (and its guidance), while networks relate to the empirical phenomenon that policy issues are solved within networks of actors (for a more elaborate discussion of this distinction, see Klijn 2008). Thus, governance networks will be used here as an indication of *more or less stable patterns of social relationships (interactions, cognitions and rules) between mutually dependent public, semi-public and private actors that arise and build up around complex policy issues or policy programmes.*[2]

Trust in governance networks: the crux of the issue

Trust is often mentioned as the core coordination mechanism of networks. Trust is often contrasted with two other forms of governance: markets and hierarchies (Thompson et al. 1991). Hierarchies are characterized by rules and central steering, while markets are dominated by the decentralized mechanism of prices as dictated by supply and demand. The discussion on trust as a core coordination mechanism in networks is often somewhat misleading and confusing in that it places networks somewhere between markets and hierarchies, when in fact this practice reveals little about networks. This placement blurs more than it illuminates because networks tend to incorporate traces of several coordination mechanisms other than trust at the same time, including rules and central steering, market mechanisms and bargaining (see Koppenjan and Klijn 2004). Given this mix, the idea of trust as the core coordination mechanism in networks is not exceedingly useful. Nonetheless, we would do well to remember that the inclusion of trust is not entirely without merit.

This chapter: the importance of trust in ensuring innovative governance network related outcomes

This chapter argues that trust is an important element of governance networks. We shall demonstrate that the function of a governance network is essentially to facilitate negotiations and reconcile different values with each other. For a network to be successful, innovative policy proposals have to be achieved within the complex interaction process. Trust is an essential component that facilitates fluent interactions, the flow of information, and other conditions necessary for actors to develop innovative solutions. However, trust does not arise automatically. It has to be consciously achieved through improvements in the interaction between actors and through dedicated network management activities (see also Huxham and Vangen 2005).

This chapter will first discuss the essence of governance networks, the value of conflicts, and their necessity in fostering innovative policy proposals. It will then discuss the importance of trust and use empirical evidence to illustrate the contributions of trust to the process. The chapter concludes with a section on how to achieve trust in governance networks.

2. The essence of governance networks: political struggle between actors with differing values

To assess the value or importance of trust in governance networks, we must first look at the essential characteristics of governance networks. It is reasonable to say that much of the literature on governance networks stresses the complexity of the governance process, and emphasizes that these processes should provide new and innovative solutions for societal problems and improve implementation (see Koppenjan and Klijn 2004; Skelcher et al. 2005; Sorenson and Torfing 2007). However, the policy problems that are addressed within governance networks are also often characterized by value conflicts and complex interaction and bargaining processes. So, although innovative policy solutions are necessary, they are not easily won since various actors favor different, often conflicting values and policy solutions.

Governance networks as wicked issues, and value conflicts

Most of the issues that are dealt with within governance networks are fairly complex. Typical projects include large infrastructure developments, water safety and water management projects, and other complex service delivery initiatives involving more than one partner. These problems are referred to in the literature as "wicked problems" (see Rittel and Webber 1973). Wicked problems are policy issues that involve many actors who often disagree about the nature of the problem and the desired solution. In addition, there is usually insufficient or controversial information surrounding these problems, which makes it difficult to interpret them and to find appropriate solutions. Wicked problems are difficult to resolve as they almost always involve tricky conflicts between values and scarce resources. Looking at decisions related to infrastructure such as the building or expansion of a road, the question of which of the following values to prioritize arises in earnest:

- transport values (prioritizing the expansion of the road so that traffic is facilitated)
- liveability values (prioritizing the values of inhabitants around the road who suffer from the negative external effects of its use and expansion)
- environmental values (prioritizing the elements of nature that will suffer as a result of the expansion of the road)

Such conflicting values make it difficult to derive a univocal criterion for good governance network outcomes (Kickert et al. 1997; Mandell 2001). In the above example, key actors who hold the differing values include environmental interest groups that promote environmental values, the ministry of transport that favors road expansion, and citizen/inhabitant groups who hold liveability-related values that drive them to protect their living environments. All the actors demand a say in the decision-making process, and their inclusion makes decision-making within the governance network immensely complex.

However, while the process may be contentious, there is little that is illegitimate about it. None of the actors typically pursues unlawful efforts, and their attempts to influence the decision-making process can be seen as a normal part of a mature democracy in which actors can articulate their interests in a relatively open decision-making process. From this point of view, the often heard complaints in the world of politics, bureaucracy and the media about lengthy decision procedures, too many interest groups, and so on seem questionable. Fault-finders (usually ministries) often protest because they feel that their values are compromised in the trade-off against the values of other stakeholders.

Governance networks as complex interactions

Given the value difference, it is not surprising that a large number of actors are part of the governance networks in which these wicked problems are dealt with. Recent research in the Netherlands shows that twelve different organizations are involved in an average environmental planning project (Klijn et al. 2010). It is typical for the network relationships to exist over a longer period of time, and to change as a result of the interactions between the actors involved and their interpretations of the problem space (for a more elaborate discussion of these ideas, see Koppenjan and Klijn 2004). Governance networks thus manifest themselves in concrete policy interactions, which can be seen as policy games that are played by the different actors. During these games, the actors attempt to influence policy issues, partly by reinterpreting the available information and the informal and formal rules that were previously generated.[3] In short, governance networks can be characterized by intense dynamism and a high degree of complexity (Teisman et al. 2009), which makes them very difficult to manage. Managers and other parties involved in the negotiations are often surprised by the many unexpected turns of events, and by the unexpected effects of the dynamic interactions between individual actors and their strategic choices.

Governance networks as a conduit for the value-driven search for solutions

The wicked character of governance network processes renders them intrinsically political in nature. Governance networks essentially present a struggle between differing values, how problems are defined, and how solutions are derived. If, following Easton (1953) (and many other Public Administration experts), we define politics as the authoritative allocation of values, the political character of processes in networks becomes clear. However, it also becomes clear that this process of authoritative allocation no longer takes place solely within representational bodies. A number of writers have argued that politics is removed from governance networks (e.g. Bovens et al. 1995) because politics has been dissolved, or at least partially dissolved, in the network itself where the struggle between all the different groups takes place (also see Klijn and Skelcher 2007). All political institutions including the lower chamber, the various city councils, the provincial states and all the political parties are entrenched in the network of actors. They no longer simply realize the public interest from far above the turmoil of battle. Thus, the often-heard complaint that networks and the interest groups involved in them are a threat to democracy essentially implies that we (i.e. as members of the media, citizens and academics) no longer recognize politics as a visible center of power.

There rarely is a cut-and-dried solution to many of the problems addressed through governance networks, no matter how eagerly the media make us believe that there is. Many of these issues involve problems of which we have little knowledge, problems that are ill-defined, and in which the basic information surrounding the issue is contested. Further, the problems addressed in governance networks rarely can be solved by quick unilateral measures. The different actors differ in their opinions about the desired solutions, and these actors may include civilians, organized groups as well as governmental bodies. The decision-making process itself is a quest for solutions involving the collection of necessary information. Actors work to determine which solutions would be acceptable for as many of the parties involved. In this way, networks can be viewed as efforts to unite various values with one another.

Governance networks: the search for innovative solutions that combine values

The inter-active nature of the network process requires that a good attempt was made to combine the values of various parties which requires new solutions. Creativity is essential to the generation of new solutions. Most of the solutions initially available for consideration are developed by parties advocating their own point of view and their own particular values. For the network to be useful, it has to be able to generate new, innovative solutions that combine information arising from different actors and their resources. But the act of sharing information and resources, and of working cooperatively toward an innovative solution, is often seen by individual actors or interest groups as being risky. None of the actors can fully predict the form that the solution will eventually take. Exchanging information with other actors can lead to a situation in which other actors use the information for their own benefit.

This situation presents a classic mix of the challenges associated with collective decision-making, strategic games and risk-taking (Axelrod 1984; Williamson 1996). Trust becomes even more essential for risk-taking when the actors have opposing perspectives on the nature of the problem, what values are relevant, and the nature of a desirable solution. Governance networks have the potential to serve as a viable means of developing trust and achieving interesting outcomes. This view of networks as a facilitator of trust differs somewhat from the more commonly held view that trust is the core coordination principle of networks, an argument that was criticized at the start of this chapter.

3. Governance networks, trust and risk

In the context of the above discussion, one can begin to see networks as a viable means of achieving collective action. Such networks serve to solidify the otherwise fluid interaction patterns between actors. Uncertainty and risk are key concepts in such governance networks. Thus, trust and managerial activities can be expected to be very important because few authoritative mechanisms exist that serve to bind actors, and the presence of multiple parties heightens strategic uncertainty. What is said in the literature about trust, and its relation to risk and uncertainty, is interesting in this context, and so in this section we further examine the relationship between trust, risk and uncertainty. But, first, we need to establish a workable definition of trust.

What is trust?

Trust is defined in multiple ways in the literature. Before we start a discussion about trust, we have to narrow the range. A few key characteristics emerge from the literature (see Edelenbos and Klijn 2007). First, when an actor trusts another actor, he is in fact taking a risk, and allowing himself to be vulnerable to opportunistic behavior. Each actor expects the other actor to refrain from opportunistic behavior, even if the opportunity for it arises (Deakin and Michie 1997; Deakin and Wilkinson 1998). He or she trusts that the partner will take their interests into account in the interaction (Rousseau et al. 1998; Nooteboom 2002). In unpredictable situations, a minimum level of trust is a prerequisite for any pro-active undertaking (Gambetta 1988; Lane and Bachmann 1998). A conscious choice has to be made to take a risk, and this is usually done with the belief that the other party can be trusted.

A working definition for trust can thus be derived as follows: "Trust refers to the actors' more or less stable, positive perception of the intentions of other actors, that is, the perception that other actors will refrain from opportunistic behavior" (Edelenbos and Klijn 2007). Although trust can be recognized from the actions of the various actors, actions are in turn a result of trust and we have to distinguish trust from the actions themselves. We also have to be careful to make a distinction between trust and institutional characteristics such as rules and norms which often serve to facilitate trustworthy behaviors. These institutional features are not the same as trust. Only the more precise, limited definition of trust can be useful in research; and, as we shall see in section 4, it allows us to measure the level of trust in governance networks by assessing perceptions of trust among network actors.

Trust and risk: a classic economic perspective

Trust does not play a role of any importance in most classical economic views of transactions and market relations. In fact, it is often seen as irrelevant to a normal market situation. Buyers and sellers are led by their own rational behavior, and simple transactions can be dealt with using classical contracts or a firm handshake. Most economic analysts see no use for the concept of trust, even in more complex situations involving specific investments and long-term relations. Although most would accept that we face a situation of incomplete contracts (and incomplete information), they would suggest means other than trust to address these concerns. Most analysts would stress that incomplete contracts should come with safeguard mechanisms to protect the contractor against other parties. Their solution to the problem of risk would more likely lie in contractual safeguards and reputation-related incentives (see Lyons and Metha 1997; Lorenz 1999). These safeguards can take the form of bonds, penalties and other contractual agreements, and should serve to prevent opportunistic behavior and facilitate the resolution of ex-post disputes between partners. An alternative to devising safeguards is vertical integration, which provides partners with an incentive to invest efficiently and reduces transaction costs if transactions are frequent, specific and uncertain.

Another way to deal with the problem of uncertainty is to describe and analyze it in terms of reputation: according to this view, actors have an interest in preserving a good reputation for the sake of future deals. This reputation argument is strongly inspired by game theory (Lorenz 1999) and is similar to the arguments of Axelrod (1984), who found that cooperation is possible in repeated prisoner's dilemma games when the gains that can be earned in future (the "shadow of the future") are great enough.

Williamson (1996), the godfather of transaction economics, goes as far as to tell us that trust is a confusing concept because it amounts to nothing more than risk-taking. He says that "*calculative relations should be described in calculative terms, to which the language of risk is exactly suited*" (Williamson 1996: 485–6). In his view, notions of trust blurs the argument, because they cause one party to accept the risk that the other party may be acting opportunistically. In his view, the notion of trust as acting in good faith (without calculation) does not add anything useful to the analysis of the situation.

Williamson distinguishes between trust at the institutional level (trust in the functioning of institutions such as the legal system) and trust at the individual level. In Williamson's neo-institutional perspective, risk-taking is reduced to the problem of calculating whether an organization will begin to work with another organization, and this can be deduced by asking: Is the balance of benefits and costs favorable enough to take the risk that another contracting party might act opportunistically? Also, what risks can an organization afford to take? These questions apply also to concerns about reputation. They allow the problem to be reduced to one in which risks are analyzed and weighed.

Trust, risk and rationality: the need for trust

Most authors on trust agree that trust is inextricably related to risk. Without risk, the notion of trust is simply unnecessary (Rousseau et al. 1998; Lyons and Metha 1997; Lane and Bachmann 1998; Nooteboom 2002). As demonstrated earlier, trust has much to do with the expectations an actor has of another actor. In contractual relations, partnerships and almost all cooperative relations involving private and public actors of various affiliations, actors are confronted with risks that can take various forms. Once we recognize the various kinds of behavioral risks being faced, Williamson's analysis allows for an immediate clarification of the problem. Under this analysis, trust is seen as almost unnecessary, and the concept is viewed as being almost synonymous with risk-taking. The risk-taking perspective assumes that a calculation can be made which then forms the basis for a rational decision. Without such a calculation, the assumption of risk becomes just as blind as trusting the other actors. However, this assumption cannot easily be squared with the idea of bounded rationality, which is also the starting point in the neo-institutional approach. If the possibility of gathering information is limited, then so are the opportunities to assess the behavioral alternatives that independent actors have. Interestingly, this argument holds even more strongly for larger governance networks with greater numbers of actors and where unexpected strategic moves take place more frequently and the possibilities are wider. The uncertainty over the strategic behavior of actors is thus much greater than the term "information insecurity" suggests, certainly as it is presented in the literature on governance networks. In her attempts to define away the social context of choices, Williamson's neo-institutional economics thus implicitly assumes the hyper-rationalism in her argument against trust – a rationalism for which she often critiques classic economic approaches.

Trust and governance networks: a perfect couple

The value of the concept of trust lies in the fact that the environment is too complex for us to foresee all the possible contingencies, reason them out or calculate them accurately (Deakin and Wilkinson 1998). It is precisely the many possible contingencies that present themselves which makes the concept of trust such an interesting one to consider when appraising the performance of governance networks (Edelenbos and Klijn 2007).

Trust provides an anchor with which actors in governance networks determine what risks actors will or will not take in cooperative relations, and it allows them to make their choices accordingly. The fact that trust is *not* the same as calculation and cannot be entirely reduced to purely rational assessments does not mean, as Williamson suggests, that it is blind. Trust does in fact have a rational basis. Most authors point to the fact that trust grows according to the actor's earlier experiences (Nooteboom et al. 1997; Lyons and Metha 1997; Rousseau et al. 1998) and that trust will not be sustained when it is repeatedly violated (Rousseau et al. 1998; Nooteboom 2002) as evidence that the decision to trust is usually well considered. Reciprocal behavior is an essential condition for trust to emerge and to be sustained. This reciprocity is precisely what happens in governance networks.

In other words, trust can only exist by virtue of dependency (Rousseau et al. 1998) and earlier interactions, and these are core features of any established governance network. Actors need each other to realize the outcomes they cannot achieve alone, and networks bring about intensifying interactions and dependencies. Interestingly, these are exactly the conditions mentioned in the literature on trust. One could therefore see networks as a vehicle for achieving trust, rather than assuming (as is done in some of the literature) that trust is an inherent characteristic of networks.

4. The value of trust in governance networks: theoretical and empirical considerations

Why would trust be a favorable condition for the functioning of governance networks and the achievement of positive outcomes in governance networks? Although not inherently written from a governance point of view, several reasons can be found in the literature on trust (see also Edelenbos and Klijn 2007):

- trust reduces transaction costs
- trust facilitates cooperation and stability in (network) relations
- trust stimulates learning and knowledge exchange
- trust stimulates innovation

We shall look at each of these arguments in turn and examine some empirical evidence that supports them.

Trust reduces transaction costs

Trust may bring about a saving in transaction costs. In his book on trust, Fukuyama argues: "Property rights, contracts, and commercial law are all indispensable institutions for creating a modern market-oriented economic system, but it is possible to economize substantially on transaction costs if such institutions are supplemented by social capital and trust" (Fukuyama 1995: 336). Because trust brings about greater predictability in the behavior of key actors, it serves to reduce the risks inherent in transactions and improve the cooperative relationship. After all, in a situation where one actor assumes good intentions on the part of the other, the likelihood of opportunistic behavior leading to unexpected interactions is smaller. But trust also serves as an alternative to contracts, or as a welcome addition to them. Writing contracts is associated with a transaction cost (Williamson 1996), and the more complex the interaction, and the more complex the desired outcomes or products, the more effort actors have to put in to draw a good contract. Not surprisingly, we do not find many contracts and formalized organizational forms emerging from governance networks (see Klijn 2009 for an elaboration of how most public–private partnerships can be seen as relative loosely coupled organizational forms). Tight contracts and heavy organizational forms do not match very well with the complexity and dynamism of the interactions and the decision-making that occurs in governance networks.

As earlier mentioned, in this environment, trust becomes a welcome addition to, or even replacement for contracts (Sako 1998; Ring and Van de Ven 1992; Nooteboom 2002). It reduces the need to include extensive clauses in the contract that cover possibilities that may arise in the future.

Trust enhances investment and stability in relations

The classical neo-economic perspective does not yet fully embrace the concept of trust. Instead it focuses very keenly on the cost aspect and remains rather static in its search for explanations, concentrating almost entirely on production costs, transaction costs, organizational costs and costs resulting from opportunistic behavior in the context of the development of a new technology. Williamson acknowledges (see Nooteboom 2002) that, even though the study of long-term interactions is far more complex, the classical perspective maintains its focus on one-off interactions. It pays little attention to profit, or the relational or investment dynamics (Ring and Van de Ven 1992; Nooteboom et al. 1996). In contrast, in the field of governance networks, long-term interaction is a large area of debate along with dependency and the creation of new innovative products or policy solutions. A greater level of attention is being paid to potential revenues than to costs, and to continuous interaction over the long term instead of to single transactions (see Sako 1998; or Parker and Vaidya 2001).

Trust increases the probability that actors will invest (with resources like money, knowledge, etc.) in cooperation, and it creates stability in the relationship. If trust is present, actors are more willing to invest despite the risks involved. Following the argument of competitive advantages in the private sector (Sako 1998; Nooteboom 2002), one could say that governance networks with a higher level of trust between the actors gain a "policy advantage" in that the lower levels of distrust and uncertainty and the stronger ties between players empower the actors to move more quickly and forcefully.

Trust stimulates learning and knowledge exchange

Much of the knowledge in modern networks, such as that related to specific routines and contacts, is tacit. It lies within specific individuals or organizations (Parker and Vaidya 2001; Nooteboom 2002) and is acquired over many years of experience. It can only be accessed through frequent exchanges and more intensive cooperation. A similar observation can be made regarding the importance of learning (Lundvall 1993). Learning and discovering new things require a high level of knowledge exchange and intensive interaction. Because actors lack the resources and knowledge to realize solutions, they have to interact to acquire them. The performance of these networks is probably strongly dependent on the extent to which they succeed in this exchange.

Needless to say, these forms of knowledge exchange require a minimum of trust to take place. Drawing up a contract in such a network of organizations is far too costly and may even be impossible, given the limited means and typically limited access that parties provide to information that they may hold (Graeber 1993; Parker and Vaidya 2001). Trust serves to facilitate and encourage the flow of information between the actors in governance networks (Edelenbos and Klijn 2007).

Trust stimulates innovation in governance networks

Last but not least is the argument that governance networks need to create innovative solutions for complex problems. As we know from the literature on research and development (R&D) partnerships, the problem with innovation is that it is as risky as it is desirable. R&D has the potential to give firms a clear competitive advantage, but it is impossible to ascertain beforehand if something valuable will come out of the R&D efforts, or if the other partner will do his or her share to further the most desirable outcome (Parker and Vaidya 2001; Lundvall 1993).

From a transaction cost perspective, vertical integration is optimal for this situation (Williamson 1996); but this, too, has its disadvantages. Vertical integration provides incentives for players to minimize their differences, but this has a negative effect on innovation. It is fair to say that the cognitive distance between partners should be neither so great that it prohibits cooperation nor so small that it prohibits innovation (Nooteboom 2000). It is these opposing forces that help explain why organizations in the private sphere increasingly choose to interact within networks (Miles and Snow 1986; Alter and Hage 1993; Lundvalt 1993; Parker and Vaidya 2001).

One of the main reasons for the emergence of governance networks is the fact that they have to deal with wicked problems that require the cooperation of many different actors who have to develop innovative solutions together. Trust is thus invaluable in governance networks as it facilitates innovation by reducing uncertainty about opportunistic behavior, and encourages the horizontal exchange of information and cooperation. One would predict that networks that demonstrate higher levels of trust would show more innovative results and perform better in solving complex policy problems.

Does trust matter in governance networks? Empirical evidence

Although there is a substantial body of research being conducted on matters of trust, this area is seldom addressed in the field of public administration and is almost completely absent in the governance literature (for exceptions, see Edelenbos and Klijn 2007; Klijn et al. 2010). From research done in business administration, especially on partnerships, we know that higher levels of trust have several positive effects, including better relations with suppliers (Nooteboom 2002), which translate into lower costs. Trust also enables relational governance between actors and facilitates cooperation. Examining the literature to determine whether trust matters, McEvily and Zaheer concluded that it does: "In most optimistic sense, we find a number of studies have produced results that are consistent with our own findings that trust enhances inter-organizational performance" (McEvily and Zaheer 2006: 294). But does this also hold for governance networks?

More recently, Klijn, Edelenbos and Steijn (2010) have looked at the relationship between trust and outcomes in governance networks. Judging from their survey of actors involved in a large environmental project, there appears to be a high correlation between the level of trust (as measured by five items) and perceived outcomes. Respondents to this survey made a clear distinction between process and content outcomes, and the researchers found in their regression analysis (which controlled for actor characteristics [e.g. public or private], phase of decision-making and the complexity of the issue) that trust has a very strong relationship with both content (Beta of .534) and process outcomes (Beta of .545). Thus, we are inclined to conclude that trust does matter in governance networks.

5. No trust without (network) managing efforts

It is clear that trust does not arise unaided. If one looks at the many case studies that have been written on governance networks, it is clear that interactions are dominated by actors following their own goals. There is typically a fair amount of distrust related to conflicting strategies, leading to deadlock and other negative outcomes (see Mandell 2001; Marcussen and Torfing 2007). These problems demonstrate a lack of trust and make two additional things clear:

1. Trust is not a characteristic which is naturally present in networks;
2. To achieve trust, it is necessary to facilitate intensive levels of interaction, and the network has to be actively managed.

Trust does not arise unaided: the need for network management

Despite the critical nature of trust, it cannot be assumed to be present in every governance network. The research actually suggests that trust is a relatively scarce commodity in many governance networks and has to be developed over time (Zucker 1986; Lane and Bachmann 1998; Edelenbos and Klijn 2007) by intensifying the interaction between actors. But the greater interaction will only lead to greater trust if the actors see real benefits arising from the interaction (see Nooteboom 2002).

The intensification of the interaction in the pursuit of the development of interesting and rewarding content is a crucial managerial task that forms a key part of the governance and supervision of any governance network. Looking at the literature, network management strategies fall into four main categories (see Agranoff and McGuire 2001; Mandell 2001; Koppenjan and Klijn 2004):

- *arranging:* this includes strategies to organize the interactions in governance networks into temporary organizational structures
- *exploring content:* exploring the varying views of different actors, the new solutions that may arise from interactions with them, and connecting the ideas of different actors
- *connecting:* securing contacts between actors, improving relations, etc.
- *process agreements:* agreements about process rules and methods of interaction between the actors

We know from a wide range of case studies that employing network managerial strategies improves the outcomes of networks (see, for instance, Marcussen and Torfing 2007). In particular, the studies of Meier and O'Toole (2001, 2007) on the Texas educational districts have large sample sizes that convincingly demonstrate the impact of network management strategies, along with other studies (see also Huang and Provan 2007; Klijn et al. 2010). But do network management strategies really enhance trust? What is the nature of the relationship between trust outcomes and network management in governance networks?

The impact of network management on trust

There are very few empirical studies of governance networks that examine the relationship between trust and network management strategies. Although several studies suggest that increasing the intensity of the interactions and employing network management strategies enhance the relations between actors in the governance network (see, for instance, Marcussen and Torfing 2007; Huang and Provan 2007), the level of trust has not been directly related to the intensity and character of the network management strategies employed.

Klijn, Edelenbos and Steijn (2010) asked actors involved in environmental projects questions about their network management strategies. They constructed sixteen items that measured the four types of network management strategies mentioned above, and found a fairly strong correlation between the number of strategies employed in governance networks and the overall level of trust. Interestingly, when the outcomes were included in the regression analysis, it was found that the relation between trust and outcomes diminishes but still remains significant. There also appears to be a significant relationship between network management strategies and outcomes.

So it can be said that both trust and the number of employed network management strategies have independent effects on network outcomes, but network management also positively connects with trust. It seems that better results are achieved in governance networks if active network management is combined with and stimulates a higher level of trust.

6. Conclusion: the value of trust in governance networks

There has been little said about the role of trust in governance networks other than that it serves as a key coordinating mechanism. However, as we have seen in this chapter, this statement is highly debatable since networks are characterized by many coordinating mechanisms. The theoretical literature in fields other than that of governance networks, particularly public administration, provides ample support for the view, as does the scarce empirical material available on the subject.

The main reason for trust's positive impact on the performance of networks lies in its beneficial effect on the cooperation between the actors in the networks and the flow of information it facilitates between actors for the purposes of innovation. Since networks are mostly formed around wicked problems that require such innovative solutions along with the resources of multiple actors, the beneficial effects of trust are clear. Trust also seems to be a promising concept for further examination in the discussion on governance and governance networks.

Notes

1 If one were to seek articles with the word "governance" in Scopus, over 8,000 articles are found. The articles fall under the category of social science, with a large number being from public administration and environmental planning. A significant rise is seen in the number of governance-related between 1996 (106) and 2007 (1193).

2 Despite the stability in the relations of the network, interactions within networks can still be capricious, because actors deploy their own strategies. For an elaboration of this point, see Koppenjan and Klijn 2004.

3 Governance networks can thus be seen as the temporarily solidified form of these policy games: the pattern of interactions at a certain moment in time, the set of perceptions of the actors (and the resemblances and differences) at that moment and the set of valid informal and formal rules at that moment.

References

Agranoff, R. and McGuire, M. (2001) "Big Questions in Public Network Management Research", *Journal of Public Administration Research and Theory*, 11: 295–326.

Agranoff, R. and McGuire, M. (2003) *Collaborative Public Management: New Strategies for Local Governments*, Washington, DC: Georgetown University Press.

Alter, C. and Hage, J. (1993) *Organizations Working Together*, Newbury Park, Calif.: Sage.

Axelrod, R. (1984) *The Evolution of Cooperation*, New York: Basic Books.

Bache, I. and Flinders, M. (eds) (2004) *Multilevel Governance*, Oxford: Oxford University Press.

Bekkers, V., Dijkstra, G., Edwards, A. and Fenger, M. (2007) *Governance and the Democratic Deficit: Assessing the Democratic Legitimacy of Governance Practices*, Aldershot: Ashgate.

Bovens, M. et al. (1995) De verplaatsing van de politiek, Amsterdam.
Deakin, S. and Michie, J. (eds) (1997) *Contract, Co-operation, and Competition: Studies in Economics, Management and Law*, Oxford: Oxford University Press.
Deakin, S. and Wilkinson, F. (1998) "Contract Law and the Economics of Inter-organizational Trust", in C. R. Lane and R. Bachmann (eds) *Trust Within and Between Organizations: Conceptual Issues and Empirical Applications*, Oxford: Oxford University Press.
Easton, D. (1953) *A Systems Analysis of Political Life*, New York: John Wiley.
Edelenbos, J. and Klijn, E. H. (2007) "Trust in Complex Decision-making Networks: A Theoretical and Empirical Exploration", *Administration and Society*, 39 (1): 25–50.
Ferlie, E., Lynn, L. E. and Pollitt, C. (eds) (2005) *The Oxford Handbook of Public Management*, Oxford: Oxford University Press.
Frederickson, H. G. (2005) "What Happened to Public Administration? Governance, Governance Everywhere", in E. Ferlie, L. E. Lynn and C. Pollitt (eds) *The Oxford Handbook of Public Management*, Oxford: Oxford University Press.
Fukuyama, F. (1995) *Trust: The Social Virtues and the Creation of Prosperity*, New York: The Free Press.
Gambetta, D. (1988) *Trust: Making and Breaking of Cooperative Relations*, Oxford: Blackwell.
Graeber G. (ed.) (1993) *The Embedded Firm: Understanding Networks. Actors, Resources and Processes in Interfirm Cooperation*, London: Routledge.
Hood, C. (1991) "A Public Management for All Seasons", *Public Administration*, 69 (Spring): 3–19.
Huang, K. and Provan, K. G. (2007) "Structural Embeddedness and Organizational Social Outcomes in a Centrally Governed Mental Health Service Network", *Public Management Review*, 9 (2): 169–89.
Huxham, C. and Vangen, S. (2005) *Managing to Collaborate: The Theory and Practice of Collaborative Advantage*, Abingdon: Routledge.
Kickert, W. J. M., Klijn, E. H. and Koppenjan, J. F. M. (1997) *Managing Complex Networks: Strategies for the Public Sector*, London: Sage.
Klijn, E. H. (2008) "Governance and Governance Networks in Europe: An Assessment of 10 Years of Research on the Theme", *Public Management Review*, 10 (4): 505–25.
Klijn, E. H. (2009) Public Private Partnerships in The Netherlands: policy, projects and lessons, *Economic Affairs*, March 2009: 26–32.
Klijn, E. H., Steijn, B., Edelenbos, J. (2010) The impact of network management strategies on the outcomes in governance networks, in Public Administration 2010 (forthcoming).
Klijn, E. H., Edelenbos, J. and Steijn, B. (forthcoming, 2010a) Trust in governance networks; its impact on outcomes, Administration and Society (forthcoming 2010a).
Klijn, E. H. and Skelcher, C. K. (2007) "Democracy and Governance Networks: Compatible or Not? Four Conjectures and Their Implications", *Public Administration*, 85.
Kooiman, J. (ed.) (1993) *Modern Governance: New Government–Society Interactions*, Newbury Park, Calif.: Sage.
Koppenjan, J. F. M. and Klijn, E. H. (2004) *Managing Uncertainties in Networks: A Network Approach to Problem Solving and Decision Making*, Abingdon: Routledge.

Lane, C. and Bachmann, R. (eds) (1998) *Trust Within and Between Organizations: Conceptual Issues and Empirical Applications*, Oxford: Oxford University Press.

Lorenz, E. (1999) "Trust Contract and Economic Cooperation", *Cambridge Journal of Economics*, 23: 301–15.

Lundvall, B. A. (1993) "Explaining Interfirm Cooperation: Limits of the Transaction-cost Approach", in G. Graeber (ed.) *The Embedded Firm: Understanding Networks. Actors, Resources and Processes in Interfirm Cooperation*, London: Routledge.

Lyons, B. and Metha, J. (1997) "Private Sector Business Contracts: The Text between the Lines", in S. Deakin and J. Michie (eds) (1997) *Contract, Co-operation, and Competition: Studies in Economics, Management and Law*, Oxford: Oxford University Press.

Mandell, M. P. (ed.) (2001) *Getting Results through Collaboration*, Westport, Conn.: Quorum.

Marcussen, M. and Torfing, J. (eds) (2007) *Democratic Network Governance in Europe*, Cheltenham: Edward Elgar.

Marks, G. and Hooghe, G. L. (2004) "Contrasting Views on Multi-level Governance", in I. Bache, and M. Flinders (eds) (2004) *Multilevel Governance*, Oxford: Oxford University Press.

McEvily, B., Zaheer, A. (2006) Does trust still matter? Research on the role of trust in inter-organisational exchange, in: R. Bachmann, A. Zaheer (eds) 2006, Handbook of Trust Research, Cheltenham: Edward Elgar Publishing.

Meier, K. J. and O'Toole, L. J. (2001) "Managerial Strategies and Behaviour in Networks: A Model with Evidence from US Public Education", *Journal of Public Administration and Theory*, 11 (3): 271–93.

Meier, K. J. and O'Toole, L. J. (2007) "Modelling Public Management: Empirical Analysis of the Management–performance Nexus", *Public Administration Review*, 9 (4): 503–27.

Miles, R. E. and Snow, C. C. (1986) "Organization: New Concepts for New Forms", *California Management Review*, 28 (3).

Nooteboom, B. (2002) *Trust: Forms, Foundations, Functions, Failures and Figures*, Cheltenham: Edgar Elgar.

Nooteboom, B., Berger, H. and Noorderhaven, N. (1997) "Effects of Trust and Governance on Relational Risk", *Academy of Management Journal*, 40 (2): 308–38.

Osborne, D. and Gaebler, T. (1992) *Reinventing Government: How the Entrepreneurial Spirit Is Transforming the Public Sector*, Reading, Mass.: Addison-Wesley.

Osborne, S. P. (2006) "The New Public Governance", *Public Management Review*, 8 (3): 377–87.

Parker, D. and Vaidya, K. (2001) "An Economic Perspective on Innovation Networks", in O. Jones, S. Conway and F. Steward (eds) *Social Interaction and Organisatonal Change: Aston Perspectives on Innovation Networks*, London: Imperial College Press.

Pierre, J. and Peters, B. Guy (2000) *Governance, Politics and the State*, Basingstoke: Macmillan.

Rhodes, R. A. W. (1997) *Understanding Governance: Policy Networks, Governance, Reflexivity and Accountability*, Buckingham: Open University Press.

Ring, P. S., and Van der Ven, A. (1992) "Structuring Cooperative Relations between Organizations", *Strategic Management Journal*, 13: 483–98.

Rittel, H. J. W. and Webber, M. M. (1973) "Dilemmas in a General Theory of Planning", *Policy Sciences*, 4: 155–69.

Rousseau, D., Sitkin, S. B., Burt, R. S. and Camerer, C. (1998) "Not So Different After All: A Cross-discipline View of Trust", *Academy of Management Review*, 23 (3): 393–404.

Sako, M. (1998) "Does Trust Improve Business Performance?", in C. Lane and R. Bachmann (eds) *Trust Within and Between Organizations: Conceptual Issues and Empirical Applications*, Oxford: Oxford University Press.

Skelcher, C., Mathur, N. and Smith, M. (2005) "The Public Governance of Collaborative Spaces: Discourse, Design and Democracy", *Public Administration*, 83 (3): 573–96.

Sorensen E. and Torfing, J. (eds) (2007) *Theories of Democratic Network Governance*, Cheltenham: Edward Elgar.

Teisman, G. R., van Buuren, A. and Gerrits, L. (eds) (2009) *Managing Complex Governance Networks*, Abingdon: Routledge.

Thompson, G. J. Frances, Levacic, R. and Mitchel, J. (1991) *Markets, Hierarchies and Networks: The Coordination of Social Life*, London: Sage.

Williamson, O. E. (1996) *The Mechanisms of Governance*, Oxford: Oxford University Press.

Zucker, L. (1986) "Production of Trust: Institutional Sources of Economic Structure, 1840–1920", *Research in Organizational Behavior*, 8: 53–111.

18

IMPLEMENTATION AND MANAGERIAL NETWORKING IN THE NEW PUBLIC GOVERNANCE

Laurence J. O'Toole, Jr and Kenneth J. Meier

Abstract

Implementing public programs and delivering public services in the era of New Public Governance call for public managers to interact externally and often collaboratively with a range of stakeholders. Such relationships, it is often argued, build support for implementation, buffer programs from unexpected and negative shocks, and induce co-productive contributions from potential partners during execution. This chapter presents empirical evidence from hundreds of public organizations about how such networking behavior, which may constitute a form of organizational social capital, influences outcomes. At the same time, internal management within hierarchies also seems to matter for results. One of the key aspects of the research agenda on the New Public Governance is to sort through these relationships for their performance-relevant implications.

The era of the New Public Governance signals considerable promise as well as substantial challenges. The latticing of horizontal linkages across actors and institutions, overlaying and potentially complicating the more familiar vertical ones, requires careful analysis. Networks of policy-involved actors often work in complex ways to shape policy choice and action (Bardach 1998; Huxham 2000; Stoker 2004; Bingham and O'Leary 2008). In some nations, corporatist arrangements and assumptions bind disparate "social partners" in processes of decision-making. Even in much less corporatist and considerably more pluralist systems, arrangements like Public–Private Partnerships and government contracting – relational and otherwise – are now commonplace. The increasing attention directed to many countries' commitment to sustainable development induces ever more intricate interweaving of policy sectors and social actors to address the cross-cutting governance needs impelled by this daunting policy agenda (Lafferty 2004). For reasons having to do with political motives, technical requirements for successful implementation, and the increasingly ambitious policy agendas of governments, webs of intertwined organizations and other institutions routinely co-produce outputs and outcomes. Successfully achieving policy *results* in such governance contexts requires that these complicated multi-actor institutional settings be managed effectively.

This chapter overviews the challenge of policy implementation in complex governance settings involving networks of interdependent actors. We first frame the implementation theme and establish the importance of its multi-actor, networked character in contemporary governance. We then review briefly some of what is known about the determinants of implementation success or failure. We concentrate in particular on one key driver of implementation performance – the actions of public managers, particularly as they interact in and with the set of interdependent actors in other organizations. In this regard we distill some of the recent research findings that bear on public management and policy implementation in complex settings, and sketch some related questions deserving of further research attention.

Policy implementation in complex settings

When considering "policy implementation" we are interested in what happens between the establishment of a governmental intention to do something – or stop doing something – and the consequent effect of that decision in the world of action. Emphasizing an era of governance implies that implementation action involves a multiplicity of actors contributing to the results of public programs, rather than merely the "lonely organization" (Hjern 1982) assumed in some early studies.

But is that so? Anecdotal and case-study evidence is abundant, and systematic data are increasingly available as well. The answer from the growing number of the latter is clear: networks of interdependent organizations – or parts of organizations – are typically involved in trying to turn policy goals into reality. Local public managers in the UK (Walker, O'Toole and Meier 2007) and the US (Agranoff and McGuire 2003) routinely report extensive connections with external actors in their environment. Swedish Public Employment Service offices and municipalities regularly interact, and policy implementation is assisted when both trust and goal congruence are present (Lundin 2007). Local networks contribute to the implementation of agricultural watershed management and the adoption of environmental best-management practices (Lubell and Fulton 2008). Dutch institutions of higher education sit in networks the characteristics of which help shape performance (Schalk Torenvlied and Allen forthcoming). Hundreds of cases of inter-organizational collaboration in numerous policy fields have been identified at the subnational level in Thailand (Krueathep, Riccucci and Suwanmala forthcoming). The great majority of new or substantially revised national public programs in the US require or strongly encourage participation by multiple organizations, governments, and often sectors in the US (Hall and O'Toole 2000, 2004). And a recent meta-analysis of 137 cases of collaborative governance including evidence from multiple countries and policy fields suggests regularities in what makes for successful operation (Ansell and Gash 2008). Networked, collaborative and interorganizational implementation settings are clearly the rule rather than the exception.

Does it matter? A number of theoretical arguments provide reasons to think so (for instance, Kickert, Klijn and Koppenjan 1997; Provan and Milward 2001; Agranoff and McGuire 2003; see also Rhodes 1997; Stoker 1999). Certainly inducements to and constraints inhibiting cooperation across organizational boundaries in networked and collaborative settings are different from – and typically more challenging than – generating successful cooperative implementation via unified organizations. Authority is typically weaker in interorganizational situations, and encouragement toward cooperation must perforce rely less on established communication channels, routines and shared worldviews than it does within hierarchical agencies. One important implication is that public management itself is likely to be even more important to successful implementation in networks than in hierarchies (O'Toole 2000a), and "management" in these cases will surely involve considerable negotiation, framing, activation (and deactivation) of connections among nodes, and trust-building across organizational lines.

Determinants of implementation success in networked settings: the role of the manager

The huge literature on policy implementation in complex multi-actor settings includes many efforts to identify key variables that shape results but often relatively little in the way of parsimonious theoretical exposition (for reviews of the research literature, see O'Toole 1986, 2000b, 2004). Exacerbating the problem has been a case-study literature that cannot in principle provide much in the way of a valid, multivariate exposition. Nevertheless, some progress has recently been made, particularly with regard to an often underemphasized contributor to implementation success in networks: public management itself.

In part to remedy this gap, we initiated a research program more than a decade ago systematically to model and explore the relationship between public management and public program performance during implementation, particularly in networked settings. After reviewing the case-study literature on managers, management, and their putative role in executing policy, we formalized some of the key ideas available into a testable model (O'Toole and Meier 1999).[1]

Our model incorporates three basic principles with regard to public management and administrative systems for delivering public program results. First, such arrays are autoregressive systems – that is, they create processes and operating procedures that tend to reproduce the same outputs over time. Second, the model is complex and nonlinear rather than strictly additive. At times variables interact in a multiplicative manner, at times the interaction is with a reciprocal function, and at other times terms add together and then interact with another variable to generate their overall impact on public program performance. Third, the model is contingent to reflect our view that what works in terms of public management is contingent on a variety of other factors. Among the most interesting contingencies are those involving networks, managerial networking, and the environment.

The model contains three different functions of management. They are efforts to manage the internal operations of the organization,[2] efforts to exploit opportunities in the interdependent environment,[3] and efforts to limit the negative impact of environmental perturbations on the administrative system.[4] The latter two functions in the second, or environmental, portion of the model are often combined.[5] Our particular focus in this chapter is this managerial function of operating outward toward and in the interdependent environment of the organization – the ability to manage in the network (thus, managerial networking). We also devote some brief attention to aspects of the first-listed managerial function, internal management in the organization, including the managerial effort devoted to handling impacts from the interdependent environment that penetrate the core organization, particularly in difficult situations.

The theory of public management and program performance that we have been developing is highly parsimonious; it contains only four variables, or variable clusters: performance, management, stability, and the environment. Recognizing that an operationalization and full testing of this model with any existing dataset is impossible, we have opted for an incremental strategy that focuses on the link between management and performance in general – and specifically on developing reliable and valid measures of management. Within this strategic approach, we have proceeded by testing discrete portions of the model and building on the results in subsequent rounds of analysis. In doing so, we have always controlled for the other two variable clusters, either statistically[6] or by holding a variable relatively constant across cases.[7] In most cases we have conducted these studies in a pooled time-series analysis of Texas school districts.[8] Unless otherwise noted, the empirical findings are generated from this database (for a scientific justification of the extensive use of this database, see Meier and O'Toole 2007).

Managers, networking and networks: evidence from a research program

Public managers coordinate and support production-oriented action inside their organizations, and they also work outward toward and in the interdependent environment as they network to build support and enhance implementation results. The latter efforts may involve managers' building support for program implementation among interested stakeholders, facilitating collaborative efforts at program execution with other involved organizations, protecting core production from threatening aspects of the organizational environment, linking or disconnecting network actors from each other to improve policy execution, or even using persuasion and bargaining skill to change the nature of the interdependent co-produced action. Such efforts by managers, especially when executed with skill, may constitute a form of organizational social capital that can be important for implementation in today's policy settings.

We have conducted extensive empirical study of this networking function and how it is related to policy outcomes. Our measure of managerial networking assumes that managers cannot engage in network-like behavior with other actors in the environment without coming into contact with them. Using the Texas School District dataset, we asked top managers to rate how frequently, from daily to never, they interact with each of a set of environmental actors (five actors in a 2000 survey, eight actors in 2002 and 2005 surveys, and ten in the 2007 survey). These items have been factor-analyzed and consistently produce a first factor that is a general networking measure with all positive loadings (at times one factor only is produced). This factor score is used as the measure of managerial networking.

In support of the networking measure

Does this measure tap managerial networking activity in a valid and reliable way? The evidence is rather strong that it does. The factor analysis of networking items shows a consistent pattern across nodes; the networked contacts are all correlated with each other, and analysis always produces a generic first factor with positive loading regardless of how many nodes are included in the analysis.[9]

The networking measure is also positively correlated with a manager's estimate of how much of her effort is directed externally rather than focused on matters internal to the organization (Meier and O'Toole 2003). The measure also shows links to performance as tapped with numerous indicators (O'Toole and Meier 2003b: 54, 56), thus demonstrating substantial empirical support and external validity.

Furthermore, a comparison of networking data between 2000 and 2002, as well as comparisons for later surveys such as 2005 and 2007, show that networking by top managers is very much a managerial choice rather than a behavior pattern forced upon managers by external actors. Networking measures for the top manager in a given organization at the two time points were essentially uncorrelated if the organization had changed managers but were strongly correlated when the same manager was in place in both time points (Meier and O'Toole 2005). Goerdel (2006) has also shown that when the manager reports pro-active (self-initiated) interactions with external nodes the link between networking and performance is more strongly positive. All these findings support the use of this measure as a way of tapping managers' activities in the networked environment in studies of interorganizational implementation and the role of managers in that process.

Is managerial networking related to implementation performance?

Estimating the relationship between managerial networking and program outcomes requires controlling for the other influences, particularly constraints and resources, that can also shape results. Accordingly, we used several years of data across all Texas school districts for which we were able to gather survey data from top managers[10] and have controlled for several resources and constraints that vary over time and across jurisdictions. Meier and O'Toole (2001: 285) and later papers showed that managerial networking was positively related to student performance on standardized tests and on high-end indicators for college-bound students. The relationship held even when controlling for past performance – a particularly tough test. Interviews with managers indicated that higher networking activity often signaled that managers were addressing problems in the organizational environment, particularly political ones, and keeping such distractions from affecting the organization's production personnel. In this sense, public education managers' networking activities are likely directed toward building interorganizational routines or trust among network members. A more detailed assessment of contents of the reported networking by managers is a research subject that still awaits exploration.

Clearly, considerable additional research is needed if we are to understand fully the ways that managerial networking matters for implementation results in various places and fields. Some of that work has begun and extends the pattern reported here for school districts to local law enforcement. Nicholson-Crotty and O'Toole (2004) created an external management scale that combined measures of contact with measures of public feedback systems and with community-oriented policing activities. They found a strong positive relationship between this measure of networking and environmental management and performance measured as crime clearance rates.

How much difference does managerial networking make? The maximum effect size is estimated at approximately 5 to 6 percent of performance.[11] In other words, managerial networking does not turn implementation disaster into brilliant success, but it makes an important and measurable difference – particularly given that other variables likely to be important in generating results, like task difficulty or financial resources, are controlled for in these analyses.

The nonlinear aspects of the relationship between managerial networking and performance have been explored in two articles (Meier and O'Toole 2001,

2003; see also Hicklin, O'Toole and Meier 2008). An interesting relationship was found in the link between managerial networking and the autoregressive character of the administrative system. Inertia can obviously help when implementation is going well, but excessive inertia indicates a rigid system; such systems have difficulty adapting to change and therefore are likely to suffer implementation deficits over time. Meier and O'Toole (2003: 696) found that at high levels of managerial networking (more than 1.5 standard deviations above the mean), the degree of autoregressivity declines rapidly. This relationship suggests that managing in the networked setting can provide a public organization with some flexibility and allow it to break away from suboptimal routines when useful. We also found greater efforts to manage externally were associated with more support from program clientele (Meier and O'Toole 2003: 693).

The second, or environmental, term of the model referenced earlier suggests that managerial networking interacts with various resources and constraints in a nonlinear fashion. Theoretically speaking, the notion here is that under certain conditions management should enhance the positive impact of resources considerably above normal or be able to mitigate the performance-dampening effect of constraints. Meier and O'Toole (2001: 289) showed that managerial networking can indeed reduce the negative impact of black and Hispanic students (measures of task difficulty regarding more disadvantaged students) as well as of noncertified teachers on performance, as expected by the theory. (On the different forms of buffering that management may be able to employ to support the core production in a public program, see O'Toole and Meier 2003a; empirical studies are reported in Meier and O'Toole 2009; Meier, O'Toole and Hicklin forthcoming). Similarly, managerial networking selectively interacts with some resources and can produce much larger gains for a unit increase in resources in organizations with high levels of managerial networking (Meier and O'Toole 2003: 696).

Managerial networking also interacts with program performance in nonlinear ways. When the data were split into quintiles based on the level of organizational performance, the relationship between management and performance varied across the five subgroups. Managerial networking matters more for units at the extremes of performance – for organizations in the highest and lowest performing quintiles (Meier and O'Toole 2001: 695). The former case is likely the more important one, since almost anything management is likely to do will improve the sorry performance of organizations at the bottom. When implementation performance is quite high, managers have the option of deploying their networking in pursuit of more, or more complicated, opportunities in the interdependent environment, thus leveraging the impact of networking more than usual.

What about the possibility of diminishing or even negative marginal returns from networking by managers? Hicklin, O'Toole and Meier (2008) investigated whether nonlinearity applied to managerial networking taken by itself. The analysis showed just such a pattern and also demonstrated that talented managers (measured as those scoring high on a measure of managerial quality: see below) seemed aware of the limits of networking, since they restricted their own efforts before they experienced negative marginal returns. In sum, networking efforts by managers provide a positive contribution to performance, nonlinearities can be documented, and such networking behavior is subject to diminishing returns.

Networks and networking: differentiated performance impacts

Much of our empirical work has focused on the behavior of public managers and the impact of what they do on the implementation of public programs. Managerial networking, for instance, is one important such behavior. But networks themselves are structural entities; we define them as patterns of two or more units, in which not all major components are encompassed within a single hierarchical array (O'Toole 1997).

We know that structural properties of implementation networks are likely to help shape policy outcomes, but estimating such impacts is difficult for methodological reasons. Detailed studies of network structures are labor-intensive, typically involve one or a few cases, and thus cannot isolate the effects of network-structural properties on policy results (for a small-N effort to make the connection, see Provan and Milward 1995). In addition, maximizing the variance in terms of network characteristics typically means examining cases from different policy fields. Since comparable performance metrics rarely span different sectors of policy, the difficulties involved in probing the network-structure-to-results linkage are even more imposing.

In an effort to explore both behavioral networking and structural properties of networks, we estimated the effects of managerial networking in more and also less networked structural settings – with the structural feature included in the analysis an aspect of the network defined in financial terms – the degree to which the school district had to depend on other levels of government for budgetary support (state and federal governments). Managerial networking is positively linked to performance both when the organization is financially dependent on others and when it is financially independent, but it is more important for performance among organizations that are dependent on others for financial support. In short, managerial networking matters more in structural networks (O'Toole and Meier 2004b: 487–8).

Networking: quantity and quality

Considerable evidence indicates that managerial networking can boost public program performance, and that more networking – to a point – generates more results. But does the *quality* of managerial efforts make a difference as well? The answer is yes.

We have developed a general measure of managerial quality and applied it to the Texas schools dataset. The measure does not isolate the quality of networking alone but rather the quality of management overall. The networking measure clearly taps only quantity of activity; the quality measure includes the quality dimension of both internal and external management. Incorporating such a measure of managerial quality in a large-N analysis presents daunting obstacles. We responded by developing a measure that incorporates the judgments of locally informed political overseers, the individual school boards, in annual decisions about remuneration for top managers. The top managers in question are relatively mobile individuals in a competitive labor market with extensive information on salaries and performance. In such a situation, the annual salary determination by a school board can be expected to include some assessment of the quality of job the manager has done. The measure essentially predicts what the manager's salary should be, based on a set of factors that are highly correlated with salary (district size, human capital investments, prior performance, etc.), and uses the difference between predicted salaries and actual salaries as an estimate of management quality (see Meier and O'Toole 2002 for details).

Analysis shows that top management quality is related to implementation results for almost all performance indicators (Meier and O'Toole 2002). And, since the quality measure and the networking-quantity measure are uncorrelated, their combined effect size is the sum of the two taken separately; for the public entities in question, this is approximately double that for the networking behavior alone.

Do all clientele win from managerial networking?

Much of the literature on networks and networking – linked as it often is to themes of co-production and collaboration – says or at least implies that when managers stimulate interorganizational linkages everyone wins. The literature certainly recognizes that sometimes it is difficult to make these networked connections, but networking per se is typically portrayed as a potentially important but also fundamentally apolitical or technocratic enterprise (for more detailed coverage, see O'Toole and Meier 2004a). But studies in administrative politics, including some venerable classics (Selznick 1949), suggest a political dimension to managers' efforts to interact with, attend to, and build bridges with external actors. We examined this question across hundreds of school districts. Because actors in the interdependent environment that are engaged in exchange relationships with a core public organization are likely to over-represent the more advantaged parties in any social setting, we explored the distributional aspect of managerial networking by seeing who benefits from this form of managerial behavior.

We found that networking was positively related to higher test scores for Anglo students (as well as overall test scores) and three measures of performance for college-bound students. However, managerial networking was unrelated to pass rates for Latinos, blacks, or low-income students (O'Toole and Meier 2004a: 688).[12] This pattern indicates the operation of a politics of public management whereby the more powerful political forces are likely to exert greater influence on management as managers increase their activities in the network. For those interested in policy implementation in interorganizational settings, accordingly, the distributional dimension of performance should be a subject of sustained attention. Operating in networks and engaging in networking constitute activities that do not suspend the patterns of exchange and influence in the broader system; they likely obscure such channels but may even amplify their impacts.

Implementation in an era of the New Public Governance: concluding notes

The foregoing coverage, drawn largely from an extended research program on the role of public management in the execution of public programs and the delivery of policy results, clearly demonstrates the importance of interorganizational patterns, and especially the networking behavior of managers, in shaping implementation results. Considerable advancement has been made. Two cautionary points should nonetheless be noted. First, for all the progress made, we do not yet know nearly enough about how networks and networking shape performance. And, second, even in a time of a New Public Governance, the *internal* management of public organizations – and perhaps the relationship between internally and externally oriented management – requires serious attention.

We know that networking matters, and also that structural features of networks have performance impacts as well. Furthermore, cross-national comparative analysis with large datasets has been initiated and should pay substantial dividends. But understanding implementation and its management in patterns resembling the New Public Governance requires additional advances and other lines of research.

The research program we have developed for the past decade offers significant findings on a host of issues important to implementation and performance, but it has also had its limits. In particular, while we have analyzed managerial behavior outward into the networked environment, we have not conducted empirical work on the management of networks themselves. There are substantial difficulties in doing so (see O'Toole 2000a for details), but the topic deserves attention. We have developed some initial theoretical ideas and sought to formalize them (Meier and O'Toole 2004), but the management of networks for implementation merits substantially more attention.

In addition, we have extended our research program beyond the network-related aspects of public management to explore the ways that internal management also contributes to policy outcomes. While a careful review of the findings would extend far beyond the reach of this chapter's theme, it is important to note that several aspects of internal management contribute positively to implementation results – and do so independently of the externally oriented aspects of management. For example, the management and development of a public organization's human capital is strongly related to performance across a wide array of outcomes (O'Toole and Meier 2009). Human resource management has also been shown to be related to the performance of local law enforcement agencies (Nicholson-Crotty and O'Toole 2004).

Internal management consists of much more than the management of human resources, of course. Other aspects of inward-directed management have also been systematically analyzed, with similarly positive effects on program results. Our studies of crisis management, whether from a sizable budget-cut or from natural disasters, show that managers make adjustments in the allocation of financial resources and staff to minimize disruptions in the implementation of their core activities (Meier, O'Toole and Hicklin forthcoming; Meier and O'Toole 2009). Management capacity, which can sometimes seem like wasted or slack resources, can contribute to results – including or especially during times of organizational stress.

Given these findings, it would be wrongheaded to proclaim an end to hierarchy or to the importance of its effective management for implementation (Olsen 2006). Indeed, our findings regarding the importance of internal management and of hierarchy are generally supportive of the evidence reviewed in hundreds of studies by Hill and Lynn (2005). Accordingly, it is likely that management of hierarchies, *as well as* of externally oriented, interorganizational management, typifies implementation in today's governance systems. The usual characterization of the "New Public Governance" being developed by observers refers to undeniably important forces, but plenty of the more venerable influences remain. Understanding the combined influences of the more complex patterns now visible should be a research priority for the field.

Acknowledgment

This chapter is part of an ongoing research agenda on the role of public management in complex policy settings. That agenda has benefited from the helpful comments of George Boyne, Stuart Bretschneider, Gene Brewer, John Bryson, Amy Kneedler Donahue, Sergio Fernández, H. George Frederickson, Carolyn Heinrich, Peter Hupe, Patricia Ingraham, J. Edward Kellough, H. Brinton Milward, Sean Nicholson-Crotty, David Peterson, Hal G. Rainey, Bob Stein and Vicky M. Wilkins on various aspects of this research program. Needless to say, this article is the responsibility of the authors only.

Notes

1 The model itself, which aims to depict the relationship among public management, institutional arrangements, and public program performance, is as follows: $O_t = \beta_1(S + M_1)O_{t-1} + \beta_2(X_t/S)(M_3/M_4) + \varepsilon_t$ where O is some measure of outcome; S is a measure of stability; M denotes management, which can be divided into three parts: M_1 management's contribution to organizational stability through additions to hierarchy/structure as well as regular operations, M_3 management's efforts to exploit the environment of the organization, M_4 management's effort to buffer the unit from environmental shocks; X is a vector of environmental forces; ε is an error term; the other subscripts denote time periods; and β_1 and β_2 are estimable parameters. In the model, S can be considered a composite of the various kinds of stability in an organizational setting. Stability means constancy in the design, functioning and direction of an administrative system over time. Some stability is induced by structure; other forms of stability have their origins in management processes and procedures. A discussion of these factors can be found in O'Toole and Meier (1999) and the various empirical works cited in this chapter.

2 This aspect of management is the M_1 function in the formal model depicted in note 1.

3 This managerial aspect is depicted as M_3 in the formal model.

4 This aspect appears as M_4 in the formal model.

5 The combination of these two functions can be formally represented by M_2, defined as the ratio of M_3 to M_4. The M_2 term can thus replace that ratio in a slightly simplified version of the formal model.

6 As with the "X" vector of resources and constraints from the environment.

7 As with the "S" term, since we have often conducted our large-N studies across structurally similar public organizations.

8 School districts in the United States are generally independent local governments with their own taxing powers. All districts in the analyses discussed in this chapter are of this type. "Independent" means that the school district is not subordinate to another unit such as a city. Independent districts have their own elected board, have the ability to tax and set budgets, and acquire bonding authority by a vote of the residents. There are roughly 14,000 school districts in the US, approximately 1,000 of which are in Texas.

9 With the school-district dataset, we have factor analyzed reported networking data involving varying numbers of nodes. The factor scores are very highly correlated with each other for a given set of survey results, a finding strongly supportive of the measure's validity and reliability. Analysis of similar survey data gathered from local-authority managers in the United Kingdom also consistently yields a first factor with a set of positive loadings (Walker, O'Toole, and Meier 2007: 750).

10 We have used time series of varying lengths, most typically four or five years, and we have surveyed several times: 2000, 2002, 2004–5, and 2007. For certain research questions, we have used up to twenty years of performance data.

11 The full maximum effect from what managers do is considerably larger than this amount. The result reported here omits, for example, effects from internal management. It also includes only the quantity of networking, not necessarily the quality; see below for some treatment of the latter. This estimate does not include any of the nonlinear impacts (see below).

12 Networking was associated with lower dropout rates, a disadvantaged indicator, but was not related to attendance rates, another low-end indicator.

References

Agranoff, Robert and McGuire, Michael (2003) *Collaborative Public Management: New Strategies for Local Governments*, Washington, DC: Georgetown University Press.

Ansell, Chris and Gash, Alison (2008) "Collaborative Governance in Theory and Practice", *Journal of Public Administration Research and Theory*, 18 (4): 543–71.

Bardach, Eugene (1998) *Getting Agencies to Work Together*, Washington, DC: The Brookings Institution.

Bingham, Lisa Blomgren and O'Leary, Rosemary (2008) *Big Ideas in Collaborative Public Management*, Armonk, NY: M. E. Sharpe.

Goerdel, Holly T. (2006) "Taking Initiative: Proactive Management and Organizational Performance in Networked Environments", *Journal of Public Administration Research and Theory*, 16 (3): 351–67.

Hall, Thad E. and O'Toole, Jr, Laurence J. (2000) "Structures for Policy Implementation: An Analysis of National Legislation, 1965–66 and 1993–94", *Administration and Society*, 31 (6): 667–86.

Hall, Thad E. and O'Toole, Jr, Laurence J. (2004) "Shaping Formal Networks through the Regulatory Process", *Administration and Society*, 36 (2): 1–22.

Hicklin, Alisa, O'Toole, Jr, Laurence, J. and Mier, Kenneth J. (2008) "Serpents in the Sand: Managerial Networking and Nonlinear Influences on Organizational Performance", *Journal of Public Administration Research and Theory*, 18 (2): 253–73.

Hill, Carolyn J. and Lynn, Jr, Laurence E. (2005) "Is Hierarchical Governance in Decline? Evidence from Empirical Research", *Journal of Public Administration Research and Theory*, 15 (2): 173–95.

Hjern, Benny (1982) "Implementation Research – the Link Gone Missing", *Journal of Public Policy*, 2: 301–8.

Huxham, C. (2000) "The Challenge of Collaborative Governance", *Public Management Review*, 2: 337–52.

Kickert, Walter J. M., Klijn, Erik-Hans and Koppenjan, Joop F. M. (1997) *Managing Complex Networks: Strategies for the Public Sector*, London: Sage.

Krueathep, Weerasak, Riccucci, Norma M. and Suwanmala, Charas (forthcoming) "Why Do Agencies Work Together? The Determinants of Network Formation at the Subnational Level of Government in Thailand", *Journal of Public Administration Research and Theory*.

Lafferty, William (2004) *Governance for Sustainable Development: The Challenge of Adapting Form to Function*, Cheltenham: Edward Elgar.

Lubell, Mark and Fulton, Allan (2008) "Local Policy Networks and Agricultural Watershed Management", *Journal of Public Administration Research and Theory*, 18 (4): 673–96.

Lundin, Martin (2007) "Explaining Cooperation: How Resource Interdependence, Goal Congruence, and Trust Affect Joint Actions in Policy Implementation", *Journal of Public Administration Research and Theory*, 17 (4): 651–72.

Meier, Kenneth J. and O'Toole, Jr, Laurence J. (2001) "Managerial Strategies and Behavior in Networks: A Model with Evidence from US Public Education", *Journal of Public Administration Research and Theory*, 11 (3): 271–95.

Meier, Kenneth J. and O'Toole, Jr, Laurence J. (2002) "Public Management and Organizational Performance: The Impact of Managerial Quality", *Journal of Policy Analysis and Management*, 21: 629–43.

Meier, Kenneth J. and O'Toole, Jr, Laurence J. (2003) "Public Management and Educational Performance: The Impact of Managerial Networking", *Public Administration Review*, 63: 675–85.

Meier, Kenneth J. and O'Toole, Jr, Laurence J. (2004) "Conceptual Issues in Modeling and Measuring Management and Its Impacts on Performance", in Patricia Ingraham and Laurence E. Lynn, Jr (eds) *The Art of Governance: Analyzing Management and Administration*, Washington, DC: Georgetown University Press.

Meier, Kenneth J. and O'Toole, Jr, Laurence J. (2005) "Managerial Networking: Issues of Measurement and Research Design", *Administration and Society*, 37: 523–41.

Meier, Kenneth J. and O'Toole, Jr, Laurence J. (2007) "Modeling Public Management: Empirical Analysis of the Management–Performance Nexus", *Public Management Review*, 9: 503–27.

Meier, Kenneth J. and O'Toole, Jr, Laurence J. (2009) "The Dog That Didn't Bark: How Public Managers Handle Environmental Shocks", *Public Administration*, 87 (3): 485–502.

Meier, Kenneth J., O'Toole, Jr, Laurence J. and Hicklin, Alisa K. (forthcoming) "I've Seen Fire and I've Seen Rain: Public Management and Performance after a Natural Disaster", *Administration and Society*.

Nicholson-Crotty, Sean and O'Toole, Jr, Laurence J. (2004) "Public Management and Organizational Performance: The Case of Law Enforcement Agencies", *Journal of Public Administration Research and Theory*, 14 (1): 1–18.

Olsen, Johan P. (2006) "Maybe It Is Time to Rediscover Bureaucracy", *Journal of Public Administration Research and Theory*, 16 (1): 1–24.

O'Toole, Laurence J., Jr (1986) "Policy Recommendations for Multi-actor Implementation: An Assessment of the Field", *Journal of Public Policy*, 6 (2): 181–210.

O'Toole, Laurence J., Jr (1997) "Treating Networks Seriously: Practical and Research-based Agendas in Public Administration", *Public Administration Review*, 57 (1): 45–52.

O'Toole, Laurence J., Jr (2000a) "Different Public Managements? Implications of Structural Context in Hierarchies and Networks", in Jeffrey Brudney, Laurence J. O'Toole, Jr, and Hal G. Rainey (eds) *Advancing Public Management*, Washington, DC: Georgetown University Press.

O'Toole, Laurence J., Jr (2000b) "Research on Policy Implementation: Assessment and Prospect", *Journal of Public Administration Research and Theory*, 10 (2): 263–88.

O'Toole, Laurence J., Jr (2004) "The Theory–practice Issue in Policy Implementation Research", *Public Administration*, 82 (2): 309–29.

O'Toole, Laurence J., Jr and Meier, Kenneth J. (1999) "Modeling the Impact of Public Management: Implications of Structural Context", *Journal of Public Administration Research and Theory*, 9 (4): 505–26.

O'Toole, Laurence J., Jr and Meier, Kenneth J. (2003a) "Bureaucracy and Uncertainty", in Barry C. Burden (ed.) *Uncertainty in American Politics*, New York: Cambridge University Press.

O'Toole, Laurence J., Jr and Meier, Kenneth J. (2003b) "*Plus ça change*: Public Management, Personnel Stability, and Organizational Performance", *Journal of Public Administration Research and Theory*, 13: 43–64.

O'Toole, Laurence J., Jr and Meier, Kenneth J. (2004a) "Desperately Seeking Selznick: Cooptation and the Dark Side of Public Management in Networks", *Public Administration Review*, 64 (6): 681–93.

O'Toole, Laurence J., Jr and Meier, Kenneth J. (2004b) "Public Management in Intergovernmental Networks: Matching Structural Networks and Managerial Networking", *Journal of Public Administration Research and Theory*, 14: 469–95.

O'Toole, Laurence J., Jr and Meier, Kenneth J. (2009) "The Human Side of Public Organizations: Internal Management and Organizational Performance", *American Review of Public Administration*, 39 (5): 499–518.

Provan, Keith G. and Milward, H. Brinton (1995) "A Preliminary Theory of Interorganizational Network Effectiveness", *Administrative Science Quarterly*, 40 (1): 1–33.

Provan, Keith G. and Milward, H. Brinton (2001) "Do Networks Really Work? A Framework for Evaluating Public Sector Organizational Networks", *Public Administration Review*, 61 (4): 414–23.

Rhodes, R. A. W. (1997) *Understanding Governance: Policy Networks, Reflexivity and Accountability*, Buckingham: Open University Press.

Schalk, Jelmer, Torenvlied, René, Allen, Jim (forthcoming) "Network Embeddedness and Organizational Performance: The Strength of Strong Ties in Dutch Higher Education", *Journal of Public Administration Research and Theory*.

Selznick, Philip (1949) *TVA and the Grass Roots: A Study in the Sociology of Formal Organization*, Berkeley, Calif.: University of California Press.

Stoker, G. (ed.) (1999) *The New Management of British Local Governance*, Basingstoke: Palgrave Macmillan.

Stoker, G. (2004) *Modernizing British Local Government: From Thatcherism to New Labour*, Basingstoke: Palgrave Macmillan.

Walker, Richard M., O'Toole, Jr, Laurence J. and Meier, Kenneth J. (2007) "It's Where You Are That Matters: An Empirical Analysis of the Networking Behaviour of English Local Government Officers", *Public Administration*, 85: 739–56.

19

FROM NEW PUBLIC MANAGEMENT TO NETWORKED COMMUNITY GOVERNANCE? STRATEGIC LOCAL PUBLIC SERVICE NETWORKS IN ENGLAND

Steve Martin

Introduction

This chapter examines the impact on local public service networks in England of a range of policies which are inspired by the concept of networked community governance. This new(ish) approach is predicated on the belief that local government need not be directly involved in the delivery of local services but that it does have a key role to play in orchestrating partnerships of local providers from across the public, private and voluntary sectors. The chapter first describes the traditional model of the local welfare state which held sway in the period immediately following World War II. Next it considers the policies pursued by the Thatcher governments of the 1980s and early 1990s which are widely seen as having been influenced by and symptomatic of the "New Public Management" (NPM). It then focuses on recent policies and their impact on local government and local governance. It argues that the increasing influence of networked community governance reflects an awareness of some of the weaknesses of previous approaches. However, it has not entirely displaced previous paradigms. Current policies blend approaches associated with traditional models of public administration, the NPM and networked community governance. They are not therefore entirely new but they have led to an increased emphasis on collaboration and "citizen-centered" services. This requires local officials and politicians to work across organizational boundaries in ways that were not expected of them in the past, and it poses challenges to traditional forms of central government oversight of local government and other service providers.

The local welfare state

In contrast to most other Western European countries, in the UK the roles and responsibilities of local government are not codified, and there are no constitutional guarantees of its existence. The national parliament is sovereign and is able to create, restructure or abolish other tiers of government at will. Local government's position is further weakened by its lack of financial autonomy. Ministries often regard local authorities simply as the delivery agents of national policies rather than as democratically elected entities with their own independent mandate and locally determined priorities. And the absence of constitutional checks and balances means that it is very easy for the executive to enact new legislation and implement organizational changes (Pollitt 2007), with the result that local authorities frequently complain of "initiative overload".

British local authorities have no direct responsibility for the delivery of healthcare, but they play a major role in the provision of most other local public services. In the period immediately following World War II, local government was seen as the main vehicle for the delivery of the newly created welfare state and in particular in the provision of state-funded education, social care and housing. The 1944 Education Act established free compulsory schooling from age 5 to 15. Central government set the overall policy framework, but within broad parameters county councils were free to decide how education was delivered locally. Some local education authorities (LEAs) chose to provide primary schooling until the age of 11, whilst others moved children from primary to middle schools at the age of 9 and then on into secondary education at 14. Some separated the most academically gifted at the age of 11 and sent them to specialist (grammar) schools. Others had nonselective systems and sent all children to mixed-ability (comprehensive) schools. Local government also oversaw post-16 and a wide range of social services including child protection, services for vulnerable adults (for example, ex-offenders and people with mental health problems, learning and/or physical disabilities) and personal care for older people. Local authorities housed a significant proportion of the population. The 1957 Housing Act placed a duty on them to evaluate housing conditions in their area and provide additional homes where necessary, and by the late 1970s councils owned almost 7 million dwellings (Wilson and Game 2006). They were also responsible for a range of public utilities as well as for consumer protection, environmental health, fire and rescue services, emergency planning, highways maintenance, transport and traffic management, leisure, arts, recreation, libraries, planning, and the collection and disposal of waste.

Councils were therefore monopoly suppliers of key local public services. They had large budgets and were major employers. For the most part, they were organized around services. Directors of education, social services, housing and other key functions ran specialist departments which often had little contact with other parts of the organization. Their activities were overseen by committees of local politicians who, like the professional staff, often became specialists in particular services. Users of services (clients, pupils and tenants) had no choice of who provided services and little direct influence over how they were run.

The fragmented local state

In the late 1960s and throughout the 1970s the combination of spiraling costs of welfare provision and a succession of economic crises began to call into question the postwar model of welfare provision. The assumption that public services should be provided directly by local authorities no longer seemed sustainable. The Secretary of State for the Environment famously informed councils that "for the time being at least, the party is over". Their budgets came under increasing pressure. The number of lower-tier (district) councils was reduced, and on the recommendation of the Bains Committee, which was established by central government to advise on the internal management of local authorities, many councils underwent significant internal restructuring. Chief executives, senior management teams, and policy and resources committees were encouraged to assert corporate priorities, and in the process began to erode the power of the large, functionally organized service departments that had been such a dominant feature of local government in the immediate postwar period.

The Conservative government that came to power in 1979 believed that Britain's future economic prosperity depended on gaining control of public spending and breaking the power of large public-sector trade unions. In pursuit of these twin objectives, it embarked on a series of policies which were inspired by the NPM and set it on a collision course with many local authorities. Hood (1991) identifies seven "doctrines" of the NPM: "hands-on professional management"; explicit standards and measures of performance; greater emphasis on output controls; the disaggregation of units; greater competition; the promotion of private-sector management practice; an emphasis on greater discipline and parsimony in resource use. Pollitt (1995: 133) offers a similar list of "core elements" of the NPM which he suggests "comprise a kind of 'shopping basket' for those who wish to modernize the public sector of Western industrial societies". He adds to Hood's list the introduction into public-sector organizations of more flexible working (including short-term contracts, performance-related pay and local bargaining) and an emphasis on service quality and responsiveness to service users. Operating at a slightly higher level of abstraction, Pollitt and Bouckaert (2000) identify four broad strategies for public services reform: the maintenance of controls on public spending; modernization of the administrative system through the introduction of private-sector management practices and reform of political and managerial structures and practices; marketization of public services through the introduction of competition; and minimization of the state through privatization and contracting out of functions.

In their attempts to reform local government, the Conservatives delved deep into the NPM shopping basket, deploying all four of Pollitt and Bouckaert's reform strategies at various times over the following two decades. The "maintenance" strategy was manifested in tight controls on local government spending. The level of grants paid to local councils by central government decreased in real terms, and ministers took new powers to restrict the amounts by which local politicians could raise local taxes.

"Minimization" was evident in the way in which local government was stripped of key functions. Councils lost control over post-16 education and training, and responsibility for regeneration programs was transferred to new bodies which were placed under the control of business people and community representatives who were directly appointed by central government. The 1988 Education Reform Act took away councils' ability to determine what was taught in their local schools and introduced a national curriculum. Schools were encouraged to opt out of local-authority control altogether and receive their funding directly from central government. Those which chose not to go down this route nevertheless received an increasing proportion of their funding in the form of central government grants that were dedicated to particular initiatives favored by ministers. Council-house tenants were given a legal right to buy their home at discounts of up to 70 per cent of the true market value. Local authorities were left with the poorest-quality accommodation, and their remaining tenants were given the option to transfer the residual housing stock to registered social landlords, subject to the outcome of ballots which used a controversial system that was widely seen as being weighted in favor of a "yes" vote.

Marketization played a key role in the government's plans to improve the economy, efficiency and effectiveness of local services. From 1980 onwards, local authorities were required by law to expose specified services to competitive tendering. A council's own workforce could only be awarded a contract if they submitted a lower bid than private-sector competitors and generated a specified return on capital. The number and range of the services to which this legislation was applied was increased over time, starting with manual services such as waste collection and housing management but eventually encompassing a wide range of professions. The attempt to expose services to competition proved deeply unpopular with councils, which regarded it as an attack on their autonomy and their employees' pay and conditions. Some engaged in elaborate maneuvers designed to abide by the letter of the law whilst making their services unattractive targets for potential bidders. Private contractors meanwhile complained of a lack of "fair competition".

Alongside these initiatives, the government also sought to "modernize" local government by introducing private-sector management techniques. As

noted above, there had already been moves to encourage
approach. Now the government sought to encourage the ac
planning and more systematic performance management. T
sion was initially created to oversee the financial auditing
but was soon charged with specifying national performan
cils had to report these data on a regular basis, and th
them to compile performance league tables.

Networked local governance

The Labour government that came to power in 1997 also had ambitious plans for reforming public services. However, unlike their immediate predecessors, ministers increased spending on public services. Local authorities received large real-terms increases in their budgets as part of a strategy which the government called "invest and reform". In return for additional resources, ministers expected to see far-reaching changes in the ways in which public services were designed and delivered. Administrative systems had, they said, to be updated, and management practices must be overhauled. In the past, services had too often been designed around the convenience of the providers. Henceforth they would need to focus on the needs of users (Cabinet Office 1999).

In the health service and in education, ministers turned to a combination of "modernization" and "marketization" to achieve improvements. Modernization initiatives included internal restructuring, the introduction of new information and communications technology and new forms of external inspection (Martin and Davis 2008; Walshe 2008). Marketization involved the encouragement of competition between service providers. Although they initially rejected the Conservatives' policy of creating an internal market in the National Health Service, Labour ministers later gave patients the option to choose the hospital at which they were treated. The theory was that, faced with the need to attract patients, hospitals would behave like businesses and in the process become more responsive to the needs and aspirations of their "customers". Similarly, the government encouraged choice between schools in the belief that this would put pressure on teachers and governing bodies to "drive up" standards in order to attract students.

In contrast to the policies that were applied to health and schools, competition was not a significant feature of New Labour's approach to reforming local government. One of its first acts was to announce the abolition of the requirement for councils to subject their services to competitive tendering. In its place ministers introduced a new duty of "Best Value", which required councils to put in place arrangements to secure continuous improvement by reviewing the efficiency and effectiveness of their services in consultation with users, citizens and other local interest groups (Martin 2001). Enforced competition was seen as having been counterproductive. Whilst it had made the costs of services more transparent", the "detailed prescription of the form and timing of competition led to unimaginative tendering, and often frustrated rather than enhanced real competition" (DETR 1998: clause 7.22). Instead, the government now wished to encourage local councils to forge long-term partnerships with private-sector companies in the provision of a wide range of frontline services such as schools and waste management and "back office" functions like legal services, asset management, HR and payrolls (Entwistle and Martin 2005).

There was a residual element of "minimization" in New Labour's approach to local government reform. Starved of funds to refurbish their remaining housing stock, local authorities were encouraged to transfer them to arm's-length management organizations. As a result, by 2004 councils held less than half the number of residential properties which they had owned in 1979. Ministers also curtailed local-authority control over schools to an even greater extent than their predecessors. Having initially toyed with the idea of abolishing LEAs, they eventually decided to retain them but to encourage schools to opt out of their control. Failing schools in inner-city areas were closed down and replaced by independent "city academies" which were partly funded by private sponsors (such as businesses, faith groups and charities) that took over control of the governing body, curriculum, staffing and management. Other secondary schools were encouraged to apply for status as "specialist schools", which took them out of local-authority control and allowed them access to private funding. By 2005 the majority had made this transition.

The centerpiece of New Labour's approach to reforming local government was through a range of policies that became known as the "modernization agenda". These were predicated on the assumption that local councils had an important role in the delivery of public services but needed to undergo what a local government white paper in 1998 called a process of "radical modernisation". There needed, it was argued, to be "a fundamental shift of culture". Councils must "break free from old fashioned practices and attitudes"; "paternalism and inwardness" had to be "swept away" (DETR 1998).

The principal agent of the modernization process was an unparalleled and apparently unbridled enthusiasm for top-down performance-monitoring. There was a huge increase in the scale, scope and intensity of external inspection of local authorities. According to the government's own calculations, the total cost of public services inspection rose steeply from £250 million in 1997–8 to £550 million by 2002–3 (OPSR 2003). By 2005 the direct costs of inspection of local government amounted to £97 million per annum (ODPM/HM Treasury 2005). The costs of inspecting education more than doubled from £88 million to £201 million. Spending on inspection of social services increased from £6 million to £11 million. The Audit Commission, which had responsibility for overseeing most other local government services, saw its budget balloon from £111 million to £217 million and its workforce grow by almost 90 percent as it recruited an army of new inspectors. For the first time all local government services were subject to external scrutiny, and inspectors no longer simply checked that services were meeting minimum standards. They were now charged with assessing a service's prospects for improvement. In 2002 the inspection framework was strengthened by the introduction of "Comprehensive Performance Assessments" (CPAs), which scored each council's overall performance and graded them on a five-point scale ranging from "excellent" to "poor" (Downe and Martin 2007). Councils at the bottom end of the resulting performance league table were subject to direct intervention, which usually involved the replacement of their senior managers and the provision of support and advice by a government-funded improvement and development agency (Martin 2002; Yapp and Skelcher 2007). The increase in external inspection of English local government was, of course, part of a much broader "audit explosion" which has been a feature of public management across many Western democracies (Power 1997). But it was particularly prominent in the UK (Hood et al. 1999). As has been widely documented, the fragmentation of the local state, associated with the NPM, led to the displacement of traditional hierarchical forms of coordination, which in turn saw policy-makers turn to the "long distant mechanics of control" offered by public services audit and inspection (Hoggett 1996).

New Labour also became increasingly concerned with improving horizontal coordination between local agencies. There was a recognition that the public was confused about who was responsible for local services and frustrated at having to deal with a multitude of providers. The solution was not, it was argued, to reinvent the local welfare state of the immediate postwar period. What was needed was for local authorities and others to work together to offer more "joined up" services. As the prime minister explained, "It is in partnership with others – public agencies, private companies, community groups and voluntary organisations – that local government's future lies" (Blair 1998: 13). Unlike the previous Conservative government's vision of minimalist local government the role of which was to oversee the outsourcing of local services, ministers were not seeking to by-pass councils or to reduce their role. They wanted to redefine it. Unlike the architects of the local welfare of the immediate postwar period, the Blairite vision of local government did not assume that it was necessary for local councils to provide local services. Henceforth their role should be "to actively steer processes of co-ordination and collective action across public, private and voluntary boundaries" (Stoker 2004). To succeed they would have to rely on, and seek to influence, the actions of other bodies. This, it was argued, would enable a more "joined up" approach which was better-suited to dealing with the "wicked" issues that cut across the responsibilities of individual service providers. This model, which became known as "networked community governance", envisaged local authorities playing a vital "community leadership" role, operating as the hubs of local service delivery networks and orchestrating the activities of health service providers, the police, training agencies, businesses and charitable organizations.

The idea of community leadership was not new. Most local politicians saw their primary duty as being to represent constituents' interests, and most councils had a long tradition of speaking up on behalf of their localities to regional bodies, national government and the European Commission. They were also used to coordinating celebrations (such as local carnivals or even international sporting or cultural events) and responses to environmental and economic crises (such as natural disasters or the closure of large local employers). However, the Blair government's formal recognition of their community leadership marked an important shift, which was manifested in three key policies – the creation of Local Strategic Partnerships, a requirement for local authorities to produce Sustainable Community Strategies, and the introduction of Local Area Agreements.

Local Strategic Partnerships consist of representatives of the private, public, voluntary and community sectors who meet regularly to review the needs of their area and formulate plans for joint action to address them. The objectives on which they agree are set out in Sustainable Community Strategies, which typically articulate a long-term (five-to-ten-year) vision. Statutory responsibility for preparing strategies rests with local authorities, but they are expected to liaise extensively with the other members of Local Strategic Partnerships. The strategies also set out plans for consulting with and reporting to local communities. Local Area Agreements are agreed between a Local Strategic Partnership and central government, and are informed by community strategies and national policy priorities. The latest round of agreements included up to fifty-three targets based on statutory performance indicators defined by central government departments plus a range of outcomes which matter locally. In return for signing up to agreements, local agencies are given greater freedom to pool the funding they receive from central government departments. They also receive performance reward grants for hitting targets.

This new approach poses formidable challenges for local authorities. They are now being held accountable for the delivery of agreed outcomes over which they often have little direct control. Local politicians and local authority officers now have to be able to work across organizational boundaries to a degree that was never expected of previous generations. Staff working in the hierarchical organizations of the past derived their authority from their formal positions and professional expertise. The emergence of networked community governance calls for officers and local politicians who are able to network with, and influence the actions of, other agencies (Sullivan and Skelcher 2002). This "boundary-spanning" behavior calls for an understanding of the often very different priorities, cultures and professional backgrounds of the diverse organizations that comprise Local Strategic Partnerships (Williams 2002), and for strong negotiating skills and powers of persuasion.

This new style of operating has also blurred traditional lines of accountability. A recent study found that one-third of the senior local authority managers surveyed believed that partnership working had made it more difficult for the public to hold local service providers in their area to account (Cowell et al. 2009). However, on the positive side, there is evidence that partnership working has made local agencies more directly accountable to each other. In the past, local politicians focused primarily on the activities of local councils. Now that local authorities are being held accountable for the achievement of a much wider range of outcomes, they are looking for ways of scrutinizing the performance of other service providers.

Partnership working of the kind engendered by Local Area Agreements also marks a change in the way in which central government holds local agencies to account. In the past, relations between central and local government were dominated by strong vertical links between individual local services and the central government department which oversaw them. LEAs, for example, reported to the Department for Education, which also oversaw the activities of the Office for Standards in Education (OFSTED) – the body with responsibility for school inspection. LEAs often had little interaction with other council services. OFSTED had minimal contact with other inspectorates. And the Department for Education had a clearly defined brief beyond which it rarely strayed far. A similar pattern was apparent in social services, housing, planning and a range of other council services. Here, too, local authority departments had strong vertical links with national inspectorates and their associated central ministries which bound together groups of practitioners and policy-makers who often came from similar professional backgrounds and had a common sense of purpose (Rhodes 1999). Policies designed to encourage "joined up" working at local level have made it much more difficult for central government and inspectors to work exclusively within these traditional "silos".

Attempts to coordinate the activities of inspectorates have included joint reviews of social services undertaken by the (then) Social Services Inspectorate and the Audit Commission, and more recently "joint area reviews". Reports by OFSTED and the inspectors of social services have also been used by the Audit Commission to compile CPAs, and there have been some mergers of inspectorates. In 2008, for example, OFSTED took over responsibility for the inspection of all children's services, adding social services to its previous responsibilities for the inspection of schools and colleges. In 2009, Comprehensive Area Assessments were introduced in an attempt to evaluate how well local agencies are working together to deliver the outcomes specified by Local Area Agreements. The aim is to bring together the judgments made by several different inspectorates into a single report.

However, this process is not easy. Different inspectorates collect different kinds of performance information in different ways, and it is not a straightforward task for them to bring together the large volume of data that they hold, let alone to combine them into an overall judgment about how well agencies are working together.

Central government departments have also experienced problems dealing in a holistic way with local partnerships. Despite the emphasis on "joined up" government, central ministries continue to be functionally organized. The services which local authorities provide cut across the responsibilities of a total of eight central government departments and more than twenty government ministers, and the mechanisms for coordinating activities across departments are weak. As a result, there were significant difficulties and delays experienced in the negotiation of the first Local Public Service Agreements, which were the forerunners of Local Area Agreements. Local authorities often found it difficult to navigate their way through the "maze" of central government departments and agreements involved. "Cross-cutting targets were particularly difficult, and revealed a lack of joined-up working between departments in central government" (Sullivan and Gillanders 2005: 563). The potential problems were magnified once it was decided to include in Local Area Agreements the services provided by a much wider range of other local agencies. To alleviate this, Government Regional Offices were used as intermediaries, and conducted the negotiations on behalf of central ministries. This solved many of the difficulties but has not entirely eliminated them, as central government departments have continued to regard agreements primarily as a means of meeting their particular departmental objectives rather than of achieving the more "joined up" policy-making and service delivery which they now require of local service networks.

Conclusion

The emergence of Local Strategic Partnerships, Sustainable Community Strategies and Local Area Agreements is, then, a very significant policy development. They are evidence of networked community governance in action, proof perhaps that the reforms of the NPM type of the 1980s and 1990s have been supplanted by a new approach inspired by a different and distinctive paradigm. In contrast to Conservative policies two decades ago, the aim is not to by-pass local government or to strip away its functions. Local authorities have in some senses been rehabilitated. But not in their former role as direct providers of local services. They are now required to work together with other local agencies to a degree that would have been almost unimaginable twenty years ago. This has changed the nature of local governance and the relationships between service providers. It also has important implications for central–local relations.

However, it is not a simple case of the previous model of local service delivery having been overturned by a new, wholly different approach. In reality English local government retains many of the features of the postwar local welfare state and of the disaggregated local state bequeathed by the NPM-inspired reforms of the Thatcher era. These two states cohabit with new policies that reflect the new(ish) concept of networked community governance. In truth, councils' service-delivery role never went away. It was diminished but not extinguished by the policies of the 1980s and 1990s. Councils continue to be big business. They still deliver a vast array of services and employ large numbers of staff – councils in England currently employ more than 2 million people, not far off 10 per cent of the total workforce. Nor has central government suddenly let go of the old levers of control. The new language of central–local "partnership" is important but it falls well short of the kind of autonomy enjoyed by subnational governments in many other European countries. Local Area Agreements have incentivized a new style of working among local public service networks, but local authorities and their partners continue to operate largely as delivery agents for national government, tied into its priorities through an elaborate system of centrally driven performance targets linked directly to their future funding.

References

Blair, T. (1998) *Leading the Way: A New Vision for Local Government*, London: IPPR.

Cabinet Office (1999) *Modernising Government*, London: The Stationery Office.

Cowell, R. J., Ashworth, R., Downe, J., Skelcher, C., Bovaird, A. G. and Chen, A. (2009) *The State of Local Democracy: The Impact of Policy Changes on Accountability and Public Confidence*, London: Department for Communities and Local Government.

Department of Environment, Transport and the Regions (1998) *Modern Local Government: In Touch with the People*, Cmnd 4014, London: The Stationery Office.

Downe, J. and Martin, S. J. (2007) "Regulation Inside Government: Processes and Impacts of Inspection of Local Public Services", *Policy and Politics*, 35 (2): 215–32.

Entwistle, T. and Martin, S. J. (2005) "From Competitive Tendering to Collaboration in Public Service Delivery: A New Agenda for Research", *Public Administration*, 83 (1): 233–42.

Hoggett, P. (1996) "New Modes of Control in the Public Service", *Public Administration*, 74: 9–32.

Hood, C. (1991) "A Public Management for All Seasons", *Public Administration*, 69 (1): 3–19.

Hood, C., Scott, C., James, O., Jones, G. and Travers, T. (1999) *Regulation Inside Government*, Oxford: Oxford University Press.

Martin, S. J. (2001) "Implementing Best Value: Local Public Services in Transition", *Public Administration*, 78 (1): 209–27.

Martin, S. J. (2002) "The Modernisation of UK Local Government: Markets, Managers, Monitors and Mixed Fortunes", *Public Management Review*, 4 (3): 291–307.

Martin, S. J. and Davis, H. (2008) "The Rise of Public Services Inspection", in H. Davis and S. J. Martin (eds) *Public Services Inspection in the UK*, London: Jessica Kingsley.

ODPM/Her Majesty's Treasury (2005) *Securing Better Outcomes: Developing a New Performance Management Framework*, London: Her Majesty's Treasury.

OPSR (2003) *Inspecting for Improvement*, London: Cabinet Office.

Pollitt, C. (1995) "Justification by Works or by Faith? Evaluating the New Public Management", *Evaluation*, 1 (2): 133–54.

Pollitt, C. (2007) "New Labour's Re-disorganization: Hyper-modernism and the Costs of Reform – a Cautionary Tale", *Public Management Review*, 9 (4): 529–43.

Pollitt, C. and Bouckaert, G. (2000) *Public Management Reform: A Comparative Analysis*, Oxford: Oxford University Press.

Power, M. (1997) *The Audit Society: Rituals of Verification*, Oxford: Oxford University Press.

Rhodes, R. A. W. (1999) *Control and Power in Central–Local Government Relations*, 2nd edn, Aldershot: Ashgate.

Stoker (2004) *Transforming Local Governance: From Thatcherism to New Labour*, Basingstoke: Palgrave Macmillan.

Sullivan, H. and Gillanders, G. (2005) "Stretched to the Limit? The Impact of Local Public Service Agreements on Service Improvement and Central–local relations", *Local Government Studies*, 31 (5): 355–74.

Sullivan, H. and Skelcher, C. (2002) *Working across Boundaries: Collaboration in Public Services*, Basingstoke: Palgrave Macmillan.

Walshe, K. (2008) "Regulation and Inspection of Health Services", in H. Davis and S. J. Martin (eds) *Public Services Inspection in the UK*, London: Jessica Kingsley.

Williams, P. (2002) "The Competent Boundary Spanner", *Public Administration*, 80 (1): 103–24.

Wilson, D. and Game, C. (2006) *Local Government in the United Kingdom*, Basingstoke: Palgrave Macmillan.

Yapp, C. and Skelcher, C. (2007) "Improvement Boards: Building Capability for Public Service Improvement through Peer Support", *Public Money and Management*, 27 (4): 285–92.

Part V

GOVERNANCE OF POLICY NETWORKS

20

POLICY NETWORKS: THEORY AND PRACTICE[1]

Tobias Jung

While the notion of policy networks can be traced back to Greek philosophy (Parry 1969; Kimber and Richardson 1974), it has its modern roots in the writings of Bentley: at the beginning of the twentieth century he described government as "networks of activity" (Bentley 1908: 261). At the time, other authors toyed with similar ideas. For example, in his *Impasse of Democracy*, Griffith (1939) advocated the concept of "whirlpools of activity" within the political system. However, it was only during the 1950s that the idea of policy networks started to gain momentum when structural and socio-political changes following World War II led to an increasing complexity in the organization of government and the governing of society. The key features of this included: a move toward a pluralist and collaborative approach to developing and implementing policies, division of labor, sectoralization, and functional differentiation (Kenis and Schneider 1991; Pappi and Henning 1998). These changes were picked up in the works of authors such as Freeman (1955), Truman (1951), Maass (1951), Dahl (1956), Schattschneider (1935) and Lindblom (1965), who, driven by a dissatisfaction with more traditional conceptions of the policy process, started to explore the idea of placing groups of actors with shared interests at the heart of policy-making. Out of this, the policy network approach, with its focus on the links between actors involved in both policy formulation and implementation, developed.

There have been lengthy and not always fruitful debates about the precise role played by the policy networks concept. While some authors appear to have argued that the concept amounts to nothing more than some sort of metaphor (Dowding 1995), others maintain that policy networks exist not only as a model but also as a real influence on the formulation of policy (Potters and Sloof 1996), acting as "links" amongst the actors in the policy field (John 1998; Lovseth 2000). Nonetheless, the policy network idea has become increasingly well established and accepted as an analytical tool (Heany 2001a; Albrechts and Lievois 2004). Because of its portable nature, the idea of policy networks can be applied to various areas of public interest (John 1998), making it an ideal framework for any policy researcher's and practitioner's toolbox; from their humble origins at the beginning of the twentieth century, policy networks have emerged as prominent themes across countries, sectors and disciplines (Robinson 2006). Even those who were strong critics in the past now argue that exploring the networks involved in the policy process is important in analyzing both policy formulation and policy implementation (Dowding 2000, 2001).

This chapter sketches the terminological pot-pourri surrounding policy networks and provides an outline of the key concepts of iron triangles, issues networks, policy communities and advocacy coalitions; it highlights the concepts' defining characteristics, their advantages and disadvantages.

Terminological confusion

Despite the widespread acceptance and prominent use of the policy network idea within academic discourse, there is a lack of agreement on networks' defining characteristics, the appropriate terminology, and the concept's correct application. Assumptions about the ontological, epistemological and methodological standing of policy networks are diverse: they range from positivistic traditions at one end, to realist and interpretative ones at the other (Marsh and Smith 2001). Those who take a positivist view try to understand networks through measures of cohesion, centrality and structure (see, for example, Knoke 1994; Dowding 1995; Milward and Provan 1998; Dowding 2001), while proponents rooted in interpretative approaches are interested in the processes and contents of interactions that take place within networks (see, for example, Marsh and Rhodes 1992; Marsh and Smith 2000; Bevir and Rhodes 2003).

In general, the literature on policy networks appears to have become preoccupied with definitional disputes, conceptual ambiguities and a proliferation of typologies (Wolman 1992; Lovseth 2000). As a result, authors have argued that a "Babylonian variety" of terms and applications has emerged within the field (Börzel 1998), a "terminological jungle in which any newcomer may plant a tree" (Barnes 1972). Alongside the aforementioned "policy whirlpools" (Griffith 1939), authors have referred to "subsystems" (Freeman 1955), "subgovernments" (Cater 1964), "triangular trading patterns" (Lowi 1962), "sloppy large hexagons" (Jones 1982), "issue niches" (Browne 1990), or "epistemic communities" (Haas 1992). The danger of such mushrooming terminology is that the explanatory power of the concept can easily be inflated (Marin and Mayntz 1991), especially given that there is no coherent school of thought, glossary of terms, or application. A large number of authors have only a vague idea of what constitutes a policy network and often fail to state their nebulous assumptions or ideas (McCool 1990; Marsh 1998). It is thus not unheard of that two different authors, while using the same term, mean two completely different things or, vice versa, that two authors using different terms do actually refer to the same thing (Börzel 1998).

For example, Peterson (2003) highlights incongruities about "advocacy coalitions" between the writings of Sabatier and Jenkins-Smith (1993) and Keck and Sikkink (1998), as well as the different conceptions of policy communities in the writings of Rhodes (1990) and Wright (1988).

The aforementioned issues are aggravated by the fact that different countries have traditionally conceived of and used the policy-network approach in different ways. There exist at least three different international schools of thought relating to policy networks: the American, the British and the European, the last of which can again be subdivided into Dutch, French and German traditions. These different perspectives can be roughly clustered under two headings: the interest intermediation school and the governance school (Börzel 1998; Marsh 1998; Marsh and Smith 2000).

The governance school perceives policy networks as an alternative form of governance that by way of its nonhierarchical coordination constitutes an alternative to markets and hierarchies (Börzel 1997, 1998). The problem with this approach is that it is idealistic, prescriptive and theoretical. The interest intermediation school, on the other hand, focuses on analyzing the role policy networks, perceived as various kinds of relationships between interested groups and the state, play in the formulation and implementation of policies. While this perception can be criticized as being overly static, it offers a practical, straightforward way of effectively identifying and outlining policy networks' characteristics (Börzel 1997, 1998; Thompson and Pforr 2005). To this end, it offers various network models. Despite the terminological disparity and variety that can be identified within the literature, these existing perspectives are essentially variations on four key models: iron triangles, issue networks, policy communities and advocacy coalitions (see, for example, Hanks 2000).

Iron triangles

Iron triangles' roots are difficult to identify (Freeman and Stevens 1987), especially as they have confusingly also been referred to as "networks", "subgovernments", "subsystems" and "whirlpools" within the literature (Browne and Paik 1993). However, it appears that the concept was originally based on research into agricultural, water and public works policies (Heclo 1978). While the actual components that are nowadays thought of as constituting an iron triangle – interest groups, committees and an executive agency – appear to have been first identified by Cater (1964) in his examination of policy-making in Washington's "subgovernments", the concept as such has become mainly associated with the work of Lowi (1962, 1969). Lowi had initially identified "triangular trading patterns" within the policy arena (Lowi 1962) and started to refer to the metaphorical concept of "iron triangles" only in subsequent work, where he expanded on his original idea of "triangular trading patterns" (Lowi 1969).

Traditionally, it has been assumed that iron triangles are very stable tripartite arrangements which operate over a long period of time with little or no outside interference; in this respect they can be considered to be almost autonomous as regards their decision-making abilities (Thurber 1991). Iron triangles normally control a very narrow and small niche within the policy field, and the relationships amongst the small number of participants are assumed to be slow-changing and "mutually advantageous" (Heclo 1978; McCool 1990). Although each member of the triangle receives some sort of benefit from the arrangement, benefits are not necessarily distributed equally (Nachamias and Rosenbloom 1980). Because of this benefit focus, iron triangles most commonly appear in the case of distributive policies, with each side of the triangle supporting and complementing the other two (Jordan 1981).

The idea of iron triangles has been considered to be analytically useful in so far as it helps to simplify complex interactional arrangements. As a consequence, it has been widely referred to. However, the real-world applicability of the concept has been questioned. First of all, it seems to be difficult to identify clearly the three key groups within iron triangles (Browne and Paik 1993). Second, the iron-like structure does not allow for a permeation of it from outside, nor does it account for any relation to the surrounding environment; rather, the iron triangle appears to be some form of secluded insular arrangement detached from everything else (Stein and Bickes 1995). However, the major criticism of the iron triangle concept has come from Heclo, who has argued that the concept of iron triangles is "not so much wrong as it is disastrously incomplete" (Heclo 1978: 88). Iron triangles cannot take into account the huge level of complexity of the policy process: researchers are trying hard to identify the three major players while missing the interactions that take place within the broader networks of people who increasingly have an impact on government (Heclo 1978).

> Use of the iron triangle metaphor – even as a "straw man" – oversimplifies political relationships so badly as to hide the very consequential local influences in Congress and its network.
>
> (Browne and Paik 1993: 1075)

Although there have been attempts to make the concept of "iron triangles" more inclusive by adding extra players, illustrated by Cerny's (2001) move from "iron triangles" to "golden pentangles", one problem with such modifications is that the defining nature of the concept is lost and the difference from some of the other concepts becomes less clear.

Issue networks

The concept of issue networks, which has also become known under a variety of terms (Heany 2001a), was proposed by Heclo (1978) as a way of addressing the shortcomings he saw with iron triangles. Although the originality and conceptual contribution of this concept has been questioned in so far as all it appears to do is to change the label of an earlier concept, "whirlpools" (Freeman and Stevens 1987), it is issue networks that have become widely known. While Heclo considers issue networks to be "almost the reverse image in each respect" of iron triangles (Heclo 1978: 102), other authors have questioned this and argued that issue networks are "not discreetly different arrangements from iron triangles" (Jordan 1981: 103). Instead it has been claimed that all they account for are iron triangles with an increased number of participants, larger disaggregation of power, less predictable participants, and both lower cohesion and lower homogeneity (Jordan 1981).

The defining trait of an issue network is the large number of participants involved, ranging from individuals to huge interest-groups. Issue networks operate at a multitude of levels, and within issue networks the number of participants is in a permanent flux. As a result, no one is really in control of the issue agenda. Whereas involvement in iron triangles is mainly driven by materialistic reasons, it is assumed that the underlying reasons for participation in issue networks are emotional or intellectual factors, with members sharing a specific interest. Although on first impression this seems to imply that issue networks amount to little more than political movements, this is not the case: policy goals are more specific in issue networks than in political movements; and, while one defining trait of political movements is uncertainty about authority within the movement, in issue networks there is no tendency for anybody to obtain perceived or legitimate authority as to what represents the public will (Heclo 1978; Salisbury 1984).

Although the major advantage of issue networks appears to have been that the concept offered an alternative to iron triangles (McCool 1990), it has also drawn attention to important aspects of the policy process. First of all, it has highlighted that policy is made in communities, the structure, nature and stability of which all influence the policy process. Second, it has drawn attention to the permanent flux within such communities because of players moving in as well as out; such changes lead to modifications in agendas, interests and linkages between various issues. Third, the concept brings to light a more decentralized understanding of power, with no one person being fully in charge (Heany 2001a).

Nonetheless, there are certain problems with issue networks as an analytical concept. It is incredibly difficult to identify a specific issue network since at any point in time only parts of the network might be active. Consequently, there is no clearly identifiable set of participants, links between participants might fade or be strengthened, and there are no clear-cut boundaries between governmental institutions and their environment. As Heclo (1978) himself recognized when trying to examine issue networks, it is virtually impossible to state where a network leaves off and its environment starts. Issue networks are therefore "more like amorphous clouds than geometric designs" (Browne and Paik 1993: 1055). As such, they do not lend themselves to academic studies.

Although the idea of issue networks has been frequently quoted and accepted (McCool 1990; Heany 2001a), only structures that display some of the features that characterize an issue network appear to have been identified within the literature (Sabatier and Jenkins-Smith 1993).

Policy communities

Initially, the idea of policy communities appears to have been a defence of pluralism against its critics and corporatist theory (Jordan 1981), and can be seen as a British reproduction and duplication of the American concepts of iron triangles and issue networks (Jordan 1990). Although it has been pointed out that at the time there was no direct application of American ideas to the British context, but that the approach taken was simply a description of structures within British policy-making with a subsequent recognition of American precedents (Richardson and Jordan 1979), others simply consider it to be a development of the US literature for Britain (Dowding 1995).

Leaving any such disputes aside, this combination of British and American schools of thought has had its own merits. While, on the one hand, policy communities follow the idea of issue networks by widening the number of participants, they also assume stable relationships that mirror the longstanding relationships within iron triangles, perceived as assisting in the negotiation process. Policy communities are thus a special case of stable networks (Jordan 1990); and, were one to draw a continuum of policy network concepts, policy communities would be placed somewhere between iron triangles and issue networks (Hanks 2000).

Within the literature, policy communities are understood to be a sort of "common culture and understanding" within specific policy domains as regards problems and decision-making processes (Dowding 1995: 138). Some of these communities are "diverse and fragmented" while others are "extremely closed and tightly knit" (Kingdon 1995: 118). These communities are made up of specialists in any given policy area (Kingdon 1995); and, if a new policy focus develops, sooner or later a new policy community will evolve around it (Jordan 1990). As a result, "policy communities are swept by intellectual fads" (Kingdon 1995: 127), so that the attention given to certain issues will fluctuate over time (Kingdon 1995): as the focus on one policy area becomes intellectually fatigued and routinized, other areas become more interesting.

One of the main difficulties with the idea of policy communities is the variety of ways in which it has been used. This makes it almost impossible to come up with a coherent picture (Campbell et al. 1989; Anderson 1990;

Rhodes 1990; Marsh and Rhodes 1992). For example, Grant et al. (1988) identify differentiation, specialization and interaction as characteristics of policy communities, whereas Rhodes (1988) in his examination distinguishes between interests, membership, resources, and horizontal and vertical interdependence. So, while in its original form the concept was "parsimonious and thought-provoking", it has been "complicated and diluted" in subsequent work (Grant 1995: 34).

More recently, the policy community approach has been dominated by the work of Rhodes (1988, 1990; Rhodes and Marsh 1992), who considers policy communities as only one sort of network amongst professional networks, intergovernmental networks, producer networks and issue networks. According to this perspective, a policy community's defining characteristics are the more restricted number of participants, high-quality interaction of all groups on all matters related to policy issues, and a dominance of economic or professional interests, with both values and membership persisting over a long period of time (Rhodes and Marsh 1992). However, these characteristics appear to be problematic. At a basic level, it is questionable whether high-quality interaction of all groups on all matters related to policy issues is even theoretically feasible, and also whether it is possible to maintain the idea of stability over time (Richardson 2000). More important, however, the assumption that only people with some form of expertise can participate in policy communities does not seem to hold, and a focus on mainly economic or professional interests is dubious, with the arising picture resembling an "elite cartel" rather than a policy community (Grant 1995): they appear as exclusionary, hidden gatherings of vested interests that use public resources for private aims (Miller and Demir 2006).

Advocacy coalitions

In order to replace the traditional triangular approach to policy networks and the conventional idea of a stagist policy-cycle, according to which policies can be understood as a set of interdependent phases through which policies go over time, Sabatier – first with Pelkey (1987) and later with Jenkins-Smith (1993) – developed the idea of advocacy coalitions. These form part of a broader framework: the advocacy coalitions framework.

According to the advocacy coalitions framework, networks of policy-makers, within this approach called policy subsystems, are made up of several competing coalitions – normally between two and four (Cairney 1997). Each of these coalitions consists of a variety of players, ranging from various governmental to private organizations, who share certain core beliefs. These core beliefs are of a fundamental normative and ontological nature, and therefore not very susceptible to change. Advocacy coalitions will try to translate these core beliefs, which act like "glue" to hold the advocacy coalition together (Sabatier and Jenkins-Smith 1993), into policies. In order to do so, they will apply various strategies, such as litigation, lobbying of elected officials, commissioning research or other ways of influencing opinions (Elliott and Schlaepfer 2001). However, opinions on these secondary, more pragmatic and instrumental aspects of how to achieve the policy goal may differ between various players within the same advocacy coalition and are open to change over time (Sabatier and Jenkins-Smith 1993).

As well as those players within the coalitions, the existence of another group of actors, the "policy-brokers", is assumed. These brokers are considered to be people, such as high civil servants, whose concern it is to keep the level of political conflict within acceptable limits so that a "reasonable" solution to a perceived problem is reached (Sabatier and Jenkins-Smith 1993). It appears that it will usually be difficult to distinguish between these brokers and "advocates" since they are based on a continuum.

Outside the policy subsystem there are two factors that provide both resources and restraints for the actors within. First of all, there are relatively stable parameters that hardly change in the short run, such as the basic distribution of the natural resources, basic attributes of the "problem" area, basic legal structure and the fundamental socio-cultural values and structures. Second, there are those aspects that are open to major changes in the short run. These include changes in socio-economic conditions, public opinion, governing coalitions as well as policy decisions, and impacts from other subsystems. It is these aspects which provide the main driving forces behind changes in policies (Sabatier and Jenkins-Smith 1993: 20–3).

Despite the fact that the advocacy coalitions framework comes with a set of "testable" hypotheses which have been tried through several case studies, the major criticism of this concept has been that it is mainly based on the American system. It is consequently difficult to apply to any political system that does not correspond to American-style pluralism (Parsons 1995: 200–3). Although an attempt at a "European" version was published in 1998 (Sabatier 1998), its usefulness is open for debate. Sabatier essentially appeared to ask European researchers to do their own work: "The real task of European researchers is to develop falsifiable hypotheses based upon the ACF" (Sabatier 1998: 121). While several studies have tried to apply the concept to European structures, mainly the EU itself (see, for example, Radaelli 1999; Warleigh 2000; Elliott and Schlaepfer 2001; Weber and Christophersen 2002), questions have arisen about the framework's applicability to a European context. For example, Warleigh (2000: 237) concludes that "Sabatier's model of the advocacy coalition . . . appears unable entirely to encapsulate the entrepreneurial dynamics of EU decision-making". However, a proper critical analysis of the extent to which the advocacy coalitions framework's original criteria can be extended to the EU is still wanting: to date, most applications of the advocacy coalitions framework within EU contexts have not so much focused on theory-testing as applied the framework as a heuristic device (Fueg 2009).

Leaving aside issues about the advocacy coalitions framework's transferability, more general problems with this concept arise out of the notion of belief systems. First of all, the grouping of people according to beliefs rather than to importance or influence is problematic. Second, the idea of core beliefs might not explain the reasons why groups form coalitions. Third, core beliefs might not shape the day-to-day operations and actions of coalitions. Fourth, the distinction between various levels of beliefs is awkward, and it will be virtually impossible to identify a coalition's core beliefs (Cairney 1997). Fifth, there are questions about whether a priori core beliefs are a valid assumption: people's beliefs and values are vague, contradictory and unstable (Hajer 1995). Sixth, since no historical context is developed as part of the advocacy coalitions framework which allows for an analysis of coalition formation (Sabatier and Jenkins-Smith 1993), the development of a coalition's core beliefs cannot be analyzed (Watt 1997). Given this lack of historical context, the advocacy coalitions framework lends itself more to established policy networks (Sabatier and Jenkins-Smith 1993), and thus does not really take into account how different topics can come on to the policy agenda; the advocacy coalitions framework might explain policy stability better than policy change (Fischer 2003).

Other prominent criticisms outlined by Parsons (1995) have addressed the distinction between "events" and "stable parameters": the question is how far the constraints and resources set for the policy subsystem by these two factors exist in a subsystem's physical environment or if they are cognitive constructs within the individuals and organizations that make up the subsystem. In addition, there is an assumption that non-elites, such as members of the general public, have "neither the expertise, nor the time, nor the inclination to be active participants in a policy subsystem" (Sabatier 1999: 202). The final concern about the extent to which the advocacy coalitions framework can contribute to a better understanding of the policy process is its methodological and epistemological limitations: it is firmly rooted in a positivist worldview (Fischer 2003).

Concluding comments

Since the 1950s, policy networks have emerged as a prominent analytical tool within academic discourses for exploring policy processes. Unfortunately, a lot of energy has been wasted on debates as to which conceptualization of policy networks is the most appropriate. What is often ignored is the complementary nature of the underlying models and the real-world practical application they offer. For example, LaPorte (1996) has drawn attention to the possibilities of approaching networks from different perspectives: from within the network, from above the network, and from the side of the network. The first is an organization-centric view that considers the network through the eyes of a key network participant looking out, up, across and down at other actors with whom it must deal. The second perspective takes an elevated position and explores a sector's contexts and structures from above. The final approach looks at the network from the side, as a player who has, as of yet, limited stakes in the network under observation but who operates from a similar institutional status level to some of those within that network. Similarly, by taking an organization-centric view, Mikkelsen (2006) has highlighted how using policy networks as a strategic, analytical tool might offer network players a better understanding of the context in which they operate, and their options for pursuing and achieving their strategic objectives. In both instances, the models of iron triangles, issue networks, policy communities and advocacy coalitions can assist. While none of the concepts is perfect, and it is unlikely that any concept will ever be, each highlights different facets of the same phenomenon (Hudson et al. 2007): they represent a continuum and should be considered as complimentary. In combination, these four concepts draw attention to aspects that range from rigid, longstanding and limited structures to open and amorphous filigrees; they address different degrees of ease of entry into a network and the level of structuration therein. As such, they are helpful in identifying and teasing out key facets of a policy network, independently as to whether one's interest in a network is of an academic or a practical nature.

Note

1 This chapter is revised and developed from one presented at the UK–Japanese Comparative Workshop on Local Governance, held in Tokyo in December 2008, with the support of the Daiwa Foundation, the GB-Sasakawa Foundation and the Japan Foundation Endowment Committee.

References

Albrechts, L. and Lievois, G. (2004) "The Flemish Diamond: Urban Network in the Making?", *European Planning Studies*, 12 (3): 351–70.

Anderson, J. E. (1990) *Public Policymaking: An Introduction*, Boston, Mass.: Houghton Mifflin.

Barnes, J. (1972) "Social Networks", *Addison-Wesley Module in Anthropology*, 26: 1–29.

Bentley, A. F. (1908) *The Process of Government*, Chicago, Ill.: University of Chicago Press.

Bevir, M. and Rhodes, R. A. W. (2003) *Interpreting British Governance*, London: Routledge.

Börzel, T. A. (1997) "What's So Special about Policy Networks? An Exploration of the Concept and Its Usefulness in Studying European Governance", *European Integration online Papers (EIoP)*, 1 (16), http://eiop.or.at/eiop/texte/1997–016a.htm

Börzel, T. A. (1998) "Organizing Babylon: On the Different Conceptions of Policy Networks", *Public Administration*, 76: 253–73.

Browne, W. P. (1990) "Organized Interests and Their Issue Niches: A Search for Pluralism in a Policy Domain", *Journal of Politics*, 52: 482–526.

Browne, W. P. and Paik, W. K. (1993) "Beyond the Domain: Recasting Network Politics in the Postreform Congress", *American Journal of Political Science*, 37 (4): 1054–78.

Cairney, P. (1997) "Policy Studies: Theory and Practice", http://www.pas.ac.uk/CPS/1997/cair.pdf [accessed 2 June 2004].

Campbell, J. C., Baskin, M. A., Baumgartner, F. R. and Halpern, N. P. (1989) "Afterword on Policy Communities: A Framework for Conceptual Research", *Governance: An International Journal of Policy, Administration, and Institutions*, 2: 86–94.

Cater, D. (1964) *Power in Washington: A Critical Look at Today's Struggle in the Nation's Capital*, New York: Random House.

Cerny, P. (2001) "From 'Iron Triangles' to 'Golden Pentangles'? Globalizing the Policy Process", *Global Governance*, 7: 397–410.

Dahl, R. A. (1956) *A Preface to Democratic Theory*, Chicago, Ill.: University of Chicago Press.

Dowding, K. (1995) "Model or Metaphor? A Critical Review of the Network Approach", *Political Studies*, 43: 136–58.

Dowding, K. (2000) "How Not to Use Evolutionary Theory in Politics: A Critique of Peter John", *British Journal of Politics and International Relations*, 2 (1): 72–80.

Dowding, K. (2001) "There Must Be End to Confusion: Policy Networks, Intellectual Fatigue, and the Need for Political Science Methods Courses in British Universities", *Political Studies*, 49: 89–105.

Elliott, C. and Schlaepfer, R. (2001) "The Advocacy Coalition Framework: Application to the Policy Process for the Development of Forest Certification in Sweden", *Journal of European Public Policy*, 8 (4): 642–61.

Fischer, F. (2003) *Reframing Public Policy: Discursive Politics and Deliberative Practices*, Oxford: Oxford University Press.

Freeman, J. L. (1955) *The Political Process: Executive Bureau–Legislative Committee Relations*, New York: Doubleday.

Freeman, J. L. and Stevens, J. P. (1987) "A Theoretical and Conceptual Reexamination of Subsystem Politics", *Public Policy and Administration*, 2 (1): 9–24.

Fueg, O. C. (2009) "The Advocacy Coalition Framework Goes to Europe. An American Theory and Its Application across the Pond", paper presented at the Annual Convention of the Political Studies Association, Manchester, 7–9 April.

Grant, W. (1995) *Pressure Groups, Politics and Democracy in Britain*, London: Harvester Wheatsheaf.

Grant, W., Paterson, W. and Whitson, C. (1988) *Government and the Chemical Industry*, Oxford: Clarendon Press.

Griffith, E. S. (1939) *The Impasse of Democracy*, New York: Harrison-Hilton.

Haas, P. M. (1992) "Introduction: Epistemic Communities and International Policy Coordination", *International Organization*, 46 (1): 1–35.

Hajer, M. A. (1995) *The Politics of Environmental Discourse: Ecological Modernization and the Policy Process*, Oxford: Oxford University Press.

Hanks, C. D. (2000) "Reexamining the Subsystem Concept", *Political Science*, Texas A&M University: 185.

Heany, M. T. (2001) "The Evolution of Interest-group Networks: A Study of the US National Health Policy Domain, 1977–2001", Department of Political Science and Harris School of Public Policy, Chicago, Ill.: University of Chicago.

Heclo, H. (1978) "Issue Networks and the Executive Establishment", in A. King (ed.) *The New American Political System*, Washington, DC: American Enterprise Institute.

Hudson, J., Lowe, S., Oscroft, N. and Snell, C. (2007) "Activating Policy Networks: A Case Study of Local Environmental Policy-making in the United Kingdom", *Policy Studies*, 28 (1): 55–70.

John, P. (1998) *Analysing Public Policy*, London: Pinter.

Jones, C. O. (1982) *The United States Congress: People, Place, and Policy*, Homewood, Ill.: The Dorsey Press.

Jordan, A. G. (1981) "Iron Triangles, Woolly Corporatism, and Elastic Nets: Images of the Policy Process", *Journal of Public Policy*, 1: 95–123.

Jordan, A. G. (1990) "Sub-governments, Policy Communities and Networks: Refilling the Old Bottles?", *Journal of Theoretical Politics*, 2: 319–38.

Keck, M. E. and Sikkink, K. (1998) *Activists beyond Borders: Advocacy Networks in International Politics*, London: Cornell University Press.

Kenis, P. and Schneider, V. (1991) "Policy Networks and Policy Analysis: Scrutinizing a New Analytical Toolbox", In B. Marin and R. Mayntz (eds) *Policy Networks: Empirical Evidence and Theoretical Considerations*, Frankfurt am Main: Campus Verlag.

Kimber, R. and Richardson, J. J. (eds) (1974) *Pressure Groups in Britain: A Reader*, London: Dent.

Kingdon, J. W. (1995) *Agendas, Alternatives, and Public Policies*, Boston, Mass.: Little, Brown.

Knoke, D. (1994) *Political Networks: The Structural Perspective*, Cambridge: Cambridge University Press.

LaPorte, T. R. (1996) "Shifting Vantage and Conceptual Puzzles in Understanding Public Organization Networks", *Journal of Public Administration Research and Theory*, 6 (1): 49–76.

Lindblom, C. E. (1965) *The Intelligence of Democracy*, New York: The Free Press.

Lovseth, T. (2000) "Informal Networks – What Matters? On Policy Networks and the New Institutionalism in Organization Theory", paper prepared for European Consortium for Political Research Joint Sessions, Copenhagen.

Lowi, T. J. (1962) *Legislative Politics USA*, Boston, Mass.: Little, Brown.

Lowi, T. J. (1969) *The End of Liberalism: Ideology, Policy, and the Crisis of Public Authority*, New York: W. W. Norton.

Maass, A. (1951) *Muddy Waters: The Army Engineers and the Nation's Rivers*, Cambridge, Mass.: Harvard University Press.

McCool, D. (1990) "Subgovernments as Determinants of Political Viability", *Political Science Quarterly*, 105 (2): 269–93.

Marin, B. and Mayntz, R. (eds) (1991) *Policy Networks: Empirical Evidence and Theoretical Considerations*, Frankfurt am Main: Campus Verlag.

Marsh, D. (1998) "The Utility and Future of Policy Network Analysis", in D. Marsh (ed.) *Comparing Policy Networks*, Buckingham: Open University Press.

Marsh, D. and Rhodes, R. A. W. (eds) (1992) *Policy Networks in British Government*, Oxford: Clarendon Press.

Marsh, D. and Smith, M. (2000) "Understanding Policy Networks: Towards a Dialectical Approach", *Political Studies*, 48 (4): 4–21.

Marsh, D. and M. J. Smith (2001) "There Is More than One Way to Do Political Science: On Different Ways to Study Policy Networks", *Political Studies*, 49: 528–41.

Mikkelsen, M. (2006) "Policy Network Analysis as a Strategic Tool for the Voluntary Sector", *Policy Studies*, 27 (1): 17–26.

Miller, H. T. and Demir, T. (2006) "Policy Communities", in F. Fischer, G. Miller and M. S. Sidney (eds) *Handbook of Public Policy Analysis*, Boca Raton, Fla: CRC Press.

Milward, H. Brinton and Provan, K. G. (1998) "Measuring Network Structure", *Public Administration*, 76 (Summer): 387–407.

Nachamias, D. and Rosenbloom, D. H. (1980) *Bureaucratic Government USA*, New York: St Martin's Press.

Pappi, F. U. and Henning, C. H. C. A. (1998) "Policy Networks: More than a Metaphor?", *Journal of Theoretical Politics*, 10 (4): 553–75.

Parry, G. (1969) *Political Elites*, London: George Allen & Unwin.

Parsons, W. (1995) *Public Policy: An Introduction to the Theory and Practice of Policy Analysis*, Cheltenham: Edward Elgar.

Peterson, J. (2003): "Policy Networks", *Political Science Series*, no. 90, Vienna: Institute for Advanced Studies.

Potters, J. and Sloof, R. (1996) "Interest Groups: A Survey of Empirical Models That Try to Assess Their Influence", *European Journal of Political Economy*, 12: 403–42.

Radaelli, C. M. (1999) "Harmful Tax Competition in the EU: Policy Narratives and Advocacy Coalitions", *Journal of Common Market Studies*, 37 (4): 661–82.

Rhodes, R. A. W. (1988) *Beyond Westminster and Whitehall*, London: Unwin Hyman.

Rhodes, R. A. W. (1990) "Policy Networks: A British Perspective", *Journal of Theoretical Politics*, 2 (3): 293–317.

Rhodes, R. A. W. and Marsh, D. (1992) "New Directions in the Study of Policy Networks", *European Journal of Political Research*, 21 (1): 181–205.

Richardson, J. (2000) "Government, Interest Groups and Policy Change", *Political Studies*, 48: 1006–25.

Richardson, J. and Jordan, G. (1979) *Governing under Pressure: The Policy Process in a Post-parliamentary Democracy*, Oxford: Martin Robertson.

Robinson, S. E. (2006) "A Decade of Treating Networks Seriously", *Policy Studies*, 34 (4): 589–98.

Sabatier, P. A. (1998) "The Advocacy Coalition Framework: Revisions and Relevance for Europe", *Journal of European Public Policy*, 5 (1): 98–130.

Sabatier, P. A. (ed.) (1999) *Theories of the Policy Process: Theoretical Lenses on Public Policy*, Boulder, Colo.: Westview Press.

Sabatier, P. A. and Jenkins-Smith, H. C. (1993) *Policy Change and Learning: An Advocacy Coalition Approach*, Boulder, Colo.: Westview Press.

Sabatier, P. and Pelkey, N. (1987) "Incorporating Multiple Actors and Guidance Instruments into Models of Regulatory Policymaking: An Advocacy Coalition Framework", *Administration and Society*, 19 (2): 236–63.

Salisbury, R. (1984) "Interest Representation: The Dominance of Institutions", *American Political Science Review*, 78 (1): 64–76.

Schattschneider, E. E. (1935) *Politics, Pressures and the Tariff*, New York: Arno Press.

Stein, R. M. and Bickes, K. N. (1995) *Perpetuating the Pork Barrel: Policy Subsystems and American Democracy*, Cambridge: Cambridge University Press.

Thompson, G. and Pforr, C. (2005) *Policy Networks and Good Governance: A Discussion*, Perth, Australia: Curtin University of Technology, School of Management.
Thurber, J. A. (1991) "Dynamics of Policy Subsystems in American Politics", in A. Cigler and B. A. Loomis (eds) *Interest Group Politics*, Washington, DC: Congressional Quarterly Press.
Truman, D. B. (1951) *The Governmental Process: Political Interests and Public Opinion*, New York: Knopf.
Warleigh, A. (2000) "The Hustle: Citizenship Practice, NGOs and 'Policy Coalitions' in the European Union: The Cases of Auto Oil, Drinking Water and Unit Pricing", *Journal of European Public Policy*, 7 (2): 229–43.
Watt, R. N. (1997) "Policy Networks in Theoretical Perspective", http://www.pas.ac.uk/CPS/1997/watt.pdf [accessed 2 June 2004].
Weber, N. and Christophersen, T. (2002) "The Influence of Non-governmental Organisations on the Creation of Naturea 2000 during the European Policy Process", *Forest Policy and Economics*, 4: 1–12.
Wolman, H. (1992) "Understanding Cross National Policy Transfers: The Case of Britain and the US", *Governance: An International Journal of Policy, Administration, and Institutions*, 5 (1): 27–45.
Wright, M. (1988) "Policy Community, Policy Network and Comparative Industrial Policies", *Political Studies*, 36 (2): 593–612.

21

POLICY NETWORKS IN PRACTICE: THE DEBATE ON THE FUTURE OF AMSTERDAM AIRPORT SCHIPHOL

Menno Huys and Joop Koppenjan

1. Introduction

The continuously growing airport Amsterdam Airport Schiphol is situated in a densely populated region near the economic heart of the Netherlands. Since the 1950s the Dutch government has struggled with the trade-off between the economic importance of Schiphol and the environmental impact of the increasing air traffic. In 1988 policy-making had reached a deadlock. Actors participating in the policy debate could not agree on the future of the airport, nor on the kind of policies that were needed to regulate environmental effects. In an attempt to break the deadlock, government formulated the so-called dual objective: the ambitious growth strategy of the airport would be combined with the simultaneous realization of environmental objectives. For the next twenty years (1988–2008), the policy discussion revolved around the translation of this dual objective into concrete policy measures.

In this contribution we analyze the policy-making process regarding Schiphol in the period 1988–2008 by using a policy network perceptive. The Schiphol case is characterized by a large set of public and private stakeholders with diverging and conflicting interests that are engaged in a highly politicized power game. The network approach provides us with a conceptual framework to describe and analyze the strategic interactions within a setting of relatively autonomous but interdependent actors, and to explain the course and outcomes of these interactions. Furthermore, using the policy network theory in the case of Schiphol seems even more appropriate, given the attempt of government to combine growth and improvement of the environment. It is network theory that suggests managing conflicts by transforming zero-sum games into win–win situations. Also, new interactive policy approaches that have been applied during the past twenty years can be viewed as forms of *network governance*, by which government involves a wider set of actors in the policy-making process. Here network theory presents itself as a governance mode, rather than as theory of governance. The normative implications of network theory are brought in practice as *network governance*: a specific policy or management style to be applied in multi-actor settings.

In short, the Schiphol case provides us with an opportunity to assess both the analytical and practical value of the network approach for complex policy-making issues.

Section 2 briefly outlines the central conceptual, theoretical, normative and prescriptive notions of the policy network theory as we apply them in our analysis of the policy-making process regarding the future of Schiphol. Subsequently, section 3 presents an analysis of the process and the outcome of the interactions among actors involved in policy-making regarding Schiphol, using concepts of the network approach as a heuristic tool. Section 4 provides an additional analysis, demonstrating the kind of explanations, evaluations and lessons that the policy network perspective provides. Section 5 wraps things up.

2. Applying the policy network approach to the Schiphol casus

The policy network approach provides a theoretical perspective for analyzing, evaluating and improving interaction process regarding complex issues within networks of mutually dependent actors. It differs from other policy approaches like rational choice or New Public Management in that it includes strategic and institutional factors in the analysis of policy-making and stresses not so much effectiveness or efficiency as important success criteria, but collaborative advantages, legitimacy and trust (Pierre 2000; Teisman 2000; Huxham 2000; Fukuyama 1995).

Analyzing policy-making in networks: the network approach as heuristic tool

Policy processes are conceptualized as political interaction processes or *policy games*, in which interdependent actors with diverging or conflicting interests, perceptions and strategies try to influence the policy process and its outcomes (Axelrod 1984; Scharpf 1997). These interactions take place in one or more *arenas*: places where actors meet, using strategies to influence policy-making (Allison 1971; Crozier and Friedberg 1980). In doing so, such actors may form *coalitions* either to support or to oppose certain policies (Sabatier 1988).

As far as these activities are embedded in earlier interactions, actors are part of a policy network and share outlooks, rules, language and trust that help them to interact and that reduce transaction costs (Rhodes 1997; Williamson 1998). However, if representatives of different policy networks meet in specific policy games, institutional features are not compatible and add to the complexity of the interaction process (Koppenjan and Klijn 2004).

The policy process does not evolve in a linear way, going through a series of logically structured stages (Parsons 1995). Rather it is a *policy game* that can be analyzed by distinguishing a number of rounds of interactions. These rounds evolve in an erratic, unstructured way (Teisman 2000). In each round, actors explore problems and solutions, and look for opportunities to reach a win–win outcome (Dery 1984). However, this is far from simple: diverging perceptions and conflicts of interest may result in a deadlock (Olson 1965). Then, again, breakthroughs may occur, which give the game new impulses and, to a large extent, determine the conditions for the next round in the policy game.

Interaction processes are considered successful if actors succeed in discovering common interests and arrive at win–win situations. In addition to substantive outcomes, interaction may produce institutional effects: improved or deteriorated relationships and levels of trust between actors, with repercussions for future interactions (Ostrom 1990).

Explaining policy-making in networks

The network perspective seeks to explain why parties succeed or fail in realizing collaboration and win–win outcomes. Four explanations are especially suggested:

1. *Social causes:* The ability or inability of actors to coordinate their go-alone strategies. This may be influenced by the quality, intensity or lack of interaction between interdependent actors, and the presence or absence of social variety. Deadlocks, for instance, may be broken by the entrance of new actors, or the formation of new coalitions (Termeer and Koppenjan 1997).
2. *Cognitive causes:* The ability of actors to discover collaborative advantages or win–win situations, e.g. by inventing new solutions, reframing the problem or changing the scope for policy-making (Rein and Schön 1992). This ability may be influenced by the lack or presence of cognitive variety: new ideas, knowledge or information (Van Eeten 1999).
3. *Institutional causes:* The lack or presence of institutions that reduce the risks and cost of interaction such as rules, shared convictions, norms and values, a shared language and trust.
4. *Management causes:* The absence or presence of adequate network governance. It is to be distinguished from Command and Control approaches, aimed at imposing one-sided solutions. It also differs from New Public Management strategies aimed at reducing interdependencies

by unbundling and contracting. Network governance consists of efforts to address the interdependencies of actors by involving them in the policy-making process and by arranging and managing this process. It includes the fulfillment of roles of process architect, facilitator, broker and mediator (see Susskind and Cruikshank 1987; O'Toole 1988; Klijn 2008).

Evaluating policy-making and lessons drawn: the policy network theory as normative approach

The policy network approach may be considered an empirical theory, aimed at describing and explaining interactions in complex network settings. As such, the theory facilitates the analysis of policy processes from a strategic perspective, paying attention to the role of perceptions, strategies and conflict, the institutional factors underlying these, and the outcomes of these power games in terms of allocation of values over various stakeholders, of which some may win and others may lose. Normative assumptions of the network theory include the consideration of win–win outcomes of network processes as success. Recommendations are aimed at realizing these: promoting interaction and collaboration, and suggesting supportive institutional arrangement and network governance to enhance these (Kickert et al. 1997; Agranoff and McGuire 2003; Keast et al. 2002; Soerenson and Torfing 2007). It is important to distinguish between the policy network approach as an empirical theory and as a prescriptive model applied in practice. As an empirical theory, the policy network approach may have a wider applicability and validity than as prescriptive model. It is quite possible to analyze the implications of hierarchical interventions or new public management strategies from a policy network perspective. Moreover, network governance strategies used in practice may well be at odds with the theoretical and normative implications of the policy network theory. So the network policy approach as empirical and normative theory may well be used to assess network governance practices.

Applying policy network theory to the Schiphol casus

Before describing and analyzing twenty years of debate about the future of Schiphol, it is important to underline the difference between network theory as empirical and as prescriptive model. Given the involvement of various interdependent actors with diverging and conflicting interests, the policy network theory seems to be an appropriate framework for analyzing the Schiphol case. As far as the application of network theory in practice is concerned, the case study displays a particular Dutch take on network governance, which is rooted in the Dutch culture of consensualism. This culture of consensus-building can be related to the specific situation of the

Netherlands. Its low lands, high water-levels and dense population called for collaboration between people in order to provide enough suitable land for building (Edelenbos 2000). Moreover, the relatively large outside world forced the small Netherlands to cooperate internally, strengthening the consensus orientation (Dijkink 1990). Over the years the lack of space has made it more and more important to attune the many different claims for infrastructure, housing, industry, nature, recreation, agriculture to one another, giving rise to several institutions for collaborative policy-making and planning (Faludi and Valk 1994). The Dutch consensualism is characterized by a high degree of corporatism, wherein a few powerful interest groups (i.e. labor unions, large multi-nationals) are included in the national policy-making processes (Van Waarden 1999). Finally, the Dutch consensualism is also highly pragmatic in nature, resulting in commonly used dispensations, policy experiments, policy evaluations and tolerance of illegal drugs and prostitution (Van Wijk 2007). It is against the background of this specific consensus-oriented culture, with hints of corporatism and pragmatism, that the particular Dutch take on network practice is to be understood.

However, this does not imply that the study has no value for other cases embedded in another context. First of all, the Schiphol case is analyzed using policy network theory as empirical and normative theory. This results in an analysis that, given the generic, international theoretical foundations of this theory, may have specific findings, but is not confined in its approach or implications to the particularities of the Dutch context. Second, although network governance matches the Dutch institutional context, which may explain the popularity of both the empirical and prescriptive variants of policy network theory among Dutch academics and practitioners, the recognition of the need of network governance and the application of these types of management strategies are not restricted to the Netherlands (Richardson 1982; Rhodes 1990; O'Toole 1988; Keast et al. 2002). As a result, the findings regarding the application of network governance in this case may hold lessons that are relevant for other settings in other countries. Third, it can be argued that the Schiphol case is a typical example of what might be labeled a critical case. In essence, a critical case can enhance the "generalizability" of case studies. Such cases often hold more information than randomly selected representative cases, because they activate more actors and more basic mechanisms in the situation studied. The critical case can be defined as having strategic importance in relation to the general problem. Such cases offer information, which permits logical deductions of the type "if this is (not) valid for this case, then it applies to all (no) cases" (Flyvbjerg 2001: 79). Of course, it is difficult to identify a critical case beforehand. There are no universal methodological principles available by which one can identify a critical case. The best thing to do is to look for a case which is likely either to confirm or falsify propositions and hypotheses (Flyvbjerg 2001; Ragin 1992).

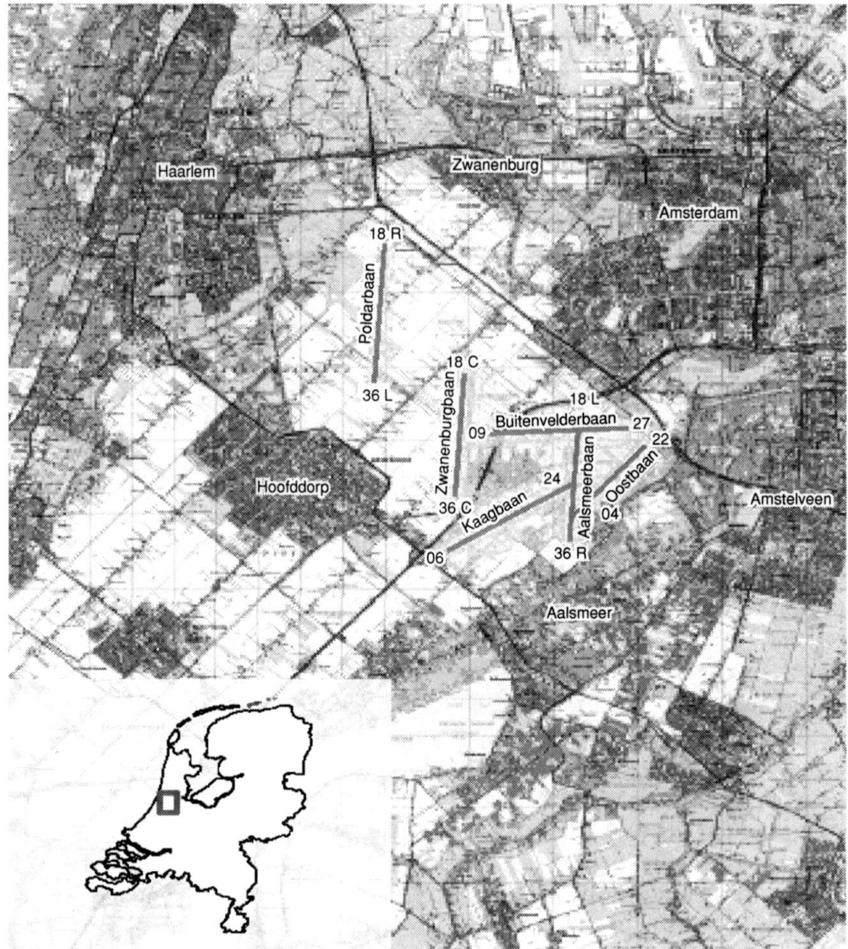

Figure 21.1 Spatial situation Schiphol region 2006.
Source: Milieu–en Natuur Planbureau, 2006.

The conflictory nature of the issues discussed in the Schiphol case and the lack of trust make it such a critical case. Several authors have commented that the Schiphol policy network is characterized by low levels of trust (cf. Van Boxtel and Huys 2005; Bröer 2006; Van Eeten 1999; Van Gils et al. 2009; RMNO 2009; Tan 2001). Trust is regarded as perceptions of the good intentions of other actors. It concerns an expectation about the intention of another actor, and that intention concerns the expectation that the other actor will respect the interests of the "trusting" actor (Koppenjan and Klijn 2004: 83; Nooteboom 2002). When expectations are repeatedly violated, the trust in another actor must be reviewed or may even disappear entirely.

A high degree of trust within networks decreases transaction costs between cooperating actors, enhances the probability that actors will exchange information, and encourages learning and innovation. In the case of wicked problems, where there is need for intensive coordination, and where levels of uncertainty are high, trust becomes an essential factor in the creation of successful governance networks. Without trust, it may be "just networks" that we are left with, holding little joint decision-making despite intensive interaction patterns (cf. Keast et al. 2005; Parker 2007). In essence, trade-offs between different spatial claims (i.e. airport infrastructure including noise protection zones and other spatial claims like housing, industrial sites, landside accessibility and green areas) need to be made in the densely populated Schiphol region owing to the lack of space (see Figure 21.1), but the high level of distrust makes it very complicated to do so in an effective and legitimate way. Given these specific characteristics of the Schiphol case, it is all the more relevant to examine the application of network governance strategies. If a specific type of network governance works for the Schiphol case, it is likely to work in less conflicted and fixated policy situations elsewhere.

In the next section we analyze the policy debate of Schiphol as a series of three rounds, using the central concepts of the policy network theory. In section 4 the success or failure of the process is established by determining to what extent win–win solutions have been created. In addition, explanations are sought by referring to cognitive, social, institutional and management causes. Next, lessons are drawn on how to improve the quality and outcome of policy debate. In addition, the case study may provide us with clues as to what extent the normative assumptions of this theory hold in practice.

3. Twenty years of debate on the future of Schiphol: three rounds of policy-making

In 1988 the Dutch government established a new policy strategy for Schiphol, the so-called mainport strategy (cf. Van Duinen 2004; Pestman 2001). Schiphol was perceived to be an important cornerstone of further economic development of the Netherlands, while at the same time it was stated that this development should not proceed at the expense of the environment (Ministry of Physical Planning 1988: 185). In 1989 the quest to translate the dual objective of the mainport strategy into concrete policy measures could begin. In this section we describe the Schiphol policy debate, distinguishing three rounds of policy-making:

1. The preparation of the Spatial Planning Key Decision (PKB) (from 1988 till 1997);
2. The drafting of the new Schiphol law (from 1998 until 2006);
3. The revision of the Schiphol law (2006 until 2008).

3.1. Round 1: The PKB (Spatial Planning Key Decision) process: 1988–97

This policy round revolved around the operationalization and implementation of the dual objective in a so-called Spatial Planning Key Decision (Planologische Kernbeslissing, PKB). The PKB procedure is an extensive decision-making procedure that results in a legally binding national spatial planning decision (Van Buuren et al. 1999). Government chose to use the ROM-method, a new participative policy approach designed to develop integral tailored plans for specific areas that could count on wide public support (Ministry of Physical Planning 1988). It consisted of two steps: developing a start covenant and translating this covenant into concrete measures. After these preparatory steps, the formal policy-making could begin.

The composition of the policy arena

During the development of the start covenant (the so-called Plan of Approach Schiphol and Surroundings, Plan van Aanpak Schiphol en Omgeving, PASO), actors from three different networks – i.e. the aviation network, the spatial and infrastructural planning network, and the local/environmental network – converged in the newly established policy arena (see Figure 21.2). The Department of the Environment (DGM) of the Ministry of VROM (Housing, Spatial Planning and the Environment) was put in charge of setting up the new arena, replacing the Ministry of Transport's Governmental Aviation Agency (Rijksluchtvaartdienst, RLD) that was hitherto in charge of the Schiphol affair (Tan 2001). From March 1989 onwards, DGM approached the main stakeholders one by one, resulting in participation of the Province of North Holland, the Municipality of Haarlemmermeer and the Schiphol Airport Authority (Driessen 1995). Only after this initial network was formed did DGM invite the RLD. DGM's strategy first to establish some goodwill amongst the other parties worked out well. This way there was some pressure for RLD to join in. These five actors established the so-called steering group, which started to prepare the start covenant.

Step 1: negotiating the start covenant

During the negotiations about the content of the covenant, Schiphol managed to make its own masterplan, with a detailed investment plan for the coming fifteen years, part of PASO. In order to do so, Schiphol had insisted on involving the Department of Economic Affairs of the municipality of Amsterdam in the Steering Group (Werther 1992). On 21 September 1989 the now seven parties of the Steering Group signed the Start Covenant. The dual objective was very much defined in terms of mainport development versus noise pollution: the airport was allowed to grow, as long as the noise

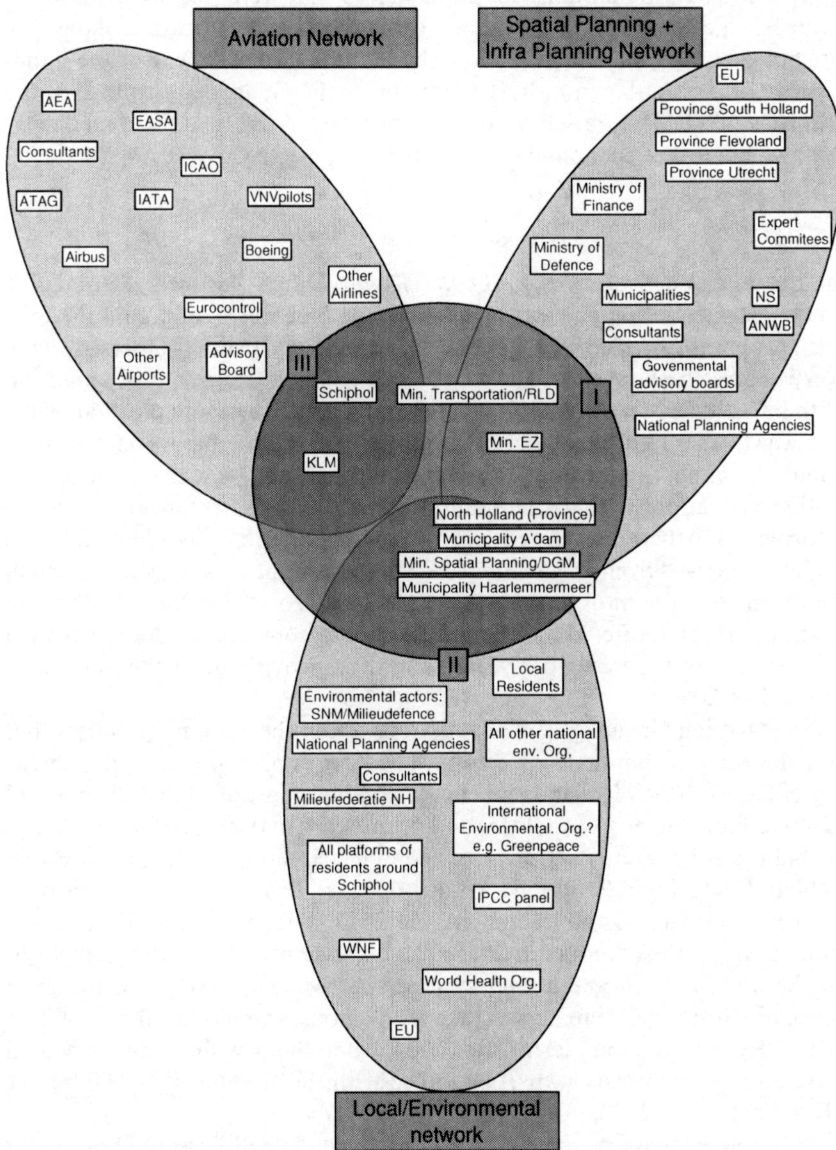

Figure 21.2 The new Schiphol policy arena (at the centre) with actors from three different networks.[1]

Source: Authors.

pollution would be diminished. Some actors that were not involved in the process, like local residents, the environmental parties (most notably the Stichting Natuur en Milieu, SNM), the Planning Department of the municipality of Amsterdam and RARO (the independent advisory council of the Ministry of VROM), raised concerns about the feasibility of the dual objective and the rather economic foundation of the perspective (PAU 2000).

Step 2: negotiating the PASO report

In the remainder of PASO, KLM (Royal Dutch Airlines, Koninklijke Luchtvaartmaatschappij) was included in the Steering Group, and the project group was extended with some airlines and municipalities (Driessen 1995). Very soon it became clear that it was impossible to reduce noise pollution with the assumed traffic growth of 6 percent a year. Therefore the dual objective was further reformulated. Earlier it was stated that Schiphol development should fit within the existing environmental standards. Now the more general notion was adopted that the quality of the living environment had to be improved. Furthermore, the criterion for noise pollution was adapted. It was no longer derived from the amount of Ke in the housing areas around Schiphol, but from the amount of houses within the 35 Ke zone.[2] Research had shown that this criterion offered more opportunities to combine the desired growth of aviation (of 6 percent per year) with an improvement of the noise situation (Ket 2000).

The Steering Group ignited negotiations about the amount of houses that was desirable within the 35 Ke zone. The environmental coalition, consisting of DGM, North Holland and Haarlemmermeer, assumed that there would be 40 million passengers in 2015, and proposed a maximum of 9,000 houses within the zone. The pro-growth or economic coalition, consisting of RLD, Schiphol, KLM and Economic Affairs, opposed this since it would frustrate further growth to 50–60 million pax. in 2015. They wanted at least 11,500 houses within the contours in 2015. The impasse was solved by distinguishing between a short- and a long-term perspective (Tan 2001). For the short term, the Steering Group agreed that 15,000 houses would be allowed within the 35 Ke. For the long term, after 2003, when the new fifth runway would have come into operation, parties agreed with the amount of 10,000 houses (Ket 2000; PAU 2000).

Still, the noise issue was not totally resolved. The discussion about night flights remained at an impasse. The pro-environment coalition argued that night flights should be ended. The pro-growth coalition stressed that such a radical measure would seriously harm the position of Schiphol vis-à-vis other European airports. As the sense of urgency to develop the final version of PASO increased, the actors decided to postpone the issue of night flights (Tan 2001). However, the province of North Holland tried to bring the issue back on to the agenda. Moreover, it called for establishing maximum transport volumes that would serve as hard limits to growth. Eventually, the Ministry of Spatial Planning (DGM) proposed to evaluate the night regime and the growth of flights in 1993. The Provincial Board hesitantly agreed with these terms, since it feared to be excluded from future rounds of Schiphol policy-making. In April 1991 the PASO covenant was signed (PAU 2000; Bureau PAU 2000). The final PASO contained 111 measures (Projectbureau Mainport and Milieu Schiphol (PMMS) 1991; VINO 1988; Werther 1992). Most important, it was agreed that a fifth runway was necessary. This runway would considerably reduce the amount of houses within the 35 Ke zone (from 16,500 to 10,000).

The formal decision-making: translating PASO proposals into the Spatial Key Decision (PKB)

Next, formal decision-making could finally begin, meant to translate PASO initiatives into a legally binding national Spatial Key Decision (Planologische Kern Beslissing, PKB). The Steering Committee remained in place, with the main difference that the secretary-general of the Ministry of Transportation took over the management role of DGM. The most important issues debated during the PKB procedure concerned the definition of a mainport and the regulation of noise pollution.

The *critical mainport barrier* referred to the minimum amount of traffic that was needed to sustain mainport operations. Different scenarios were developed. The Steering Group decided on 6 April 1993 that the lowest critical mainport barrier would be used as the point of departure for the remainder of the PKB process. The growth levels were much lower than those made by Boeing, KLM or in Schiphol's Masterplan, but this scenario offered the best possibilities for reconciling the environmental (i.e. noise pollution) and mainport objectives.

As regards the discussion on noise nuisance, a distinction was made between the short-term four-runway system and the mid-term five-runway system. For the short-term four-runway system, the environmental objective was solely defined in terms of noise pollution: if there were fewer than 15,000 houses within the 35 Ke zone, the environmental objective was achieved. For the five-runway system (after 2003) the noise criterion was adapted (i.e. the level of noise pollution should be improved in comparison with 1990) and additional limits for external safety, air pollution and stench would come into operation (PKB, pt 4, 1995: 8). The noise limits were calculated for 235 points that made up the contour. For each point, the amount of decibels had to be lower than 35 Ke during daytime, and no more than 15,100 houses were allowed within the 35 Ke zone. During night-time (2300–0600), only 10,100 houses were allowed within the area exposed to more than 26 decibels.

However, it proved impossible to fit the desired mainport development within the noise limits, especially during daytime (15,000 houses within 35 Ke zone). The solution for the noise problem popped up from a rather unexpected side. A new calculation model for noise was developed. This new model registered the actual flight routes of the airplanes by their radar tracks. The old model calculated these flight tracks. By a lucky coincidence, this resulted in different noise contours wherein only 14,900 houses fell into the zone (Ket 2000). As regards the five-runway system, it was argued that all of the new criteria would be met (PKB, pt 4, 1995). The environmental parties, especially SNM, repeatedly questioned the noise norms used and the way the contours were calculated, but with no effect whatsoever. Another environmental party, Milieudefensie (Environmental Defence), adopted a more radical strategy. Besides organizing several protests, they bought a strategic piece of cropland in April 1994, just where the fifth runway was to be located. From November 1994 onwards, they started to plant trees there and created the Bulderbos (Bulder Forest). This forest was to prevent the possibility for expropriation (De Kruijf 2002).[3]

The outcome of the PKB process and its aftermath

At the end of 1995 the PKB was politically ratified. The Lower House was not totally convinced about the rather low growth that was assumed in PKB. In the end it was decided that capacity limits would be introduced to prevent unfettered growth. Passenger numbers were not allowed to exceed 44 million in any year, and cargo tonnes were not allowed to exceed 3.3 million in any year. In the PKB of 1995 it was agreed that the noise limits would become effective from 1997 onwards, to give the sector parties sufficient time to adapt their daily operations.

Schiphol immediately exceeded the limits of several enforcement points in 1997 and 1998. In an evaluation report of the PASO/PKB process it was concluded that the forecasts were unrealistic (far too low), and probably used because they made the dual objective possible (Algemene Rekenkamer 1998 see also CPB 1998). The local residents and the environmental parties did not tolerate the excesses and started the first of many juridical procedures that would heavily frustrate further decision-making. In Figure 21.3 the structure of the policy arena is presented.

Still, the amount of houses within the daytime zone (12,800) was far below the maximum (15,000). This discrepancy was to be attributed to the specific shape of the calculated and legally binding noise zone. The In't Veld Committee, which was to assess the effectiveness of the current noise system (TK 25466, Nr 9), indicated that it was rather inefficient that the 35 Ke zone was exceeded at a few points, especially points where nobody lived (the so-called pastureland), whereas at most other points a lot of space was left. If these "absurdities" were to be repaired, noise pollution could be reduced and capacity could be increased. In practice, this implied a yearly increase of 20,000 flights, starting in 1997 (360,000), and resulting in 460,000

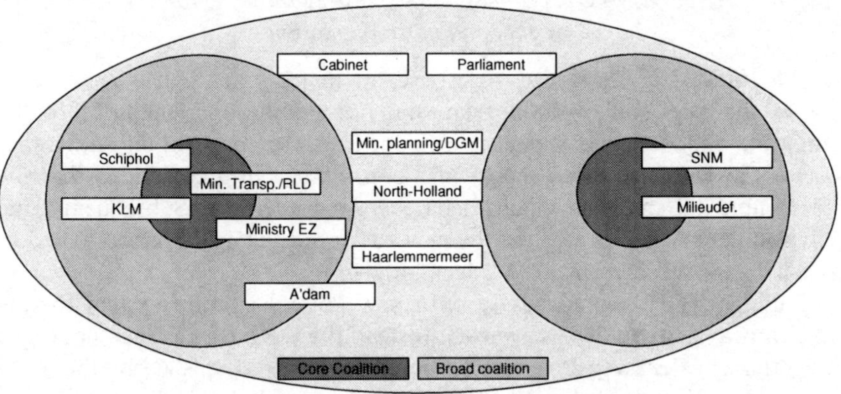

Figure 21.3 Schiphol policy arena anno 1997 with Schiphol growth coalition (left) and environmental coalition (right).
Source: Authors.

flights in 2002 (TK 25466, Nr 9). Therefore, a new noise regulative system was called for, which signaled the beginning of a new comprehensive round of policy-making.

3.2. Round 2: the new Schiphol Law: 1998–2006

During 1998 the relationships between the sector, on the one hand, and environmental parties and residents, on the other, deteriorated rapidly. In order to "clear the air", in September 1998 the Ministry of Transport initiated a new interactive policy approach: the Interim Debate on Schiphol (Tijdelijk Platform Overleg Schiphol, TOPS) was established (Tweede Kamer 1998; TK 25466, Nr 27).

The composition of the policy arena

TOPS was one of the first attempts to give environmental and nature conservation groups a formal place in an early stage of political decision-making (cf. Glasbergen 2002; Weggeman 2003). Participants in the TOPS process were sector parties (Schiphol, KLM, Martinair and BARIN = organization of airlines), environmental parties (Milieudefensie, SNM, Milieufederatie Noord Holland), central government (the Ministries of Transport and Spatial Planning and Environment), regional authorities (the Province of North Holland and the municipalities of Amsterdam, Haarlemmermeer and Aalsmeer) and local residents (the Platform Leefmilieu Regio Schiphol, Platform Environment Schiphol Region, PLRS). The final TOPS had fifteen members, but Schiphol, KLM, Milieudefensie and SNM did the actual negotiations.

The TOPS process: impasses regarding extra flights and noise regulation

TOPS' first assignment was to advise on making the yearly increase of 20,000 flights possible without increasing noise pollution. Schiphol took the initiative and designed a new noise zone in close cooperation with other sector parties. A research report of a consultancy firm concluded that the environmental situation would deteriorate considerably. Subsequently the environmental parties rejected the new zone, and the TOPS actors failed to reach an overall agreement (Weggeman 2003).

Initially, TOPS would advise on a new noise regulative system for the five-runway system (2003 onwards). Instead the ONL (Onderzoek nationale Luchthaven, Research Program National Airport) established by the RLD (Ministry of Transport) in March 1999 took over the initiative. In order to make sure that the new system could be put into force by 2003, a first design had to be ready at the end of 1999. In September 1999, ONL presented its alternatives for a new system, which were rejected by the sector. The sector, especially Schiphol, did not want to discuss the issue within TOPS (Weggeman 2003). As RLD and Schiphol negotiated the new regulative system, TOPS was sidelined.

At first, ignoring TOPS was not likely to be an efficient strategy, considering that Milieudefensie owned pieces of land where the new runway was to be constructed. However, the Cabinet had created a new emergency law, Noodwet Procedures Vijfde Baan (Emergency Act Procedures Fifth Runway), in January 1999 (Ministry of Transportation 2002). As such, Schiphol was legally empowered to acquire the missing pieces of land from Milieudefensie. Furthermore, the Cabinet opted for designing an entirely new Schiphol law, instead of a new PKB decision. This allowed for a less comprehensive procedure than the PKB (TK 27603, Nr 6/2000, p. 7).

The preparation of the new law

In the Cabinet's report *Future of the National Airport* (*Toekomst van de Nationale Luchthaven*, TNL 1999) the new regulative system was presented. It is stated that the new system offers *equal* protection to the PKB system that it comes to replace (TNL 1999: 6). In the new system, still no enforcement points were located in the outer areas. The Lower House had some serious doubts about the level of equivalence between the old and the new systems. In a response, the Cabinet installed a new independent committee of noise experts, chaired by Professor Berkhout (Commissie Deskundigen Vliegtuiggeluid, CDV) (*Staatscourant*, 20 juni 2000).

However, the CDV was very critical of the new noise system. As a consequence, the CDV was sidelined. The Minister of Transportation argued that the committee meddled in affairs for which others were responsible

(Berkhout 2003). However, the Environmental Impact Assessment Committee (EIA committee) also expressed its doubts about the value of the new noise system. The environmental actors and the local residents responded by developing an alternative Schiphol Act, the Citizen Initiative Act (Burgerinitiatief wet, 2001). Since the Lower House held some serious doubts, the minister agreed to add fifty new enforcement points within the 35–20 Ke zone (the outer areas) as a matter of compromise (ONL, 2001, Nr 9). The Upper House ratified the new Act in July 2002 (cf. EK 27603), but demanded that the new system be evaluated within three years (2006) (motion Baarda, 2002). Schiphol and KLM were satisfied with the new Act since it allowed them to put the new fifth runway (Polderbaan) needed further to facilitate hub-development into operation in February 2003.

The outcome of this round of policy-making

In February 2003 the Polderbaan was opened, and the Schiphol Act came into effect. The new regulative system did not work out very well, though. The amount of complaints about noise annoyance increased. Schiphol, KLM and ATM complained that it hampered mainport development, because the rigid flight rules did not allow for flexible runway use, so the additional capacity could not be optimally used (TK 29665, Nr 13/2005). The Committee Regional Discussion Schiphol (Commissie Regionaal Overleg Schiphol, CROS)[4] that was established in 2003 to negotiate about the development of concrete noise-reducing measures indicated that measures for reducing noise hindrance could not be implemented within the regulative system. In essence, just as with the old PKB system, the new system was not based on the actual flight routes, resulting in the exceeding of limits in some enforcement points. The rigid law made it impossible to adjust the system to the actual flight patterns, which could result in more capacity and less noise (see Figure 21.4).

In its evaluation report on the new Schiphol Act, the Cabinet concluded that the criterion of equality of protection in the old and the new regulatory system was met, but that improvements should be made regarding the use of the airport (i.e. facilitate more flights) and the reduction of noise nuisance, especially in the outer areas (Evaluation Report, 2006). Figure 21.5 shows the structure of the Schiphol policy arena anno 2006.

3.3. Round 3: revising the Schiphol law (2006–8)

At the beginning of 2006, the Cabinet announced that they would frame a covenant in close consultation with the aviation sector, in which firm and maintainable agreements would be made for reducing noise hindrance, while increasing capacity (Cabinet 2006: 5). As a response to this announcement, the sector (i.e. Schiphol Group, KLM), the regional authorities (Haarlemmermeer, Amsterdam and Province of North Holland) and the

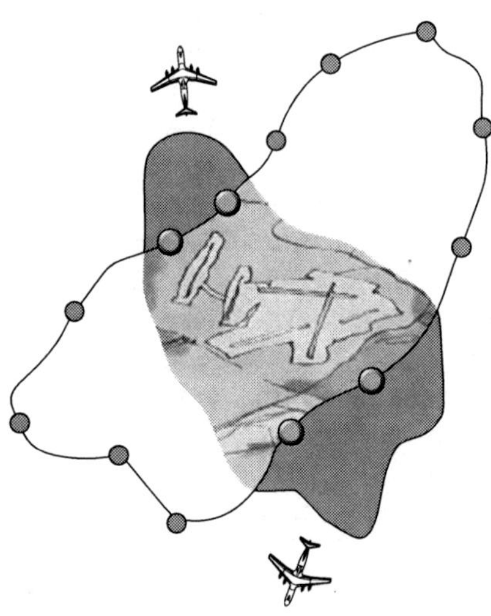

Figure 21.4 Mismatch between calculated, legally embedded noise contours (dots) and actual noise pollution (grey area) around Schiphol, 2003–6.
Source: Schiphol Group, 2007.

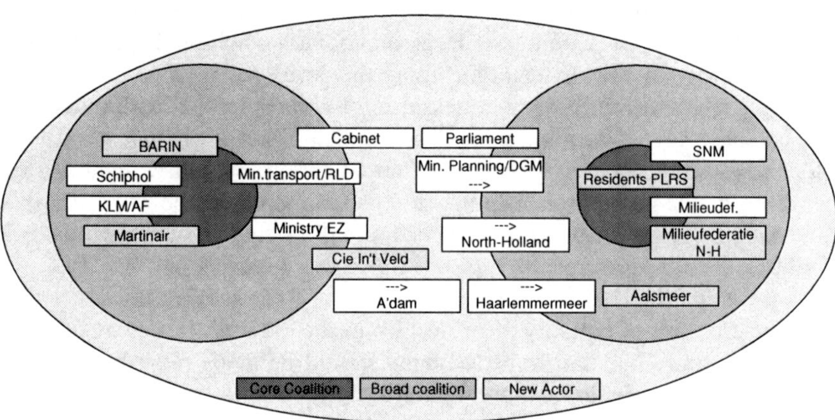

Figure 21.5 Schiphol policy arena anno 2006 with Schiphol growth coalition (left) and environmental coalition (right).
Source: Authors.

CROS claimed that this was a regional instead of a national responsibility (Letter of Region, 16 May 2006). Even the sector parties signed the letter. They apparently sensed an increasing urgency to improve the troubled relationship with the region (especially the residents) (cf. the sector report "Working to Improve the Region" of 2005). A new comprehensive interactive round of policy-making was bound to begin.

The composition of the arena in this round

In 2006 central government installed the so-called Alders table, named after its chairman Hans Alders. Actors gathering around this negotiation table were the sector parties (Schiphol Group, KLM/AF, ATM), the regional and local authorities (North Holland, Amsterdam, Haarlemmermeer, but also the municipalities of Amstelveen, Uitgeest), the CROS, and the Ministries of Transport and of Spatial Planning. The CROS insisted on two places for local residents, which added an innovative element to the forms of network governance used so far: for the first time, local residents were included in the formal negotiations about the future of Schiphol. The environmental parties did not take part in the negotiations. After TOPS they revived their old strategy of protesting, lobbying and taking legal action. This time, the Cabinet did not run formal policy trajectories alongside the table. Just as in 1999, the first assignment was to find short-term solutions for revising the existing noise system, of which noise limits had been exceeded in a few enforcement points in 2006 and 2007 (TK 29665, Nr 43/2007). As in all other years, excesses were tolerated by the Cabinet, relating the breaches to *force majeure* and in an anticipation of the revision of the rigid system (TK 29665, Nr 43/2007; TK 29665, Nr 68/2007; TK 29665, Nr 103/2008).

The table of Alders in action: preparing the advice for the short term and the long term

Schiphol suggested five alternatives for future development, which would serve as a point of departure for the negotiations (Startnotitie MER 2007).[5] The two most prominent alternatives were based on facilitating further growth to 600,000 flights. The local residents formulated a sixth alternative, aiming for qualitative growth. Only the hub-operations of AF/KLM were allowed to grow to a maximum of 500,000 flights. Freight traffic and charters were to be removed to the regional airports of Lelystad and Eindhoven, no adjustments to the prevailing limits of noise pollution were tolerated, and an improvement of noise protection of residents in the outer areas was called for. Schiphol agreed to include the alternative in the EIA, mainly to avoid early frustration of the process.

In June 2007 the Alders table presented its advice for the short term.[6] Among other things, it was proposed to allow some more pollution at some and less pollution at other enforcement points of the Airport Planning Decree (Luchthavenverkeersbesluit), so 480,000 flights will become possible in 2010 (with 435,000 in 2007). The Cabinet was content about the advice since it was unanimous and since it secured further growth for the short term.

Before the second Alders round began, the collection of platforms of local residents (Vereniging Gezamenlijke Platforms, VGP) indicated that they were not adequately represented by the two CROS members (who were thought to represent all residents). One implication of the short-term advice was that it would result in considerably more noise pollution in some of the outer areas (VGP letter to the Cabinet, 25 June 2007). Therefore, the Cabinet decided that the VGP was to be included at the Alders negotiations for the mid-term (TK 29665, Nr 70/2007).

The negotiations about the mid-term revolved around the most desirable development scenario for 2018/2020, of the six presented in the EIA of 2007, and two updated covenants on noise hindrance reduction and spatial quality for the mid-term. However, since two renowned knowledge institutes, NLR (Airspace Laboratory) and the MNP (Environmental Planning Agency), could not agree upon the validity of the new calculation methods for determining the new limits for the enforcement points, the Alders table was asked to develop a new system.

The outcome of the Alders table: unprecedented unanimity

In October 2008, the Alders table presented its final report about the mid-term development. There were two main conclusions. First, Schiphol was allowed to grow to 510,000 aircraft movements in 2020, with a maximum of 32,000 flight movements during the night regime. Furthermore, additional air traffic – approximately 70,000 flight movements – was to be removed to the regional airports of Lelystad and Eindhoven. More specifically, all hub-related traffic would be concentrated on Schiphol, whereas the freight carriers and the charters were to be removed to the regional airports. Second, the actors agreed that the only way to get rid of the endless technical discussions regarding noise nuisance was to get rid of the enforcement points, including the complicated calculation methods and the hampering maintenance system (i.e. every year a new reason was found to tolerate the seven excesses in ten years' time). In the new system noise is to be regulated through the development of new and flexible rules for runway use, restricted flight paths and flight heights, designed to ensure the lowest amount of noise pollution, a maximum amount of flight movements (510,000), and limits for the amount of houses and people exposed to serious pollution. In some areas no measures can be developed to reduce noise pollution. By means of compensation, the Cabinet has reserved 10 million euros for improving the quality of life in these areas.

In the end, almost all actors were pleased with the agreement. By allowing only hub-related traffic, AF/KLM would get sufficient possibilities to expand in the near future (Van Gils et al. 2009). The regional public authorities were also very pleased, since the selective development sits comfortably with their so-called metropolitan strategy, which they developed from 2003 onwards (cf. BRS 2006) The local residents were also pleased because additional flights would be removed to other airports. Still, the other part of the agreement (i.e. about the new noise system) initially caused disagreement among the residents. The VGP wanted to cling to the old procedures, stating that the new system offered even less legal protection. At first, the VGP had left the negotiations, but after the feedback still two-thirds of the twenty-seven platforms supported the agreement. Those platforms indicated that they wanted to be a part of the further elaboration of the new system and the future negotiations (TK 29665, Nr 110). The other platforms that refused to sign the covenant argued that they were blackmailed by Alders: if they would not sign, they were to be excluded from all future decision-making (Interview Griese, 2009). Schiphol itself was only mildly pleased with the advice, because they had assumed much higher growth rates in their own future plans. The much lower actual growth rates of air traffic, due to the economic recession that hit the world from 2007 onwards, implied that the agreement provided the airport with sufficient capacity until 2020. Besides, Schiphol Group owns both regional airports; so, as long as they are allowed to facilitate most traffic, it does not matter that much at which airport. In Figure 21.6 the structure of the Schiphol policy arena anno 2008 is presented.

Owing to this almost unprecedented unanimity, the Cabinet (i.e. the Cabinet did not respond to the blackmail accusation of the VGP members that had not signed) was very eager to take over the advice completely. However, the first problems for actually implementing the advice (in a new round of policy-making) have already emerged. It will prove to be very difficult to allow for extra flights at both the regional airports since existing spatial plans and

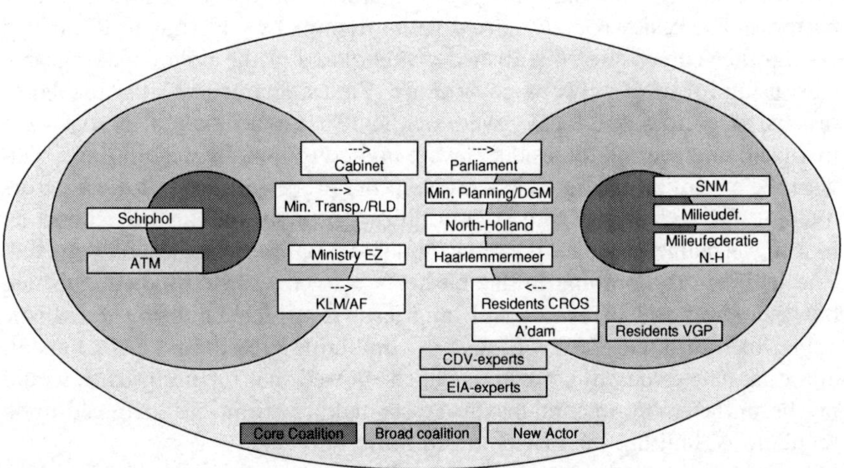

Figure 21.6 Schiphol policy arena anno 2008 with Schiphol growth coalition (left) and environmental coalition (right).
Source: Authors.

appointments about noise pollution do not allow for any further expansion. The first protests groups have already emerged (e.g. the platform of alarmed residents of Flevoland, VIVF, around Lelystad airport). The actors around the regional airport think it is rather strange that decisions are made without their involvement. Second, the airlines that are supposed to leave Schiphol, like EasyJet (which is the second-largest carrier at the airport), do not have any intention to do so. Finally, it can be argued that the expected traffic growth (580,000 in 2020) is rather low. A report commissioned by the Ministry of Transport published in 2006 expected around 720,000 flights in 2020. Just as in 1995, it seems that a rather low projection was needed to enable an agreement between the dual objectives.

4. Analyzing process, outcomes and governance strategies

In this section the success or failure of the policy debate concerning the future of Schiphol is discussed from a policy network perspective. This is done by asking to what extent the actors succeeded in engaging in forms of collaboration, resulting in win–win solutions, more specifically in realizing the dual objective aimed at reconciling growth with preservation of the quality of the environment. In addition, explanations are sought by referring to cognitive, social, institutional and management causes. Finally, the implications of these findings are discussed. Which lessons can be drawn?

4.1 The process and the outcome of the policy game assessed

The three subsequent rounds of policy-making followed more or less similar patterns. The policy rounds started with attempts by government to involve yet another category of dissatisfied stakeholders in the policy-making process, using forms of network governance. First, the arena was broadened to involve provincial and local governments; next, environmental parties were involved; and eventually residents were invited to join the negotiations. Yet, with the exception of the Alders table, in the processes that followed, actors did not succeed in carrying collaboration through and instead ended up in a power game in which the environmental coalition was outmaneuvered. The inability to combine both objectives was concealed by distinguishing between short-run measures and long-term solutions; choosing unrealistic scenarios that fitted the perspective of combining growth and environment; adapting new calculating methods which showed that further growth would not harm the environmental performance; making exceptions to agreed-upon regulations; limiting the discussion to noise only, etc.

In contrast with the dual objective, the result was systematically biased: the trade-off between growth and environment always ended up in favor of the first. The failure to reach agreements and to enforce the agreed-upon environmental measures repeatedly resulted in impasses and all-time lows of distrust in both the national government and its policy framework. So, from a policy network perspective, the interaction process and the network governance efforts were far from successful, as was the substantive outcome of the process. Recently, however, actors seem to have become more successful in collaboration and reaching mutually agreed upon outcomes, although this was also to be attributed to a "blackmail" strategy (i.e. residents had to sign at the expense of being excluded from the policy arena), external forces (i.e. the economic recession led to lower growth in traffic volumes, making the sector agree to lower growth alternatives), and removing part of the problem to other airports that were not included in the negotiations.

4.2 Explaining the policy game and its outcomes

Cognitive cause: limited policy space and lack of substantive variety

An important explanation for the way the policy process evolved lies in the limited policy space for realizing win–win situations during most of the time. As a result, old assumptions, arguments, research findings and delineations were continuously reproduced, reducing the room for innovative ideas. For example, the main assumptions underlying the growth–noise debate – i.e. the possibility of the dual objective, the conceptualization of the environmental effects in terms of noise, the conceptualization of noise hindrance in terms of decibels, the presentation of air-traffic growth as something inevitable – were never questioned during the twenty years of discussion. During the Alders table the scope of the debate was widened in a geographical way: shifting flights to regional airports. The future has to prove whether this scope change will result in win–win situations, but since the underlying assumptions have remained intact, still leading to a narrow framing of the problem (growth versus noise), it can be expected that the old feuds will come to the fore once again in the near future.

Social causes: power games reproducing impasses and distrust

The policy debate revolved around two rather stable coalitions (one pro-growth and one anti-growth). The introduction of new actors did not change this divide. This lack of social variety reinforced the cognitive fixation mentioned above. Furthermore, despite the opening up of the arena for newcomers, attitudes remained adversarial, resulting in a power game, reproducing and enhancing opportunistic behavior, impasses and distrust. Only during the third round did social variety emerge: new coalitions were formed, and actors used adapted different strategies, e.g. residents replacing protest by a pro-active attitude. It seems that both sector and region have become more aware of their interdependence, resulting in a more collaborative stance.

However, a deeper understanding of the negotiations works to nuance this collaborative stance: local residents were put under pressure to support the agreement; the economic recession made Schiphol lower its growth expectations; and the removal of the problems to local airports was only possible owing to the exclusion of those airports and the airlines involved during the negotiations.

Institutional causes: networks in the background

In the policy process, representatives of three policy networks met: the international aviation network (Schiphol, KLM, and other airlines and their allies), the spatial development and infrastructure network (the national, regional and local governments), and the local network (environmental parties and [platforms of] local residents). Since they did not have a joint institutional background, they had a hard time finding ways to interact constructively. Furthermore, proposals to regulate Schiphol lagged behind the investment decisions on further growth, taken in the aviation network. As such, Schiphol and KLM were always a step ahead of the actors in the regulatory arena, determining its agenda, rather than being regulated by it. The relationships were further biased by the asymmetrical division of resources (e.g. management skills, capacity, expertise and information) among participants, the members of the aviation sector having a clear advantage compared to the other parties. The collaboration between Schiphol and the regional actors during the third policy round is an indication of the gradual incorporation of Schiphol Airport and its traditional allies into a larger and extending regulatory network. The consensus over shifting growth on to other regions is exactly what "traditional, closed" policy networks are expected to do: dividing the gains of collaboration internally and transferring the cost to outsiders not represented within the network (Jordan 1990). For Schiphol and KLM, collaboration meant trading off autonomy against the advantages of a negotiated environment.

Management causes

The inconsistent way central government applied network governance methods contributed to the failed collaboration and unbalanced outcomes. This inconsistency stemmed from the involvement of different (parts of) ministries, each representing different networks and interests, which successively dominated the management of the process (e.g. the Environmental Agency of the Ministry of Housing, Physical Planning and the Environment, the RLD of the Ministry of Transport and the Ministry of Economic Affairs). Especially the gap between the promises of central government about regulating noise nuisance and the failure to enforce these generated further distrust. Moreover, the Ministry of Transport was committed to the growth objective, and was not prepared to refrain from the old practice of taking one-sided decisions, supportive of the sectors' growth ambitions, thus marginalizing the interactive policy arena. Only during the last period did central government operate coherently by waiting for proposals from the Alders table, thus contributing to its success.

4.3 Lessons to be drawn

Building on the above analyses from a policy network perspective, one of the lessons to be drawn is that network governance should focus on further resolving the cognitive and social fixations in the debate, a process already started during the Alders table. Introducing variety is a way to achieve this, for instance by furthering reflection on the basic assumptions underlying the Schiphol debate (e.g. by changing the agenda by asking questions like: Is the dual objective still desirable? Is environment only about noise nuisance? Is growth self-evident?). And by further broadening the arena to include regional actors in the policy-making process, who will be affected by the shift of flights to regional airports. The analysis also emphasizes the role of trust as a precondition for collaboration. Building and maintaining trust is a cornerstone of network governance. As argued in section 2, without trust it may be "just networks" that we are left with, holding little joint decision-making despite intensive interaction patterns (cf. Keast et al. 2005; Parker 2007). For government, this means that it should find a way of dealing with its substantive commitment to specific interests, on the one hand, and the need of impartiality that is related to the role of process manager, on the other. Prerequisites are not imposing solutions on other stakeholders, not marginalizing interactive arenas, managing expectations and preventing differences between stated and revealed preferences (Koppenjan and Klijn 2004). Another cause of distrust to be dealt with is the in-transparency of technological models and the role of experts, making it hard for non-experts to judge research results and the impacts of policy measures. Reverting to technocratic models may be a way of drawing up a smokescreen behind which unpopular decisions can be made by the national government. Moreover, as we have seen, it might result in a world of calculations that does not match real-world developments. This greatly enhances distrust. The specific framing of the debate (i.e. growth v. noise) does not work to restore relationships of trust, either. This framing narrows the solution space and prevents the development of longstanding agreements, making it almost impossible for interactive governance arrangements to succeed.

Finally, the case study also illustrates that engaging in network collaboration and network governance is a long-term process, which only starts paying off after a while, since all parties involved have to go through a learning curve, by which they only gradually and often reluctantly internalize the new ways of acting and thinking that are required.

5. Conclusion

Applying the policy network approach to the Schiphol case has resulted in an assessment of the policy-making process regarding Schiphol Airport as almost a twenty-year stagnating interaction process, in which parties failed at reconciling growth ambitions with environmental objectives. Only recently have actors seemed to develop some new ideas and ways of doing that might open up new opportunities for future policy-making. The analysis also provides us with explanations: the asymmetric power-relations, the opportunistic strategies of Schiphol Airport, and the inconsistent way central government applied network governance methods contributed to the failed collaboration and unbalanced outcomes. As a result, initiatives to attempt to build trust were frustrated, and this seriously hindered the development of successful network practices. The Schiphol case shows that the win–win outcomes the policy network theory advocates are sometimes hard to realize. The positive turn the process recently took may be explained by changes in strategy on the side of Schiphol and the government, owing to ongoing societal pressure, growing awareness of interdependencies and learning behavior owing to ongoing interactions. A more skeptical approach would state that the broadening of the scope to regional airports should be considered a shift of the cost of ongoing growth to new stakeholders. This was made possible under representation of the interests of these stakeholders in the interactive arenas of the Alders table. This could be considered a shortcoming of the network governance mode used and a lesson for improvement.

However, the analysis is not conclusive in determining whether this lack of success can be attributed to the inappropriate *application* of network governance practices or to the inappropriateness of *network governance itself*. In the first situation, efforts to improve network governance practices are to be considered. In the latter situation it would be wise to give up further attempts to reconcile growth and noise nuisance. It may well be that certain situations simply lack a common ground for the development of such outcomes. Perhaps this uncovers an important limitation of network governance and policy network theory. The persistency of actors to stick to deliberation and interaction despite the repeated failure of these governance strategies may indeed support the idea of a typical Dutch take on network practice in this case.

On the other hand, merely using win–win situations as evaluation criteria for interaction in network-like settings may be too rigid. Given the growth of the airport, the standstill regarding the environmental impacts may be considered as an accomplishment, which would not have been realized without the double objective. Seen in this way, the double objective should rather be seen as a management tool than as a performance measure. This objective framed the policy debate, increasingly forcing the pro-growth coalition to pay attention to the environmental impacts of their activities. The willingness of actors to remain involved in the policy-making process, despite frustrations and disappointment, indicates that they themselves value these interaction processes as worthwhile and see them as an opportunity for safeguarding their interests. What is more, the transformation of the troublesome interaction into a more or less genuine network is reason for a more positive judgment. The prolonged and not always fruitful interactions resulted at least to a certain extent in durable relationships and common understandings, offering improved conditions for jointly addressing problems in future policy-making rounds.

As stated in section 2, we perceive Schiphol as a critical case, a typical example of a wicked problem concerning competing values like economy and ecology that can be found in many other sectors and many other countries today. Its critical character makes us argue that if the network approach as management approach works for Schiphol, then it has potential to work for other (similar) cases, too. Of course, institutional conditions (e.g. a multiparty system, a history of collaboration and neo-corporatism, a culture of consensualism and depoliticized, pragmatic conflict-solving) may constrain the application of network governance strategies to certain settings, but not in such a rigid way that these governance modes should be considered to be an exclusive Dutch practice.

However, as far as the success of network governance in the Schiphol case is concerned, our analysis is not conclusive. Before making decisive statements on the applicability of network governance practices in the Schiphol case and beyond, it would be wise to compare the performance of Schiphol in terms of growth and environmental performance with airports in other countries, regulated by more hierarchical or New Public Management orientated governance modes.

Notes

1 Acronyms: AEA = Association of European Airlines; EASA = European Aviation Safety Agency; IATA = International Air Transport Association; ICAO = International Civil Aviation Organisation; ATAG = Air Transport Action Group; ATM = Air Traffic Management; VNV = Vereniging Nederlandse Vliegeniers (pilots); NS = Nederlandse Spoorwegen (Dutch Railways); ANWB = Algemene Nederlandse Wielrijders Bond; WNF = Wereldnatuurfonds (World Nature Fund); IPCC = Intergovernmental Panel on Climate Change; EU = European Union.

2 Since the 1960s noise pollution is expressed in Ke (Kosten eenheid – cost unit) in the Netherlands, where 35 Ke coincides with approximately 60 decibels.

3 Places with special environmental, monumental or ecological value are more difficult to expropriate in the Netherlands.

4 The CROS consisted of all municipalities that fell within the 20 Ke zone (although represented in nine clusters), nine local residents, the Province and the sector parties (CROS 2003).

5 Startnotitie MER "Verder werken aan de toekomst van Schiphol en de regio", April 2007, SG en LVNL.

6 See letter of Hans Alders to the Ministers of Transportation and of Spatial Planning, 13 June 2007.

References

Agranoff, R. and McGuire. M. (2003) *Collaborative Public Management: New Strategies for Local Governments*, Washington, DC: Georgetown University Press.

Algemene Rekenkamer (1998) *Groeicijfers Schiphol*, Den Haag: Sdu Uitgeverij.

Allison, G. T. (1971) *The Essence of Decision*, Boston, Mass.: Little, Brown.

Axelrod, R. (1984) *The Evolution of Cooperation*, New York: Basic Books.

Berkhout, G. (2003) *Dossier Schiphol: Relaas van een falend democractisch process*, Value report.

Boxtel, M. van and Huys, M. G. (2005) "Unraveling Decision Making about the Future Development of Amsterdam Airport Schiphol", paper presented at 45th European Regional Science Association, Amsterdam, 23–7 August.

Bröer, C. (2006) *Beleid vormt overlast, hoe beleidsdiscoursen de beleving van geluid bepalen* [*Policy Shapes Annoyance: How Policy Discourses Shape the Experience of Aircraft Sound*], Amsterdam: Aksant.

BRS (Bestuurlijke Regiegroep Schiphol) (2006) Middellange termijn visie ontwikkeling Schiphol en Omgeving. Haarlem.

Bureau PAU (2000) *Schiphol en de Ruimtelijke Ordening: De ontwikkeling van het Schipholcomplex 1980–2000*, Groningen/Den Haag.

Buuren, P. J. J. van, Backes, C. W. and de Gier, A. J. J. (1999) *Hoofdlijnen Ruimtelijk Bestuursrecht*, Deventer: Kluwer.

Centraal Planbureau (1998) Toekomstige Ontwikkeling vervoersontwikkelingen op Luchthaven Schipol: een second opinion. CPB Externe notitie 98/23, The Hague.

Crozier, M. and Friedberg, E. (1980) *Actors and Systems: The Politics of Collective Action*, Chicago, Ill./London: University of Chicago Press.

Dery, D. (1984) *Problem Definition in Policy Analysis*, Lawrence, Kan.: University Press of Kansas.

Dijkink, G. J. (1990) *Beleidenissen, politieke en ambtelijke cultuur in Nederland 1965–1990*, Groningen: STYX Publications.

Driessen, P. P. J. (1995) "Activating a Policy Network: The Case of Schiphol", in P. Glasbergen (ed.) *Managing Environmental Disputes: Network Management as an Alternative*, Dordrecht: Kluwer.

Duinen, L. van (2004) "Planning Imagery", PhD thesis, PrintPartners Ipskamp.

Edelenbos, J. (2000) *Proces in vorm; procesbegeleiding van interactieve beleidsvorming over locale ruimtelijke projecten*, Utrecht: Lemma.

Eeten, M. van (1999) *Dialogues of the Deaf: Defining New Agendas for Environmental Deadlocks*, Delft: Eburon.

Faludi, A. and van der Valk, A. J. (1994) *Rule and Order: Dutch Planning Doctrine in the Twentieth Century*, Dordrecht: Kluwer.

Flyvbjerg, B. (2001) Making Social Science Matter. Cambridge University Press.

Fukuyama, F. (1995) *Trust, the Social Virtues and the Creation of Prosperity*, New York: The Free Press.

Gils, M. K. A. van, Huys, M. G. and de Jong, B. (2009) *De Nederlandse Mainports Onder Druk*, Spectrum: Speuren naar ontwikkelkracht Uitgeverij, Houten.

Glasbergen, P. (2002) "The Green Polder Model: Institutionalizing Multi-stakeholder Processes in Strategic Environmental Decision-making", *European Environment*, 12 (6): 303–15.

Huxham, C. (2000) "The Challenge of Collaborative Government", *Public Management Review*, 2: 337–57.

Jordan, G. (1990) "Sub-governments, Policy Communities and Networks: Refilling the Old Bottles?", *Journal of Theoretical Politics*, 2 (3): 319–38.

Keast, R., Brown, K. and Mandell, M. (2002) "Getting the Right Mix: Unpacking Integration Meanings and Strategies", *International Public Management Journal*, 10 (1): 9–33.

Keast, R., Mandell, M., Brown, K. and Woolcock, G. (2005) "Network Structures: Working Differently and Changing Expectations", *Public Administration Review*, 64 (3): 363–71.

Ket, M. R. (2000) "Geluidshinderonderzoek en het Schipholbeleid", in Bureau PAU, *Schiphol en de Ruimtelijke Ordening: De ontwikkeling van het Schipholcomplex 1980–2000*, Groningen/Den Haag.

Kickert, W. J. M., Klijn, E. H. and Koppenjan, J. F. M. (eds) (1997) *Managing Complex Networks: Strategies for the Public Sector*, London: Sage.

Klijn, E. H. (2008) *"It's the Management Stupid!" On the Importance of Management in Complex Policy Issues*, The Hague: Lemma.

Koppenjan, J. F. M. and Klijn, E. H. (2004) *Managing Uncertainties in Networks: A Network Approach to Problem-solving and Decision-making*, London: Routledge.

Kruijf, A. de (2002) *Het Bulderbos: Verzet tegen uitbreiding van Schiphol 1993–2002*, Amsterdam: Mets & Schilt.

Ministry of Physical Planning (1988) *Fourth Memorandum on Spatial Development*, Den Haag, 1988.

Ministry of Physical Planning (1995) *PKB Schiphol en Omgeving*, Deel 4, Den Haag.

Ministry of Transportation (1997) *Integrale Beleidsvisie van het kabinet "Hoeveel ruimte geeft Nederland aan luchtvaart?"*, Den Haag.

Ministry of Transportation (1998) *Strategische beleidskeuze toekomst luchtvaart*, Den Haag.

Ministry of Transportation (1999) *Toekomst Nederlandse Luchtvaart*, Den Haag.

Ministry of Transportation (2002) PKB Voortgang 2002. The Hague.

Ministry of Transportation (2006) *Eindrapport evaluatie Schipholbeleid*, Den Haag.

Ministry of Transportation, Physical Planning and Economic Affairs (2006) *Cabinets Perspective Schiphol*, Den Haag.

Nooteboom, B. (2002) *Trust: Forms, Foundations, Functions, Failures and Figures*, Cheltenham: Edward Elgar.

Olson, M. (1965) *The Logic of Collective Action: Public Goods and the Theory of Groups*, Cambridge, Mass.: Harvard University Press.

Ostrom, E. (1990) *Governing the Commons: The Evolution of Institutions for Collective Action*, Cambridge: Cambridge University Press.

O'Toole, L. J. (1988) "Strategies for Intergovernmental Management: Implementing Programs in Interorganisational Networks", *Journal of Public Administration*, 25 (1): 43–57.

Parker. R. (2007) "Networked Governance or Just Networks? Local Governance of the Knowledge Economy in Limerick (Ireland) and Karlskrona (Sweden)", *Political Studies*, 55: 113–32.

Parsons, W. (1995) *Public Policy: An Introduction to the Theory and Practice of Policy Analysis*, Cheltenham: Edward Elgar.

Pestman, P. (2001) "In het spoor van de Betuweroute", PhD thesis, Amsterdam: Rozenburg Publishers.

Pierre, J. (ed.) (2000) *Debating Governance: Authority, Steering and Democracy*, Oxford: Oxford University Press.

Projectbureau Mainport and Milieu Schiphol (PMMS) (1991) *Integrale versie Plan van Aanpak Schiphol en Omgeving*. Den Haag: Sdu Uitgeverij.

Raad voor Ruimtelijk, Milieu–en Natuuronderzoek (RMNO) (2009) *Duurzame Ontwikkeling en Schiphol: Naar een creatieve confrontatie*, Den Haag: RMNO.

Ragin, Charles C. (1992) " 'Casing' and the process of social inquiry", in Charles C. Ragin and Howard S. Becker (eds) *What Is a Case? Exploring the Foundations of Social Inquiry*, Cambridge: Cambridge University Press.

Rein, M. and Schön, D. (1992) "Reframing Policy Discourse", in F. Fischer and J. Forester (eds) *The Argumentative Turn in Policy Analysis and Planning*, Durham, NC: Duke University Press.

Rhodes, R. A. W. (1990) "Policy Networks: A British Perspective", *Journal of Theoretical Politics*, 2 (3): 293–317.

Rhodes, R. A. W. (1997) *Understanding Government*, Buckingham: Open University Press.

Richardson, J. J. (ed.) (1982) *Policy Styles in Western Europe*, London: Allen & Unwin.

Sabatier, P. (1988) "An Advocacy Coalition Model of Policy Change and the Role of Policy-oriented Learning Therein", *Policy Sciences*, 21: 129–68.

Scharpf, F. W. (1997) *Games Real Actors Play: Actor-centered Institutionalism in Policy Research*, Boulder, Colo.: Westview Press.

Soerenson. E. and Torfing, J. (eds) (2007) *Theories of Democratic Network Governance*, Basingstoke: Palgrave Macmillan.

Susskind, L. and Cruikshank, J. (1987) *Breaking the Impasse: Consensual Approaches Resolving Public Disputes*, New York: Basic Books.

Tan, G. (2001) *Urgentie, leiderschap en kennisontwikkeling: verklaringen voor drie besluitvormingsronden over Schiphol tussen 1989 en 1991*, Amsterdam: Uitgeverij Lemma.

Teisman, G. R. (2000) "Models for Research into Decision-making Processes: On Phases, Streams and Decision-making Rounds", *Public Administration*, 78: 937–56.

Termeer, C. J. A. M. and Koppenjan, J. F. M. (1997) "Managing Perceptions in Networks", in W. J. M. Kickert, E. H. Klijn and J. F. M. Koppenjan (eds) *Managing Complex Networks: Strategies for the Public Sector*, London: Sage.

Tweede Kamer (1998) File 25466, Nr. 19. Letter from the Minister of Transportation to the Lower House.

Van Wijk, M. (2007) Airports as Cityports in the Cityregion. Netherlands Geographical University Press.

Waarden, F. van (1999), "European Harmonization of National Regulatory Styles?", in J. A. E. Vervaele et al. (eds) *Compliance and Enforcement of European Community Law*, Deventer: Kluwer.

Weggeman, J. (2003) *Controversiële besluitvorming*, Utrecht: Lemma.

Werther, P. (1992) *De uitbreiding van Schiphol: invloed op de besluitvorming van 1989 tot 1991*, Vrije Universiteit, Amsterdam.

Williamson, O. E. (1979) "Transaction Costs Economics: The Governance of Contractual Relations", *Journal of Law and Economics*, 22 (2): 233–61.

Williamson, O. E. (1998) "Transaction Costs Economics: How it Works, where is it Headed", *De Economist*, 146 (1): 23–58.

22

GOVERNANCE, NETWORKS AND POLICY CHANGE: THE CASE OF CANNABIS IN THE UNITED KINGDOM[1]

Beatriz Acevedo and Richard Common

Introduction

The two coterminous concepts of governance and policy networks have been reasserted in public management studies in the wake of the recent decline in the popularity of the so-called New Public Management (NPM) movement. The concepts appear to be inter-related with the notion of the policy network offering a perspective on efforts to "join up government", which is also derived from "governance" approaches (DeLeon 2005). While this chapter focuses on these concepts, it is clear that an understanding of networks is vital to the aspirations of the proponents of joined-up government in terms of achieving joined-up *governance.* It is also assumed that *governance* goes beyond top-level policy coordination to where the public sector coordinates and cooperates with nonstate actors, such as firms and voluntary organizations, to deliver policy outcomes.

Policy networks have enjoyed acceptance and popularity amongst scholars of public management for describing the complexity of the policy process in modern states. Policy networks refer to the diversity of actors and relationships in the policy process beyond political bureaucratic relationships (Atkinson and Coleman 1992: 156). Furthermore, the network concept has been defined and used in different ways. However, there is a broad agreement that it is a meso-level concept, which provides a link between the micro-level of analysis, which deals with the role of interests and government in relation to particular policy decisions, and the macro-level of analysis, which is concerned with broader questions regarding the distribution of power (Marsh and Rhodes 1992: 1). The link with governance is that an understanding of networks provides a basis for horizontal approaches to service delivery and provides an alternative approach to that of NPM (Klijn 2005: 260).

This chapter examines the case of drugs policy in the United Kingdom in order to examine the usefulness of network approaches. Several studies about drugs regulations have focused on its social and historical developments (Becker 1953, 1963; Berridge 1990, 2005; Mills 2000). Contemporary research on drugs policy has evolved from the 1960s, adopting a more international perspective (Dorn et al. 1996; Boekhout van Solinge 2002) and analyzing drugs policy in the context of criminal policy in the UK (McLaughlin and Muncie 1994; Murji 1998). However, very few attempts at analysis from a public management perspective have been made (Marlow 1999). The fact that drugs policy is managed by a variety of actors at international, state and local level, and that major tensions arise when agencies are required to cooperate with each other while competing for resources, means that drugs policy has enormous potential for assessing the utility of network analysis. We examine these issues based on current research about drug policy in the United Kingdom, particularly the analysis of the decisions around the reclassification of cannabis in the regulatory system of drugs during the last seven years. We use this example to provide practical and empirical insights for the discussion about the utility of the enhanced policy network analysis proposed by Atkinson and Coleman (1992), in addition to developments in conceptualizing different types of networks as posited by Rhodes (1997). The chapter will also use this case to examine the view of governance presented by networks. What is clear is that the rational or evaluative concerns of NPM cannot be applied to policy areas such as drugs.

The chapter is divided as follows: in the first section, we discuss some of the theoretical and conceptual aspects of the main topics of this chapter: "policy networks", "policy communities" and "governance". In the second section, we present an overview of drugs policy in the United Kingdom, pointing out the difficulties in regulating cannabis use. The application of policy network analysis to the case of cannabis reclassification is the subject of the third section. In the fourth section we focus on the different "appreciations" of the cannabis problem emerging from the previous analysis of the policy networks involved in the drugs policy discussion. We argue that the "appreciative system", as proposed by Rhodes, combined with the differential influence of certain policy networks, does determine decision-making in drugs policy. Taking into account these important considerations, we shall present some of the implications that such issues have for public-sector management, in particular the challenges that are faced in managing networks of actors to achieve policy outcomes. Differing perceptions, and the imbalance of power within networks, present obstacles for the neat horizontal governance that prescriptive approaches to network management seem to imply (Richards and Smith 2002). Finally we offer some conclusions regarding the utility of the central concepts of this chapter.

1. Policy networks and governance in the United Kingdom

Policy networks

Although beset by definitional squabbling, policy network analysis appears to provide a useful empirical metaphor for understanding the complexity of contemporary policy processes:

> The metaphor of a network or community seeks to focus on the pattern of formal and informal contacts and relationships, which shape policy agendas and decision-making as opposed to the interplay within and formal policy making organizations and institutions. . . . Network analysis is based on the idea that a policy is framed within a context of relationships and dependences.
>
> (Parsons 1995: 185)

In Britain the network metaphor has provided a framework to understand policy-making in democratic regimes. Richardson and Jordan (1979: 23) stated that the policy-making map of Britain was characterized by a fragmented collection of subsystems – a "series of vertical compartments of segments, each segment inhabited by a different set of organized groups and generally impenetrable by 'unrecognised groups' or by the general public" (p. 74). With the increasing complexity of policy issues, the participation of networks in decision-making processes has defined a broad area to understand.

Rhodes has provided an extensive approach to network analysis, stressing the continuity in the relations between interest groups and governmental departments (Rhodes 1988, 1997). Drawing on the European literature, he takes a different approach from that of Richardson and Jordan, defining policy networks with regard to interorganizational relations rather than to subgovernments, emphasizing the structural relationship between political institutions rather than interpersonal relations (Rhodes 1997: 36). Thus, he defines a policy network as a cluster or complex of organizations connected to one another by resources dependencies. The types of networks are to be distinguished by their degree of integration, stability and exclusiveness. In addition, Rhodes identifies four dimensions along which networks vary: interests, membership, interdependence and resources (p. 39). In his typology, at one end of a continuum are policy communities that have stable and restricted memberships, which are highly integrated within the policy-making process. Issue networks, in contrast, represent a much looser set of interests, are less stable and are non-exclusive, and have much weaker points of entry into actual policy-making. In the middle we have professional networks, intergovernmental networks and producer networks (pp. 37–8).

To enhance the advantages of using policy networks, Atkinson and Coleman's analysis suggests including three additional aspects: the macro political context, the international dimension and the dynamic of political change. In the first place, they question whether by disaggregating the state in different policy networks there would be little incentive to reconstitute the state or conceive of it as anything other than an assembly of organizational actors. They also argue that the concept of a "policy network" has been developed primarily to assess national policy-making from a domestic point of view. Whether the studies are comparative or limited to one country, the stress is on the identification of constellations of national or subnational state agencies, politicians, interest groups and political parties; they acknowledge that an increasing number of political areas are now determined at the international level (Rhodes 1997: 168).

Taking into account the complex nature of drugs policy, it is possible to evaluate the potential of using policy network analysis in understanding certain processes of policy-making involving multiple agencies. As drug policy making in the United Kingdom involves multiple actors, it is difficult to point to a dominant agency for either the formulation or the implementation of related policies. Duke (2003) uses policy networks to analyze the relationship between prisons and drugs policy. She accounts for how different groups dispute authority over managing the drugs problem inside prisons, whilst emphasizing different values and appreciations concerning diverse institutions and groups involved in tackling this problem.

In addition to the multi-agency approach, a second element in this analysis is provided by the use of the notion of governance. Although it appears that the main characteristic of the drugs policy network corresponds to that of an "issue network" in the classification of Marsh and Rhodes (1992), the attempt to steer networks in the managerialist interpretations of governance still suggests the manipulation of targets and strategic planning to reach the policy outcomes formulated by central government. As Klijn (2005) points out, there are two managerialist interpretations of governance on offer. One is the NPM variant offered by Marsh and Rhodes (1992); the other is the joined-up-government approach. Although Pollitt (2003a: 65–7) adds a considerable list of weaknesses to the network approach, he concedes that within the context of governance it is capable of offering an analysis of inter-organizational dynamics.

Governance

Many contemporary debates about public management revolve around the concept of governance. Much of its current attractiveness to both politicians and policy-makers is that governance implies obtaining a much wider range of policy outcomes than those provided by the state. Although the term is not new, governance has evolved from the shortcomings of NPM, involving non-state actors in service delivery and the shift away from hierarchical organization in the public sector toward networks (Eliassen and Sitter

2008). In the case of many policy areas, including drugs, governance implies a wider analysis of the outcomes delivered by policy that go beyond the mechanistic assessments and the tinkering with inputs implied by the public management approach. In addition, the association with networks is clear owing to the centrality of multiple and often conflicting stakeholders at the core of governance approaches to policy management.

Wälti et al. (2004: 86) emphasize the importance of "governance" in their analysis of Swiss drug policy:

> "Governance", "networks" and "partnerships" are widely used concepts to denote changes in the way public policies are managed. They capture transformation in the nature of coordination among agencies and in their relationship with society. They imply that public action takes place in self-organizing networks that govern without recourse to hierarchy, or at least, with a significant degree of autonomy from the state, and that public and private organizations cooperate and compete in a socio-cybernetic, horizontal and inter-organizational system of actors.

They highlight some aspects in the operation of policy networks in terms of actors and relationships that are useful for understanding the British case. For example, they present how media and social opinion play an important role in any decision on the drug policy, and how drug policy networks might be enhancing the representation of marginalized actors such as drug users. A similar situation can be evidenced in the British discussion about cannabis policy, as will be analyzed in this chapter.

Clearly, there are limitations to political science interpretations of policy networks under the rubric of "governance". Rhodes (1997: 50) also recognizes this when he identifies "governance as a socio-cybernetic system" as one possible use of "governance". Although this term presents different interpretations, it can be assumed that it is in the interest of governance to keep a balance between maintaining control over political decisions and empowering policy networks by consultation, restitution or direct decentralization.

For this analysis, our first question is whether the object of governance is the management of complex networks, which in theory reinforces subsystem autonomy enabling networks to resist central control; and autonomy is enhanced further because networks possess specialist knowledge and control of "street-level" implementation (Taylor 2000: 52). Thus, the point here is to find out to what extent networks can effectively have autonomy to influence policy-making and not just at the level of implementation or consultation.

Drugs policy represents an opportunity to analyze the extent of influence of networks over policy formulation. In the case of cannabis, a number of networks have had representation in the "advisory councils" or the "commissions" in the different governmental agencies. They can be defined as taskforces, and hence they may seem to be the "response of the Labour government to the demands of central coordination of intergovernmental relations: the epitome of government steering rather than rowing" (Taylor 2000: 53–4). With regard to this point, Atkinson and Coleman argue that if policy networks exchange relationships, then the question would be: What is the structural context in which these exchanges take place? Are there relationships of power and dependency that transcend and color individual transactions?

> If the answer is yes, then we will have to reach beyond transactional analysis to posit the structural conditions in which interaction occurs. . . . To bridge the gap it will be necessary to focus on institutional variables such as the level of centralization and professionalism that characterize organizations in a network, and on ideological variables, such as the intellectual foundations of dominant worldviews in particular policy areas.
>
> (Atkinson and Coleman 1992: 157)

The next question is whether policy network analysis can provide a comprehensive framework for drug policy understanding by reviewing the evolution of the network approach. The analysis will also attempt to map the various vertical and horizontal interdependencies to emphasize the problems of managing complex networks and to assess the extent to which interorganizational relationships are a necessary and potentially enduring feature of governance. To carry out this analysis, first we provide an overview of drugs policy in the United Kingdom, focused on the case of cannabis.

2. Drugs policy in the United Kingdom

The development of drugs policy in Britain has been determined by a combination of, on the one hand, the different perceptions of the problem of drugs and, on the other hand, the international conventions regulating these substances (Acevedo 2007). In the United Kingdom, the responsibility for dealing with the "drugs problems" has been disputed between the medical profession, who argue for a public health approach, and the criminal justice system, responsible for the application of the legislation and the administration of penalties for drugs offences (Berridge 1990; Stimson and Lart 2005; Bean 2002).

In particular, current UK drugs policy emerges as the product of both domestic discussions about the "problem of drugs" during the 1960s and the formalization of the international approach to narcotic drugs, articulated in the Single International Convention of 1961. The result was formalized by the Misuse of Drugs Act of 1971, which proposed a classification of drugs based on their level of individual and social harmfulness; hence defining

Table 22.1 Classification of illegal drugs in the United Kingdom, based on the Misuse of Drugs Act, 1971

Class	*Including (amongst others)*	*Penalties for possession*	*Penalties for supply*
A	Cocaine, crack cocaine, ecstasy and related compounds, heroin, LSD, "magic mushrooms" or psilocybin, methadone, morphine and opium	Seven years' imprisonment or unlimited fine	Life imprisonment or unlimited fine
B	Amphetamines, barbiturates and codeine Cannabis (herbal and resin) – after 29 January 2009 returns from Class C to Class B.	Five years' imprisonment or unlimited fine	Fourteen years' imprisonment or unlimited fine
C	Anabolic steroids, benzodiazepines and bupronorphine. Minor tranquillisers are classified as C, yet possession is illegal without a prescription	Two years' imprisonment or fine	Five years' imprisonment or fine

different penalties for each substance. It divides drugs into three classes (Table 22.1).

The Misuse of Drugs Act of 1971 remains the most important output in UK drugs policy-making. The Act also placed the Advisory Council on the Misuse of Drugs (ACMD) as the relevant scientific body to consider any further legislative changes. Throughout nearly four decades there have been remarkably few changes, given that the drug market and the pattern of consumption have changed dramatically. In contrast, new agencies have appeared to address the drugs problem. However, it was only as recently as 1995 that a comprehensive strategy was finally proposed. The initiative "Tackling Drugs Together" emanated from the Department of Health and seemed to apply a "multi-agency" approach. When Labour was elected in 1997, they drew upon this strategy, emphasizing a "partnership" approach and acknowledging the experience gained in previous years. Therefore, it was not surprising that:

> drugs were moved to the centre of the political stage. Drugs policy was to be "joined up" in the sense that a holistic multiagency approach was to be adopted. Intervention was to be "evidence-based" and closely monitored to ensure that it constitutes "best value".
>
> (Marlow 1999: 1)

A number of changes to this strategy were also implemented by the new Labour government, articulated in "Tackling Drugs Together: To Build a Better Britain". Amongst these changes, the government first insisted on a cross-cutting approach to drugs by appointing the UK Anti-Drug Coordinator, more popularly known as the Anti-Drug Tsar. Located in the Cabinet Office, the UKADC Unit was responsible for the coordination and implementation of the drugs strategy (Blair 1998). The strategy was coordinated and driven across government by the Cabinet Sub Committee on Drug Misuse, to which the Anti-Drugs Coordinator reported. Delivery at local level continued through Drug Action Teams (DATs) and their Drug Reference Groups (DRG), formed under the previous Conservative government. However, this "joined-up" experience in coordinating drugs policy was rather short-lived: Labour's second term of office saw the Home Office wresting control of drugs policy from the "cross-cutting" unit of the Cabinet Office, which was terminated.

In June 2001, the Home Office retook the task of managing drugs policy while maintaining DATs. At the same time, the Home Office proposed a revision of cannabis policy by asking the ACMD for its opinion on the harmful aspects of cannabis. This development represents a milestone in UK drugs policy, and it is our main focus here. Indeed, despite a previous call for a revision of the status of cannabis in the legislation, the political context in 2001 provided a window of opportunity for policy change. A possible explanation is the role of policy networks and the growing popularity of governance approaches to so-called "wicked" social problems (Pollitt 2003: 68). The set of questions posed by governance and public management in regard to other contemporaneous Labour initiatives such as "best value" and "joined-up government" influenced a traditional value-driven issue. The result was a policy revision called "What Is Working in the Government Drugs Strategy" (House of Commons 2002). On the other hand, it is possible to say that this initiative was part of the Home Secretary's strategy to regain control over the drug issue, after the brief but high-profile tenure of the UK anti-drugs tsar. The process of cannabis reclassification appeared to be an extensive consultative process, taking into account the variety of actors involved. Figure 22.1 aims to "visualize" the complexity of actors, networks, institutions and agencies involved in the policy-making debate.

3. Cannabis reclassifications: from B to C and back again

We use the case of cannabis reclassification as a representative example for our analysis of policy networks. In doing so, first we explain the process of downgrading and upgrading cannabis, and the role of different agencies, networks, institutions and actors in the public debate and in the policy-making process. The process of reclassifying cannabis and returning it again to its former class can be understood within changes to the Misuse of Drugs

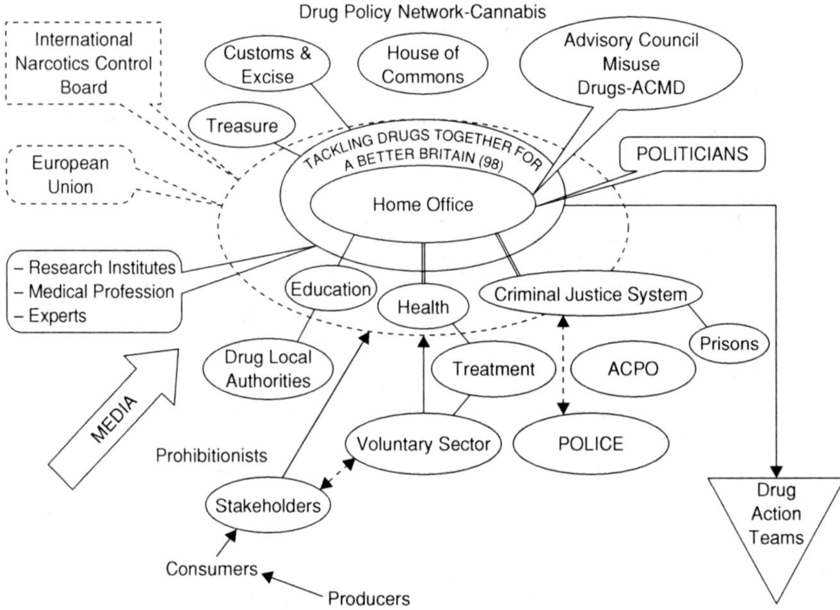

Figure 22.1 International agencies, governmental institutions and diverse actors involved in the debate about cannabis policy in the United Kingdom.

Act, 1971. The first decision was to downgrade cannabis from class B to class C. This decision was officially implemented in 2004 as the result of extensive consultation involving an appraisal by the ACMD (ACMD 2002: I). The decision to downgrade cannabis was based on a range of competing arguments, but amongst them was the fact that by 1998 there were 100,000 arrests for cannabis, although almost 50 percent of them only resulted in a caution. It was also argued that, in comparison with harder drugs, cannabis use should not be criminalized but treated with less severe penalties. In this way, it was possible to redirect resources toward more dangerous drugs (May et al. 2002).

The government stressed that the downgrading of cannabis did not mean decriminalization. However, its implications were interpreted by public opinion as a step toward legalizing cannabis, which was still unacceptable to many.[2] Increasing media pressure, the voice of the international community (INCB 2002) and some sections of the police who did not want to give up the practice of stopping and searching people for cannabis possession challenged this decision. However, the real implications in terms of penalties for cannabis offences were not radical: by moving cannabis to class C, the only real effect was that penalties for possession were two years' imprisonment instead of five. As a class C drug, penalties for supplying should have decreased to seven years; however, penalties for supplying class C drugs were actually increased to fourteen years. At the implementation level, a wide range for discretion was also given to the police.

Following reclassification, wide-ranging commentary about cannabis began to appear in the media. One line of opinion was that the nature of the cannabis available has changed (dominated by a stronger variety called "skunk"), which was more likely to be detrimental to mental health. On the other hand, new scientific evidence contested the reclassification by suggesting that cannabis use was also linked to certain forms of psychosis (Castle and Murray 2004). Although this link is not new, the argument gained prominence in the media and it added to the pressure against a relaxation on cannabis as perceived in relation to its downgrading.[3] On the other hand, some official surveys suggest that the downgrading of cannabis in 2004 actually discouraged its use amongst young people rather than encouraged its consumption (Sian et al. 2007: 58). In 2008, in spite of this evidence and responding to increasing media pressure, the Home Office called for a second round of consultations to evaluate this new evidence. The result of this review was contradictory: the ACMD (as the relevant body of experts responsible for evaluating the evidence) recommended keeping cannabis as class C; the government took the decision of upgrading it back to class B. In the next section, we apply network analysis to explain this apparent policy reversal.

4. Applying policy network analysis

Although the concept of policy networks for analyzing drugs policy issues is beset by definitional problems, drugs policy appears to display the characteristics of "issue networks", which are unstable, have large numbers of members and "limited vertical interdependence" (Rhodes 1997: 38). Drugs policy also appears as an "intergovernmental network" at the subnational level, particularly as it is based on an "extensive constellation of interests". In the case of drugs, these constellations of interests are also articulated in national strategies, while at the same time there are international agencies also to be taken into account. Particularly in the case of the cannabis debate, several types of policy networks participated. As defined by Rhodes, they are described in Table 22.2.

In Table 22.2, it seems that "issue networks" may well describe the process of policy-making in the case of cannabis. An issue network tends to have many participants, fluctuating interactions, limited consensus, interaction based on consultation, unequal power relationship and few resources (Rhodes 1997: 45). In the case of cannabis reclassification, it can be demonstrated that the great variety of opinions mean that, although there is a remarkable process of consultation, this is not leading to a *real* negotiation, and politicians retain their discretion in final decisions which are unlikely to change core values

Table 22.2 Policy networks involved in the policy-making on cannabis in the United Kingdom

Type of network	*Participants*
a. Policy community	Police, Home Office, Health Department, criminal justice system
b. Professional network	NHS, treatment system, medical doctors and psychologists
c. Intergovernmental networks	Drug action teams
d. Producer networks	Not present in the debate, but active in the cannabis market
e. Issue networks	Activists, media, parents, campaigners, Advisory Council on the Misuse of Drugs (AMCD)

in the consideration of drugs. In fact, the analysis must include the distinction between insider and outsider groups. Although the wide range of participants and groups were incorporated in the discussion, at the end access to final decisions is only given to insider groups but only if they "fit" political thinking on the issue (Dunleavy and O'Leary 1987: 163).

Another interesting aspect of this typology is the definition of a "producer network"; which would be crucial for an analysis of a legal economic activity. However, in the case of drugs, the presence of "producers" is unclear, since they remain illegal and organized by criminal gangs or "cottage industries". Nonetheless, they are an important actor in the drugs economy, since home-grown cannabis provides approximately 50 percent of local consumption (Hough et al. 2003), and this trend has increased owing to the proliferation of cannabis "factories" (Home Office 2008). In the United Kingdom, cannabis production does not present sufficient signs of cohesion or integration to be defined as a "network". In any case, the analogy is useful, as a kind of "consumer network" does exist, given the increased use of cannabis. However, cannabis consumers do not have direct representation as a "consumer network" group, but their influence on drugs policy decisions should not be diminished by their "invisibility".

Table 22.2 suggests that changes in drugs policy could have been influenced by different groups, to various degrees. Smith (1993: 51) argues that policies that emanate from the state do not always reflect the demands of groups or classes but are the result of how state actors *perceive* their interests, and how they perceive particular problems and their solutions. During the discussion about cannabis reclassification from 2002 to 2009, several appreciations regarding the cannabis problem can be identified. Some networks define it as a matter of public policy in which the principles of NPM can be applied. This appreciation is characteristic of the original arguments supporting cannabis reclassification, such as the House of Commons evaluation on drugs policy (House of Commons 2002), ACMD (2002, 2008) opinion, and an independent group of experts commissioned by the Police Foundation (Runciman 1999). On the other hand, cannabis is also defined as a matter of public health, emphasizing the risks associated with cannabis use involving physical and mental harm. In particular, "cannabis psychosis" has reinforced medical views on the problem of cannabis. Consequently, professional networks of medical practitioners, psychologists and psychiatrists claim their authority on dealing with this issue. More generally, cannabis use has been mainly defined as a matter of criminality. This view is supported by the general perception of British society in which cannabis is associated with violence and deviance, and reinforced by the number of news items pointing out this connection (Acevedo 2007). In terms of policy networks, this appreciation is expressed by policy community networks and intergovernmental networks, such as the Association of Chief Police Officers (ACPO 2003), the Home Office, the criminal justice system, and the International Narcotics Control Board. Finally, other networks, including activists and campaigners representing users, have claimed that cannabis use should be regarded as a "medicinal practice", and for others it is a "recreational" practice (Parker et al. 1998). These views have been supported by reports commissioned by the government (i.e. The Police Foundation 1999; House of Lords Selected Committee on Science and Technology 1998, 2001). The public debate on cannabis reclassification illustrates the coexistence of these different appreciations in defining the "problem of cannabis". However, their existence as policy networks in our analysis does not guarantee that they are equally represented in the process of decision-making.

Atkinson and Coleman suggested that the identification of different policy networks should be complemented by the consideration of wider issues. First, they recommend considering the issues of change and dynamism in politics. The case of cannabis evidences how the government's interest and attention can change throughout time; thus, the initial impulse to the downgrading of cannabis has been transformed in an actual opposition to the measure. Further, some interesting data have contested the government view about cannabis consumption following the reclassification in 2004. For instance, figures for 2007 show a decline in the level of consumption of this substance amongst the British population. The proportion of 16–59-year-olds taking cannabis has decreased from 2002–3 when it reached 10.09 percent toward 8.2 percent in the latest British Crime Survey of 2006–7 (Sian et al. 2007: 58). Indeed, only 24.8 percent of young people aged between 16 and 24 years old took cannabis during 2004–5 (after the reclassification of cannabis in January 2004) compared to 23.5 percent in 2003–4 within the same age group (Roe 2005). Against this, it is possible to conclude that, although the consumption is in decline, the visibility of the problem has provoked an increase of arrests

(Sian et al. 2007); hence the initial objective of diverting resources to class A drugs may not have been achieved.

In view of this evidence, decisions on cannabis policy should consider both the facts and expert advice. However, as Atkinson and Coleman remind us, it is important to include the macro-political context. In this sense, considering the volatile levels of popularity of New Labour, it seems that politicians would not risk taking a stand against a rooted view on drugs as a matter of criminality and violence. In contrast to this view, the ACMD evaluated the government idea of returning cannabis to class B by reviewing the evidence, consulting with different stakeholders, and calling a number of meetings and conferences. The result of this extensive process was for cannabis to remain as class C. However, the government managed to return cannabis to class B early in 2009. This reversal undermined expert opinion, since in this case it seems the decision was taken based on the influence of a few "insider" groups rather than being informed by scientific advice or based on evidence. Thus, the very nature of an "evidence-based" policy, guided by expert advice and scientific research, as proclaimed by NPM, is seriously questioned in this case.

Rhodes (1997: 39) offers an explanation by stating that "although decision-making within the organisation is constrained by other organisations, the *dominant coalition* retains some discretion. In this sense, it can be said that *political communities* tend to retain the power and they may act as those 'dominant coalitions'". With regard to this, Rhodes relates the idea in which the "appreciative system" of the dominant coalition does influence which relationships are seen as a problem and which resources will be sought. The notion of appreciation is crucial in understanding how certain problems are defined, and thus how decisions are taken (Vickers 1995). Atkinson and Coleman (1992: 174) observe that relevant knowledge may prevail when defining political problems. Consequently, policy network analysis may benefit from a consideration of the diverse appreciative systems within different policy networks. It is also important to consider that expert opinion is not unified and different appreciations exist; this characteristic emphasizes the importance of professional networks in defining drug problems. Moreover, Atkinson and Coleman consider the international context, which in the case of drugs policy includes institutions such as the International Narcotics Control Board. The Board wields considerable power when approving or disapproving any change in national policies concerning commitments acquired by governments under international conventions (Acevedo 2007).

Although it is difficult to apply, we cannot dismiss the lingering NPM variant of governance when analyzing networks (Klijn 2005: 260). In this interpretation, different opinions should be taken by following a rational evaluation of the evidence and the advice of experts. However, this view ignores the power configuration and influences of some groups over others. In this way, the role of the ACMD is crucial in the process of decision-making since not only do they represent the expert advice but they are also responsible for the consultation process. Notwithstanding, the decision to return cannabis to class B contradicts this "rational" view and suggests that complex dynamics of power actually can challenge the logic of NPM. The case of cannabis illustrates how the opinion of dominant groups inside the policy networks can actually determine the development of the policy by disregarding evidence and expert advice in favor of decisions perceived as "popular", such as a hard policy on drugs. Furthermore, an analysis of drugs policy stands outside market rationality, given the unorganized nature and criminality of producers and the diverse nature of consumers.

In synthesis, the case of cannabis policy evidences the importance of including the dimension of power in the process of policy-making. However, it is not only a matter of influencing decisions but also of the way that problems and subjects are constructed by the interaction of power and knowledge. Thus far, we have shown how different appreciations of the problem of cannabis are shaped in the process of policy-making. Following Rhodes, these appreciations determine how certain problems are defined in terms of public policy, and therefore influence the type of solutions, institutions and actions for addressing that problem. Thus, it is possible to argue that changes proposed in the case of drugs policy will depend heavily on cultural values, institutional interests and prevailing discourses about the drugs problem. As a result of this reflection, a challenging aspect for the policy networks analysis is the consideration of power in relation to knowledge, and its relationship with further aspects of governmentality (Foucault 1991).

5. Implications for public management

The final aim of the chapter is to assess the utility of the network concept for public management. The case of drug policy, and particularly the recent example of cannabis reclassification, shows the complexity of this issue when analyzing it through policy networks. Atkinson and Coleman's (1992) critique of the network approach, as demonstrated in this chapter, provides important insights for enhancing the quality of policy network analysis. The rhetoric of NPM in Labour's approach also seems to be tested in the case of cannabis reclassification. Although originally the proposal was based on the principles of value for money, efficiency in the use of resources, and evidence-based policies, this aim is hampered by the contrasting appreciations of the drug problem. Hence, when policy networks discuss their appreciations of the problem of cannabis, it must be clarified that they are not necessarily sharing the principles of NPM, but they are wrestling their own views within the political context. This further demonstrates the fundamental weaknesses of NPM in many policy areas.

As argued above, the results of the first phase of cannabis reclassification (2002–6) show a decrease in terms of cannabis consumption, indicating a certain level of success of the strategy. Despite these results, the issue became contingent, and the government proposed the reversal on this measure. Ignoring the recommendation of the ACMD, and wishing to show a tough approach, the government returned cannabis to class B. However, the point here is to analyze to what extent the advice of the experts is really taken into account when dealing with "wicked" issues such as drugs policy. Following policy network analysis it is clear that external networks, such as pressure groups, mass media and so forth, although not necessarily responsible for making political decisions, continue to play a crucial role in shaping "appreciations" of problems. Consequently, politicians tend to respond to these pressures rather than following expert advice or evidence-based information.

Clearly the implications for public management are very different from the NPM approach. The strategic role of the public manager horizontally across the network will defy the control structures wedded to the target-based and performance management systems found across large swathes of the public sector. Network management (including partnerships) looks very different from the managerialist solutions of NPM. A normative literature has been developing around this theme for some time (for example, Lawton 1999; Joyce 2000). The emphasis is on professional knowledge, managing relationships and understanding the nature of networks. The organizational fragmentation and competition for resources under NPM would undermine any notion of a coherent drugs strategy.

However, the usefulness of the network approach is compromised by systems of policy evaluation that focus on outcomes, which are attributable to individual organizations. The ability of networks to learn by practice and through the acquisition of shared knowledge defies managerialist approaches to dealing with policy problems such as drugs. Institutionalized learning within the network may run contrary to the strategic intent of policy-makers as the network, in time, becomes highly resistant to change, forcing elected politicians either to "reinvent" policy or to "negotiate and persuade" through networking (Pollitt 2003b: 47). A clear implication for public management is to recognize and accommodate stakeholders, a core tenet of the governance approach (Loffler 2009).

6. Conclusions

Policy network analysis has received both wide attention and criticism, although it remains of value as a heuristic device for analyzing complex policy processes. Drugs policy represents one of the more extreme cases, in which policy network analysis can be enhanced by introducing the three aspects offered by Atkinson and Coleman: macro-political context, policy change and the international dimension. Following this framework, our analysis of drug policy shows that the dynamics of networks may be influenced by key state actors who have considerable command over resources and thus dominate policy within the network. Macro-political aspects, in which apparently pluralist systems may advocate for participation and extended consultation, remain dominated by insider groups and by an elite perspective on public affairs. Nevertheless drugs remain a value-driven issue; thus, political decisions are likely to be influenced by public opinion, and the particular action of stakeholders over a certain period of time. In this sense, the presence of international pressure at the level of supranational structures, international agencies, and lobbyists and campaigners adds complexity to this analysis.

In addition, governance principles advocate wider participation and empowerment of community partnerships. These principles, although difficult to put into practice, are generating changes in the evaluation of drugs policy, and they are actually influencing political decisions. The case of cannabis shows how governance approaches are supported by politicians, who traditionally do not like to be seen as "soft on drugs", in this particular case. Interactions between network members and participants, and where "state boundaries" are broken down, tend to be fairly unique to particular networks, and drugs policy is no exception. An enduring feature of the governance approach is that it offers an explanation of network behavior to the public manager which contrasts sharply with the rationalist approach of NPM. Moreover, Le Grand (2003) argues that governance rather than NPM-inspired systems of policy delivery are more likely to be robust in the long term. It is the same difference as between classical and processual approaches to strategic management.

Third, it is clear that managerialist approaches to policy analysis will be strictly limited within such a fluid environment where the drugs issue has such a high political saliency. However, it must be acknowledged that, whilst locating drugs as a problem to be managed, the debate may cut loose from a criminalized approach and its questionable results in time. Likewise, when emphasizing managerialism, some aspects related to the practicalities of drug policy may be incorporated into drug policy-making, in terms of a learning process. However, in some other cases it seems that managerialism might continue to be an obstacle rather than a facilitator for practitioners and public officials in dealing with this complex issue.

In conclusion, we recommend complementing the analysis of policy networks by stressing the importance of the "appreciative systems" within policy networks, which are indeed determined by certain dynamics of power and knowledge (Foucault 1991). As demonstrated in this chapter, the rhetoric of NPM in defining problems as a matter of rational management is contested by the appreciations that different policy networks have about that particular issue and their power in influencing final decisions. In this case, the role of media and social pressure is crucial in influencing the debate, while politicians are driven by electoral purposes rather than by evidence-based figures or expert advice. In this context, the rationale of NPM within the

Labour approach is questioned by the "appreciative system" and the differential power of some actors and networks within the policy-making process.

Notes

1 This chapter is expanded and developed from B. Acevedo and R. Common (2006) "Governance and the Management of Networks in the Public Sector: Drugs Policy in the United Kingdom and the Case of Cannabis Reclassification", *Public Management Review*, 8 (3): 395–414.

2 A *Guardian* poll in 2002 showed that 53 percent of Britons opposed the measure. See A. Travis (2002) "Cannabis Relaxation Opposed by Majority", *The Guardian*, 31 July 2002. Available at http://www.guardian.co.uk/uk/2002/jul/31/drugsandalcohol.immigrationpolicy [accessed 15 January 2009].

3 For an extensive historical analysis of the origin of the link between cannabis and madness in the context of colonial practices in India, please refer to J. Mills (2000) *Madness, Cannabis and Colonialism*, New York: St Martin's Press.

References

Acevedo, B. (2007) "Understanding Cannabis Policy in the United Kingdom: A Systems and a Post-structuralist Approach", PhD thesis, University of Hull.

Advisory Council on the Misuse of Drugs (2002) *The Classification of Cannabis under the Misuse of Drugs Act 1971*, London: Home Office.

Advisory Council on the Misuse of Drugs (2008) *Cannabis: Classification and Public Health*, available at http://drugs.homeoffice.gov.uk/publication-search/acmd/acmd-cannabis-report-2008 [accessed 29 March 2009].

Association of Chief Police Officers of England, Wales and Northern Ireland (2003) *Cannabis Enforcement Guidance*, London: ACPO.

Atkinson, M. and Coleman, W. (1992) "Policy Networks, Policy Communities and the Problem of Governance", *Governance*, 5 (2): 154–80.

Bean, P. (2002) *Drugs and Crime*, Uffculme: Willan.

Becker, H. S. (1953) "Becoming a Marihuana User", *The American Journal of Sociology*, 59: 395–403.

Becker, H. S. (1963) *Outsiders: Studies in Sociology and Deviance*, New York: The Free Press.

Berridge, V. (ed.) (1990) *Drug Research and Policy in Britain*, Aldershot: Gower.

Berridge, V. (2005) "The 'British System' and Its History: Myth and Reality", in J. Strang and M. Gossop (eds) *Heroin Addiction and the British System*, Vol. 1, *Origins and Evolution*, Abingdon: Routledge.

Blair, T. (1998) "A Personal Statement from the Prime Minister", in *Tackling Drugs Together: To Build a Better Britain*, London: Home Office.

Boekhout van Solinge, T. (2002) *Drugs and Decision Making in the European Union*, Amsterdam: Mets & Schilt.

Castle, D. and Murray, R. (eds) (2004) *Marijuana and Madness: Psychiatry and Neurobiology*, Cambridge: Cambridge University Press.

DeLeon, L. (2005) "Public Management, Democracy and Politics", in E. Ferlie, L. Lynn, Jr and C. Pollitt (eds) *The Oxford Handbook of Public Management*, Oxford: Oxford University Press.

Dorn, N., Jepsen, J. and Savona, E. E. (1996) *European Drug Policies and Enforcement*, London: Macmillan Press.

Duke, K. (2003) *Drugs, Prisons and Policy Making*, Basingstoke: Palgrave Macmillan.

Dunleavy, P. and O'Leary, B. (1987) *Theories of the State*, Basingstoke: Macmillan.

Eliassen, K. and Sitter, N. (2008) *Understanding Public Management*, London: Sage.

Foucault, M. (1991) "On Governmentality", in G. Burchell, C. Gordon and P. Miller (eds) *The Foucault Effect: Studies in Governmentality*, Hemel Hempstead: Harvester Wheatsheaf.

Home Office (2008) *Drugs: Protecting Families and Communities*, available at http://drugs.homeoffice.gov.uk/publication-search/drug-strategy/drug-strategy-2008 [accessed 29 March 2009].

Hough, M., Warburton, H., Few, B., May, T., Lan Ho, M., Witton, J. and Turnbull, P. (2003) *A Growing Market: The Domestic Cultivation of Cannabis*, York: Joseph Rowntree Foundation.

House of Commons, United Kingdom (2002) *Third Report: The Government's Drug Policy: Is It working?*, London: House of Commons.

House of Lords, United Kingdom (1998) *Cannabis: The Scientific and Medical Evidence*, London: House of Lords Select Committee on Science and Technology.

House of Lords, United Kingdom (2001) *Second Report: Therapeutic Uses of Cannabis*, available at http://www.publications.parliament.uk/pa/ld200001/ldselect/ldsctech/50/5001.htm [accessed 15 January 2009].

International Narcotics Control Board (2002) *Report of the International Narcotics Control Board for 2002*, Vienna: United Nations, available at http://www.incb.org/incb/annual_report_2002.html [accessed 15 January 2009].

Joyce, P. (2000) *Strategy in the Public Sector*, Chichester: John Wiley.

Klijn, E. H. (2005) "Networks and Inter-Organizational Management: Challenging, Steering, Evaluation, and the Role of Public Actors in Public Management", in E. Ferlie, L. Lynn, Jr and C. Pollitt, C. (eds) *The Oxford Handbook of Public Management*, Oxford: Oxford University Press.

Lawton, A. (1999) "Managing Networks", in A. Rose and A. Lawton (eds) *Public Services Management*, Harlow: FT Prentice Hall.

Le Grand, J. (2003) *Motivation, Agency and Public Policy*, Oxford: Oxford University Press.

Loffler, E. (2009) "Public Governance in a Network Society", in T. Bovaird and E. Loffler (eds) *Public Management and Governance*, 2nd edn, Abingdon: Routledge.

McLaughlin, E. and Muncie, J. (1994) "Managing the Criminal Justice System", in J. Clarke, A. Cochrane and E. McLaughlin (eds) *Managing Social Policy*, London: Sage.

Marlow, A. (1999) "Joined-up Thinking: Youth and Drugs Policy at the Millennium", in A. Marlow and G. Pearson (eds) *Young People, Drugs and Community Safety*, Lyme Regis: Russell House.

Marsh, D. and Rhodes, R. A. W. (1992) *Policy Networks in British Government*, Oxford: Clarendon Press.

May, T., Warburton, H., Turnbull, P. J. and Hough, M. (2002) *Times They Are a-Changing: Policing of Cannabis*, York: Joseph Rowntree Foundation.

Mills, J. (2000) *Madness, Cannabis and Colonialism*, New York: St Martin's Press.

Mills, J. (2003) *Cannabis Britannica: Empire Trade and Prohibition 1800–1928*, Oxford: Oxford University Press.

Murji, K. (1998) *Policing Drugs*, Aldershot: Ashgate.

Parker, H., Aldridge, J. and Measham, H. (1998) *Illegal Leisure: The Normalization of Adolescent Recreational Drug Use*, London: Routledge.

Parsons, W. (1995) *Public Policy: An Introduction to the Theory and Practice of Policy Analysis*, Aldershot: Edward Elgar.

Pollitt, C. (2003a) *The Essential Public Manager*, Maidenhead: Open University Press.

Pollitt, C. (2003b) "Joined-up Government: A Survey", *Political Studies Review*, 1 (1): 34–9.

Provan, K. and Milward, H. (1995) "A Preliminary Theory of Interorganizational Network Effectiveness: A Comparative Study of Four Community Mental Health Systems", *Administrative Science Quarterly*, 40: 1–33.

Rhodes, R. A. W. (1988) *Beyond Westminster and Whitehall: The Sub Central Governments of Britain*, London: Unwin Hyman.

Rhodes, R. A. W. (1997) *Understanding Governance: Policy Networks, Governance, Reflexivity and Accountability*, Buckingham: Open University Press.

Richards, D. and Smith, M. (2002) Governance and Public Policy in the UK, Oxford: Oxford University Press.

Richardson, J. J. and Jordan, A. G. (1979) *Governing under Pressure: The Policy Process in a Post-parliamentary Democracy*, Oxford: Martin Robertson.

Roe, S. (2005) *Drugs Misuse Declared: Findings from the 2004/05 British Crime Survey England and Wales*, London: Home Office Statistical Bulletin 16/05.

Runciman, R. (1999) *Drugs and the Law: Report of the Independent Inquiry into the Misuse of Drugs Act 1971*, London: The Police Foundation.

Sian, N., Kershaw, C. and Walker, A. (2007) *Crime Survey England and Wales 2006/2007*, London: Home Office Statistical Bulletin.

Smith, M. (1993) *Pressure, Power and Policy*, Hemel Hampstead: Harvester Wheatsheaf.

Stimson, G. V. and Lart, R. (2005) "The Relationship between the State and Local Practices in the Development of National Policy on Drugs between 1920–90", in J. Strang and M. Gossop (eds) *Heroin Addiction and the British System*, Vol. 1, *Origins and Evolution*, Abingdon: Routledge.

Taylor, A. (2000) "Hollowing out or Filling in? Task Forces and the Management of Crosscutting Issues in British Government", *British Journal of Politics and International Relations*, 2 (1): 46–71.

Vickers, G. (1995) *The Art of Judgement: A Study of Policy Making*, Thousand Oaks, Calif.: Sage.

Wälti, S., Kübler, D. and Papadopoulus, Y. (2004) "How Democratic Is 'Governance'? Lessons from Swiss Drug Policy", *Governance: An International Journal of Policy, Administration and Institutions*, 17 (1): 83–113.

23

CONCLUSIONS

Public governance and public services delivery: a research agenda for the future

Stephen P. Osborne

The introductory chapter to this volume explored the argument that public policy implementation and public services delivery have evolved across three regimes over the past century – from Public Administration (PA), through the New Public Management (NPM) and hence on to what has been termed here "the New Public Governance" (NPG) in the contemporary state. The subsequent chapters of this volume have then explored the reality of this regime shift in current public policy and public services delivery.

It is argued here that these chapters have demonstrated that public governance is indeed a significant paradigm for contemporary public services delivery, embracing policy-making and a range of interorganizational and network-based modes for public services delivery. It is also argued here that the NPG, by its very nature, requires a broader engagement with the environment of public policy and public services than has perhaps been the case in the past. This, in turn, requires greater attention to the issues of sustainability – not only in terms of public policies, public service organizations and public services themselves, but also in terms of the impact of these elements upon broader issues of societal and environmental sustainability (Ball 2005).

It is debatable perhaps whether this is genuinely "new" – but public governance is certainly a reality in our modern fragmented public policy and public services delivery landscape. This concluding chapter now sets out an agenda to frame both public policy implementation and managerial practice within the NPG and "state of the art" research about its impact upon public policy and public services delivery.

It is important at this stage to re-emphasize that the NPG regime is not being posed here either as a normative, policy alternative to PA and the NPM nor as "the one best way" (Alford and Hughes 2008) by which to manage public policy implementation and public services delivery. Rather it is offered as a conceptual model that can both help us understand and evaluate the reality of public policy implementation and public services

Table 23.1 An exploratory model of the interaction of public policy implementation and public services delivery regimes and managerial practice

Policy and service regime	*Focus of managerial action*		
	Policy	*Organization*	*Environment*
PA	Street-level bureaucracy	Professional practice	Political management
NPM	"Costs of democracy"	Organizational performance	Competitive market behavior
NPG	Stakeholder management	Boundary spanning and boundary maintenance	Sustainable public policy and services

delivery in the twenty-first century and clarify what the core challenges are for public service managers within this "brave new world".

It is also worth reiterating that the reality of "actually existing" public policy implementation and public services delivery is far more complex than a simple set of discrete implementation and delivery regimes or paradigms. In practice, these regimes will invariably coexist and interact rather than serially replace each other. Thus, it has been argued here that the NPG has become the dominant regime of public policy implementation and public services delivery, with a premium being placed upon the development of sustainable public policies and public services and the governance of inter-organizational relationships. However, that does not take away either the importance of the public policy process or the necessity to manage individual organizational resources and performance in an efficient and effective manner. The world has simply become more complex, and we need to recognize this in the conceptual models that we build. The bare bones of a more sophisticated approach are suggested, in a purely exploratory way, in Table 23.1. This explores the interplay of the policy and delivery regime and the focus of managerial activity.

This more sophisticated approach is perhaps a model to be developed further in the future. The intention here is more modest: to explore the new questions that we need to start asking in order to understand and evaluate the impact and import of the NPG for public policy implementation and public services delivery – and subsequently to use this knowledge to encourage evidence-influenced public policy and managerial practice in the future. Accordingly, this chapter will consider the seven "new questions" that were articulated at the outset of this volume, as the core direction for future research upon public policy implementation and public services delivery. These questions are:

- What should be our basic unit of analysis in exploring public policy implementation and public services delivery – and what are the implications of this for theory and practice? *(the fundamentals question)*
- What organizational architecture is best-suited to delivering public services in the plural state? *(the architectural question)*
- How do we ensure sustainable public service systems – and what does sustainability mean? *(the sustainability question)*
- What values underpin public policy implementation and services delivery in such systems? *(the values question)*
- What key skills are required for relational performance? *(the relational skills question)*
- What is the nature of accountability in fragmented plural and pluralist systems? *(the accountability question)*
- How do you evaluate sustainability, accountability and relational performance within open natural public service delivery systems? *(the evaluation question)*

The new questions

The fundamentals question

Within PA, the unit of analysis was the public policy system as a *closed system*, with a focus upon the efficacy and impact of this system in its own right.[1] The key questions in this regime were about the effectiveness of the policy-making process and the extent to which public policy implementation addressed the aspirations of the resultant extant public policies (see, for example, Parsons 2003; Hill and Hupe 2009). A key concept here was that of the *implementation gap* – concerned with why policy implementation might fail. Often in this work, public managers were seen as "the villains of the piece", who intentionally or unintentionally subverted these aspirations (Schofield 2001).

Within the NPM, the unit of analysis shifted to the individual public service organizations (PSOs) as *open rational systems* and to individual public service managers within these systems. It models public services delivery as an intraorganizational process that turns inputs into outputs (services) within a mediating environment, and with an emphasis upon the economy and efficiency of public services delivery. As noted in our introductory chapter, the NPM asked questions about the management and performance of such organizations and managers. Even when issues of interorganizational working were addressed, these were inevitably from the perspective of the individual organization (for example, O'Toole et al. 2005).

Our argument is that such a discrete focus is no longer suitable for the study of contemporary public services. Rather a *systemic* approach is required that views public services delivery from an *open natural systems* perspective.

This focuses attention upon the institutional and external environmental pressures that enable and constrain public policy implementation and the delivery of public services within such a plural and pluralist system. Borrowing from the services management literature (for example, Gronroos 2007; Normann 2007), it is suggested here that the fundamental unit of analysis should be *the public service system*. This includes not just the public policy process and PSOs (including their personnel and hard and soft service delivery technologies), but also the involvement of services users as the *co-producers* of public services (Pestoff et al. 2006) and the wider institutional and environmental contingencies of public services delivery. Such an approach moves beyond the concept of "simple" interorganizational networks as the focus of attention for analysis, as in open rational systems. Rather it moves our attention to the inter-relationships between a number of interdependent elements of the public service system.

Co-production is a core element here. Public management theory has traditionally drawn upon theory from the business sector derived primarily from manufacturing. However, there is a coherent body of theory about services management that may well be far more relevant to public services than this manufacturing-derived theory. This body of theory is focused both upon this element of co-production in services and also upon the relational nature of services that require governance rather than management (Gronroos 2007).

In this context, the key "fundamentals" questions for our research agenda include:

- What can we learn from the services management literature that will help to illuminate the nature of public delivery within the NPG regime or paradigm?
- What are the core elements of the service delivery system and how do they inter-relate?
- What types of public service systems are there – and do they require a differential approach to their management and governance?
- What are the implications of the implicit element of user co-production within public service systems?
- What is the role of PSOs and of networks of PSOs in delivering public services?

The architectural question

The architecture of public services delivery within PA was relatively straightforward. This involved all elements of service provision being vertically integrated within PSOs – and with these bodies invariably being part of the government sector. The structure and functioning of these governmental bodies was broadly similar for all services.

Within NPM, the architecture became more complex, with the plural provision of public services both from a range of PSOs and from a range of societal sectors (government, the third sector and the private sector). The architecture of these organizations could vary in size, structure and functions, but was often broadly similar within societal sectors. Moreover, the market acted as an isomorphic force to encourage homogeneity between organizations providing similar services.

Such vertically integrated and sectoral approaches to organizational architecture have broken down as the fragmentation and pluralism of the NPG has progressed. Increasingly the unit of analysis is not distinct organizations. Now it includes networks of both public managers and PSOs working in concert to provide public services (O'Toole et al. 2007) and *hybrid organizational forms* that do not neatly fit within one distinctive societal sector and that have a fragmented and intermingled architecture (Evers 2008).

Now, the concept of hybrid organizations is not a new one. There has been a longstanding debate about "publicness" in PSOs and the blurring of the boundaries between public and private organizations. What is distinctive now is the growing complexity of this hybridity. It is not simply a blurring of the boundaries between the public and the private. Rather it is the evolution of genuinely new forms of organizational architecture that are not bound by sectoral limitations and that engender new forms of accountability. Social enterprises are one example of such hybrid organizations that mix social ends with a business orientation to income generation (Vidal 2008).

In this world, there is no "one best way" or prescribed approach to organizational architecture. It becomes a contingent process. Such new architecture needs us to ask questions such as

- What organizational architecture is best suited to deliver what sorts of public services?
- What are the key contingencies of the contemporary architecture of PSOs, and what are their implications for public services delivery?
- How do PSOs develop organizational architecture that goes beyond simple organizational survival to tackle the issues of "boundary spanning" and "boundary maintenance" in sophisticated service delivery systems that rely upon multiple elements for the successful delivery of public services to local communities?

The sustainability question

To date, sustainability has often been viewed in public services delivery research either as concerned with the organizational ecology of PSOs and the sustainability of individual PSOs or as concerned with issues of environmentalism and ecological sustainability. The contemporary architecture of public services, as discussed above, requires a more sophisticated approach. This needs to consider sustainability across a number of dimensions:

- The development of sustainable income streams and funding for public services, and the impact of these income streams upon their wider environment (perhaps through ethical investment strategies);
- The ecology of PSOs and their sustainability as discrete entities;
- The sustainability of services delivered by PSOs and public service delivery systems, and their impact upon their users and host communities; and
- The effect of public services delivery systems upon environmental and ecological sustainability.

Some preliminary questions in this area are:

- What is sustainability? There is a need to move beyond the simple definitions of the Brundtland report.
- What are the key dimensions of sustainability for public service delivery systems? Are the ones suggested above the correct ones, or are there alternatives or additional ones?
- To what extent is sustainability a marginal or mainstream issue for PSOs – and is it being "backwards incorporated" into existing service-led agendas from the NPM paradigm?
- How has the concept and practice of sustainability evolved over the period of PA–NPM–NPG?

The values question

The discussion about the role of values in public services has a long lineage. Within PA, there was an assumption of distinctiveness in the values of public- as opposed to private-sector management – and often an assumption of moral hegemony of the former. One of the first statements of the "public value thesis" was Sayre (1958); and the argument was developed by, among others, Rainey et al. (1976) and Murray (1975) – though the classic statement was probably Allison (1984), who argued that "public and private management are at least as different as they are similar, and that the differences are at least as important as the similarities" (p. 234).

As market and business disciplines came to have a greater influence on public management within the NPM, however, this hegemony of public values was challenged. A number of studies argued that public- and private-sector values and managerial practice were either not as differentiated as had earlier been argued or were converging (e.g. Posner and Schmidt 1996; Boyne 2002). Several studies also argued that public values had been replaced by new public-sector entrepreneurial values (Llewellyn et al. 2007), whilst

Mark Moore has coined the term "public value" as the equivalent of "shareholder value" within public organizations (Moore 1997).

Within the field of public governance, however, the debate about values has become a contested one. Hoggett (2006: 192) has argued that PSOs now have 

> multiple tasks which are often in contradiction; they are certainly beset by conflicting notions of what they should be doing and . . . for some organizations, paradoxically, it is important that they fail in order to maintain their contested legitimacy by serving the public's unresolved ambivalence.

Because of this contested terrain in which PSOs now operate, and also because of the hybridity discussed above, public values have also become contested. Further, the evolution of the co-production of public services, as discussed in this volume by Pestoff and Brandsen, also poses new challenges both for the way that service users are perceived by the staff of PSOs and for the value base of PSOs themselves. The competing discourses of "client", "consumer", "customer" and "citizen", to name but a few, all imply different modes of service delivery for PSOs and a different set of values underpinning this service production.

For managers working in hybrid organizations, their values may need to span different societal sectors and be able to embrace the paradoxicality of their new organizational architecture and logic. Thus, for example, Poole et al. (2006) found both convergence and divergence in public- and private-sector managerial practice and values, whilst feminist critics have challenged the public and private dichotomy as irrelevant in contemporary society (Nickel and Eikenberry 2006). As a consequence of these critiques, it is important now to ask some fundamentally new questions about public values within the plural state and within public service systems:

- What values do public service managers and public service users hold, and how can the potential contradictions between these be governed?
- Does co-production require a distinctive set of values to underpin public services delivery – and what might the basis of these values be?
- What is the impact of contested values within public service systems upon the delivery and use of these services?
- Do individual public services have distinctive values, and how can these be negotiated in complex service delivery systems?

The relational skills question

The development of the human resources[2] of PSOs has undergone substantial transformation over the last thirty years, and been subject to substantial research in its own right. The intention here is to describe the broad trajectory of change over this period and to consider what questions we need to be asking now about the place and impact of human resources upon and within the NPG.

The approach to human resources under the dominant mode of PA was well characterized by Farnham and Giles (1996: 118–19), reflecting upon the practice prior to 1979:

> Traditional people management practices and institutions of industrial relations in the public services had distinctive features and were broadly universalistic. These . . . were largely influenced by the characteristics of the British state and government's role as a "model" and "good practice" employer, assumed since at least 1917. This role originated from the state's need to harmonise and improve the effectiveness of public services provision nationally, enhance its political accountability and contain public expenditure as the public services expanded . . . the state's objectives were to provide terms and conditions necessary to attract, retain and motivate the most skilled and professional staff, ensure harmonious and equitable employment practices across the public sector, and promote stable employment relations.

This "model employer" role was first articulated by the Tomlin Commission in 1929 and was subsequently refined by the Priestley Commission in 1956. This emphasized the benefits of stability and continuity in employment against those of higher rates of pay. Human resources were centrally controlled in this period, with pay and conditions often decided by central government and monitored through civil service departments. Local discretion was extremely limited (Farnham and Giles 1996).

As the NPM regime developed, one began to see changes in this approach. In its very nature, the NPM was antithetical to the "old" people management approach of PA. Increasingly staff became a human resource to be managed within the organization and with a strong emphasis upon the importation of private-sector managerial and human resource practices into PSOs. Training began to be seen as a significant element of public services delivery with an explicit focus upon the skills necessary for effective service delivery by the organization (Farnham and Giles 1996).

Central to this approach to training and skills development was the competencies model that developed out of the work of David McClelland (1975). This approach sought to identify the distinctive skill competencies required to undertake a specific task or post, and subsequently to use these competencies as the basis for recruitment and ongoing training. This was subsequently developed by Boyatzis (1982) to specify twenty areas of core competencies for effective management across all sectors of the economy. Ironically, whilst the competency approach adopted within government was intended both to try to match current resources to future needs and explicitly link these competencies to performance, the competencies adopted were invariably rooted within current, not future, practice. As Daley (2002) has noted in the US context, many competencies became fixed objectives and were rarely re-evaluated in terms of the changing needs of PSOs.

This has become an especial problem as the issue of managing PSOs and public services in the fragmented state has evolved. Current competencies invariably emphasize the tasks of organizational and service management, and their links to performance. However, the reality of contemporary public service management is that it is an interorganizational and collaborative activity, and requires the governance of complex systems and interorganizational processes. Despite this, training has often remained rooted in organizational needs rather than embracing the requirement to develop skills in managing the complex processes of interorganizational, network and systems governance.

The evidence base to begin this shift is growing. Within the private sector, the burgeoning literature on relational capital is making extant both the contribution of individuals to interorganizational working and the skills that they need to be effective in this (e.g. Kale et al. 2000). Some work has also begun to explore the competencies required for collaborative working (e.g. Huxham and Vangen 2005; Getha-Taylor 2008). Work is also needed on the nature of leadership within public service delivery systems, as opposed to within individual PSOs (see Crosby and Bryson 2005; Mandell and Keast 2009). However, this work is still at the margins of the field. In the mainstream, research continues to be dominated by concerns about the training and incentives required to enhance organizational performance. If our research community is to provide research that can meet the challenges of the new regime and provide a basis for evidence-influenced policy and practice, then we need to be asking new research questions about the skills required for relational performance. These will include:

- What are the core elements of relational performance?
- How do you identify, develop and sustain the relational capital of a PSO?
- What key competencies are required for relational performance, and how best can these be facilitated?
- What are the links between such "boundary-spanning" activity and the "boundary-maintenance" activity required for organizational survival – and what are the implications of this leadership within public service delivery systems?

The accountability question

Accountability is, and has been, a recurrent concern for public administration and public management. It continues to be within public governance – but the context has become that much more intricate. Traditional theories of public accountability with public administration were concerned with the formal lines of accountability, linking politicians and the political process to the delivery of public services by public officials and governmental organizations (Day and Klein 1987).

Within public management, the discussion became far more complicated – now accountability concerned not just the accountability of politicians for public policy implementation but also the accountability relationships between governmental commissioners of public services and PSOs and their managers based outside government – in both the commercial and the third sectors (e.g. Cutt and Murray 2000; Cribb 2006).

Public governance has brought these two issues together. By focusing on public service systems, it links both the role of politicians and political accountability in these systems and the accountability of nongovernmental service providers for the delivery of public services. It also links into the issue of sustainability discussed earlier and the need for accounting systems that go beyond traditional formal accounting approaches and focus (e.g. Gray 2002). Key questions here now include:

- What is the focus of accountability?
- How do you establish accountability in fragmented public service delivery systems – how can you hold interorganizational systems and networks accountable for the delivery of public services?
- How can you build sustainability into the accounting process?
- What is the interaction between the value base of public services, the relationship of these services to their users (and/or co-producers) and the accountability required by these services?

A key issue for the implementation of accountability in a fragmented state is discussed further below.

The evaluation question

In many respects, performance evaluation and management are a true child of the NPM. It would be a gross overstatement to say that services were never evaluated within the PA regime. They clearly were. However, the framework was one of the hegemony of the professional paradigm – services were evaluated against professional standards and service objectives, and rather more rarely against resources or strategy (Broadbent and Laughlin 2002).

As Hood (1991) has made clear, though, performance management and performance metrics were at the heart of the NPM. Subsequently, a whole generation of researchers around the world have developed significant research agendas exploring this issue (e.g. Boyne 1999; Boyne et al. 2003). The core of this approach to the management of public services and of PSOs has been their conceptualization as open rational systems that process resources within a constrained environment in order to produce public services. Importantly, the focus has been upon PSOs as the unit of analysis rather than upon more complex service delivery networks or systems.

The classic model of this approach has to be the "production of welfare" model developed by Knapp (1984). Highly innovative in its time, this model explored the production of social care services precisely as such an open rational system, where inputs were transformed into service outputs and produced outcomes for their users. Interestingly, Knapp argued against attempts to try to evaluate outcomes for service users. This was in part because the timescales required to do so properly were too long to be useful for managing public services in real time. However, it was also because of the difficulty of determining whether a particular outcome was directly attributable to a specific service, owing to the effect both of the intervening variables in the environment and of the intrinsic characteristics of service users themselves (see, for example, DoH 1991).

Partly because of the influence of Knapp's work and partly because service outputs lent themselves more easily to the sort of quantitative analysis that began to fuel public policy-making in the 1980s and beyond, the "accounting logic" (Broadbent and Laughlin 2002) of performance management became deeply embedded within public services management as part of the NPM regime. It drove both the strategic planning process within PSOs and their accountability to local and central government for delivering public services to the local community.

It can be argued that this performance management culture is one of the lasting legacies of the NPM – and, indeed, in some countries (for example, England) this has been extended over subsequent years from the "straightforward" use of indicators to evaluate organizational and service performance and toward the use of performance targets and indicators as a way to control the delivery of public services. They have become part of a regulatory, rather than simply a performance-oriented, state (Jayasuriya 2004). For the research community, this effect is seen most strongly in the recent ESRC Public Services Programme, which has had at its heart the whole issue of organizational and service performance management and performance metrics.

Our argument is that this fixation upon the metrics of organizational and service performance is now at odds with the reality of public services delivery in contemporary society. Again, as has been emphasized several times before on other elements of the service system, this is not to say that such performance evaluation of organizations and services is now irrelevant. It manifestly is not – and individual PSOs and public services will always need to monitor and evaluate their performance against their available resources and their strategic objectives. However, the reality of public service systems, as discussed above, has moved on from the "service silos" of the 1980s and

1990s. Performance management and performance metrics have not moved on with them, but rather have remained locked within the open rational systems of the NPM. To take one example, efforts to use performance metrics to integrate sustainability into the core of public services management have to date been thwarted by the resilience of the service focus of local government in England. Rather sustainability has been reinterpreted and backwardly integrated into existing performance metrics, emasculating its potential for transformational change (Ball 2005).

This is not to say that there are not already models of performance management and accounting that could drive forward such a new approach. The social accounting tradition (Gray 2002) has the potential to reframe the approach to performance within public services to include broader issues than service and financial performance alone. It has certainly begun to influence performance evaluation in some parts of the world (for example Italy – see Marcuccio and Steccolini 2005), whilst some have also argued strongly for its potential to advance "an agenda for the social justice dimension of sustainability" (Ball and Seal 2005: 471). Elsewhere, work has also begun on evaluating the performance of collaborative networks, rather than of the constituent organizations (Head 2008; Mandell and Keast 2008).

There are thus a raft of new issues that need to be addressed in using performance management to address the new challenges of the delivery of public services within the NPG regime. These are issues located within an open natural systems approach discussed previously, which emphasizes the inter-relationship of the organization and its environment, the fragmentation of services delivery within contemporary society, the primacy of systems logic and the pre-eminence of values. It is also necessary to move beyond the simple (?) evaluation of individual PSOs and to ask some fundamental questions about how you evaluate multi-organizational performance and co-production in public service delivery systems. These questions include:

- How do you evaluate performance of a multi-organizational service system, as opposed to a single organization or service, and which system includes service users as co-producers?
- How do you evaluate "relational performance" in the sense of the performance of collectivities of PSOs and service users that co-produce public services within service delivery systems?
- How do you evaluate the effectiveness of PSOs in working together in terms of both their ability to create and sustain relational capital within their organizations and to work effectively with other PSOs (that is, the evaluation of the process of interorganizational working, rather than its outputs or outcomes)?
- Is it possible to evaluate outcomes in a meaningful way that provides information that can be used in the planning and management of public services?

- How do you actually evaluate the sustainability of public services and PSOs and their contribution to societal sustainability in its widest sense – and in a way that allows transformational change in service delivery systems?
- How do you integrate public values into performance evaluation so that issues such as equity and social justice can be part of the judgment of service systems, as well as economic performance?
- How can you use performance metrics to open up the debate about contestability within public services – in terms of service goals, values and impacts?

Conclusions

This volume began by questioning the extent to which a "new public governance" exists or not. The evidence presented here, notwithstanding Hughes's healthy skepticism, is that public governance does indeed exist and is a defining element of public service delivery systems in the twenty-first century. Its meaning may continue to be contested; and, at its worst, it can mean "all things to all people". Nonetheless the concept does capture the challenges of the delivery of public services within fragmented service delivery systems around the world. The challenges may not be the same in all parts of the globe, but relational values are at their core.

This chapter has suggested that a new research agenda is required to capture fully the complexity and diversity of public governance in this global context. It is an ambitious one. However, the argument here is that it is one that must be embraced if we are to move forward and consider the realities of public policy implementation and public services delivery within public governance. Again, this is a not a "boosterist" agenda that argues for the NPG as the "one best way" to implement policy and deliver public services. Nor does it suggest that the need for effective public policy processes and for effective organizational management has gone away. Rather it asks how these challenges can be approached within the fragmented, interorganizational and contested space that now comprises "the public sector".

This concluding discussion has suggested what these new questions might be. It is certainly not intended to be either exhaustive or conclusive. Rather it is intended as a contribution to fire a debate about the research agenda on public governance for the next decade and beyond. The research community must embrace this new research agenda if it is to stop asking "old questions" that do not reflect the reality of public services in the twenty-first century. The "new questions" suggested here do not, of course, negate the need to continue exploring some of these "old questions" – but rather to do so in a context that reflects the new context of public governance. These "new questions" are ones that must be addressed in order to drive forward evidence-influenced public policy implementation and public services delivery in the twenty-first century.

Notes

1 For a broad discussion of systems approaches see Scott (1992).
2 The appropriate term to use here is also a subject of dispute, with each variation having its own discourse. Thus, for example, you will find the field described variously as "human resource management", "people management", "personnel management" and, perhaps more narrowly, "workforce planning".

References

Alford, J. and Hughes, O. (2008) "Public Value Pragmatism as the Next Phase of Public Management", *American Review of Public Administration*, 38 (2): 130–48.

Allison, G. (1984) "Public and Private Administrative Leadership: Are They Fundamentally Alike in All Unimportant Respects?", in *Leadership and Organizational Culture*: 214–39.

Ball, A. (2005) "Environmental Accounting and Change in UK Local Government", *Accounting, Auditing and Accountability Journal*, 18 (3): 346–73.

Ball, A. and Seal, W. (2005) "Social Justice in a Cold Climate: Could Social Accounting Make a Difference?", *Accounting Forum*, 29: 455–73.

Boyatzis, B. (1982) *The Competent Manager*, New York: John Wiley.

Boyne, G. (1999) "Processes, Performance and Best Value in Local Government", *Local Government Studies*, 29 (3): 1–15.

Boyne, G. (2002) "Public and Private Management: What's the Difference?", *Journal of Management Studies*, 39 (10): 98–122.

Boyne, G., Farrell, C., Law, J., Powell, M. and Walker, R. (2003) *Evaluating Public Management Reforms*, Buckingham: Open University Press.

Broadbent, J. and Laughlin, R. (2002) "Public Service Professionals and the New Public Management", in K. McLaughlin, S. Osborne and E. Ferlie (eds) *New Public Management: Current Trends and Future Prospects*, London: Routledge.

Cribb, J. (2006) *Being Accountable*, Wellington: Institute of Policy Studies.

Crosby, B. and Bryson, J. (2005) *Leadership for the Common Good*, San Francisco, Calif.: Jossey-Bass.

Cutt, J. and Murray, V. (2000) *Accountability and Effectiveness Evaluation in Non-profit Organizations*, London: Routledge.

Daley, D. (2002) *Strategic Human Resource Management*, Upper Saddle River, NJ: Prentice Hall.

Day, P. and Klein, R. (1987) *Accountabilities*, London: Tavistock.

Department of Health (DoH) (1991) *Assessing Outcomes in Child Care*, London: The Stationery Office.

Evers, A. (2008) "Hybrid Organisations: Background, Concepts, Challenges", in S. Osborne (ed.) *The Third Sector in Europe*, London: Routledge.

Farnham, D. and Giles, L. (1996) "People Management and Employment Relations", in T. Sergiovanni and J. Corbally (eds) *Managing in the New Public Services*, published by University of Illinois Press, Chicago p. 425.

Getha-Taylor, H. (2008) "Identifying Collaborative Competencies", *Review of Public Personnel Administration*, 28 (20): 103–19.

Gray, R. (2002) "The Social Accounting Project and 'Accounting Organizations and Society': Privileging Engagement, Imaginings, New Accountings and Pragmatism over Critique?" *Accounting Organizations and Society*, 27 (7): 687–707.

Gronroos, C. (2007) *Service Management and Marketing*, Chichester: John Wiley.
Head, B. (2008) "Assessing Network-based Collaborations: Effectiveness for Whom?", *Public Management Review*, 10 (6): 733–50.
Hill, M. and Hupe, P. (2009) *Implementing Public Policy*, London: Sage.
Hoggett, P. (2006) "Conflict, Ambivalence and the Contested Purpose of Public Organizations", *Human Relations*, 59 (2): 175–94.
Hood, C. (1991) "A Public Management for All Seasons?", *Public Administration*, 69 (1): 3–19.
Huxham, C. and Vangen, S. (2005) *Managing to Collaborate*, London: Routledge.
Jayasuriya, K. (2004) "The New Regulatory State and Relational Capital", *Policy and Politics*, 32 (4): 487–501.
Kale, P., Singh, H. and Perlmutter, H. (2000) "Learning and Protection of Proprietary Assets in Strategic Alliances: Building Relational Capital", *Strategic Management Journal*, 21 (3): 217–37.
Knapp, M. (1984) *The Economics of Social Care*, Basingstoke: Macmillan.
Llewellyn, N., Lewis, P. and Woods, A. (2007) "Public Management and the Expansion of the Entrepreneurial Ethos?", *Public Management Review*, 9 (2): 253–68.
McClelland, D. (1975) *A Competency Model for Human Resource Management Specialists to Be Used in the Delivery of the Human Resource Management Cycle*, Boston, Mass.: McBer.
Mandell, R. and Keast, R. (2008) "Evaluating the Effectiveness of Inter-organizational Relations through Networks: Developing a Framework for Revised Performance Measures", *Public Management Review*, 10 (6): 715–32.
Mandell, M. and Keast, R. (2009) "A New Look at Leadership in Collaborative Networks", in J. Raffel, P. Leisink and A. Middlebrooks (eds) *Public Sector Leadership*, Cheltenham: Edward Elgar.
Marcuccio, M. and Steccolini, I. (2005) "Social and Environmental Reporting in Local Authorities: A New Italian Fashion?", *Public Management Review*, 7 (2): 155–76.
Moore, M. (1997) *Creating Public Value: Strategic Management in Government*, Cambridge, Mass.: Harvard University Press.
Murray, M. (1975) "Comparing Public and Private Management: An Exploratory Essay", *Public Administration Review*, July–August: 364–71.
Nickel, P. and Eikenberry, A. (2006) "Beyond Public vs. Private: The Transformative Potential of Democratic Feminist Management", *Administrative Theory and Praxis*, 28 (3): 359–80.
Normann, R. (2007) *Services Management*, Chichester: John Wiley.
O'Toole, L., Meier, K. and Nicholson-Crotty, S. (2005) "Managing Upward, Downward and Outward: Networks, Hierarchical Relationships and Performance", *Public Management Review*, 7 (1): 45–68.
O'Toole, L., Walker, R., Meier, K. and Boyne, G. (2007) "Networking in Comparative Context", *Public Management Review*, 9 (30): 401–20.
Parsons, W. (1995) *Public Policy*, Cheltenham: Edward Elgar.
Pestoff, V., Osborne, S. and Brandsen, T. (2006) "Patterns of Co-production in Public Services", *Public Management Review*, 8 (4): 591–6.
Poole, M., Mansfield, R. and Gould-Williams, J. (2006) "Public and Private Sector Managers over 20 Years: A Test of the 'Convergence Thesis'", *Public Administration*, 84 (4): 1051–76.

Posner, B. and Schmidt, W. (1996) "The Values of Business and Federal Government Executives: More Different than Alike", *Public Personnel Management*, 25 (3): 277–89.

Rainey, H., Backoff, R. and Levine, C. (1976) "Comparing Public and Private Organizations", *Public Administration Review*, March–April: 233–44.

Sayre, W. (1958) "Premises of Public Administration", *Public Administration Review*, 18 (2): 102–5.

Schofield, J. (2001) "Time for a Revival? Public Policy Implementation", *International Journal of Management Reviews*, 3 (3): 245–63.

Scott, W. (1992) *Organizations: Rational, Natural and Open Systems*, Upper Saddle River, NJ: Wiley/Prentice Hall.

Vidal, I. (2008) "The Role of Social Enterprises in Europe: A Core Element or a Distraction in the Provision of Public Services?", in S. Osborne (ed.) *The Third Sector in Europe*, London: Routledge.

INDEX

Theories

Regulation theory (p. 38)

Theories of governing / NPM

Capability theory (p. 42)

Lightning Source UK Ltd.
Milton Keynes UK
UKOW020659111011

180102UK00003B/13/P